THE PAN–PEARL RIVER DELTA

The Pan–Pearl River Delta

An Emerging Regional Economy in a Globalizing China

Edited by

Y. M. Yeung and Shen Jianfa

The Chinese University Press

The Pan–Pearl River Delta: An Emerging Regional Economy in a Globalizing China
  Edited by Y. M. Yeung and Shen Jianfa

© **The Chinese University of Hong Kong**, 2008

ISBN: 978–962–996–376–7

THE CHINESE UNIVERSITY PRESS
The Chinese University of Hong Kong
SHA TIN, N.T., HONG KONG
Fax: +852 2603 6692
     +852 2603 7355
E-mail: cup@cuhk.edu.hk
Web-site: www.chineseupress.com

Printed in Hong Kong

Contents

List of Figures and Tables

Figures

Tables

Preface

This is the fifth book by the Urban and Regional Development in Pacific Asia Programme of the Hong Kong Institute of Asia-Pacific Studies at The Chinese University of Hong Kong tracking China's rapid development consequent to the adoption in 1978 of a policy of openness and reform. The books in this series have been conceived in tandem with important policies promulgated by the central government that have affected various parts of the country at different times. The four previous books, all published by The Chinese University Press, have focused on Guangdong (1994, 1998), Shanghai (1996), Fujian (2000) and China's Western region (2004). This book is on the Pan–Pearl River Delta (Pan-PRD) region, a grouping that came into being following the inaugural Pan–Pearl River Delta Regional Cooperation and Development Forum held in June 2004.

Fully convinced of the significance and impact of the new regional grouping on the development of the region and beyond, the programme was quick to respond with a variety of research initiatives. With the Central Policy Unit (CPU) of the HKSAR government, the programme jointly organized a large-scale conference held at the Hong Kong Convention & Exhibition Centre and in the University in December 2004, which was attended by a large number of participants, including government officials, businessmen, academics and the public. The theme of the conference was to explore how Hong Kong could interactively work with the relevant provincial units in a greatly enlarged hinterland for the benefit of all parties concerned. A book arising from the papers presented at the conference has been published by the Institute. The programme has also worked systematically on a couple of issues that should matter a great deal to Hong Kong from the viewpoint of enhanced cooperation and development. In 2005 and 2006, a series of research papers were published, also by the Institute, on infrastructure development within the Pan-PRD region, from which a book was published in 2007. In addition, another series of research papers has been launched, concentrating on new prospects and opportunities for cooperation between Hong Kong and the provincial units within the Pan-PRD grouping under the Eleventh Five-year Plan.

This book project was launched in early 2005. Many of the contributors to this book are Mainland Chinese scholars who had participated in the December 2004 conference. The fieldwork that had been undertaken for the earlier books has greatly facilitated the putting together of this volume. The first editor, for example, has travelled to all of the provinces in China, including all of the spatial units covered in this volume. He has also been able to draw upon his personal collection for pictures to illustrate this book. From the beginning, he participated in all of the major meetings of the regional grouping. He has represented Hong Kong at the four annual Pan-PRD Forums in 2004, 2005, 2006 and 2007. At the inaugural Pan-PRD Forum held in Macao on 2 June 2004, he spoke as an academic representative from Hong Kong. At the 2006 Pan-PRD Forum held in Kunming, he spoke as a member of the infrastructure panel. In addition, he has served as the Chairman of the Pearl River Panel of the CPU in 2003 and 2004, and of the Pan-Pearl River Panel since 2005. This has enabled his understanding of the region to grow, as the region evolves and progresses with regard to regional cooperation and development.

This being the fifth book in the series, we have followed certain useful templates. We aspire to be as up-to-date and comprehensive as possible, by tracking information and data from published materials, the internet and other sources. Chinese names are provided with characters, for the convenience of the reader. By and large, the style and format of this book correspond with those of the previous volumes.

As in previous volumes, this book has been completed in a relatively short period of time because of the devotion and hard work of a strong team. As always, Janet Wong 汪唐鳳萍 was her dependable self, overseeing the project by assisting to correspond with the contributors, liaising with The Chinese University Press and, generally, managing the project. Gordon Kee 紀緯紋 has been a competent and versatile research assistant. He not only helped with the overall research needs of this project, but also contributed to two chapters as the second author. Moreover, he diligently learned and mastered the techniques of computer cartography and has drawn and redrawn most of the maps. The reader can judge the quality of his artistic creations. Some of the maps and figures, however, have been provided by the contributors; hence the different styles of presentation across the chapters. Lu Yifei 盧一飛 came on board the production team at a late stage but provided helpful assistance. Thanks are due to two anonymous referees for their constructive comments on the draft manuscript and we have responded to the extent possible.

Finally, we wish to express our thanks and appreciation to the contributors, who have shared with us their knowledge of the region and responded to our requests for data, information and follow-ups with cooperation, understanding and forbearance. We are responsible for any remaining errors and shortcomings in the book.

The editors
February 2008

Abbreviations and Acronyms

ACFTA	ASEAN-China Free Trade Area
ADB	Asian Development Bank
APEC	Asia-Pacific Economic Cooperation
APO	Association of Southeast Asian Nations Plus One
APT	Association of Southeast Asian Nations Plus Three
ASEAN	Association of Southeast Asian Nations
ASEM	Asia-Europe Meeting
BRR	Bohai Rim Economic Region
CA	certificate authority
CAAC	(The) General Administration of Civil Aviation
CAB	Constitutional Affairs Bureau
CCP	China Communist Party
CEECs	Central and Eastern European Countries
CEPA	Closer Economic Partnership Arrangement
CEZs	Comprehensive Economic Zones
CITIC	China International Trust and Investment Company
CPLP	Comunidade dos Paises de Lingua Portuguesa, or Community of Portuguese Language Countries
CPU	Central Policy Unit
CV	coefficient of variation
DDN	digital data network
DICJ	Director of the Gaming Inspection and Coordination Bureau
DWT	dead weight tons
EAFTA	East Asian Free Trade Area
EHP	(The) Early Harvest Programme
EHV	extreme high voltage
EMS	Express Mail Service
EMU	Economic and Monetary Union
EU	European Union

Expressway =	Superhighway
FDI	foreign direct investment
FIE	foreign-invested enterprises
FT	full-time
FTAA	free trade area of the Americas
FTAs	free trade areas
FYP	Five-year Plan
GATS	General Agreement on Trade in Services
GATT	General Agreement on Tariffs and Trade
GDP	gross domestic product
GMS	Greater Mekong Sub-region
GPRD	Greater Pearl River Delta
ha	hectare 1 ha = 15 *mu*
HDI	Human Development Index
HE	Higher Education
HKIAPS	Hong Kong Institute of Asia-Pacific Studies
HKSAR	Hong Kong Special Administrative Region
HKTDC	Hong Kong Trade Development Council
HP	hydropower
IDD	international direct dial
IT	information technology
ITC	information technology communication
km	kilometer
LNG	liquefied natural gas
LSE	lower secondary education
LSS	lower secondary school
MFA	Multi Fibre Agreement
MICE	meeting, incentive, convention and exhibition
MNCs	multinational corporations
MOC	(The) Ministry of Communications
MOF	China's Ministry of Finance
mu or mou =	666 2/3 sq m
NAFTA	North America Free Trade Agreement
NEPZ	Nanchang Export Processing Zone
NIEs	newly industrializing economies
3PL	Third Party Logistics
Pan-PRD	Pan–Pearl River Delta
PATA	Pacific Asia Travel Association
PC	personal computer

PLA	People's Liberation Army
PPP	purchasing power parity
PRC	People's Republic of China
PRD	Pearl River Delta
R&D	research and development
RCA	revealed comparative advantage
RHQs	regional headquarters
ROs	regional offices
RMB (or *yuan*)	renminbi
RTAs	regional trade agreements
SAD	Single Administrative Document
SAR	Special Administrative Region
SARS	Severe Acute Respiratory Syndrome
SECB	Singapore Exhibition and Convention Bureau
SEZ	Special Economic Zone
SMEs	small and medium enterprises
ST	substitute
STDM	Sociedade de Turismo e Diversoes de Macau, S.A.
TEUs	twenty-foot equivalent units
TFP	total factor productivity
TFR	total fertility rate
TSEs	time-space envelopes
TVEs	township and village enterprises
UN	United Nations
UNDP	United Nations Development Programme
UNESCO	United Nations' Economic, Scientific and Cultural Organization
USA	United States of America
USE	upper secondary education
USS	upper secondary school
VTE	vocational/technical education
WTO	World Trade Organization
YRD	Yangzi River Delta

1

Introduction

Y. M. Yeung

Completely *sui generic* in scale and scope, different from everything that came before, the most dramatic event of the century, China "matters" in a way that no other emergent market has.[1]

The above quotation is employed to underscore the special and unprecedented nature of contemporary China's development, not only in the present century, but also in the past quarter century when China embarked on a bold trajectory of openness and economic reform. What is germane to this introductory discussion is the formation of the Pan–Pearl River Delta (Pan-PRD) 泛珠江三角洲 regional grouping in June 2004, an association that is innovative in its scale, form and substance.

The Pan-PRD regional grouping was born in June 2004 after top leaders from Guangdong 廣東 and the surrounding eight provinces of Guangxi 廣西, Yunnan 雲南, Sichuan 四川, Guizhou 貴州, Hainan 海南, Hunan 湖南, Jiangxi 江西 and Fujian 福建, together with those of the Special Administrative Regions (SARs) 特別行政區 of Hong Kong 香港 and Macao 澳門, met in Hong Kong, Macao and Guangzhou amid much publicity and fanfare — hence the shorthand of "9+2" for the new regional grouping. The leaders put their seal to an ambitious and creative regional cooperation framework that had no precedent in any country, or for that matter, in any part of the world.

The new regional grouping is so large that it comprises an area equivalent to one-fifth of China's land area, one-third of its population, 40% of its GDP and 58% of its foreign direct investment (FDI)[2] (Figure 1.1). It embraces essentially Greater South China, the Greater Southwest, Central China and Southeast China. It may be viewed as a microcosm of China, especially in a historical and cultural sense (Chapter 2, Lau Yee-cheung). The prefix "Pan" to PRD, in fact, denotes the inclusion of any province with the potential to establish economic and trade links with the PRD region, aside from those provinces immediately surrounding Guangdong.[3] As Zhang Li (Chapter 3) explains, there is a geographical basis to the regional grouping. The Pearl River drains Yunnan, Guangxi, Guangdong and part of Jiangxi, and originates in the vicinity of Kunming 昆明 in Yunnan.

The underlying theme of this book is the interaction of processes of globalization and regionalization that found spatial expression in the establishment of a new regional grouping. These processes are amply discussed, directly or indirectly, in the individual chapters that follow. The strategic design behind the establishment of the Pan-PRD grouping is to

Figure 1.1   The Pan-PRD Region in Its Geographical Setting

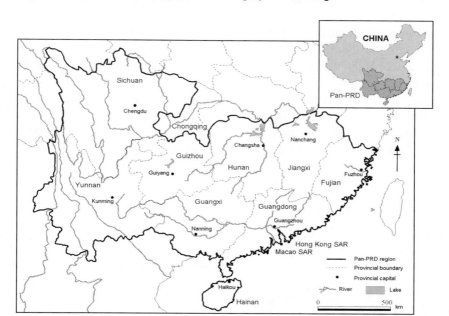

strengthen the new regional economy, minimizing economic and social disparities within it. This also echoes the aim of lessening regional disparities that was an inherent objective of the Western Development Strategy promulgated in 1999.[4]

Following the format of *Developing China's West,*[5] this book is divided into two parts. The first part consists of nine chapters that provide thematic surveys and analyses of the overriding issues that confront the region in its path to development. They are intended to deepen the reader's understanding of the region before the individual regional units are addressed. The second part presents 11 chapters designed to bring out the most important characteristics and vital development issues of the 9+2 spatial units. In all cases, every attempt has been made to ensure that the latest data and information have been used. As in previous volumes, Chinese names are rendered for the convenience of the reader.

This introductory piece is intended to help the reader become acquainted with the subject with the greatest ease. First, a sketch of the Pan-PRD in general context is provided, enabling the reader to gain a glimpse of the region before delving into the body of the book. Second, the economic and planning rationale of the regional grouping is laid out, tracing why and how it came about. Third, a physical and human mosaic is described, with the aim of highlighting the extraordinary diversity within the region. Fourth, a succinct progress report is attempted of what the new regional grouping has achieved in its lifespan of almost four years. The final section focuses on challenges faced by the new regional set-up and the opportunities available to it, taking a forward-looking perspective. Frequent references are made to the subsequent chapters because tantalizing pointers may prompt the reader to read on and gain a holistic perspective.

Contextualizing the Pan-PRD

The enormous size of the Pan-PRD is obvious from Figure 1.1. It is approximately half the area of the 25 countries of the expanded European Union and, with 455 million people, on par with it in population.[6] Yet Table 1.1 reveals that, on a national basis, the provinces within the regional grouping are far from notable in land area or population. Only Sichuan (5), Jiangxi (8), Guangxi (9) and Hunan (10) are within the top ten in land area, and Sichuan (3), Guangdong (4), Hunan (7) and Guangxi (10) in population. In GDP, only Guangdong (1) and Sichuan (9) rank among the top ten, and in per capita GDP, only Guangdong (6) and Fujian (7). Finally, only Guangdong (2) and Fujian (7) are among the top ten in actual FDI. From these sets of figures, it can be deduced that provinces within the Pan-PRD hardly stand out nationally in land area or population, but that Guangdong and Fujian, as two provinces where China first experimented with policies of openness and economic reforms since the early 1980s, have done well economically and in attracting foreign investment.[7]

When Table 1.1 is further examined, it is apparent that the SARs of Hong Kong and Macao, notwithstanding their miniscule land area and relatively small population, are economic juggernauts in their own ways. They are comparable in their level of per capita GDP, at approximately 10 times Guangdong's, which is far greater than that of other Pan-PRD provinces. At US$34.04 billion, Hong Kong's actual FDI is 63.6% that of Mainland China's, and its success in the Hong Kong Stock Exchange during the past two years has been making headlines worldwide. Macao's (Chapter 20, Kwan Fung and Lee Pak-kuen) miraculous economic growth has also continued, largely propelled by a gaming business that since 2002 has been

Table 1.1   Selected Comparative Statistics for the Pan-PRD Region, 2004
(National Ranking in Parentheses)[1]

	Land area (1,000 sq m)	Population (million)	GDP (RMB billion, at current prices)	GDP per capita (RMB)	Actual FDI[2]	
					Amount (US$ million)[3]	As % of China
Guangdong	186,000 (15)	83.04 (4)	1,603.95 (1)	19,707 (6)	7,822.94 (2)	14.62
Guangxi	236,300 (9)	48.89 (10)	332.01 (17)	7,196 (28)	418.56 (16)	0.78
Fujian	120,000 (23)	35.11 (18)	605.31 (11)	17,218 (7)	2,599.03 (7)	4.86
Jiangxi	166,600 (8)	42.84 (13)	349.59 (16)	8,189 (22)	1,612.02 (9)	3.01
Hunan	210,000 (10)	66.98 (7)	561.23 (12)	9,117 (20)	1,018.35 (12)	1.90
Sichuan	488,000 (5)	87.25 (3)	655.6 (9)	8,113 (23)	412.31 (17)	0.77
Yunnan	394,000 (8)	44.15 (12)	295.95 (19)	6,733 (29)	83.84 (25)	0.16
Guizhou	170,000 (16)	39.04 (15)	159.19 (26)	4,215 (31)	45.21 (26)	0.08
Hainan	34,000 (28)	8.18 (28)	76.94 (28)	9,450 (18)	421.25 (15)	0.79
Nine provinces	2,004,900	455.48	4,639.77	10,187	14,433.51	26.98
National[1]	9,600,000	1,299.88	13,687.59	10,561	53,504.67	100.00
Hong Kong	1,100	6.92	1,372.03[4]	199,348[4]	34.04 billion	—
Macao	30	0.47	85.52[5]	187,145[5]	484.38	—

Notes: 1. Data for Hong Kong and Macao are not included.
2. US$100 to RMB827.68.
3. FDI data in 2003, except Hong Kong and Macao.
4. HK$100 to RMB106.23, US$100 to HK$778.8.
5. RMB100 to MOP96.93, US$100 to MOP802.26.

Sources: *Zhongguo tongji nianjian 2005*; *Zhonghua Renmin Gongheguo xingzheng quhua*, http://www.gov.cn/test/2005-06/15/content_18253.htm; *Hong Kong Annual Digest of Statistics 2006*; *The Statistics and Census Service of Macao*, http://www.dsec.gov.mo.

greatly expanded and up-scaled. By 2006, Macao had surpassed Las Vegas to become the world's largest gaming capital, as total earnings from the gaming industry reached MOP 55.0 billion or about US$6.9 billion.[8]

The comparative advantages between the nine provinces within the Pan-PRD on the one hand, and the two SARs on the other, are implicit in the figures in the table. They are made explicit by the trade and investment figures in Chapter 19 (Y. M. Yeung and Shen Jianfa). Table 19.5 (p. 540) shows that in 2003, almost one third of the total exports of the nine provinces passed through Hong Kong, as opposed to 17.41% for the nation as a whole. Likewise, more than half of the total foreign investment in the nine provinces in 2003 originated from Hong Kong, compared to 34.76% for the nation (Table 19.4, p. 538). The critical importance of Hong Kong to China's trade and foreign investment, and to the provinces within the Pan-PRD grouping in particular, is indisputable.

Yet the nine provinces are resource-rich, geographically diverse and have a long history of development, with many people famous for their achievements in many walks of life having come from these provinces. One of the most effective ways of understanding the character of the Pan-PRD region is Lau Yee-cheung's (Chapter 2) division of the region into four sub-regions. First is the Southwest Heartland of Yunnan, Guizhou and Sichuan, notable for the blending of the cultures of the indigenous and *Zhongyuan* people, the Ancient Tea-Horse Road 茶馬古道 from Kunming to Tibet and India via Dali 大理, and the high level of economic and cultural achievements in ancient Sichuan. The Central Corridor is the second sub-region, comprising Hunan and Jiangxi. Both provinces have been more prominent in the past, producing numerous leaders of national renown in literature, politics, philosophy and other fields. For centuries Jiangxi was the transit centre of north-south traffic and trade, but its economic fortunes waned after Shanghai and Guangzhou rose to national prominence. The third sub-region is the Second Tier Littoral, with Guangxi and Hainan playing second fiddle to other provinces more centrally located in relation to the locus of political power. Finally, the pioneering seafaring provinces of Fujian and Guangdong are famous, respectively, for their links with Southeast Asia through the overseas Chinese and for producing forward-looking reformers and revolutionaries whose thoughts and actions have affected the course of modern China and its people.

Taking into account comparative strengths in contemporary economic structure and natural resources, along with geographical endowments, another scholar has proposed a three-fold division of the Pan-PRD to achieve long-term development potential. The first is the southeastern coastal sub-region, consisting of Guangdong, Fujian, Hainan and Guangxi, which are well positioned to cooperate in developing a marine economy, including coastal industries, port development and marine resources. The second is the southern stretch of land following the Jing-Guang 京廣 (Beijing 北京-Guangzhou 廣州) and Jing-Jiu 京九 (Beijing-Kowloon 九龍) Railroads, encompassing Guangdong, Jiangxi and Hunan, which can cooperate in the production, processing and development of agricultural products, non-ferrous metals and specialized products. The third is southwestern sub-region, involving Guangdong, Yunnan, Sichuan and Guizhou, which can cooperate in the energy, minerals, tourism and Chinese medicine industries. In contrast to the previous classification of sub-regions, these three sub-regions include Guangdong in every instance, implying its leadership role in this set-up.[9] It should also be noted that in most of the chapters in Part II, the resource endowments of the provinces, whether natural, mineral, timber, energy, human, agricultural or geopolitical, are repeatedly stressed.

Given the thinking behind the last-mentioned division of regions, it is not surprising that Guangdong has been the prime mover in the Pan-PRD movement. The concept of the Pan-PRD region was first advocated in July 2003 by Zhang Dejiang 張德江, the then Party Secretary of Guangdong. This was followed by a year of intensive preparatory activities before the landmark regional cooperative framework agreement was signed on 3 June 2004.[10]

The formation of the Pan-PRD grouping should also be seen against the backdrop of China's emergent global role in trade and production, especially after its accession to the World Trade Organization (WTO) in late 2001. Since China joined the WTO, its economic development has continued to broaden and deepen. In 1999, when the US-China WTO agreement was concluded, China reported that its total global trade was about US$360 billion. In 2006, the figure approached US$1.7 trillion. In the period 1999–2006, China's contribution to world trade soared from 4% to 10%.[11] In terms of global output, China accounted for 4% in 2000, and is anticipated to increase to 11% of world GDP by 2025.[12] In preparation for playing an enhanced role in world trade and production, China has been intensifying its activities, investment and networks, especially at the international level under the United Nations. Within the country, Chinese authorities have seized the opportunity to strengthen regional economies through promoting inter- and intra-regional cooperation, with the Pan-PRD as a forerunner in strengthening regionalization to counter globalization.

Economic and Planning Rationale

As a straightforward intra-regional framework, one reason that has been advanced for the birth of the Pan-PRD grouping is the sharp decline that has taken place over the past 15 years in the economic indicators of the PRD relative to those of the Yangzi River Delta (YRD) 長江三角洲. For instance, whereas in 1990, the PRD accounted for US$2.19 billion of China's realized FDI versus the YRD's US$402 million, by 2004, their relative scores and importance were reversed at US$10.15 billion and US$25.4 billion, respectively. In percentage terms of national share, the PRD saw a sharp decline from 33.14% to 16.75% in the period in question, whereas the YRD witnessed a phenomenal growth from 6.09% to 41.96% (see Table 3.7, p. 78). With the rapid emergence of the YRD as a strong regional growth centre, it was necessary, from the perspective of Guangdong, to strengthen the "dragon head" role of the PRD, and hence the crusade led by Zhang Dejiang to create the Pan-PRD grouping.

Indeed, the dragon head role of the PRD is built around Guangdong, Hong Kong and Macao, which, in a decade or two, could become one of the most thriving and dynamic regions in the world. Guangdong is on the way to become a manufacturing powerhouse, having attracted 404 of the *Fortune 500* enterprises; Hong Kong is already one of the world's leading logistics and financial centres; and Macao has transformed itself since 2002 to become a world-class gaming-cum-tourist destination. Consequently, in order for these dragon head functions to radiate over a wider region, Hong Kong must strengthen its cooperation with the Pan-PRD members in its acknowledged service functions. Moreover, the PRD must scale up its cooperation with member provinces outside Guangdong in manufacturing industries. Finally, cooperation within the regional grouping in hardware and software development must be accelerated with a view towards achieving a unified market.[13] In fact, Guangdong Governor Huang Huahua expressed hopes that the Pan-PRD grouping would go one step further than this to become a common market like the European one.[14]

China's large national market is fragmented and "cellularized" along administrative, notably provincial, boundaries, with the inevitable consequence of intra- and inter-regional competition (Chapter 3). Undue competition has had the following negative effects: duplication of infrastructure projects, ineffective utilization of limited land resources, and a segmented cross-regional market created by various forms of local protectionism. Through the theme of "Prosperity Through Partnership" adopted in the 2004 Pan-PRD Forum, the plan is for reforms to be deepened in the Pan-PRD region and the penetration of global forces increased, to eventually raise the overall competitiveness of the region.

Yet the form of regionalism embodied in the Pan-PRD framework is a loose format that may be described as bottom-up approach and one that is probably against the normative principles of economic groupings (Chapter 4, Tsang Shu-ki). The mode of operation is akin to the time-honoured norms adopted by the Association of Southeast Asian Nations (ASEAN), that is, "voluntarism, consent, non-inference and informality." Hong Kong's exemplary and facilitative role in the framework has been duly recognized, as reflected in the pattern of trade and investment linkages of the nine provinces with Hong Kong. Hong Kong is considered to be an effective window for the provinces to "go out," meaning to go global via the Hong

Kong stock market and beyond. Consequently, the Closer Economic Partnership Arrangement (CEPA) signed between Hong Kong/Macao and the central government in 2004, is a vital institutional framework to guide cooperation between the two SARs and the provinces. Hong Kong has participated fully in the 10 domains for cooperation that were identified in the 2004 Pan-PRD Forum, namely infrastructure, investment, business and trade, tourism, agriculture, labour, education and culture, information and technology, environmental protection, and public health and the prevention of infectious diseases.[15] CEPA is a form of "regional trade agreement," or more precisely a "free-trade area" (FTA) approved by the WTO that may be viewed as building blocks rather than stumbling blocks to globalization. There is also an external dimension to the regional grouping, as it is seen to offer geopolitical links to Southeast Asia via the ASEAN-China FTA (ACFTA), which was reached in 2002.[16] Guangxi and Yunnan, two provinces that share land borders with ASEAN countries, are assigned special roles in this regional integration.

CEPA came into being soon after China's accession to the WTO. The institutional framework is widely seen as an instrument that will enable Hong Kong and Macao to enter the mainland market ahead of other countries. Provisions for the entry of the latter are to be provided after the first five years of China's accession to the WTO in 2001. However, with this policy framework in the context of the Pan-PRD, one can read a meaning into the participation of the two SARs in the new regional grouping. With Hong Kong and Macao admitted to membership of the Pan-PRD, they will be fully integrated with the mainland, giving concrete substance to the "one country, two systems" concept. The potential for Hong Kong and the nine provinces to cooperate for their mutual benefit is immense.[17]

Although different regions within China have developed informal regional structures since the early 1980s,[18] the Pan-PRD is the first regional bloc approved by the central government. As highlighted in Chapters 7 (Chun Yang and Haifeng Liao) and 9 (Mingjei Sun and Cindy Fan), the new regional grouping is predicated on the fact that disparities among members exist along many economic and spatial dimensions, on which detailed data and analyses are offered. Their varied comparative advantages provide plenty of scope for cooperation and this is a major rationale for the formation of the regional framework. It has been observed, on the other hand, that, over time, the coastal provinces, with the exception of Guangxi, have remained leaders in development, whereas inland provinces are generally laggards. Guangdong and Fujian have pulled away from the others, with Guizhou falling further behind. The large gaps in regional disparity may threaten the soundness of the concept of regional collaboration. Only deliberate policy attention and a heightened sense of the need to alleviate present disparities will launch the region on the path of more even and balanced development.

Finally, it will be helpful to invoke Saskia Sassen's latest discourse on interdependence and globality to give meaning to the Pan-PRD. The establishment of the new regional grouping may be viewed both as a foundational change arising from inside complex systems as well as a consequence of external forces. The transformation inside the nation-state is one foundational factor in the current global era. This involves changes in territory, authority and rights — three key concepts that underpin Sassen's globalization thesis. In the context of the Pan-PRD, these elements have been re-assembled into novel denationalized configurations that may operate at the global, national or sub-national levels.[19]

A Physical and Human Mosaic

To gain a better understanding of the newly constituted Pan-PRD, reference to its geographical basis is instructive (Chapter 3). Apart from being drained by the Pearl River, as referred to earlier, other pertinent factors are its immense size, the economic relations among its spatial units, the coastal-inland dichotomy, divergent strategic locations, and the geographical continuity of the Greater PRD (GPRD, i.e., PRD plus Hong Kong and Macao). Figure 1.1 shows that the region under review lies south of the Yangzi River, accounts for much of the China coast south of Shanghai, shares borders with Vietnam, Laos and Myanmar in the south and southwest, and encompasses at the northwestern corner several large rivers that thunder down from the Tibetan Plateau through the Southwest Heartland.

Within the Pan-PRD, there are huge physical contrasts in landform. In the southwest, Guangxi, Yunnan, Guizhou and Sichuan are often mentioned in one breath because they are part of the Western Development Strategy enunciated in 1999. In that sense, they have been members of a larger regional framework and have benefited from policy measures and resource allocations that came with this strategic development. Within the Pan-PRD framework, Guizhou, Yunnan and Guangxi have accelerated their West-East Hydro Power Transmission Project, with Guangdong as the destination. Guizhou (Chapter 13, Peng Xianwei and Maggi Leung) has thus intensified the development of its energy sector, as well as of its tourism, mineral resources, medicinal herbs and specialty food processing sectors. The province has been struggling against poverty. The earlier intensive "input phases" during 1953–1957 and 1966–1970 that resulted in the introduction to Guizhou of the aviation and aerospace, and electronic industries, unfortunately, had little "trickling-down" effect on the populace. Guizhou still had 7 million people mired in poverty in 2004, or about 10% of the national total.

Yunnan (Chapter 12, Yang Xianming and Ng Wing-fai) is sometimes dubbed the "water tower of Asia" because of its energy reserves, which are important for Southeast Asia. It is China's gateway to Southeast Asia and South Asia. Consequently, Yunnan's importance lies in its plentiful natural resources in minerals, biological varieties, tourism, ethnic culture and location. Its strategic location could enable the Pan-PRD region, and more broadly China, to deepen relationships with the Greater Mekong Sub-region (GMS). Yunnan can provide land crossings from China to Southeast Asia; recent investments in infrastructure have accordingly been geared towards that objective.

Likewise, in Chapter 11, Huang Yefang emphasizes the strategic border location of Guangxi. After the inaugural China-ASEAN Expo held in Nanning in 2004, Guangxi was assigned a special role in China's expanding economic and political ties with ASEAN. This is over and above the central government's decision to construct a sea passage in Southwest China in 1992, with a focus on Guangxi. This province has also been actively involved since the 1980s in regional cooperation in Southwest China. Jiangsu and Guangxi have collaborated in the central government's paired assistance programme, in which one strong province is paired with a weaker one. Guangxi's cooperation with Guangdong dates back many centuries, and has been outstanding.

Sichuan (Chapter 14, Dai Bin, Qian Zhihong and Chung Him) is the largest province in China's Southwest, in land area and population, and has long been renowned for its economic and cultural vitality. Known as the "Land of Heaven on Earth" 天府之國, its contemporary development capitalizes on its abundant natural and human resources, and a judicious balance between within-province sub-regional integration and regional cooperation with areas outside of the province. Chengdu 成都 has emerged as a key metropolis within Southwest China, particularly with regard to its convention and exhibition industry.

One conundrum in the Pan-PRD jigsaw revolves around the absence of Chongqing 重慶 in the regional grouping. Two plausible reasons have been put forward to explain the omission. One is the fact that the city occupies a vital role in the Yangzi River Basin, especially its upper reaches. Thus it is more logical, so the argument goes, for Chongqing to be affiliated with the YRD. Another explanation relates to the city's special status since 1997, when it was elevated to a Special Municipality, with a ranking equivalent to that of a province. Its inclusion in the new regional set-up would lead to undue competition with Guangdong. Since Chongqing has been left out of the regional grouping and since it was part of Sichuan prior to 1997, some chapters (Chapters 8 and 9) have presented adjusted statistics for meaningful comparisons.

In terms of economic relations, it should be remembered that Hong Kong and Guangdong account for half of the GDP of the Pan-PRD region. With regard to GDP, the group can be divided into four tiers: Hong Kong and Macao first, followed by Guangdong and Fujian, then Hainan and Hunan, and finally the other provinces. In this connection, it is pertinent to note the transformation of Guangdong's economy in the past 25 years, as reflected in the ratios among the primary, secondary and tertiary sectors of the economy: from 29.8:46.6:23.6 in 1978 to 7.8:55.4:36.8 in 2004. From an economy based on agriculture, Guangdong has transformed itself into a manufacturing powerhouse and into an economy that has a variety of service industries. Guangdong accounted for approximately one-tenth of China's GDP and one-seventh of its fiscal revenue, and is on track to become a moderately well-off society in 5–15 years (Chapter 10, Liang Guiquan, You Aiqiong and Gordon Kee).[20]

As for the other provinces, their geographic location and comparative advantages mean that they can make varied contributions to the Pan-PRD region. Following a prolonged eclipse in economic importance, Hunan (Chapter 15, Hu Wuxian and Joanna Lee) and Jiangxi (Chapter 16, Zhou Guolan, Huang Shuhua and Lin Hui) are poised for a resurgence. Hunan is becoming the main supplier of agricultural products and migrant labour to the PRD. It is also ready to receive industries seeking to relocate from the PRD as a result of structural changes within the delta and more stringent environmental controls. Similarly, Jiangxi aspires to develop its locational, ecological and resource advantages, and to make a great leap forward in its industrial development. Fujian (Chapter 17, Zheng Daxian, Hu Tianxin, Tang Xiaohua and He Chenggeng) is strategically located in relation to Taiwan and, as one of the first provinces to develop under the policy of openness adopted after 1980, is well positioned economically and culturally to contribute to the collective development of the Pan-PRD region, particularly considering its strong overseas Chinese connections.[21] Finally, Hainan (Chapter 18, Yang Guanxiong and Matthew Chew) is unique in that it has a tropical climate, oceanic resources of oil and gas, and is an island. The types of tourism and agricultural products that are being exploited in Hainan have no competitor or parallel in the Pan-PRD region or, in fact, in China.

The highly varied physiography and history of the units that make up the Pan-PRD grouping have endowed the region with a range of naturally beautiful and culturally diversified tourism attractions. Some of the more famous are Sichuan's Sanxingdui 三星堆, Dujiangyan 都江堰 and Jiuzhaigou 九寨溝, Guizhou's Huangguoshu Falls 黃果樹大瀑布, Yunnan's Shilin 石林 and Lijiang 麗江, Guangxi's Guilin 桂林, Hunan's Zhangjiajie 張家界, Jiangxi's Lushan 廬山 and Hainan's Sanya 三亞. The physical and human geography of the new region offers so many contrasts that it invites exploration. Many places in the region are comfortable to live in because of their temperate climate. The long coastline promises high accessibility; the region's geopolitical position is favourable; and the abundant opportunities that come with a growing market and continuing rapid economic growth makes the region a natural target for foreign investment. The scope for regional cooperation is immense.

From the viewpoint of population, the Pan-PRD is a region of perpetual change and endless fascination. In 2000, its ethnic minority population numbered 58.15 million, comprising about 55% of China's total ethnic minority population (Chapter 8, Shen Jianfa). Of the 17 minority nationalities with a population of at least one million each in China, 13 were found in this region. Considering the rapid economic development in Guangdong and Fujian, it is not surprising that these provinces attracted the largest number of migrants in the period 1995–2000, totalling 12.18 million and 8.41 million, respectively. Migration within the nine provinces in the Pan-PRD region has been greater than between the region and non-Pan-PRD provinces. This is indirect evidence of the coherence of the new regional grouping.

Progress to Date

At the time of writing, the Pan-PRD grouping had been established for about three years. Much has been achieved, as in recent years, cross-boundary integration has been seriously pursued by the Hong Kong with Guangdong authorities under the GPRD framework, as part of the annual Joint Guangdong-Hong Kong Consultative Conference. This mechanism, along with CEPA and the individual visit scheme implemented since 2003, has effectively been continued against the background of the Pan-PRD framework.

From the outset, the set-up has been established at three levels in order for the coordinating mechanism of the Pan-PRD to be effective: (1) the highest level, involving the top leaders of 9+2, where key policy decisions are made at the annual Forum; (2) a secretariat consisting of provincial secretaries-general and Development and Reform Commission chairmen promoting regional cooperation; and (3) a special committee, formed in August 2004 under the Joint Guangdong-Hong Kong Consultative Committee, tasked to work on Pan-PRD regional coordination. This coordinating level is assisted by departmental and operating offices in the different jurisdictions.[22] For Hong Kong, overall coordination of Pan-PRD affairs is the responsibility of the Constitutional Affairs Bureau (CAB; renamed Constitutional Mainland Affairs Bureau, CMAB, in 2007). In order to provide improved on-the-scene services, the Hong Kong Economic and Trade Office in Guangdong based in Guangzhou was expanded in April 2006 to cover five provinces, namely Guangdong, Guangxi, Jiangxi, Fujian and Hainan. In September 2006, another representative office was opened in Chengdu, covering Sichuan, Hunan, Yunnan and Guizhou. In this way, all nine provinces within the Pan-PRD are fully covered.

In the first review, undertaken in June 2005, of what was achieved in the Pan-PRD region in one year, Hong Kong was found to have participated in a wide range of cooperative activities covering the 10 domains of regional cooperation as identified by the 2004 Pan-PRD Forum. Under the category education and culture, as many as 24 distinct activities were held between Hong Kong and Pan-PRD members, mostly led by Guangdong. Trade, infrastructure and planning, research and overseas promotion received the greatest attention in the first year. Reciprocal visits of government officials to set up personal contacts and networks and to discover potential areas for cooperation also took place.[23]

From the latter half of 2005, from Hong Kong's standpoint regional cooperation was focused more on specific sectors, particularly financial services, tourism and infrastructure planning. To promote Hong Kong's advantages in financial services, two high-level delegations led by the Secretary for Financial Services and Treasury visited Fujian in September 2005 and Hunan in September 2006. On 1 May 2006, the individual visit scheme was extended to all provincial capitals of the Pan-PRD. Close cooperation and frequent meetings helped ensure steady progress on several large-scale infrastructure projects involving Hong Kong and the PRD.[24]

Including the inaugural summit, four Pan-PRD Forums have been held in 2004, 2005, 2006 and 2007. In the 2005 and 2006 Forums held in Chengdu and Kunming, respectively, Hong Kong's Chief Executive, Mr Donald Tsang, led the Hong Kong delegation, along with selected policy secretaries. The Chief Executive has also led special delegations to Guangxi, Hunan, Guizhou and Jiangxi, during which agreements were signed on cooperation in specific and general areas. These were also opportunities for Hong Kong businessmen and professionals to size up prospects for investment and partnership.[25]

With a view to being in tune with the nation's Eleventh Five-year Plan (FYP), the Pan-PRD grouping has collectively prepared five special sectoral plans, namely integrated transport, energy, technology, informationalization and environmental protection. These plans were reviewed and approved at the 2006 Forum held in Chengdu. Hong Kong has followed up on its implementation.[26]

As a positive response to the Eleventh FYP, an Economic Summit on "China's Five-Year Plan and the Development of Hong Kong" was held on 11 September 2006, in which government officials and 33 prominent business leaders and professionals participated. In the Summit, the discussions were organized among four Focus Groups: Trade and Business, Financial Services, Information and Technology and Tourism — the four pillars of Hong Kong's development. In January 2007, an action agenda was made public, in which a large number of recommendations were made, many of them involving the Pan-PRD region.[27]

Although the CEPA that was put into practice in 2004 is a policy instrument applicable nationwide, many in the Pan-PRD region have benefited from it. By the end of 2006, the HKSAR had cumulatively issued 19,033 Certificates of Hong Kong Origin, entitling applicants to zero tariffs on exports of goods to the mainland, involving a total amount of RMB620 million.[28]

During the first half of 2006, imports and exports of all provinces within the Pan-PRD region totalled US$280.15 billion, accounting for 35.2% of the figure for the entire country. Of this amount, exports accounted for US$160.6 billion, an increase of 26.7% over the same period, versus imports of US$119.5 billion, an increase of 19%. The increase in exports exceeded that of imports by 7.7%. The trends in the import and export trade showed that Sichuan and Jiangxi recorded the highest increase, although all provinces within the region reported respectable growth. Moreover, Hong Kong, the U.S.A. and the EU constituted the three leading markets for the exports of the Pan-PRD region, with Hong Kong accounting for US$48.35 billion, or a 30% growth over the previous half year. Finally, the value of the transshipment trade via Hong Kong and Macao from the Pan-PRD region totalled US$50.98 billion and US$0.93 billion, respectively, accounting for 18.2% and 0.3%, respectively, of the total transshipment trade of the regional grouping. Nevertheless, they represent an impressive increase of 26.3% and 51.9% over the figure for the previous six months.[29]

Apart from the above statistical profile that shows Hong Kong's growing integration with the Pan-PRD through trade and investment, the influx of mainlanders into Hong Kong as tourists and visitors has been massive and palpable. By January 2007, as many as 49 cities in the mainland, many of them in the Pan-PRD region, had been included in the individual visit scheme. The tourists have significantly narrowed the physical and psychological distance between mainlanders and Hong Kong people. Mainlanders account for more than half of the tourists visiting Hong Kong, giving Hong Kong's economic recovery since mid-2003 a big boost. Thus, in addition to the substantial increase in tangible exchanges between Hong Kong and the Pan-PRD region over the past three years, the vastly enlarged opportunities for exchanges of information, personal contacts and mutual understanding have been a critical element bringing the people of the two places ever closer.

To summarize three years of progress under the Pan-PRD framework, Guangdong Governor Huang Huahua highlighted seven achievements: the establishment of two annual platforms in forum and trade; the formation of a multi-level coordinating mechanism; the institutionalization and implementation of regional development plans; the strengthening of regional infrastructure development; the promotion of the construction of an open and equitable market; the enrichment and extension of domains of cooperation; and the amplification of the impact of regional cooperation. Efforts have been made to realize concepts, plans, programmes, mechanisms, brand names and services.[30]

Implications and Prospects

As a new and fledgling regional grouping, marked more by virtual bonds than physical reality, the Pan-PRD has been going through a period of teething problems and challenges. Two aspects are especially worthy of mention.

Based on the experience of other countries, the role of infrastructure in spearheading regional development cannot be in doubt. Chapter 5 (Y. M. Yeung and Gordon Kee) shows that in all key sectors of infrastructure development, the Pan-PRD has fared well, in keeping with recent national investment and prospects for furthering domestic flows of people, goods and information. The administrative restructuring of port management in Fujian and the decentralization of airport management following the 2002 Civil Aviation Reform are two important systematic changes made to rationalize and improve infrastructure development. There is considerable room for infrastructure development to be used as a lever to accelerate economic growth, as revealed by the fact that within the Pan-PRD region, the annual average growth of passenger traffic (6.52%) and freight traffic (6.84%) is far below the annual average growth rate of regional GDP (12.6%) and national gross industrial output (21.58%). Rapidly growing demands on infrastructure services have yet to be met.

Education and manpower training (Chapter 6, Jin Xiao) represent another sector that presents many challenges and opportunities. For the past half century, China has been struggling with few resources to transform 80% of its illiterate population into educated citizens and an educated workforce. Even at present, the level of illiteracy or of those who have received only a primary level of education ranges from 20–30% (Guangdong, Hainan and Jiangxi) to 40–50% (other provinces). Females still face the dual disadvantage of fewer opportunities in education and jobs. Rural-urban disparities in both aspects are huge and not easily bridged. The region faces the prospect of a large and ever-growing tide of people from rural areas who lack an adequate education pouring in from the western provinces.

The prospects for regional cooperation are promising but the odds against achieving such cooperation are also great, at least in the near future. The obstacles include diverse administrative systems (two SARs, two SEZs and other provinces) and multiple currencies (the renminbi, the Hong Kong dollar and the Macao pataca), economies that are only slowly becoming more market-oriented, poor regional transport and communication networks, overlapping economic structural trends, Guangdong's inadequacies in spreading around the fruits of its economic growth and in providing support in services, and varied cultural backgrounds leading to different behavioural and societal constraints.[31] There are also differences in administrative systems, officials' attitudes towards regional integration and methods of raising funds for development.

It is not surprising, therefore, that the provinces themselves hold different views of the regional grouping and their roles in it. It has been generally observed that Guangdong, as a prime mover in the regional design, and Hong Kong and Macao as two targets for integration being SARs, are fully supportive of the cooperation framework. At another level, Hunan and Jiangxi have exhibited the greatest enthusiasm to pursue regional cooperation. Both provinces are relatively close to Guangdong and areas beyond, and land transport in these provinces is well developed. The four leading source provinces of Guangdong's temporary population of 15 million were Hunan (22.1%), Sichuan (18.9%), Guangxi (14.7%) and Jiangxi (10.7%).[32] In addition, Hainan's staunch support for the regional grouping is reflected in the exceptionally large official delegation it sent on a study tour of the region prior to the 2004 Pan-PRD Forum and then in the large trade delegation the province sent to explore business opportunities (Chapter 18). On the other hand, Yunnan, Fujian and Sichuan have reportedly responded in a lukewarm manner to proposals for regional cooperation (Chapter 3). Among the contributors to this book, Tsang Shu-ki (Chapter 4) views the regional grouping as a "talk show," while Lau Yee-cheung (Chapter 2) assesses it to be a "worthwhile enterprise." In any event, Zhang Li (Chapter 3) concludes that the real benefit of the Pan-PRD regionalization will be skewed in favour of the economic core. Laggard provinces will face a struggle to attract investors in a competitive global economy. Another scholar has highlighted the need to pursue cooperation with provinces not included in the regional grouping, as well as intra-regional cooperation, lest the goal of establishing a unified national market be jeopardized.[33]

There have been other developments that have cast doubt on the viability of the regional grouping. When the Eleventh FYP was released in the spring of 2006, promoters of the Pan-PRD concept were disappointed to see that it made no provisions for the regional grouping. Inclusion would have meant the allocation of resources to the grouping and a degree of permanency for it. As things stand, the new regional design is still in its infancy and going through a period of experimentation. In addition, the Plan contains a proposal to organize the country into eight comprehensive economic zones within the period 2006–2010 (see Table 3.9, p. 82). Some of these zones include provinces of the Pan-PRD. This raises questions about the cohesiveness of the new regional grouping.

It is too early to judge the success or otherwise of the Pan-PRD region as a framework for regional cooperation. All indications to date are positive, since, as outlined earlier, much has been achieved. The proponents of the regional concept are realistic in their objectives and pragmatic in their approach. At the 2005 Pan-PRD Forum, a two-stage cooperative development plan was endorsed: in 2005–2010, to build up the infrastructure and network for regional cooperation; and in 2011–2020, to achieve coordinated industrial development, open and competitive markets, and regional competitiveness (Chapter 4).

In truth, after only three years of the existence the Pan-PRD as a regional grouping, it is gaining a favourable reputation within China and is becoming known to overseas investors. It is not only planners, developers and academics within the country who are watching with keen interest the fast-paced and ever-changing development within region; international investors and observers are no less enthusiastic about the prospects for new markets and opportunities for cooperation. Should the Pan-PRD region continue achieving successes and expanding its spheres of activity, it will be a model for emulation within the country and will draw closer scrutiny from other countries and regions around the world.

Notes

1. Jonathan Anderson, "China's True Growth: No Myth or Miracle," *Far Eastern Economic Review*, September 2006, p. 10.
2. Yue-man Yeung, "Emergence of the Pan-Pearl River Delta," *Geografiska Annaler*, 87B, 2005, pp. 75–79.
3. Xie Pengfei 謝鵬飛, Li Zibiao 李子彪 and Zeng Muye 曾牧野 (eds.), *Fan Zhusanjiao quyu hezuo yanjiu* 泛珠三角區域合作研究 (Pan–Pearl River Delta: Research on Regional Cooperation) (Guangzhou: Guangdong renmin chubanshe 廣東人民出版社, 2004), p. 10.
4. Y. M. Yeung and Shen Jianfa (eds.), *Developing China's West: A Critical Path to Balanced National Development* (Hong Kong: The Chinese University Press, 2004).
5. Ibid.
6. Yeung, "Emergence of the Pan-Pearl River Delta" (see note 2).
7. For a systematic analysis of the achievements and challenges of development in these provinces, see Y. M. Yeung and David K. Y. Chu (eds.), *Guangdong: Survey of a Province Undergoing Rapid Change* (2nd ed.; Hong Kong: The Chinese University Press, 1998); and Y. M. Yeung and David K. Y. Chu (eds.), *Fujian: A Coastal Province in Transition and Transformation* (Hong Kong: The Chinese University Press, 2000).
8. *Ming Pao* (24 January 2006) reported that Macao had vastly increased its gaming revenue in 2006 by 22%, with a rapid increase in the number of hotels and casinos in the SAR. More, in fact, are under construction and will be ready for business in 2007 and 2008. Some 80% of the gaming visitors to

Macao are from the mainland. MOP stands for Macao pataca, the currency of Macao. US$100 is equivalent to MOP802.26. It should be noted that "Macao" and "Macau" are often used interchangeably. As "Macao" is the spelling preferred by the SAR government, it is used consistently in this book.

9. Liang Guiquan 梁桂全 (ed.), *Fan Zhujiang quyu hezuo: zouxiang da zhanlüe* 泛珠江區域合作：走向大戰略 (Pan–Pearl River Delta Regional Cooperation: Towards Large Strategies) (Guangzhou: Guangdong renmin chubanshe, 2004), p. 3.

10. See Table 3.5, p. 74, for a detailed breakdown of the stages in the formative process in the establishment of the Pan-PRD grouping.

11. "China's Re-emergence and Role in Global Trade," *China Daily*, 28–29 October 2006, p. 11. An excerpt of a speech by Charlene Barshefsky at the Beijing Forum.

12. Anderson, "China's True Growth" (see note 1, p. 14). China's rapid rise in global output has been impressive, but the figures can be compared with Asia's historical performance. In 1965, Japan, the Asian tigers and ASEAN collectively accounted for exactly 4% of global GDP; 20 years later, in 1985, the share had increased to 13%, and, by 1990 to more than 16%.

13. Xie Pengfei, "Quyu hezuo zhong de longtou zuoyong" 區域合作中的龍頭作用 (The Dragon Head Role of Regional Cooperation), *Wen Wei Po*, 24 August 2004, p. 32.

14. The Hong Kong Foreign Office's six-month report for January–June 2004, paragraph 80.

15. HKSAR Government, *Hong Kong 2004* (Hong Kong: Government Logistics Department, 2005), p. 15.

16. See Yue-man Yeung, "The Pan-PRD and ASEAN-China FTA as Agents of Regional Integration in Pacific Asia," Occasional Paper No. 13, Shanghai–Hong Kong Development Institute (Hong Kong: Hong Kong Institute of Asia-Pacific Studies, The Chinese University of Hong Kong, 2006).

17. See Y. M. Yeung and Shen Jianfa (eds.), *Fan Zhusanjiao yu Xianggang hudong fazhan* 泛珠三角與香港互動發展 (The Pan–Pearl River Delta and Its Inter-active Development with Hong Kong) (Hong Kong: Hong Kong Institute of Asia-Pacific Studies, The Chinese University of Hong Kong, 2005). Also the Democratic Alliance for Betterment of Hong Kong (DAB) 民建聯, *Xianggang zai Fanzhu quyu hezuozhong de qianjing, wenti yu duice* 香港在泛珠區域合作中的前景、問題與對策 (Prospects, Problems and Strategies of Enhancing Hong Kong's Role in Pan-PRD Cooperation) (Hong Kong: DAB, 2006).

18. See Yue-man Yeung, "China's Urbanizing Population and Regional Integration: Challenges and Opportunities in the Era of Globalization." Paper presented at the Beijing Forum, 27–29 October 2006.

19. Saskia Sassen, *Territory, Authority and Rights: From Medieval to Global Assemblages* (Princeton and Oxford: Princeton University Press, 2006), p. 406.

20. See also Yeung and Chu, *Guangdong* (see note 7).

21. See also Yeung and Chu, *Fujian* (see note 7).

22. *Fanzhu hezuo jieshao* 泛珠合作介紹 (Introducing Cooperation in the Pan-PRD Region), via http://www.pprd.org.cn/ziliao/jieshao. Accessed on 2 February 2007.

23. Information for this and the last paragraph came from the "Progress Report on Regional Cooperation in the Pan-PRD–HKSAR." Report prepared by the Constitutional Affairs Bureau, June 2005.

24. See "Progress Report on Regional Cooperation within the Pan-PRD." Report prepared by the Constitutional Affairs Bureau, November 2006.

25. "Xingzheng zhangguan zongjie Jiangxi kaocha huodong" 行政長官總結江西考察活動 (Overview by the Chief Executive of His Reconnaissance Visit to Jiangxi), 20 January 2007 (in Chinese).

26. "Progress Report …" (see note 23).

27. *Our Way Forward: Action Agenda (Report on Economic Summit on "China's Five-year Plan and the Development of Hong Kong")* (Hong Kong: Central Policy Unit, January 2007). See also Yeung Yue-man, Shen Jianfa and Zhang Li, *China's 11th Five-year Plan: Opportunities and Challenges for Hong Kong* (Hong Kong Institute of Asia-Pacific Studies, The Chinese University of Hong Kong, 2006). Final report prepared for the Bauhinia Foundation.

28. CEPA under the Trade and Industry Department, HKSAR, via http://www.tid.gov.hk/english/cepa/statistics/cocepa_statistics.html. Accessed on 29 January 2007. Also *Fanzhu quyu lianjie wu zhang'ai* 泛珠區域連接無障礙 (Seamless Connection with the Pan-PRD), via http://www.pprd.org.cn/shuju/cy/200701/t20070123_14195.thm. Accessed on 29 January 2007.

29. "Jiu shengqu zuixin chunyun zixun" 九省區最新春運資訊 (The Latest Trade Figures in the Nine Provinces), via http://www.pprd.org.cn/haiguan/shuju/200608/t20060811_10441.htm. Accessed on 30 January 2007.

30. Wu Wenshen 伍文深, *Fanzhu datupo, Xianggang ying genjin* 泛珠大突破, 香港應跟進 (Breakthroughs in the Pan-PRD Region; Hong Kong Should Follow Suit), *Wen Wei Po*, 12 January 2007, A21.

31. Liang, *Pan–Pearl River Delta* (see note 9), pp. 211–22.

32. *Henan renkou waichu renkou shi duoshao?* 河南人口外出人口是多少？ (How Many People from Henan Go Outside?). See http://zhidao.baidu.com/question/7557553.htm. Accessed on 1 February 2007.

33. Li Siming 李思名, *Fan Zhusanjiao: yiguo zhinei de jingji quyuhua? Jianlun Xianggang zai Zhusanjiao suo dandang de juese* "泛珠三角"：一國之內的經濟區域化？兼論香港在珠三角所擔當的角色 (Pan-PRD—Economic Regionalization with a Country. Discussion of Hong Kong's Role in the Pan-PRD). Occasional Paper No. 62, The Centre for China Urban and Regional Studies, Hong Kong Baptist University, 2006.

PART I

THEMATIC PERSPECTIVES

2

Historical and Cultural Diversity

Lau Yee-cheung

Introduction

The Chinese culture has pluralistic origins, having evolved from the cultures
of various ethnic groups, each with their own distinctive traits. From the
eighth to third centuries B.C., the south including the Pan–Pearl River Delta
(Pan-PRD) 泛珠江三角洲 region, most of which is situated south of the
Yangzi River 長江, gradually came under the cultural sphere of *Zhongyuan*
中原, the central plains along the Yellow River 黃河, as a result of territorial
expansion by northern states. Subsequent cultural contacts and exchanges
among various parts of China forged the Chinese culture as we know it.
The founding of the Qin 秦 empire (221–206 B.C.) with its conquest of the
south and resulting north-south integration characterized China's nation-
building process. People in the north continued to move southwards
throughout the centuries, spurring remarkable economic growth and social
development in the south and the country as a whole. By the Tang 唐-Song
宋 transition (ca. tenth century), China's political centre shifted to the east
and north, and the economic and cultural heartland to the south, especially
the Yangzi River and the Pearl River 珠江 regions.

Southern China's contacts with the outside world began two millennia
ago with overland routes linking Sichuan 四川 with Xinjiang 新疆 and
southwestern China with India and Myanmar, and sea routes linking the
southeastern coastal region, especially Guangdong 廣東 and Fujian 福建,
with places overseas. During the Ming 明 (1368–1644) and Qing 清 (1644–
1912) periods, people from these two coastal provinces sought economic
opportunities in Southeast Asia; in the process, they contributed
tremendously to the development of their adopted homeland. Two hundred
years ago, especially following the Opium War (1840–1842) between China
and Britain, the two provinces emerged at the forefront in China's quest for
modernization, owing to their early contacts with the West. In the late
twentieth century, they again led the country in implementing economic
reforms and the open-door policy. These policies were aimed at saving the
country from the brink of economic bankruptcy, a situation it faced following
the depredations of the "Great Proletariat Cultural Revolution" of 1966–
1976.

China's quest for modernization began around the mid-nineteenth
century, when it was thrust open to the outside world by the West. At first
it started as a strenuous endeavour since China had for centuries considered
itself self-sufficient. It turned out that China's path to modernization was
zigzagging, often moving one step forward and two steps backward.

However, as soon as the national leaders became acutely aware of the critical importance of reform and modernization, they made an all-out effort towards its realization. Political movements including the Hundred Days Reform (1898), the constitutional reform (1900s), the republican and the communist revolutions (the first half of the twentieth century) have all geared towards achieving the goals of modernization. Tribute must be given to generations of Chinese people for having turned China from a largely medieval empire to a modern nation-state in the past one-and-a-half centuries.

Due to foreign aggression including the Japanese invasion (1931–1945) and successive civil wars, China's initial fruits of modernization, limited as they were, had been more or less wiped out by 1949 when the People's Republic of China was founded. Soon afterwards, the new regime embarked upon a new wave of economic development by launching the Four Modernizations in the 1950s. The blueprint, however, was not followed through, when pragmatic and well-conceived economic plans gave way to hastily-conceived programmes, aiming at surpassing both Great Britain and the United States in three decades. The Great Leap Forward economic programme, together with natural disasters, drove millions of people into starvation. A more pragmatic approach was adopted in the early 1960s by Liu Shaoqi 劉少奇 and Deng Xiaoping 鄧小平 who helped save the country from economic bankruptcy.

However, political storms descended soon afterwards and ushered in the so-called Great Proletariat Cultural Revolution with Mao Zedong 毛澤東 as its architect, at the expense of modernization and economic development with pragmatists condemned as capitalist roaders. The ten-year political trauma (1966–1976) drove the country to the brink of disaster and near collapse and the Communist regime's loss of the mandate to rule the country. It was only after Mao's death and the arrest of the "Gang of Four" in September and October 1976, respectively, was the policy turned around. With Deng Xiaoping in command and his "cat adage" adopted for economic development, China has once again begun its long search for modernization.

It was against this historical backdrop the Pan-PRD framework has been conceptualized and put into implementation in the beginning of the new millennium. The core of the framework lies in the Pearl River Delta (PRD) 珠江三角洲, which has been one step ahead of the rest of the country in adopting new economic policies. Indeed, the PRD in the past three decades has completely changed its economic landscape from a largely rural area into the most bustling industrial zone of China.[1] "Taking full advantage of its proximity to and excellent connections with Hong Kong 香港, the delta region has been allowed to move ahead of the nation in attracting foreign investment and developing a market economy. Two of China's four Special Economic Zones were established in the delta. In 1985, the entire delta was officially designated an Open Economic Region. Growth and development have been phenomenal ever since. Capital investment has been flowing in from Hong Kong and overseas; joint ventures and cooperative trade enterprises have been established and expanded rapidly; numerous bridges, freeways, ports and harbours have been and are being built; and new farming systems and technology are being practised. The delta, increasingly intertwined with Hong Kong, has quickly emerged as one of the fastest growing and most dynamic regions in the western Pacific Rim."[2] It has also spearheaded the rest of the country in its quest for modernization. With the PRD as its industrial heartland, Guangzhou 廣州, Hong Kong and Macao 澳門 are the trio-engine for the region's economic growth and development. The Pan-PRD framework has further pushed forward the momentum of industrialization and modernization for this part of the country.

Due to both topographical differences and an uneven distribution of natural resources, the Pan-PRD region has a mosaic of ethnic groups, each possessing a distinctive culture. Most of China's 55 minority nationalities are found here. In the province of Yunnan 雲南, for instance, there are 25 minority nationalities with a population numbering 4,000 or more each.[3] The degree to which the various minority nationalities of the Pan-PRD region have assimilated into Han 漢 culture varies. Some, due to their relative geographical isolation, have retained many of their cultural traits including social organization, courtship rituals, language and religion; while others have largely assimilated. With its rich cultural assets, the region is highly diverse, and some areas have been designated world cultural heritage sites by the United Nations' Economic, Scientific and Cultural Organization (UNESCO).

The Southwest Heartland: Yunnan (Dian 滇), Guizhou 貴州 (Qian 黔) and Sichuan (Chuan 川)

The peoples of the north introduced agriculture, handicrafts and Confucianism to Yunnan. Moreover, the ruling state of Nanzhao 南詔-Dali 大理 (738–1254), constituted predominantly of the Bai 白 nationality of Diqiang 氐羌 ethnic origin, adopted Tang's (618–907) political institution, culture and language. This facilitated Yunnan's later integration into

China.[4] Situated at the junction of China, Southeast Asia and South Asia bordering Myanmar, Laos and Vietnam, Yunnan from ancient times had contact with the outside world. For instance, the ancient Indian Road linked Yunnan with India, Central Asia and Arabia; one could also journey on the *chama gudao* 茶馬古道 (the ancient Tea-Horse Road), which started from Kunming 昆明, to Tibet 西藏 and India via Xiaguan 下關 and Dali. The latter route played an important role in economic and cultural exchanges between Yunnan and Tibet.[5] In short, Yunnan under the Nanzhao-Dali state witnessed the blending of the indigenous Diqiang culture with those of the *Zhongyuan*, Tibet and Southeast Asia, to form a unique Yunnan culture.[6]

Since the pre-Qin period, Yunnan had received influences from the *Zhongyuan* culture, especially that of the Chu 楚 (841–223 B.C.) and Shu 蜀 (3,000 ca.–316 B.C.). Emperor Wu 武 (141–87 B.C.) of the Han 漢 (206 B.C.–220 A.D.)[7] dynasties, seeking to promote Confucianism, established government schools in Yunnan. During the Tang and Song (960–1279) periods, Confucianism, Legalism and Taoism flourished in the region. More government schools were founded with the *Zhongyuan* language as the teaching medium. During the subsequent Yuan 元 (1279–1368), Ming and Qing periods, the degree of Chinese cultural influence was greater than ever before, as more schools and Confucian temples were established and civil service examinations were held in Yunnan. By the late Ming period, the *Zhongyuan* culture had become part of the fabric of the province.[8]

Guizhou came firmly under Chinese rule during the reign of Emperor Cheng 成 (33–7 B.C.) of the Han dynasty, when its state of Yelang 夜郎 was annexed.[9] The region, administered through native officials in the name of the central government, was brought under the control of the central bureaucracy during the Ming dynasty, when more central government officials were appointed and given daily administrative responsibilities for the province. Subsequently, Guizhou became an integral part of China.[10] Guizhou's indigenous Luoyue 駱越 ethnic group,[11] together with incoming Miao 苗, Yi 彝 and Hui 回, brought cultural diversity to Guizhou, including such aspects as language, literature, music, dance, folk customs, clothing and religion.[12]

Owing to their long-lasting relations with neighbouring provinces, including Hunan 湖南, Sichuan and Guangxi 廣西, the people of Guizhou were influenced by the cultures of people living in these provinces. During the Tang dynasty, more exchanges occurred between the Guizhou culture and those of its neighbouring regions and *Zhongyuan*.[13] Song emperors welcomed the pledges of loyalty from Guizhou's leading households; and the Yuan regime incorporated the province within its nationwide administrative structure. Schools were established during the Song dynasty, a period when both Buddhism and Taoism were first introduced to the area.[14] With officials directly appointed by the central government as local administrators during the Ming and Qing periods, further interaction between the native Guizhou culture and outside ones became possible.[15]

Since the Ming dynasty, the ethnic Han Chinese population gradually outgrew other ethnic groups. To consolidate their control over the southwest, both the Ming and Qing regimes encouraged immigration to Guizhou and established military units charged with dual responsibilities of frontiers defence and land cultivation. This turned Guizhou into a strategic area, occupying a key political and military position for frontier defence. The *Zhongyuan* culture thus became the mainstream culture in Guizhou, and its language emerged as the lingua franca among the ethnic Hui, Bai and Tujia 土家 peoples.[16]

Because of the establishment of a network of postal routes, centrally appointed officials in charge of local administrative duties and large-scale immigration, Guizhou experienced substantial development during the Ming and Qing periods.[17] A network of five major postal routes was constructed, with the capital city Guiyang 貴陽 as the centre, linking the province to Hunan, Yunnan, Sichuan and Guangxi. Due to its strategic position, Guizhou became in 1413 one of the country's 13 provincial administrative regions.[18]

Guizhou was the birthplace of the Wang Yangming 王陽明 (1472–1529) School of Confucianism or *xinxue* 心學 in early sixteenth century. Wang in Guizhou developed his own perception of Confucian thought, expounding on that of Lu Jiuyuan 陸九淵 of the Southern Song 南宋 (1127–1279) period. Wang's teachings offered an alternative to Zhu Xi's 朱熹 (1130–1200) interpretations of Confucianism. Wang and his disciples' educational endeavour, teaching and promotion of scholarship turned Guizhou into a flourishing ground of learning and scholarship.[19]

The people of the province of Sichuan came into contact with the *Zhongyuan* during the late Shang 商 and early Zhou 周 dynasties (ca. 1200–1000 B.C.). It was conquered by Qin in 316 B.C. and the region was brought into the Chinese sphere.[20] Named the "heavenly state on the earth (*tianfuzhiguo* 天府之國)" by Zhuge Liang 諸葛亮 (231–284 A.D.) for its rich natural endowments, Sichuan attracted migrants from the middle reaches of the Yangzi valley, Yunnan, Hubei 湖北 and Hunan,[21] who brought along their respective cultures. Since the Shang and Zhou dynasties, both the *Zhongyuan* culture and the Chu culture have left their imprints on Sichuan's culture. Sichuan's impressive economic prosperity and cultural achievements have been attributed to its receptiveness of immigrants and their cultures.

As part of the process of becoming integrated with the *Zhongyuan* during the Qin period, Sichuan imported social institutions and technology, including that of river control, the construction of city walls, handicrafts, iron smelting, salt mining and the opening of wells. In the Han dynasty, Sichuan became the most prosperous province in the empire. Its bountiful agricultural yields and flourishing handicrafts industries spurred population growth and urban development. Schools were founded to promote cultural and educational activities, and they produced such literary geniuses as Sima Xiangru 司馬相如 (ca. 180–117 B.C.) and Yang Xiong 揚雄 (53 B.C.–A.D. 18), both natives of Chengdu 成都. Artistic creativity, illustrated by the production as seen in depiction on sculptures and miniature terra cotta figures, attracted wide attention and patronage. The world's earliest examples of mining works and utilization of natural gas were found in Sichuan. The Dujiangyan 都江堰 Dam, constructed by Li Bing 李冰 and his son, has been in use as Sichuan's major system of agricultural irrigation since the Qin.[22]

Several major trunk routes linked Sichuan with the outside world. To the north, the famous Shu Road was constructed during the late Shang (18th–12th century B.C.) dynasty, and by the Warring States Period, a network of at least six major Shu Roads was in use: three starting from the Sichuan basin northwards and another three starting from the Hanzhong 漢中 Basin and cutting through the Qin Mountain Ranges 秦嶺 and into the Guanzhong 關中 Plains.[23] To the south, there existed two major routes: one linking Chengdu and Dali in Yunnan, and the other linking Yibin 宜賓 with Kunming and Dali, with a branch line going southeastwards into Bijie 畢節 and Anshun 安順 in Guizhou. Two additional routes provided direct links between the province (in Puling 涪陵 and Yibin) and Guizhou (in Bijie and Zunyi 遵義). Thanks to its numerous navigable rivers, Sichuan had a sophisticated water transport network, with the Yangzi River as the trunk line supplemented by the Minjiang 岷江, the Tuojiang 沱江, the Jialingjiang 嘉陵江, the Pujiang 涪江, the Qujiang 渠江 and the Wujiang 烏江. The eastward-flowing Yangzi River served as Sichuan's key route of communication with the outside world.[24]

The famous Southwest Silk Road began in Sichuan, passing through Yunnan, Myanmar, India, Pakistan and Central Asia, before finally entering

Europe (Figure 2.1). The *Sanxingdui* 三星堆 historical site and its accompanying findings testify to Sichuan's extensive exchanges with the outside world that were taking place as early as four millennia ago.[25] The southwestern heartland also boasts many famous tourist attractions, including Yunnan's red rock mountains and Guizhou's Huangguoshu 黃果 樹 Falls.

The Mongol invasion of China in the early thirteenth century devastated the province; by 1290, wanton massacres by the invaders reduced Sichuan's population from 6.6 million in 1223 to less than one-tenth of that figure. In the Ming dynasty, Sichuan's economy gradually recovered to its previous level, and its population rose to 3.1 million by 1578. However, 80 years of successive warfare in the late Ming period again led to a tremendous loss of life and ruined the province's economy. By 1661, Sichuan's population had been reduced to only 80,000! Government efforts to encourage immigration from Hubei, Hunan, Jiangxi 江西, Fujian, Guangdong and Shaanxi 陝西 led to a demographic and economic recovery. By 1851, 44 million resided in Sichuan, making it the most populous province in China. The great influx of people from various provinces in China made Sichuan a melting pot of distinctive cultures.[26] In China's recent past, the three southwestern provinces together served the country and its people well by acting as the last citadel in China's war of resistance against the Japanese invasion in 1937–1945.

The Central Corridor: Hunan (Xiang 湘) and Jiangxi (Gan 贛)

The Hunanese people descended from intermarriages between the native Miao and other ethnic groups and those migrating from the *Zhongyuan*. Culturally, Hunan was an amalgam of the native Chu culture and that of the incoming Han.[27] In the Spring and Autumn and Warring States Periods 春秋戰國, Hunan and Hubei had been the base of the powerful Chu state, which had defeated 48 smaller states to the south of the Yangzi River, and thereby contributed significantly to what would later become the Chinese empire.[28] The territorial expansion of the state of Chu also facilitated the formation of a new culture blending together the cultures of the various states before their absorption by Chu.

The Chu culture, noted for its creativity and originality, left imprints on those of the *Zhongyuan*, Bashu 巴蜀, Wuyue 吳越 and Lingnan 嶺南 as evidenced by archeological finds in these areas.[29] The gold coins issued by

Figure 2.1 The Southern Silk Road, Jiangxi's Position in North-South Communication, Jiangxi's Major Commercial Centres in the Ming Dynasty and the Lingqu Canal

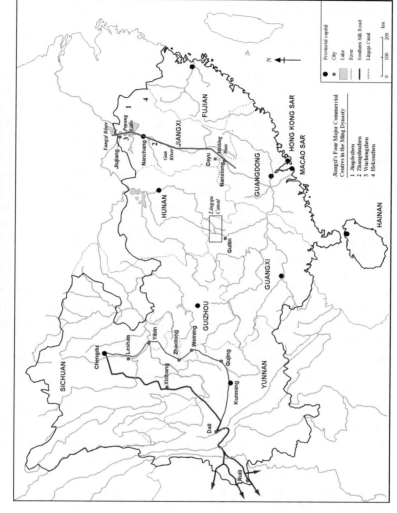

the state of Chu, the only state to use them as currency at that time, circulated widely in nine provinces, including Jiangsu 江蘇, Henan 河南, Shaanxi, Hubei, Shandong 山東, Zhejiang 浙江 and Anhui 安徽. The Chu state invented the local administrative unit of the *xian* 縣, or county, which came directly under the supervision of the central government. This was the forerunner of Qin's local government *jun-xian* 郡縣 structure.

The literary works produced during the Chu period were famous for their romantic flavour, and had left an impact on the development of Chinese literature. *Chu Ci* 楚辭, the poetry of Chu, with its distinctively beautiful style, language and powerful messages best illustrated by the works of the poet Qu Yuan 屈原 (ca. 343–277 B.C.), stands among the greatest of China's literary achievements.[30] The paintings produced during the Chu period are also unique containing religious myths and legends, blending together themes of heaven and the human world, and expressing imagination and reality with the heavy use of colour to produce a comprehensive religious world.[31] Chu also produced its own music characterized by a touch of coarseness and infused with folk religious practices, as well as by the use of the unique musical instrument, the *bianzhong* 編鐘, the bell serial.[32]

The medical expert Zhang Zhongjing 張仲景 (168–196) developed Chinese medicine to a sophisticated level. He authored *On Typhoid and Miscellaneous Illnesses* (*Shanghan zabinglun* 傷寒雜病論).[33] Since the Song and Ming dynasties, a unique embroidery has also been developed in Hunan which, together with those of Jiangsu and Guangdong, ranks among the best in China. Various kinds of animals, birds and beasts, especially the phoenix and dragon, were favourite decorations on Hunanese clothing, with the phoenix being the symbol of the Chu people.[34]

From the Spring and Autumn and Warring States Periods to the Former Han 前漢 (206 B.C.–8 A.D.), Hunan had been a centre of Taoism, whose founders Laozi 老子 and Zhuangzi 莊子 had strong ties with the region.[35] Originating from the south, Taoism represented a significant philosophical alternative to Confucianism. The province also became the birthplace of the Chan 禪 School of Buddhism.[36]

Towards the end of the Later Han 後漢, the province emerged as a centre of learning. The Yuelu 嶽麓 Academy, founded in 976 A.D. (during the early Song), produced such illustrious graduates as Wang Fuzhi 王夫之 (1619–1692), Wei Yuan 魏源 (1794–1857), Zeng Guofan 曾國藩 (1811–1872) and Zuo Zongtang 左宗棠 (1812–1885).[37] Wang Fuzhi's philosophy, in particular on statecraft and the ethnic difference between Chinese and barbarians, had a direct influence on both the Qing reforms of the nineteenth century and the subsequent republican revolution. Wei Yuan, a fellow Hunanese statecraft scholar, pioneered the epochal movement of learning from the West.

In the past two centuries, Hunan played a pivotal role in the making of modern China. The pioneers of what became a century-long reform movement emerged from the province. They included Tao Shu 陶澍 (1779–1839), He Changling 賀長齡 (1785–1848), Wei Yuan and others. In the mid-nineteenth century, the Qing regime faced its arch rebels — the Taiping 太平 Army led by Hong Xiuquan 洪秀全 (1814–1864), who came very close to overthrowing the dynasty. It was a group of Hunan literati including Zeng Guofan, Zuo Zongtang, Guo Songdao 郭嵩燾 (1818–1891) and many others who played a pivotal role in defeating the rebel regime.

In the closing years of the nineteenth century, Hunan emerged as a model for reforms in China under Governor Chen Baozhen 陳寶箴 (1831–1900), assisted by his brilliant lieutenants Huang Zunxian 黃遵憲 (1848–1905)[38] and Liang Qichao 梁啟超 (1873–1929) among others. The reform efforts were cut short by a *coup* at the court, backed by the Empress Dowager Cixi 慈禧 (1835–1908).[39] During the republican revolution, Hunanese again played a significant role, with leaders such as Huang Xing 黃興 (1874–1916) and Song Jiaoren 宋教仁 (1882–1913), and influential polemicists such as Chen Tianhua 陳天華 (1875–1905).[40] After 1921, Hunanese including Mao Zedong (1893–1976), Liu Shaoqi (1898–1968) and Peng Dehuai 彭德懷 (1898–1974) played a pivotal role in the Communist revolution leading to the founding of the People's Republic of China in 1949.

Jiangxi in the Han period experienced rapid development with the arrival of more *Zhongyuan* immigrants, who brought with them advanced production technology and iron instruments. The population of the province soared from 351,965 in the Former Han to 1,668,906 in the Later Han.[41] Successive waves of northern immigrants turned the province into a major grain producer when its Poyang 鄱陽 Lake area was further opened up. It was spared the social disorder and political upheavals that swept over other parts of the country during the period of division in the Tang-Song interregnum.[42]

Jiangxi continued to enjoy economic prosperity during the Song, Yuan, Ming and Qing periods from the mid-tenth century to the mid-nineteenth century, due to its strategic location in north-south traffic and transportation networks, rapid agricultural growth, and flourishing handicrafts industry and commerce. To elaborate on the first factor, Jiangxi, lying south of the

Yangzi River, was situated in a key position for north-south communication, partly because of the Gan and Zhang 章 Rivers, which flow through the province. Once entering Poyang Lake from the Yangzi River, travellers were able to continue their journey south by sailing on the Gan and Zhang Rivers before disembarking in Dayu 大庾, whence they travelled through the famous Meiling 梅嶺 Pass and entered Nanxiong 南雄 in Guangdong (Figure 2.1). For 900 years, this well-trodden route was one of the busiest thoroughfares in the country, especially in the Ming and Qing periods when a ban on seafaring was decreed. Chinese and foreign merchants, diplomats and missionaries from Southeast Asia and Europe would arrive at Canton (Guangzhou), then continued their journey north on this key route. On the return journey, they took the same route in the reverse direction.[43]

Jiangxi's agriculture reached a sophisticated level in terms of the opening up of arable land and the productivity of the land. As land on the plains became fully cultivated, low-lying hills were terraced. By the Yuanfeng 元豐 reign (1078–1085) in the Northern Song (960–1127) dynasty, the total amount of arable land in Jiangxi was 452,000 ha, which was about the limits of what was possible and similar to the amount that is under cultivation there today. The province continued to be a major producer of grain during the Yuan dynasty.[44]

Jiangxi's kilns have long been famous for turning out the best porcelain in China. Jingdezhen 景德鎮 became its nationwide production centre, and porcelain figured prominently in China's trade with other countries. Jiangxi paper was also famous. Cotton was introduced into the province during the Yuan dynasty, which bolstered the province's weaving industry. The weaving industry was brought to a new height in the Ming, with the use of weaving machines. In addition, by the Ming dynasty, Jiangxi's iron smelting industry was producing more than 40% of the total output of the nation.[45]

Trade flourished in Jiangxi with the emergence of many commercial centres. In the Ming dynasty, besides the porcelain trade of Jingdezhen, Zhangshuzhen 樟樹鎮 became known for its trade in Chinese medicine; Wuchengzhen 吳城鎮, strategically located at the mouth of the Gan River by Poyang Lake and thus a key transit centre for all kinds of riverine transport, was a prominent centre for trade in timber and rice; and Hekouzhen 河口鎮, situated at a transport junction for the four provinces of Jiangxi, Fujian, Zhejiang and Anhui, was known for its paper and tea trade (Figure 2.1). Jiangxi experienced further economic growth during the Qing dynasty until the Opium War of 1840–1842. Thereafter, the centre of foreign trade shifted from Guangzhou to Shanghai 上海 (Figure 2.2), and Jiangxi began to lose its strategic position in trade. The subsequent construction of the Beijing-Hankou 漢口 Railroad and the Hankou-Guangzhou Railroad reduced the importance of riverine transport in the country. Consequently, the previously flourishing Jiangxi route and its pivotal position in north-south traffic and transport suffered further decline. [46]

Jiangxi became the birthplace of many distinguished scholars and high officials, with more than 10,400 *jishi* 進士, holders of the highest civil service examination degree, hailing from this province.[47] Brilliant playwrights, poets, calligraphers and scientists also emerged from the province. The most famous writer was Tang Xianzu 湯顯祖 (1550–1616), the Chinese counterpart of William Shakespeare for his *Four Dreams of Linchuan* (*Linchuan simeng* 臨川四夢) including the ever renowned *Mudan Ting* 牡丹亭 (Peony Pavilion).[48] The great scientist Song Yingxing 宋應星 (1587–1664) and his *A Compendium of Science and Technology on Agriculture and Industry* (*Tiangong kaiwu* 天工開物), first published in 1637, was the earliest Chinese volume containing finely executed illustrations and scientific explanations of both the production processes and key technologies in the Chinese agriculture and handicraft industries. For Song's brilliant contribution to Chinese science and technology, Joseph Needham considered him the Chinese counterpart of Georgius Agricola (1493–1555).[49]

During Jiangxi's long history of relative stability and prosperity, especially during the Song and Ming dynasties, a high level of material wealth as well as achievements in the arts, philosophy and statecraft was achieved. The province's illustrious scholar-officials, philosophers, scientists and artists have bestowed China with fine cultural assets.

The Second-tier Littoral: Guangxi (Gui 桂) and Hainan 海南 (Qiong 瓊)

Guangxi became an integral part of the *Zhongyuan* when the First Emperor of the Qin sent troops to conquer the Lingnan region. To facilitate transportation of troops and provisions for the military campaigns, he ordered that a canal be constructed in 219 B.C. When its construction was completed four years later, the famous Lingqu 靈渠 Canal, linking the upper reaches of the Xiangjiang 湘江 with the Lishui 漓水 (the Lijiang 漓江), resulted in a merger of the Yangzi River transport network and the Pearl River (Figure 2.1). This canal, itself an engineering feat and uniting the

Zhongyuan and Lingnan, was a milestone in China's history of nation-building. It enabled more Han immigrants with their advanced culture and technology to enter the region. After Qin's conquest of the Lingnan region, three local administrative regions, or *jun* 郡, were established, namely Guilin 桂林, Nanhai 南海 and Xiang 象. Guangxi acquired its present name when the Yuan regime first set it up as a separate administrative unit in 1363.[50]

A series of illustrious scholars emerged from Guangxi including the late Later Han Buddhist scholar Mouzi 牟子, who was well versed in both Confucian and Taoist learning applying both in interpreting Buddhist thought; three Tang poets and scholar-officials Cao Ye 曹鄴, Cao Tang 曹唐 (847–873) and Zhao Guanwen 趙觀文; the Qing dynasty Confucian scholar and statesman Chen Hongmou 陳宏謀 (1696–1771). Ji Han 嵇含 (263–307) of the Western Jin 西晉 (280–317) dynasty and Zhou Qufei 周去非 of the Southern Song dynasty, authored two important works drawing from their experiences of serving as officials in Guangxi. Ji's *On the Plants in the South* (*Nanfang caomuzhuang* 南方草木狀) was a scientific study of 80 kinds of plants found in Guangxi. With this work, Ji laid the foundation for the study of botany in China. Zhou's *An Answer from Beyond the Five Mountain Ranges* (*Lingwai daida* 嶺外代答), was a comprehensive volume on the ethnography, natural resources and various other aspects of a region comprising today's Guangxi, the Leizhou 雷州 Peninsula of Guangdong and Hainan. Zhou's encyclopaedic work remains an essential reference for a thorough understanding of Guangxi.[51]

Ever since the construction of the Lingqu Canal in the Qin era, both riverine and overland transportation in Guangxi underwent steady development. The river network and coastal transport greatly facilitated communication and exchanges between Guangxi and the rest of China and beyond. People began travelling to Southeast Asia using the sea route, embarking in Hepu 合浦 and Xuwen 徐聞 as early as during the reign of Emperor Wu of the Han dynasty. At this time, Guangxi's shipbuilding industry had already reached an advanced level, thus contributing to a prosperous maritime trade, both internal and foreign. Over a long period of time, beginning from the Spring and Autumn and Warring States period, a comprehensive overland transportation network in the province also developed. By the Qing period, eight major overland routes serving traffic coming and going from all directions between Guangxi and various provinces in China and Vietnam were well established. Mention should also be made of a species of horse from Guangxi, which was invaluable for military, economic and social purposes for about 1,900 years.[52]

Guangxi's various ethnicities including the Zhuang, Yao 瑤, Miao, Yi and Shui 水, exhibited a wide range of costumes of distinctive designs, colours and symbolic meaning. They also contributed to the many varied folk customs and religious beliefs in the province. Its special native musical instrument, the intricately decorated brass drum (*tonggu* 銅鼓), reflected its people's history and religious beliefs.[53] In Guangxi were also found the earliest manufactured porcelains in China. The region has a rich tradition of plays, dramas and music from its various ethnic groups, such as Zhuang drama, the native *nuo* 儺 masked drama, Dong 侗 music, and so forth. Plays and dramas of neighbouring Hunan and beyond also found their way into Guangxi, influencing the indigenous ones; *Zhongyuan* drama and itself undergoing transformation. For instance, Gui drama, the major school of Guangxi drama, which originated with Kunshan 崑山 drama, imported via Hunan during the Qianlong 乾隆 (1736–1795) and Jiaqing 嘉慶 (1796–1820) reigns of the Qing dynasty. It underwent indigenization and developed into a new school of drama performed in the local Guilin dialect.[54]

From both socioeconomic and spatial perspectives, Guangxi occupies a unique position in the Pan-PRD. Over a long period of time, it had an extended network of communication with those provinces that comprise the hinterland half of the Pan-PRD, namely Yunnan, Guizhou, Sichuan, Hunan and Jiangxi on the one hand; and the littoral half of the Pan-PRD, i.e., Fujian, Guangdong, Hainan, Hong Kong and Macao on the other. With its abundant human resources, rich natural endowments, good transportation networks, and strategic location in what will be China's "10+1" Free Trade Area with the ASEAN member states by 2010, Guangxi, under the Pan-PRD framework of collaboration, should expect to play a unique role in bringing about a win-win situation for all members of the grouping.

Hainan, formerly under the jurisdiction of Guangdong, became a separate province in 1988. Its major ethnic group in the province, the native Li 黎 people, probably descended from the Nanyue 南越 ethnic group. The island came under the influence of Han culture when Emperor Wu established the Zhu-yai 珠崖 and Dan-er 儋耳 *jun* in 110 B.C. However, the control of successive *Zhongyuan* regimes was nominal, since native officials appointed by the central government exercised local government functions. During the sixth century, central rule strengthened when Madam Xian (*Xianfuren* 冼夫人), the legendary heroine who had ruled the island for about half a century, secured *de facto* control of the island for the *Zhongyuan* Han regime.[55] By pledging loyalty to the Han regime, she contributed to the further acculturation of Hainan's native Li with the Han people.[56]

During the Tang and Song periods, Hainan, given its frontier location and as a distant outpost, became a destination for officials demoted for holding different political views. Altogether, about 50 court officials of board president rank, including 21 of prime ministerial rank, were exiled to Hainan.[57] They left a rich cultural legacy on the island. Among them was Su Dongpo 蘇東坡 (1037–1101), who arrived in Danzhou 儋州 in 1097 and spent three years on the island. During this period, he made invaluable contributions to its cultural growth both by establishing schools and teaching. His efforts attracted students from other areas of Hainan such as Qiongshan 瓊山 and Haikou 海口, and from across the strait in Guangdong and Fujian. Thereafter, formal education through the establishment of *shuyuan* 書院, or colleges, became widespread in Hainan. Thus, Su Dongpo's pioneer endeavour in this regard was a milestone in the history of the development of Hainan's culture and civilization. Consequently, Hainan's culture and education underwent steady development, and the island was able to produce a total of 105 *jinshi* degree holders during the Song-Ming-Qing periods.[58]

By the fifteenth century, Hainan had produced its first brilliant scholar-official, Qiu Jun 邱濬 (1421–1495) of Qiongshan county. He served four Ming emperors and was retained by the court as the monarch's trusted counsel reaching the rank of a prime minister. Qiu produced a highly esteemed treatise on statecraft, *A Supplement to the Interpretation of the Great Learning* (*Daxue yanyibu* 大學衍義補), consisting of 161 volumes (*juan* 卷), and 1.2 million words. The treatise, a comprehensive "handbook" on all aspects of statecraft, paid special attention to economic theory including such aspects as finance, currency, commerce, population, social relief, maritime transportation, forestry and the opening up of waste land for cultivation. It had considerable influence on the art of statecraft, and has remained a classic since it was first published.[59]

Another legendary figure was Hai Rui 海瑞 (1514–1587), also of Qiongshan county. For discharging his responsibilities throughout his public career, and particularly for his dealings with monarchs, his name became synonymous with uprightness and fearlessness. Hai Rui also published a work, *A Collection of Memoranda* (*Beiwangji* 備忘集), which reflected his philosophy on statecraft and addressed practical approaches to the daily management of state affairs.[60] He has come to personify incorruptibility and justice of the highest standard in traditional Chinese public service.[61]

Hainan had been able to produce quality sugar cane, sweet potatoes, coconuts, fruits, cotton and rice. In the Ming and Qing, tobacco, pineapples, peppers, pumpkins, tomatoes, onions and tea were introduced there. In the late nineteenth century, rubber and coffee were first planted on the island. Since before the Tang dynasty, Hainan had been exporting its products overseas, and foreign trade grew in the Song dynasty, when merchant ships from Southeast Asia and Arabia began to dock on the island. During the Ming-Qing transition, merchant ships from Hainan loaded with silk products made frequent trading trips to Japan. Handicrafts including woven materials, pottery, brewed drinks, and the production of salt and sugar, first developed before the Tang dynasty, became regular trade items in the late Song and the early Yuan period. During the Ming and Qing eras, Hainan was also famous for its shipbuilding industry.[62] Haikou, the commercial, cultural and political centre of Hainan, was made a treaty port in 1858, under the terms of the Treaty of Tianjin 天津.[63]

The Pioneer Seafaring Provinces: Fujian (Min 閩) and Guangdong

In 334 B.C., the Yue 越 people began entering northern Fujian by crossing the border of Zhejiang. Intermarriages between the native Min people and the Yue immigrants led to the birth of an ethnic Minyue 閩越 people.[64] When the Qin unified China, Fujian was absorbed into the *Zhongyuan* state structure, although it was administered by the native Minyue regime. It had come under the influence of the Han culture since Emperor Wu of the Han dynasty conquered the Minyue state and established direct imperial rule there. During the Wei 魏 and Jin periods (220–420), more Han people migrated to Fujian, further blending the native Minyue culture with that of the *Zhongyuan*. As the *Zhongyuan* culture, with its more advanced production technology and management know-how, made inroads into the province, Fujian's economy experienced steady growth, especially in shipbuilding, porcelain and weaving industries.[65] In the Sui 隋-Tang era, large numbers of migrants arrived in Fujian. Scholarship and learning began to flourish, and more than 50 *jinshi* degree-holders were produced in the Tang dynasty. In the Tang-Song interregnum, under Wang Shenzhi's 王審知 (862–925) regime during the state of Min, Fujian, which was unscathed by the political disorder and social upheaval that wracked much of the rest of the country, continued growing economically and culturally. Foreign trade flourished with Fuzhou 福州 and Quanzhou 泉州 as two major ports in trade with Korea, Southeast Asia, India, Arabia and beyond (Figure 2.2).[66] However, Fujian's economy suffered a series of setbacks due to the rise of anti-foreign sentiments in Quanzhou in the late Yuan period. Ming Emperor Yongle 永樂 (Zhu Li, 朱隸, 1360–1424) sent Admiral Zheng He 鄭和 (1371–1433) on missions to Southeast Asia and beyond. Zheng's unprecedented naval feats contributed to the revival of Quanzhou's formerly flourishing maritime trade, as both tributary ships and foreign merchant vessels again made their way to China.[67] When Quanzhou's harbour began to silt up and decline, the port of Yuegang 月港 port in Zhangzhou 漳州 (Figure 2.2), also in southern Fujian, emerged as a leading centre for foreign and maritime trade.[68]

Scholarship and culture in Fujian experienced splendid growth during the Qing era, when almost 300 colleges (*shuyuan*) were established there. *Shuyuan*, prototypes of the modern university and research institute, first appeared in the Tang period. Both public and private educational endeavours in the province thrived due to Fujian's relative political stability, economic growth, rise of population and the promotion of these endeavours by both the central and local governments.[69] Towards the end of the Qing, modern colleges and schools were founded by provincial governments and Christian churches, bringing education in these institutions in line with the latest trends in modern learning.[70]

During Southern Song period, when the political centre of China shifted to the southeast, Fujian's economy reached a historical peak. The province enjoyed prosperous maritime trade, and Quanzhou, the Chinese end of the Maritime Silk Road, emerged as the busiest port in the country, where merchants from more than 40 countries congregated. With Quanzhou unscathed by the dynastic wars between the Song and the Yuan, and its maritime trade reaching yet another new height in the establishment of commercial links with more than 100 countries, Fujian's economy during the Yuan period enjoyed further growth. In the same period, Confucian learning flourished in Fujian as evidenced by the rise of Min learning (*Minxue* 閩學), or Neo-Confucianism (*Lixue* 理學) with emphasis on studying Confucian classics, promoting Confucian morality and stressing Confucian ethics. The province topped in the nation in producing 5,985 *jinshi* degree-holders. During the Shaoxing 紹興 and Chunxi 淳熙 reigns of the Southern Song period, Min learning matured. Zhu Xi consolidated various Neo-Confucian ideas, which had begun to develop in the Northern Song period, thus establishing himself as the spokesman of Neo-Confucian thinking. His writings had an enormous impact on thought and society in the Ming and the Qing periods.[71] With Zhu Xi's *Interpretation on the Four Confucian Classics* (*Sishu jizhu* 四書集注) made official text for the civil service examinations, his teaching greatly influenced the Ming-Qing society.

Figure 2.2   Fujian's Cities, Guangdong's Cultural Zones, the Five Treaty Ports and Guangxi's Cities

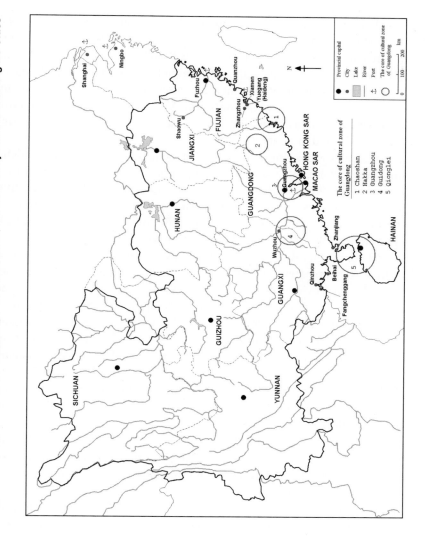

Consequently, *Minxue* became further enriched as more scholars concentrated on its development, and Fujian emerged as a Mecca of Neo-Confucianism.[72]

Following the Qing state's conquest of Taiwan 台灣 and its successful unification of China, the ban on seafaring was lifted. When maritime trade was resumed, Chinese merchant vessels sailed to Southeast Asia. Xiamen 廈門 then emerged as the centre of foreign trade (Figure 2.2).[73] Fujianese people have been known for their adventurousness in seeking economic opportunities abroad, with Southeast Asia as their major destination. Consequently, today about 90% of overseas Chinese of Fujianese origin are concentrated in Southeast Asia.[74]

With its various ethnic groups and branches of the Han people including the Hakka 客家 in its western region, Fujian has a colourful mixture of regional folk cultures, religious beliefs, literature, performing arts, sculpture, stone inscriptions and architecture. The unique earthen houses found in the province have attracted considerable attention. They are simple, environmentally friendly and for multi-purposes.

Major world religions found their way into Fujian at different periods of time. Taoism entered the province in the Later Han, and spread widely in the Tang, as evidenced by erection of many temples. It reached its peak of influence during the Song, when more temples were built. Beginning in the Qing, more Taoist "clergymen" became professional religious workers, performing various religious services for people. Among the many mountains in Fujian noted for their concentration of Taoists, Wuyi mountain 武夷山 is the most famous. It has a long history as a Taoist centre, has been the home of many distinguished Taoist teachers and contains a large number of temples. It was also the birthplace of the Taoist Shenxiao 神霄 Sect and the South Sect.[75]

Buddhism arrived in Fujian in the Western Jin dynasty (265–316) and underwent steady growth thereafter. Four-fifths of the country's monasteries and temples were located there. Among Buddhism's various influential sects, the Chan sect became the most popular, having produced a number of esteemed monks. The province also made unique contribution to the publishing, acquisition and circulation of Buddhist classics. The flourishing of Buddhism in Fujian has been attributed to the promotion of the religion by the ruling class of the province, the large landholdings of the Buddhist temples in Fujian and the arrival of many learned monks from outside the province. Buddhism greatly influenced the thought of Fujian literati, and the province's music, dances and plays. In addition, many notable monuments of Buddhism, including statues and temples, remain.[76]

Islam experienced considerable growth in Fujian, especially in Quanzhou, where the tombs of four Arab Islamic missionaries who came to China in the seventh century are located.[77] During the Yuan era, Quanzhou received a great number of Muslims from abroad owing to its strategic location as the Chinese end of the Maritime Silk Road.[78] Muslims in Fujian succeeded in uniting Han cultural traditions and Islamic social customs and reached an advanced degree of acculturation by intermarrying with the Han ethnic group and valuing achievement in the civil service examinations.[79] There are also a large number of mosques and Islamic tombs and pavilions in the province.[80]

Christianity entered Quanzhou and Fujian during the Yuan dynasty, and Quanzhou became one of the two Christian dioceses in China at the time.[81] During the process of evangelizing, Christian churches and missionaries founded schools, hospitals, orphanages, newspapers and magazines. Together, they made a significant contribution to China's modernization.[82] Christian schools in Fujian produced numerous talented young people with various fields of expertise.[83]

Guangdong, inhabited by the local Yue ethnic people, was officially absorbed into China in 214 B.C. when the First Emperor of Qin conquered Lingnan. People from the *Zhongyuan* began migrating there in large numbers, bringing an advanced culture. The local Yue people steadily acculturated with the incoming Han. Since the Wei and Jin dynasties, Guangdong has experienced social and economic growth. During the Tang and Song eras, maritime traffic and commerce brought Guangdong's economy, culture and education to new heights; the subsequent Yuan and Ming period witnessed further growth in these areas. In the mid-Qing, Guangdong emerged as a centre of China's efforts to address the new influences coming from the West.[84]

There are many regional cultures in Guangdong including those of Guangzhou, Chaoshan 潮汕, the Hakka, Qionglei 瓊雷, Guidong 桂東 and of minority ethnic groups (Figure 2.2). Guangzhou culture, centring on Guangzhou in the Pearl River Delta — an important port for foreign trade since the Qin-Han eras — is characterized by its distinctive dialect (resulting from mixing of the languages of the native Yue people and migrants from the north), opera, music and embroidery. Value is placed on education, literary creativity and scholarly research.

The Chaoshan culture, centring in the Han River 韓江 Delta to the east of Guangzhou, was heavily influenced by southern Fujianese culture because of the area's geographical proximity to Fujian. The Chaoshan people, speaking a dialect closely related to that of southern Fujian, are known all over the China coast and Southeast Asia, Thailand in particular, for their business acumen. The Chaoshan culture is also noted for its fine opera, music, sculpture, tea and cuisine.

The Hakka people, who are concentrated in northeastern Guangdong, the East River, the North River and in the central and western parts of the province, consider Meixian 梅縣 to be their centre. They speak a dialect that developed from interactions between migrants from North China and native people, and developed their own distinctive cuisines and earthen homes. Owing to the scarcity of arable land at home, they often went abroad to Southeast Asia and as far as the Caribbean in search of economic opportunities.

The centre of the Qionglei culture is the Leizhou Peninsula and Hainan Island. The culture formed when the native Luoyue people came into contact with and intermarried incoming Han people who arrived by sea from southern Fujian and Chaozhou 潮州. The Qionglei people speak the Leizhou and Hainan dialects, which are closely related to the southern Fujianese dialect. They are also known for their business acumen as well as for their artistic achievements in songs and opera.

Owing to its location on the borders of Guangdong and Guangxi, Guidong has both Yue and Gui flavours. The dialects of Guilin, Guangzhou, the Hakka and minority peoples are all spoken here. Minority ethnic groups, namely the Zhuang, Yao, She 畲, Hui and Manzhou 滿洲, with their respective languages, clothing and customs, add to the spectacular spectrum of Guangdong culture.[85]

Since the Qin period, Guangdong has been at the receiving end of migration from North China. The successive waves of migration have produced a people imbued with courage and the spirit of adventure. Beginning in the late Tang period, Guangdong people began seeking economic opportunities abroad due to both the shortage of arable land in the province and a decline in foreign trade resulting from political and social upheavals.

Because of Guangdong's continuous economic and cultural communications with the outside world and its distance from the centre of power, Guangdong culture is also characterized by the spirit of boldness and open-mindedness. For instance, Ge Hong 葛洪 (284–364) of the Eastern Jin period founded a school of Taoism, Hui Neng 惠能 (638–713) of the

Tang dynasty founded the Chan School of Buddhism, Chen Xianzhang 陳 獻章 (1428–1500) of the Ming developed his own school of Confucianism focusing on valuing nature, a breakthrough from the limitations and restrictions imposed by the Cheng 程-Zhu School of Neo-Confucianism. In modern times, Guangdong has produced such reformers and revolutionaries as Hong Xiuquan, Kang Youwei 康有為 and Sun Yat-sen 孫逸仙 (1866–1925), who changed the path of modern Chinese history. The spirit of open-mindedness has been demonstrated by overseas Chinese of Guangdong origin, who upon returning to China founded various modern industries and enterprises, modern schools and hospitals. The Guangdong culture is also a pragmatic one, owing in part to the long tradition in Guangdong of making profits through foreign trade.[86]

On Guangdong's foreign links with the outside world, the Maritime Silk Road enabled the region to establish communications, conduct trade and maintain contact with the outside world for more than two millennia. Guangdong became the window for China partly because of its harbours. Compared with other harbours along the China coast, the distance between Guangdong and Southeast Asia, South Asia, West Asia, Africa and Europe was shorter; compared with the Silk Road in Northwest China, rates were cheaper and distances shorter for the transport via sea of major trade goods produced in southeastern China such as silk, porcelain and tea. Moreover, a comprehensive network of riverine and maritime transportation routes linking Guangdong and the rest of the country made Guangzhou a centre for the reception and distribution of both imports and exports. Finally, owing to its relative remoteness from the centre of power, Guangdong generally provided a stable environment for foreign traders and visitors.[87]

Guangzhou's links with the outside world began in the Qin-Han period, when it became a destination in the Maritime Silk Road and established a shipbuilding industry. The major trade commodity at this time was silk, which was shipped to South India and then carried to Arabia, Egypt and Europe by Persian and Roman merchants.[88] Maritime traffic increased during the subsequent Wei-Jin and Northern and Southern dynasties when the Roman Empire became divided and the overland route was blocked. Guangzhou became the first port of call for foreign merchants, diplomats and Buddhist missionaries. Buddhist monks also transmitted Indian philosophy, literature, medicine, astronomy, music, painting, sculpture and architecture, significantly influencing Chinese culture.[89]

In the Sui-Tang period, Guangzhou emerged as the key transit centre and a popular destination for sojourners travelling between China and the

Islamic world under the Arabian empire. In Guangzhou, the Chinese government established a foreign quarter, *fanfang* 番坊, wherein foreigners lived according to their own customs and practised their own religious beliefs, including Islam, Judaism, Christianity and Zoroastrianism.[90] During the Song and the Yuan dynasties, Guangzhou continued to serve as the busiest port city in China for foreign trade. Since East-West contacts relied heavily on the Maritime Silk Road, Guangzhou and Quanzhou to the north were two major centres of global trade at the time.[91]

In the Ming and Qing eras, Guangzhou remained China's window to the outside world. Twice Guangzhou became the sole trading port for China's foreign trade, after the closure of three other ports, Yuntaishan 雲台山 in Jiangsu, Ningbo 寧波 (later transferred to Dinghai 定海) in Zhejiang and Zhangzhou in Fujian, where such trade had been permitted.[92] This was during a period of great geographical discoveries, with an ever-increasing number of travellers, merchants, diplomats and Christian missionaries from the West making their way to China. Guangzhou and adjacent areas became their first ports of call. Among missionaries to China, Francisco Xavier of Spain was the first Jesuit, reaching Shangchuan 上川 Island in Guangzhou prefecture in 1552.[93] In 1553, Portuguese merchants succeeded in securing permission from a Ming local official to stay in Macao, thus laying the foundation for Guangdong's further opening to the West.

Because of its two millennia of foreign connections, Guangdong played a pioneer role in China's efforts to modernize by learning from the West. Via Guangdong, Christian missionaries helped to introduce modern science and technology, medicine and education to China following the Opium War. Guangdong entrepreneurs established modern industries and imported advanced facilities and technology, while its intellectuals explored avenues for social and political change. The province is still one of the vanguards in China's new Long March to become a full member of a globalized world in the new millennium.[94]

The Special Administrative Regions: Macao and Hong Kong

For the past four and a half centuries, Macao and Hong Kong have served as a breeding ground for China's modernization. Between 1553 and 1557, by means of pleading and bribing Chinese local officials, Portuguese merchants managed to secure Macao as a base where they were permitted to reside and trade. In 1849, the Portuguese authorities tightened their control over Macao. They closed the Chinese customs office, evicted Chinese officials and stopped paying the land tax. They turned Macao into a *de facto* colony, although the Chinese government never conceded its sovereignty to Portugal.[95] On 20 December 1999, in accordance with the Sino-Portuguese Joint Declaration on Macao's Future signed in 1987, the Macao Special Administrative Region (SAR) came into existence.

Macao played a pioneer role in bringing China into the world economic system. From the mid-sixteenth to the mid-nineteenth centuries, Macao was a key link in a world trade network including the Macao-Nagasaki, Macao-Philippines (Manila)-Mexico-Spain and Macao-Malacca-India (Goa)-Portugal routes. As an early port in Sino-foreign trade, it contributed to Chinese foreign trade and economic growth. During these three centuries, Macao served as the main venue for East-West interactions. Christian missionaries arriving in Macao brought Western science and technology to China and also introduced Chinese culture to the West.[96]

Macao's pivotal position in the global marketplace was challenged when the British emerged as the master of the seas, both by Hong Kong's rise since 1842 as the meeting point between East and West and by the subsequent opening up of China to the outside world.[97] Macao then began to rely heavily upon opium smuggling and the illicit coolie trade.[98] An estimated half a million Chinese were smuggled out of Macao by coolie traders between the late 1840s and 1875.[99] Following the prohibition of the coolie trade, Macao developed a gambling industry first legalized in 1847. By the early twentieth century, income from the gambling industry, together with opium trade, accounted for 90% of the Macao government's revenues. In 1961, the Portuguese government designated Macao as a tourist area, giving the colony special permission to operate gambling operations as an entertainment industry.[100]

Macao's economy became more diversified after the Korean War. Garments, porcelain, rubber, firecrackers, joss sticks, incense and matches began to be produced in Macao. Beginning in the 1970s, Macao's economy grew steadily. It was spurred by Hong Kong's economy, the proclamation of the *Regulations on the Organization of Macao* by the Portuguese government in 1976 allowing greater autonomy for Macao and the Macao government's subsequent emphasis on building infrastructure to improve the climate for investment. The implementation of reforms and an open-door policy in China since the late 1970s also boosted economic growth in Macao. Since the 1980s, Macao's economy has diversified into manufacturing, imports and exports, tourism, construction, finance and commerce.[101]

Hong Kong Island became a British colony in 1842 under the Treaty of Nanjing 南京. Under the Treaty of Beijing 北京 signed in 1860, the Kowloon 九龍 Peninsula was ceded to the United Kingdom (U.K.), and in 1898 the New Territories was leased to the U.K. for 99 years. On 1 July 1997, in accordance with the Sino-British Joint Declaration of 1984 between the governments of the People's Republic of China and the U.K., the Hong Kong SAR was created. Hong Kong, an entrepot since 1842, had been an outpost where from the British guarded their imperial interests in Asia and China, as well as a bridgehead for entry of Western merchants into China. Following the founding of the People's Republic of China and the outbreak of the Korean War, Hong Kong served as a haven for merchants, capitalists, labourers and refugees. With the influx of capital, entrepreneurs and labour from China, Hong Kong began a new stage of economic development.[102] Such industries as textiles, wigs, plastics, electronics and electrical appliances developed in the territory in the 1950s and 1960s. By the 1970s, after two decades of economic growth, Hong Kong had transformed itself from an entrepot into an international financial, communication and shipping centre. With a capitalist economy and free society, it has emerged as China's most modern city.

Having undergone a metamorphosis[103] since the mid-twentieth century and with the rule of law firmly established, Hong Kong possesses sound institutions including a clean government, a competent civil service and a free marketplace. It is ready to lend its strengths to fellow members of the Pan-PRD region framework in their endeavours to achieve economic growth and social enhancement. When China becomes more open to the outside world, and forges closer links with the international marketplace, Hong Kong, hailed as a development model for coastal cities,[104] may contribute to the rise of a transformed social structure required for China's modernization. The Hong Kong SAR could help China absorb the most vital aspects of foreign culture, thus enriching Chinese culture with fresh ideas.[105] Hong Kong entrepreneurs, together with their Taiwanese and overseas Chinese counterparts, have invested handsomely in China. Hong Kong may also continue to play an important role in South China and Southeast Asia by offering special assistance to the region, encouraging the indigenous elites of these areas to collaborate with overseas Chinese to establish stable investment links in coastal cities in south China.[106] Eventually, as Hong Kong forges close partnerships with fellow Chinese on Taiwan, Hong Kong, Macao and the coastal region of South China, the economies of these areas will become integrated. Thus, the Chinese along the coast, including Hong Kong people, should actively develop a "Greater China" economic sphere, using it as a base to extend their economic power into China's heartland and Southeast Asia.[107]

Having been heavily influenced by both East and West, Macao and Hong Kong have a rich historical and cultural heritage. Recently, Macao received a world cultural heritage award from the United Nations for its museum-type of city layout.[108] Hong Kong has also become increasingly aware of the importance of preserving its historic sites, both Chinese and Western, especially Victorian, styles of architecture. In China's overall development, Macao and Hong Kong play their respective roles. Macao, because of its geographical proximity to western Guangdong and Southwest China, will play a strategic role in stimulating economic growth in those areas. While Hong Kong, because it possesses comprehensive social, economic and legal institutions that are crucial for a large and sustainable economy, is destined to play a role in promoting national growth. Hong Kong's reunion with China in 1997 must be seen as a golden opportunity for the territory to develop into an international metropolis for the whole of China. With Hong Kong's status as an international financial and shipping centre closely linked to economic growth in China, its remarkable vitality and international competitiveness can be maintained only if it serves China well as its metropolis.[109]

Conclusion

In terms of natural endowments and topography, the Pan-PRD region appears to be a microscopic version of the country. Both the region and the country contain developed and fast-developing coastal areas, as well as a hinterland ripe for development. Yunnan, Guizhou and Sichuan have enormous potential in natural resources. Sichuan is also an important base in China for modern science and technology as well as higher education; while Yunnan has a booming floral industry and Guizhou is blessed with immense potential in hydraulic energy.[110] Yunnan is strategically located for the conducting of trade relations with ASEAN under the "10+1" Free Trade Area framework. The three provinces are equipped with both natural resources and talent; it remains to be seen how they can be best put to use.

Guangxi, bordering Vietnam, is another gateway from China to member countries of ASEAN, while Hainan is strategically located for tapping the opportunities presented by the future "10+1" Free Trade Area framework.[111] Guangxi and Hainan are respectively endowed with a network of riverine transportation networks and rich natural resources. Sound government policies and rational strategic plans for development would guarantee the two provinces to reap the fruits to be born under the Pan-PRD framework.

Both Hunan and Jiangxi, also endowed with rich natural resources, have a glorious history of intellectual and cultural achievements. People from these provinces have contributed significantly to China's economic, social and political progress. About a century ago, Hunan stood at the forefront of China's quest to become a modern nation. Drawing on past experiences and lessons, and with proper direction, wise leadership and a sound policy-making apparatus, the two provinces are ready for the opportunities and challenges of growth.

With their long history of foreign contacts, Fujian and Guangdong have been the first to benefit from China's latest reforms and the implementation of its open-door policy. Ahead of the rest of the nation, the region is ready for an economic take-off in China's quest for modernization. Guangdong, in close collaboration with Macao and Hong Kong in the Greater Pearl River Delta framework, stands at the threshold of starting the engine for the Pan-PRD venture, economic and otherwise. Fujian, strategically located especially in view of cross-Taiwan Strait relations, is expected to draw upon its contacts with the outside world to further develop its trade with Taiwan and Southeast Asia. Fellow provincials and overseas Chinese of Fujian and Guangdong origin have achieved economic success and established themselves as respectable citizens of their adopted countries in Southeast Asia, the South Pacific and the Oceanic Islands, South Africa, the Americas and the Caribbean. The two provinces would serve the Pan-PRD region and China well in the nation's efforts to achieve economic growth and modernization.

For historical reasons, Macao and Hong Kong have served as the testing ground for China's experiments with cultural, economic, social and political reforms. The two special administrative regions are seizing the opportunities that have arisen in the wake of rapid economic growth of the rest of China. They are collaborating with Guangdong to serve as an engine of economic growth for South China and the Pan-PRD.[112] Within the Pan-PRD framework, in addition to providing financial services and raising capital for China's commercial and industrial ventures, Hong Kong should build on its strengths and, by offering professional services in law, accountancy and other fields of expertise, develop into China's centre for commerce and services. Hong Kong should aim to become China's most important metropolis,[113] as it possesses sound institutions governing commerce, trade, consumption and the tourism industries, which will be useful to China in its latest modernization efforts.[114]

For the whole Pan-PRD region, Hong Kong plays the role of an engine spearheading economic growth and development, with other cities including Fuzhou, Xiamen, Chaozhou, Shantou 汕頭, Guangzhou, Zhanjiang 湛江, Beihai, Fangchenggang and Haikou playing an auxiliary role in pushing forward modernization. According to "the port metropolis-transportation route-hinterland" trio spatial relationship modernization paradigm, which, according to Wu Songdi, has determined the pattern of China's economic geography ever since the mid-nineteenth century, Hong Kong, together with other port cities, will shoulder the role of development engine for the region's modernization, with the whole region as the hinterland. Whether it is able to make good the responsibility depends on the degree of comprehensiveness of collaboration and far-sightedness of planning efforts by the 11 member players of the Pan-PRD region. Indeed, the Pan-PRD framework of regional collaboration is a historically unprecedented attempt on China's modernization in terms of its area and population involved.[115] Economic growth and development also depend on parallel advances made in social, legal, political and other sectors of the region.

The Pan-PRD, as a microcosm of the whole of China, may likewise rise to the forefront of national economic growth and development. The Pan-PRD, as an entity for regional collaboration, aims at increasing interaction and collaboration among eastern, central and western China on the one hand, and the nine provinces and the special administrative regions of Hong Kong and Macao on the other. It also hopes to achieve close collaboration with ASEAN, as two of its members, Yunnan and Guangxi, have common borders with member states of ASEAN.[116] The Pan-PRD region is rich in both natural resources and cutting-edge talent in many fields and disciplines. It possesses excellent tourist attractions with its world cultural heritage sites and diverse cultural and ethnic traditions, and has an illustrious record of communication and contact with foreign countries. Its success would be a useful reference for China in the nation's efforts to modernize. From this perspective, the Pan-PRD is a worthy enterprise both for the interests of its members and for China as a whole.

Notes

1. George C. S. Lin, *Red Capitalism in South China: Growth and Development*

of the Pearl River Delta (Vancouver: UBC Press, 1997), especially chapter 5.

2. Ibid., p. 77.

3. Ou Kunbo 歐鵾渤, *Dianyun wenhua* 滇雲文化 (Yunnan Culture) (Shenyang 瀋陽: Liaoning jiaoyu chubanshe 遼寧教育出版社, 1998), pp. 15–16.

4. Ibid., pp. 6 and 120.

5. Ibid., p. 156. Bin Yang stated that, "… the study of Yunnan, a seemingly peripheral area but indeed a bridge connecting several civilizations, would help us understand volumes and degrees of civilizational interactions. And it is these interactions that eventually formulated the 'ecumenical world system.'" … "I argued that the Southwest Silk Road had played an active and dynamic role in long-distance trade between China, Southeast Asia and South Asia for over two thousand years.… Moreover, I argued that three Silk Roads had constituted a network (or, if not a network, at least they connected to each other), supplementing each other temporarily and spatially, which would shed light on the understanding of Sino-foreign/East-West communications and thus the whole Eurasian continent. Finally, in terms of Yunnan, I argue that Yunnan should be seen as part of Southeast Asia and the Indian Ocean until the 'modern' period. The cowry money system in Yunnan has demonstrated that the successful incorporation of the Chinese could not be understood until Yunnan had been examined in a global perspective." See Bin Yang, "Horses, Silver, and Cowries: Yunnan in Global Perspective," *Journal of World History*, Vol. 15, No. 3 (September 2004), pp. 22, 26–27. http://www.historycooperative.org/journals/jwh/15.3/yang.html, registered on 17 August 2005.

6. Ou, *Dianyun wenhue* (see note 3), pp. 154–55.

7. There occurred in the Han dynasty with an interregnum of the Xin 新 dynasty 8–25 A.D., founded by Wang Mang 王莽.

8. Ou, *Dianyun wenhue* (see note 3), pp. 337–42.

9. Huang Diming 黃滌明, *Qian Gui wenhua* 黔貴文化 (Guizhou Culture) (Shenyang: Liaoning jiaoyu chubanshe, 1998), p. 3.

10. Ibid., pp. 5–6.

11. Guizhou is the fifth in terms of the number of minority nationalities living in a province or an autonomous region, with Yunnan, Xinjiang, Qinghai and Guangxi, in that order, as the four populated by most numbers of ethnic groups. Shi Jizhong 史繼忠, *Guizhou wenhua jiedu* 貴州文化解讀 (An Explanation of the Guizhou Culture) (Guiyang: Guizhou jiaoyu chubanshe, 2000), p. 35.

12. For instance, *Zhongyuan*'s Spring Festival celebrations was practically observed by other ethnic groups; and ancestral worship or paying respect to ancestors also became a major festival celebration. Huang, *Qian Gui wenhua* (see note 9), p. 8.

13. Huang, *Qian Gui wenhua* (see note 9), p. 7.

14. Increasing contact and communication among various ethnic groups resulted in their acceptance of *Zhongyuan* culture. Shi Jizhong, *Guizhou wenhua jiedu* (see note 11), pp. 126–36.
15. Huang, *Qian Gui wenhua* (see note 9), p. 7.
16. Shi, *Guizhou wenhua jiedu* (see note 11), pp. 42 and 144.
17. Ibid., pp. 143–44.
18. Ibid., pp. 137–40.
19. Huang, *Qian Gui wenhua* (see note 9), pp. 58–83. The province subsequently produced illustrious scholar-officials, including the diplomat Li Shuchang in the late nineteenth century.
20. Yuan Tingdong 袁庭棟, *Bashu wenhua* 巴蜀文化 (Bashu Culture) (Shenyang: Liaoning jiaoyu chubanshe, 1991), pp. 3–11.
21. Ibid., pp. 44–45.
22. Ibid., pp. 58–65.
23. Ibid., pp. 46–48.
24. Ibid., pp. 49–55.
25. Ibid., pp. 70–71.
26. Ibid., pp. 79–88.
27. Wang Jianhui 王建輝 and Liu Senmiao 劉森淼, *Jingchu wenhua* 荊楚文化 (Hubei-Hunan Culture) (Shenyang: Liaoning jiaoyu chubanshe, 1992), p. 3.
28. Ibid., pp. 8–9.
29. Ibid., pp. 58–61.
30. Ibid., pp. 9–10, 115–17.
31. Ibid., p. 180.
32. Ibid., pp. 128, 131–37.
33. Ibid., pp. 173–74.
34. Ibid., pp. 219–25.
35. Ibid., pp. 92–10.
36. Ibid., pp. 109, 279–84.
37. Ibid., photo caption opposite page 1.
38. Both Chen Baozhen and Huang Zunxian were of Hakka ethnic origin. Chen's son Sanli 三立 also served as his father's trusted lieutenant in pushing for reforms.
39. Tan Sitong 譚嗣同 (1865–1898), a Hunan reformer with close ties to Kang Youwei 康有為 (1858–1927) and Liang Qichao, who was determined to sacrifice his life for the cause of reform, declined an opportunity to escape after the *coup*.
40. Chen drowned himself while studying in Japan in protest against Japanese regulations for Chinese students. Chen wanted to arouse the patriotism of his fellow Chinese students and awaken in them a determination to save China from further weakening at the hands of foreign aggressors.

41. Zhou Wenying 周文英, et al., *Jiangxi wenhua* 江西文化 (Jiangxi Culture) (Shenyang: Liaoning jiaoyu chubanshe, 1993), pp. 12–13.

42. Ibid., pp. 16–20.

43. Ibid., pp. 20–21.

44. Ibid., p. 22.

45. Ibid., pp. 23–24.

46. Ibid., p. 24. According to a conversation between the author and Professor Luo Yong 羅勇, dean of the Hakka Research Institute of the Gannan Normal University 贛南師範學院 in Ganzhou 贛州, during the International Conference on Hakka Folk Beliefs and Local Society held at the University on 23–27 November 2007, the Beijing–Kowloon Railroad, making a stop in Jiujiang 九江, has been a boost for Jiangxi's economic development

47. They included Tao Yuanming 陶淵明 (365–427), Yan Shu 晏殊 (991–1055), Ouyang Xiu 歐陽修 (1007–1072), Zeng Gong 曾鞏 (1019–1083), Wang Anshi 王安石 (1021–1086), Yan Jidao 晏幾道 (1030–1106), Huang Tingjian 黃庭堅 (1045–1105), Yang Wanli 楊萬里 (1127–1206), Jiang Kui 姜夔 (ca. 1155–1235), Lu Jiuyuan, Wen Tianxiang 文天祥 (1236–1283), and Wu Cheng 吳澄 (1249–1333).

48. The other three are *Zicaiji* 紫釵記, *Nankeji* 南柯記 and *Handanji* 邯鄲記. Zhou et al., *Jiangxi wenhua* (see note 41), pp. 60–61, 106–12 and 220–21.

49. Zhou Wenying et al., *Jiangxi wenhua* (see note 41), pp. 241–61; Georgius Agricola was a "German mineralogist, metallurgist and author, commonly regarded as the father of mineralogy." See Patrick Hanks et al. (eds.), *Collins Dictionary of the English Language* (London & Glasgow: William Collins Sons & Co., Ltd., 1986), p. 29.

50. Pan Fudong 盤福東, *Bagui wenhua* 八桂文化 (Guangxi Culture) (Shenyang: Liaoning jiaoyu chubanshe, 1998), pp. 21–26. Guilin was made the provincial capital of Guangxi in the Qing dynasty. In the Republican period, the capital shifted between Guilin and Nanning. In 1949, with the founding of the People's Republic of China, the latter was finally picked to be the provincial capital. Pan Fudong, *Bagui wenhua*, pp. 27–28. The three *jun* of Guilin, Nanhai and Xiang included, respectively, today's Guangxi *Zhuang* 壯 Nationality Autonomous Region, Guangdong and a small portion of the Guangxi Autonomous Region.

51. Ibid., pp. 83–114.

52. Ibid., pp. 145–59.

53. Ibid., pp. 182–89, 238–45.

54. Ibid., pp. 351–59.

55. Guan Wanwei 關萬維, *Qiongzhou wenhua* 瓊州文化 (Hainan Culture) (Shenyang: Liaoning jiaoyu chubanshe, 1998), pp. 3, 202–205.

56. Ibid., pp. 205–13.

57. Ibid., p. 216.

58. Ibid., pp. 220–25; Wang Wanfu 王萬福, *Hainan wenhua lunji* 海南文化論集 (A Collection of Essays on Hainan Culture) (Taipei 台北: Lingnan congshu bianzuan weiyuanhui 嶺南叢書編纂委員會, 1992), p. 36.

59. Guan, *Qiongzhou wenhua* (see note 55), pp. 225–34.

60. Ibid., pp. 243–44.

61. In 1965, the Ming historian, also a deputy mayor of Beijing, Wu Han 吳晗, was severely criticized by Yao Wenyuan for his play, *Hai Rui's Dismissal from Office*. Yao's unusually harsh criticism of the play turned out to be the first gunshot setting off the "Great Proletarian Cultural Revolution," a 10-year-long upheaval that brought the country to the brink of collapse. Wu was criticized for likening Peng Dehuai, the Chinese defence minister before his dismissal in 1959, to Hai Rui, and for attacking Mao Zedong's handling of Peng. Hainan also produced a famous poet, Wang Zuo, whose unique works, characterized by an emphasis on serene beauty and tenderness, has won him the reputation of being one the best poets from the island. Guan, *Qiongzhou wenhua* (see note 55), pp. 247–48.

62. Guan, *Qiongzhou wenhua* (see note 55), pp. 258–60.

63. Ibid., pp. 258–63.

64. He Mianshan 何綿山, *Bamin wenhua* 八閩文化 (Fujian Culture) (Shenyang: Liaoning jiaoyu chubanshe, 1998), p. 6

65. Ibid., pp. 7–11.

66. Ibid., p. 16.

67. Marco Polo, the great Italian traveller and merchant, who served at the Yuan court, sailed from Quanzhou in 1291. He remarked that, "Zatong (Quanzhou) was one of the largest ports in the world packed with huge groups of merchants and piles of goods. The busy transactions of business reached a state beyond one's imagination," quoted in He Mianshan, *Bamin wenhua* (see note 64), p. 20. See also Zhongguo hanghai xuehui, Quanzhoushi renmin zhengfu 中國航海學會、泉州市人民政府 (eds.), *Quanzhou gang yu hai shang sichou zhi lu san: jinian Zheng He xia Xiyang liubai zhounian lunwenji* 泉州港與海上絲綢之路三：紀念鄭和下西洋六百週年論文集 (Quanzhou Harbour and the Maritime Silk Road III: A Collection of Essays in Commemoration of the Sexcentenary of Zheng He's Voyages to the South Seas) (Beijing: Chinese Social Sciences Press 中國社會科學出版社, 2002), pp. 15–16, 555–56.

68. He, *Bamin wenhua* (see note 64), p. 22; Lau Yee-cheung and Lee Kam-keung, "An Economic and Political History," in *Fujian: A Coastal Province in Transition and Transformation*, edited by Y. M. Yeung and David K. Y. Chu (Hong Kong: The Chinese University Press, 2000), p. 27.

69. For instance, Wang Shengzhi made education compulsory for all children of school age. The total number of *shuyuan* was far larger than that of government schools in the province. Great scholars such as Zhu Xi often undertook teaching duties in *shuyuan*, turning them, by Song times, into places of learning,

research, publication, scholarly exchanges, and of the making of sacrifices to Confucius and other scholar-sages of the past. He, *Bamin wenhua* (see note 64), pp. 14, 411–420.

70. Worth mentioning here is a special genre of culture that was found in the locality of Houguan 侯官 in modern Fuzhou, the native place of such illustrious personages as Lin Zexu 林則徐 (1785–1850), Shen Baozhen 沈葆楨 (1820–1879), Lin Changyi 林昌彝 (1803–1876), Yan Fu 嚴復 (1853–1921), Lin Shu 林紓 (1852–1924), Liu Buchan 劉步蟾 (1852–1895), Lin Yongsheng 林永升 (1853–1894), Ye Zugui 葉祖珪, Sha Zhenbing 薩鎮冰 (1858–1952), Fang Shengdong 方聲洞 (1886–1911), Lin Juemin 林覺民 (1887–1911) and Lin Xu 林旭. A "Houguan culture" emerged as a social network of relationships and solidarity forged among men from Houguan county. This cohort included statesmen, military strategists, educationalists, literary giants, diplomats, thinkers and translators. Individually and together as a group, they contributed immensely to various aspects of the country's modernization. He, *Banmin wenhua* (see note 64), pp. 24–25.

71. He, *Bamin wenhua* (see note 64), p. 17.

72. Ibid., p. 20.

73. Ibid., p. 23.

74. The reasons why Southeast Asia became the most popular place for Fujianese to settle overseas include its relative geographical proximity to Fujian and the fact that the region has historically been a major trading partner of Fujian. He, *Bamin wenhua* (see note 64), pp. 29–31.

75. Ibid., pp. 63–65.

76. Ibid., pp. 42–63.

77. According to the *Minshu* 閩書 (The Book of Min), four Arab Islamic missionaries, known as the Four Sages, arrived in China during the region of the first emperor, Gaozu 高祖, of the Tang dynasty (618–626) at the prophet Mohammed's behest. Sages One (Yi Xian 一賢) and Two (Er Xian 二賢) stayed in Guangzhou and Yangzhou 揚州, respectively, propagating their faith. Both Sages Three (San Xian 三賢) and Four (Si Xian 四賢) did likewise in Quanzhou, where they were buried after death. Their graves became known as the Islamic Holy Tomb. The graves of Arab Muslims who came to Quanzhou during subsequent dynasties were buried nearby. Sources: http://qz.wmf.com.cn/listinfo.asp?classid=20041103101122093&info_id=20040211155953468 (accessed on 7 August 2006); http://www.fjgov.cn/PubInfoDo/pageDefineAct.do?pageDefineKey=720&containerKey=13493 (accessed on 7 August 2006). Miss Mui Pik-chu, assistant director of the Chinese Islam Research Division, Alliance Bible Seminary, helped to locate the above two websites.

78. Muslims in northern Fujian, especially in Shaowu 邵武, are descended from generals and soldiers who were stationed in the area after the Yuan dynasty. Those in central Fujian, especially in Fuzhou, are descendants of the Muslims

who arrived in Fujian from Gansu 甘肅, Ningxia 寧夏, Shaanxi, Shandong, Henan and Hebei 河北 for various reasons, including accepting invitations to teach Islam, to be united with relatives, and to take up government positions. Some later migrated from Fujian to neighbouring provinces, to Taiwan and abroad. He, *Bamin wenhua* (see note 64), pp. 109–112.

79. Rich historical records on Islam in Fujian, including gazetteers, genealogies, and inscriptions provide invaluable sources for the study of Islam in China. Ibid., pp. 113–16.

80. Ibid., pp. 116–18.

81. Another diocese was in Beijing. He, *Bamin wenhua* (see note 64), pp. 78–79.

82. Ibid., pp. 78–109.

83. Among them is the prominent historian of modern China, Professor Liu Kwang-ching. Professor Liu related to me some of his experiences during his days as a student at the Christian school in Fuzhou, during one of his visits to Hong Kong in 1997 when the International Studies Programme at The Chinese University of Hong Kong was celebrating the 25th anniversary of its founding.

84. Yuan Zhongren 袁鍾仁, *Lingnan wenhua* 嶺南文化 (Lingnan Culture) (Shenyang: Liaoning Educational Press, 1998), pp. 3–16.

85. Ibid., pp. 17–22.

86. Ibid., pp. 25–27.

87. Ibid., pp. 76–78.

88. Ibid., pp. 78–80.

89. Ibid., pp. 83–86.

90. Ibid., pp. 86–89.

91. The Maritime Silk Road thrived because of hindrances on the overland route and the rise of the State of Xixia 西夏. Ibid., pp. 90–93.

92. The Ming regime imposed restrictions on maritime trade and travel. These were reinforced in 1522–1576, in response to resistance against the restrictions by the Chinese people living along the south coastal region, including Jiangsu, Zhejiang, Fujian and Guangdong. Guangzhou was decreed to be the only port permitted to receive tribute missions from vassal and other states. Beginning in 1578, two trade fairs were held in Guangzhou, one each in January and June. Foreign merchants conducted trade transactions there, using Macao as a place to store goods. Starting from 1580, Portuguese merchants were allowed into Guangzhou twice a year to engage in trade. During 1757–1842, the Qing regime under the Qianlong emperor limited the conducting of foreign trade to Guangzhou alone, because of the violation by James Flint, an employee of the British East India Company, of the Chinese rule that prohibited foreigners from sailing north of the Yangzi River. See Yuan Zhongren, *Lingnan wenhua* (note 84), pp. 95–97; Zhang Wenqin 章文欽, "Dai Yixuan xiansheng

zhuanlüe," 戴裔煊先生傳略 (An Outline Biography of Mr Dai Yixuan), in *Aomenshi yu zhongxi jiaotong yanjiu* 澳門史與中西交通研究 (Macao's History and the Study of Sino-Western Communications), edited by Cai Hongsheng 蔡鴻生 (Guangzhou: Guangdong gaodeng jiaoyu chubanshe 廣東高等教育出版社, 1998), pp. 287–337, especially pp. 316–17, 323–24; Li Youhua 李友華 and Chen Yue 陳曜, "Zhongguo diyige ziyou maoyiqu tanyuan — Aomen ziyou maoyiqu tanyuan" 中國第一個自由貿易區探源：澳門自由貿易區探源 (On the Origins of the First Chinese Free Trade Area: The Origins and Development of Macao's Free Trade Area," in *Aomen jingji xuehui xuebao Aomen jingji: Aomen ziyou maoyiqu tanyuan* 澳門經濟學會學報澳門經濟：澳門自由貿易區探源 (Macao Economics, Journal of the Macao Economics Society), Vol. 19 (December 2004), pp. 46–55.

93. Due to the Chinese ban on foreigners residing on the mainland, Xavier was not allowed to set foot in Guangzhou and took refuge on Shangchuan Island off the coast. He soon died there, having suffered from freezing weather and heavy rainstorms, while lying in a make-shift shed.

94. Lau Yee-cheung, "History," in *Guangdong: Survey of a Province Undergoing Rapid Change*, edited by Y. M. Yeung and David K. Y. Chu (Hong Kong: The Chinese University Press, 1998), pp. 465–83.

95. The Portuguese government made use of the ambush of Governor Joao Maria Ferreira do Amaral by Chinese people as the pretext to secure greater control over Macao.

96. Dai Yixuan and Zhong Guohao 鍾國豪, *Aomen lishi gangyao* 澳門歷史綱要 (An Outline History of Macao) (Beijing: Zhishi chubanshe 知識出版社, 1999), p. 1; Jonathan Porter, *Macao: The Imaginary City: Culture and Society, 1557 to the Present* (Boulder, Colo.: Westview Press, 1996), pp. 141–42.

97. Macao also provided the Chinese government with handsome revenues, for instance, one billion taels of silver were imported to Macao from Portugal, Spain and Japan between 1573 and 1644; and between the mid-seventeenth century and the 1820s, four billion Mexican pesos were imported to Macao. Chinese merchandise accounted for 63% of Mexican imports in the late eighteenth century. Li Youhua and Chen Yue (see note 92), especially pp. 52–54.

98. Macao registered very slow growth in foreign trade from 1800 onwards. Its trade value grew from 23.855 million dollars in 1800 to 25.4284 million dollars in 1886 — a rate of 6.6% in 86 years. The figure rose to 32.2264 million dollars in 1908. Dai and Zhong, *Aomen lishi gangyao* (see note 96), pp. 246–47.

99. Ibid., pp. 156–99.

100. Ibid., pp. 249–50.

101. Ibid., pp. 291–93.

102. Wang Gungwu 王賡武, "Jielun pian: Xianggang xiandai shehui" 結論篇：

香港現代社會 (Concluding Chapter: Hong Kong's Modern Society), in *Xianggang shi xinbian* 香港史新編, edited by Wang Gungwu (Hong Kong History: New Perspectives) (Hong Kong: Joint Publishing Co., Ltd., 1997), pp. 859–67, especially pp. 862–64.

103. The term "metamorphosis" is borrowed from Denis Bray, *Hong Kong: Metamorphosis* (Hong Kong: Hong Kong University Press, 2001).

104. It has been proposed by Deng Xiaoping that more "Hong Kongs" should be created out of the coastal cities.

105. Wang (see note 102), pp. 865–66.

106. Ibid., p. 866.

107. Ibid., p. 867.

108. Liu Benli 劉本立, "Fan Zhusanjiao jingji fazhan zhanlüe yu Aomen de xinjihui" 泛珠三角經濟發展戰略與澳門的新機會 (Strategy for the Economic Development of the Pan-PRD and the New Opportunities for Macao), in *Aomen jingji xuehui xuebao Aomen jingji* (Macao Economics, Journal of Macao Economics Society), Vol. 19 (December 2004), pp. 9–23.

109. Indeed, Macao, Hong Kong and Mainland China, especially Guangdong, have combined to form a commonwealth of destinies under "the one-country, two-systems" framework. At the same time, Hong Kong's political, economic and social development is helping to shape China's future; thus Hong Kong is a part of the integral strength of China. Zhang Bingliang 張炳良, "Xianggang zai bianyuanhua?" 香港在邊緣化？ (Is Hong Kong Becoming Marginalized?), *Ming Pao Daily* 明報 (Hong Kong: 19 April 2006 (p. A30 Forum)).

110. The source of the information on hydraulic energy and the flower industry was an interview with Professor Tuan Chyau 段樵 by Ms Law Wing-fai 羅詠暉, a news reporter with Radio Television Hong Kong (channel 1), which aired on 2 June 2006.

111. When the port facilities of Guangxi's three harbours, namely Fangchenggang 防城港, Qinzhouwan 欽州灣 and Beihai 北海, are further developed and brought up to date, the Zhuang Nationality Autonomous Region economy growth will boom. In 2005, the largest amount of capital invested in Guangxi was from Hong Kong, at US$3.8 billion. Most of that sum was invested in land for commercial use and in infrastructure, and accounted for 45% of total investment from outside the autonomous region. Interview reported by Ms Law Wing-fai, news reporter with Radio Television Hong Kong (channel 1), aired on 1 June 2006.

112. Zhang, "Xianggang zai bianyuanhua?" (see note 109).

113. To quote former chief executive of the Hong Kong SAR, Tung Chee-hwa 董建華, "Beikao zuguo, mianxiang guoji" 背靠祖國 面向國際, or "Hong Kong Faces the World with the Fatherland as Its Strong Backer," in Zhang, "Xianggang zai bianyuanhua?" (see note 109); interview with Professor Tuan Chyau (see note 110); interview with Professor Anthony G. O. Yeh 葉嘉安

by Ms Law Wing-fai, news reporter with Radio Television Hong Kong (channel 1), aired on 2 June 2006; and Wang, "Jielun pian: Xianggang xiandai shehui" (see note 102).

114. Interview with Professor Yeh. Ibid.

115. Wu Songdi 吳松弟, "Gangkou—fudi he Zhongguo xiandaihua kongjian jincheng yanjiu gaishuo" 港口——腹地和中國現代化空間進程研究概說 (Harbour-hinterland and Spatial Development of China's Modernization), *Zhejian xuekan* 浙江學刊 (Zhejiang Academic Journal) (Hangzhou 杭州: Zhejiang Academy of Social Science 浙江省社會科學院, 2006), pp. 25–35.

116. Interview with Guangdong governor, Huang Huahua 黃華華, reported by Cheng Manqing 程滿清 and three other news reporters with the *Nanfang Daily* 南方日報, Guangzhou, 2 June 2006, p. A02.

3

Geographical Background and Strategic Networking

Zhang Li

Introduction

Deepening reforms and a greater penetration of global forces in the Chinese economy in the last two decades have redrawn the map of China's geo-economy — reinforcing a spatial clustering of the economy, widening regional disparities, and causing the segregation of domestic markets. Since the 1980s, China has become increasingly integrated into the global market system. As a result, certain regions along its Pacific coast, notably the Pearl River Delta Economic Region 珠江三角洲經濟區 (hereafter, PRD), the Yangzi River Delta Economic Region 長江三角洲經濟區 (hereafter, YRD) and the Bohai Rim Economic Region 渤海灣經濟區 (hereafter, BRR),[1] have become the agglomerative centres for a variety of Fordist style manufacturing operations and are often labelled "world factories" (Figure 3.1).[2] The formation of these manufacturing clusters has mainly been driven by the development of the new international division of labour and reflects a good match with the strategy of multinational corporations (MNCs) of relocating manufacturing operations to places with low production costs. Concurrently, external forces leading to the formation of manufacturing clusters have been reinforced by preferential national and regional policies to establish different types of economic open zones or industrial parks,[3] and also by efforts to increase region-wide synergies.[4] Consequently, the above-mentioned regions have led China in such economic indicators as gross domestic product (GDP) growth, import and export volumes, foreign direct investment (FDI), disposable income, and retail sales. They are also platforms for China's growing integration with the global economy.

Strong outward linkages propelled by economic globalization and open policies are the major engine of growth in certain Chinese regions, mainly coastal cities with good access to ports. Early commercial and industrial development in coastal China led to the rise of cities such as Guangzhou 廣州, Shanghai 上海, Tianjin 天津, and Qingdao 青島, where foreign imperial powers played an important role until 1949. Beginning in 1978, China adopted a policy of openness aimed at attracting FDI and promoting foreign trade. Those coastal cities thereupon became major destinations of FDI due to their locational and competitive advantages. Regional disparities are observed to have widened, because the development impact of foreign-driven and export-led industrialization is location-selective.[5] Foreign capital investments in China have mainly focused on export-oriented but low-end (low-technology and labour-intensive) assembly and processing

Figure 3.1 The Geographical Location of Three Economic Regions in China

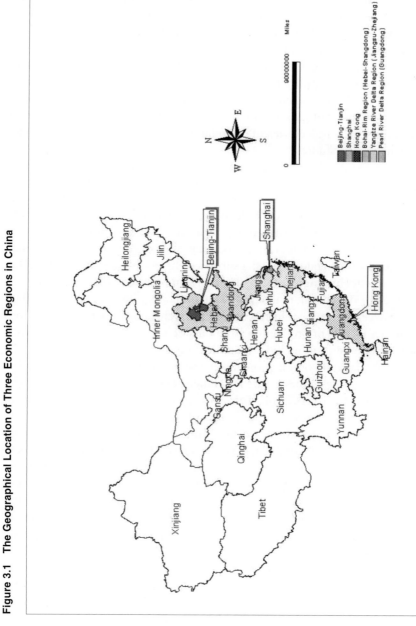

operations.[6] Foreign-invested enterprises are largely concentrated in several
coastal areas with easy access to international markets, thereby limiting
their developmental effect to a small geographic space and intensifying
tendencies towards polarization in the national economy.[7] Regions
inaccessible to international markets and therefore less attractive to foreign
investors have lagged badly in development. Most backward regions are
located in the central and western parts of the country. Poor regional
economic linkages and cooperation have limited the development-diffusing
effect of the developed regions and have further exacerbated regional
disparities. The trajectories of regional disparities have been documented
in a number of studies.[8]

Meanwhile, the national market has become increasingly fragmented
as an inevitable consequence of intra-regional and inter-regional
competition. In the wake of reforms aimed at achieving economic
decentralization, every local bureaucracy sought to expand its revenues by
competing to offer investment opportunities. Despite different levels of
development and comparative advantages, most regions of China share
similar resource endowments: a surplus of labour but a scarcity of capital,
and a low technological level. This, in combination with the bottom-up
strategy of development that has been both a requirement and a corollary
of the decentralization reforms, has led to severe competition among regions
to attract factors of production from outside sources. The negative effects
of such competition include: a duplication of infrastructure projects as a
result of a lack of coordination and cooperation, the ineffective utilization
of limited land resources to lure investment, and a segmented cross-regional
market arising from various forms of local protectionism. In empirical
investigations of the "commodity wars" of the late 1980s and 1990s, many
studies have demonstrated that China's domestic market has been
"cellularized" along administrative boundaries.[9] By examining changes to
the pattern of provincial economic structures, Young has suggested that
during much of the reform period China markets were becoming less
integrated.[10] Huang agreed with this thesis of increasing market fragmentation in China.[11] Watson et al. argued that rampant regionalism, referring to
local governments intervening in markets to protect local interests, was a
rational outcome of economic decentralization that created clearly defined
and independent local interests.[12] The increase in the power of local governments to generate and retain revenue from their own economic activities
offered them incentives to pursue developments that did not take into account
the interests of other localities. Some studies found that the greater

involvement of Chinese provinces in international trade coincided with a low level of specialization and a decrease in the magnitude of domestic trade, reflecting a tendency towards fragmentation of the national market.[13]

In the context of economic polarization, market fragmentation, and undue regional competition, the formation of an economic bloc with a common market has been conceived of as a strategic solution to establish a vibrant regional economy and to alleviate the problems of undue regional competition. The assumption is that a common market arrangement would enhance competitiveness and lead to economic complementarities by widening the space for development and expanding market potential. With the aim of promoting regional cooperation and narrowing regional disparities, China also launched new regional development strategies in the Tenth Five-year Plan (2001–2005), with the focus on encouraging better linkages between developed and underdeveloped regions of the country. The establishment of the Pan–Pearl River Delta Region (hereafter, Pan-PRD) 泛珠江三角洲 represents an unprecedented attempt to develop better cross-regional coordination and cooperation in China. Against this backdrop, this chapter first reviews the formation of the Pan-PRD, laying out the basic geographic background of such an economic grouping. It then outlines the economic rationale for a Pan-PRD network. Based on such a review, we perceive that while the Pan-PRD initiative sounds economically logical and attractive, the implementation and realization of this ambitious initiative will be a great challenge.

The Geographical Setting of the Pan–Pearl River Delta Regional

The Pan-PRD, also known as the "nine plus two" cooperation, comprises nine mainland provinces — Fujian 福建, Jiangxi 江西, Hunan 湖南, Guangdong 廣東, Guangxi 廣西, Hainan 海南, Sichuan 四川, Guizhou 貴州, and Yunnan 雲南 and two special administrative regions (SARs) — Hong Kong 香港 and Macao 澳門. Geographically, it is a very large region. Membership in this super economic bloc is based on physical and economic considerations.

One of the geographical bases of the Pan-PRD is the catchment area of the largest river system in South China — the Pearl River 珠江. The Pearl River is formed by the confluence of three tributary rivers — the Xijiang 西江, Beijiang 北江, and Dongjiang 東江. The Xijiang has its headwaters in the Nanpan River 南盤江 and the Beipan River 北盤江 in the Wumeng

Mountain Area 烏蒙山區 of Yunnan, and runs through Yunnan, Guizhou, and Guangxi before flowing into the South China Sea. The Beijiang starts in the southern part of Hunan and Jiangxi. The Dongjiang has its source in southern Jiangxi. The three rivers meet in Guangdong, fanning out as a large estuary between Hong Kong and Macao and flowing into the South China Sea through eight outlets, mainly at Humen 虎門, Jiaomen 蕉門, Hongqimen 洪奇門, Hengmen 橫門, Modaomen 磨刀門, Jitimen 雞啼門, Hutiaomen 虎跳門, and Yamen 崖門. By converging on three rivers, the Pearl River links Yunnan, Guizhou, Guangxi, Hunan, Jiangxi, Guangdong, Hong Kong, and Macao.

Another loose geographic factor contributing to the formation of the Pan-PRD is its geographical contiguity to the Greater Pearl River Delta Region (GPRD) 大珠江三角洲, the economic core of the Pan-PRD. Since the introduction of economic reforms in China in the late 1970s, the GPRD, which consists of the Hong Kong SAR, the Macao SAR, and the Pearl River Delta Economic Region of Guangdong province, has emerged as one of the world's most dynamic economic regions. Having received a large amount of FDI, the GPRD has become a big provider of non-agricultural jobs, and attracts a large number of migrant workers from other parts of China. The integration of Hong Kong, Macao, and the PRD has contributed significantly to the Guangdong's prosperity.[14] The Pan-PRD is a further extension of the GPRD. Several members of the Pan-PRD, such as Hainan, Guangxi, Hunan, Jiangxi, and Fujian, are geographically adjacent to the GPRD and are perceived to be able to benefit from their attachment to this economic powerhouse.

Apart from being part of a fluvial network and geographical contiguity, membership in the Pan-PRD would also seem to be based on economic relations. Most obvious is the case of Sichuan. Although not a part of the Pearl River basin and lying distant from Guangdong, Sichuan is included in the Pan-PRD grouping. This is due largely to the province's close economic ties with Guangdong, the advocator of the Pan-PRD concept.[15] Guangdong is regarded as a major gateway for Sichuan to international markets.[16] It is also well known that Sichuan, one of the most populous provinces in China, has been a major provider of labour to Guangdong's labour-intensive industries during the past two decades.[17] In 2004, 7.4 million Sichuan labourers worked in other provinces, 76% of them in coastal regions, with Guangdong being one of the major destinations. Remittances sent home by Sichuan migrant workers have played a vital role in Sichuan's development. It has been reported that remittances sent by migrant labourers from rural areas of Sichuan amounted to RMB57.6 billion in 2004, or about RMB3,300 per labourer.[18]

By adopting multiple criteria for membership, the Pan-PRD has become the largest economic bloc in China, far surpassing similar economic groupings. By 2004, the region had a total land area of about 2 million sq. km and an aggregate population of 463 million, accounting for 21% and 36%, respectively, of the country's total, (Table 3.1), several times larger than other economic regions on both counts (Table 3.2). The population of the Pan-PRD is roughly the same as that of the European Union.[19] The territorial immensity of the Pan-PRD means that geographical conditions inside the area are diverse. Table 3.3 summarizes its diversity.

The Pan-PRD region spans different geographic zones generally characterized from east to west by a dichotomy between coastal and inland areas. Some members of the grouping, such as Guangdong, Fujian, Hong Kong, and Macao, border on the South China Sea, and have long coastal lines and alluvial plains, a moist monsoon climate, and a high population density.[20] Guangdong and Fujian contained the most important ports in Chinese history and had a close connection to the "Maritime Silk Road." Hong Kong and Macao also later became famed port cities. The populations of Guangdong and Fujian have strong ties to ethnic Chinese overseas. Such geographical features provide favourable conditions for the development of an internationally oriented economy. In contrast, some members of the grouping, such as Guizhou, Yunnan, Guangxi, and Sichuan, possess much stronger "interior" topographical characteristics, with highlands, mountains, and basins making up their main landforms. Nonetheless, those provinces have relatively abundant natural resources such as water, diverse species of plants, and non-ferrous metals. However, they are remote to sea routes. Guizhou and Yunnan are also noted for their high ethnic diversity. Other members of the grouping, such as Jiangxi and Hunan, are situated in the so-called central economic region, the regional division that the Chinese government used to formulate its regional policies during the period of the Seventh Five-year Plan (1986–1990). Many areas of both provinces are hilly and are linked by tributaries of the Yangzi River. Their topography is characterized by interspersed mountains and valleys. Differences in their geographical conditions, particularly in natural resource endowments, indicate the possibility of complementary areas of development and the potential for cooperation among the Pan-PRD members.

Certain members of the Pan-PRD region possess strategic locations with a wide range of geo-political implications for their development. Being adjacent to international borders, for example, means that the prosperity of southwestern members of the Pan-PRD region is always linked to the state

Table 3.1   Land and Population of the Pan-PRD, 2004

	Land area		Population		Population density (persons/sq km)
	Size (10,000 sq km)	% of China[1]	No. (million)	% of China[1]	
Guangdong	18.0	1.9	83.04	6.4	461
Guangxi	23.7	2.5	48.89	3.8	206
Fujian	12.1	1.3	35.11	2.7	290
Jiangxi	16.7	1.7	42.84	3.3	257
Hunan	21.2	2.2	66.98	5.2	316
Sichuan	48.5	5.1	87.25	6.7	180
Yunnan	39.4	4.1	44.15	3.4	112
Guizhou	17.6	1.8	39.04	3.0	222
Hainan	3.5	0.4	8.18	0.6	234
Nine provinces	200.7	20.9	455.48	35.0	227
Hong Kong	0.11	0.0001	6.88[2]	0.5	6,880
Macao	0.003	<0.0001	0.46[2]	0.04	1,533

Notes: 1. National data do not include the figure for Hong Kong, Macao and Taiwan.
2. Mid-year population in 2004.

Sources: National Bureau of Statistics (NBS) 國家統計局, *Zhongguo tongji nianjian 2005* 中國統計年鑒2005 (China Statistical Yearbook 2005) (Beijing: Zhongguo tongji chubanshe, 2005). Department of Comprehensive Statistics on the National Economy, National Bureau of Statistics (NBS) 國家統計局國民經濟綜合統計司, *Xinzhongguo wushiwunian tongji ziliao huibian 1949–2004* 新中國五十五年統計資料彙編1949–2004 (New China Compendium of Statistics 1949–2004) (Beijing: China Statistics Press, 2005).

Table 3.2   Comparison of the Physical and Economic Size of Major Economic Regions, 2004

	BBR	YRD	PRD	Pan-PRD
Land area (1,000 sq km)	374.2	109.6	41.5	2,007.0
As of national total (%)	3.9	1.1	0.4	20.9
Population (million)	185.06	82.12	24.51	455.48
As of national total (%)	14.2	6.3	1.9	35.0
GDP (RMB billion)	3,147.47	2,877.54	1,339.40	4,639.78
As of national total (%)	23.0	21.02	9.79	33.9
GDP per capita (RMB/person)	17,008	35,040	54,639	10,187
Exports (US$ billion)	80.48	208.30	182.22	238.60
As of national total (%)	13.6	35.1	30.7	40.2
Realized FDI (US$ billion)	15.88	25.44	10.153	14.433
As of national total (%)	26.19	41.96	16.75	26.98

Sources: Compiled from *Zhongguo tongji nianjian 2005*. International Statistical Information Centre of the NBS, *Changjiang he Zhujiang Sanjiaozhou ji Gangao tebie xingzhengqu tongji nianjian 2005* (see note 30).

Table 3.3 Major Features of the Physical Geography of the Nine Mainland Provinces

Province	Average altitudinal level	Climate	Land characteristics	Major mineral resources
Guangdong	Step 3 of China's terrain; < 500 m above sea level	Subtropical monsoon climate; warm and humid	25% hills; 33% mountains; 23% plains; 19% tableland	Coal, iron ore, kaolin, peat, metallurgical gangue, germanium, antimony, silver, lead, bismuth, thallium, uranium, monazite, glass silicon
Guangxi	Step 2 of China's terrain; between 1,000 m and 2,000 m above sea level	Subtropical monsoon climate	85% hills and mountains; 15% plains	Tin, antimony, silver, bauxite, tantalum, tungsten, titanium, lead, mercury, niobium, chromium, cobalt, beryllium, yttrium, scandium
Fujian	Step 3 of China's terrain; < 500 m above sea level	Subtropical maritime climate; warm and humid	90% hills and mountains	Gold, silver, lead, zinc, manganese, kaolin, limestone, granite, alunite, pyrophyllite, sulfur, quartz-sandstone
Jiangxi	Step 3 of China's terrain; < 500 m above sea level	Subtropical monsoon climate; warm and humid	42% hills; 36% mountains; 22% plains and water body	Copper, tungsten, gold, silver, uranium, thorium, niobium
Hunan	Step 3 of China's terrain; < 500 m above sea level	Subtropical monsoon climate; warm and humid	80% mountains and hills; 20% plains	Wolfram, bismuth, antimony, fluorite, barite, feldspar, sepiolite, kaolin, albeit, manganese, vanadium
Sichuan	Step 2 of China's terrain	Subtropical monsoon climate in the Sichuan basin; Plateau climate in the Western Sichuan Plateau	Basin and rough plateau	Oil, natural gas, coal, iron, copper, lead, zinc, aluminum, platinum, gold, nickel, asbestos, phosphorus
Yunnan	Step 2 of China's terrain	Three climate zones (temperate, subtropical and tropical) from north to south	93% hills and mountains	Tin, zinc, titanium, copper, antimony, phosphorous
Guizhou	Step 2 of China's terrain	Subtropical humid climate	93% mountains and plateaus	Coal, phosphorus, mercury, aluminum, manganese, antimony, gold, barite
Hainan	Step 3 of China's terrain; < 500 m above sea level	Tropical and maritime monsoon climate	13% hills; 25% mountains; 33% mesa; 29% savanna	Oil, natural gas, iron-ore arenaceous quartz, zirconium, nitrogenous fertilizer rock, titanium

Sources: Compiled from the statistical yearbooks of the various provinces.

of China's foreign relations and to border trade. Guangxi and Yunnan share borders with several Southeast Asian developing countries, such as Vietnam, Laos, and Myanmar, making these two provinces particularly important in efforts to achieve both national security and economic cooperation with Southeast Asian nations. At the same time, Guangdong's leading position in economic development is a direct consequence of its coastal position, which provides it with easy access to Hong Kong and to international markets. In fact, since China's centrally planned economy shifted to a reorientation towards the world economy, Hong Kong has been the main source of FDI in the country. Finally, being located on one side of the Taiwan Strait, Fujian can boost its economy by linking its future to China's unification with Taiwan 台灣.

Given its huge territory and diverse geopolitical conditions, it is not surprising that the Pan-PRD is a heterogeneous grouping, with uneven levels of development and international linkages (Table 3.4). The general pattern of economic development is that of a steep decline from east to west, with provinces that lie further from China's coast lagging behind. This feature is illustrated in Table 3.4. Although they are certainly not large in land area and population, the two SARs are much richer than the other members of the grouping in terms of per capita GDP. Table 3.4 also shows that the nine mainland provinces of the Pan-PRD together accounted for about 34% of the nation's GDP and 40% of its exports, and received 27% of the nation's FDI. However, Guangdong alone accounted for 35% of total GDP and 81% of the exports generated by the nine provinces. Meanwhile, about 54% of the foreign investment in the nine provinces went to Guangdong.[21] Provinces located in the southwestern part of China only attracted a small fraction of China-bound FDI. Whereas the two SARs and Guangdong top the region in economic indicators and form the economic core of the region, the other participants are economic laggards and peripheral members. Their per capita GDP is lower than the national average. In fact, Guizhou and Yunnan are two of the poorest provinces in China.

The principles behind the formation of the Pan-PRD and the geographical setting of the group's members suggest that, to a great extent, the regionalization of the grouping goes against the normative principles in China for creating economic groupings. With the aim of maximizing trans-regional comparative advantages, China has introduced various economic regionalization schemes and has organized different multi-provincial macro-economic regions 大經濟區 or economically coordinated regions 經濟協作區 since the period of socialist planning. Conventionally,

Table 3.4   Selected Economic Indicators of the Pan-PRD, 2004

	GDP (RMB billion, at current prices)	GDP per capita (RMB)	GDP composition (%)			Imports (US$ billion)	Exports		Retail sales of consumer goods (RMB billion)	Actual FDI[3]	
			Primary	Secondary	Tertiary		Amount (US$ billion)	As % of its GDP[2]		Amount (US$ million)	As % of China[1]
Guangdong	1,603.95	19,707	7.8	55.4	36.8	170.94	192.4	96.3	637.04	7,822.94	14.6
Guangxi	332.01	7,196	24.4	38.8	36.8	2.5	2.3	5.6	97.34	418.56	0.78
Fujian	605.31	17,218	12.9	48.7	38.4	19.3	30.6	40.6	199.58	2,599.03	4.9
Jiangxi	349.6	8,189	20.4	45.6	34.0	2.2	2.6	6.0	105.99	1,612.02	3.0
Hunan	561.23	9,117	20.6	39.5	39.9	2.9	3.1	4.4	206.98	1,018.35	1.9
Sichuan	655.60	8,113	21.3	41.0	37.7	3.2	3.5	4.3	238.40	412.31	0.77
Yunnan	295.95	6,733	20.4	44.4	35.2	1.7	2.0	5.4	88.49	83.84	0.16
Guizhou	159.19	4,215	21.0	44.9	34.1	1.1	1.3	6.6	51.76	45.21	0.08
Hainan	76.94	9,450	36.9	23.4	39.7	2.1	0.8	8.3	22.02	421.25	0.79
Nine provinces	4,639.78	10,187				205.94	238.6	41.3	1,647.60	14,433.51	26.98
National[1]	13,687.59	10,561	15.2	52.9	31.9	561.23	593.33	34.8		53,504.7	100.0
Hong Kong	1,516[4]	220,342[4]	0.1	10.3	89.6	270.66[4]	258.86[4]	137.2			
Macao	85.17[5]	186,394[5]	0.0	13.1[3]	91.2[3]	3.37[5]	2.7[5]	27.3			

Notes: 1. Data for Hong Kong and Macao are not included.
2. US$100 to RMB803
3. Data in 2003.
4. HK$100 to RMB103, US$100 to HK$780.
5. MOP100 to RMB103, US$100 to MOP828.

Source: *Zhongguo tongji nianjian 2005.*

the delimitation of a subnational economic region emphasizes geographical propinquity, similar natural attributes, similar levels of economic and social development, and long-standing historical ties among the members of that grouping. Having a leading centre in the economic region and being of a manageable size is also regarded as conducive to cooperation and integration among the members of such a grouping, and therefore to its success. Because of its immense size and diversity, the Pan-PRD is a larger and more complex spatial structure than other regional groupings in China, with various economic and social interactions taking place among territorial units that are at different levels of development.

The Economic Rationale behind the Pan-PRD Strategic Network

The concept of the Pan-PRD was first advocated by the then Guangdong Communist Party Secretary Zhang Dejiang 張德江 in July 2003. Centring on the GPRD and falling under the framework of the Closer Economic Partnership Arrangement (CEPA) pacts between the mainland and the two SARs, the aim behind the Pan-PRD concept is to facilitate large-scale regional cooperation and integration. Functioning as an economic powerhouse rather than as a political big brother, Guangdong has taken the lead in pushing forward the concept. Guangdong invited neighbouring provinces to participate in this economic bloc. After a series of preparatory meetings and round-table discussions, nine provinces plus the two SARs jointly signed "the Pan-PRD Regional Cooperation Framework Agreement" in June 2004, officially unveiling the establishment of the Pan-PRD. Table 3.5 highlights the timeline and major events in the formation of the Pan-PRD region. Under the principle of "the market leads, the government facilitates," the members of the Pan-PRD have agreed to form closer ties, in an open and fair manner, in 10 different business sectors to achieve a "win-win" situation. These business sectors include infrastructure, industry and investment, commerce and trade, tourism, agriculture, labour, science, education and culture, information technology, environmental protection, and public health (Table 3.6). The members of the grouping have also agreed to remove trade barriers within the region.

Guangdong's motive for promoting the ambitious concept of the Pan-PRD lies in the constraints it faces on sustainable industrialization. These constraints include the province's weak capabilities in R&D, producer and professional services that do not meet international standards, and the

Table 3.5 Timeline of the Formation of the Pan-PRD

24 July 2003	Guangdong Party Secretary Zhang Dejiang first advocated the concept of the Pan-PRD.
8-9 August 2003	Officials of the Development and Planning Commission of the nine provinces met in Guangzhou to reach a preliminary consensus on the establishment of the Pan-PRD.
September 2003	Guangdong Party Secretary Zhang Dejiang, Guangdong Governor Huang Huahua 黃華華 and Guangdong Standing Vice-governor Zhong Yangsheng 鍾陽勝, approved the report presented by the Guangdong Development and Reform Committee on accelerating the formation and development of the Pan-PRD Economic Region.
8 October 2003	Relevant governmental officials of the nine member provinces met in Foshan 佛山 to discuss the establishment of cooperative mechanisms for the Pan-PRD.
3 November 2003	In the "2003 Guangdong International Consultative Conference," Guangdong Party Secretary Zhang Dejiang first disclosed the plan for the Pan-PRD regional cooperation to international delegates.
11 November 2003	"The framework of technological cooperation in the Pan-PRD" was put forward in Guangzhou 廣州.
28–29 November 2003	Governmental representatives of the candidate provinces met in Guangzhou to discuss strengthening regional cooperation in the development of highway networks.
2-3 December 2003	Representatives from the Academies of Social Sciences of the nine candidate provinces plus Chongqing 重慶, Beijing 北京, Hebei 河北 and Ningxia 寧夏 attended the first workshop on the economic cooperation of the Zhujiang (i.e. Pearl River) Valley Region.
2 January 2004	The Guangdong government sent requests to the State Development and Reform Commission, the Hong Kong and Macao Office of the State Council and the Centre of Development Research of the State Council, respectively, for guiding instructions on cooperation and development in the Pan-PRD. In their letters of reply, the three government units supported the idea of the Pan-PRD and agreed to become the members of the guiding committee for the Pan-PRD Regional Cooperation and Development Forum.
6–7 March 2004	In Beijing, Guangdong Party Secretary Zhang Dejiang and Guangdong Governor Huang Huahua met with the Macao SAR's Chief Executive Ho Hau-wah 何厚鏵 and the Hong Kong SAR's Chief Executive Tung Chee-hwa 董建華 to exchange views on the Pan-PRD. The decision was made to hold the Pan-PRD Regional Cooperation and Development Forum in July in Hong Kong, Macao and Guangzhou.
18 March 2004	Representatives of the Investment Promotion Organizations of the candidate provinces attended a seminar on cooperating in efforts to promote investment in the region.
8 April 2004	The preparatory meeting for the Pan-PRD Regional Cooperation and Development Forum was organized by the Guangdong Development and Reform Committee.
20 May 2004	The Plenary Session of the Organizing Committee of the Pan-PRD Regional Cooperation and Development Forum was held in Guangzhou.
1 June 2004	Governors of the member provinces and the Chief Executives of two SARs attended the Pan-PRD Regional Cooperation and Development Forum in Hong Kong.
3 June 2004	Leaders of the members signed the Pan-PRD Regional Cooperation Framework Agreement in Guangzhou.

Source: Compiled from "The Pan-PRD Regional Cooperation and Development Forum," 中國新聞網 http://www.chinanews.com.cn/n/2004-05-31/40/332.html; China Today, http://www.chinatoday.com.cn/china/2004/0408/32.htm.

Table 3.6   Areas of Cooperation in the Pan-PRD

Area	Cooperation content
Infrastructure	• Establishing networks for transmitting energy resources from resource-rich provinces to areas of high consumption; • Building up intra-regional transportation network, including road, railway, water transport, as well as cooperation between airports in the Region
Industry and investment	• Creating a fair, open and attractive investment environment; • Establishing a transparent, helpful and standardized investment promotion mechanism; • Supporting cooperation in technology, products and investment to form complementary industrial structures
Commerce and trade	• Eliminating intra-regional trade barriers; • Cooperating in setting product standards; • Mutually recognizing product testimonials, inspections, and registrations or certifications
Tourism	• Cooperating in the formulation of regional tourism development and marketing strategies; • Setting up a database on regional tourism and an e-tourism platform; • Developing and promoting fine tour routes;
Agriculture	• Establishing a stable marketing mechanism for agricultural products; • Opening regional "barrier-free channels" for agricultural products; • Cooperating in the establishment of a regional system on food safety
Labour and manpower	• Establishing an information system on labour markets; • Facilitating the intra-regional mobility of labour; • Coordinating to protect labour rights; • Mutually recognizing the qualifications for technical skills
Science and culture	• Propelling cooperation among higher education and research institutions; • Establishing a platform for regional technological cooperation and the commercialization of research outcomes
Information technology	• Forging regional networks for the exchange of information; • Strengthening and standardizing e-commerce rules and regulations; • Cooperating in research on information technology and in its application
Environmental protection	• Establishing a mechanism for regional coordination in environmental protection; • Drawing up plans for regional environmental protection; • Strengthening ecological protection in upstream areas of the Pearl River
Sanitation and the prevention of epidemics	• Coordinating to circulate the latest information on epidemics; • Advancing technology in the prevention and control of epidemics

Source: The Pan-PRD Regional Cooperation Framework Agreement, see China Today, http://www.chinatoday.com.cn/china/2004/0408/25.htm.

keen competition among PRD cities and their increasing reluctance to cooperate with each other.[22] Because of successful economic reforms and its proximity to Hong Kong, the PRD, the core of Guangdong's development, grew rapidly in the 1980s and 1990s, ahead of other major economic regions such as the YRD and the BRR in terms of GDP growth, the intake of FDI, and export volumes. Driven mainly by investment from Hong Kong and having benefited from a division of labour in the Hong Kong–Guangdong linkage,[23] the PRD cities have come to lead the world in such industries as electronics, household appliances, telecommunications and computer equipment, toys, timepieces, lamps and light fixtures, garments, footwear, plastic products, and ceramics.[24] In just over two decades, the PRD has successfully transformed itself from an agricultural backwater to a world juggernaut in light manufacturing.

However, this "world factory" has been formed largely by a combination of foreign investment, technology, and business services, and an almost inexhaustible pool of cheap labour from inland provinces. It has so far been sustained by price-competitive rather than innovative products.[25] Although it has a strong capacity for manufacturing certain goods, the PRD itself has few of its own internationally known brand names. This development pattern is a result of low levels of research and education in the PRD and little R&D.[26] In fact, the PRD's fast economic growth in the past two decades has been based mainly on its advantages of cheap land and labour, and on foreign capital and technology, resulting in a "buyer-driven" industrialization.[27]

A focus on low value-added manufacturing has caused the PRD's economy to be at the very low end of a global value chain. Perhaps due to comparative weakness in human capital and business know-how, value creation in the PRD has mainly been confined to buyer-driven production. Although 37% of the PRD's GDP is currently derived from the tertiary industry and over 70% of its utilized FDI is in the manufacturing industry,[28] there has not been enough advanced producer and business services in the PRD to attract and sustain higher value-added manufacturing. While a global productive cluster has already emerged in the PRD, high-level supporting services that add value to manufacturing and enhance productivity are only slowly being developed.

Undue competition has created another constraint on the PRD's development. The PRD is not an entirely uniform economic entity but rather a constellation of discrete jurisdictions with different levels of administration and development. However, within a relatively small geographic space, the PRD's jurisdictions do not have heterogeneous and supplementary resource endowments. Such a similarity of resource endowments, in combination with locally self-financing development as a result of decentralization, seems to offer a justification for intercity competition for outside investment. Indeed, each jurisdiction in the PRD has its own development agenda that shows little concern for the development plans of neighbouring cities.[29] The provincial government suffers from a lack of resources and has little authority to coordinate local development, as most development projects are initiated and financed at the local level. Although competition among the cities of the PRD have in part contributed to its dynamic growth, the lack of effective cooperation among them has also created many problems, such as redundant infrastructure and development projects, and the offer of free land to lure investment. After years of extensive growth and over-competition, PRD cities are beginning to experience, to various degrees, bottlenecks in land and a shortage of resources, including in the supply of labour, particularly skilled labour.

While the PRD continues to experience growth, the pace has slowed recently, allowing other regions to catch up. In recent years, the YRD and the BRR have been challenging the PRD in GDP and export growth (Table 3.7).[30] This process has been reinforced by a geographical shift in FDI from the PRD to the YRD and the BRR (Table 3.8). It should be noted that it is difficult to compare the economic indicators shown in Tables 3.7 and 3.8 because the regions differ in size. Nonetheless, the tables show that the YRD and the BRR have been growing very dynamically in recent years. They have become other magnets for FDI (Table 3.8). The rapid rise of the YRD and the BRR as major growth poles in the country has aroused the

Table 3.7   Selected Economic Indicators of Three Major Economic Regions in China, 2004

	Population (million)	GDP (RMB billion)	GDP per capita (RMB/ person)	Foreign trade (US$ billion)	Exports (US$ billion)	Realized FDI (US$ billion)
National total	1,299.88	13,687.59	10,560	1,154.55	593.32	60.63
BRR	185.06	3,147.47	17,008	170.75	80.48	15.88
YRD	82.1	2,877.54	35,040	401.23	208.30	25.44
PRD	24.5	1,339.40	54,639	341.78	182.22	10.15

Note: National figures do not include figures for Hong Kong, Macao and Taiwan.
Source: *Zhongguo tongji nianjian 2005.*

Table 3.8   Realized FDI, by Economic Region, 1990–2004

Region	1990	2000	2002	2003	2004
Amount (US$ millions)					
National total	6,596	40,715	52,743	53,505	60,630
BRR	502	6,500	8,223	10,706	15,880
YRD	402	10,708	23,514	21,716	25,440
PRD	2,186	8,387	14,236	10,117	10,153
National Share (%)					
National total	100.0	100.0	100.0	100.0	100.0
BRR	7.61	15.96	15.59	20.01	26.19
YRD	6.09	26.3	44.58	40.59	41.96
PRD	33.14	20.6	26.99	18.91	16.75

Note: The national total does not include the figures for Hong Kong, Macao and Taiwan.

Sources: Compiled from *Zhongguo tongji nianjian 2005*. International Statistical Information Centre of the National Bureau of Statistics 國家統計局國際統計信息中心, *Changjiang and Zhujiang Sanjiaozhou ji Gangao tebie xingzhengqu tongji nianjian*, various years (see note 30); Shandong Provincial Bureau of Statistics 山東省統計局, *Shandong tongji nianjian 2005* 山東統計年鑒2005 (Shandong Statistical Yearbook 2005) (Beijing: Zhongguo tongji chubanshe, 2005); Hebei Provincial Government 河北省人民政府, *Hebei jingji nianjian 2005* 河北經濟年鑒2005 (Hebei Economic Yearbook 2005) (Beijing: Zhongguo tongji chubanshe, 2005); and Secretariat of the 21st Forum on Statistics and Information 第二十一屆統計信息交流會秘書處, *Zhixiashi, fushengjishi, jingji tequ he yanhai kaifang chengshi tongji ziliao huibian 2004* 直轄市，副省級市，經濟特區和沿海開放城市統計資料彙編2004 (The Collection of Statistics for Cities Directly under the Central Government, Vice-provincial Cities, Special Economic Zones and Coastal Open Cities 2004).

concern among Guangdong's policy-makers for the future of the PRD. It is perceived that the major disadvantages of the PRD, compared with its rivals, are its less versatile factors of production, lack of sophisticated producer services, and a small and uneven hinterland, economically speaking.[31] The small geographic size of the PRD is regarded as the main constraint in efforts to achieve economies of scale and larger markets. If the PRD wants to retain its dynamism and, most importantly, its leading position in the country, it has to explore new markets and offer new opportunities for development. On the one hand, it needs to increase integration with Hong Kong to upgrade its industries; on the other, it needs to expand its hinterland to a size at least on a par with other competitors. This premise is at the basis of Pan-PRD cooperation.

Whatever the economic rationale behind the formation of the grouping, the idea of the Pan-PRD is attractive, as such a grouping could bring the complementary advantages of the regional members into full play. It is said that the notion of the Pan-PRD is in line with the strategy set by the central government for promoting coordinated regional development.[32] It will help to boost Hong Kong's economy, which is facing many challenges from the restructuring of its economy under globalization. Through closer ties and cooperation, the proposed objective of this strategic regionalization is to remove the obstacles of administrative boundaries and to create a common market within the region. In this common market, trade barriers between members will be removed and the free flow of factors of production (capital, labour, etc.) will be facilitated. The aim is to achieve better utilization of resources and eventually to enhance the region's competitiveness. At the same time, Hong Kong can gain access not only to a larger and more diverse Chinese market, but also a more integrated one. More specifically, the Pan-PRD region would provide more opportunities for Hong Kong's capital and service sectors, and ease the pressure on Hong Kong as it restructures its economy.

Prospects of a Pan-PRD Network

Judging from the current scheme, the Pan-PRD is simply a loose economic bloc that emphasizes complementary comparative advantages and mutual economic benefits in the development process as the basis for the grouping. For the time being, the essence of cooperation among the Pan-PRD members is "prosperity through partnership," the theme of the Pan-PRD Regional Cooperation Forum held in June 2004 in Hong Kong. What the Pan-PRD aims to achieve is to raise the overall competitiveness of the region through better and closer cooperation. The signatories to the cooperation framework agreed to participate on a voluntary basis in all or some of the areas of cooperation outlined in Table 3.6. Given its extensive geographic coverage, non-rigid and informal organizational nature, existing differences in resources, economic structures and stages of development, and the lopsided economic benefits to the members, the region faces several challenges to realizing its high-minded rhetoric on regional cooperation.

Institutionally, the Pan-PRD is a very loose cooperative organization. At least at the initial stage, it is not intended to be a rigid and formal organization or agreement like the European Union (EU) or the North American Free Trade Agreement (NAFTA). This is because the Pan-PRD is not a new cascading tier of administrative units mandated by the central government. Although the central government has taken a positive attitude towards the idea of the Pan-PRD, the idea itself did not come from the central authorities but from Guangdong. It is a kind of agreement between provincial administrations of the same administrative ranking, and its members are not bound by a strong central authority. It should be noted that no central preferential policies were granted to the Pan-PRD and no-vice premier attended the first Pan-PRD Regional Cooperation and Development Forum. This is rare for such events, and indicates that the central government played little role in facilitating the formation of this grouping. Politically, no member is regarded as constituting the centre of the region with the authority to play a leadership role in this new setup. Fundamentally, economic incentives define the basis of the Pan-PRD grouping. Consequently, the implementation of such a province-led and economic regionalization is entirely free from political provisos or commitments. In the absence of political obligations and against the background of various overlapping regionalization arrangements, it is uncertain if the current members share the same mindset on Pan-PRD regionalization or can be strongly bound by it. Furthermore, the factors that delimit the region are rather stable over time. Indeed, the regionalization of the Pan-PRD is a different idea from the one very recently proposed by a state think-tank for the Eleventh Five-year Plan (2006–2010) in a plan for coordinated regional development. The State Council's Centre of Development Research has suggested that the country be organized into eight Comprehensive Economic Zones (CEZs) 綜合經濟區, in which members of the Pan-PRD will be designated into different CEZs (Table 3.9).

This brings up the related issue of the enthusiasm of the members in participating in the grouping and the cohesiveness of the grouping. Not all members of the Pan-PRD are active proponents of the idea because most members have only loose economic ties. In addition, some members of the grouping would stand to gain much more from the regionalization of the Pan-PRD than others. While the economies of Guangdong and Hong Kong are inextricably linked with each other and are becoming more integrated other time, such bilateral or multilateral links and integration are nearly absent in other parts of the region. Indeed, it is very difficult for other parts of the Pan-PRD to match the distinctive combinations and complementarities that have contributed to the growth of Guangdong and Hong Kong. Some participants, such as Yunnan, Jiangxi, Fujian, and Sichuan, are half-hearted

Table 3.9   Organization of Comprehensive Economic Zones (CEZs) for the Eleventh Five-year Plan (2006–2010)

Northeast CEZ	Liaoning 遼寧, Jilin 吉林, Heilongjiang 黑龍江
Northern coastal CEZ	Beijing 北京, Tianjin 天津, Hebei 河北, Shandong 山東
Eastern coastal CEZ	Shanghai 上海, Jiangsu 江蘇, Zhejiang 浙江
Southern coastal CEZ	Fujian, Guangdong, Hainan
Yellow River middle-reaches CEZ	Shaanxi 陝西, Shanxi 山西, Henan 河南, Inner Mongolia 內蒙古
Yangzi River middle-reaches CEZ	Hubei 湖北, Hunan, Jiangxi, Anhui 安徽
Great southwest CEZ	Yunnan, Guizhou, Sichuan, Chongqing 重慶, Guangxi
Great northwest CEZ	Gansu 甘肅, Qinghai 青海, Ningxia 寧夏, Xizang 西藏, Xinjiang 新疆

Source: http://news.sina.com.cn/c/2005-06-14/01036161586s.shtml.

about becoming part of the region, as they are also informally part of several other economic groupings and are not fixed members of any defined economic region.[33] While leading economic players such as the two SARs and Guangdong stand to benefit greatly from a much broader hinterland for their products and services and can shift their production from high-cost to low-cost places, other economically peripheral members may have to wait a long time for development to spill over and for industries to relocate from the core region — a process that has yet to happen. It is interesting to note that the largest relative gains have gone to the core part of the region. Currently, members of the Pan-PRD have not reached an agreement on the specific role that each member must play to accomplish closer cooperation. Such an agreement is hard to achieve because of rival provincial interests.[34] It is, therefore, not surprising that the provinces that are more geographically distant from the core area show more passivity and less enthusiasm about being drawn into the group than those in the core area. They have kept a relatively lower profile and have not aired detailed proposals for putting the idea of regionalization into practice.

The vast Pan-PRD also presents a dilemma for economic cooperation among the members of the grouping. In theory, complementarities in development can be enhanced among members of that vast territorial entity. Regional integration can create a larger market that can provide opportunities for economies of scale to all members who had previously been confined to more limited markets. However, two interrelated facts mean that conditions for cooperation in the Pan-PRD are not quite as favourable as anticipated.

First, resource endowments in the Pan-PRD are undoubtedly diverse but are not necessarily complementary. In reality, infrastructure problems will have to be overcome if the diverse resources are to be utilized. Certain provinces are not contiguous and are currently not linked by well-developed transport systems, which means that huge infrastructure investment and transport costs will be involved before the benefits of regionalization can be realized. Members of the Pan-PRD are widely separated and several of them occupy locations peripheral to the economic core of the Pan-PRD. Except for energy resources, the members have not relied heavily upon one another's resources but instead have traded mainly finished manufactured goods. The coastal enterprises of the Pan-PRD currently import raw materials mainly from abroad rather than from provinces in the interior. This is an indication that the resource advantage of the underdeveloped provinces has not been integrated into the production chains of the developed provinces.

Second, the collective market in the Pan-PRD is large but far from integrated. Lingering restrictions on intraregional movements of the factors of production remain, as individual members compete for outside investment and introduce non-tariff barriers to the flow of goods across their boundaries. Even economic policies inside the PRD are far from harmonious and the integration within the PRD is not yet complete. Rampant local protectionism constrains the economies of scale that the Pan-PRD regionalization is expected to bring about. It will take years before the Pan-PRD can be become an integrated economic entity.

Conclusion

The formation of the Pan-PRD is not a top-down process of regionalization that has political significance. Instead, it is a voluntary, bottom-up course of economic action. This grand strategy can be readily understood against the background of intensified economic concentration in certain favoured locations under globalization; increased competition among those economic clusters, notably the PRD, the YRD and the BRR; and the fragmentation of the national market caused by local protectionism. Moved by the fear that it will fall behind the YRD and the BRR, and concerned about its lack of a hinterland, Guangdong has shifted the focus of its development from the promotion of an export-oriented economy to one based on economic cooperation, if not full economic integration, with neighbouring provinces. The Pan-PRD has been put forward as the means by which members can become better connected economically and, consequently, through the integration of regional markets, expand their economic space. Although the main purpose of the Pan-PRD seems to be the promotion of regional development, the plan needs to be regarded in two ways. It can be seen as part of an effort among the members of the grouping to achieve regional cooperation, or as part of a strategy among the leading economic players to expand their hinterland.

Theoretically, geographic contiguity, complementary economic structures, equal stages of development, distinctive regional identities, and existing economic relations among the regional actors will determine how regional integration is going to proceed. The immensity of the Pan-PRD presents an intriguing paradox, largely because of geographical incongruity, enormous disparities in development, and loose interaction among the regional actors in that vast territory. On the positive side, this grand scheme of regionalization provides opportunities for its members to make better use of their own comparative advantages. However, space and infrastructure constraints must first be overcome before the region's comparative advantages can be utilized. Furthermore, the real benefit of the Pan-PRD region will be skewed in favour of the economic core. The assets that the laggard provinces possess, such as natural resources and lower costs of production, are not sufficient to attract investors in today's competitive global economy. Obviously, much needs to be done if the aims behind the formation of the Pan-PRD are to be realized.

Notes

1. The geographical delineation of economic regions in China has varied from study to study. Here, we adopt the definition used by China's National Bureau of Statistics. The Pearl River Delta Economic Region is comprised of Guangzhou 廣州, Shenzhen 深圳, Zhuhai 珠海, Foshan 佛山, Jiangmen 江門, Dongguan 東莞, Zhongshan 中山, Huizhou urban district 惠州市區, Huiyang 惠陽, Boluo 博羅 county, Zhaoqing urban district 肇慶市區, Gaoyao 高要 and Sihui 四會. The constituent units of the Yangzi River Delta Economic Region include Shanghai 上海, Nanjing 南京, Suzhou 蘇州, Wuxi 無錫, Changzhou 常州, Zhenjiang 鎮江, Nantong 南通, Yangzhou 揚州, Taizhou 泰州, Hangzhou 杭州, Ningbo 寧波, Jiaxing 嘉興, Huzhou 湖州, Shaoxing 紹興, Zhoushan 舟山 and Taizhou 台州. The Bohai Rim Economic Region

consists of Beijing 北京, Tianjin 天津, Hebei 河北 and Shandong 山東. See Fig. 3.1 for the locations of these economic regions.

2. V. F. S. Sit, "Increasing Globalization and the Growth of the Hong Kong Extended Metropolitan Region," in *Globalization and the Sustainability of Cities in the Asia Pacific Region*, edited by F. Lo and P. Marcottullio (Tokyo: United Nations University Press, 2001), pp. 199–238; Wang Jici 王緝慈, *Chuang xin de kongjian: qiye jiqun yu quyu fazhan* 創新的空間：企業集群與 區域發展 (Innovative Spaces: Enterprise Clusters and Regional Development) (Beijing: Peking University Press 北京大學出版社, 2001).

3. Susan M. Walcott, *Chinese Science and Technology Industrial Parks* (Aldershot, England: Ashgate Publishing Company, 2003).

4. Simon X. B. Zhao and L. Zhang, "Foreign Direct Investment and the Formation of Global City-regions in China," *Regional Studies*, Vol. 41, No. 7 (2007), pp. 979–94.

5. Francoise Lemoine, *FDI and the Opening Up of China's Economy* (Paris: Centre d'Etudes Prospectives et d'Informations Internationales, Working Papers 2000-11, 2000).

6. Jiang Xiaojuan, *FDI in China: Contributions to Growth, Restructuring and Competitiveness* (New York: Nova Science Publishers, 2004).

7. Tao Qu and Mulford B. Green, *Chinese Foreign Direct Investment: A Subnational Perspective on Location* (Aldershot, England: Ashgate, 1997).

8. For example, see Wang Shaoguang and Hu Angang, *The Political Economy of Uneven Development: The Case of China* (Armonk: M. E. Sharpe, 1999); Barry Naughton, "Provincial Economic Growth in China: Causes and Consequences of Regional Differentiation," in *China and Its Regions: Economic Growth and Reform in Chinese Provinces,* edited by Mary-Francoise Renard (Cheltenham, United Kingdom: E. Elgar, 2002), pp. 57–86; Lin Yifu 林毅夫 and Cai Fang 蔡昉, *Zhongguo jingji: gaige yu fazhan* 中國經濟：改 革與發展 (Chinese Economy: Reform and Development) (Beijing: Zhongguo caizheng jingji chubanshe 中國財政經濟出版社, 2003).

9. A. Watson, C. Findlay and Y. Du, "Who Won the Wool War?" *The China Quarterly*, No. 118 (1989), pp. 213–41; X. Zhang, W. Lu, K. Sun, C. Findlay and A. Watson, *The "Wool War" and the "Cotton Chaos": Fibre Marketing in China* (Working Paper 14, Chinese Economy Research Unit, University of Adelaide, 1991); K. Foster, *China's Tea War* (Chinese Economy Research Unit, University of Adelaide, 1991); J. W. Longworth and C. G. Brown, *Agribusiness Reforms in China: The Case of Wool* (Wallingford: CAB International, 1995); C. G. Brown, J. W. Longworth and S. A. Waldron, *Regionalisation and Integration in China: Lessons from the Transformation of the Beef Industry* (Ashgate, 2002).

10. A. Young, "The Razor's Edge: Distortions and Incremental Reform in the

People's Republic of China," *Quarterly Journal of Economics,* No. 115 (2000), pp. 1091–1136.

11. Huang Yasheng, *Selling China: Foreign Direct Investment during the Reform Era* (Cambridge, United Kingdom: Cambridge University Press, 2003).

12. A. Watson, H. X. Wu, and C. Findlay, "Regional Disparities in Rural Development," in *China's New Spatial Economy: Heading Towards 2020,* edited by G. J. R. Linge (Hong Kong: Oxford University Press, 1997), pp. 167–90.

13. M. Enright, E. E. Scott and Chang Ka-mun, *Regional Powerhouse: The Greater Pearl River Delta and the Rise of China* (Singapore: John Wiley & Sons, 2005).

14. M. Enright and E. E. Scott, *The Greater Pearl River Delta* (Hong Kong: Invest Hong Kong of the HKSAR Government, 2003).

15. Although located between Guizhou and Sichuan, the municipality of Chongqing 重慶市 has been excluded from the Pan-PRD. It is reported that Guangdong did not invite Chongqing to join when the concept of the Pan-PRD was initiated (*Chongqing Evening News*, 4 June 2004). It is interesting to speculate just why this was so. One possible reason for excluding Chongqing is that the municipality of Guangzhou is now competing for hub status for the Pan-PRD and intends to minimize the number of potential competitors. Chongqing is perceived as a strong competitor. Another possible reason is that Guangdong does not want to create the impression that the formation of the Pan-PRD is an attempt to undermine the hinterland of Shanghai municipality, as Chongqing is geographically and historically part of the Yangzi basin 長江流域 (see One Country Two Systems Research Institute, *Cooperation between Hong Kong and the Pan-PRD Region: A Background Report* [Hong Kong, 2004], accessible in www.info.gov.hk/cup/english/papers/200405%20Pan-PRD.pdf).

16. Ibid.

17. Sichuan Provincial Government 四川省人民政府, *Sichuan nianjian 2004* 四川年鑒 2004 (Sichuan Yearbook 2004) (Chengdu: Sichuan Yearbook Press, 2004), p. 125.

18. Sichuan Provincial Government, *Sichuan nianjian 2005* (Chengdu: Sichuan Yearbook Press, 2005), p. 132.

19. Yue-man Yeung, "Emergence of the Pan-Pearl River Delta," *Geografiska Annaler, Series B*, Vol. 87, No. 1 (2005), pp. 75–79.

20. Hainan was part of Guangdong until the mid-1980s. The First Session of the Seventh National People's Congress adopted a proposal to establish Hainan Province on 13 April 1988.

21. During the 1980s, Guangdong absorbed nearly one-half of all FDI in China. In the 1990s, when a significant portion of FDI flowed into the YRD, the province was still attracting more than one-quarter of the FDI in the nation.

See Markus Taube and Mehmet Ögütçü, *Main Issues on Foreign Investment in China's Regional Development: Prospects and Policy Challenges* (Organization for Economic Cooperation and Development, 2002).

22. Yue-man Yeung, Shen Jianfa and Zhang Li, *The Western Pearl River Delta: Growth and Opportunities for Cooperative Development with Hong Kong*, Research Monograph No. 62 (Hong Kong: Hong Kong Institute of Asia-Pacific Studies, The Chinese University of Hong Kong, 2005).

23. The division of labour between the PRD and Hong Kong is often referred to as *qian dian hou chang* 前店後廠 (the shop at the front, the factory at the back). Hong Kong functions as the shop and the PRD acts as the factory.

24. Yue-man Yeung, "Integration of the Pearl River Delta," *International Development and Planning Review*, Vol. 25, No. 3 (2003), pp. iii–viii; Enright et al., *Regional Powerhouse* (see note 13).

25. Li Luoli 李羅力, "Da Zhusanjiao quyu jingji zhenghe nan zai nali?" 大珠三角區域經濟整合難在哪裏？ (Where Are Difficulties in Economic Reorganization in the Greater Pearl River Delta?), *Naoku kuaican* 腦庫快參 (Think-tank Quick Reference), No. 28 (2004). www.cdi.com.cn.

26. Qiao Guodong 喬國棟 and Chen Dong 陳東, "Zhusanjiao de jingzhengli weishenme xiajiang le?" 珠三角的競爭力為什麼下降了？ (Why Has the Competitiveness of the PRD Declined?) *Zhongguo jingji shibao* 中國經濟時報 (China Economy Times, 19 July 2003).

27. "Buyer-driven" industrialization refers to a process of industrialization in which brand-name companies, especially those in light consumer goods industries, have relocated their manufacturing operations to wherever the production costs are low. Firms in newly industrialized countries compete for contracts based on low fees and produce products in developing countries based on the specifications and designs provided by the buyers. Such relocation of production has led to trade-led industrialization in developing countries. See Gary Gereffi, "Capitalism, Development and Global Commodity Chains," in *Capitalism and Development*, edited by L. Sklair (London and New York: Routledge, 1994), pp. 211–31. For the case of the PRD, see *Ming Pao* 明報, *Yue tisheng chanye, difujiazhi qiye shiwei; Zhusanjiao siwan gangshang mianlin biqian* 粤提升產業，低附加值企業勢危；珠三角四萬港商面臨逼遷 (Guangdong Upgrades Its Industries and the Fate of Low Value-added Enterprises Is Critical; Forty Thousand Hong Kong Businessmen in the Pearl River Delta Face Forced Moves), 18 April 2006.

28. Guangdong Provincial Bureau of Statistics 廣東省統計局, *Guangdongsheng tongji nianjian 2005* 廣東省統計年鑒 2005 (Statistical Yearbook of Guangdong Province 2005) (Beijing: China Statistics Press, 2005).

29. Guangdong Development and Planning Commission, *Zhujiang Sanjiaozhou shuaixian jiben shixian xiandaihua guihua huibian* 珠江三角洲率先基本

實現現代化規劃彙編 (Compilation of Plans for the PRD to Achieve Modernization) (Internal document, 2003).

30. International Statistical Information Centre of the National Bureau of Statistics 國家統計局國際統計信息中心, *Changjiang he Zhujiang Sanjiaozhou ji Gangao tebie xingzhengqu tongji nianjian 2005* 長江和珠江三角洲及港澳特別行政區統計年鑒 2005 (Yangzi River Delta and Pearl River Delta and Hong Kong and Macao SAR Statistical Yearbook 2005) (Beijing: China Statistics Press, 2005).

31. Guangdong Provincial Bureau of Statistics, *Guangdongsheng tongji nianjian 2005* (see note 28).

32. Ibid.

33. One Country Two Systems Research Institute, *Cooperation between Hong Kong and the Pan-PRD Region: A Background Report* (see note 15).

34. See *Fanzhu hezuo: chanye zhuanyi yu liyi fenpei shangshu nanti* 泛珠合作：產業轉移與利益分配尚屬難題 (The Cooperation of the Pan-PRD: Industrial Relocation and the Allocation of Interests Are Still Difficult Problems) (Beijing: *The First Financial Daily*, 9 June 2006).

4

The Economic Basis of Regionalization

Tsang Shu-ki

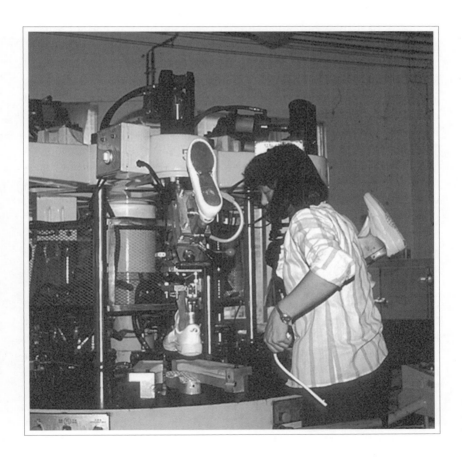

Introduction

In 2003, the Hong Kong and Macao special administrative regions (SARs) both entered into their respective Closer Economic Partnership Arrangement (CEPA) with mainland China. In June 2004, nine mainland provinces — Guangdong 廣東, Fujian 福建, Jiangxi 江西, Guizhou 貴州, Sichuan 四川, Yunnan 雲南, Hunan 湖南, Hainan 海南, and the Guangxi Zhuang Autonomous Region 廣西壯族自治區, together with the Hong Kong 香港 and Macao 澳門 SARs, signed the "Pan Pearl River Delta Regional Cooperation Framework Agreement" (the so-called "9+2 Agreement"). The aim behind these two sets of arrangements, initiated mainly by government authorities, is to achieve trade liberalization and economic integration at different levels. The operational targets are a reduction in tariff and non-tariff barriers to trade, enhanced investment and a more efficient flow of resources, as well as strengthened regional cooperation in various aspects of development.

From the macro perspective, economic integration in the Pan–Pearl River Delta (Pan-PRD) 泛珠江三角洲 region, like economic globalization, appears to conform to the major historical tendencies that are unfolding all over the world. While member economies of the "9+2" Agreement have individual characteristics, they also have remarkable aggregate attributes. Together, they have a combined population of 450 million and occupy an area of 2 million sq km, representing a respective 35% and 21% of China's total. The Pan-PRD contributes about 40% of the nation's GDP, which would rank it among the 20 largest economic entities in the world. Also, the potential for complementary efforts in capital construction, transportation, energy and other natural resources, manufacturing industries, and services seems to be great. If regional cooperation progresses well, a win-win situation for all parties concerned can be achieved.

Nevertheless, that the Pan-PRD could form an economic region with explicit coordination was not expected by many a few years ago, despite the already close relationship between Guangdong and the two SARs of Hong Kong and Macao. Geographically, all of the constituent economies (with the exception of parts of Sichuan) are located south of the Yangzi River 長江. In itself, this "natural" feature is not an automatic qualification, however, and the transportation network outside Guangdong is as yet not extensive and efficient. At the same time, some have pointed to the conundrum of why Chongqing 重慶, in the heart of Sichuan, was not included in the Agreement, despite being a municipality under the direct control of the central government. The diversities in the levels and modes of development of the member economies might be regarded as potential complementarities; on the other hand, they could become serious obstacles to cooperation and interaction.

Interesting questions naturally arise concerning this new experiment in regionalism. The earlier economic interaction between Guangdong and Hong Kong–Macao was largely market-led in the sense that private enterprises from the latter took the initiative, and shouldered the risks of investing in southern China and engaging in outward processing from the 1980s onwards without the blessing or help of their respective colonial governments. The mainland authorities were largely receptive with regard to policy. CEPA, however, is a proactive step taken by the central government, apparently in an effort to boost the economies of Hong Kong, and in conjunction, Macao. This "top-down" or "statist" approach contrasts with the evolutionary process that had been followed so far.

Is the Pan-PRD campaign, like CEPA, politically motivated? Or is it, also like CEPA but with less significance attached to the fact, based on sound economics? How are the member economies supposed to work towards the realization of the Framework Agreement or even towards the further deepening of integration?

The Pan-PRD Framework Agreement as a Loose Form of Regionalism

According to the WTO, "Regionalism is described in the Dictionary of Trade Policy Terms, as 'actions by governments to liberalize or facilitate trade on a regional basis, sometimes through free-trade areas or customs unions'."[1]

The Pan-PRD framework agreement is clearly a further step towards achieving sub-national liberalization (or regionalization) arrangements within China following the launching of CEPA. The WTO has classified the CEPAs between Mainland China and Hong Kong and Macao as constituting "free trade areas" (FTAs). FTAs are one of two major types of "regional trade agreements" (RTAs), the other being "customs unions," e.g., the European Common Market. RTAs are monitored and regulated under by Article XXIV of GATT, the 1979 Decisions, as well as Clause V of GATS (General Agreement on Trade in Services).[2]

To put things in the proper perspective, the Pan-PRD cooperation agreement is supposed to work within the overall frameworks of "one country, two systems" and CEPA. Hong Kong and Macao are independent customs areas. In the short to medium term, it is not easy for the two SARs to do what the European Union (EU) has done, that is, to establish a common market, to unify tariffs on foreign goods (CCT); or to establish a so-called "Single Administrative Document" (SAD) with the mainland or any part of it. In addition, a common market is not equivalent to economic unification. After establishing the Common Market, Europe proceeded to push forward the Economic and Monetary Union (EMU). While the EU expanded its membership in 2004 to 25, 12 states abolished their domestic currencies and switched to the euro. As is well known and despite recent setbacks, the EU's ultimate objective is comprehensive political unification.

In any event, China need not follow the footsteps of other countries. The "9+2" Framework Agreement put forward the following 10 key areas of collaboration: (1) infrastructure; (2) industry and investment; (3) commerce and business; (4) tourism; (5) agriculture; (6) labour; (7) science, education, and culture; (8) informatization construction; (9) environmental protection; and (10) sanitation and disease control. Many proposals are project-based programmes for cooperation, rather than a matter of calculative or broad-brush "formal liberalization." Clause 2 of the "Framework Agreement" stipulates the following "Cooperation Principles": "Based on the common desire for development, all parties participate voluntarily in Pan-PRD regional co-operation and enjoy equal status and rights of development in the Cooperation Framework. In accordance with laws, policies and needs, the Hong Kong and Macao SAR governments and the other agreeing parties have the right to participate in all or parts of the cooperation projects."[3]

The major modes of operation under the Framework Agreement have been forums, symposiums, exhibitions, trade fairs, investment gatherings, agreements, plans to build platforms, and so forth. Some are multilateral with general purposes and involve all member economies (e.g., the annual Pan-PRD Regional Cooperation and Development Forum, the second of which was held in Chengdu 成都 in July 2005); others are multilateral or bilateral with a specific agenda within the 10 areas of cooperation.[4]

Pan-PRD Guidelines for a two-stage cooperative development plan were laid out in a concluding document of the second annual Pan-PRD Regional Cooperation and Development Forum: (1) 2005–2010: to build up the infrastructure and network for regional integration, to develop a good institutional environment for regional factor and product markets through the public administrative functions of governments, and to construct an important platform for economic cooperation between China and Association of Southeast Asian Nations (ASEAN); (2) 2011–2020: to achieve coordinated industrial development in the region through market allocations, to establish open and competitive factor and commodity markets, to raise the region's international competitiveness and influence, to form a setting for interactive and coordinated development among the eastern, the middle, and the western regions, and to enhance the level of exchange with ASEAN.[5]

These are rather general principles and directions. In other words, the Agreement and its implementation provide for a high degree of flexibility. The mode of operation sounds more like the time-honoured ASEAN norms of "voluntarism, consent, non-interference, and informality"[6] instead of formal commitments with explicit incentives and sanctions. It appears to some to be a wise choice as a first step, given practical realities in China as well as the Pan-PRD.[7] However, Okfen's warning may also be relevant: "Interaction does not lead *per se* to a positive attitude among those who interact with each other." Quite a number of commentators have argued that ASEAN is actually an example of procrastination, if not outright failure. Although the member countries share common attributes, there are significant political, economic, and cultural barriers and resistance to integration. Over-interaction has led to "forum fatigue."

Diversity versus Complementarity

Any economic region must possess some similarities and affinities. Otherwise, a certain degree of coherence cannot be established, even over the long term. On the other hand, if there is no diversity within such a region, there can be no meaningful division of labour, cooperation and virtuous competition among the constituent members. Hence, diversity and complementarity are linked in complicated ways.

For a start, the Pan-PRD appears to be a more closely-knit region than, say, the Asia-Pacific Economic Cooperation (APEC) grouping: There are no long distances or significant cultural differences among the member economies. Nevertheless, various political and administrative barriers do exist, as the mainland provinces are still undergoing reforms at an uneven pace, while Hong Kong and Macao are arguably among the "freest" market economies in the world.

Moreover, diversity surely exists, as can be seen from Table 4.1. Size-wise, Guangdong and Hong Kong are the largest and second-largest economies among the 11 members, while Hainan and Macao are the smallest, at less than 10% of the size of the former. In terms of level of development, the unevenness is rather striking. Hong Kong's per capita GDP in 2004 was nearly 50 times that of Guizhou, the poorest, whose GDP at about RMB10,000 was less than half the average of the mainland provinces in the Agreement (i.e., the Pan-PRD excluding Hong Kong and Macao).

Regarding the economic structure, the contrast between the service economies of Hong Kong and Macao on the one hand, and the agriculturally based economies of most mainland provinces (with the exception of Guangdong and Fujian) on the other, is remarkable. The biggest difference, however, is in the degree of outward orientation of the economies. The ratio of total foreign trade (total imports and exports) to GDP in 2004 was 325.5% and 187.7% in Hong Kong and Guangdong, respectively, but only around 10% for most of the other provinces (with the exception of Fujian and Hainan).

Of course, one can take all these contrasts as potential complementarities, as emphasized by a consultancy report of the HKSAR Government in its first monthly report: "From an economic development point of view, the Pan-PRD is a necessary and reasonable regional formation. The development and economic conditions of the "9+2" constituents vary substantially, ranging from Guangxi, Yunnan, Guizhou, Sichuan, Jiangxi, Hunan and Hainan which are well endowed with natural resources and labour, but lacking balanced development, to relatively developed coastal economies of Guangdong and Fujian, to Hong Kong and Macao SARs that are well exposed to the international market. These diversities make it particularly efficient for provinces/regions in the Pan-PRD to leverage on their comparative advantages to support and complement each other's development and achieve a win-win situation for all."[8]

Trade and Investment Linkages with Hong Kong

One interesting question is why the mainland provinces should have incentives to strengthen economic relationships with Hong Kong. The answer is straightforward: Hong Kong so far has played a rather unique role in the Pan-PRD. First, it is the most important intermediary in international trade for the nine mainland provinces. Hong Kong's economic relationship with Guangdong has, of course, always been very significant. Hong Kong's trade with other provinces is also noteworthy. At present,

Table 4.1 Economic Statistics on the Pan-PRD Provinces and Regions (2004)

	Fujian	Jiangxi	Hunan	Guang-dong	Guangxi	Hainan	Sichuan	Guizhou	Yunnan	Mainland[a] Total/Average	Hong Kong	Macao
Nominal gross domestic product (RMB100mn)	6,053	3,496	5,612	16,039	3,320	790	6,556	1,592	2,959	46,417	13,492	854
Per capita gross domestic product (RMB)	17,241	8,161	8,379	19,316	6,791	9,408	7,514	4,078	6,703	10,187	196,100	186,868
Industrial structure:												
Primary (%)	12.9	20.4	20.6	7.8	24.4	36.4	21.3	21.0	20.4	15.8	0.1[b]	0.0
Secondary (%)	48.7	45.6	39.5	55.4	38.8	25.5	41.0	44.9	44.4	47.1	10.8[b]	12.6
Tertiary (%)	38.4	34.0	39.9	36.8	36.8	38.2	37.7	34.1	35.2	37.2	89.1[b]	87.4
Yearly average wage (RMB)	14,310	10,521	12,221	19,986	11,953	10,397	12,441	11,037	12,870	12,860	121,202	63,989
Retail sales of consumer goods (RMB100mn)	1,996	1,060	2,070	6,371	973	219	2,384	518	884	16,475	2,039	78
Total external trade (US$100mn)	499.4	48.2	60.8	3,636	48.3	29.0	66.8	23.8	37.4	4,449	5,303.3	62.9
Total external trade/GDP (%)	68.2	11.4	9.0	187.7	12.0	30.4	8.4	12.4	10.5	79.4	325.5	63.0
Value of exports (US$100mn)	305.7	26.1	31.4	1,925	23.1	8.2	34.8	12.8	20.2	2388	2,592.6	28.1
Value of imports (US$100mn)	193.7	22.1	29.4	1,710	25.2	20.7	32.0	11.0	17.2	2061	2,710.7	34.8
Trade balance (US$100mn)	112.0	4.0	1.9	21.5	–2.0	–12.5	2.8	1.8	3.1	326.2	–118.1	–6.7
Tourism foreign exchange receipts (US$100mn)	10.7	0.8	3.1	53.8	2.9	0.8	2.9	0.8	4.2	80.0	117.9[c]	33.9[c]
Utilized FDI (RMB100mn)	53.2	20.5	14.2	100.1	3.0	6.4	7.4	0.6	2.2	206.8	6,284.0[d]	N.A.
Bank loans (RMB100mn)	3,838	2,550	3,900	20,126	2,320	870	5,910	1,710	2,956	44,180	266,200	367
Companies listed in Hong Kong	2	1	1	30	0	1	5	0	2	42	1,096[e]	N.A.

Sources: Central Policy Unit (2005); State Statistical Bureau of China; Hong Kong Monetary Authority; Census and Statistics Department, Hong Kong SAR Government; Statistics and Census Service, Macao SAR Government (http://www.dsec.gov.mo/).

Notes: [a]Pan-PRD ex Hong Kong and Macao; [b]figures for 2003; [c]total tourism receipts; [d]derived from the change in "direct investment" statistics of Hong Kong's IIP (international investment position); [e]the total number of companies listed on the Main Board and the GEM of Hong Kong's Stock Exchange; N.A. – not available. Exchange rates used for conversion are HKD/USD = 7.788; MOP/USD = 8.02; RMB/USD = 8.28.

Hong Kong is Fujian's fourth-largest export market, and the province's trade with Hong Kong accounts for about 20% of its total foreign trade. If transshipment is included, Hong Kong-related trade would reach 50%. In 2003, Hong Kong was the largest trading partner of Jiangxi (with a share of 16.5%), Hainan (over 80%), and Guizhou (50%). Hong Kong was also the second-largest trading partner of Yunnan (15%) and the third-largest of Sichuan (6%), while trade with Hong Kong made up 8.3% of Hunan's external trade.[9]

According to Hong Kong's Trade Development Council (HKTDC), in 2003 trade between the nine provinces and Hong Kong and Macao amounted to US$65.1 billion, or 72% of the total volume of trade between mainland China and the two SARs.[10] In the first half of 2004, the nine provinces exported goods worth US$32.31 billion to Hong Kong and Macao, up 28.2%, and imported goods worth US$2.97 billion from these two places, up 5.3%. Hence the former showed a surplus of US$29.34. This indicates the fact that the provinces are main suppliers of primary and resource-intensive products to Hong Kong and Macao, but import relatively little in return.

However, according to the Department of Foreign Trade and Economic Cooperation of Guangdong, in the same period the total exports to and imports from Hong Kong of Guangdong alone amounted to US$29.10 billion and US$2.74 billion, respectively.[11] It appears that these two sets of figures are not strictly consistent (in the light of Table 4.1 and the report of the CPU (2004)). The numbers for Guangdong imply higher levels of total imports and exports between the nine provinces and Hong Kong-Macao than have been reported by the HKTDC, although Guangdong-Hong Kong trade should comprise the lion's share of foreign trade between the nine provinces and Hong Kong and Macao. The issues involved are likely to be those of statistical definitions and the recording of the general trade in goods versus total trade including outward processing. The latter is much larger in gross value and the basis of classification might affect statistics on general trade.[12]

In any case, Hong Kong has undoubtedly been serving as the dominant port for the region. During the first six months of 2004, for example, the nine provinces exported goods worth US$23.85 billion via Hong Kong, up 12% and accounting for 23.1% of their total exports; and imported goods worth US$60.52 billion via Hong Kong, up 28.4% and accounting for 65.9% of their total imports. Interestingly, exports to ASEAN via Hong Kong and Macao amounted to US$2.02 billion, while imports from ASEAN via Hong Kong and Macao amounted to US\$8.62 billion, up 23.5%. Hence, the total volume of the import and export trade of the nine provinces with ASEAN via Hong Kong and Macao reached US\$10.64 billion, which represented nearly 60% of their trade with ASEAN.

Second, foreign investment in the nine provinces has mainly come from Hong Kong. Hong Kong investment accounted for over 50% of foreign direct investment in Guangdong, Jiangxi, and Hunan. In 2003, the nine provinces absorbed US\$7.8 billion in direct investment from Hong Kong and Macao, accounting for 43% of direct investment made by the two SARs on the mainland.[13]

On the other hand, as a result of China's accession to the WTO and the implementation of CEPA, the number of mainland enterprises coming to invest in Hong Kong and "going global" through Hong Kong has also increased significantly. They include companies from Guangdong and other Pan-PRD provinces. As shown in Table 4.1, the number of enterprises from the Pan-PRD listed in Hong Kong's stock exchange stood at 42 at the end of 2004, of which 30 were from Guangdong alone.

The Pan-PRD in the Context of Globalization and Regionalization

With trade and investment linkages already established, why is there a need to further expand economic relationships through regionalization? What is the shared long-run vision, if any, of the Pan-PRD as an economic region? Should the region be outwardly oriented, led by Guangdong and Hong Kong, in an attempt to further participate in the world economy? Or should more effort be directed to promoting the intra-regional market, given its diversity and supposed complementarities? It is easy to pay lip service to all aspects of the grouping and only the persistent implementation of promises and the realization of vague principles will reveal the actual emphasis of the grouping, by design or default.

While regional economic cooperation is a multi-faceted research topic, some initial observations can be made. Economic globalization and regional economic integration are historical trends, but their interactions are complex. Both are not irreversible and do not provide guarantees for success. The Pan-PRD is a regional bloc within the Chinese economy. It is also part of the global economic network. Hence, economic integration is a two-pronged process. Attention must be paid to both internal consolidation and promotion on the one hand, and external extension on the other. Insofar as a region can attain economies of scale and scope through meaningful consolidation, it will be a more powerful competitor in the international and global arena. The EU is one such example.

Why should regional economic blocs be formed and how does the Pan-PRD region fit into the patterns observed with previous and existing regional blocs? In the recent literature on development economics and international political economy, regionalism can be viewed as both positive and negative. Regarded positively, it can be a way of gaining economies of scale and scope so as to permit more effective engagement and participation in globalized production and competition. These developments are often termed "new regionalism" or "open regionalism." As Bergsten, the concept "represents an effort to resolve one of the central problems of contemporary trade policy: how to achieve compatibility between the explosion of regional trading arrangements.... The concept seeks to assure that regional agreements will in practice be building blocks for further global liberalization rather than stumbling blocks that deter such progress".[14]

In contrast, regionalization can also be a fallback position or a viable retreat from over-extended globalization. The "resistance model" is often not purely economic in perspective. It emphasizes the difficulties of maintaining local economic and social institutions and arrangements in the face of globalization and the importance of regional collective action to act as safeguard. Kurzer, for example, argued that the future of national social democratic systems and policies in Europe hinges on the successful development of the EU.[15]

Another variant of the debate is concerned with consequences, not intentions. The relevant question here is whether the proliferation of RTAs in recent years is providing "building blocks" or throwing up "stumbling blocks" to globalization (suspending for the moment our assessment of the merits of either globalization or regionalization). Although these two "schools" are often considered to promote opposing approaches to super-national economic development, the empirical evidence is much more mixed. Wei and Frenkel, for example, confirm that East Asia indeed practised open regionalism during 1970–1992, which is "Pareto-improving for world welfare". But so did Western Europe, albeit to a much lesser extent.[16]

In theory, an economic region cannot be successfully launched if it does not possess a set of special attributes that outside areas do not share to any significant extent. Imagine a small plain in a large flatland where people and cargo can freely move in and out. At best it can become a transit point.

Of course, a region may not be integrated if internal barriers and resistance are too large to prevent the smooth flow of human and physical resources among member economies.

In the more concrete context of increasingly globalized production and marketing, a region needs to be of a size that would allow for a substantial division of labour among parts that have different comparative advantages. In other words, it should facilitate a certain degree of vertical segmentation of the production process. Some areas within it should be richly endowed with natural resources, others with efficient or quality labourers, and yet others with entrepreneurial, capital, or financial prowess. Hence, the region has to be heterogeneous rather than homogeneous. But equally, in order for the vertical division to be viable, resources must flow across different parts with relative ease and at a lower cost than would be the case in other arrangements. Hence, a FTA involving countries and territories with various endowments at different stages of development, yet with appropriate proximity and affinity, could become an ideal economic region in an era of globalization.

In the latter context, the recent literature has focused on discussions of the so-called "old versus new regionalism." Questions have been raised on the choices between (1) shallow and deep integration; and (2) the extension of RTAs between developing and developed countries, and so forth.[17]

Economic Globalization versus Regional Economic Cooperation?

The proliferation of bilateral and multilateral preferential trade agreements and the extension of regions seem to be viable and desirable trends, given the globalization of production and consumption. According to information provided by the World Trade Organization (WTO), RTAs are an emerging wave. "By July 2005, only one WTO member — Mongolia — was not party to a regional trade agreement. The surge in these agreements has continued unabated since the early 1990s. By July 2005, a total of 330 had been notified to the WTO (and its predecessor, GATT). Of these: 206 were notified after the WTO was created in January 1995; 180 are currently in force; several others are believed to be operational although not yet notified."[18]

However, regional multilateralism or multiple regionalism[19] could backfire and has its critics. Okfen, for example, has argued that organizations such as APEC and the Asia-Europe Meeting (ASEM) are too loose to be effective, and that ASEAN's norms of "voluntarism, consent, non-interference and informality" do not always generate positive attitudes towards the formation of "community spirit."[20] One might wonder whether many of the members signing up to join RTAs are "natural trading partners." Practically speaking, if member countries of an RTA are involved with multiple RTAs, which involve countries outside the RTA, the costs of implementing restrictive rules of origin will increase, hence reducing the trade creation benefits of the arrangement.

Indeed, there is a certain tension between globalism and regionalism. Ideally, in a truly and completely globalized world, there is little need for regionalism. Yet, the reality is far from the ideal. Even the United States, the most prominent (if not always the most consistent) advocate of globalism, faces the dilemma of having to choose between globalism and regionalism and has to deal with many conflicting interests. Yamada has highlighted the political-economic dimension of the problem.[21] The United States (U.S.) has not been one-sidedly globalist in its trade policies. As much as its top economic elites, represented by the MNCs, want to have a global reach, other domestic interests in the country are more eager to preserve their relative positions through (anti-globalist) protectionism or more expedient regionalist approaches. From the 1990s onwards, moreover, environmental groups and non-governmental organizations have become increasingly vocal and visible in opposing globalization, particularly at international forums (such as the WTO meeting in Seattle). Yamada has argued that since it is becoming increasingly difficult to push through these kinds of multilateral trade talks and since such talks have become ever more subject to adverse publicity, even the U.S. government is torn between regionalism and multilateralism.[22] As a result, the U.S. has shown some keen interest in striking regional trade agreements such as the North America Free Trade Agreement (NAFTA) and the Free Trade Area of the Americas (FTAA).

The Pan-PRD as an Economic Region: Internal and External Considerations

Some economists are of the view that China's development strategy has so far been overtly outward-oriented, perhaps excessively so. The motto has often been "open first, reform later." This characteristic is a result of not only the major trends in the global economy towards free trade, but also of the existence of internal administrative and economic barriers — or local protectionism — within the country.

China's degree of openness, in terms of the ratio of total trade (imports and exports) to GDP, has risen remarkably, from less than 13% in 1980 to 38.3% in 1995, and 59.8% in 2004.[23] A level of 60% is about 50% higher than the world average of 41% in 2004 and substantially above that of around 20% for the United States, Japan, and India. Certainly there are problems in computing such a ratio because of the problems of purchasing power parity (PPP),[24] the remaining distortions in the exchange rate, multiple counting arising from China's outward processing activities, and so forth. However, it is clear that in the past decade there has been a steeply rising trend of openness in trade.

In any case, such a trend, if it persists, may lead to problems. Already China's increasing trade surplus against the United States has given rise to friction. Moreover, the presumption of ever-increasing world trade may be dangerous. In fact, the world's economic and trade patterns in the past two hundred years have shown two "long waves." In the second half of the nineteenth century, the ratio of global total trade (imports plus exports) to total output value rose rapidly, from less than 10% to over 20% by 1913. However, thereafter, because of the world wars, the collapse of the gold standard, and the spread of protectionism, the ratio dropped significantly to below 10%. Only in the 1970s did it move back to the peak of the 1910s.[25] In recent years, the trend has accelerated, and the ratio recently climbed above 40%. In other words, economic globalization is by no means a linear process, and the twists and turns over the long run have been remarkable. Therefore, it would be wishful thinking to pin all hope of economic development on the provision of external resources and the permanent expansion of foreign demand.[26]

Nevertheless, degrees of openness within different parts of China are highly uneven, as can be seen in Table 4.1 and in our discussions above. Viewed more broadly, with the largest population in the world, China arguably possesses more of a "continental" type of economy, and the promotion of the internal economy may be a more viable development strategy than other approaches. Yet, as a result of the persistence of administrative barriers, the degree of internal economic integration in various large regions within the country, whether the PRD, the Yangzi Delta 長江三角洲, or the Bohai Region 渤海地區, is still far from significant. Because of this, the "open first, reform later" strategy, which has produced short-term gains, has led to the unpalatable phenomenon of structural convergence among those regions, which value low-efficiency competition more than the far-sighted nurturing of complementarities; for example, localities compete for FDI by legally or illegally lowering effective taxation rates and business costs as well as by offering extra incentives.

In any event, the lessons of the East Asian financial crisis must be learned. In recent years, some emphasis is being placed on stimulating domestic demand. This has provided a useful reference for the formulation of future development strategies.

Given the national developmental priorities that have been revealed, the design of the Pan-PRD under CEPA is still rather outwardly oriented. Not enough attention has been paid to promoting internal development and interactions. While this may be optimal for the PRD (Guangdong, Hong Kong, and Macao), it is probably problematic for the whole Pan-PRD to follow the lead of the core economies. Even Guangdong is reconsidering its strategy of "front shops, back factory" and is keen to engage in industrial upgrading.

This view does not imply the neglect of the outward orientation of the Pan-PRD. After all, the core of the Pan-PRD is very outward oriented. Hong Kong and Macao are independent customs areas, with well-established linkages to English and Portuguese-speaking countries around the world. In addition, Guangxi, Hainan, Sichuan, Guizhou, Yunnan, and Fujian could help in the effort to develop economic connections with ASEAN countries. All in all, a balance between internal and external considerations needs to be struck.

Outward Orientation to Where? ASEAN?

If the Pan-PRD should become an open region and further participate in world trade and global economic relations, what external area(s) should it primarily engage with? One apparent answer is ASEAN, given the close proximity between many of the member countries of ASEAN and the nine provinces on the mainland. Hong Kong, on the other hand, has also been playing a useful part in trade between ASEAN and the Pan-PRD. As mentioned above, in the first half of 2004, the volume of the import and export trade of the nine provinces with ASEAN via Hong Kong and Macao reached US$10.64 billion, representing nearly 60% of the total. China and ASEAN are, of course, promoting the development of the ASEAN-China Free Trade Area (ACFTA). The Pan-PRD would be best positioned as one core on the Chinese side of the equation. The emphasis of the external linkage to ASEAN was also contained in the concluding document of the second development forum of the Pan-PRD held in Chengdu in July 2005.[27]

Nevertheless, the further enhancement of trade between the Pan-PRD and ASEAN may run into a relative lack of genuine complementarities, as a result of similarities in resources and production levels. In a wider context, Wong and Chan have expressed skepticism about the prospects for China-ASEAN free trade: "The China-ASEAN Free Trade Agreement has been hailed as a landmark pact in pushing for freer trade between China and the ASEAN countries. With the establishment of the free trade zone, trade and investment between the Chinese and ASEAN economies are expected to increase significantly; but while the economic benefits are inexorable, the extent of gains derived from closer integration hinges on the Sino-ASEAN economic relationship, which is both complementary and competitive in nature. At the present stage of development, China and ASEAN are more competitive than complementary, given the similarity in their trade and industrial structures. ASEAN and China are also direct competitors for foreign investment, rather than significant investors in each other's economies. Despite these challenges, the prospects for bilateral trade to flourish are bright if both China and ASEAN can interlock their economies through deeper integration in the long term."[28]

Historically, East Asian trade has been driven by what Kawai has called the "FDI-trade nexus," under which the formation of regional supply chains and networks by multinational corporations is the dominant feature.[29] The specialization and fragmentation of production sub-processes in different East Asian nations based on comparative advantage — factor proportions and technological capabilities — then increase trade among them. This strategy is consistent with the "new regionalism" discussed above. It has induced vertical intra-regional and intra-industry trade in East Asia.[30] Of course, there is a competitive element in that the countries are trying to attract as much FDI as possible and the pattern of the regional division of labour is not fixed. From this angle, one of the key problems with ACFTA is that the "FDI-trade nexus" may not be very strong.

Views similar to those Wong and Chan have been put forth by Sussangkarn,[31] who has found evidence of a great deal of competition between Thailand and China in external trade. Apart from prima facie trends of China's relative rise and Thailand's relative decline especially after the East Asian financial crisis (not just in trade but also in the absorption of FDI), detailed analyses of empirical data include the latter's RCA (revealed comparative advantage) rank correlations with various countries (including China) and its rank correlations with China within different product groups. Based on those findings, Sussangkarn has emphasized the need for ASEAN countries to improve their competitiveness so as to attract more FDI especially from Japan, which has a more complementary trade and investment structure with Thailand than do other countries, as well as an already significant production and investment presence.[32]

Nevertheless, both China and ASEAN have been keen to pursue an economic relationship. One possibility for enlarged opportunities may be the rapidly rising demand for resources on the part of the Chinese, including relatively resource-poor Guangdong. In contrast, ASEAN has a relatively large supply of natural resources. Negotiations on the establishment of ACFTA by 2010 were launched in October 2001. The "Early Harvest Programme" (EHP) focusing on agricultural and some industrial products were agreed upon and implemented in 2004. Under the Trade in Goods Chapter, tariffs for most goods were reduced starting from July 2005 (with a 40% reduction involving about 7,000 items as a kick-off), with the target of eliminating "all" tariffs by 2010 for the ASEAN Six and by 2015 for the other four new members.

It remains to be seen whether the FTA will be fruitful. A somewhat interesting observation is that Hong Kong does not seem to be very concerned about ACFTA. According to a newspaper report in Hong Kong in July 2005, most local enterprises were not aware of the imminent reduction of tariffs under the Trade in Goods Chapter.[33] In view of our discussion above, this is not surprising. Hong Kong, after all, is rather different from Japan. Since the second half of the 1980s, most of Hong Kong's manufacturing industries have been relocated to the Pearl River Delta and a process of structural transformation has turned Hong Kong into a service economy with little interest in the acquisition of physical resources. Unlike Japan, and to a lesser extent Taiwan and South Korea, no notable industrial upgrading has taken place and most of Hong Kong's recent large-scale investments in the mainland have been in the infrastructure and service sectors. Hence, the potential FDI-induced trade that has been generated is much weaker than that by Japan. Hong Kong may not be a very effective leader in the development of a new regionalism.

What, then, does the saying that Hong Kong can serve the Pan-PRD to "reach the world" mean? It seems to focus on information and market connections with the United States, Europe, and Japan. An aspect of this is Hong Kong's fund-raising capability as an international financial centre. In fact, Hong Kong is now the mainland's most important outside platform for stock listings because of the concentration in the SAR of multinational financial institutions, including investment and merchant banks and stock brokerage firms. At the end of October 2005, the number of H-shares listed in the Hong Kong Stock Exchange totalled 78, with a market capitalization of HK$1,115.592 billion, accounting for 14.8% of Hong Kong's total capitalization. The number of "red chips" was 85, with a market capitalization of HK$1,602.078 billion and a share of 21.24%.[34] Together they constitute one-third of Hong Kong's total market capitalization!

Internal Consolidation?

From one perspective, the potential complementarities within the Pan-PRD are probably higher than those between the Pan-PRD and ASEAN. Resources can be transferred from the western provinces to the eastern industrial core of the PRD, while industries and enterprises from the latter can move westwards. Such intra-regional trade and investment should in theory be more cost effective than external trade and investment.

However, the major problem will be one of political economy rather than pure economics. Cooperation and competition between various member economies and their respective positionings will emerge as delicate issues. As a region, there is bound to be a division of functions in the form of clusters, hinterlands, and hierarchies of production and services. Certainly, there can be more than one development centre (or core of clusters), leading various hinterlands. These centres can also form a hierarchy of overlapping sub-regions with different functions and levels of cooperation and competition. However, which area is going to be the "dragon head" — Hong Kong or Guangzhou 廣州? Which areas would be satisfied with being a hinterland or periphery led of another area?

In the wider context of China's economic development and global trends, these may not be crucial questions. After all, any regional classification within the country is bound to be arbitrary to a certain extent. China may assign eight or more "major economic regions." But where would the boundaries lie? And what would be the rationale for drawing such boundaries? For example, why should Sichuan be inside or outside the Pan-PRD? Should it not belong to the Yangzi belt? In any case, in a dynamic world, the relationship between a core and the periphery is not a static one. It is evolving all the time and the division of labour and interactions with optimized resource allocations constantly need to be updated.

Nevertheless, as the author has frequently stressed in analyzing developments in the Hong Kong economy, there are risks and hopefully returns involved in any regional integration through the removal of resource barriers. There is the controversy between the so-called "resource mobility view" versus the "local advantage view." CEPA, like globalization, enhances resource mobility and freedom of movement. At the same time, it may imply a net outflow (rather than a net inflow) of quality resources, including high-end physical, financial, and human capital. This is why ASEAN countries understand that ACFTA is a double-edged sword. In short, the China factor is both a blessing and a curse.[35]

Therefore, before an area's economic "frontiers" or floodgates are opened up, questions must be asked about the strengths and weaknesses of that area and whether there is likely to be a net inflow to or outflow of quality resources from that area. Would opening up be a mutually beneficial matter? Would the area be playing the role of the core or a periphery in a cluster?[36] In any case, the opening of any area, particularly one with no clear niche, must at the same time involve the promotion of the "local advantage" of that area. Such an area may eventually experience an economic revival arising from a process of regional cooperation and competition, for example, the so called "backyard" strategy advocated by some economists for Kunshan 昆山 vis-à-vis Shanghai 上海 and Zhenjiang 鎮江 vis-à-vis Nanjing 南京.[37] Otherwise, they could face the danger of "hollowing out" or becoming "marginalized" (apparently a worry of Hainan).[38]

Coordination or Competition?

Could the Pan-PRD deteriorate into a talk show, because of a lack of persistence in pursuing efforts to implement integration and coordination under a top-down approach, given the diversity among the members of the grouping? The signs are that the authorities are strenuously trying to avoid that prospect, but the outcome is far from certain.

A revealing speech was given by Donald Tsang, the new Chief Executive of the Hong Kong SAR, in the Second Pan-PRD Economic Cooperation and Development Forum, held in Chengdu on 25 July 2005, in which he stressed the need to avoid "unnecessary competition" in infrastructure investments within the region.[39] That such a plea should have been made is in itself significant, and may point to the problems of designing such a regional economic bloc from day one.

A sobering experience relating to this crucial point is Hong Kong's role as the logistics centre of the Pan-PRD. Hong Kong has been the number one container port in the world since 1992, and has only once been overtaken by Singapore, in 1998. It regained its supremacy in 1999. With CEPA and the "9+2" Framework Agreement, one would have thought that its position as the world's busiest port would be further enhanced. Unfortunately, that did not turn out to be the case. Right in the first quarter of 2005, total throughput in Hong Kong amounted to only 5.123 million twenty-foot equivalent units (TEUs), representing a year-to-year decline of 1.5%, which was lower than Singapore's 5.523 million TEUs.

For the year 2005 as a whole, Hong Kong's container throughput rose by a mere 2% to 22.42 million TEUs, while Singapore's jumped 8.7% to 23.19 million TEUs, to retake the number one position in the world. Hong Kong's growth rate of 2% was 5.5% lower than the 7.5% registered in 2004.

Moreover, Hong Kong is now under tremendous competitive pressure from Shanghai and Shenzhen, the world's third and fourth busiest container ports, respectively. Shanghai's throughput shot up 24.3% to 18.08 million TEUs, while Shenzhen's climbed 18.6% to 16.20 million TEUs. Many analysts are predicting that in a few years Hong Kong will be overtaken by the two Chinese ports.

This paradoxical phenomenon reflects, on the one hand, the high operating costs of Hong Kong's container port. Including land transport costs and port handling charges, a shipper has to pay nearly US$300 more per TEU of goods, compared with using Shenzhen. Hong Kong's remaining advantages lie in its efficiency, reliability, and international connections (with a global reach). However, the high costs are increasingly becoming a drag as globalized production is very much characterized by cost reduction. The siphoning off of port businesses from Hong Kong to the cheaper ports of Shenzhen and Shanghai is threatening Hong Kong's position as the primary logistics centre of the Pan-PRD, despite some governmental efforts to address the complaints of shippers.[40]

On the other hand, with regard to infrastructure, there also seem to be more conflicts of interests. Shanghai and Shenzhen are in the process of frantically building ports and transportation networks, often with heavy government involvement. However, the Hong Kong SAR Administration still prides itself on practising the principle of "big market, small government." This reflects what the author has called "asymmetry in government behaviour".[41]

Hong Kong's weakening position is a direct result of competition from Shanghai and Shenzhen, which have been investing heavily in upgrading their transportation facilities. This casts doubt on the ability of the various ports to engage in coordination in the development of infrastructure and on Donald Tsang's plea to avoid "unnecessary competition."

Structural Incongruence and a Lack of Common Interests

Guangdong, the other core economy of the Pan-PRD, has been facing its own problems with upgrading after more than 20 years of low-value-added and processing-driven growth and increasing competition from other regions in the country. Its rising costs and tightening resource constraints, as reflected in energy shortages (in electricity and gasoline) and in a drying up of the supply of cheap labour in recent periods, are a testimony to the dilemma faced by the province. Despite past linkages, Hong Kong as a service economy is not in much of a position to offer assistance in developing high-tech industries and in upgrading industries in Guangdong. What it can offer are mainly "soft goods and services." Hence, in future, there could be a lack of common interests.[42]

In Guangdong's Eleventh Five-year Plan released in late 2005, the provincial authorities stressed the need to "adjust and optimize the economic structure" and to "comprehensively enhance the quality of industries." A number of key industries were highlighted in the Plan for promotion. The Plan emphasized on the need to: strengthen the two "pillar industries" of the electronic IT and petrol-chemical industries; speed up the development of the two "leading sectors" of automobile and equipment manufacturing; actively nurture the three "strategic industries" of bio-engineering, new materials, and new energy generation; reform and enhance the three "traditional sectors" of textiles and garments, food and beverages, and construction materials; and finally to quicken the development of Chinese medical treatments and pharmaceuticals.[43]

It is apparent that most of Hong Kong's manufacturing industries that were relocated to the PRD belong to the "traditional sectors," which are supposed to be reformed and enhanced. They are not "pillar," "leading," or "strategic" in nature. Moreover, most of the 60,000 plus factories set up by Hong Kong businessmen in the PRD, unlike many of the plants set up by Taiwanese, Japanese and those from other countries, are small and medium in size, scattered in terms of location, and lacking in economies of scale. In the increasingly land-scarce province of Guangdong, the problem of consolidation may have to be faced, before genuine reforms and enhancements can be implemented. The author was told by a member of a Guangdong think-tank that the provincial and local governments are pinning their hopes on the possibility that the Hong Kong factories will move voluntarily out of the crowded south into the relatively spacious northern and western parts of the province, leaving more room for industrial consolidation and upgrading.

The structural incongruity between the developmental directions of the two potential "dragon heads" of the Pan-PRD might spell trouble in the future for efforts at coordination.

Concluding Remarks

Economic globalization and regional economic integration are major historical trends, but they not irreversible and certainly do not guarantee success. Their interactive relationships in different contexts are also complex. The Pan-PRD is part of the Chinese and global economic system. Hence, both internal and external linkages need to be carefully handled.

Based on the reality of the Pan-PRD, where development and integration is uneven, but where there is good potential for complementarities, priority should be given to the construction of the hardware, software, and networking infrastructure. However, further down the road, the issues of cooperation and the division of labour, as well as the positioning of constituent economies (within hierarchies of clusters, consisting of cores and hinterlands), will pose a challenge for the authorities, particularly given the asymmetry in governmental behaviour on the two sides of the border with the mainland and the proliferation of local objectives and mini-plans. How to avoid unnecessary competition between the various areas of the Pan-PRD and to ensure structural congruence as well as the formation of common interests are key issues this experiment in regionalization.

Notes

1. "Regional Trade Agreements: Scope of RTAs," WTO web page: http://www. wto.org/english/tratop_e/region_e/scope_rta_e.htm.
2. These three sets of rules are available from the WTO web page: www.wto. org/english/tratop_e/region_e/regrul_e.htm.
3. This is the author's own translation of the clause. The Chinese text of the Framework Agreement can be found in http://www.info.gov.hk/info/9+2/chi/ agreement.pdf. An English summary of the 10 areas of co-operation is provided in Central Policy Unit, HKSAR Government, *Consultancy Study on Socio-Economic-Political Trends in Pan Pearl River Delta Region, Part I and Part*

II, First Monthly Report, (Hong Kong: HKSAR Government, 2004, posted on www.info.gov.hk/cpu/english/papers/PPRD%20A01.pdf and www.info.gov.hk/cpu/english/papers/PPRD%20A02.pdf), Appendix I.

4. See, for example, Memorabilia of Pan-PRD Regional Co-operation. Central Policy Unit, HKSAR Government, *Consultancy Study on Socio-Economic-Political Trends in Pan Pearl River Delta Region, Part I and Part II, Twelfth Monthly Report* (Hong Kong: HKSAR Government, 2005, posted on http://www.cpu.gov.hk/english/documents/new/press/pan-prd%20A12.pdf and http://www.cpu.gov.hk/english/documents/new/press/pan-prd%20B12.pdf), Part I, pp. 58–59; Part II, p. 51.

5. See the extract of the document in Chinese on http://hm.people.com.cn/GB/42273/3566416.html.

6. Nuria Okfen, *Towards an East Asian Community? What ASEM and APEC can tell us* (U.K.: Centre for the Study of Globalization and Regionalization, Warwick University, 2003, Working Paper No. 117/03, www2.warwick.ac.uk/fac/soc/csgr/research/workingpapers/2003/wp11703.pdf/).

7. Tsang Shu-ki, "PPRD Economic Integration: Opportunities or Challenges?" *Hong Kong Economic Journal Monthly*, 2004c (331), pp. 12–14 and 16 (in Chinese).

8. Central Policy Unit, *Consultancy Study on Socio-Economic-Political Trends* (see note 3).

9. The Information is adapted from Section VI of Central Policy Unit (see note 3), supplemented by reports available on the Foreign Trade and Economic Relations and Section of the official Pan-Pearl River Delta Co-operation website http://www.pprd.org.cn/waijingmao.

10. "New Opportunities for Hong Kong in PPRD," *Business Alert—China*, Issue 2, 2005 (1 February), Trade Development Council, Hong Kong (http://www.tdctrade.com/alert/cba-e0502pp1.htm#).

11. Statistics available on http://www.gddoftec.gov.cn/en/Statistical/200406/9.htm and http://www.gddoftec.gov.cn/wjmtj/index.html.

12. According to a mainland report, in the first half of 2005, "general trade" (of imported and exported goods) of the nine provinces amounted to US$69.04 billion, but their "processing trade" totalled double at US$138.77 billion (http://www.southcn.com/news/gdnews/gdtodayimportant/200507250529.htm).

13. "New Opportunities for Hong Kong in PPRD" (see note 10).

14. C. Fred Bergsten, *Open Regionalism* (Washington, D.C.: Institute for International Economics, 1997, Working Paper 97-3), p. 1.

15. P. Kurzer, *Business and Banking: Political Change and Economic Integration in Western Europe* (Ithaca: Cornell University Press, 1993).

16. "A Western European country tended to trade 10% more with everyone than otherwise similar countries. Interestingly, East Asia was even more open than Europe even though it also had a very high intra-regional bias. An East Asian

country traded 100% ... more with a country outside the region than two random countries both outside East Asia.... What they mean is that, for both regions, the formation of (an implicit, if not explicit) trade bloc has not led to a substantial amount of trade diversion from countries outside the regions. Indeed, the trade blocs in these regions appear to have promoted their openness in general, even though trade among themselves may have grown even larger." See Wei Shang-jin and Jeffrey A. Frankel, *Open Regionalism in a World of Continental Trade Blocs* (U.S.: NBER, 1995, Working Paper 5272), pp. 23–24.

17. Mary E. Burfisher, Sherman Robinson and Thierfelder, "Regionalism: Old and New, Theory and Practice." Paper presented at the International Agricultural Trade Research Consortium Conference, Capri, Italy, 2003, http://www.ifpri.org/pubs/confpapers/2003/burfisherrobinsonthierfelder.pdf.

18. Information from the WTO web pages: http://www.wto.org/english/thewto_e/whatis_e/tif_e/bey1_e.htm and www.wto.org/english/tratop_e/region_e/region_e.htm.

19. Paul Bowles, "ASEAN, AFTA and the 'New Regionalism'," *Pacific Affairs*, Summer, 1997, pp. 219–33.

20. Okfen, *Towards an East Asian Community?* (see note 6).

21. Atsushi Yamada, *Between Regionalism and Multilateralism: New Dilemmas in U.S. Trade Policy* (IDE APEC Study Centre, 2002, Working Paper Series 01/03 - No. 5, http://www.ide.go.jp/English/Publish/Apec/pdf/apec13_wp5.pdf).

22. Ibid.

23. The figures are computed on the basis of the revised GDP statistics released after the 2004 Economic Census in China.

24. The ratio is formed by dividing total trade (largely internationally priced) by GDP (underestimated because of the remnants of planning and market distortions). Hence, the denominator is dubiously small although the numerator is acceptable; and the ratio may be exaggerated.

25. For the historical statistics and analyses, see Alan M. Taylor, *Globalization, Trade and Development: Some Lessons from History* (U.S.: NBER, 2002, Working Paper 9326) and Antoni Estevadeordal, Brian Frantz and Alan M. Taylor, "The Rise and Fall of World Trade, 1870–1939," *Quarterly Journal of Economics*, Vol. CXVIII, No. 2 (2003), pp. 359–407.

26. It is worth attention that during the Great Depression of 1929–1935, China was under the Silver Standard and was relatively segregated from the international economy. Many scholars are of the opinion that it was a major reason why China was spared of serious repercussions. A recent example of this kind of analysis can be found in Lai Cheng-chung and Gau Joshua-shiang, Jr., "The Chinese Silver Standard Economy and the 1929 Great Depression," *Australian Economic History Review*, Vol. 43, No. 2 (2003), pp. 155–68.

27. See the extract in Chinese posted on: http://hm.people.com.cn/GB/42273/3566416.html.

28. John Wong and Sarah Chan, "China-ASEAN Free Trade Agreement: Shaping Future Economic Relations," *Asian Survey*, Vol. 43, No. 3 (2003), p. 507.

29. Masahiro Kawai, "Trade and Investment Integration for Development in East Asia: A Case for the Trade-FDI Nexus" (Paper presented to the East Asia Session at the ABCDE Europe Meeting in Brussels, 2004, wbln0018. worldbank.org/eurvp/web.nsf/Pages/Paper+by+Kawai/$File/KAWAI+ABCDE+EUROPE+05-07-2004.PDF), p. 1.

30. Ibid, pp. 2–4.

31. Wong and Chan, *China-ASEAN Free Trade Agreement*, (see note 28); Chalongphob Sussangkarn, "Emergence of China and Asian Revitalization." (Paper presented to the East Asia Session at the ABCDE Europe Meeting in Brussels, 2004, wbln0018.worldbank.org/eurvp/web.nsf/Pages/Paper+by+Sussangkarn/$File/SUSSANGKARN.PDF).

32. Ibid.

33. See the report in Chinese on *Hong Kong Commercial Daily*, 3 July 2005, page A01.

34. H-share and "red chips" are both groups of stocks listed in the Hong Kong Stock Exchange. "Red chips" are firms incorporated in Hong Kong but whose main businesses are in China; while H-shares refer to those mainland enterprises with a secondary listing in Hong Kong.

35. Tsang Shu-ki, "Hong Kong's Economic Strategy Reconsidered" (2003, http://www.hkbu.edu.hk/~sktsang/Devt_Strategy(e).pdf).

36. Tsang Shu-ki, "A Note on Spatial Perspectives: Tacit Knowledge, Embeddedness and Clusters" (2004a, www.hkbu.edu.hk/~sktsang/SpatialClusters.pdf).

37. An example of such strategic thinking is provided in Zhang Huilai 張會來, *Changsanjiao shangyan "houhuayuan" zhi zheng: chengjie fushe cuowei jingzheng* 長三角上演 "後花園" 之爭 —— 承接輻射錯位競爭 (The Competition for Serving as 'Backyard' in the Yangzi Delta—Receiving the Radiating Effect and Competition from the Unusual Position), posted on the web-page of the *Xinhua wang Zhejiang pindao wangye* 新華網浙江頻道網頁 (Zhejiang Channel of Xinhua Net), 7 May 2004 http://big5.xinhuanet.com/gate/big5/www.zj.xinhuanet.com/business/2004-05/07/content_2085796.htm.

38. See Wang Xiaolin 王曉林, *Hainan yousi yu di sanci jiyu* 海南憂思與第三次機遇 (Hainan's Worries and the Third Opportunity), *Ershiyi shiji jingji daobao* 21世紀經濟導報 (21st Century Economic Report), 7 June 2004.

39. The speech, in Chinese only, is available on the website of the Hong Kong SAR Government: http://www.info.gov.hk/gia/general/200507/25/07250107.htm.

40. See the report in Chinese on *Wen Wei Po* 文匯報, Hong Kong, December 2005, p. B04.

41. Tsang Shu-ki (2004b), "The Economic Development Strategy and Fiscal Budget of the SAR," *Hong Kong Economic Journal Monthly*, 2004b (325), pp. 4–6 (in Chinese).
42. Tang Sheng 唐盛, Xiao Tian 曉甜 and Xiao He 曉河, *Quyu jingji bianzou: Chang Zhusanjiao jingji jianshu shi guaidian haishi qiji?* 區域經濟變奏：長珠三角經濟減速是拐點還是契機？(Changes in Regional Economic Development Tempo: Is the Slowing Down of the Economies of the Yangzi Delta and the Pearl River Delta a Turning Point or an Opportunity?), 13 August 2005, posted on *Zhongguo jingji wang* 中國經濟網 (China Economic Net) (http://www.ce.cn/new_hgjj/guonei/dqjj/200508/13/t20050813_4417032.shtml).
43. See the proposed plan approved by the Guangdong CCP in late October and posted on: http://finance.dayoo.com/gb/content/2005-11/01/content_2280599.htm.

5

Infrastructure and Economic Development

Y. M. Yeung and Gordon Kee

For a region as large as half of the size of the expanded European Union, massive infrastructure facilities and services are required for the economic and social development of the Pan–Pearl River Delta (Pan-PRD) 泛珠江三角洲 region. Although a great deal of infrastructure has been built in recent years, the region's varied geography and economic diversity have created a sizeable gap in infrastructure development needs between coastal and inland provinces and between urban and rural areas.[1] For example, the differences in the density of expressways, in capital investment, and in the quality of transport and energy supply are huge. The wealthy and highly urbanized coastal areas possess superior infrastructure. However, despite improvements in infrastructure in the region as a whole, there is a long way to go before the region achieves maturity in this area.

Against the background of globalization and regionalization, the Pan-PRD cooperation framework was established in 2004, the aim of which is to strengthen the regional economy and interactions among the members of the grouping. Here, the relationship between infrastructure and economic development is crucial.[2] The relationship is at once close and important, but unclear. The World Bank examined the issue of infrastructure and development and wrote in the *World Development Report 1994* that, infrastructure represents, if not the engine, then the "wheels" of economic activity.[3] In the early twenty-first century, the Asian Development Bank (ADB) and China's Ministry of Finance (MOF) expressed the view in a technical assistance report that "infrastructure projects can play a major role in generating economic and social benefits, supporting rural and regional development, and reducing poverty and regional disparities."[4] Various empirical studies have also suggested that investment in good infrastructure can reduce costs, and raise the productivity of national and regional economies.[5] Nevertheless, "the precise linkages between infrastructure and development are still open to debate," with the causal relationship between the two remaining unclear.[6]

Although the relationship between infrastructure and economic growth has yet to be defined, the ADB and MOF report presented four principal economic roles that they believe investment in infrastructure will play in China. They are: (1) investments to respond to unmet infrastructure demands and needs resulting from past economic growth; (2) investments to anticipate future development and to stimulate investment in other sectors and economic growth in future years; (3) investments to shape the distribution of growth, individual activity and settlement within regional systems, and (4) investments used by governments as a counter-cyclical instrument to compensate for weaknesses in aggregate demand in other sectors. The report argued that the first role is the most important while the fourth role has become very prominent in the past few years in China. However, it considered that the fourth role can be sustained for a few years and will play a diminishing role as a counter-cyclical device. On the other hand, the second and third roles could take on greater prominence in the coming years.[7]

Setting aside the fourth role for the time being because it is subject to debate, the first three roles do play a significant part in the development of the Pearl River Delta 珠江三角洲 (PRD), the leading region in the Pan-PRD. The development of infrastructure has kept pace with economic development. In the 1980s, economic growth as well as infrastructure development were relatively slow. Entering the 1990s, both economic growth and investment in infrastructure took off. The construction of expressways and ports in Shenzhen 深圳 are outstanding examples. Shenzhen's economy and urban development have literally exploded because of sound infrastructure development. Similarly, the economies of many rural villages have improved vastly after these villages were connected to highways and supplied with telephone and electricity services. From the regional perspective, infrastructure is a tool to narrow economic and social disparities between the eastern, central and western parts of the Pan-PRD region. It is widely anticipated that the strong economies of the eastern Pan-PRD will stimulate growth and investment in the central and western Pan-PRD through improvements in regional infrastructure networks and flows. For instance, the newly completed expressway from Chongqing 重慶 to Guangdong 廣東 is likely to promote the development of the logistics industry in the western Pan-PRD. Likewise, the West-East Power Transmission 西電東送 grid can boost the electricity generation and construction industries in Yunnan 雲南, Guizhou 貴州, and Guangxi 廣西.

To be sure, regional development is hardly a new subject in China. Soon after the establishment of the People's Republic of China in 1949, the "inland development" strategy was adopted. More recently, the Western Region Development Strategy was launched in 1999. Infrastructure, specifically transport, communication, and energy infrastructure to enhance regional connections and flows, plays a critical role in regional development. In the age of globalization, the emphasis on flows — logistics — makes infrastructure even more important to a region. The wide application of high technology in infrastructure allows quality facilities and services to serve the region, with positive effects on regional development and competitiveness.

In the next section, the current conditions in transport, communication and energy infrastructure in the Pan-PRD region are surveyed. The discussion will then focus on new technologies that can improve infrastructure in the new regional economy. The final section evaluates the development of infrastructure in the Pan-PRD.

Provision of Infrastructure

The Pan-PRD framework is widely regarded as the brainchild of Zhang Dejiang 張德江, the Communist Party secretary of Guangdong since 2003. From the outset, infrastructure was assigned a pioneering role in regional development. In early 2004, as a precursor to the establishment of the Pan-PRD region, a road transport cooperation agreement was signed by the nine mainland Pan-PRD members and Chongqing. Outline plans for the building of transport (expressways and waterways) and energy infrastructure in the Pan-PRD were drafted in March 2006. The aim was to establish a coordinated and comprehensive infrastructure network for the region from period of the Eleventh Five-year Plan (11th FYP, 2006–2010) to 2020.

In 2004, passenger traffic in the Pan-PRD region totalled 6.71 billion, or almost 38% of the nation's total. The Pan-PRD region also handled one-fourth of the nation's freight traffic (Table 5.1). These figures attest to the Pan-PRD's significant contribution to transport flows in China. From 2000 to 2004, the Pan-PRD, excluding Hong Kong 香港 and Macao 澳門, invested RMB413.37 billion in capital construction for the "Production and Supply of Electric Power, Gas and Water" and RMB615.38 billion in "Transport, Storage, Post and Telecommunication Services." An extra RMB88.99 billion and RMB209.20 billion, respectively, were earmarked for innovations in these two sectors. The sums poured into these two categories of investment over this period were RMB502.36 billion and RMB824.58 billion, accounting for 14.53% and 23.85%, respectively, of the total investment by the nine Pan-PRD members in these categories.[8]

Highways

In China, highways have developed to be the most important mode of transport, with over 90% of passengers and 70% of goods being transported by highway over the past five years. In 2004, 6.31 billion passengers and 3.40 billion tonnes of freight were transported by highway in the Pan-PRD, or 38.84% and 27.33%, respectively, of the nation's total, as well as

Table 5.1   Passenger and Freight Traffic in the Pan-PRD Region, 2004

	Passenger traffic (million persons)			
	Total	Railways	Highways	Waterways
Pan-PRD	6,709.43	297.48	6,308.98	102.97
% of the nation	37.96%	26.62%	38.84%	54.08%
% of the Pan-PRD region	100.00%	4.43%	94.03%	1.53%

	Passenger-km (billion passenger-km)			
	Total	Railways	Highways	Waterways
Pan-PRD	505.64	169.31	334.03	2.31
% of the nation	31.00%	29.64%	38.18%	34.84%
% of the Pan-PRD region	100.00%	33.48%	66.06%	0.46%

	Freight traffic (million tonnes)			
	Total	Railways	Highways	Waterways
Pan-PRD	4,370.25	484.79	3,402.70	482.76
% of the nation	25.61%	19.47%	27.33%	25.76%
% of the Pan-PRD region	100.00%	11.09%	77.86%	11.05%

	Freight tonnes-km (billion tonnes-km)			
	Total	Railways	Highways	Waterways
Pan-PRD	1,100.26	405.69	248.14	446.43
% of the nation	15.84%	21.03%	31.64%	10.78%
% of the Pan-PRD region	100.00%	36.87%	22.55%	40.57%

Source: By the authors' calculation. National Bureau of Statistics of China, *China Statistical Yearbook 2005* (Beijing: Zhongguo tongji chubanshe, 2005), p. 556–59.

94.03% and 77.86%, respectively, of the total passenger and freight traffic of the region (Table 5.1). Notwithstanding the importance of highway transport in traffic flows in the Pan-PRD region, the region still lacks a complete network of expressways. Dead-end expressways are commonly found between provinces, and even within a province. This drawback has severely set back the goal of achieving heavy regional flows of people and goods.

An early plan for a national highway network comprised of five North-South and seven East-West 五縱七橫 trunk lines was issued in the early 1990s. When completed, it is estimated that the total length of the network will be over 35,000 km, and all 12 lines have been in use by late 2007. The National Expressway Network Plan announced in September 2004 will strengthen what is still a limited highway network. This much-enlarged plan consists of 7 lines with Beijing 北京, the capital, as the origin; 9 North-

South lines and 18 East-West lines (in short, the "7918 Network"). The estimated length of the expressway network is over 85,000 km, and 319 cities with a population of 200 thousand or more will be served.[9] The plan provides for an improved basic highway network that can carry more road traffic by the end of 11th FYP period. By 2010, there will be total of 2.3 million km of highway, with an increase of 380 thousand km. The construction of regional transportation links will be enhanced.[10]

By the end of 2004, there was a total of 12,163 km of expressways in the Pan-PRD, or 35.47% of the total for China.[11] The Pan-PRD Regional Transport (Highways and Waterways) Infrastructure Outline Plan, based on the "7918 Network, was announced in March 2006. A regional expressway network of 10 radial lines originating from major cities in the Greater PRD (GPRD), six North-South lines, five East-West lines, six international corridors and three inter-city expressway networks will be established by 2020 (Figure 5.1). The estimated total length of this network is 37,300 km. Sixteen major nodes and another 49 secondary nodes are planned. The region aims to complete 25,000 km of expressways before 2011. The central role of Guangzhou 廣州 will be consolidated, and the flows within the PRD region, the Chengdu 成都-Chongqing region, and Hainan Island 海南島 will be enhanced by the inter-city expressway networks.[12]

One basic emphasis of both plans is to facilitate an increasing flow of people and goods. Once the network is completed, starting from Hong Kong, it will be possible to reach the following seven Pan-PRD provincial capital cities within 24 hours: Guangzhou, Fuzhou 福州, Nanchang 南昌, Changsha 長沙, Haikou 海口, Nanning 南寧, and Guiyang 貴陽. Two other Pan-PRD provincial capital cities, Chengdu and Kunming 昆明, and Chongqing, Shanghai 上海, and Xi'an 西安, will be reachable within another 24 hours. The embarrassing situation of dead-end highways will probably be eliminated.[13] Not only will intra-Pan-PRD connections be strengthened, but six highway corridors with Myanmar, Laos, and Vietnam will further enhance the connections and flows with these Southeast Asian countries. The strategic role of Yunnan and Guangxi in the ACFTA (ASEAN-China Free Trade Area) development will be more prominent.

Out of 10 radial lines, two start from Hong Kong and Macao. The Zhuhai 珠海-Macao section is also part of the Beijing-Hong Kong/Macao Line in the "7918 Network". On the other side, the Shenzhen Western Corridor 深港西部通道, opened on 1 July 2007, will serve as a major section between Shenzhen and Hong Kong of this national expressway. The Hong

Figure 5.1   The Pan-PRD Regional Expressway Network Plan

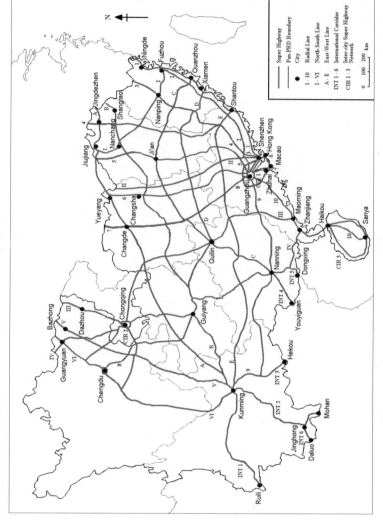

Source: The Pan-PRD Regional Transport (Highways and Waterways) Infrastructure Outline Plan, http://www. Pan-PRD.org.cn/ziliao/zhengce/20060303030014.htm.

Kong—Shenzhen—Guangzhou Expressway, the Guangzhou—Zhuhai—Macao Expressway, and the Hong Kong-Zhuhai-Macao Bridge are three sections that constitute the PRD inter-city expressway network. The aim behind the construction of the Hong Kong-Zhuhai-Macao Bridge, which is now undergoing final feasibility studies, is to connect the two sides of the delta and drive economic growth in the western PRD. It is expected to be an irreplaceable section of the PRD inter-city expressway network once it is completed by the Twelfth FYP period.

Railways

As the vice-minister of the Ministry of Railways noted in 2004, the prevailing conditions of the railways in Pan-PRD of low and saturated capacity, slow running speeds, low railway standards, and insufficient lines were hindering the provision of good railway services and economic development.[14] Nevertheless, the Pan-PRD's railways still handled 26.62% and 19.47%, respectively, of the passenger and freight transport of the country in 2004. Although the absolute numbers of passengers and freight carried by railways cannot compare to those transported by highway, passenger traffic by railway measured in passenger-km and freight traffic in tonne-km made up one-third of the total for the region (Table 5.1). Inter-provincial freight traffic has also been on the rise over the past decade, showing that the links between Guangdong and the southwestern provinces have been increasing.[15] In addition, Guangzhou is the site of one of four passenger railway hubs in the country, handling a large number of passengers on two major lines — the Beijing-Guangzhou Line and the Beijing-Kowloon 九龍 Line. The connections between Guangdong and provinces within the Pan-PRD grouping continue to grow.

Both the central and provincial governments have made sizeable investments in railway transport in recent years, and adopted parallel policies and plans to respond to the dynamic socio-economic changes and demands that have emerged. Work on electrification, double-tracking, and raising the running speed of trains by five times provided a sound foundation on which to build the National Railway Network consisting of eight North-South and eight East-West Lines 八縱八橫. The plan was launched in 2001, with half of the 16 lines to serve the Pan-PRD region. Over the past five years, the Pan-PRD region has chalked up remarkable progress, such as the electrification of the Chengdu—Kunming Line and the rise in the running speed of the Beijing—Guangzhou Line and the Beijing—Kowloon Line.[16]

The National Railway Network has led to an expanded and long-term railway development plan for the country. In January 2004, the central government approved the Medium-to-Long-Term Railway Network Plan. A target of 100,000 km of railways, split between passenger and freight lines, with half of the railways double-tracked and electrified, is to be achieved by 2020. The general running-speed of passenger lines will be raised to 200 km/hour.[17] The short-term goal in the 11th FYP period is to construct 19,800 km of railways, with 9,800 km devoted to passengers, and 8,000 km to be double-tracked and 15,000 km fully electrified.[18]

Under this plan, a brand-new railway network will be constructed in the Pan-PRD region. Eight new railways will be built by 2010, and major projects include the Pan-PRD Regional Express Railway Network, the Beijing—Guangzhou (Shenzhen) Passenger Line, the Hangzhou 杭州—Shenzhen Passenger Line, the Nanjing 南京—Chengdu Passenger Line, and the Hangzhou-Changsha (Zhe-Gan 浙贛) Passenger Line (Figure 5.2). Approximately 10,000 km of railway in the Pan-PRD will be constructed, for a total length of over 29,000 km. In many cities, a frequent and speedy daily public railway service will be introduced.

As the heart of the Pan-PRD, cities in the PRD region will be connected by a new inter-city railway network. Their connections with Hong Kong and Macao will be vitalized by the new Guangzhou-Shenzhen-Hong Kong Line and the Guangzhou-Zhuhai Line. Shenzhen will probably become the second railway hub after Guangzhou in Guangdong, by functioning as the interchange station of the Hangzhou-Shenzhen Passenger Line and the Guangzhou-Shenzhen-Hong Kong Line. Consequently, Hong Kong's hinterland will be vastly expanded through these new railways. Through this new network, Guangdong will be connected by railway with all peripheral provinces, including Hainan Island. In the northwest, Chengdu will be directly connected with Shanghai by new railways. The expected travel time will be greatly shortened from the present 35 hours to only 10 hours. In the southwest, the Pan-Asian Railway will be built and three alignments have been proposed. The China section of the Pan-Asian Railway begins in Kunming; with the eastern alignment having been chosen, the railway will proceed to Vietnam and end up in Singapore, totalling over 5,500 km in length. Besides the eastern alignment, the Yunnan section of the central and western alignments of the Pan-Asian Railway should also be built to increase the number of international corridors leading to and from Yunnan.[19]

Figure 5.2   Medium-to-Long-term Railway Network Plan

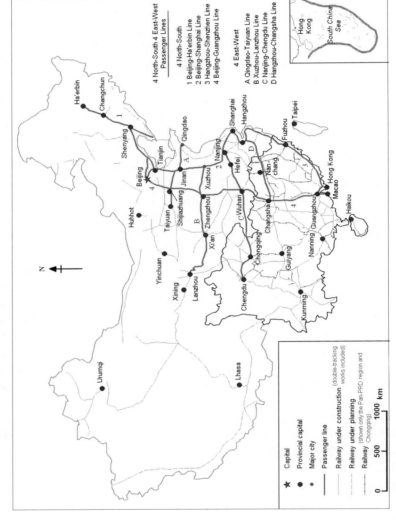

Source: Yeung and Kee, 2005b, p. 17.

Ports

Together, mature river systems spreading across the region and the long coastline have made it possible to develop successful and highly effective regional and international water transport links. Hong Kong Port, Shenzhen Port, and Guangzhou Port are world renowned, partly owing to their favourable locations at the intersection of two major international shipping routes.[20] In 2004 Hong Kong Port and Shenzhen Port ranked first and fourth in the world, respectively, in terms of container throughput, and Guangzhou was sixth in the world by volume of goods handled. The strong trend of increase in throughput, especially in Shenzhen and Guangzhou, is well supported by their vigorous export trade.

In Fujian 福建, Xiamen Port 廈門港 and Fuzhou Port — two of the top 10 ports in China — provide the most direct connections to Taiwan 台灣. There has been direct transport between the two sides of Taiwan Strait for some years, operated on a trial basis, and the preliminary results have been fruitful. People are now clamouring for regular direct transport services to be established. The Xi River 西江, the Lancang River 瀾滄江, and others are major conduits for regional river transport and international trade with Southeast Asian countries. Canalization works has been carried out in the Lancang River—Mekong and river ports such as Jinghong Port 景洪港 and Simao Port 思茅港 have been upgraded to handle the increase in international trade. Although water transport is not a major mode in the region (Table 5.1), water transport in the Pan-PRD, especially with regard to passenger traffic, is a major contributor to the nation. In total, waterway traffic made up 40.57% of the freight tonne-km of the region.

The Ministry of Communications' (MOC) 11th FYP targets and the Pan-PRD Regional Transport (Highways and Waterways) Infrastructure Outline Plan are very ambitious with regard to the development of coastal water transport and infrastructure. The MOC is striving to perfect the spatial structure of the ports, to construct transshipment systems for container, coal, oil, and iron ore, to expand the capacity of ports, to improve navigation channels, and so on.[21] Eight ports and three port authorities in Xiamen Bay have been integrated. The daily management of the eight ports, all navigation channels, and water transport is now the responsibility of the Xiamen Port Authority. Officials strongly believe that this is an important step to achieving better planning and a better allocation of resources in the Bay area, thereby enhancing the capacity and importance of all ports in question. It is, at the same time, a positive step to advancing Fujian's economy.

Following such administrative restructuring, ports in Fujian's Meizhou Bay 湄洲灣 will be similarly integrated.[22]

On the other hand, in order to manage the increasing volume of goods needing to be shipped, major coastal ports in each province, such as Fangchenggang Port 防城港 in Guangxi, Nansha Port 南沙港 and Yantian Port 鹽田港 in Guangdong, and Xiamen Port in Fujian, will be expanded with new deep-water ports to handle container shipments, oil shipments, and so forth. As a result, by 2020 the container throughput and overall port capacity of the region, excluding Hong Kong and Macao, is expected to rise to 110 million TEUs and about 2.3 billion tonnes, respectively.[23] As the leading port in the region, Container Terminal 9 of Hong Kong Port came into full operation in 2004. Hong Kong Port now possesses 24 berths for container use and an annual processing capacity of up to 14.4 million TEUs.[24] Serious consideration is being given to the construction of Container Terminal 10, prompted by increasing concerns over regional coordination. The fear is that, if Hong Kong does not continue to expand its port capacity, it will be left behind in the process.

With regard to river transport and ports, the improvement of port facilities and navigation channels are major ongoing tasks. For example, modifications will be made to the Gan River in Jiangxi and the Xiang River 湘江 in Hunan 湖南 to make it possible for 300 DWT vessels to navigate these rivers. The canalization of the Jialing River 嘉陵江 is underway. However, the Pan-PRD Regional Transport (Highways and Waterways) Infrastructure Outline Plan conveys the impression that the top priority is the development of the Pearl River System. The plan includes the completion of a network of high-class channels in the PRD and improvements to the navigation channel of Xi River, inclusive of the canalization of the You River 右江. Nanning Port, Guigang Port 貴港, Foshan Port 佛山港, and others have been designated to be major river ports in the Pan-PRD.[25] Figure 5.3 highlights the plan to construct class 3–5 navigation channels in the Pearl River.

Airports

The demand for air transport is rising rapidly. As people become increasingly affluent, they have been flying more for work and leisure. A changing consumer market is also making the speedy delivery of goods more critical. In 2004, the 10 busiest intra-Pan-PRD routes together handled 7.25 million passengers (Table 5.2), an increase of 2.37 million passengers over the

Figure 5.3 Major Rivers and Navigation Channels in the Pan-PRD Region

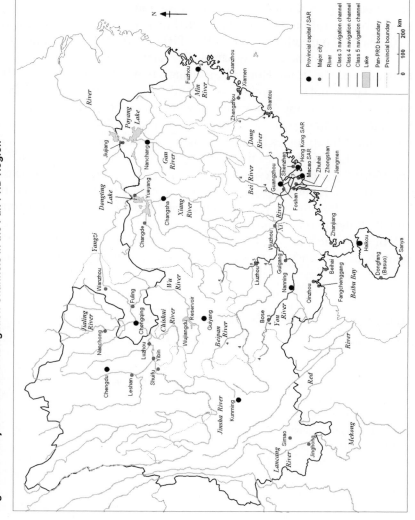

Source: Yeung and Kee, 2005c, p. 3.

previous year, when numbers were down due to the outbreak of Severe
Acute Respiratory Syndrome (SARS). The Guangzhou–Haikou Line was
the only route to transport over one million passengers, and ranked seventh
among all domestic routes in China. Two conclusions may be drawn from
these figures. First, Guangzhou's pre-eminent role as a national hub partly
arises from the role it plays in the Pan-PRD region. Among domestic routes
in China, its connection with two Pan-PRD provincial capitals tied for
second place, and the route to Sanya 三亞, another tourist destination in
Hainan, ranked seventh. However, its connection with the third Pan-PRD
provincial capital — Kunming — ranked only 12th. On the other hand,
Chengdu and Kunming airports are growing in importance and popularity.
Second, two intra-provincial routes did not make the list of the 10 busiest
intra–Pan-PRD air routes in 2003, including the Chengdu-Jiuzhaigou 九寨
溝 Line and the Kunming-Lijiang 麗江 Line, which handled only 114,522
and 166,195 passengers, respectively, that year. However, these two routes,
along with the Xishuangbanna 西雙版納-Kunming Line now on the top 10
list, can be classified as tourism routes, and provide proof of the strong
growth of the tourism industry in Sichuan 四川 and Yunnan in 2004.

In the same year, 33 major airports in the Pan-PRD (each with a
throughput of at least 100 thousand passengers), including the Hong Kong

Table 5.2   The Ten Busiest Intra-Pan-PRD Air Routes, 2004

Route	Frequency	Passenger traffic (person)	Freight traffic (tonnes)
1. Guangzhou-Haikou	9,799	1,169,699	9,015.4
2. Guangzhou-Chengdu	7,644	918,964	31,886.0
3. Chengdu-Jiuzhaigou*	6,108	782,778	48.3
4. Chengdu-Shenzhen	6,511	729,054	21,019.3
5. Xishuangbanna-Kunming*	6,122	693,832	3,152.1
6. Chengdu-Kunming	5,905	691,606	12,990.9
7. Guangzhou-Sanya	5,985	690,475	1,626.8
8. Haikou-Shenzhen	4,926	659,915	1,329.8
9. Kunming-Shenzhen	3,851	497,133	12,845.4
10. Kunming-Lijiang*	3,937	412,492	208.0
17. Guangzhou–Hong Kong	3,845	353,554	4,080.0

Remarks: Hong Kong and Macao included.
* Intra-provincial routes.
Source: *China Transportation and Communications Yearbook 2005* (see note 10),
         p. 686.

International Airport and the Macao International Airport, together handled 137.10 million passengers and 5.08 million tonnes of goods, or 48.63% and 57.46%, respectively, of the nation's total.[26] Of the 33 airports, the Hong Kong International Airport was the busiest, with 36.29 million passengers and 3.09 million tonnes of goods handled in 2004, followed by the Guangzhou Baiyun International Airport 廣州白雲國際機場 and Shenzhen International Airport. As with other modes of transport, the supply of air services cannot fully meet the huge emerging demand, especially for the most popular routes and during peak periods. Under such conditions, delays or flight cancellations are common, resulting in large economic losses.

In response to the increasing demand for air transport services, the construction of new airports or the upgrading of existing ones is a major element of infrastructure development. Indeed, a significant component of the 11th FYP is the strengthening of airport infrastructure. In the 10th FYP period, a total of RMB94.7 billion was invested in air transport and 21 airports were built. A large number of airports were also expanded.[27] In the PRD, the new Guangzhou Baiyun International Airport replaced the old airport in August 2004. Its potential is partly reflected in at the fact that it is 3.6 times the size of the old airport, or 231 hectares larger than Hong Kong International Airport.[28] Shenzhen International Airport is now building a second runway. In view of the large number of airports in the region, a new air transport development strategy calls for any new airport being built to pay full heed to a coordinated spatial layout, taking into account scale, functions, and facilities. Consequently, a new international airport in Kunming will be constructed in parallel with the new town of Kunming. It will serve as a hub for southwest China and a gateway to the ASEAN countries. In the GPRD region, the Hong Kong Airport Authority, which is not governed by the General Administration of Civil Aviation (CAAC), recently unveiled a HK$4.5 billion plan to upgrade a series of facilities and to enhance capacity at the Hong Kong International Airport by 2010.[29] The Hong Kong International Airport is already one of the busiest and the best airports in the world.[30] The enhancement works will further consolidate its status as an international hub in the region and will go some way towards smoothing cooperation with Guangzhou International Airport, Shenzhen International Airport, Macao International Airport, and Zhuhai Airport in the GPRD region.

In addition, better coordination between airports is contingent on the implementation of relevant policies and continuous reforms in the air transport industry. In fact, these are also the main targets to be fulfilled in the 11ᵗʰ FYP period. In the 10ᵗʰ FYP period, the basic hub-and-spokes network was constructed in Yunnan. For example, Kunming Airport has been functioning well as a key link in intra- and inter-provincial routes. The frequent flights between Kunming Airport and over 10 Yunnan local airports such as Lijiang Airport, Dali Airport 大理機場, and Xianggelila (Shangri-la) Airport 香格里拉機場 have greatly enhanced Yunnan's tourism industry, and have enabled the province to export the products of its horticultural and agricultural industries to the international market. Such positive developments owe much to the decentralization of airports in China, with the exception of the airports of Beijing and Tibet 西藏, that took place following the Civil Aviation Reforms of 2002. As a result of the reform policy, the assets, ownership, and daily management of China's airports, which were formally controlled by CAAC, have been localized. Each province manages its local airports by setting up enterprises. The decentralization of airport management may be viewed as a giant step forward, as it allows each province to manage and develop its own airports. The result has been improved spatial coordination and airport connectivity.

However, a hub-and-spokes network has yet to be formed in other Pan-PRD provinces such as Sichuan and Guizhou, which are also rich in tourism potential and natural resources. In Guizhou, Xingyi Airport 興義機場 was opened in 2004, Liping Airport 黎平機場 in 2005 and Libo Airport 荔波機場 in 2007. The hope is that a proper network will form between the Guiyang Airport (the hub) and these local airports (the spokes). As important as the hub-and-spokes network (the function and role), the extent to which these airports are utilized should be an indicator of their value and contribution. As Yeung and Kee (2006a) have emphasized, only an airport favoured by airlines and passengers can generate income and support its development. Therefore, in planning an airport, it is essential for the governments and enterprises involved to factor in its attraction to airlines and passengers, to say nothing of coordinating with other airports. For the five airports in the GPRD region, coordination has become a top priority. A regional governance structure is not to be found in the letter of the law. In an attempt to come to grips with the problems of coordination, the A5 Forum was established in 2001, and four meetings have been held so far. Important decisions of coordination such as the re-arrangement and management of flight paths have yet to be made. Hong Kong International Airport's continuing cooperation with Shenzhen International Airport and Zhuhai Airport are positive initial steps, but many obstacles to coordination remain.

Communication and Telecommunications

Communication and telecommunications play a critical role in building a new national economy and in fostering the integration of the Pan-PRD region. By the end of 2005, over 111 million people in China had access to internet services, with 37.50 million households having accessed the internet by broadband networks. On the other hand, the number of registered mobile phone users in the country increased by 58.60 million for a total of 393.43 million users.[31] Within the Pan-PRD region, there were five categories of digital subscribers, accounting for between 22.09% to 41.61% of the total number of users in the nation in 2004, with two internet categories comprising 36.84% and 37.63% of the national total.[32] Internet and mobile communication services are becoming popular; in fact, for some people, they have become daily necessities.

As can be seen from the above brief background sketch, if the country is to sustain its new economy, it must construct and improve its infrastructure. In 2004, RMB219.91 billion was invested in the telecommunications industry. Since 1998, the whole country has been under the coverage of a network consisting of eight North-South and eight East-West 八縱八横 fibre cables, with an initial capacity in 2.5Gb/s.[33] Six North-South and three East-West fibre cables are operating in the Pan-PRD region. Intra-provincial networks and local networks are being extended to include more towns and villages, especially those in coastal areas that have been wired to the virtual world. By the end of 2005, the total length of fibre cables laid in China reached 4.05 million km.[34] The latest figure for China on the informationalization composite index is 30.6%, still a far cry from the situation in industrially advanced countries.[35] Although the general figure is much lower in some provinces, especially those in southwest China, the figure for some cities, such as those in Guangdong, is over 60%, or even 80%, reaching the level of developed countries.

Rapid development was seen in the communication and information industry during the 10th FYP period, and its contribution to the national GDP increased. Living standards improved, especially in rural areas. For example, at the end of the 10th FYP some 95% of the villages in China had telephone services, compared to 89.2% five years earlier. In the 11th FYP period, the industry has been singled out as a major technological industrial sector for expansion and for the construction of large-scale infrastructure. Apart from the provision of infrastructure, the government plans to promote and enhance electronic services, such as e-government, e-commerce, e-education, e-medical treatment, and so on. Even traditional sectors have been encouraged to adopt new communication devices and information technology.[36]

Within the Pan-PRD, enhanced cooperation is being facilitated via the construction of public virtual platforms and infrastructure, as well as by the development of an IT industry. An outstanding example is the construction of the homepage of the Pan-PRD (www.Pan-PRD.org.cn). It is a comprehensive information platform that provides much information on the 11 Pan-PRD members. The information provided ranges from governmental issues to development trends in various business sectors and investment opportunities. The site also carries daily news and annual statistics, as well as tourism information and links to other topics. It is a convenient gateway for individuals, enterprises, investors, and travellers with different interests to approach the Pan-PRD region. Unfortunately, so far only people able to read Chinese can access this gateway. The Pan-PRD Office should at least provide an English homepage for the benefit of foreigners who are not proficient in Chinese. There is also another homepage on information relating to investment, tourism, and on the nine Pan-PRD provincial capitals. To be sure, electronic business, the exchange of business information, software, and certificate authority (CA) are among the major means of communication within those business and industrial sectors that focus on development.

Energy

Insufficient supplies of energy are hindering economic and social development in China. In China, especially in the coastal provinces, there is a great imbalance between supply and demand for energy resources.[37] Within the Pan-PRD region, Guangdong is the leader by far in both the generation and consumption of power, and frequently experiences serious energy shortages. Not surprisingly, the current development strategy of the country is to actively explore natural resources in western China to secure a more stable supply of energy to the coastal region. There is almost an ideal match between the eastern and the western regions of the country, based as it is on fulfilling reciprocal needs and making use of comparative advantages for mutual benefit.[38] The West-East Power Transmission Project and the West-East Gas Pipeline Project 西氣東輸 were launched in 2000 under this simple economic logic.

While the West-East Gas Pipeline Project is an engineering feat entailing the construction of an almost endless run of pipelines from Xinjiang 新疆 to Shanghai, the West-East Power Transmission Project consists of three parts, with a southern line directing supplies of energy to the Pan-PRD region.

In addition to the progress that has been made in the 10th FYP period on individual projects in the coal and oil industries, significant headway has been made in the area of electricity supplies, with many projects having been completed ahead of schedule, such as the Longtan Power Station 龍灘水電站 in Guangxi, Nayong Power Plant One 納雍一廠 in Guizhou, and the Gui-Guang (Guizhou-Guangdong) 500 kV direct current (DC for short) cable. The basic southern power grid, completed in September 2004, should be mentioned as being one of the most important projects (Figure 5.4). This power grid network is providing Guangdong, Guangxi, Guizhou, and Yunnan with a more stable and reliable power supply than before, and will allow the West-East power transmission to run at a maximum load of 11 million kW.

Between now and 2020, Pan-PRD governments are committed to undertaking a series of hydropower projects and to constructing coal power plants in order to enhance the West-East transmission of power. In Guangxi, the Qinzhou Power Plant 欽州電廠 and the Fangchenggang Power Plant are now under construction. In Yunnan, two mammoth projects, the Xiaowan Power Station 小灣水電站 and the Nuozhadu Power Station 糯扎渡水電站 are being built, along with six other dams and power stations in the middle reaches of Lancang River. The hydropower that will be generated will be transmitted not only to local areas and to Guangdong, but also to Southeast Asia. Along the Jinsha River 金沙江, which divides Yunnan and Sichuan provinces, the plan is to build eight power stations in the middle reaches. In the lower reaches, four more gigantic power stations will be constructed, namely the Xiluodu 溪洛渡, Xiangjiaba 向家壩, Wudongde 烏東德 and Baihexi 白鶴溪 stations. When all four power stations are operating simultaneously, the maximum amount of power generated could reach 38. 50 million kW, twice the power generated by the Three Gorges Power Station.

Besides coal and hydropower, the governments involved have been developing other means of generating power to meet the rapid growth in energy consumption. To date, nuclear power contributes only 2.3% of the supply of energy, mainly because governments have invested only modestly in developing in nuclear power. However, the 11th FYP actively provides

Figure 5.4   Southern Power Grid, 2004

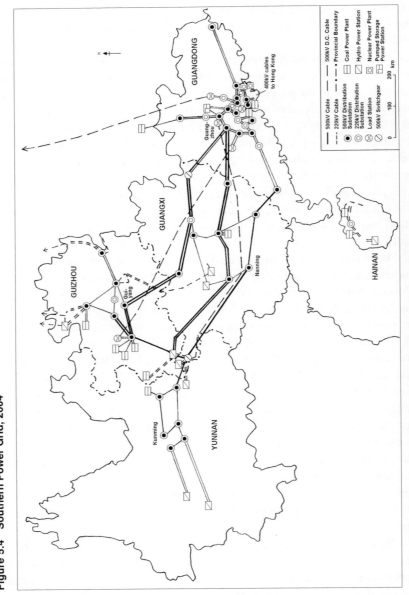

Source: EHV Power Transmission Company (www.spsc.com.cn/map.htm).

for the country to expand its use of nuclear power. It is anticipated that the country will increase its nuclear power capacity by four times, from 8.7 million kW to 36 million kW, in the coming 15 years.[39] Therefore, nuclear power will likely contribute about 6% of China's electricity by 2020.[40] As power plants have very specific locational requirements and require government support to be built in the Pan-PRD region, most nuclear power plants are found in Guangdong. These plants include the Ling'ao 嶺澳 Phase Two, to be completed by 2010; and the Yangjiang 陽江 nuclear power plant. The latter is a US$8 billion project involving the installation of six sets of one million kW power generators. It should be the largest project to date and should be completed by 2012. Two more nuclear power plants on a similar scale are in consideration and will probably be located in Jiangmen 江門 and Shanwei 汕尾. When all of these projects are completed, Guangdong will have nuclear power generators with a capacity of 24 million kW.[41]

The increasing consumption of power has forced the China Southern Power Grid Company to expedite the installation of 800 kV and 1000 kV extreme high voltage (in short, EHV) cables. The EHV technology can support a stable and powerful supply of power on a larger, regional scale. During a meeting of Pan-PRD members, contracts were signed between Guangdong and Yunnan and Guizhou. In addition, in the 11th FYP period Yunnan and Guizhou will ensure the stable West-East transmission of power to Guangdong, and with increased investment, speed up the work of constructing in these two provinces coal power plants and hydropower stations as well as the necessary accessories. Moreover, a contract for combining the southern power grid and the Hainan power grid has been signed (Figure 5.4). This combined power grid will increase the stability of power transmissions, reduce power wastage, and will be favourable for the environment.

Infrastructure and the New Economy

As Yeung and others have highlighted, the New Economy, predicated on the production, acquisition, and transmission of new information, has arrived following a battery of technological advances driven by telecommunications, robotics, and other innovations.[42] As an economic powerhouse, China is tackling the difficulties posed by the New Economy. Opening up from a closed market, the widespread problems of poor infrastructure, local protectionism, and ineffective laws and regulations are hindering economic development. Improving infrastructure facilities and services is a necessary first step. Moreover, in the New Economy, logistics is not simply about the transporting of goods. It is a technologically oriented system of management and monitoring, including the processing of the transport of goods. Information technology is widely applied in this industry.

Since the Pan-PRD region accounts for some 40% of the nation's exports, a huge volume of goods is being transported between coastal ports and inland provinces. Therefore, improving the flow of goods, enhancing efficiency and effectiveness, and developing modern logistics systems are matters of high priority. In 2004, the total expenditure on logistics in China was RMB2,911.4 billion, an increase of 16.6% over the previous year. China's expenditure on logistics was 21.3% of national GDP, as against about 10% in developed countries such as the US and Japan, indicating that there is much room for improvement in this industry in China.[43]

Based on an upgraded transport and communication infrastructure, information technologies can be widely used to manage and monitor freight transport, to coordinate transshipments, and to provide on-schedule and safe services. The aim is to utilize transport services effectively to provide a seamless, just-in-time and time-saving flow of goods from origin to destination. This objective is reflected in the Agreement of the Cooperative Development of Modern Logistics in the Pan-PRD Region. The agreement provides for the enhanced connection of logistics nodes (cities), the construction of inter-provincial infrastructure, and a simplified and one-stop check as practical measures to be carried out in the region. For the last item mentioned, the agreement calls for encouraging enterprises to adopt information technology in their logistics management, to construct a logistics information feedback system and an alarm system in all relevant government departments. Guangdong and Hong Kong are the two members of the Pan-PRD grouping with the most advanced and flourishing logistics industries. Developing intertwined infrastructure and information exchange platforms, and ensuring that they run smoothly, are priorities. Inevitably, infrastructure development is going to play a decisive role in regional development.

Concluding Remarks

The Pan-PRD is a very large and diverse region of China, where it is extremely challenging to construct and maintain transport, tele-communications and energy infrastructure. To enhance regional connectivity and accessibility, the Southwest Corridor (Chongqing-Zhanjiang 湛江), the Beijing-Zhuhai Expressway (the Hunan and Guangdong section), the Tong-San 同三 Expressway (the Fujian and Guangdong sections), the Qian-Gui 黔桂 Railway, the Beijing-Guangzhou Railway, and the Chengdu-Kunming Railway, to name a few, have been constructed and bear the responsibility of fostering regional development. On the other hand, the Five Fixed Train services, Green Corridors for agricultural products, and Barrier-Free Travel are being promoted to foster the development of multi-modal transshipment and logistics systems, the transport of agricultural products, and regional tourism in the Pan-PRD.

Notwithstanding the achievements in providing infrastructure that have been realized so far, the Pan-PRD is a brand-new framework under which a satisfactory level of coordination among members must await time and trial. Successful cooperation in developing infrastructure can come only after trial and error. To move the agenda for cooperation forward, the remaining discussion can focus on the following problems.

First, as a novel framework for regional cooperation in which the members of the grouping are bound by goodwill rather than by the letter of the law, the Pan-PRD did not figure in the National 11th FYP. To begin with, the region is characterized by very different political systems and provincial economies at very different levels of development. Different administrative systems among the governments involved, diverse official attitudes towards regional integration, and varying degrees of success in raising funds are among the barriers to achieving coordination in the development of infrastructure. A proper regional mechanism and appropriate government departments in each province have yet to be created. In addition, covert practices widespread in governments at the bottom level should be eliminated. Infrastructure that has been constructed without having undergone the proper approval procedures cannot fit in with the regional infrastructure plan and should be prohibited.

Second, infrastructure that was developed prior to the formation of the Pan-PRD generally suffers from a lack of coordination in terms of spatial layout, scale, and timing; the result is poor economic and social efficiency. The annual average rates of growth of passenger traffic (6.52%) and freight traffic (6.84%) in the Pan-PRD from 2000 to 2004 are much lower than the average GDP growth rate for the region (12.66%) and the national gross industrial output (21.58%). Consequently, the growing demand for transport services cannot be fully satisfied. The construction of new infrastructure under the Pan-PRD framework should improve this situation. A well-managed comprehensive regional infrastructure network should be an impetus for development.

Third, similar to the case of Western Region Development that was studied by Yeung and others,[44] the transport, energy, and telecommunications sectors are those that have received the most attention and captured the most investment in the development of that region of China, while other sectors have been allocated less resources. Infrastructure related to ecological protection, disaster prevention, or the most basic provision of water and hygiene, especially in rural areas and in southwest China, should be an obvious focus for immediate attention. Fortunately, Guangxi, Sichuan, Guizhou, and Yunnan can capitalize on both the favourable policies of Western Region Development and the Pan-PRD framework to make great progress in constructing infrastructure and to possibly leapfrog to cutting-edge standards for such infrastructure.

Indeed, the Pan-PRD is a region full of resources, comparative advantages, and opportunities. In the two Pan-PRD forums held in 2004 and 2005, RMB57.08 billion and RMB20.8 billion, respectively, of infrastructure projects were signed; the projects signed after the first Pan-PRD Forum were worth RMB453.5 billion. To sustain the development of regional infrastructure, three conditions must be achieved and maintained.

There is an urgent need to establish a mechanism for coordinating infrastructure projects. Ideally, this should be a permanent body with the power to coordinate government authorities on such issues as the timing, scale, and other technical issues of all regional infrastructure developments, such as in the building of comprehensive transport and energy infrastructure. Moreover, it should be a body that can coordinate the operation and maintenance of infrastructure.

In addition, an active market in transport and energy can foster the development of infrastructure. In this respect, the participation of the private sector and the adoption of market mechanisms are prerequisites. Not only does the role of various levels of government and the private sector need to be well defined, but a healthy regional market with unambiguous regulations, and a smooth and unimpeded flow of information should also be created.

Last, but not least, investment in infrastructure has been wholly the prerogative of governments until recently. However, the infrastructure market has changed sharply, with the role of government being supplemented by new channels and opportunities for attracting capital from different sources. The result is that investments in infrastructure and the management of infrastructure services have become much more diversified and effective. The outcome is a more favourable situation in which the development of infrastructure can be used as a lever to accelerate regional development.

Notes

1. See Chapter 3 for a discussion of the geographical background of the Pan-PRD region, Chapter 4 on its economic basis, and Chapter 9 on the issue of regional disparities in the region.
2. Y. M. Yeung, Jin Fengjin and Zeng Guang, "Infrastructure and the New Economy," in *Developing China's West: A Critical Path to Balanced National Development*, edited by Y. M. Yeung and Shen Jianfa (Hong Kong: The Chinese University Press, 2004), p. 108.
3. World Bank, *World Development Report 1994* (New York: Oxford University Press, 1994), p. 14.
4. Asian Development Bank (ADB) and Ministry of Finance (MOF), China, *Strengthening Public Infrastructure Investment Policy in the People's Republic of China: Strategic Options for Central, Provincial and Local Government. Executive Summary Report* (Manila: Asian Development Bank, 2002), p. 5.
5. Such as Emiel A. Wegelin, "The Urban Management Programme and Integrated Urban Infrastructure Development," in *Integrated Urban Infrastructure Development in Asia*, edited by Kulwant Singh, Florian Steinberg and Nathaniel von Einsiedel (New Delhi: Oxford and IBH Publishing Co. Pvt. Ltd., 1996), p. 49; World Bank, *World Development Report* (see note 3), p. 2; Chen, Jiyu, Cao Yong and Liu Jie, "Bridges, Tunnels and Their Relationship to the Economic Development on Both Sides of Taiwan Strait," *Marine Georesources and Geotechnology*, Vol. 21 (2003), pp. 261–67; Tuan Chyau and Linda Ng, *A Miracle via Agglomeration: The HK-PRD connection* (Hong Kong: Department of Decision Sciences and Managerial Economics, The Chinese University of Hong Kong, 2003).
6. ADB and MOF, *Strengthening Public Infrastructure Investment Policy* (see note 4), p. 4.
7. Ibid.
8. By the authors' calculation. Year 2004 figures for Yunnan are not available; therefore, the figures are not complete. National Bureau of Statistics of China, *China Statistical Yearbook 2001–2004* (Beijing: China Statistics Press, various years); *Statistical Yearbook 2005* of Fujian, Jiangxi, Hunan, Guangdong, Guangxi, Hainan, Sichuan and Guizhou.
9. ADB and MOF, *Strengthening Public Infrastructure Investment Policy* (see note 4), p. 108.

10. "Jiaotongbu jiang zai 'shiyi wu' qijian ban cheng jiaotong shiye liu jian da shi" 交通部將在"十一五"期間辦成交通事業六件大事 (MOC to Complete Six Transport Businesses in the 11th FYP Period). 中央政府門戶網站 (The Chinese Central Government's Official Web Portal) (www.gov.cn), 16 January 2006.

11. *Zhongguo jiaotong nianjian 2005* 中國交通年鑒 2005 (China Transport Yearbook 2005) (Beijing: Zhongguo jiaotong chubanshe 中國交通出版社, 2005), p. 652.

12. "Fan Zhusanjiao quyu hezuo gonglu shuilu jiaotong jichu sheshi guihua gangyao" 泛珠三角區域合作公路水路交通基礎設施規劃綱要 (Pan-PRD Regional Highways and Waterways Infrastructure Outline Plan), 泛珠三角合作信息網 (Pan-PRD Information Net) (www.Pan-PRD.org.cn), 3 March 2006.

13. Y. M. Yeung, Y.M. 楊汝萬 and Gordon Kee Wai-man 紀緯紋, *Fan Zhusanjiao jichu jianshe fazhan yanjiu xilie, I. Gaosu gonglu* 泛珠三角基礎建設發展研究系列, I. 高速公路 (Basic Infrastructure Development in the Pan–Pearl River Delta Research Series, I. Highways) Occasional Paper No. 153 (Hong Kong: Hong Kong Institute of Asia-Pacific Studies, The Chinese University of Hong Kong, 2005a), p. 14.

14. Y. M. Yeung, and Gordon Kee Wai-man, *Fan Zhusanjiao jichu jianshe fazhan yanjiu xilie, II. Tielu* 泛珠三角基礎建設發展研究系列, II. 鐵路 (Basic Infrastructure Development in the Pan–Pearl River Delta Research Series, II. Railways) Occasional Paper No. 155 (Hong Kong: Hong Kong Institute of Asia-Pacific Studies, The Chinese University of Hong Kong, 2005b), p. 14.

15. Ibid., p. 9.

16. Yeung et al., "Infrastructure and the New Economy" (see note 2), p. 113; see also Yeung and Kee, *Fan Zhusanjiao jichu jianshe fazhan* (see note 14), p. 15.

17. Yeung and Kee, *Fan Zhusanjiao jichu jianshe fazhan* (see note 14), p. 16.

18. "Tielu queding shiyi wu guihua liu da mubiao, jiang jian xinxian 19,800 gongli" 鐵路確定十一五規劃六大目標, 將建新線19,800公里 (Six Railway Targets in the 11th FYP Period, 19,800 km of New Railway Will Be Constructed), 中央政府門戶網站 (The Chinese Central Government's Official Web Portal) (www.gov.cn), 21 February 2006.

19. Yeung and Kee, *Fan Zhusanjiao jichu jianshe fazhan* (see note 14), p. 22.

20. See Chapter 10 p. 286.

21. See notes 10 and 12.

22. "Fujian dazao quanxin Xiamen Gang, tongshi zujian Xiamen Gangkou Guanliju" 福建打造全新廈門港, 同時組建廈門港口管理局 (Fujian Has Established a New Xiamen Port and a New Xiamen Port Authority), 交通部新聞 (Ministry of Communications News) (www.moc.gov.cn), 4 January 2006.

23. See note 12.

24. Y. M. Yeung and Gordon Kee Wai-man, *Fan Zhusanjiao jichu jianshe fazhan yanjiu xilie, III. Gangkou ji hangdao* 泛珠三角基礎建設發展研究系列, III. 港口及航道 (Basic Infrastructure Development in the Pan–Pearl River Delta Research Series, III. Ports and Waterways) Occasional Paper No. 158 (Hong Kong: Hong Kong Institute of Asia-Pacific Studies, The Chinese University of Hong Kong, 2005c).

25. See note 12; also see Yeung and Kee, *Fan Zhusanjiao jichu jianshe fazhan* (see note 24).

26. Yeung, Y. M. and Gordon Wai-man Kee, *Fan Zhusanjiao jichu jianshe fazhan yanjiu xilie, IV. Jichang he minhang* 泛珠三角基礎建設發展研究系列, IV. 機場和民航 (Basic Infrastructure Development in the Pan–Pearl River Delta Research Series, IV. Airports and Civil Aviation) Occasional Paper No. 163 (Hong Kong: Hong Kong Institute of Asia-Pacific Studies, The Chinese University of Hong Kong, 2006a), p. 8. In mainland Chinese statistics, air routes between mainland Chinese cities and the two SARs (Hong Kong and Macao) are not included as domestic flights. However, for reasons of simplicity, in this regional study (Pan-PRD), all flights within the Pan-PRD region are treated as domestic flights.

27. "Zhongguo minhang 'shi wu' chengjiu he 'shiyi wu' zhanwang" 中國民航 "十五"成就和"十一五"展望 (The Achievements of the Civil Aviation Administration of China in the 10th FYP Period and the Prospects for the 11th FYP), 中國民用航空總局 (CAAC news) (www.caac.gov.cn), 14 February 2006.

28. Yeung and Kee, *Fan Zhusanjiao jichu jianshe fazhan* (see note 26) p. 5. The new Baiyun Airport was constructed under the standard of a hub airport, and its size is 1,456 ha.

29. "$4.5 billion to Enhance Airport Capacity and Facilities," Hong Kong Airport Authority news, 26 January 2006.

30. Yeung and Kee, *Fan Zhusanjiao jichu jianshe fazhan* (see note 26), p. 9. Hong Kong International Airport ranked first in the handling of international cargo and fifth in the number of international passengers in 2004. It received the world's "Best Airport Award" from Skytrax Research for the fifth consecutive year (2001–2005). It was also named Best Airport Worldwide in the AETRA survey in 2005.

31. "Wo bu fabu 2005 nian tongxin ye fazhan tongji gongbao" 我部發佈2005年通信業發展統計公報 (The MII Has Released the 2005 Statistical Report of the Information Industry), 信息產業部 (Ministry of Information Industry) (www.mii.gov.cn), 9 February 2006.

32. *Zhongguo jiaotong nianjian 2005* (see note 11), p. 705. The two internet categories are "digital subscribers with dial-up access" and "digital subscribers with leased-line access." The number of people with "broadband Internet access" has yet to be included.

33. Wu Hequan 鄔賀銓, "Zhongguo guangxian chuansong wang de fazhan" 中國
    光纖傳送網的發展 (The Development of a Fibre Cable Network in China),
    通信專業網站 (www.c114.net), 7 September 2000.
34. Ministry of Information Industry (see note 31).
35. "Jie du 'shiyi wu'" 解讀"十一五" (Figuring out the 11th FYP), 中國信息產業
    網 (China Information Industry Net), 29 December 2005.
36. Ibid.
37. Y. M. Yeung and Gordon Kee Wai-man, *Fan Zhusanjiao jichu jianshe fazhan
    yanjiu xilie, V. Dianli* 泛珠三角基礎建設發展研究系列, V. 電力 (Basic
    Infrastructure Development in the Pan–Pearl River Delta Research Series,
    V. Electricity) Occasional Paper No. 167 (Hong Kong: Hong Kong Institute
    of Asia-Pacific Studies, The Chinese University of Hong Kong, 2006b); also
    see Yeung et al., "Infrastructure and the New Economy" (see note 2), p. 119.
38. Yeung et al., "Infrastructure and the New Economy" (see note 2), pp. 119–20.
39. "Zhongguo mei nian jiang jian yige Daya Wan" 中國每年將建一個大亞灣
    (China to Build One Daiya Bay-scale Nuclear Plant Each Year), *Wen Wei Po*
    文匯報, 10 February 2006, A8.
40. "Zhongguo jiang tou siqianyi jian hedian" 中國將投四千億建核電 (China to
    Invest 400 Billion in Nuclear Power), *Wen Wei Po*, 7 June 2005, A8.
41. Yeung and Kee, *Fan Zhusanjiao jichu jianshe fazhan* (see note 37).
42. Yeung et al., "Infrastructure and the New Economy" (see note 2), p. 121.
43. China Federation of Logistics and Purchasing (eds.), *China Logistics Yearbook
    2005* (Beijing: China Logistics Publishing House, 2005), pp. 128–29 (in
    Chinese).
44. Yeung et al., "Infrastructure and the New Economy" (see note 2), p. 127.

6

Education and Manpower Training

Xiao Jin

Manpower Issues and Education for Development

The rise of China through a strategy of concentrating scarce resources in the Special Economic Zones (*jingji tequ* 經濟特區, hereafter SEZs) has put Guangdong 廣東 in the spotlight since the early 1980s.[1]

Taking advantage of "disequilibria" across neighbouring regions has been the key to rapid economic take-off in the Pearl River Delta region (*Zhujiang sanjiaozhou* 珠江三角洲, hereafter PRD). Factors in the success of the PRD include cheap labour, low land costs, preferential policies in the SEZs, mature assembling and manufacturing technology, and ready access to international markets through Hong Kong, an entrepôt for trade into and out of China.[2] The rapid rise in wage levels attracted both the best-educated young people for managerial and professional jobs and millions of young rural labourers from neighbouring provinces for frontline jobs.[3] Those of the floating population possessing an average of at least 9 to 12 years of education were sufficiently large in number to have easily resolved the issue of manpower needs at the take-off stage. Up to 2003, China's economy had been growing at an annual rate of over 9%, with trade growing at more than 20% per year.[4] However, such rapid economic growth has given rise to both admiration and alarm.

Under the "Go West" policy of the late 1990s, the economic activities taking place across provinces appear to be changing the monolithic central-provincial relationship to one of regional cooperation.[5] Such an orientation might strengthen the connection across provinces in South China. For instance, the hinterland provinces of Yunnan 雲南, Guizhou 貴州, and Guangxi 廣西 are becoming a frontier for production and trade with Southeast Asian countries.

With the economies of all of the neighbouring provinces growing rapidly, labour issues and manpower needs have become acute concerns. First, the concept of the "economic development centre" is now being used as a model by various localities, and the migrant labourers that once seemed to flock to the PRD in endless numbers now have multiple job options near their hometowns. For instance, several coastal provinces experienced labour shortages in 2004.[6] Liu Kaiming has stated that the "drought in floating labour" is rooted in a "drought in education." A study of the participation and non-participation of employees in Shenzhen in job-related education and training found that a large majority of frontline workers, who are mostly undereducated, are kept from participating in job-related training; and that such non-participation prevents employees from reaping economic benefits from the formal job sector.[7] Unfortunately, the issue of the lack of education and training for the rural population as well as for migrant labour in more wealthy urban areas has not been made part of the ambitious forward-looking blueprints that have been drawn up by business sectors and governments.[8] With their large populations, growing needs, and the process of reform still unfolding in the Western regions, the nine provinces on the Pan–Pearl River Delta 泛珠江三角洲 (Pan-PRD) region[9] represent enormous economic potential, but such potential is accompanied by many challenges. The issue of labour needs raises the problem of the lack of education and skills training for the population.

There have been three recent developments that have led to the promotion of compulsory "Education for All" in China. First, in March 1990, delegates from 155 countries and about 150 organizations gathered in Jomtien, Thailand and signed the *World Declaration on Education for All*. The effort continued with the *Dakar Framework for Action, Education for All* in 2000 when collective global commitments were required to be made for the provision of basic education for disadvantaged children and adults. Receiving education to a level adequate enough for one to acquire the knowledge and skills necessary for gainful employment and full participation in society has been declared a fundamental human right.[10] About one-sixth of the world's population did not have such access to proper education. Governments are held to their obligation to ensure that the targets of the Education for All are reached.

In late 2001, China gained entry to the World Trade Organization (WTO), which is spurring the country to further open up its economy to international competition. The importance of improving the general quality of the population through education has captured the attention of policy-makers in China as well. Human capital theory[11] claims that the skills, knowledge and values that individuals have acquired in formal schooling can raise their productive capacity in the workplace and benefit them over a lifetime. A large number of studies have documented the existence of a positive relationship between education and productivity in developed countries.[12] Investment in education has been regarded as one of the major strategies for enhancing the economic competitiveness of firms and nations.[13]

Third, economic growth in China over the last two decades has increased household incomes, especially in the cities. At the same time, the rural population sees education as a ticket to urban employment. The rapid expansion of secondary education has led to demands for more education at the next level. Much weight is given in human resource strategies to the training of professionals and skilled workers.[14]

In order to understand the extent to which manpower issues can be resolved through education and training, this chapter reviews human resource development in the nine provinces of the Pan-PRD. First, a profile of the educational attainments of the population will be presented. Then, the provision of compulsory education for both rural and urban populations is reviewed. Following this are sections on upper secondary education (USE) and higher education, which are considered a form of quality control for the population entering the job market. Finally, adult and workforce training will be examined. The data are from government education and labour statistics.[15] A literature review of empirical studies and interviews of firms will be used to substantiate the government data.

Educational Attainment of the Population

China's education reforms began in 1985.[16] An overall review of its impact after two decades on the quality of the population with regard to education is first presented.

Table 6.1 shows the attainment of 12 years of education by those aged 15 and above in the nine provinces and three cities of the Pan-PRD. In Hainan 海南, established as a new province and an SEZ in 1988, the percentage of the population with 12 years of education reached 15.2% in 2003 from 10.7% in 1997. Jiangxi 江西 and Hunan 湖南 are doing well with much larger populations. In contrast, Guangdong and Fujian 福建, supposedly the wealthiest provinces in the Pan-PRD, are not doing better than Jiangxi and Hunan. Therefore, we suppose that besides the factor of wealth, provision of education has an impact on the allocation of resources for education. Sichuan 四川 and Guangxi rank next. Not surprisingly, Guizhou and Yunnan, the two poorest, are at the bottom. The provision of education in the poorest provinces are definitely a matter of concern.

For those provinces that saw a rise in the percentage of the population with 12 years of education, it is observed that the proportion of students enrolled in concurrent years to the total population was maintained at 17% to 20%. This indicates that these provinces are making a financial effort to provide education to their populations.

Let us trace the issue of educational attainment to educational provision. In Hong Kong, the capacity of secondary education is equal to that of primary education. In Guangzhou, they became equalized in the six-year

Table 6.1 Population and Educational Attainment

Province	Year	Total population (thousand)	Population aged 15 and over with 12 years of education (%)	Proportion of students (%)	Province	Year	Total population (thousand)	Population aged 15 and over with 12 years of education (%)	Proportion of students (%)
Hainan	1997	7,430	10.7	20.2	Jiangxi	1997	41,500	8.8	17.2
	2003	8,110	15.2	20.5		2003	42,540	14.9	17.8
Guangdong	1997	70,510	10.6	20.0	Sichuan	1997	84,300	7.8	13.7
	2003	79,540	12.4	21.1		2003	87,000	10.0	15.3
Fujian	1997	32,820	7.5	19.8	Guizhou	1997	36,060	5.3	17.8
	2003	34,880	12.7	17.8		2003	38,700	7.9	19.2
Guangxi	1997	46,330	6.1	19.3	Yunnan	1997	40,940	5.3	16.0
	2003	48,570	10.5	17.4		2003	43,760	4.4	16.3
Hunan	1997	64,650	9.7	18.1	Shenzhen	1998	3,950	39.2	8.2
	2003	66,630	13.7	16.0		2003	5,574	36.7	12.5
Hong Kong	1998	6,544	21.8	17.4	Guangzhou	1998	6,741	N.A.	21.3
	2003	6,803	26.4	16.8		2003	7,252	N.A.	27.2

Sources: *Zhongguo tongji nianjian, 1998*, p. 107; *2001*, p. 92; *2004*, p. 96 (Beijing: Zhongguo tongji chubanshe); Census and Statistics Department 2004, *Hong Kong Annual Digest of Statistics*. Hong Kong SAR, p. 267; *Shenzhen tongji nianjian, 2000*, p. 93; *2004*, pp. 53, 274; *Guangzhou tongji nianjian, 1999*, p. 498; *2001*, p. 54; *2004*, pp. 63, 598.

period from 1997 to 2003. Both metropolises have solid government budgets to provide school places for their populations.

In sharp contrast, the lower secondary schools, offering three years of education, can provide places for about one-third of the primary students in nine provinces. The capacity of upper secondary schools is one-third that of the lower secondary schools. Finally, Higher Education (hereafter, HE), including both junior colleges and four-year universities, represents in most cases around 2%, or less, of all the student population enrolled.

It is obvious that the bottleneck in the provision of education starts at lower secondary education (LSE). Even Hainan, Guangdong and Fujian, the pioneers of economic reforms, are very far from achieving nine years of education for their entire population! But in terms of administrative responsibility, the great divide in the provision of education is urban versus rural. The following sections will compare the provision of education in city, townships, and rural areas.

Provision of Primary Education

In 1985, China announced that nine years of education was compulsory. The central government handed over the responsibility for financing primary and secondary education to counties and townships.[17] In 1993, the central government set up a national goal with "two basic targets" (*liangji* 兩基): to "basically eliminate illiteracy among the young and middle-aged adults in rural areas, and to basically achieve nine years of education for youth by 2000."[18] The compulsory education target was easily achieved in cities by 2000, but the issue of the financing of rural education has persisted, with local resources being diverted to urban areas.[19]

To understand education in rural areas, we need to see how schooling is organized. About 60% of the population in China live in the countryside and another 15% in small towns called *xiangzhen* 鄉鎮. In most cases, there are about a dozen to a few dozen school-aged children in a natural village (*zirancun* 自然村). A village school tends to consist of primary grades one to three, with one or two teachers. Children in the fourth grade and above have to walk for more than 5 km through footpaths to a central school. In our nine provinces, a majority of villages are located in mountains.

With the intention of improving the quality of education in the countryside, the central government launched in 2001 an experiment in reforming the taxes and fees (*shuifei gaige* 稅費改革) for rural areas. It consolidated administrative power at the county level. However, this financial arrangement did not increase the overall resources available for education.

Because of the division of responsibilities over fiscal control and financial resources, basic education is administered at three levels. Schools funded by municipal governments are called urban schools. Schools funded through the revenues of county governments are called town schools. Finally, rural schools are funded by local funds collected through rural taxes and fees. In order to reduce costs and improve the quality of teaching as well as management efficiency,[20] school merger occurred. Most provinces saw about 35% of their rural schools closed down by 2004 as compared to the number in 1997. Guangxi, Sichuan, Guizhou and Yunnan are mountainous provinces. School mergers are a serious issue for children aged about 7 to 12 because they have to walk for over an hour to school in the early morning when it is still dark, and through unlit country paths or fields.[21] Poverty, insufficient food, a lack of shoes, and a low motivation to make the long trek to school all eventually become barriers that such children have to face; the result is a higher dropout rate than before.

Table 6.2 compares school resources in terms of the student/school ratio, teacher/school ratio, student/teacher ratio, and the number of full-time (FT) teachers and substitute (ST) teachers in each school. Urban schools have a capacity to enroll several hundred students, town schools a couple of hundred, and rural schools 100 to 150 students.

With regard to the ecology of schools in rural societies, it should be remembered that, rural schools are located in mountainous areas and are often barely within walking distance. Thus, it would be misguided to plan mergers solely with economies of scale or efficiency in mind. Sending children to boarding schools in towns has increased the cost for both families and schools.

The average number of FT teachers per urban school in the nine provinces was 24 in 1997, 26 in 2000, and 37 in 2003. In comparison, there were 16, 17, and 28 teachers per town school and 5, 6, and 7 teachers per rural school for the years 1997, 2000, and 2003, respectively. In western provinces such as Guangxi, Guizhou, Sichuan, and Yunnan, the numbers were smaller. With regard to the student/teacher ratio, in urban schools each teacher takes care of 21 students, in township schools 22 students, and in rural schools 24 students. With fewer teachers per school site, we can understand that the teaching staff capacity is limited. The ratio of FT teachers to total staff shows that in each school, the number of support staff is limited to around 0.1. Rural schools rely heavily on ST teachers to make

Table 6.2 Primary School and Class in School, 2003

Province	Total Enrol-ment (million)	Urban						Town						Rural					
		As % of total enrol-ment	Students/ per school	FT teachers per school site	Students/ FT teachers	FT teachers/ staff	ST-PT teachers/ FT teachers	As % of total enrol-ment	Students/ per school	FT teachers per school site	Students/ FT teachers	FT teachers/ staff	ST-PT teachers/ FT teachers	As % of total enrol-ment	Students/ per school	FT teachers per school site	Students/ FT teachers	FT teachers/ staff	ST-PT teachers/ FT teachers
Hainan	1.0	13.5	852	39	22	0.8	1.1	22.8	757	39	19	0.9	2.2	63.7	179	9	21	0.9	5.6
Guangdong	10.4	26.4	977	35	28	0.8	13.3	17.7	818	34	24	0.9	3.8	55.9	282	10	27	0.9	14.4
Fujian	3.1	15.1	623	32	19	0.9	1.8	29.7	460	25	19	0.9	1.2	55.1	126	8	17	1.0	3.5
Guangxi	4.9	8.8	518	28	19	0.9	6.2	15.9	506	28	18	0.9	9.1	75.2	123	5	27	0.9	44.1
Hunan	4.7	12.9	643	34	19	0.9	1.5	20.8	427	24	18	0.9	0.8	66.4	127	7	18	1.0	2.3
Jiangxi	3.9	8.7	883	45	20	0.9	1.5	32.4	257	13	20	1.0	3.1	58.8	164	8	20	1.0	4.5
Sichuan	7.6	7.9	994	47	21	0.9	2.8	19.6	863	39	22	0.9	2.5	72.4	154	6	25	0.9	12.5
Guizhou	4.8	7.5	689	32	21	0.9	3.3	14.9	600	28	21	0.9	3.3	77.6	204	7	29	0.9	16.6
Yunnan	4.4	4.6	730	37	20	0.9	0.4	13.0	382	22	18	0.9	2.2	82.5	97	5	20	0.9	14.7

up for staff shortages. The proportion of ST teachers varies greatly, from a small percentage to over 30%; with over 14% being common.

Estimations based on these statistics reveal a demand for additional teachers: 13,915 for urban schools, 20,957 for township schools, and 164,654 teachers for rural schools, or a total of 199,526 teachers. In comparison, the total number of students who graduated from normal universities and junior colleges in 2003 was 39,764.

Secondary Education and Human Resource Development

Secondary education consists of two levels: three years of general education at lower secondary school (LSS), and another three years at upper secondary school (USS). The number of years of compulsory education is nine, including primary school and LSS. Basic education is termed the completion of 12 years of education, up to graduation from USS. USS is comprised of two tracks: general as well as vocational/technical education (VTE). USS places are limited. General USSs admit students who score at the upper percentiles in examinations at graduation from LSS, and VTE takes the rest.[22] Based on statistics on the total student population in the nine provinces, the proportion of students enrolled in primary education was 56.6% in 2003, 28.6% in the LSSs, 7.4% in general USSs, 4% in VTE, and 3.5% in higher education.

The provision of nine years of compulsory education to all of the population by the year 2000 became a national goal.[23] For the ordinary population, entry into a USS means an opportunity to one day enter the skilled labour market through HE. In this section, we will find that as long as a scarcity of financial resources remains an issue, disparities in the provision of education will continue to put the rural population at a disadvantage.

The Capacity to Provide General Education

In administration, LSSs and general USSs are often combined into one at the county level, and teachers could be asked to teach courses at both the LSS and USS sectors. Therefore, we examine the two levels of secondary schools together.

LSSs in both urban areas and towns admitted more students to their first grade than the number of students who graduated from primary schools in the same locality that year. In contrast, rural LSSs admitted to their first grade about 60% to 80% of primary school graduates that year. That is because rural families pay to put their children into town schools and families in towns pay to send their children to urban schools, in order to increase their opportunities of being admitted into a university in the future.

In 1997, urban USSs in all nine provinces could provide places for about half of the graduates in urban LSSs. In 2000, their capacity increased. By 2003, urban USSs in three provinces — Jiangxi (1.05), Hunan (0.96) and Sichuan (1.05) — reached full capacity; while Fujian, Guangxi, Guizhou, and Yunnan were able to admit 80% of the LSS graduates in the same locality. However, Guangdong and Hainan, two wealthy provinces, provide USS places to less than 59% of their LSS graduates. USSs in towns are in a weaker position, being only able to provide places for 30% to 40% of LSS graduates. In most cases, only a small percentage of rural LSS graduates could be admitted into USSs.

Allocation of Teachers in General Schools

Table 6.3 provides information about how students are organized and the FT teachers that are available to students.[24] These statistics show that all schools have large classes, with an average of 53 students in LSSs and 52 in USSs in urban areas; and 56 and 55, respectively, in LSSs and USSs in towns/rural areas. For each class, there are 3.3 FT teachers in both LSSs and USSs in urban cities. In town/rural schools, there are 2.8 FT teachers for each class at the LSS level and 3.4 at the USS level.

By calculation, the average student/teacher ratios in LSSs among urban, town, and rural schools were 15.1, 18.0, and 19.5, respectively, in 1997; 16.3, 19.1, and 22.0 in 2000; and 17.6, 20.4, and 20.8 in 2003. That is, teachers in rural LSSs take care of more students than teachers in town schools, and that teachers in urban schools have the fewest students on average. At the USS level, the student/teacher ratio is considerably lower than that at the LSS level. On average, the student/teacher ratios among urban, town, and rural schools were 14.0, 14.8, and 12.6, respectively, in 1997; 15.8, 17.0, and 15.2 in 2000; and 17.5, 18.8, and 18.3 in 2003.

Nevertheless, schools are short of teachers. In order to make courses available according to curriculum guidelines, schools have been hiring substitute or contract teachers at a low cost, which has implications for the quality of the teaching being offered at the schools.[25] These substitute or contract teachers are paid at a rate of about one-fifth to one-sixth of the salary of a FT teacher.[26] In 1997, these teachers made up the equivalent of

Table 6.3   General Secondary School Capacity, 2003

Province	Total FT teachers (thousand)		Urban				Town and rural				Substitute and contract teachers			
			Students per class		Teacher/class ratio		Students per class		Teacher/class ratio		As % of FT teachers	% in urban schools	% in town schools	% in rural schools
	Lower	Upper	Lower	Upper	Lower	Upper	Lower	Upper	Lower	Upper				
	(1)	(2)	(3)	(4)	(5)	(6)	(7)	(8)	(9)	(10)	(12)	(13)	(14)	(15)
Fujian	100	36	50.5	48.0	3.0	3.3	52.6	43.0	2.7	2.6	3.3	22.8	38.9	38.3
Jiangxi	117	39	53.7	51.8	3.3	3.0	60.3	59.7	3.0	3.1	2.8	27.4	39.2	33.4
Hunan	203	56	57.5	35	3.2	1.9	60.0	62.1	3.2	3.3	2.1	26.7	28.8	44.6
Guangdong	205	66	53.8	53.1	2.8	3.2	57.7	56.6	2.7	3.3	4.7	43.3	28.2	28.4
Guangxi	116	29	52.1	56.1	2.8	2.9	58.8	61.7	2.7	3.1	8.1	13.2	55.1	31.7
Hainan	20	5	54.8	52.2	2.9	3.1	59.4	60.5	2.8	3.1	2.7	43.7	42.2	14.2
Sichuan	188	59	51.9	59	3.2	3.3	56.8	62.3	2.8	3.1	3.3	18.9	37.3	43.8
Guizhou	88	19	51.6	53.0	2.9	2.8	58.7	59.1	2.5	2.9	4.9	15.8	27.5	56.6
Yunnan	99	21	52.7	55.7	3.1	3.4	56.1	56.6	2.9	3.3	2.3	7.8	31.1	61.1

7.1% of FT teachers, 4.5% in 2000, and 3.8% in 2003, on average among the nine provinces.

Provision of Secondary Vocational Technical Education

The percentage of the total student population enrolled in theVTE track at the USS level was 3.3% in 1997, 3.5% in 2000, and 4.0% in 2003. The VTE enrolment to general USS student enrolment ratio was 1.0 in 1997, 0.8 in 2000, and 0.5 in 2003, a pattern of decline from the "50%-to-50%" as reinforced by the central government in 1993.[27] VTE schools are a national strategy to train skilled workers before they enter the job market and, at the same time, to reduce the pressure on universities. VTE is divided into three tracks. The first of these is specialized secondary education, which used to be under the administration of various ministries. The second track is the technical worker schools, most of which were established in the late 1950s and early 1960s to train skilled workers. These schools were often affiliated with enterprises. The third track is the vocational schools, which were started in 1985 when the central government pushed to restructure USS education into both general and VTE tracks, with each enrolling 50% of students.[28] The vocational schools are under the administration of the educational bureau. In recent education reforms, specialized USSs and technical worker schools have been moved to the administration of educational bureaux at the provincial level.[29] The specialized USSs admit students into technician programmes. Technical worker schools and vocational schools have almost all been merged together to train skilled workers. Thus, in this chapter, VTE is classified into the two current tracks of specialized schools and vocational education schools for consideration.

First, let us examine the patterns of enrolment and teachers in specialized schools. With regard to enrolment, with the exception of Sichuan and Hunan, all of the other seven provinces saw an increase over six years. The average size of specialized secondary schools is over 1,000. Over the six years from 1997 to 2003, student/teacher ratios increased. On the one hand, enrolment increased and, on the other hand, many teachers left. This has been a longstanding issue. Teaching staff in specialized fields are considered professionals and many have "jumped into the sea of business" and taken up highly paid jobs. It is very difficult to retain good teachers. In 2003, specialized schools hired many ST teachers or teachers on contract to help out.

Vocational enrolment in cities increased in three provinces in 2000 compared with 1997; and in town schools, enrolment increased in six provinces. Both vocational education schools in urban areas and in towns make up less than 50% of the total VTE enrolment, and are much smaller in size than specialized secondary schools, ranging from a couple of hundred to a few hundred. Student/teacher ratios are very small, at less than 20 students, and averaging about 15. This has made it difficult for these schools to offer a large range of courses. After 2000, there was an expansion mostly in specialized schools; at the same time, the merger of schools since the late 1990s resulted in the closing of many vocational schools, leaving fewer in the towns. This may lead to another problem of the urban population being favoured with easy access to VTE while rural students are forced to shoulder higher costs for schooling.

Secondary School Completion Rates

Secondary education is important because it lays a foundation for knowledge and helps to determine a person's future social status. As for those who have had only an LSS education, they will later mostly be denied entry into even adult HE programmes.

In the late 1990s, the government encouraged school-aged drop-outs to go back to school, in order to realize the goal of compulsory education to children by 2000. Primary schools in seven provinces did manage to maintain a 100% school completion rate. In the case of Hainan, primary schools in 2003 had been able to maintain the capacity to graduate 96% of the students admitted in 1997; while Fujian only graduated about 87% of the students admitted in 1997.[30] With regard to urban and town schools respectively, there were six provinces and four provinces, respectively, that did not have full completion rates by 2003.

For general education at the LSSs and USSs in cities, the rate of completion in 2000 over admissions in 1997 is about 90%. There were five provinces (i.e., Fujian, Guangdong, Guangxi, Hainan, and Guizhou) with a completion rate in 2003 of over 1, higher than the number of students admitted in 2000. This might be because students transferred from other areas to urban schools. In contrast, the other four provinces (i.e., Jiangxi, Hunan, Sichuan, and Yunnan) had completion rates of between 0.85 to 0.90 in 2003 over the number admitted in 2000 as compared to the rates for 1997/2000, which were above 0.95. This might indicate that there are more dropouts during the period 2000–2003 than previously.

Completion rates in town schools for both LSS and USS education were mostly around 0.80.[31] Completion rates in rural schools in the same province were usually much lower. For rural LSSs, the completion rates for 2000 over those admitted in 1997 and 2003 over those admitted in 2000, respectively, were 0.94 and 0.99 (Fujian), 0.81 and 0.80 (Jiangxi), 0.88 and 0.86 (Hunan), 0.50 and 0.66 (Guangdong), 0.78 and 0.33 (Guangxi), 0.82 and 0.31 (Hainan), 0.86 and 0.85 (Sichuan), 0.79 and 0.56 (Guizhou), and 0.89 and 0.77 (Yunnan). Rural USSs show the same trend of completion rates for 2003 over those admitted in 2000 being lower than the rates for 2000 over those admitted in 1997. And both are lower than those in LSSs. It should be remembered that rural students are often transferred to town schools in order to increase their chances of getting into university. This would lead to a substantial increase in the town completion rates. At the same time, rural dropout rates increase when another group of students sees that the chances of climbing to the next level of education are slim. Students drop out mostly when faced with two situations: (1) when their family is unable to scrape up the necessary cash to pay school fees, and (2) when students, taking mock examinations, are aware that they cannot hope to attain the necessary scores to enter the next level of schooling. With regard to VTE, completion rates are no more satisfactory than those for rural USSs. This is due to changes in government policies, a population desperate to receive a general education, and the irrelevance of VTE programmes to the labour market.[32]

A Great Leap in Higher Education

HE started to undergo reform and expansion after 1995. The rapid expansion of secondary education and an increase in household incomes both culminated in a mounting demand for HE. China's entry into the WTO in 2001 has become another impetus in the development of a competent workforce.

HE institutions can be classified into three types in terms of financial situation. The regular HE institutions provide USS graduates with four years of university education or three years of an associate degree programme. These institutions are under the direct administration and funding of the government. The second type is adult HE, which provides professional or four-year programmes for adults. Such institutions could be an adult education institution run by a local government bureau or by an institution affiliated with a university's evening programmes, a broadcasting and VT university or a sub-institute (*erji xueyuan* 二級學院), or an independent institution run by professionals. The third type is the private HE institution or "people run" (*minying* 民營) institution.[33] The last two types of institution may start out with different financial resources, but their main source income is from learners admitted to programmes. This section will only cover HE institutions funded by the government, the first type. The next section will cover other institutions providing education and training for adults.

Table 6.4 presents statistics on regular HE institutions in the nine provinces of the Pan-PRD region. The first column shows an increase in the number of HE institutions over six years. Guangdong saw an increase of 35 new HE institutions, from 42 to 77; and Jiangxi of 23, from 31 to 54. These two provinces experienced a great leap in the number of HE institutions. The two laggards were Fujian and Yunnan, with the number of HE institutions increase from 30 to 39 and from 26 to 34, respectively. Column 2 presents enrolment in 1997 as the baseline and growth rates in 2000 and 2003. Among the nine provinces, three were ranked at top: Hunan with 143,700 students in 1997, Guangdong with 174,700 students, and Sichuan with 150,100 students. Guizhou and Yunnan were at the bottom, with 38,500 and 57,400 students, respectively, in 1997. Nevertheless, enrolments in all nine provinces tripled in 2003. As a result, HE institutions grew in size from a capacity of 2,000 to 3,000 students in 1997 to a large size of over 4,000 as advocated by Tsang and Min in 1992.[34]

This rapid increase in enrolment has brought about many challenges. Column 5 shows that, in 1997, the student-teacher ratio was about 7 to 9. By 2003, the ratio had nearly doubled. The dilution of resources at universities due to increased enrolment has become a big issue; the rapid expansion that has taken place in a very short time is making it impossible for universities to offer a quality education.

Adult Education and Workforce Training

In addition to formal schooling, China has an almost equivalent system of adult education that provides various education and training programmes from literacy programmes and primary and secondary programmes to HE for adults, whether working or unemployed. This system emerged from the revolutionary tradition of mass education for workers and peasants before 1949 and was expanded into full-scale literacy programmes all over China in the 1950s.[35] Since the early 1990s, this system of adult education has seen a new horizon in the provision of education and training for the adult population. In the last decades, new jobs have been replacing old occupations, and firms are facing competition from the international market.

158   *Xiao Jin*

Table 6.4　Capacity of Regular Higher Education

Province	Year	Institutions (1)	Enrolment (thousand) and growth (2)	Average enrolment (3)	Professors/ total teaching staff (%) (4)	Students/ teaching staff (5)	Students/ professors (6)
Fujian	1997	30	78.1	2,603	36.0	9	26
	2000	28	1.8	4,924	37.4	14	38
	2003	39	3.3	6,600	41.2	16	39
Jiangxi	1997	31	88.3	2,848	33.9	9	27
	2000	32	1.7	4,643	35.2	14	41
	2003	54	4.1	6,641	35.1	16	47
Hunan	1997	46	143.7	3,123	37.5	9	24
	2000	52	1.9	5,112	38.5	13	34
	2003	73	3.7	7,359	39.4	16	41
Guangdong	1997	42	174.7	4,160	37.3	10	28
	2000	52	1.8	5,885	40.7	15	37
	2003	77	3.4	7,633	36.6	15	40
Guangxi	1997	26	70.6	2,714	32.6	9	28
	2000	30	1.8	4,124	32.0	13	41
	2003	45	3.2	5,050	31.9	16	51
Hainan	1997	5	12.8	2,557	32.5	9	28
	2000	5	1.5	3,839	34.6	12	35
	2003	11	3.4	3,954	36.8	16	44
Sichuan	1997	43	150.1	3,490	36.8	8	22
	2000	42	1.6	5,849	45.4	13	29
	2003	62	3.4	8,269	38.4	16	43
Guizhou	1997	20	38.5	1,924	28.3	7	24
	2000	23	2.1	3,471	41.5	11	27
	2003	34	3.9	4,395	31.9	13	40
Yunnan	1997	26	57.4	2,209	33.4	7	22
	2000	24	1.7	3,996	45.3	10	23
	2003	34	3.1	5,155	36.9	14	39

Sources: *Zhongguo jiaoyu tongji nianjian 1997, 2000, 2003* (Beijing: Renmin jiaoyu chubanshe).

It is becoming a challenge for firms to develop human resources to match their business strategies in order to maintain a niche in the market. Therefore, firms are providing or subsidizing education and training of various types for employees to attend within or outside the firm. Employees are also individually seeking education and training outside their work units to meet their own occupational aspirations. This section will examine two aspects of the workforce: first, the workforce profile of educational attainment; second, a full array of education and training programmes available for adults.

The Workforces and Their Educational Attainments

The total workforce in each province is about 50% of the total population. In coastal provinces like Fujian and Hainan, the workforce is less than 50% and, in Guangdong, it is just above 50%. The figure for Jiangxi is also low. The remaining provinces, hinterland areas like Hunan and the three provinces of the western region, have a larger proportion in the workforce, up to 55%. These provinces have a low proportion of their workforce in the manufacturing and tertiary industries. In wealthy provinces, the urban workforce would make up a larger proportion. In Fujian, the figure was 25% in 2000; in Guangdong, 28%; and in Hainan, 33%.

Consider registered specialized personnel (*zhuanye renyuan* 專業人員, including cadres, professionals and technicians) in the urban workforce, which are those with formal household registrations with the government. To train a large number of specialized personnel has been a goal explicitly expressed in policy papers since the early 1980s. Employees with educational qualifications at or above the secondary specialized education are ranked as specialized personnel in payrolls. In most urban areas, up to 25% and sometimes even more than 30% of the urban workforce fell into this group in 2003. However, we must remember that the urban workforce dropped in 2003, so that this increased proportion could be the result of unskilled employees leaving the urban workforce, rather than due to increased recruitment. Next, it is not surprising to see that female specialized personnel comprise 40% of the urban workforce.

We can break down the category of specialized personnel by the ownership of work units into state-owned, collectively owned, or other new emerging forms of ownership. Among the three groups of ownership entities, the state and its affiliated work units have between 80% to 90% of the well-trained personnel, and the rest work in collectively owned and newly emerging joint ventures or foreign enterprises. That the best-trained human resources are still concentrated in government organizations and state-owned enterprises is a matter of great concern. Studies conducted in China and other countries have all shown that skill formation and economic performance are socially constructed and experienced within social institutions, and can be organized in different ways.[36] As specialized personnel are concentrated in state-owned enterprises, or as state-owned enterprises still employ the majority of such personnel, this is not conducive to the diffusion of knowledge and technology into other economic sectors. Alternatively, this situation might be a hindrance to improving the efficiency of the non-government sector and to expanding job opportunities for the population as a whole.

Figure 6.1 gives a picture of how much education the overall workforce received before entering the labour market. For comparison, Hong Kong provides a metropolitan case. In Guangdong, females made up about 45.5% of the labour market. About 4.2% of the females and 1.2% of their male counterparts were illiterate; and that 33% of the females and 21% of the males had a primary education. Of females and males respectively, 45% and 50% had an LSE, and 13% and 20% had a USE. Respectively, 6% of the females and 8% of the males had HE. Obviously, males had an advantage in formal education. Among provinces, labourers in Guangdong, Hainan, and Hunan have the best profile in terms of education received. Following them are Guangxi, Sichuan, Fujian, and Jiangxi. Yunnan and Guizhou, not surprisingly, are at the bottom.

Figure 6.1   Educational Attainment of the Workforce, 2002

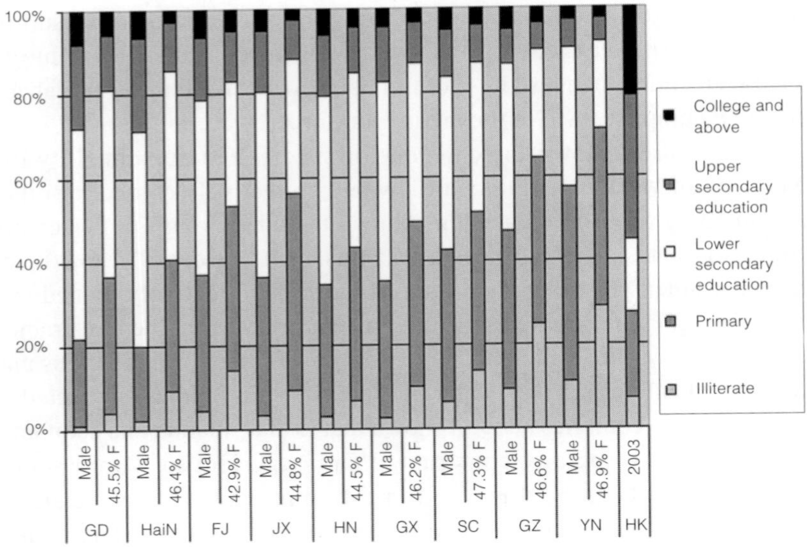

Adult Education and Training for the Workforce

There are two ways by which adults, whether employed or unemployed, can receive education and training. The first is through on-the-job training, where programmes are provided to meet the needs of the workforce. The second is through institutions that work parallel with the formal system, and whose programmes and enrolments government education bureaus monitor.

It is found that Guangdong provided the most training to its workforce, about 12% in 1997. Fujian and Jiangxi followed, with about 10% of the workforce having received training in 1997. Hainan ranked next, with 7% of its workforce having received training in 1997. In Hunan, Guangxi, Guizhou, and Yunnan, about 4% to 5% of the workforce had an opportunity to receive training. Sichuan, with a large population, provided training to only 2% of its workforce. The coastal provinces provided more training to their workforces, due to pressure from the labour market. Those inland were slower to respond to the demand for training. With regard to gender difference, males were favoured in Guizhou and Yunnan, with only 29% and 38% of those who had received training in these two provinces respectively being females. In the other seven provinces, among those who had received training an average of 43% were females. The unemployed, both young people and those who had been laid off, made up about 60% of those who had received training. Therefore, it is evident that the issue of unemployment has received the most attention.

China has gradually developed another tradition of providing opportunities to those who have been denied by the formal system.[37] This tradition started in the 1950s. As up to 80% of the population had not received any education, adult schools and literacy programmes that operated in parallel to the formal system at different levels of education were set up for people from all walks of life, including peasants, workers, cadres. This tradition is called the "two-legs-walking" strategy: one leg being formal education and the other being adult education. The adult system includes schools under the administration of ministries, with courses offered through the radio/TV, evening sections affiliated with regular universities, and other programmes.

There are three major institutions that provide such education. The first are those that provide a junior college education. They include radio/TV universities, worker/peasant colleges, normal colleges, and cadre colleges. This whole group of institutions has the capacity to enrol a couple of thousands to a few tens of thousands of adults. The second group is comprised of programmes run by the evening sections of regular universities. Their programmes include junior-college equivalency programmes and short courses to obtain a professional certificate. They also enrol a few dozen to several tens of thousands of adults, and sometimes even up to a hundred thousand adult learners in a province. The third type is those institutions that have received permission from the Ministry of Education to provide certificate programmes in specialized areas or to prepare adults for entrance examinations.[38] Together, these three types of programmes provided a level of enrolment that was equivalent to or exceeded that in the formal system in both 1997 and 2000, before the formal system underwent expansion.

There is also a parallel to the formal system of secondary schools, consisting of specialized schools, technical workers schools, and general education schools. These institutions are under the administration of education bureaus, but the provision of their programmes is largely dependent on fees charged to adult learners. Of the three groups, technical schools enrolled the majority of the learners, ranging from 80% to 99% in most of the nine provinces. Therefore, we can say that technical schools have become a major avenue for the training of skilled workers. Courses are most often short-term courses, lasting just a few months and can respond quickly to market needs. The total enrolment is very impressive, comparable in size to the formal system. Certainly, course quality is always a concern as quality inspection or control over teaching staff and curriculums is lacking.

Discussion and Conclusion

China has cultivated a dual system of providing education that serves the country's young population as well as its adult population. This approach to dealing with the huge need for education and training for socialist construction has "Chinese characteristics." The dual system is rooted in a history in which China sought, with limited resources, in the 1950s to transform a population that was 80% illiterate into educated citizens and an educated workforce. The long-standing issues of a rising demand for education and a scarcity of resources remain unresolved in the twenty-first century.[39] Although progress has been made through the expansion of the education system since 1985, the dilemma remains, as we have seen from an examination in this chapter of the situation in the nine provinces. The state's capacity to provide nine years of compulsory education to the whole population is very limited. A huge rural population without adequate education continues to pour into the Greater Pearl River Delta region and to serve as an indispensable component of the workforce.[40] The situation is more serious in the provinces in the western regions. This flow of migrant labour into urban areas has become a social and structural issue that needs to be addressed.

This study has shown that male working adults who are illiterate or who have received only a primary level of education make up about 20% to 30% of the workforce in Guangdong, Hainan, and Jiangxi; the figure as high as 40% to 50% in other six provinces. For female working adults, the figure is up to 50% to 75%. Disparities are apparent. First, about half of the population has not completed nine years of compulsory education as required by central policy. Second, females are substantially disadvantaged with regard to educational opportunities or to job opportunities. Third, economically wealthy provinces are providing more educational opportunities to their population, while poor provinces are lagging behind.

Judging by the fact that the annual progress in the effort to lift the educational attainment of the workforce to above the level of primary education was 1.6% for males and 1.4% for females during the period 1997–2003, it is expected that about another 20 years will be required to reduce this illiterate/primary education group as a percentage of the total workforce to 25–30%.[41] The annual rate at which educational attainment was lifted to nine years of secondary education is estimated to have been 1.0% for males and 1.3% for females during the period 1997–2003. It costs more to provide secondary education, and the dropout rate is high when youths approach the age of 15, when the opportunity costs of staying in school are high. In any case, secondary education is critical because it is a stage during which one builds up one's foundation for learning to allow one to continue learning over a lifetime.

Education and manpower training is a social component under a macro socioeconomic structure. The strategy of hiring cheap labour has made rapid growth possible. Employers, both state-owned and private enterprises, will continue to hire cheap workers, most often the least educated ones, for low-skilled jobs until their products face competition. The problem is that this strategy is unsustainable over the long term, which leads to other issues.[42] The first reason is the high rate of turnover and its cost. A study in 2005 found that out of the 503 sampled firms, 41% were short of employees. In the spring of 2005, firms were only able to hire about 58.6% of the skilled workers they needed. Without adequate salaries and welfare policies, workers frequently resort to the option of quitting to search for a better job. From the viewpoint of firms, the poor quality of the labour and their lack of commitment make hiring difficult and orderly production problematic. In particular, firms are short of skilled employees such as mechanics, technicians and professionals. It should be kept in mind that most skilled technicians and professionals are concentrated in state-owned units. Compared to state-owned units which offer the secured welfare package, collective and private enterprises are at a disadvantage in recruiting. Therefore, solving the issue of a shortage of skilled labour will require the wisdom of both the government and enterprises. It is necessary to provide incentives for the implementation of the minimum wage policy and welfare packages, and to monitor compliance. The firms have to assure that working conditions continue to improve. At the same time, public resources should be allocated to train a skilled workforce.

As long as the rural population serves as a cheap pool of labour for the urban sector, migrant labour will be a phenomenon, boosting economic growth or counterbalancing the gains made in the economy. At the heart of the issue is the transfer of rural youth to non-farming work. Education, although important, is only one of the variables in building one's capacity to make the transition from school to work. Under a macro social structural framework, in addition to variables such as the geographical location of a province, rural-versus-urban residential registration, gender, type of work unit, and type of education received, other variables all matter, such as the relevance of the curriculum, the nature of a personal transition from studying to working, and the economic transition that the nation is going through. Therefore, a few more variables should be added to smooth the process of transition into the world of work and life.

First, school curriculums in China are notorious for their lack of relevance to work and life. When there is a mismatch between the knowledge that schools transmit and what the labour market requires, entry into the workforce is hindered.[43] Improving employability involves improving the relevance of school curriculums and school-firm linkages.

Second, nowadays workplaces frequently require employees to learn new skills because enterprises are continuously upgrading their technology.[44] In order to cope with a changing workplace, many firms now offer on-the-job training programmes for their workforce as part of a strategy to upgrade their human capital.[45] The other is vocational and credential programmes for working adults offered through different adult education institutions. These programmes offered are more closely related to the work and life of adults. This chapter also found that this non-formal education alternative is prevalent in the Pan-PRD. As skills are best learned through practice and have to be upgraded in the workplace, China should continue to strengthen adult and continuing education, which have served as a complementary component in building up the competence of the workforce.[46]

The third issue is that jobs are no longer permanent for young people. Instead, they often "jump" among jobs or between their rural farming and urban jobs. This makes the transition from studying to getting established in the workplace even more complicated. As all cities in China have set up a physical market for employers and prospective employees to meet,[47] the occupation centre could offer career guidance and training programmes for young people from rural areas.

The fourth issue is the exclusion of disadvantaged social groups from training programmes. There are two typical situations. In rural China, there are few opportunities for the population to receive education and training, as illustrated in this chapter.[48] In Shenzhen, a very developed city, employees at the low end of the job ladder and with the least education are also excluded from training programmes.[49] These people fall into a vicious trap out of which they are denied the opportunity to lift themselves. As rural life and farming will remain a substantial part of the occupation of a large proportion of population, community cultural centres (*shequ wenhua zhongxin* 社區文化中心) are necessary to provide training programmes for the rural population.[50] In the urban sectors, the government could provide subsidies to NGOs, firms, and professionals to reach out to the most disadvantaged through adult education programmes.

The fifth issue is secondary VTE. Many skills required in the workplace cannot be taught in a classroom. They are best learned through practice in the workplace together with other employees. Actually, practice gives one real experience for understanding theory in context or the inspiration to come up with theories that can guide practice. Internships can be arranged for learners at secondary VTEs.

For some occupations, Hong Kong has developed world-standard codes of occupation and behaviour. The Pan-PRD can recruit Hong Kong expertise to develop training programmes. Hong Kong firms and manufacturing companies in the Pan-PRD can also take the lead in modelling workplace mentorship programmes and in offering adequate compensation to employees. This would set an example in building up sustainable competence. Companies based in Hong Kong can send professionals to disseminate knowledge and information on world-standard criteria for conducting business. For instance, quality control and accounting systems are most urgently needed in many companies. Hong Kong expertise can also be used to coordinate training programmes with firms and adult education centres in the Pan-PRD to improve the quality of training programmes.

In short, the challenges arise from how to play up the merits of China's dual system, which has an infrastructure to serve both the young generation and the working population. At the heart of the manpower issues is who can obtain the opportunities to participate in the economic life. Structural obstacles linked to social inequalities need to be overcome. Research and policy analysis is needed on feasible options to share with the disadvantaged the country's growing economic wealth. Tearing down discrimination against rural inhabitants with education subsidies to the disadvantaged is imperative to improving equity in the workforce. However, policies, whether public or private, should be devised to encourage firms to commit to developing the skills of their employees and to building up an organization that can face the challenges of competition. Only with complementary inputs from the education/training sector, the government, and the economic sector, will it be possible to find a way to sustain economic growth by allowing the disadvantaged to participate to the benefit of the whole population.

Notes

1. OECD, 1986, *China's Special Economic Zones*; Deng Shuxiong 鄧樹雄 and Hu Dun-ai 胡敦靄 (eds.), *Maixiang ershiyi shiji Gang'ao guanxi* 邁向二十一世紀港澳關係 (On the Hong Kong-Macao Relationship in the Twenty-first Century), *Xueshu yantaohui lunwenji* 學術研討會論文集 (Proceedings of the Conference) (Hong Kong: Hong Kong Baptist College, 1990); Michael J. Enright, "Globalization, Regionalization and the Knowledge-based Economy in Hong Kong," in *Regions and the Knowledge Economy*, edited by John Dunning (Oxford: Oxford University Press, 2002), pp. 381–406.
2. Liu Guoguang 劉國光, *Shenzhen jingji tequ de fazhan zhanlüe* 深圳經濟特區的發展戰略 (Development Strategies for the Shenzhen Special Economic Zone) (Shenzhen: Shenzhen jingji yanjiu zhongxin 深圳經濟研究中心, 1985); Liu Guoguang, *Shenzhen jingji tequ jiushi niandai fazhan zhanlüe* 深圳經濟特區九十年代發展戰略 (Strategies of Economic Development for the Shenzhen Special Economic Zone in 1990s) (Beijing: Jingji guanli chubanshe 經濟管理出版社, 1992).
3. Sung Yun-wing, Liu Pak-wai, Wong Yue-chim, Richard and Lau Pui-king,

The Fifth Dragon: The Emergence of the Pearl River Delta (Singapore: Addison Wesley, 1995), pp. 112–19.

4. Michael J. Enright, Edith E. Scott and Chang Ka-mun, *Regional Powerhouse: The Greater Pearl River Delta and the Rise of China* (Singapore: John Wiley & Sons (Asia), 2005), pp. 1–5.

5. Li Shantong 李善同, Hou Yongzhi 侯永志 and Feng Jie 馮傑, "Zhongguo quyu jingji hezuo de xingeju: sitiao hengguan dongxi de jingjidai" 中國區域經濟合作的新格局：四條橫貫東西的經濟帶 (A New Horizon of Regional Collaboration in Economic Development in China: Four East-west Economic Zones), *Diaocha baogao* 調查報告 (Investigation Report) (27 March 2003), pp. 1–18.

6. Liu Kaiming 劉開明, " 'Mingonghuang' de beihou" "民工荒"的背後 (Behind the "Shortage of Labour"), *Zhongguo laogong yanjiu zhiyuan wangluo luntan* 中國勞工研究支援網路論壇 (Forum on a Supporting Network for Research on Labour in China), Vol. 8 (2004), p. 6.

7. Xiao Jin 肖今 and M. C. Tsang, "Determinants of Participation and Non-participation in Job-related Education and Training in Shenzhen, China," *Human Resource Development Quarterly*, Vol. 15, No. 4 (2004), pp. 389–420.

8. Fan Zhujiang Sanjiaozhou fazhan yanjiuyuan 泛珠江三角洲發展研究院, "Fan Zhusanjiao jingjiqu hezuo jizhi yanjiu baogao" 泛珠三角經濟區合作機制研究報告 (Report on the Pan–Pearl River Delta Collaboration Mechanism), *Zhujiang jingji* 珠江經濟 (Pearl River Economy), Vol. 9 (2004); HKGCC, April 2003, *Mainland/Hong Kong Closer Economic Cooperation Arrangement HKGCC's Position on the Consultation* (www.chamber.org.hk); Luisa Tam, (ed.), *The Confluence of Affluence: The Pearl River Delta Story* (Hong Kong: SCPM Book Publishing, 2005).

9. The Pan-PRD Region includes Hong Kong, Macao and the nine provinces of Guangdong, Fujian, Jiangxi, Hunan, Guangxi, Hainan, Guizhou, Sichuan and Yunnan.

10. Dakar Framework for Action, Education for All: Meeting Our Collective Commitments. UNESCO has Monitored Education for All Actions around the World since 2002. See http://www.unesco.org/education/efa/ed.

11. T. W. Schultz, "Investment in Human Capital," *American Economic Review*, Vol. 51 (1961), pp. 1–17.

12. E. Cohn and J. Addison, "The Economic Returns to Lifelong Learning in OECD Countries," *Education Economics*, Vol. 6, No. 3 (1998), pp. 253–307.

13. L. Thurow, *The Future of Capitalism* (New York: Penguin Books, 1996).

14. Zhongguo jiaoyu yu renli ziyuan wenti ketizu 中國教育與人力資源問題課題組, *Cong renkou daguo maixiang renli ziyuan qiangguo* 從人口大國邁向人力資源強國 (Advance from a Country Characterized by a Tremendously Large Population to One Characterized by Strong Human Resources) (Beijing:

Gaodeng jiaoyu chubanshe 高等教育出版社, 2003); Jiaoyubu 教育部, "2000–2005 quanguo rencai duiwu jianshe guihua gangyao" 2000–2005年全國人才隊伍建設規劃綱要 (Guidelines to the National Development of Professional Personnel for the Period 2000–2005), *Jiaoyubu zhengbao* 教育部政報 (Policy of the Ministry of Education), Vols. 7/8 (2002), pp. 293–300; Guowuyuan 國務院, *Guowuyuan guanyu jichu jiaoyu gaige yu fazhan de jueding* 國務院關於基礎教育改革與發展的決定 (Decision on the Reform and Development of Basic Education). Beijing: *Guofa (2001) 21* 國發 [2001] 21號 (State Council Document No. 21, 2001). Please see http://www.moe.edu.cn/.

15. *Zhongguo jiaoyu tongji nianjian 1997* 中國教育統計年鑑1997 (Educational Statistics Yearbook of China 1997), *Zhongguo jiaoyu tongji nianjian 2000* (Educational Statistics Yearbook of China 2000) and *Zhongguo jiaoyu tongji nianjian 2003* (Educational Statistics Yearbook of China 2003) (Beijing: Renmin jiaoyu chubanshe 人民教育出版社, 1997, 2000 and 2003); *Zhongguo laodong tongji nianjian 1998* 中國勞動統計年鑑1998 (Statistical Yearbook on Labour in China 1998); *Zhongguo laodong tongji nianjian 2000* (Statistical Yearbook on Labour in China 2000) and *Zhongguo laodong tongji nianjian 2003* (Statistical Yearbook on Labour in China 2003) (Beijing: Zhongguo tongji chubanshe 中國統計出版社, 1998, 2000 and 2003). These are the sources from which the tables and figures in this chapter have been drawn, unless further details are shown.

16. Zhonggong zhongyang guowuyuan 中共中央國務院, "Zhongguo jiaoyu gaige he fazhan gangyao" 中國教育改革和發展綱要 (1993年2月13日) (A Guide to China's Education Reform and Development, 13 February 1993), *Zhonghua Renmin Gongheguo jiaoyu falü fagui zonglan* 中華人民共和國教育法律法規總覽 (Educational Laws and Regulations of China) (Beijing: Falü chubanshe 法律出版社, 2000), pp. 2–13; Jiaoyubu, "Mianxiang ershiyi shiji jiaoyu zhenxing xingdong jihua" 面向21世紀教育振興行動計劃 (A Plan to Revitalize Education for the Twenty-first Century), *Jiaoyubu zhengbao*, Vol. 3 (1999), pp. 99–106.

17. Zhonggong zhongyang, "Zhonggong zhongyang guanyu jiaoyu tizhi gaige de jueding" 中共中央關於教育體制改革的決定 (1985年5月27日) (Decision by the Central Committee of the CPC on the Reform of the Education System, 27 May 1986), *Zhonghua Renmin Gongheguo jiaoyu falü fagui zonglan* (Educational Laws and Regulations of China) (Beijing: Falü chubanshe, 2000), pp. 2–7.

18. Zhonggong zhongyang guowuyuan, "Zhongguo jiaoyu gaige he fazhan gangyao" (see note 16).

19. Guowuyuan, "Guowuyuan guanyu jichu jiaoyu gaige yu fazhan de jueding" (see note 14).

20. Guowuyuan, "Guowuyuan guanyu jichu jiaoyu gaige yu fazhan de jueding" (see note 14). Article 13 in this document proposes that the allocation of schools

should be considered. Zoning should be applied to school enrolment for both primary and lower secondary schools. That would make the best use of educational resources and appropriately re-allocate schools. Please see http://www.moe.edu.cn/.

21. Xin sanpian diqu jichu jiaoyu fazhan shuiping yanjiu ketizu 新三片地區基礎教育發展水平研究課題組, "Guangxi nongcun jichu jiaoyu diaoyan baogao" 廣西農村基礎教育調研報告 (Research Report on Basic Education in Rural Guangxi), *Jiaoyu yanjiu* 教育研究 (Education Research), Vol. 4 (2003), pp. 24–29; Xiao Jin, "Xiandaihua jinchengzhong yanzhong zhihou de cunluo: xibu nongcun de shehui huanjing" 現代化進程中嚴重滯後的村落：西部農村的社會環境 (Villages Lagging Behind: The Social Environment of the Countryside), *Zhanlüe yu guanli* 戰略與管理 (Strategy and Management), Vol. 2, No. 63 (2004), pp. 21–31; Field notes of interviews in 60 villages in "Gaoyuan County," in *Yunnan* by Xiao Jin.

22. For more detailed information, please see Xiao Jin, "Education Expansion in Shenzhen, China: Its Interface with Economic Development," *International Journal of Educational Development*, Vol. 18, No. 1 (1991), pp. 3–19; M. C. Tsang, "The Structural Reform of Secondary Education in China," *Journal of Educational Administration*, Vol. 29, No. 4 (1998), pp. 65–83.

23. Zhonggong zhongyang guowuyuan, "Zhongguo jiaoyu gaige he fazhan gangyao" (see note 16).

24. Town schools and rural schools have almost the same ratios because both are under the direct administration of the county government. Therefore, they are placed together for consideration.

25. Liu Li 劉理 and Tu Yanguo 塗豔國, "Nongcun zhong xiaoxue jiaoshi duiwu zhuangkuang wenti diaocha baogao" 農村中小學教師隊伍狀況問題調查報告 (A Study Report of Schoolteachers in Rural Areas), *Jiaoyu fazhan yanjiu* 教育發展研究 (Educational Development Research), Vol. 4 (2005), pp. 8–14. The total number of ST teachers is under-reported in the government statistics. In the case in Yunnan, my student who was conducting field research in an economically well-off county with a population of 590,000 found a total of about 750 substitute and contract teachers. There are 128 counties in Yunnan.

26. Teachers on contract received a monthly salary of about RMB106, and ST teachers about RMB96. Field studies found salaries to be even lower than those in other provinces.

27. Zhonggong zhongyang guowuyuan, "Zhongguo jiaoyu gaige he fazhan gangyao" (see note 16); Jiaoyubu, "Mianxiang ershiyi shiji jiaoyu zhenxing xingdong jihua" (see note 16).

28. Zhonggong zhongyang, "Zhonggong zhongyang guanyu jiaoyu tizhi gaige de jueding " (see note 17).

29. Xiao Jin, "Zhuanxing shiqi de Zhongguo jiaoyu gaige: zhuanxiang hefang?" 轉型時期的中國教育改革——轉向何方？ (Education Reform in a Period of

Transition: Which Direction?), in *Hongfan yanjiu* 洪範研究, edited by Wu
Jinglian 吳敬璉 and Jiang Ping 江平, Vol. 3, No. 2 (June 2006), pp. 144–83.

30. The mushrooming of enterprises in coastal areas attracted students away from
schools because of the chance to make quick money. Therefore, the realization
of nine years of compulsory education has become a difficult job. Xiao Jin
and Leslie Lo, "Education," in *Fujian: A Coastal Province in Transition and
Transformation*, edited by Y. M. Yeung and David K. Y. Chu (Hong Kong:
The Chinese University Press, 2000), pp. 401–29.

31. There are a few cases in which the rates approach 200% or above. These
cases include (a) Guangxi, Hainan and Guizhou for admission in 2000 and
graduation in 2003 in LSS town schools; (b) Sichuan for admission in 2000
and graduation in 2003 in USS rural schools, and (c) Jiangxi, Guangdong,
Hainan, Sichuan and Yunnan for admission in 2000 and graduation in 2003 in
urban vocational technical schools. The statistics have been triple-checked.
There are at least two possible explanations for these high rates. One is the
unreliability of the statistics and the other is the merging of schools in the
early 2000s. The mergers might also have led to a mishandling of the statistics.

32. M. C. Tsang, "The Structural Reform of Secondary Education in China,"
Journal of Educational Administration, Vol. 29, No. 4 (1991), pp. 65–83;
Qian Jingfang 錢景舫, "Heyi miandui pugaore" 何以面對"普高熱" (How to
Face the Demand for Higher Education), *Jiaoyu cankao* 教育參考 (Education
Reference), Vol. 5 (1997), pp. 26–27; Xiao Jin, "Education Expansion in
Shenzhen, China: Its Interface with Economic Development," *International
Journal of Educational Development*, Vol. 18, No. 1 (1998), pp. 3–19.

33. For details, see Xiao, "Zhuanxing shiqi de Zhongguo jiaoyu gaige" (see note 29).

34. M. C. Tsang and W. F. Min, "Expansion, Efficiency and Economics of Scale
in Higher Education in China," *Higher Education Policy*, Vol. 5, No. 2 (1992),
pp. 61–66.

35. Xiao Jin, "Higher Adult Education in China: Redefining Its Roles," in
Higher Education in the Post-Mao Time, edited by M. Agelasto and
B. Adamson (Hong Kong: Hong Kong University Press, 1998), pp. 189–210;
and see note 29.

36. See note 7; H. Lauder, "Innovation, Skill Diffusion, and Social Exclusion," in
High Skills: Globalization, Competitiveness, and Skill Formation, edited by
P. Brown, A. Green and H. Lauder (New York: Oxford University Press, 2001),
pp. 161–203.

37. Xiao Jin, *Fazhan jingji zhong de renli ziben — qiye de celüe* 發展經濟中的人
力資本——企業的策略 (Human Capital Development in a Period of Economic
Transition in China: Firms' Strategies) (Beijing: Beijing shifan daxue
chubanshe 北京師範大學出版社, 2004), Chapter 8.

38. See note 29, particularly the section on higher education.

39. Xiao Jin, "Zhongguo jiaoyu zhidu mianlin de tiaozhan" 中國教育制度面臨的

挑戰 (Challenges to China's Education System), *Ershiyi shiji* 二十一世紀 (Twenty-first Century), Vol. 64 (2001), pp. 9–18.

40. Li Luoli 李羅力 (ed.), *ShenGang fazhan yu Da Zhusanjiaozhou lianhe* 深港發展與大珠三角洲聯合 (Development in Shenzhen-Hong Kong and Collaboration in the Pearl River Delta) (Beijing: Zhongguo jingji chubanshe 中國經濟出版社, 2005). See Chapter 11, "Da Zhusanjiaozhou quyu wailai laodongli yanjiu" 大珠三角洲區域外來勞動力研究 (Migrant Labourers in the Greater Pearl River Delta Area), pp. 129–38.

41. Hong Kong launched its nine-year compulsory education scheme in 1979. It took it about 30 years to reduce the illiterate/primary group down to 25% in 1997. Hong Kong is an urban economy. It has been 20 years since China started its nine-year compulsory education programme. The issue in China is how to educate people in rural areas.

42. *Diaocha baogao* 調查報告 (Investigation Report), *Zhusanjiao rengran nan zhaodaogong* 珠三角仍然難招到工 (It Is Still Difficult to Recruit in the Pearl River Delta), *Zhongguo laogong yanjiu zhiyuan wangluo luntan*, Vol. 13 (June 2006), pp. 16–19.

43. Xiao Jin, "Rural Classroom Teaching and Non-farm Jobs in Yunnan," in *Education and Social Change in China: Inequality in a Market Economy*, edited by Gerald Postilione (New York: M. E. Sharpe, 2006), pp. 111–35.

44. Xiao Jin, "Redefining Adult Education in an Emerging Economy: Complements to Development," *International Review of Education*, Vol. 49, No. 5 (2003), pp. 487–508.

45. J. Benson and Y. Zhu, "The Emerging External Labour Market and the Impact on Enterprise's Human Resource Development in China," *Human Resource Development Quarterly*, Vol. 13, No. 4 (2002), pp. 449–66; also see note 29.

46. Xiao Jin, "Redefining Adult Education in an Emerging Economy: Complements to Development" (see note 44).

47. In every city, there is a physical market for manual labourers (*laodong shichang* 勞動市場) and a market for professionals and technicians (*rencai shichang* 人才市場). The former is under the administration of the Bureau of Labour and the latter is under the administration of the Bureau of Professionals.

48. Guan Ruijie 關銳捷, Wu Zhigang 武志剛 and Wei Xu 魏旭, "Zhongguo nongcun laodongli suzhi zhuangkuang fenxi ji jianyi" 中國農村勞動力素質狀況分析及建議 (The Quality of Labour in Rural China: Analysis and Suggestions), *Jingji yaocan* 經濟要參 (Economic Reference), Vol. 25 (2003), pp. 10–16; see Xiao Jin in note 21.

49. See note 7.

50. Xiao Jin, "Nongcun jiaoyu he peixun yingwei shequ jianshe fuwu" 農村教育和培訓應為社區建設服務 (Education and Training in Rural Areas Should Serve Rural Construction), *Huazhong shifan daxue xuebao* 華中師範大學學報 (Journal of Huazhong Normal University), Vol. 2 (2006).

7

Urban and Regional Development*

Chun Yang and Haifeng Liao

Introduction

The Pan–Pearl River Delta (Pan-PRD) region 泛珠江三角洲 has experienced uneven development on a provincial basis, while its cities have been centres of rapid change and development. This chapter examines patterns of urban and regional development in the Pan-PRD region. It explores the establishment of the Pan-PRD regional bloc in the context of globalization and regionalization, especially the institutionalized integration that is occurring in East Asia. It is argued that the Pan-PRD has emerged as a result of regional competition and cooperation in China during the post-reform period. It then investigates the comparative advantages, existing patterns, and the future balance of urban and regional growth in the Pan-PRD region.

This chapter is divided into four parts. In the first, an overview of inter-provincial relations in China in the context of dialectic globalization and regionalization is provided, to establish a conceptual framework for an empirical analysis of the Pan-PRD. In the second, patterns of regional competition and cooperation in China, the backdrop to the establishment of the Pan-PRD, are analyzed. Patterns of economic inequality among the provinces and regions of the Pan-PRD are examined in the third part, in terms of comparative advantages, economic levels, paths of economic development and rural-urban disparities. This is then followed with an exploration of urbanization and urban systems in the Pan-PRD. The chapter concludes with some preliminary observations on patterns of urban and regional development in the Pan-PRD and on the policy implications for the governments concerned.

Regional Cooperation in China in the Context of Globalization and Regionalization

New Trends of Regionalization in East Asia

Concurrent with globalization, there has been a resurgence of political and economic regionalization around the world over the past two decades.[1] Regionalization implies global homogenization and takes different forms across time and space. It is a complex process of changes taking place simultaneously at various levels: the structure of the world system as a whole, interregional relations, and the internal patterns of a single region. This last can, in turn, be divided into the individual nations as well as subnational and transnational micro-regions.[2] The need for various approaches to integration has become even more pressing with the simultaneous growth of complex supranational organizations and the burgeoning of small-scale regional entities.[3]

The European and North American experience of cross-border integration have been primarily based on supranational institutions, namely, the European Union (EU) and North American Free Trade Agreement (NAFTA). Economic integration in East Asia, however, has largely occurred in the absence of a formal institutional framework, and has been more market-driven.[4] Policies such as preferential arrangements have traditionally not played much of a role in the integration of the region. The 1990s witnessed a paradigm shift from non-preferential to preferential routes towards trade liberalization; it was at this time that more formal preferential agreements began to be made in the Asia-Pacific region.[5] Growing economic regionalism in the world economy since the mid-1980s is helping to push East Asia towards a regional grouping. In recent years, two proposals calling for institutionalized efforts at regional economic cooperation in East Asia have attracted both regional and global attention. One is a call for the construction of an East Asian Free Trade Area (EAFTA) on the basis of the Association of Southeast Asian Nations (ASEAN) Plus Three (APT) framework. The other is for the establishment by ASEAN of free trade agreements with China, Japan, and South Korea within the framework of an ASEAN Plus One (APO) forum. China is the first country with which ASEAN has reached a free trade agreement (FTA).

In the context of the changing nature of regional integration in East Asia, a pattern of institution-based economic integration has been emerging since the early 2000s between the mainland, especially the Pearl River Delta (PRD), and Hong Kong, and particularly since the establishment of the Closer Economic Partnership Arrangement (CEPA) 更緊密經貿關係安排 in June 2003.[6] Following CEPA, the Pan-PRD, a free trade regional bloc, was established in June 2004 as a response to ASEAN-China regional cooperation. This may, to some extent, push forward the trend towards institution-based integration in China.

Changing Inter-provincial Relations in the Post-reform Period

Over the past two decades, a rich body of literature has been devoted to the relationship between the central government and local governments in

China,[7] more specifically, with the government of Guangdong 廣東.[8] These studies have primarily focused on the economic decentralization that has been taking place since the early 1980s, and its impact on economic development in China. The prevailing view is of weakened central control.[9] In comparison with the considerable amount of literature on central-local relations in the vertical dimension, there have been few efforts to examine the horizontal dimension to inter-provincial relations. With regard to the issues of regional competition and cooperation, inter-provincial relations in the post-reform period are still poorly understood.

Since launching the move to open up to the outside world and implement economic reforms, China has decentralized its fiscal and planning authority to lower levels of provincial government. Although this has provided lower-level governments with the enormous incentive and autonomy to pursue regional development, it has also resulted in strong regionalism and territorial confrontations. Widespread and fierce localism and a weakening of the central control have already led to an alarming level of political tension in China. For instance, the percentage of total consumer imports originating from other provinces fell from 38% in 1979 to 29% in 1986.[10] Since the 1990s, the call to "battle against localism and maintain national unity and stability" has become the focus of annual meetings of the Central Committee of the Party and the State Council on "Central Economic Work".[11]

There are two main reasons for the surge in localism. The most immediate is the "industrial convergence" that has been taking place among provinces since the early 1980s. Because of financial incentives and price distortions in favour of manufactured goods, China's provinces have tended to develop similar industries biased towards the manufacturing sector. The advantages of trade have thus been reduced among provinces with similar economic structures.[12] The second reason has to do with the anti-trade policies of the provincial governments. Although the reform has achieved remarkable success in moving the nation towards the development of a free market economy, some provincial and local governments in China are still trying to maintain economic blockades on trade routes, to prevent the outflow of scarce local raw materials as well as the sale of non-locally produced goods within their areas.[13] Furthermore, there are institutional and political dimensions to the problem. Since local officials are often appointed by the central government on tenures of only a few years, during their terms many tend to take a short-term approach to tackling problems.

In many cases, they set up inter-provincial trade barriers in order to maintain employment levels within their jurisdiction. Although efficiency gains from specialization and exchange would ultimately exceed the net benefits of erecting trade barriers, local protectionism was still rampant in China until the early 2000s. Many local authorities of provinces, counties, cities, and even villages have imposed various restrictive standards and regulations on business coming from outside. These include the imposition of sales quotas for locally made consumer goods on locally-controlled stores and shops, prohibiting non-local manufacturers from opening direct sales offices or shops, and ordering local institutions or enterprises to buy goods from local factories. The central government has been attempting for many years to break down inter-regional barriers on trade. In 1993, the central government enacted the "Anti-Unfair Competition Law of the People's Republic of China" 《中華人民共和國反不正當競爭法》,[14] which prohibits the erecting of inter-regional trade barriers. In 2001, a set of "Regulations of the State Council for Eliminating the Regional Barriers in Market Economic Activities" 《國務院關於禁止在市場經濟活動中實行地區封鎖的規定》 came into force.[15] The regulation states that no unit or individual is allowed to stop or interfere in the sale and purchase of products and services from other parts of the country.

In order to break down local protectionism in China, the most essential issue is to develop inter-provincial cooperation based on the competitive advantages of the provinces and to promote the transition from an "Administrative Zone-based Economy" 行政區經濟 to an "Economic Zone-based Economy" 經濟區經濟.[16] Nevertheless, in the context of regional development in China, inter-provincial relationships have shifted significantly, particularly after the launching of reforms in 1979. This is mainly due to a change in the attitude of the central government towards inter-provincial cooperation. The development of inter-provincial relationships in China after 1949 can be generally divided into three periods. The first was from 1949 to the late 1970s, i.e., the pre-reform period. In this period, inter-provincial relationships were tightly controlled by the central government and based on the arrangements of a planned economy, the ideology of egalitarianism, and considerations of national defence.[17]

The second period ranged from the early 1980s to the late 1990s. During that period, the central government advocated a policy of decentralization. Meanwhile, the economy shifted dramatically from a planned to a market economy. During this period of transition, regional protectionism and localism became rampant, consistent with the increasing incentives and autonomy for regional development being handed to the localities. At the same time, the central government also encouraged uneven regional development, by offering preferential policies for specific coastal provinces.[18] The economic disparities between provinces grew significantly. Most had been attempting to develop the same kinds of "profitable" manufacturing enterprises and to attract more of the same types of FDI.[19] Provinces competed fiercely with each other, often ignoring attempts by the central government to reassert control.

The third period started from the late 1990s and extends to the present. The policy of balanced development was again advocated, based on new realities in the development of China's regions. In fact, early into the "Ninth Five-year Plan" (1996–2000) the central government proposed to introduce policies against uneven development. Yet the project of promoting inter-provincial cooperation was not implemented until 1999, with the launching of Western Region Development project 西部大開發.[20] In 2003, the policy of regional coordination and regional cooperation was put forward in the "five coordination" 五個統籌 strategies[21] proposed by the General Secretary of the Communist Party of China, Hu Jintao 胡錦濤, on 14 October 2003 at the Third Plenary Meeting of the 16th Central Committee of the Communist Party of China 中國共產黨第十六屆中央委員會第三次全體會議. Since then, inter-provincial cooperation began to be highlighted at the national level. In fact, the inter-provincial cooperation that is taking place in the current transitional market economy is not the same as the cooperation found in the period of the centrally planned economy. The resurgence of regional cooperation efforts in this current period is a result of the will of the provincial authorities, and is not just something ordered by the central government. Actors such as firms and local governments are willing to take part positively in the regional cooperation efforts, not just passively as before. With the voices for regional co-operation coming from the provinces themselves, such as the nine provinces in the Pan-PRD, it is clear that the provinces realize the disadvantages of an economy based on provincial administrative zones.[22] Along with the emergence of complementary competitive advantages, it is evident that the inter-provincial relationship is one that has not been designed only by the central government and the local governments. In consequence, this "bottom-up" form of regional cooperation is proving to be more applicable to the current transitional market economy than a "top-down" form would have been.

Coexistence of Regional Competition and Cooperation in China

Emergence of Regional Competition in China

An important part of the background to the formulation of the Pan-PRD is the increasing competition coming from other fast-growing regions of China since the early 2000s, such as the Yangzi River Delta (YRD) 長江三角洲, centred around Shanghai 上海; and the Bohai Bay 渤海灣, centred around Beijing 北京, Tianjin 天津, and Tangshan 唐山 (Table 7.1).

Table 7.1   Main Economic Indicators of Three Leading Regions, 2002

Major indicators	PRD	YRD	Bohai Bay
Total population (million persons)	40.95	83.06	224.50
Shares of national total (%)	3.2	6.5	17.5
Land area (1,000 sq km)	41.7	99.6	523.4
Proportion of national total (%)	0.4	1.0	5.5
GDP (RMB billion)	938.61	1,998.33	2,738.67
Shares of national total (%)	9.0	19.2	26.8
Per capita GDP (RMB)	34,295	22,538	12,203
Financial revenue (RMB billion)	76.9	187.3	201.8
Exports (US$ billion)	112.61	92.45	62.32
Shares of national total (%)	34.6	28.4	19.14
Actualized foreign investment (US$ billion)	15.02	18.28	12.31
Shares of national total (%)	27.3	33.2	22.4
Total fixed-asset investment (RMB billion)	288.66	759.07	971.29

Source: Compiled from G. Liang (2004).[23]

The PRD and the YRD are the most important regions of the Chinese economy, and were among the first to open to the world. Since the late 1990s, the competition between the YRD and the PRD has been intensive. The YRD economic zone includes Shanghai, southern Jiangsu 江蘇, and north-eastern Zhejiang 浙江. It comprises 16 key cities above the local level, and is situated at the intersection of China's eastern coastal area and dense industrial areas along the Yangzi River. The YRD enjoys the advantage of being located midway between North and South China, where rivers meet the ocean. It ranks among China's most important industrial, commercial, and trade bases. In 2003, the YRD's GDP reached RMB2,380 billion (20.39% of the national total), while that of the PRD was just half that of the YRD's, at RMB1,133 billion (9.71% of the national total).[24] However, the GDP of the Greater Pearl River Delta (GPRD) 大珠三角, which consists of the PRD in Guangdong and the two Special Administrative Regions (SAR) of Hong Kong and Macao, is still larger than that of the YRD, although the gap has narrowed in recent years (Figure 7.1). "In face of the enormous development potential of the YRD, there is a need for the PRD to further integrate with neighbouring provinces/regions, in order to expand its economic hinterland to form a stronger economic entity that may compete with the YRD."[25] This was the broad background to the establishment of the Pan-PRD.

Regional Integration: Expansion from the PRD to the Greater PRD and the Pan-PRD

The Pan-PRD regional cooperation effort is regarded as a powerful and meaningful way of fighting against regional protectionism, at least to some extent. According to the "Pan-PRD Regional Cooperation Framework Agreement" 《泛珠三角區域合作框架協定》,[26] one of the main aims of the Pan-PRD regional cooperation effort is to eliminate regional barriers to the movement of goods, labour, technology, and investment. The Pan-PRD regional cooperation grouping also aims to establish a unitary market in order to develop a cross-boundary region in the context of globalization

Figure 7.1   Comparison of the GDPs of the YRD, the PRD and the Greater PRD

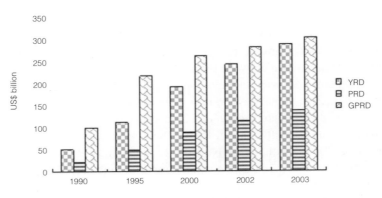

Source: Compiled from the *Yangzi River Delta and Pearl River Delta and Hong Kong and Macau SAR Statistical Yearbook* (2003 and 2004 editions) (see note 23).

and regionalization. In the Pan-PRD, provinces and SARs have realized the importance of regional cooperation and coordination, and are willing to set up a win-win base for the economic activities taking place in the region. "Each party is committed to enhance coordination, create an investment environment, which is fair, open and attractive, and to establish a mechanism to promote transparent, convenient and standardized investment systems."[27]

The emergence of the Pan-PRD is closely linked to increasing demands for regional cooperation, and Pan-PRD is the first regional bloc in China to be approved by the central government. The PRD is a region based on a natural and economic geography. The administrative sphere of the PRD Economic Zone 珠江三角洲經濟區 designated by the Guangdong provincial government in 1994 includes Guangzhou 廣州, Shenzhen 深圳, Foshan 佛山, Zhuhai 珠海, Dongguan 東莞, Zhongshan 中山, Jiangmen 江門, Huizhou 惠州 (just the urban district 市區, Huiyang 惠陽, Huidong 惠東, and Boluo 博羅) and Zhaoqing 肇慶 (just the urban district, Gaoyao 高要 and Sihui 四會). The intensive social and economic interactions between the PRD and Hong Kong over the past two decades has led to the integration of the two entities into a cross-border region, the so-called Greater PRD (GPRD), which has been widely accepted by both academic researchers and policy-practitioners.[28] Furthermore, in June 2003, CEPA, the first bi-lateral free trade agreement, was signed between the central government and the Hong Kong SAR 香港特別行政區 government. It represents the institutionalization of the economic integration that has occurred between the mainland and Hong Kong.[29] Immediately following the establishment of CEPA, in September 2003 the Guangdong provincial government proposed the creation of a "Pan-PPD" region. The first Pan-PRD Regional Cooperation and Development Forum was held in June 2004 in Hong Kong, Macao and Guangzhou. The goals of the Forum are to expand the Delta's hinterland and to participate more actively in both regional integration and economic cooperation efforts (Figure 7.2).

From the national perspective, another objective of the Pan-PRD cooperation effort is to use Guangdong and the Pan-PRD to strengthen cooperation with ASEAN, and to link up with the ASEAN+China free trade area. The China+ASEAN free trade area was first proposed in November 2001, at the "10+3" (ASEAN countries plus China, Japan, and South Korea) national leaders meeting. On 14 May 2003, detailed agreements on the ASEAN+China free trade area such as the goals, principles, content of cooperation, and timetable, were discussed in Beijing. According to the

Figure 7.2   Expansion from the PRD to the Greater PRD and the Pan-PRD

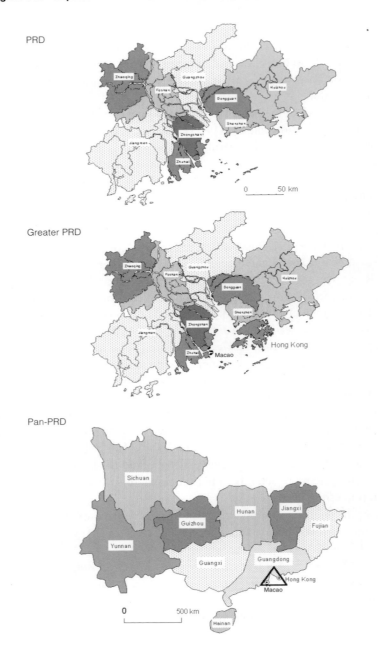

Table 7.2 Selected Economic Indicators of the PRD, Guangdong, Greater PRD, Hong Kong, Macao, YRD and China, 2002

	PRD	Guangdong	Hong Kong (HK)	Macao (MA)	Greater PRD (PRD+HK+MA)	YRD	China
Land area (sq km)	40,165	179,757	1,102	26.8	41,294	100,200	9,597,000
Registered population 2002 (million persons)	23.65	76.49	6.79	0.44	30.88	75.71	1,284.53
Census (PRC) or actual (Hong Kong, Macao) population 2000 (million persons)	40.77	85.23	6.73	0.44	47.94	82.28	1,265.83
GDP (US$ billion)	113.75	142.15	161.51	6.73	281.99	230.98	1,265.59
Primary industries (%)	4.90%	8.80%	0.10%	—	2.00%	5.80%	15.40%
Secondary industries (%)	49.80%	50.40%	12.40%	12.60%	27.50%	51.90%	51.10%
Tertiary industries (%)	45.30%	40.80%	87.50%	87.4%	70.60%	42.30%	33.50%
GDP per capita (US$ 2002) (2001 for the YRD)	4,142	1,815	23,797	15,356	—	2,722	988
GDP 2002 / registered population 2002	4,810	1,858	23,800	15,242	—	3,051	985
GDP 2002 / Census population 2000	2,790	1,668	23,998	15,466	5,883	2,807	1,000
Real annual GDP growth rate 1980–2002	16.1%	13.40%	5.20%	4.90%	12.6%	12.5%	9.50%
Real annual GDP growth rate 1990–2002	17.4%	14.00%	4.00%	3.10%	11.1%	13.5%	9.70%
Retail sales of consumer goods (US$ billion)	42.05	60.55	22.67	0.65	65.37	75.45	494.09
Gross industrial output (US$ billion)	170.6	197.8	22.1	2	194.7	324.7	1,337.90
Value added of gross industrial output (%)	26.30%	26.63%	31.00%	23.67%	26.80%	25.62%	29.78%
Imports (US$ billion)							
Estimated imports from economies other than Hong Kong, Macao, China (US$ billion)	98.39	102.63	207.62	2.53	308.52	82.81	295.17
Exports (US$ billion)							
Estimated exports to economies other than Hong Kong, Macao, China (US$ billion)	111.55	118.46	200.1	2.36	314.01	92.4	325.6
Utilized FDI (US$ billion)							
Estimated utilized FDI from sources other than Hong Kong, Macao, China 2002 (US$ billion)	11.62	13.11	9.68	0.38	21.68	17.85	52.74

Source: Compiled from the website of the Department of Foreign Trade and Economic Cooperation of Guangdong (http://www.thegprd.com/about/economic.html)

proposed arrangements, in the next 10 years both China and ASEAN will work hard to develop an intimate relationship of cooperation with each other. The region will become the largest free trade area among the developing countries, comprising 1.7 billion consumers and a total GDP of US$2,000 billion.[30] In the context of the development of the ASEAN+China free trade area, Guangdong, especially the PRD, will realize enormous opportunities in this area, together with neighbouring provinces, the Hong Kong SAR and the Macao SAR.

Regional Inequality in Economic Development in the Pan-PRD

Comparative Advantages of the Provinces in the PRD

The Pan-PRD is a necessary and reasonable regional formation based on the complementarities of the comparative advantages of each province and region. The development and economic conditions of the "9+2" constituents vary substantially, ranging from those provinces that are well endowed with natural resources and labour but lacking in balanced development, namely Guangxi 廣西, Yunnan 雲南, Guizhou 貴州, Sichuan 四川, Jiangxi 江西, Hunan 湖南, and Hainan 海南, to the relatively developed coastal economies of Guangdong, Fujian 福建, Hong Kong, and Macao that are well exposed to international markets.[31] Yeung (2005) has pointed out that "for the different units that are the components of the new regional framework, they need to be realistic as to what the framework can or cannot do for them. As many provinces and units are at different levels of development, with diverse socioeconomic make-up, there is goodness-of-fit for them to cooperate for their mutual advantage."[32] In particular, each province/region has its competitive advantages, as shown in Table 7.3. Based on these, 10 sectors have been identified and selected to develop close cooperation in the areas of infrastructure, industry and investment; commerce and business; tourism; agriculture; labour; science education and culture; information construction; environmental protection; sanitation; and disease control.[33]

Provincial Variations in Economic Development

The Pan-PRD region encompasses 21% of China's total land area, and 35% of its population. In 2003, the nine provinces of the Pan-PRD accounted

Table 7.3 Renowned Competitive Advantages in the Pan-PRD

Province/Region	Major renowned advantages
Guangdong	Location (adjacent to Hong Kong and Macao), capital, world-famous manufacturing base, foreign trade
Fujian	Location adjacent to Taiwan, harbours, growing manufacturing activities
Jiangxi	Resources, energy, location (pivot of the Three Deltas including the YRD, PRD, Min River Delta)
Guangxi	Location, resources, policies of autonomy
Hainan	Sole tropical tourism resources in China
Sichuan	One of the largest populated provinces in China, natural resource-based heavy industry
Guizhou	Resources advantages, energy and mineral resources, tourism resources, ethnic pharmaceuticals, characteristic eco-agriculture
Yunnan	Location (geared to the ASEAN countries) resources, tourism, tobacco-manufacturing
Hong Kong SAR	International centre of finance, logistics, commerce and service, as well as tourism
Macao SAR	International centre of gambling and tourism

Source: Compiled by the authors.

for over 33% of China's GDP; if Hong Kong and Macao are included, the figure would be over 40% of total national GDP.[34]

In such a huge economic region, the economic disparities are significant. First, in total economic volume the nine provinces of the Pan-PRD vary considerably from each other. The top province is Guangdong, with a GDP of RMB1,363 billion in 2003, more than twice that of the second province, Fujian, which had a total GDP of just RMB523 billion. In GDP, Guangdong has almost caught up with Hong Kong, whose total GDP was HK$1,291 billion in 2003. In fact, Hong Kong and Guangdong accounted for over 50% of the total GDP of the Pan-PRD region. In addition, according to the coefficient of variation (CV) of GDP, it is obvious that economic disparities have grown over the past two decades. The value of CV rose from just 0.53 in 1980 to 0.89 in 2003 (Table 7.4).

Second, economic disparities in the Pan-PRD are also significant when measured in terms of per capita GDP. The per capita GDPs of Hong Kong and Macao are much higher than those of any of the nine provinces of the Pan-PRD; and among these nine provinces the differences were also dramatic. Guangdong and Fujian were the most developed regions, with

Chun Yang and Haifeng Liao

Table 7.4 Growth of GDP in the Nine Provinces of the Pan-PRD, 1980–2003

Provinces/GDP (RMB billion)	1980	1985	1990	1995	2000	2003
Guangdong	24.97	57.74	155.90	573.40	966.22	1362.59
Sichuan	22.93	42.12	89.10	250.50	401.03	545.63
Fujian	8.71	20.05	52.23	216.05	392.01	523.22
Hunan	19.17	34.99	74.44	219.57	369.19	463.87
Jiangxi	11.12	20.79	42.86	124.51	200.31	283.05
Guangxi	9.73	18.10	44.91	160.62	205.01	273.51
Yunnan	8.43	16.50	45.17	120.67	195.51	246.53
Guizhou	6.03	12.39	26.01	61.07	99.35	135.61
Hainan	2.89	4.33	10.25	36.42	51.85	67.09
MEAN	12.66	25.22	60.10	195.87	320.05	433.46
Coefficient of variation	0.61	0.66	0.71	0.81	0.85	0.89

Source: Compiled from the *China Statistical Yearbook (2004)*.[35]

per capita GDPs of over US$2,000 in 2003. Hainan and Hunan, where the figure was over US$1,000, are in the second tier. Finally, Jiangxi, Sichuan, Guangxi, Yunnan, and Guizhou, all had per capita GDPs of less than US$1,000 in 2003, and can be regarded as the relatively undeveloped provinces in the region (Figure 7.3).

Third, the disparities in economic structure are also notable among the various provinces of the region (Table 7.5). In Hong Kong and Macao, tertiary industries accounted for more than 80% of the local GDP in 2003. This means that both of these places have developed into post-industrialized societies, whereas tertiary industries accounted for just 38.4% of GDP in Guangdong. More importantly, the disparities in industrial structure among the nine provinces are remarkable. The economies of Guangdong and Fujian depend mainly on secondary industries, particularly on manufacturing. For most of the inland provinces including Jiangxi, Hunan, Sichuan, Guizhou, and Yunnan, primary (agricultural) industries made up almost 20% of GDP. In Guangxi, primary industries accounted for 23.8% in 2003, the second highest among the nine provinces. Finally, for Hainan, primary and tertiary industries accounted for more than 70% of the province's GDP. In summary, the disparities in industrial structure show the potential for complementary benefits in regional cooperation.

Figure 7.3   Provincial Variations in GDP Per Capita in the Pan-PRD, 2004

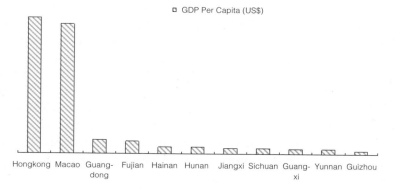

Note: *China Statistical Yearbook (2005)* (see note 35); the exchange rates used in the
       table is: US$1 = HK$7.8 = RMB 8.28 = MOP 8.02.

Table 7.5   Industrial Structure of the Pan-PRD by Region, 2003 (% of total GDP)

Province/Region	Primary industries (%)	Secondary industries (%)	Tertiary industries (%)
Hong Kong	0.1	11.8	88.1
Macao	0	12.6	87.4
Guangdong	8	53.6	38.4
Fujian	13.3	47.6	39.1
Hainan	37	22.5	40.5
Hunan	19.1	38.7	42.2
Jiangxi	19.8	43.4	36.8
Sichuan	20.7	41.5	37.8
Guangxi	23.8	36.9	39.3
Yunnan	20.4	43.4	36.2
Guizhou	22	42.7	35.3

Source: Compiled from the *China Statistical Yearbook (2004)* (see note 35).

Different Paths of Economic Development

The nine provinces of the Pan-PRD region differ significantly from each other in the paths that they have taken in economic development. In Sichuan, Guizhou, Guangxi, and Yunnan, economic development has depended greatly on state-owned enterprises. During the pre-reform period, large state-owned enterprises were set up in these western provinces based on a national strategy to achieve even development and on the "Third Front" 三線 policy (a policy to develop industries based on national defence considerations).[36] However, since 1979, the uneven development policy that has been followed has greatly affected economic development in these provinces. The pace and extent of the transition from a centrally planned economy to a socialist market economy in these provinces have been much slower than in coastal provinces. Moreover, due to their distant inland location and insufficient infrastructure and transportation networks, they did not receive large inflows of foreign investment until the early 2000s. Since 2000, because of the implementation of the Western Region Development project, the central government has invested a great deal in these provinces, and foreign investment has followed.

By contrast, in the last two decades, Guangdong, Fujian, and Hainan have rapidly developed economies dominated by foreign investment. Of these three provinces, Hainan is the most undeveloped. After Hainan was separated from Guangdong in 1988 and made into a province, its economy has development mainly along the lines of tourism and agriculture. But, although Hainan is the largest Special Economic Zone in China, its economy has not developed as rapidly as that of other special economic zones, such as Shenzhen and Zhuhai. As for Fujian, which was also opened early to the outside world, economic growth has fluctuated during the past two decades. Like Guangdong, industrialization in Fujian has also been based on foreign investment, and on township and village enterprises (Figure 7.4). In fact, since 2002, Fujian's GDP has maintained double-digit growth (e.g., 11.5% in 2003 and 10.5% in 2002). The industries in which Fujian is strong are somewhat similar to those of Guangdong, such as microcomputer manufacturing. Future economic growth in Fujian will be probably based on its high-quality harbours as well as on the development of the Min River 閩江 Delta and on the achievement of a breakthrough in cross-strait economic relations. Finally, Guangdong leads the Pan-PRD provinces in economic development. Since 1979, Guangdong has become a leading industrial province of China with its sectors featuring a strong capability in producing, processing and assembling. Its accelerated industrialization was supported by a flood of foreign investment, mainly from Hong Kong and Taiwan and, in recent years, by the rapid development of local enterprises. Although Guangdong has historically not been one of Mainland China's manufacturing bases, manufacturing has become Guangdong's leading industry. In 2002, Guangdong ranked first among all of Chinese provinces in gross value of industrial output (RMB1,638 billion), industrial added value (RMB432 billion), income from products sales (RMB1,625 billion), sales profits (RMB77 billion), and profit payments and tax turnover (RMB138 billion).[37] In 2003, Guangdong achieved an industrial added value of RMB636 billion, an increase of 19.8% over the previous year. Many industrial products of Guangdong play an important role in China — the province is the country's leading producer of home electric appliances, construction ceramics and computers.[38]

In addition to the disparities among various provinces, income disparities between residents in rural and urban areas are also remarkable in the Pan-PRD. Using an index to measure income disparities, provincial variations in disparity in the quality of life of inhabitants in rural and urban areas of the Pan-PRD are examined in Figure 7.5. The nine provinces all had an index reading of over 0.5, which indicates that the disparity in life quality between rural areas and urban areas is still significant in the Pan-PRD. The highest index reading was 0.78 in Yunnan, and the lowest was 0.63 in Fujian.

Figure 7.4 Utilized Foreign Direct Investment in the Pan-PRD, 2003

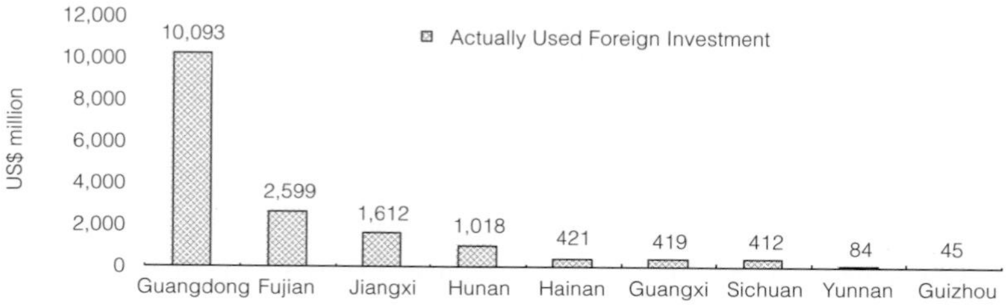

Source: Compiled from the *China Statistical Yearbook* (1987, 1991, 1996, 2001, and 2004 editions) (see note 35) and the *Provincial Statistical Yearbook 2004* of the respective nine provinces of the Pan-PRD.[39]

Figure 7.5   Rural-urban Income Disparities in the Pan-PRD, 2003

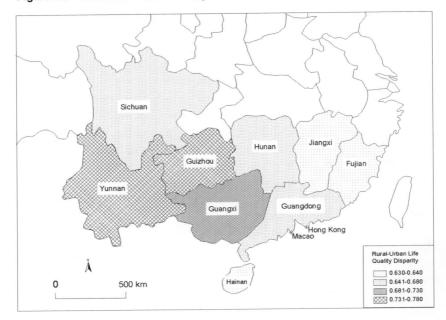

Note: S = 1-I1/I2
         S: Index for the disparity of income between rural and urban residents;
         I1: Rural per capita annual net income; I2: Urban per capita annual disposable
         income
Source: Compiled from the Central Policy Unit, Hong Kong SAR government (2004),
         Consultancy Study on Socio-Economic-Political Trends in Pan-Pearl River Delta
         (see note 25).

Urbanization and Urban Systems in the Pan-PRD

Provincial Variations in Levels of Urbanization

In 2003, the level of urbanization in the Pan-PRD as measured by the
percentage of the non-agricultural population was only 24.7%, lower than
the national average level of 27.89%. This was due to the lower-than-average
levels of urbanization in some provinces of the region, e.g., Guizhou,
Yunnan, and Guangxi (Table 7.6). According to data from the national
population census of 2000, the urbanization level of the Pan-PRD was
33.8%, lower than the national average level of 36.1% (Table 7.7).

In general, in urbanization levels the provinces of the Pan-PRD can be divided into three groups. The first group consists only of Guangdong. Due to foreign investment and the rapid development of rural enterprises, Guangdong's level of urbanization, which rose to 47.7% in 2003, was much higher than that of the other eight provinces in the Pan-PRD. The second group consists of Fujian, Hainan, Jiangxi, Hunan, and Sichuan, with

Table 7.6 Employment Structure of the Provinces of the Pan-PRD, 2003

Provinces	Employment structure (%)			Urbanization level (based on non-agricultural population, %)	Density of cities (Unit/10^5 sq km)
	Primary	Secondary	Tertiary		
Fujian	42.5	27.8	29.8	29.7	18.99
Jiangxi	50.1	17.8	32.1	24.9	12.50
Hunan	57.4	15.5	27.1	21.4	13.71
Guangdong	37.9	27.9	34.2	47.7	24.88
Guangxi	59.8	10.7	29.4	18.3	8.86
Hainan	59.5	9.8	30.7	27.3	24.11
Sichuan	54.5	16.8	28.6	21.0	5.67
Guizhou	62.6	9.6	27.7	15.6	7.38
Yunnan	72.7	8.9	18.3	16.3	4.42
Total	54.0	17.3	28.8	24.7	10.37

Source: Compiled from the *China Statistical Yearbook (2004)* (see note 35).

Table 7.7 Urban and Rural Population in the Provinces of the Pan-PRD, 2000

	Total population	Urban population (million persons)	Rural population	Proportion (%)	
				Urban	Rural
National	1,263.33	455.94	807.39	36.1	63.9
Fujian	34.71	14.43	20.28	41.6	58.4
Jiangxi	41.4	11.46	29.94	27.7	72.3
Hunan	64.4	19.16	45.24	29.8	70.3
Guangdong	86.42	47.53	38.89	55.0	45.0
Guangxi	44.89	12.64	32.25	28.2	71.9
Hainan	7.87	3.16	4.71	40.1	59.9
Sichuan	83.29	22.23	61.06	26.7	73.3
Guizhou	35.25	8.41	26.84	23.9	76.1
Yunnan	42.88	10.02	32.86	23.4	76.6
Sub-total of Pan-PRD	441.11	149.04	292.07	33.8	66.2

Source: Compiled from the *China Statistical Yearbook (2001)* (see note 35).

urbanization levels of more than 20% in 2003. The third group includes Guangxi, Guizhou, and Yunnan, with levels of urbanization below 20%.

The process of urbanization can also be exemplified by the transformation of employment from the primary to the secondary and tertiary industries. In 2003, the proportion of those employed in primary (agricultural) industries was still 54% in the nine provinces. In Guangdong, Fujian, and Guangxi, the proportion was lower than the national level of 50%. Moreover, considering the industrial structure of the nine provinces shown in Table 7.6, those provinces in which the proportion of those employed in the agriculture sector was more than 50%, including Jiangxi, Guangxi, Hunan, Sichuan, Guizhou, and Yunnan, were more likely to have experienced slow urbanization in the past two decades.

The density of cities demonstrated the general situation of the contribution of the urban economy to regional development. Based on Table 7.6 and Figure 7.6, the density of cities was very closely related to the level of urbanization. The coastal provinces enjoyed a higher density of cities, and the figures declined gradually from east to west. Of the nine provinces, Guangdong again ranked top in density of cities, exceeding the national density (6.8) and even far outstripping the average (19.7) for the eastern region of mainland China.

In conclusion, provincial disparities in levels of urbanization are significant in the Pan-PRD, where the density mainly declined from east to west and decreased from coastal areas to inland regions. Disparities in urbanization were closely related to disparities in economic development and industrialization among the nine provinces. In addition, disparities in the quality of life between rural and urban areas were still notable, and have become an important impetus for urbanization.

Hierarchy of the Urban System

A province's level of urbanization only describes the total number of people in that province who live in urban areas; it does not indicate whether the urban population is concentrated in one large centre or spread proportionally throughout the urban system within the province. This study of the urban system of the Pan-PRD aims to examine the evolution of the rank-size model in the region. The future spatial distribution of the cities in the Pan-PRD will be predicted.

The evolution of the urban system in the Pan-PRD indicates that large and extra-large cities have developed more rapidly than smaller ones,

Figure 7.6 Distribution of Urbanization Levels in the Pan-PRD, 2003

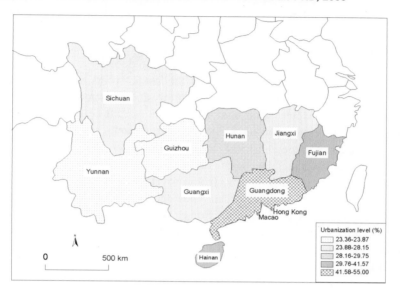

Figure 7.7 Density of Cities in the Pan-PRD

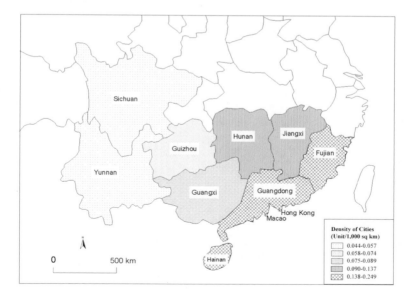

although the national policy for urban development is that the development of extra-large and large cities should be controlled and the development of medium and small cities should be encouraged. As the only world city in the Pan-PRD, Hong Kong still stands at the top of the urban system in the Pan-PRD, with a strong economy and large population.

Next, it should be observed that, in the last ten years, cities in the nine provinces of the Pan-PRD have grown rapidly and attracted a large number of rural people. Many medium-sized cites and small cities have become large cities and even extra-large cites. The total number of large cities and extra-large cities in the Pan-PRD increased from 12 in 1995 to 131 in 2003, with an annual average growth rate of 34.8%. At the same time, the number of super-large cities rose sharply from only 1 in 1995 to 7 in 2003 (Table 7.8 and Table 7.9). During the same period, the total population of these largest cities increased rapidly. For example, the total population of Guangzhou was 6.47 million in 1995, and 7.25 million in 2003, for an annual average growth rate of 1.4%.

Finally, it should be pointed out that a situation exists among the provinces of the Pan-PRD of an unbalanced development of cities.

Table 7.8   Urban System of the Pan-PRD, 1995

Region	Number of cities	Grouped by population in urban districts (million persons)				
		>2 Super-large city	1–2 Extra-large city	0.5–1 Large city	0.2–0.5 Medium city	<0.2 Small city
National Total	640	10	22	43	192	373
Fujian	23	0	0	1	5	17
Jiangxi	20	0	1	0	7	12
Hunan	28	0	1	1	9	17
Guangdong	53	1	0	3	24	25
Guangxi	17	0	0	2	4	11
Hainan	7	0	0	0	1	6
Sichuan	35	0	1	0	14	20
Guizhou	12	0	1	0	3	8
Yunnan	16	0	1	0	2	13
Total	211	1	5	7	69	129

Note: From 2001 onwards, the criterion used to classify cities in Mainland China was changed to that of grouping them by the total population of the urban districts rather than by the urban population in the city.

Source: Compiled from the *China Statistical Yearbook (1996)* (see note 35).

Table 7.9   Urban System of the Pan-PRD, 2003

Region	Number of cities	Grouped by population in urban districts (million persons)				
		>2 Super-large city	1–2 Extra-large city	0.5–1 Large city	0.2–0.5 Medium city	<0.2 Small city
National total	660	33	141	274	172	40
Fujian	23	1	5	7	10	0
Jiangxi	21	0	3	11	5	2
Hunan	29	0	7	13	8	1
Guangdong	44	4	18	12	10	0
Guangxi	21	0	5	8	5	3
Hainan	8	0	1	4	2	1
Sichuan	32	1	11	15	5	0
Guizhou	13	0	2	4	7	0
Yunnan	17	1	1	4	8	3
Pan-PRD	208	7	53	78	60	10

Source: Compiled from the *China Statistical Yearbook (2004)* (see note 35).

Guangdong had 22 extra-large cities and super-large cities in 2003, most of them located in the PRD. Sichuan, which ranked second, had only 12 extra-large cities and super-large cities. Fujian, Hunan, Guangxi and Sichuan have also experienced fast growth in the number of super-large cities and extra-large cities. However, in Hainan, Guizhou, Yunnan, and Jiangxi, the increase in the number of such cities was relatively slow.

Urban Primacy: Who Is the Dragon Head of the Pan-PRD?

According to the figures on urban primacy in the nine Pan-PRD provinces shown in Figure 7.8, in 2002 the index readings for Sichuan, Guizhou, and Yunnan were more than 2.[40] This means that the urban development in these three provinces is unbalanced, with the urban population concentrated in the province's top city. This "one-city" pattern is called primacy distribution and it is probably caused by social disequilibrium resulting from rapid economic growth in the middle stage of economic development.[41] By contrast, urban development was more balanced in the other six provinces of Guangdong, Guangxi, Hunan, Jiangxi, Fujian, and Hainan, with most of these provinces having at least two largest cities.

In the Pan-PRD regional cooperation framework, "Hong Kong's

Figure 7.8   Urban Primacy of the Provinces of the Pan-PRD

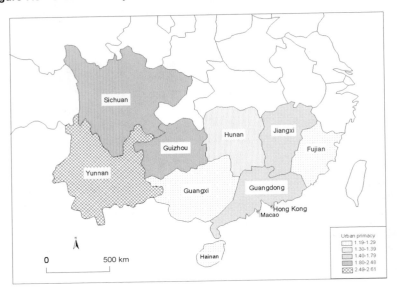

comparative advantages clearly include its status as a centre for international finance, trade, transport, communications and tourism, its manpower resources, management expertise, legal system and extensive experience in market operation and competition."[42] In the future, not only will Hong Kong be one of the top cities in the Pan-PRD, but it will also play a crucial role in regional cooperation between ASEAN and China. Furthermore, Guangdong's competitive advantage mainly lies in its production capabilities, especially in manufacturing. As the leading province in the Pan-PRD, Guangdong will become more closely integrated with Hong Kong with the implementation of CEPA. With respect to the urban system, based on the concept of the GPRD, the cities in the PRD and Hong Kong have developed into an emerging global city-region,[43] one of the three major city regions in mainland China (the other two are the YRD and Bohai Bay). According to theories of global city regions, the hierarchies of the urban system tend to be weaker inside than outside the metropolis, and the cities tend to be distributed spatially in a network structure rather than in a rank-size structure, this probably leading to the emergence of several comparative poles in the region.[44] To date, the emergence of the GPRD city region has mainly been based on two poles, namely the Guangzhou-Foshan metropolitan region and the Shenzhen-Hong Kong metropolitan region. In the future, the Zhuhai-Macao metropolitan region will likely emerge as a third pole, and the city region of the GPRD should be regarded as the head of the urban system in the Pan-PRD.

Urban Agglomerations in the Pan-PRD

Besides provincial variations in urban systems in the Pan-PRD, the cities of the Pan-PRD are unevenly distributed, being mainly concentrated in the coastal provinces, as shown in Figure 7.9. With an increase in the number and size of the cities, the urban agglomerations in the region have led indirectly to advances in the urban economy and development. Meanwhile, although urban agglomerations in China are still at an incipient phase of development, research on their delimitations and gradations has been active.[45] The latest study on the subject was conducted by Fang et al.[46] The study divided 28 current urban agglomerations in China into 3 grades based on a comprehensive index of degrees of development encompassing 14 sub-indexes. With regard to the spatial distribution pattern of cities in the Pan-PRD, the major urban agglomerations and their grades are identified in Table 7.10, according to Fang's calculations.

Within these major urban agglomerations in the Pan-PRD, the most developed urban agglomeration is the Greater PRD. In 2002, the population of the Greater PRD region reached 30.53 million, with a land area of 41,294 sq km.[47] Since 1980, apart from Guangzhou, the cities in the east and west wing of the PRD have expanded very rapidly. All of the sub-regional cities in the PRD including Foshan, Zhongshan, Jiangmen, Zhuhai, and Zhaoqing in the western wing; and Huizhou, Dongguan, and Shenzhen in the eastern wing have developed into a huge network of cities. The intimate interaction among these cities plus the three core cities including Hong Kong, Guangzhou, and Shenzhen has generated a three-pole urban agglomeration. Moreover, the fast pace of urbanization in the PRD is mainly based on the area's advantageous location adjacent to Hong Kong and Macao, and on its rapid industrialization supported by rural enterprises and foreign investment. Together with the YRD and Baohai Bay, the GPRD is regarded as a first-level urban agglomeration at a national scale.

Some other urban agglomerations in the second layer should also be emphasized (Table 7.10), i.e., the Chengdu Plain Urban Agglomeration, the Xia-Zhang-Quan Urban Agglomeration, the Chang-Zhu-Tan Urban

Table 7.10   Major Urban Agglomerations in the Pan-PRD

Grade	Region	Index of development	Number of cities	Major cities	Core cities
1	Greater PRD Urban Agglomeration 大珠三角城市群	9.924	11	Hong Kong, Macao, Guangzhou, Shenzhen, Zhuhai, Foshan, Huizhou, Zhaoqing, Jiangmen, Dongguan, Zhongshan	Hong Kong, Guangzhou, Shenzhen
2	Xia-Zhang-Quan Urban Agglomeration 廈漳泉城市群	3.991	3	Xiamen 廈門, Zhangzhou 漳州, Quanzhou 泉州	Xiamen
2	Chengdu Plain Urban Agglomeration 成都平原城市群	2.809	10	Chengdu 成都, Deyang 德陽, Mianyang 綿陽, Guangyuan 廣元, Yibin 宜賓, Leshan 樂山, Luzhou 瀘州, Nanchong 南充, Zigong 自貢, Dazhou 達州	Chengdu
2	Chang-Zhu-Tan Urban Agglomeration 長株潭城市群	2.495	3	Changsha 長沙, Zhuzhou 株洲, Xiangtan 湘潭	Changsha
2	Nan-Bei-Qin-Fang Urban Agglomeration 南北欽防城市群	2.471	4	Nanning 南寧, Beihai 北海, Fangchenggang 防城港, Qinzhou 欽州	Nanning, Beihai
3	North Jiangxi Urban Agglomeration 贛北城市群	1.744	5	Nanchang 南昌, Jiujiang 九江, Jingdezhen 景德鎮, Yingtan 鷹潭, Shangrao 上饒	Nanchang
3	Central Yunnan Urban Agglomeration 滇中城市群	1.688	4	Kunming 昆明, Qujing 曲靖, Yuxi 玉溪, Chuxiong 楚雄	Kunming
3	Central Guizhou Urban Agglomeration 黔中城市群	1.485	5	Guiyang 貴陽, Zunyi 遵義, Anshun 安順, Duyun 都勻, Kaili 凱里	Guiyang

Notes: The index of development degree is calculated based on 14 sub-indexes, namely the sub-index of GDP per capita, sub-index of transportation, sub-index of communication, Gini coefficient, density of cities, city primacy, industrial location quotient, sub-index of urban district area, sub-index of the performance of enterprises, sub-index of internal consumer goods, location quotient of primary, secondary, territory industries, sub-index of economic openness, and sub-index of industrialization.

The three grades are designated as, Grade 1: Index of development>5, Grade 2: Index of development>2 and <5, Grade 3: Index of development<2.

Source: Compiled from Fang et al. (2005)[48].

Agglomeration, and the Nan-Bei-Qin-Fang Urban Agglomeration. As with the GPRD, these four urban agglomerations are mainly located either in coastal areas or in plains with plentiful resources and good harbours. They have a high density of population and abundant agriculture or a high level of industrial production. In particular, the Chengdu Plain Urban

Agglomeration has historically been on of the important agricultural and commercial centres in China. Moreover, within these four secondary urban agglomerations, the Chengdu plain Urban Agglomeration and the Xia-Zhang-Quan Urban Agglomeration seem to be more important in the Pan-PRD. The Chengdu Urban Agglomeration mainly consists of Chengdu, Deyang, and Mianyang. The land area of the Chengdu Urban Agglomeration is 19,450 sq km, with 10 cities. The Xia-Zhang-Quan Urban Agglomeration in Fujian is centred on Xiamen, and the index reading of the development degree of this urban agglomeration is second to that of the GPRD (Table 7.10).

In comparison with the Chengdu Plain and Xia-Zhang-Quan urban agglomerations, the Chang-Zhu-Tan and Nan-Bei-Qin-Fang Urban Agglomerations are smaller. It is notable that the Chang-Zhu-Tan Urban Agglomeration is much larger than the Nan-Bei-Qin-Fang Urban Agglomeration surrounding the Beibu Wan 北部灣. The total population of the Chang-Zhu-Tan Urban Agglomeration was 12.50 million in 2002, while that of Nan-Bei-Qin-Fang Urban Agglomeration was just 8.55 million.[49] Besides the five major urban agglomerations mentioned above, the other cities in the Pan-PRD tend to co-locate along major transportation routes. This is because, first, many cities are located along the coast, such as Shantou 汕頭, which is east of Guangdong. Second, some cities tend to be located along a major river, such as Jiujiang of Jiangxi, which is on the Yangzi River. Third, other cities tend to be located along railway routes, especially the Beijing-Guangzhou railway and major transportation intersections, such as Chenzhou 郴州 in Hunan.

It is predicted that cities in the Pan-PRD will keep expanding in the near future, due to rapid urbanization. The size and number of large and extra-large cities will likely keep growing. The development of urban agglomerations will certainly contribute to urban and regional development and eventually become the primary motor for continued rapid urbanization in the Pan-PRD. According to current urban agglomerations, to trends in urban development in the region over the past 10 years, and to urban planning projects in each province and infrastructure construction projects in the Pan-PRD, the development of urban agglomerations will probably focus on the following three levels in the Pan-PRD region.

Primary Level Urban Agglomeration

1. Greater PRD, including Hong Kong and Macao — the leading region in the Pan-PRD

Secondary Level Urban Agglomeration

1. Coastal Cities in Fujian
2. Cities in the Chengdu Plain
3. Changsha-Zhuzhou-Xiangtan cities
4. Coastal cities around the Beibu Wan of Guangxi, linking with the coastal cities in west Guangdong and Haikou 海口 in Hainan

Tertiary Level Urban Agglomeration

1. Ganbei 贛北 (North Jiangxi) in Jiangxi
2. East wing of Guangdong, including Shantou, Shanwei 汕尾, Chaozhou 潮州, and Jieyang 揭陽
3. Ganzhou 贛州-Shaoguan 韶關-Chenzhou (called *Hongsanjiao* 紅三角 Red Delta)
4. Central Yunnan centring on Kunming
5. Central Guizhou centring on Guiyang
6. Wuzhou 梧州, Guilin 桂林, Liuzhou 柳州 (Regional core cities in Guangxi)
7. Sanya 三亞 and surrounding cities in Hainan

Conclusion

This chapter has examined patterns of urban and regional development in the Pan-PRD in the context of the coexistence of regional cooperation and competition in China. The urban and regional development of the Pan-PRD seems to be consistent with the emerging institutionalization of economic integration in East Asia since the late 1990s. The comparative advantages, economic disparities, and the different paths of economic development followed by the provinces and regions of the Pan-PRD have provided a solid foundation for cross-boundary cooperation in the region. The disparity in levels of urbanization in the Pan-PRD has been found to be remarkable. On the one hand, the present level of urbanization in the Pan-PRD is lower than the national average, owing to the fact that urbanization has lagged in such provinces of the region as Guizhou, Yunnan, and Guangxi. On the other hand, the PRD is one of the most promising metropolitan regions in China. Moreover, Hong Kong is well known as an international city. The Pan-PRD is characterized by its attractive location for inter-provincial migration. Guangdong is the leading province in terms of immigrants, while Sichuan, Hunan, Jiangxi, and Guangxi are the largest source of migrants in China. From this viewpoint, free cross-boundary flows of population and labour will be essential for the future development of the Pan-PRD as a regional bloc and for enhancing regional integration among the provinces of the region.

Acknowledgements

*Financial support for this study was received in the form of a Competitive Earmarked Research Grant (HKU7238/04H) from the Research Grants Council of the Hong Kong Special Administrative Region Government, and in a Seed Funding for Basic Research grant (2006) (10206763/20373/04500/302/01) from The University of Hong Kong.

Notes

1. S. Breslin, C. W. Hughes, N. Phillips and B. Rosamond (eds.), *New Regionalisms in the Global Political Economy* (London and New York: Routledge, 2002).
2. A. Hurrell, "Explaining the Resurgence of Regionalism in World Politics," *Review of International Studies*, Vol. 21 (1995), pp. 331–58.
3. J. Häkli and D. H. Kaplan, "Learning from Europe? Borderlands in Social and Geographical Context," in *Boundaries and Place: European Borderlands in Geographical Context*, edited by D. H. Kaplan and J. Häkli (Oxford: Rowman & Littlefield, 2002), pp. 1–17.
4. C. P. Chu, "Regionalism and Regional Integration in the Asia-Pacific and the European Union," in *Northeast Asian Regionalism: Learning from the European Experience*, edited by C. M. Dent and W. F. Huang (London: Routledge Curzon, 2002), pp. 34–64.
5. Z. Zhang, "Regional Integration, Trade and Investment Expansion in the Asia-Pacific," *Papers in Regional Science*, Vol. 82, No. 3 (2003), pp. 303–7.
6. C. Yang, "From Market-led to Institution-based Economic Integration: The Case of the Pearl River Delta and Hong Kong," *Issues & Studies*, Vol. 40, No. 2 (2004), pp. 79–118.
7. L. J. C. Ma, "Modelling Central-local Fiscal Relations in China," *China Economic Review*, Vol. 6 (1995), pp. 105–36; L. Y. Zhang, "Chinese Central-local Fiscal Relationships, Budgetary Decline and the Impact of the 1994 Fiscal Reform: An Evaluation," *China Quarterly*, No. 157 (1999), pp. 122–42.
8. P. T. Y. Cheung, "Changing Relations between the Central Government and Guangdong," in *Guangdong: Survey of Province Undergoing Rapid Change*

(2nd edition), edited by Y. M. Yeung and D. K. Y. Chu (Hong Kong: The Chinese University Press, 1998), pp. 23–61.

9. L. Brandt and X. Zhu, "Redistribution in a Decentralized Economy: Growth and Inflation in China under Reform," *Journal of Political Economy*, Vol. 108 (2000), pp. 422–39; A. Feltensteina and S. Iwata, "Decentralization and Macroeconomic Performance in China: Regional Autonomy has Its Costs," *Journal of Development Economics*, Vol. 76 (2005), pp. 481–501; H. Jin, Y. Qian and B. R. Weingast, "Regional Decentralization and Fiscal Incentives: Federalism Chinese Style," Working Paper (Maryland: Department of Economics, University of Maryland, 1999); B. Naughton, *Growing Out of the Plan: Chinese Economic Reform, 1978–1993* (New York: Cambridge University Press, 1995); S. Yusuf, "China's Macroeconomic Performance and Management during Transition," *Journal of Economic Perspectives*, Vol. 8 (1994), pp. 71–92.

10. Y. Huang, "Central-local Relations in China during the Reform Era: The Economic and Institutional Dimensions," *World Development*, Vol. 24, No. 4 (1996), pp. 655–72.

11. J. Oi, "The Role of Local State in China's Transitional Economy," *China Quarterly*, Vol. 144 (1995), pp. 1132–49; S. X. B. Zhao and L. Zhang, "Decentralization Reforms and Regionalism in China: A Review," *International Regional Science Review*, Vol. 22, No. 3 (1999), pp. 251–81.

12. Huang, "Central-local Relations in China during the Reform Era" (see note 10).

13. P. K. Lee, "Local Economic Protectionism in China's Economic Reform," *Development Policy Review*, Vol. 16, No. 3 (1998), pp. 281–303.

14. The National People's Congress of the People's Republic of China, *Zhonghua Renmin Gongheguo fan buzhengdang jingzheng fa* 中華人民共和國反不正當競爭法 (Anti-unfair Competition Law of the People's Republic of China) (Beijing: The National People's Congress of the People's Republic of China, 1993), http://www.competitionlaw.cn/show.aspx?id=133&cid=32, accessed on 7 July 2005.

15. State Council of the People's Republic of China, *Guowuyuan guanyu jinzhi zai shichang jingji huodong zhong shixing diqu fengsuo de guiding* 國務院關於禁止在市場經濟活動中實行地區封鎖的規定 (Regulations of the State Council for Eliminating the Regional Barriers in Market Economic Activities) (Beijing: State Council of the People's Republic of China, 2003), http://www.competitionlaw.cn/show.aspx?id=213&cid=32, accessed on 7 July 2005.

16. Lin Qiping 林其屏, "Cong xingzhengqu jingji xiang jingjiqu jingji zhuanhua: woguo quyu jingji kuaisu fazhan de biran xuanze" 從行政區經濟向經濟區經濟轉化：我國區域經濟快速發展的必然選擇 (Shift from "Administrative Zone-based Economy" to "Economic Zone-based Economy": The Necessary

Choice of the Regional Economic Development in China), *Jingji wenti* 經濟 問題 (Economic Issues), Vol. 2 (2005), pp. 2–4.

17. C. Fan, "Of Belts and Ladders: State Policy and Uneven Regional Development in Post-Mao China," *Annals of the Association of American Geographers*, Vol. 85, No. 3 (1995), pp. 421–49.

18. Ibid.

19. Huang, "Central-local Relations in China during the Reform Era" (see note 10).

20. Y. M. Yeung and J. Shen (eds.), *Developing China's West: A Critical Path to Balanced National Development* (Hong Kong: The Chinese University Press, 2004).

21. "Five coordination" (五個統籌) refers to the coordination of rural and urban development, coordination of regional development, coordination of social economic development, coordination of a balance of human and natural development, and coordination of internal development and opening.

22. Liu Junde 劉君德, "Zhongguo zhuanxingqi tuxian de 'xingzhengqu jingji' xianxiang fenxi" 中國轉型期凸現的'行政區經濟'現象分析 (Emergence of "Administrative Zone-based Economy" in the Transitional Economy in China), *Lilun qianyan* 理論前沿 (Theories Perspectives Review), Vol. 10 (2004), pp. 20–22; Shu Qing 舒慶 and Liu Junde, "Yizhong qiyi de quyu jingji xianxiang—xingzhengqu jingji" 一種奇異的區域經濟現象——行政區經濟 (An Unusual Economic Phenomenon in China: Administrative Zone-based Development) *Zhanlüe yu guanli* 戰略與管理 (Strategies and Management), Vol. 5 (1994), pp. 82–87.

23. Liang Guiquan 梁桂全, *Fan Zhujiang quyu hezuo: zouxiang da zhanlüe* 泛珠 江區域合作：走向大戰略 (Cooperation of Pan-PRD: Towards a Prominent Future) (Guangzhou: Guangdong renmin chubanshe 廣東人民出版社, 2004).

24. International Statistical Information Centre of National Bureau of Statistics (ed.), *Yangtze River Delta and Pearl River Delta and Hong Kong and Macau SAR Statistical Yearbook* (2003 and 2004 editions) (Beijing: China Statistics Press, 2003, 2004).

25. Central Policy Unit, Hong Kong SAR Government, *A Consultancy Study on Socio-Economic-Political Trends in Pan-Pearl River Delta Region, First Monthly Report* (Central Policy Unit, Hong Kong SAR Government, November 2004), p. 8.

26. Central Policy Unit, Hong Kong SAR government, *A Consultancy Study on Socio-Economic-Political Trends in Pan-Pearl River Delta Region, First Monthly Report* (see note 25 above), pp. 100–3.

27. Ibid.

28. C. Yang, "The Pearl River Delta and Hong Kong: An Evolving Cross-boundary Region under 'One Country, Two Systems'," *Habitat International*, Vol. 30, No. 1 (2005), pp. 61–86; Y. M. Yeung, "Integration of the Pearl River

Delta," *International Development Planning Review*, Vol. 25, No. 3 (2003), pp. iii–viii.

29. Yang, "From Market-led to Institution-based Economic Integration" (see note 6).

30. Liang, *Fan Zhujiang quyu hezuo: Zouxiang da zhanlüe* (see note 23).

31. Central Policy Unit, *A Consultancy Study on Socio-Economic-Political Trends in Pan-Pearl River Delta Region* (see note 25), p. 7.

32. Y. M. Yeung, "Emergence of the Pan-Pearl River Delta," *Geografiska Annaler (Series B: Human Geography)*, Vol. 87, No. 1 (2005), pp. 75–79.

33. Central Policy Unit, *A Consultancy Study on Socio-Economic-Political Trends in Pan-Pearl River Delta Region* (see note 25), pp. 100–3.

34. Central Policy Unit, *A Consultancy Study on Socio-Economic-Political Trends in Pan-Pearl River Delta Region* (see note 25), p. 7.

35. National Bureau of Statistics (NBS) (ed.), *China Statistical Yearbook* (1987, 1991, 1996, 2001, 2004 and 2005 editions) (Beijing: China Statistics Press, 1987, 1991, 1996, 2001, 2004, 2005).

36. Fan, "Of Belts and Ladders" (see note 17).

37. Guangdong Provincial Bureau of Statistics (ed.), *Guangdong Statistical Yearbook 2003* (Beijing: China Statistics Press, 2003).

38. Invest Hong Kong (IHK) and Department of Foreign Trade and Economic Co-operation of Guangdong Province (DFEG), *Greater Pearl River Delta Advantages* (IHK and DFEG, 2004), http://www.thegprd.com/advantages/index.html (accessed on 7 July 2005).

39. Guangdong Provincial Bureau of Statistics (ed.), *Guangdong Statistical Yearbook 2004* (Beijing: China Statistics Press, 2004); Fujian Provincial Bureau of Statistics (ed.), *Fujian Statistical Yearbook 2004* (Beijing: China Statistics Press, 2004); Jiangxi Provincial Bureau of Statistics (ed.), *Jiangxi Statistical Yearbook 2004* (Beijing: China Statistics Press, 2004); Hunan Provincial Bureau of Statistics (ed.), *Hunan Statistical Yearbook 2004* (Beijing: China Statistics Press, 2004); Hainan Provincial Bureau of Statistics (ed.), *Hainan Statistical Yearbook 2004* (Beijing: China Statistics Press, 2004); Guangxi Provincial Bureau of Statistics (ed.), *Guangxi Statistical Yearbook 2004* (Beijing: China Statistics Press, 2004); Sichuan Provincial Bureau of Statistics of Guangdong (ed.), *Sichuan Statistical Yearbook 2004* (Beijing: China Statistics Press, 2004); Yunnan Provincial Bureau of Statistics (ed.), *Yunnan Statistical Yearbook 2004* (Beijing: China Statistics Press, 2004); Guizhou Provincial Bureau of Statistics (ed.), *Guizhou Statistical Yearbook 2004* (Beijing: China Statistics Press, 2004).

40. Guojia tongjiju chengshi shehui jingji diaocha zongdui 國家統計局城市社會經濟調查總隊 (ed.), *Zhongguo chengshi tongji nianjian 2003* 中國城市統計年鑑 2003 (Urban Statistical Yearbook of China 2003) (Beijing: China Statistics Press, 2003).

41. X. Q. Xu and A. G. Yeh, "Provincial Variation of Urbanization and Urban Primacy in China," *Annals of Regional Science,* Vol. 18, No. 3 (1984), pp. 1–20.

42. Central Policy Unit, Hong Kong SAR Government, *A Consultancy Study on Socio-Economic-Political Trends in Pan-Pearl River Delta Region, First Monthly Report,* p. 8 (see note 25).

43. C. Yang, "Cross-boundary Integration of the Pearl River Delta and Hong Kong: An Emerging Global City-region in China," in *Globalization and the Chinese City,* edited by F. Wu (London and New York: Routledge, 2005), pp. 125–46.

44. A. J. Scott, J. Agnew and E. W. Soja, "Global City-regions," in *Global City-regions: Trends, Theory, Policy,* edited by A. J. Scott (New York: Oxford University Press, 2001), pp. 11–32; P. Hall, "Global City-regions in the Twenty-first Century," in *Global City-regions: Trends, Theory, Policy,* edited by A. J. Scott (New York: Oxford University Press, 2001), pp. 59–77.

45. S. M. Yao, "The Urban Agglomeration of China," in *Chinese Cities and China's Development: A Preview of the Future Role of Hong Kong,* edited by G. O. A. Yeh et al. (Hong Kong: Centre of Urban Planning and Environmental Management, The University of Hong Kong Press, 1995); Dai Hezhi 代合治, "Zhongguo chengshiqun de jieding jiqi fenbu yanjiu" 中國城市群的界定及其分佈研究 (A Study on the Determination and Distribution of Urban Agglomerations in China), *Diyu yanjiu yu kaifa* 地域研究與開發 (Journal of Areal Research and Development), Vol. 17, No. 2 (1998), pp. 40–43, 55.

46. Fang Chuanglin 方創琳, Song Jitao 宋吉濤, Zhang Qiang 張薔 and Li Ming 李銘, "Zhongguo chengshiqun jiegou tixi de zucheng yu kongjian fenyi geju" 中國城市群結構體系的組成與空間分異格局 (The Formation, Development and Spatial Heterogeneity Patterns for the Structures System of Urban Agglomerations in China), *Dili xuebao* 地理學報 (ACTA Geographica Sinica), Vol. 60, No. 5 (2005), pp. 827–40.

47. See notes 35 and 37.

48. See note 46.

49. See note 40.

8

Population Distribution and Growth

Shen Jianfa

Introduction

As a large regional block in China 中國, the Pan–Pearl River Delta 泛珠江三角洲 (Pan-PRD) region had a large population of 462.86 million in 2004, accounting for 35.41% of the total in Mainland China, Hong Kong 香港, and Macao 澳門 (Table 8.1).[1] The quantity and quality of a population, and its structure, distribution, growth, and migration are important elements of a regional system. Population is the source of the labour force. As consumers, a population with various levels of income and different preferences have major implications for economic activities, especially distribution and services. As active agents in society, people form vast social networks that are important in migration, trade, and flows of information and capital.

To a large extent, many of the population attributes of a region mirror the status of, and the potential for, the development of that region. They reflect the stages and levels of industrialization, urbanization, modernization, and national and international integration. Indeed, population data from censuses and other surveys provide a key and reliable source of information for studying a society in general and regional development in particular. For example, the respective percentage shares of the urban and rural population out of the total population indicate the level of urbanization of a region.

On the other hand, the status of the population has major implications for social, economic, and regional development. Reliable population data provide important information for urban and regional planning, and for solving various social and economic problems. For example, the age structure of the population provides clues on labour force supply and on the situation regarding the ageing of the population.

Many of the population-related issues mentioned above are closely related to many of the topics discussed in various chapters of this book. This chapter focuses on four main aspects, i.e., population growth and distribution, population structure, urbanization and migration. While population structure and distribution have important implications for regional development, urbanization and migration are the most dynamic parts of a population system. This chapter shows that the level of urbanization declines from the core to the peripheral areas of the Pan-PRD region. A regional migration system has been formed in the Pan-PRD region centred on the Pearl River Delta 珠江三角洲 (PRD), with important demographic links between Guangdong 廣東–Hong Kong–Macao.

Table 8.1 Population Growth in the Pan-PRD Region, 1952–2004

Area	Population (million)				Percentage growth (%)		
	1952	1982	2000	2004	1952–1982	1982–2000	1982–2004
Guangdong	29.10	53.63	86.42	83.04	84.27	61.14	54.84
Guangxi	19.43	36.42	44.89	48.89	87.44	23.26	34.24
Yunnan	16.95	32.55	42.88	44.15	92.04	31.74	35.64
Guizhou	14.90	28.55	35.25	39.04	91.61	23.47	36.74
Sichuan	64.11[1]	72.65	83.29	87.25	N.A.	14.65	20.10
Hunan	32.71	54.01	64.40	66.98	65.11	19.24	24.01
Jiangxi	16.56	33.18	41.40	42.84	100.36	24.77	29.11
Fujian	12.59	25.87	34.71	35.11	105.45	34.17	35.72
Hainan	2.59	5.67	7.87	8.18	118.92	38.80	44.27
Hong Kong	2.02[2]	5.32	6.71	6.92	163.96	26.17	30.01
Macao	0.19[3]	0.26	0.43	0.47	39.38	64.88	77.79
9+2	211.15[1]	348.11	448.25	462.86	64.86[4]	28.77	32.96
Mainland, Hong Kong, and Macao	577.02	1013.81	1272.97	1307.26	75.70	25.56	28.95
9+2 share (%)	36.59[1]	34.34	35.21	35.41	85.69[4]	112.53	113.88

Notes: 1. Including Chongqing in 1952.
2. Refers to mid-year of 1951.
3. Refers to the 1950 census figure.
4. These figures are not precise, as Chongqing's population is included in 1952.
5. The data for the nine provinces refer to year-end in 1952 and 2004, and to the period of the censuses of 1982 and 2000. Hong Kong data refer to mid-year in 1951 and to year-end in other years. The Macao data refer to the period of the census of 1950 and to the year-end in 1982, 2000 and 2004.

Sources: Department of Comprehensive Statistics of NBS, *Comprehensive Statistical Data and Materials on 50 Years of New China* (Beijing, China Statistics Press, 1999), p. 112; Guojia tongjiju renkou tongji si 國家統計局人口統計司 (ed.), *Zhongguo renkou tongji nianjian 1990* 中國人口統計年鑒1990 (China Population Statistics Yearbook 1990) (Beijing: Kexue jishu wenxian chubanshe 科學技術文獻出版社, 1991), p. 42; Guojia tongjiju renkou he shehui keji tongji si 國家統計局人口和社會科技統計司 (ed.), *Zhongguo renkou tongji nianjian 2001* (China Population Statistics Yearbook 2001) (Beijing: Zhongguo tongji chubanshe, 2001), p. 53; NBS, *2005 China Statistical Yearbook*, http://www.stats.gov.cn/tjsj/ndsj/2005/indexeh.htm, accessed on 28 June 2006; CSD (Census and Statistics Department), "Population by Sex" (2005), http://www.censtatd.gov.hk/showtableexcel2.jsp?tableID=001, accessed on 28 June 2006; C. P. Lo, "The Population: A Spatial Analysis," in *A Geography of Hong Kong* (2nd edition), edited by T. N. Chiu and C. L. So (Hong Kong: Oxford University Press, 1986), p. 160; Tong Chi-kin 唐志堅, Aomen renkou qianxi 澳門人口淺析 (Preliminary Analysis of the Population in Macao), in *Aomen fazhan de renkou tiaojian yu renkou zhengce* 澳門發展的人口條件與人口政策 (Proceedings of a Symposium on Population Conditions and Population Policy for the Development of Macao) edited by Aomen daxue chuban zhongxin 澳門大學出版中心 and Aomen yanjiu zhongxin 澳門研究中心 (Macao: Aomen daxue chuban zhongxin, 1996), pp. 55–62; Statistics and Census Service of the Macao SAR, "Estimates of Population, Birth and Death, Marriage and Divorce," http://www.dsec.gov.mo/english/indicator/e_dem_indicator_1.html, accessed on 28 June 2006.

Population Growth and Distribution

The population in the Pan-PRD region grew from 211.15 million in 1952 to 448.25 million in 2000 and 462.86 million in 2004 (Table 8.1). Because of the issue of whether to include or exclude migrants without a *hukou* 戶口 (household registration) in the region, the population data for the nine provinces in the Pan-PRD in 2004 contained in the *China Statistical Yearbook 2005* are not very accurate.[2] Thus, the population data from the 2000 census were also given in Table 8.1. For convenience, the discussion in this chapter will focus on changes in the population in the periods 1952–1982 and 1982–2000. The periods 1952–1982 and 1982–2000 were chosen to reflect population growth in the pre- and post-reform periods, respectively. The year 1982 was chosen instead of 1979, as more accurate population data on the nine provinces for 1982 were available from the 1982 census than for the earlier year. Growth rates for the period 1982–2004 are also given for reference in Table 8.1.

According to Table 8.1, population growth in the Pan-PRD region closely followed that of China (including Hong Kong and Macao) as a whole in the period 1952–1982. In this period, the population in the Pan-PRD region increased by 64.86%, for an annual growth rate of 1.71%, while the population of China increased by 75.70%, for an annual growth rate of 1.93%. It is noticeable that population growth in Hong Kong was the most rapid during that period, increasing by 163.96%, mainly due to migration from Mainland China.[3] This was followed by 100–120% growth in Hainan 海南, Fujian 福建, and Jiangxi 江西, and 84–92% growth in Yunnan 雲南, Guizhou 貴州, Guangxi 廣西, and Guangdong. In the period 1952–1982, Hunan 湖南 and Macao had the lowest growth rate in population, at 65.11% and 39.38% respectively. Overall, most provinces in the Pan-PRD region had similar population growth rates.

Due to the introduction of family planning policies in the whole country after the early 1970s, population growth in China slowed down significantly in the period 1982–2000.[4] The annual rate of population growth in the Pan-PRD region declined from 1.71% in 1952–1982 to 1.38% in 1982–2000. This reduction was smaller than that for China as a whole. The population in the Pan-PRD region increased by 28.77% from 1982 to 2000.

In the reform period 1982–2000, the population growth rate varied significantly among various areas in the Pan-PRD region. Macao had the largest percentage rate of growth, at 64.88%, followed by Guangdong at 61.14%. The growth in both places was fuelled by the arrival of migrants from other parts of China. On the other hand, the population in Sichuan

四川 increased by only 14.65% during the same period, due to significant migration to the eastern parts of China, especially Guangdong. Population growth in other areas ranged from 19% to 39%. Due to a declining fertility rate and tight controls over migration to Hong Kong, population growth in Hong Kong slowed down significantly. Hong Kong's population grew by 26.17% in 1982–2000, just slightly below the 28.77% of the Pan-PRD region.

Apart from migration, which will be examined later in this chapter, birth and death are two important components of population change. Table 8.2 presents two commonly used measures of fertility and mortality: total

Table 8.2   Total Fertility Rate and Life Expectancy in the Pan-PRD Region, 2000

Area	TFR	Life expectancy at birth (Years)	
		Males	Females
Guangdong	0.94	70.3	73.6
Guangxi	1.54	69.0	72.2
Yunnan	1.81	64.8	67.8
Guizhou	2.19	66.3	69.3
Sichuan	1.23	68.4	71.7
Hunan	1.27	69.2	72.4
Jiangxi	1.60	69.5	72.4
Fujian	1.03	69.8	72.7
Hainan	1.54	69.1	72.3
Hong Kong	0.93	78.4	84.6
Macao	1.04	79.0 (Males and Females)	
Mainland China	1.22	70.0	73.5

Notes: 1. Hong Kong data refer to the year 2001.
2. The Macao TFR figure refers to 2003 and excludes foreign labour populations, and the life expectancy figure refers to 1999–2002.

Sources: Guowuyuan renkou pucha bangongshi 國務院人口普查辦公室 and Guojia tongjiju renkou he shehui keji tongji si, *Zhongguo 2000 nian renkou pucha ziliao xiace* 中國2000年人口普查資料下冊 (Tabulations on the 2000 Population Census of the People's Republic of China, Vol. 3) (Beijing: Zhongguo tongji chubanshe, 2002), p. 1696; You and Zheng, *Zhongguo renkou de siwang he jiankang* (see note 5), pp. 40 and 56–57; CSD, *Demographic Trends in Hong Kong*, pp. 30 and 53; *Macao in figures 2005*, http://www.dsec.gov.mo/index. asp?src=/english/indicator/e_mn_indicator.html, accessed on 21 July 2005; Cheng Qiyun 程綺雲 and Li Huibing 李慧冰, *21 shiji de Aomen nüxing laodong renkou* 21世紀的澳門女性勞動人口 (Female Labour Population in Macao in the 21st century), paper presented at the Conference on 21st Century Population Changes in Mainland China, Taiwan, Hong Kong and Macao: Challenges and Opportunities, organized by the Social Science Division of the Hong Kong University of Science & Technology, 19–21 November 2004, Hong Kong.

fertility rate (TFR) and life expectancy for various areas. Except for Hong Kong and Macao, the data are for the year 2000. The life expectancy data for provinces in Mainland China were estimated in a recent study based on model life tables.[5] The TFR was below 2.2 in all areas in the Pan-PRD region. The TFR in Hong Kong, Macao, Guangdong, and Fujian was around 1, while the highest TFR was 2.19 in Guizhou. The TFR data for nine provinces in Mainland China were from the 2000 census and had been considered under-estimated due to under-reporting.[6] The TFR of the non-*hukou* population in Guangdong was particularly low, only 0.64, according to the 2000 census.[7] The TFR in Guangdong should have been 1.41 if the existing family planning regulations of the province had been fully implemented, while the actual TFR was 1.8 in 2000.[8] Both were greater than the figure of 0.94 from the 2000 census. But generally, it can be assumed that the TFR in Mainland China has been reduced to a low level, possibly below 2 for Mainland China as a whole. A strict family planning policy has been implemented in China since the late 1970s, and this policy is being continued in the twenty-first century. The declining fertility rate may help to reduce population pressure on land and natural resources.[9] In the near future, attention should be paid to the side effects of family planning and low fertility such as a high gender ratio and an ageing population.

The life expectancy figures for Hong Kong and Macao were high, close to those for Japan. In 2001, the figures for Japan were 78.1 years for men and 84.9 years for women.[10] Life expectancy in mainland provinces also reached a high level, generally over 68 years for men and 71 years for women. Life expectancy was lowest in Yunnan, at 64.8 years for men and 67.8 years for women. Life expectancy levels in Mainland China were higher than in other developing countries at a similar level of development.

Table 8.3 presents information on population distribution and population density in the Pan-PRD region. Sichuan, Guangdong, and Hunan were the three most populous provinces, accounting for 18.85%, 17.94% and 14.47%, respectively, of the Pan-PRD population in 2004. Indeed, Guangdong's share of the Pan-PRD population increased significantly in the period 1982–2004, while those of Sichuan and Hunan declined slightly. Several provinces, including Guangxi, Yunnan, Guizhou, Jiangxi, and Fujian, accounted for 7.5–10.6% of the Pan-PRD population in 2004. Hainan, Hong Kong, and Macao had the smallest populations in the Pan-PRD region, accounting for 1.77%, 1.49%, and 0.10%, respectively, of the Pan-PRD population in 2004. The share of the population of most areas was stable in the period 1982–2004. Thus, the regional distribution of the

Table 8.3 Population Distribution in the Pan-PRD Region, 1952–2004

Area	Population share (%)			Population density (persons per km^2)		
	1952	1982	2004	1952	1982	2004
Guangdong	13.78	15.41	17.94	164	301	467
Guangxi	9.20	10.46	10.56	82	154	207
Yunnan	8.03	9.35	9.54	43	83	112
Guizhou	7.06	8.20	8.43	85	162	222
Sichuan[1]	30.36	20.87	18.85	113	150	180
Hunan	15.49	15.52	14.47	154	255	316
Jiangxi	7.84	9.53	9.26	99	199	257
Fujian	5.96	7.43	7.59	104	213	289
Hainan	1.23	1.63	1.77	76	167	241
Hong Kong	0.95[2]	1.53	1.49	1,819	4,801	6,242
Macao	0.09[3]	0.08	0.10	6,828	9,517	16,920
9+2[1]	100.00	100.00	100.00	105	174	234
Mainland, Hong Kong and Macao				60	106	137
9+2 share[1] (%)				175.30	164.49	170.77

Notes: 1. Including Chongqing in 1952.
2. Refers to mid-year of 1951.
3. Refers to the 1950 census figure.

Sources: Calculated by the author from population data in Table 8.1 and area data from Guojia tongjiju renkou he shehui keji tongji si (ed.), *Zhongguo renkou tongji nianjian 2001*, p. 40; Planning Department, "Broad Land Usage," http://www.info.gov.hk/planning/index_e.htm, accessed on 19 July 2005; Macao in figures 2005.

population in the Pan-PRD region can be regarded as a stable and fundamental factor of development.

Generally, as the Pan-PRD region is located in the southern part of China and has a good climate and land resources, the density of its population is 70% higher than the average for China. Due to past population growth, population density in the Pan-PRD region increased from 105 persons per km^2 in 1952 to 174 persons per km^2 in 1982 and 234 persons per km^2 in 2004. As important cities in the Pan-PRD region, Macao and Hong Kong had the highest population densities, at 16,920 and 6,242 persons per km^2 in 2004, respectively. The nine provinces generally had large rural areas and much lower population densities than Macao and Hong Kong. In 2004 Guangdong had a high population density of 467 persons per km^2 and Yunnan had the lowest population density of 112 persons per km^2. The population density of other provinces was in the range of 180–316 persons per km^2. It is clear that a growing population is placing increasing pressure in the Pan-PRD region, especially on arable land and forests. As China has been able to produce enough food for the whole country in recent years, there is no imminent food supply problem in the Pan-PRD region, except in some poor areas.[11] For the region as a whole, the key to solving the population problem is to accelerate industrialization, urbanization, and development by facilitating domestic and foreign trade and investment.

Population Structure

This section will examine the structure of the population in the Pan-PRD region by gender, age, level of education, and composition of ethnic minorities, using the most recent data from the 2000 census in Mainland China and the 2001 census in Hong Kong and Macao. For the Pan-PRD region as a whole, the gender ratio was 108 males per 100 females, which was greater than the 106 for China as a whole in 2000.

Guangxi and Hainan had the largest gender ratio in the Pan-PRD region, at 113, while other seven provinces in the Mainland China had gender ratios of between 104 and 110. An abnormally high gender ratio was observed in the population aged zero and 1–4 in all nine provinces. The gender ratio of the population aged zero reached 137 in Hainan, 131 in Guangdong, and 127 in Guangxi and Hunan, respectively, while the gender ratio of the population aged between one and four reached 137 in Jiangxi and 136 in Hainan, respectively, in 2000. For the nine provinces as a whole, the gender ratio of the population aged zero and 1–4 was 120 and 123, respectively, higher than for Mainland China as a whole. Indeed, the high gender ratio in the Chinese population has generated a myth of "missing girls in China." According to a recent comprehensive review of gender ratios in China, the gender ratio at birth rose dramatically from 107.6 in 1982 to 116.9 in 2000. The high gender ratio in China was mainly caused by gender-selective abortions stemming from the desire to have boys, both to carry on the family name and also as a means for support in old age.[12] Under-reporting did not significantly affect the figures on the gender ratio.[13] According to a study in Guangdong, the abandoning of infants and infanticide has also played a role in producing unbalanced gender ratios. Among 1,728 abandoned children adopted by the social welfare home (*shehui fuliyuan* 社會福利院) of Yangjiang 陽江 City in 1995–2002, 1,657 were girls, accounting for 96% of the total.[14] Geographically, in 2000 Jiangxi and Guangdong had the highest gender ratios at birth in China, at 138.0 and 137.8, respectively. More developed areas like Guangdong were more likely to adopt the method of selective abortion, especially in rural areas, and for successive births. For example, the gender ratio at birth in Guangdong in 2000 was 117.3 for the first child, 179.7 for the second child, and over 180 for successive children.[15] Such an unbalanced population in terms of gender may have significant social consequences.[16] The key to the solution of the problem is the promotion of education, gender equality, and the tight implementation of the law on population and family planning, which outlaws the carrying out of gender-selective abortions.[17]

Hong Kong and Macao had normal gender ratios for people aged 0–4, but Hong Kong had a low gender ratio of 96 in the total population, according to the 2001 census. The low gender ratio in Hong Kong was due to the presence of a large number of foreign maids and legal migrants from Mainland China. The 2001 census found that the gender ratio was only 49 males per 100 females among the 0.27 million new migrants who had arrived from Mainland China to Hong Kong within the past seven years.[18] The gender ratio of one-way permit holders declined from 92 males per 100 females in 1981 to 53 males per 100 females in 2001.[19] Indeed, the gender ratio of the 2.26 million people who were born in the mainland and Macao was 97, slightly higher than that for the total population in Hong Kong.[20] This is due to the fact that the migrants from the mainland in the 1950–1970s were mainly males, and they were compensated for by female migrants in subsequent years through cross-border marriages. It is foreign maids who brought the gender ratio of the remaining population in Hong Kong down to 96, as the gender ratio of the 4.00 million people who were born in Hong Kong was 105. The gender ratio of ethnic minorities was as low as 32, but rose to 96 if the over 0.2 million foreign maids are excluded.[21]

Macao had the lowest gender ratio of 92 according to the 2001 census. The situation was similar to that of Hong Kong, but the impact of foreign maids was much smaller than that of migrants from Mainland China. The gender ratio of the 0.19 million people who were born in Macao was at a very normal level of 105, while the gender ratio of the 0.21 million people who were born in the mainland was only 79.[22] The gender ratio of people who were born in the Philippines was as low as 54, but there were only 3,455 female Filipinos in Macao.

Although the phenomenon of an ageing population will become serious in the future, the age structure of the population in the Pan-PRD region in 2000 did not show any problem with ageing. The share of population aged over 65 ranged from 5.97% in Guizhou to 11.14% in Hong Kong. The share was much lower than that seen in many developed countries such as the 16.4% in Germany, 17.2% in Japan, and 17.4% in Sweden in 2000.[23] Due to the low fertility rate in Hong Kong, the share of population comprised by those aged 0–14 was the lowest, at 16.54%, while the comparable figure was 21–30% in other parts of the Pan-PRD. The share of population aged 15–64 was relatively high, at over 63%, in all parts of the Pan-PRD.

The age structures in the city, town and rural populations in the Pan-PRD region in 2000 are also examined. The focus is on the nine provinces in the mainland, as Hong Kong and Macao are considered cities. Their city and town populations are based on the city proper and town proper boundaries as defined by the 2000 census, in an attempt to tally the urban population of China accurately.[24] The rural population had the highest share of the population in the 0–14 and 65+ age ranges, while the city population had the highest share of the population aged 15–64 in all nine provinces in 2000. The higher fertility rate in rural areas explains why such areas had a higher share of the population aged 0–14, while the migration of young population from rural to urban areas is responsible for the fact that rural areas have a higher share of the elderly population than urban areas. If such trends continue, it is expected that the rural population rather than the urban population will experience an ageing problem earlier and faster than the urban population.

The quality of human resources is a key indicator of population. It can be approximately revealed by the various levels of education in the population. Table 8.4 presents the share of population aged 15 and above by educational attainment in the Pan-PRD region in 2000. Overall, males had a higher level of education than females in all areas of the Pan-PRD region, as indicated by the higher proportion of males than females with senior secondary education and above. The gender gap was smaller in Hong Kong and Macao than in the other nine provinces. For the Pan-PRD region as a whole, the average level of educational attainment was below the average for China, as indicated by the fact that a lower proportion of population had senior secondary education and above in the Pan-PRD region than in China as a whole. In the Pan-PRD region, 4.76% of the male population aged 15 and above had received junior college education and above, 15.16% a senior secondary education, and 41.42% a junior secondary education in 2000.

The populations of Yunnan and Guizhou had the lowest level of education in the Pan-PRD region. Over 11% and 28% of the male and female populations, respectively, in these two provinces had not attended

Table 8.4 Share of the Population Aged 15+ by Educational Attainment, 2000 (%)

Area	Below primary education	Primary education	Junior secondary education	Senior secondary education	Junior college	University and above
Males						
Guangdong	2.23	23.14	48.24	20.39	3.92	2.08
Guangxi	2.80	33.70	44.68	14.79	2.83	1.20
Yunnan	11.75	44.43	30.72	9.81	2.18	1.11
Guizhou	11.19	42.37	33.51	9.53	2.28	1.12
Sichuan	6.97	40.21	37.95	10.95	2.54	1.38
Hunan	3.52	31.73	43.77	16.32	3.20	1.46
Jiangxi	4.08	30.27	44.81	16.12	3.22	1.49
Fujian	5.84	28.13	44.62	16.28	3.27	1.85
Hainan	4.25	22.55	46.42	20.96	4.00	1.82
Hong Kong[1]	4.60	20.40	22.46	34.77	3.84	13.93
Macao[2]	2.98	38.82	27.52	20.73	1.82	8.06
9+2	5.49	33.20	41.42	15.16	3.04	1.72
Mainland, Hong Kong and Macao	5.94	28.10	44.03	16.31	3.54	2.08
Females						
Guangdong	10.14	29.83	42.99	13.65	2.41	0.97
Guangxi	11.48	40.69	34.48	10.99	1.82	0.55
Yunnan	28.48	41.37	20.21	7.83	1.47	0.63
Guizhou	34.98	38.01	18.49	6.50	1.46	0.56
Sichuan	17.98	41.00	29.91	8.67	1.74	0.69
Hunan	11.38	36.29	37.47	12.08	2.09	0.69
Jiangxi	14.58	40.81	32.52	9.87	1.62	0.60
Fujian	16.57	37.92	31.87	11.10	1.76	0.77
Hainan	17.31	29.52	37.23	13.13	2.03	0.79
Hong Kong[1]	11.96	20.61	15.64	36.68	3.66	11.46
Macao[2]	8.97	36.61	27.48	18.28	2.52	6.11
9+2	16.49	37.06	32.59	11.95	1.92	0.92
Mainland, Hong Kong and Macao	16.16	32.65	34.92	12.92	2.49	1.18

Notes: 1. Hong Kong data refer to 2001. Matriculation education is counted as higher secondary school; a non-degree course as a junior college education, and a degree course as equivalent to a university education and above.

2. Macao data refer to 2001. A non-degree course is counted as a junior college education, and a degree course as a university education and above. Some 118 males and 63 females with special education are not counted.

Sources: Guowuyuan renkou pucha bangongshi and Guojia tongjiu renkou he shehui keji tongji si, *Zhongguo 2000 nian renkou pucha ziliao shangce* 中國 2000人口普查資料上冊, pp. 593–602 and various volumes of Tabulations on the 2000 Population Census of various provinces; CSD, *2001 Population Census Main Tables*, p. 29; Census Service of Macao SAR, EXCEL File (Statistical Tables), Table 14 (see note 22).

primary school. These areas face more challenges than other provinces in the path towards development and modernization. The populations of Hong Kong and Macao had the highest levels of education. For example, 13.93% and 8.06% of the male population aged 15 and above had received a university education and above (degree courses) in Hong Kong and Macao, respectively, in 2001. This was far higher than the highest proportion of 2.08% in Guangdong among the nine provinces in Mainland China. Clearly, much has to be done to improve levels of education in all areas of the Pan-PRD region. This is necessary in order to achieve sustainable social and economic development in an age of the knowledge economy, information society, and globalization.

The Chinese population consists of Han Chinese (*hanzu* 漢族) and 55 other minority nationalities (*shaoshu minzu* 少數民族). A minority nationality is defined as a group of people who share a common territory, bodily structure, language, religion, customs, and livelihood. Some minority nationalities such as the Bouyei 布依族 and Tujia 土家族 are found entirely within China, while others such as the Mongolians 蒙古族 are also found in other countries such as Mongolia 蒙古. The concentration of ethnic minorities in particular areas has major implications with regard to culture, education, and social and economic policies.[25] The distribution of ethnic minorities in the Pan-PRD region is outlined in this section. The focus is on the nine provinces in the mainland, as no detailed data are available for Kong Kong and Macao. The latter are international cities, where statistical efforts on the composition of the population have focused on the Chinese and foreign nationalities. In 2001, Hong Kong had a population of 0.37 million foreign nationals.[26] Apart from the approximately 0.15 million Filipinos maids, there were about 10–25 thousand foreign nationals from each major Western country and Japan. The foreign population in Macao was much smaller, at only 21,035 persons in 2001.[27]

The nine provinces in the Pan-PRD region had an ethnic minority population of 58.15 million, accounting for 55.26% of the total ethnic minority population in Mainland China in 2000. Ethnic minorities accounted for 13.39% of the total population in the nine provinces of the Pan-PRD region. Furthermore, the ethnic minorities were concentrated in Guangxi, Yunnan, and Guizhou, comprising 38.38%, 33.42%, and 37.84%, respectively, of the total population in these provinces in 2000.

In 2000, there were 17 minority nationalities with a population of at least one million each in Mainland China. In the same year, there were 13 minority nationalities in the Pan-PRD region with a population of one million each. Indeed, the Pan-PRD region was the main area of settlement for 10 minority nationalities, including the Zhuang 壮族, Miao 苗族, Yi 彝族, Bouyei, Dong 侗族, Yao 瑶族, Bai 白族, Hani 哈尼族, Li 黎族 and Dai 傣族. For these nationalities, the Pan-PRD region was the home of over 90% of their total population. In addition, over 53.42% of the Tujia population were concentrated in the Pan-PRD region.[28] The main areas of settlement of the Tibetans (Zang) 藏族 were Tibet 西藏 and Qinghai 青海, while the main area of settlement of the Hui 回族 was Ningxia 宁夏. But there were also 1.41 million Tibetan people and 1.24 million Hui people in the Pan-PRD region in 2000. The population of each ethnic minority was concentrated in just one, two, or three provinces. For example, 87.81% of Zhuang people were concentrated Guangxi in 2000. The spatial concentration of ethnic minorities makes it convenient to introduce specific policies to promote the development of their areas of settlement.

Overall, the key issues in the areas with large concentrations of ethnic minorities include the preservation of their culture and language, the development of infrastructure, the introduction of advanced technology, economic development, and the fight against poverty. The cultural heritage and beautiful natural landscapes in ethnic areas are also important resources for the development of tourism. Some provinces in the Pan-PRD region have great potential in this regard. Due to space limitations, these issues will not be elaborated upon in much detail in this chapter.

Population and Urbanization

The distribution of the population by urban and rural areas reflects the advancement and level of urbanization. In the Pan-PRD region, Hong Kong and Macao are cities in their own right. The focus of this section is on the nine provinces in the Pan-PRD region. However, no consistent and reliable annual data on the level of urbanization in China's provinces are available. This situation is caused partly by changes in the definition of the urban population in Chinese censuses and partly by changes in the criteria for designating cities and towns. Furthermore, in the reform period the government has adopted a new pro-urbanization strategy, which has led to the emergence of a new mode of dual-track urbanization.[29]

The *hukou* system was introduced in China in the 1950s. A person's *hukou* stipulates his/her place of residence and *hukou* category, that is, whether one considered a member of the agricultural population or non-agricultural population. In 1964 census, the urban population was formally defined as including only the non-agricultural population in urban areas. This definition had been in use for 18 years until the 1982 census. The growth of the non-agricultural population was called state-sponsored urbanization, as the non-agricultural population was entitled to certain privileges in employment, housing, education, and social welfare, from which the agricultural population was excluded. A single track of state sponsored urbanization prevailed in China before 1978.

A new track of spontaneous urbanization emerged in the reform period. This refers to the rural urbanization led by TVEs (township and village enterprises) and to the migration of a "temporary population" into urban areas.[30] Thus, along with continuing state-sponsored urbanization, a dual track mode of urbanization has emerged. Many people employed by TVEs in small towns and members of the "temporary population" in cities still hold *hukou* status indicating that they are members of the "agricultural population." Many scholars have argued that such people should be counted as belonging to the urban population.[31] The 1982, 1990 and 2000 censuses took some steps to count some or all of them as part of the country's urban population.

Following the notion of dual-track urbanization, a previous study estimated a data set of the provincial urban population for the inter-census years 1982 to 2001 using the 1982 and 2000 census results as benchmarks.[32] These data were consistent in the sense that the differences in the definition of the urban population and the undercounting of the population in the 1982 and 2000 censuses were removed by adjustment. The 1990 census data were not used because the definition of the urban population in that census differed significantly from that used in the 1982 and 2000 censuses. The urban population data for the nine provinces of the Pan-PRD region in the period 1982–2001 were extracted from this data set (Table 8.5). For the nine provinces as a whole, the share of urban population was lower than the average for Mainland China in the same period.

The level and speed of urbanization varied dramatically among the nine provinces. In 1982, the share of the urban population was over 19%, close to the average in Mainland China, in four provinces, including Guangdong, Guizhou, Jiangxi and Fujian. But the share of the urban population was below 15% in other five provinces in the same year. By 1990, the share of the urban population for the nine provinces as a whole reached 23.17%. The share of the urban population in Guangdong and Fujian reached 36.82% and 29.20%, respectively, well ahead of the other provinces in 1990. But the gap in the share of the urban population had narrowed

Table 8.5 Estimated Share of the Urban Population in the Total Population, 1982–2001 (%)

Region	1982	1985	1990	1995	2000	2001
Guangdong	19.76	24.68	36.82	54.25	55.66	56.02
Guangxi	12.12	14.47	17.51	24.09	28.16	28.95
Yunnan	13.27	15.85	17.75	20.10	23.38	23.82
Guizhou	19.39	21.05	21.02	23.31	23.96	24.20
Sichuan	14.45	16.97	19.65	24.95	27.09	27.59
Hunan	14.56	16.86	19.84	23.53	27.50	27.88
Jiangxi	19.93	21.33	23.00	25.15	27.69	28.57
Fujian	21.71	25.27	29.20	36.45	41.96	42.72
Hainan	12.68	N.A.	24.44	31.14	40.68	42.19
Nine provinces	16.40	19.18	23.17	30.00	33.71	34.37
Mainland China	21.39	24.72	28.27	33.28	37.04	37.71

Note: The figure for Hainan in 1985 is included in Guangdong and the data for Sichuan in 1985–1995 includes Chongqing.

Source: http://ihome.cuhk.edu.hk/~b890706/publish.html, accessed on 28 July 2005. For details of the estimation method, see note 32.

among other provinces. The share of the urban population increased significantly in Guangxi, Yunnan and Hainan, while that in Guizhou and Jiangxi increased only slightly in the period 1982–1990. Clearly, Guangxi and Hainan had benefited from the coastal development strategy in the 1980s.

In the period 1990–2001, the level of urbanization increased further in all nine provinces, but most dramatic growth took place in Guangdong, Fujian and Hainan. By 2001, the share of the urban population in these provinces reached 56.02%, 42.72%, and 42.19%, respectively, well over the average for Mainland China. A polarized spatial pattern of urbanization emerged in the Pan-PRD region: Guangdong, Fujian and Hainan became highly urbanized while the other provinces in the Pan-PRD lagged behind in urbanization.

It is interesting to further examine the respective contributions of state-sponsored urbanization and spontaneous urbanization in the Pan-PRD region. The share of the non-agricultural population in the total population was calculated to indicate the contribution of state-sponsored urbanization. The number of TVE employees in rural industries and that of the non-*hukou* population were used as approximate indicators of spontaneous urbanization.[33] The data on TVE employment in various provinces in 1982

Table 8.6   Share of the Non-agricultural Population in the Urban Population, 1982–2001 (%)

Area	1982	1985	1990	1995	2000	2001
Guangdong	66.17	64.33	58.35	53.20	47.99	46.95
Guangxi	69.54	68.20	65.91	63.54	61.11	60.61
Yunnan	59.82	59.13	57.98	56.81	55.64	55.41
Guizhou	46.73	48.81	52.30	55.75	59.16	59.83
Sichuan	61.37	64.39	64.47	64.44	65.19	65.38
Hunan	67.73	68.13	68.79	69.45	70.10	70.23
Jiangxi	60.51	63.26	67.65	71.75	75.52	76.23
Fujian	56.08	54.30	51.32	48.33	45.36	44.77
Hainan	82.55	N.A.	73.50	66.52	58.73	57.10
Nine provinces	61.89	62.39	61.53	59.68	57.58	57.16
Mainland China	67.23	67.13	67.09	66.53	65.89	65.70
Share of the nine provinces in the mainland	92.06	92.95	91.72	89.70	87.39	87.00

Note: The figure for Hainan in 1985 is included in Guangdong and the data for Sichuan in 1985–1995 includes Chongqing.

Source: See Table 8.5.

are not available and have been estimated according to national TVE employment in 1982 and the spatial distribution by provinces in 1990, adjusted by the changing levels of TVE revenues in various provinces from 1982 to 1990.[34]

According to Table 8.6, the share of the urban non-agricultural population in the urban population in nine of the Pan-PRD provinces declined slightly from 61.89% in 1982 to 57.16% in 2001. But it was over 50% in the whole period. This indicates the continuing importance of state-sponsored urbanization, although state sponsorship of people with non-agricultural *hukou* was reduced in the reform period.[35] It is interesting to note that in Guangdong and Fujian, the provinces with the highest levels of urbanization, the share of the urban non-agricultural population in the urban population was the lowest. Clearly, spontaneous urbanization contributed significantly to the high level of urbanization in these two leading provinces.

The growth of TVE employment reflects rural urbanization to some extent. According to Table 8.7, the nine provinces in the Pan-PRD region accounted for about 30% of TVE employees in Mainland China. The total number of TVE employees in these provinces increased from 9.37 million in 1982 to 27.73 million in 1990 and 41.33 million in 2000. Hunan,

Table 8.7 Non-*hukou* Population and TVE Employees, 1982–2000 (million)

Area	TVE employees			Non-*hukou* population		
	1982	1990	2000	1982	1990	2000
Guangdong	2.06	6.58	9.28	0.34	3.60	23.00
Guangxi	0.73	1.99	3.53	0.15	0.78	2.62
Yunnan	0.62	1.48	2.71	0.10	0.55	3.27
Guizhou	0.25	1.07	1.41	0.11	0.91	1.88
Sichuan	1.90	7.06	6.10	0.23	1.54	4.95
Hunan	1.86	4.18	9.39	0.21	3.71	3.20
Jiangxi	1.05	2.33	3.07	0.17	1.35	2.36
Fujian	0.91	2.79	5.56	0.24	1.29	4.97
Hainan	N.A.	0.25	0.28	N.A.	0.20	0.89
Nine provinces	9.37	27.73	41.33	1.54	13.93	47.15
Mainland China	31.13	92.65	128.20	6.57	20.55	109.01
Share of the nine provinces in the mainland	30.12	29.93	32.24	23.45	67.81	43.25

Notes: 1. The TVE figure for Hainan in 1982 is not estimated. The TVE employees for Sichuan in 1982–1990 include those of Chongqing.

2. The non-*hukou* population in Hainan is included in the figure for Guangdong and the non-*hukou* population in Sichuan includes that of Chongqing in 1982.

3. The non-*hukou* population in 2000 excludes the non-*hukou* population from the urban area proper of the same city.

Sources: The data on the TVE employment of various provinces for 1982 are estimated by the author; see the text for details. Other data on TVEs are from NBS, *China Statistical Yearbook 2001* (Beijing: Zhongguo tongji chubanshe, 2001), p. 111; and Benshu bianweihui, Zhongguo *Xiangzhen qiye nianjian 1991*, p. 140. The data on the non-*hukou* population is from Guojia tongjiju renkou tongjisi, *Zhongguo renkou tongji nianjian 1990*, p. 45; Guowuyuan renkou pucha bangongshi and Guojia tongjiju renkou tongjisi, *Zhongguo 1990 nian renkou pucha ziliao* 中國1990年人口普查資料1 (Tabulations on the 1990 Population Census of the People's Republic of China, Vol. 1) (Beijing: Zhongguo tongji chubanshe, 1993), p.6; Guowuyuan renkou pucha bangongshi and Guojia tongjiju renkou he shehui keji tongji si, *Zhongguo 2000 nian renkou pucha ziliao shangce*, pp. 14–15.

Guangdong, and Sichuan had the largest number of TVE employees in the period 1982–2000. In the 1990s, Hunan caught up with Guangdong in the development of TVEs. TVE development in Guizhou, Fujian, and Guangxi was also rapid in the period 1982–2000. Their TVE employees grew by five times during that period.

The growth of the non-*hukou* population was largely a result of spontaneous rural-to-urban migration. The nine provinces of the Pan-PRD region had a non-*hukou* population of 1.54 million in 1982. This increased to 13.93 million in 1990. But the really dramatic growth in the non-*hukou* population took place in the 1990s. By 2000, the non-*hukou* population reached 47.15 million in the nine provinces of the Pan-PRD region. It is clear that the non-*hukou* population led the spontaneous urbanization in the 1990s, while the development of TVEs made the most significant contribution in the 1980s.

The pattern of spontaneous urbanization as indicated by the non-*hukou* migration was quite different from that of TVE employees. Guangdong had the largest non-*hukou* population in 2000, accounting for about 50% of the non-*hukou* population in the nine provinces of the Pan-PRD region.[36] Fujian and Sichuan also had a non-*hukou* population of about five million each in 2000. The concentration of the non-*hukou* population in these three provinces took place in the 1990s, when the pace of both inter-provincial and intra-provincial migration accelerated. The migration flows in the Pan-PRD region will be examined in the next section.

Migration Flows

The Pan-PRD region consists of provinces and cities at different levels of development. Migration has been a key link between them. Migration from the nine provinces to Hong Kong and Macao is governed mainly by immigration policies set up by two SARs. Legal migration to Hong Kong and Macao is mainly from Guangdong and Fujian. Guangdong's share of the total number of one-way permit holders moving to Hong Kong rose from 46.8% in 1991 to 72.6% in 2001.[37] Fujian's share was 27.3% in 1991 and 6.4% in 2001. Among the 36,772 people who migrated from the mainland to Macao in the period 1996–2001, 22,730 were from Guangdong and 10,549 from Fujian.[38]

Migration among the nine provinces in the Pan-PRD region has been driven by the labour market and is also influenced by the household registration system.[39] Guangdong has been famous for being the destination of many migrants since the late 1980s, while several provinces in the Pan-PRD region such as Hunan, Sichuan, and Guangxi are keen to send labour migrants to Guangdong. Indeed, labour migration is an important item in the agenda of Pan-PRD cooperation. In 2004, the provincial governors of Jiangxi and Hunan formally proposed making their provinces a base for labour exports in the Pan-PRD region.[40] An analysis of migration data will reveal this aspect of the relationship among provinces in the Pan-PRD region.

The 2000 census data will be used in this section to examine migration patterns among the nine provinces of the Pan-PRD region. The migration data are based on 9.5% sample population who were required to complete a long form in the 2000 census. The data have been adjusted for this sampling ratio and the official under-enumeration rate of 1.81%.[41] The data refer to the most recent migration that took place between 1 November 1995 to 1 November 2000, and between two places including a township, a town, or a street. Multiple migrations other than the most recent migration are ignored. The data differ from another data set that counts migration according to a change in a person's usual residence on 1 November 1995 and 1 November 2000. In such a data set, multiple migrations other than the earliest migration are ignored in the five-year period. The data on the most recent migration are used here as they include information on the origin of the migrants, including villagers' committees and residents' committees. These committees are set up in specific areas where people's hukou is registered. They have been grouped into three types, including the villagers' committees of townships and towns, town residents' committees, and street residents' committees. The residents' committees of towns and streets are set up in core urban areas and migration from these areas represents the migration of an urban population with a local *hukou*.

Table 8.8 presents the total migration flows to and from various areas in the period 1995–2000. During that period, there were a total of 33.47 million intra-provincial migrants, 16.89 million inter-provincial migrants to the nine provinces, and 16.10 million inter-provincial migrants from the nine provinces. The ratio of inter-provincial in-migration or out-migration to intra-provincial migration was about 0.5. Among inter-provincial migrants, 11.16 million moved among the nine provinces. Some 5.73 million migrants moved from the non-Pan-PRD region to the Pan-PRD region, while 4.94 million migrants moved from the Pan-PRD region to the non-Pan-PRD region, resulting in a net migration of 0.79 million migrants from the non-Pan-PRD region to the Pan-PRD region in the period 1995–2000. This indicates that the Pan-PRD region forms an independent regional migration system in China with only a small net migration from outside. This is also true even if Hong Kong and Macao are included, as Guangdong and Fujian are their major sources of migrants.

In the period 1995–2000, Guangdong was the destination of the largest number of inter-provincial migrants in the Pan-PRD region. The province received 12.18 million such migrants, 8.41 million from the Pan-PRD region and 3.77 million from other provinces in the mainland. Fujian was the

Table 8.8 Migration to and from Various Provinces in the Pan-PRD Region, 1995–2000 (thousand)

Area	Intra-province	To various provinces			From various provinces		
		Nine provinces	Other provinces	Mainland China	Nine provinces	Other provinces	Mainland China
Guangdong	9,446	8,411	3,770	12,181	338	237	575
Guangxi	3,021	240	95	335	1,873	125	1,999
Yunnan	2,923	563	274	836	203	246	449
Guizhou	2,002	212	104	317	845	525	1,369
Sichuan	5,798	226	505	731	2,588	1,869	4,457
Hunan	3,777	217	212	429	3,014	476	3,489
Jiangxi	2,669	167	148	315	1,852	1,058	2,911
Fujian	3,345	956	533	1,489	339	368	707
Hainan	494	164	87	252	105	35	140
Nine provinces	33,474	11,157	5,728	16,885	11,157	4,940	16,097
Other provinces	64,500	4,940	13,780	18,720	5,728	13,780	19,508
Mainland China	97,975	16,097	19,508	35,605	16,885	18,720	35,605

Note: The migration data for the total population are calculated by considering the sampling ratio of 9.50% for migration questions in the long table of the 2000 census. They are also adjusted for an under-enumeration rate of 1.81%.

Source: Guowuyuan renkou pucha bangongshi and Guojia tongjiju renkou he shehui keji tongjisi, *Zhongguo 2000 nian renkou pucha ziliao xiace*, pp. 1797–812.

destination of the second largest number of inter-provincial migrants, at
1.49 million. Of these, 0.96 million were from the Pan-PRD region and
0.53 million from other provinces in the mainland. On the other hand,
Sichuan was the largest source of inter-provincial migrants in the Pan-PRD
region. The province sent 4.46 million inter-provincial migrants, 2.59 million
to the Pan-PRD region and 1.87 million to other provinces in the mainland.
Hunan was the second largest source, with 3.49 million inter-provincial
migrants, 3.01 million to the Pan-PRD region and 0.48 million to other
provinces in the mainland. Guangxi and Jiangxi were also the sources of
about two and three million migrants, respectively, and over 1.8 million
from each province went to the Pan-PRD region.

According to Table 8.9, the average intra-provincial migration rate in
the nine provinces of the Pan-PRD region was 7.59%, slightly below the
average of 7.74% for the mainland as a whole. Only the two most developed
provinces, Guangdong and Fujian, had a higher intra-provincial migration
rate than the average for the mainland. The average inter-provincial in-
migration and out-migration rates of the nine provinces were 3.83% and
3.65%, respectively, much greater than the average of 2.81% for the
mainland but still much lower than the 8% inter-state migration rate in the
United States in the same period.[42] Guangdong had the highest inter-
provincial in-migration rate of 14.09%, followed by 4.29% for Fujian.
Jiangxi had the highest inter-provincial out-migration rate of 7.03%,
followed by over 5% for Hunan and Sichuan.

Overall, Guangdong had the highest net-migration rate of 13.43%,
followed by 2.25% in Fujian. Jiangxi, Hunan, and Sichuan had the largest
negative net-migration rates of –6.27%, –4.75% and –4.47%, respectively.
Figure 8.1 presents the relationship between net migration rate and GDP
per capita in 2000. Generally, developed provinces such as Guangdong
had a positive net-migration rate while less-developed provinces had a
negative net-migration rate.[43] Yunnan is an exception. With a low level of
development, it still had a positive net-migration rate of 0.90%. The province
attracted large flows of 263,000 and 146,000 migrants from Sichuan and
Guizhou, respectively, while out-migration from the province was limited.

Out of the total levels of inter-provincial in- and out-migration,
66.08% and 69.31% were from and to the Pan-PRD region, respectively,
in the period 1995–2000. Over 69% of inter-provincial migrants to
Guangdong and Guangxi came from the Pan-PRD region, while only
30.94% to Sichuan came from the Pan-PRD region. Over 86% of inter-
provincial migrants from Guangxi and Hunan went to the Pan-PRD region.

Table 8.9 Various Migration Indicators in the Pan-PRD Region, 1995–2000

Area	Migration rate (%)			Net migration rate (%)	Share of the nine provinces in total inter-provincial migration (%)		Ratio of inter-provincial migration to intra-provincial migration	
	Intra-provincial migration	Inter-provincial in-migration	Inter-provincial out-migration		In-migration	Out-migration	In-migration	Out-migration
Guangdong	10.93	14.09	0.67	13.43	69.05	58.76	1.29	0.06
Guangxi	6.73	0.75	4.45	-3.71	71.63	93.73	0.11	0.66
Yunnan	6.82	1.95	1.05	0.90	67.28	45.11	0.29	0.15
Guizhou	5.68	0.90	3.88	-2.99	67.09	61.69	0.16	0.68
Sichuan	6.96	0.88	5.35	-4.47	30.94	58.07	0.13	0.77
Hunan	5.86	0.67	5.42	-4.75	50.54	86.37	0.11	0.92
Jiangxi	6.45	0.76	7.03	-6.27	53.07	63.64	0.12	1.09
Fujian	9.64	4.29	2.04	2.25	64.22	47.91	0.45	0.21
Hainan	6.28	3.20	1.78	1.42	65.27	75.02	0.51	0.28
Nine provinces	7.59	3.83	3.65	0.18	66.08	69.31	0.50	0.48
Other provinces	7.82	2.27	2.37	-0.10	26.39	29.36	0.29	0.30
Mainland China	7.74	2.81	2.81	0.00	45.21	47.42	0.36	0.36

Source: Calculated by the author.

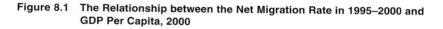

Figure 8.1 **The Relationship between the Net Migration Rate in 1995–2000 and GDP Per Capita, 2000**

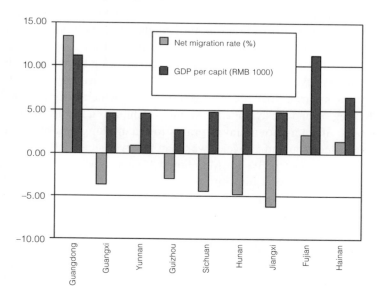

As a major source of migrants in the Pan-PRD region, Sichuan, Hunan, and Jiangxi received over 46% of inter-provincial migrants from non-Pan-PRD regions. On the other hand, as a major destination of migrants from the Pan-PRD region, only 58.76% and 47.91%, respectively, of inter-provincial migrants from Guangdong and Fujian went to the Pan-PRD region. Yunnan also sent over 54% inter-provincial migrants to the non-Pan-PRD region. It is clear that Yunnan's migration links with other provinces of the Pan-PRD region, especially Guangdong, are not well developed.

The migrants' level of education gives an approximate indication of the quality of the human resources that are redistributed through migration. Due to well-established social and educational differences among residents living in villagers' committees, town residents' committees, and street residents' committees, inter-provincial migrants from villagers' committees comprised the greatest proportion of those with a primary level of education and below, while inter-provincial migrants from street residents' committees made up the greatest proportion of those with a university education and above. For example, 11.18% of inter-provincial migrants to Guizhou from street residents' committees had received a university education and above.

Regarding inter-provincial migrants to Guangdong, the most popular destination in the Pan-PRD region, they made up a small percentage of those who had received both the lowest and highest level of education. Only 0.94% of inter-provincial migrants to Guangdong had received less than a primary level of education and 14.41% had a primary education. Both figures are lower than the average for inter-provincial migrants in the Pan-PRD region and the average for Mainland China as a whole. Similarly, only 1.64% of inter-provincial migrants to Guangdong had obtained a university education and above, lower than the average of 3.01% for the Pan-PRD region and 5.83% for Mainland China as a whole. This means that a high percentage of inter-provincial migrants to Guangdong had a secondary education.

Large-scale labour migration from less-developed provinces to Guangdong has contributed to economic development in both the areas of origin and destination. Similar to other countries, there is emerging evidence in China that migrants are adopting a strategy of "earning money in the city while spending in the village."[44] Remittances play an important role in maintaining the links between migrants and their home areas. In a survey of migrant workers in a factory in Fuzhou 福州, 49.1% indicated that they wanted to go home after saving some money.[45] Furthermore, Ma found that improvements in the skills and entrepreneurial ability of the migrants facilitated changes in occupation after the return home to rural areas.[46] In a case study of two counties in Jiangxi, Murphy found that returned migrants are important agents of transfers of information, entrepreneurship, and change.[47] Of any province, Hunan sent the largest number of migrant labourers to Guangdong. Having a reserve of millions of returned migrants with industrial skills and experience has become an advantage in attracting investment to Hunan. Remittances from Guizhou's migrant workers in Guangdong amounted to RMB1.9 billion in 2003, contributing significantly to rural development in Guizhou.[48] The remittances in the past 10 years from Guangdong to various provinces are estimated to have amounted to RMB240 billion.[49]

Jiangxi has adopted an active approach to the exporting of migrant workers. Many migrants had been given training before leaving the province, and in 2004 many migrated to various destinations according to formal arrangements. To address the problem of shortages of skilled labour in the PRD region, the government of Sichuan province allocated RMB4 million from its budget in 2003 to provide on-line training to 1.5 million migrant labourers.[50] This training proved to be effective at improving the quality of migrant labour, as the content had been chosen according to the needs of employers and the market. An on-line job interview system was also established to make it easier for migrant workers to apply for jobs and to be recruited, especially from 50 counties designated as bases for the export of migrant labour.

The impact of migration to destinations such as Guangdong has been both positive and negative. Large-scale migration to Guangdong mainly involves the non-*hukou* population — whose *hukou* is still with their hometowns. The non-*hukou* population from other provinces increased from 2.67 million in 1990 to 4.90 million in 1995 and 10.23 million in 2000. The average annual rate of increase was 14.37%, much greater than the average annual rate for the *hukou* population, at 1.89% per year, in the period 1990–2000.[51] In 2000, Shenzhen 深圳 and Dongguan 東莞 had the largest non-*hukou* population of any city in Guangdong, at 5.85 million and 4.92 million, respectively.[52] Thus, large-scale migration is supplying the huge labour force that is required by the booming economy in the PRD. Migrants have contributed to economic growth, industrialization, and urbanization in Guangdong. The recent concern of various companies in the PRD about labour shortage indicates the importance of migrant labour for the PRD economy. It was estimated that in the summer of 2004 there was a shortage of over one million migrant workers in the PRD.[53] The main negative impacts of migration are increasing pressure on education and housing in the destination areas, as well as worsening public security. Over 80% of crimes in the PRD were committed by the non-*hukou* population.[54]

Due to rising incomes in rural areas and declining household sizes in the areas of origin, the number of migrants who are willing to move to Guangdong may decline. First, grain prices increased by 26.4% in China, which helped to increase incomes in rural areas in 2004.[55] Second, due to family planning in the past 20 years, households have declined significantly in size. Many rural households may only have one to two children, and may not be willing to allow children to work far away from home. According to the 2000 census, Sichuan had a population of 8.93 million aged 25–29, 8.93 million aged 30–34, and 6.74 million aged 35–39. But it only had a population of 5.18 million aged 15–19 and 5.30 million aged 20–24.[56] The population entering working age has declined by several million each year.

In the future, poverty-stricken areas where the population pressure is high and economic opportunities are few may be targeted in the recruitment of migrant labour. Indeed, one of the poorest provinces in the Pan-PRD region, Guizhou, has a low inter-provincial out-migration rate (see Table 8.9). Furthermore, migrant workers should be encouraged to settle down in Guangdong. Further reforms in the *hukou* system are necessary to narrow the gap between the *hukou* population and the non-*hukou* population.[57] The wages of migrant workers should be gradually increased to reflect family living costs rather than individual living costs. Many efforts should be made to improve the education and training of migrant workers as well as their children.

Conclusion

This chapter examined population growth and distribution, population structure, urbanization, and migration in the Pan-PRD region. The key findings can be summarized as follows. First, the nine provinces of the Pan-PRD region experienced similar rates of population growth in 1952–1982, while the population growth in Hong Kong was the most rapid. In the reform period 1982–2000, the population growth rate varied significantly among various areas in the Pan-PRD region. Macao and Guangdong had the largest percentage growth in that period, fuelled by migrants from other parts of China.

Second, the gender ratio of the Pan-PRD region was greater than the average for China in 2000. The gender ratio of the population aged zero was over 127 males to 100 females in Hainan, Guangdong, Guangxi and Hunan. More developed areas like Guangdong were more likely to adopt selective abortion, especially in rural areas and for successive births. Hong Kong and Macao had normal gender ratios for people aged 0–4.

Third, the average educational attainment in the Pan-PRD region was below the average level for China. The populations of Yunnan and Guizhou had the lowest level of education in the Pan-PRD region, while the populations of Hong Kong and Macao had the highest level of education. The gender gap in education was also smaller in Hong Kong and Macao than in the other nine provinces.

Fourth, ethnic minorities accounted for 13.39% of the total population in the nine provinces in the Pan-PRD region, higher than the average for Mainland China. Ethnic minorities were concentrated in Guangxi, Yunnan and Guizhou. The Pan-PRD region is home to over 90% of the total population of 10 minority nationalities.

Fifth, the level and speed of urbanization have varied dramatically among the nine provinces. A polarized spatial pattern of urbanization has emerged in the Pan-PRD region. Guangdong, Fujian and Hainan have become highly urbanized provinces in the mainland. The urban population in these provinces reached over 42% by 2001. Other provinces in the Pan-PRD lagged behind in urbanization. In the period 1982–2001, the urban non-agricultural population comprised more than 50% of the urban population, indicating the continuing importance of state-sponsored urbanization. The non-*hukou* population led spontaneous urbanization in the 1990s, while the development of TVEs made the most significant contribution in the 1980s.

Sixth, a regional migration system has formed in the Pan-PRD region, centring on the PRD and with important demographic links between Guangdong and Hong Kong/Macao. There is plenty of evidence that migration links among the nine provinces are stronger than migration between the Pan-PRD region and non-Pan-PRD region. The scale of inter-provincial migration within the Pan-PRD region was about 50% greater than the scale of migration between the Pan-PRD region and the non-Pan-PRD region. This provides strong support for the concept of the Pan-PRD region, although economic links between some provinces remain weak.

With a large population and uneven level of development, migration is a key link between the various areas of the Pan-PRD region. Since the early 1980s, labour resources have been re-deployed from less-developed areas to more-developed areas in the Pan-PRD region. This is beneficial to both the origin and destination regions. However, three problems remain to be solved.

First, some less-developed provinces such as Yunnan have not established strong migration links with developed provinces such as Guangdong. Within a province, those with the least education in poor areas are not able to participate in the process of labour migration. Only people with a secondary education and above may successfully engage in labour migration. Second, with shrinking household size and rising levels of income in the areas of origin of labour migration, it has become a challenge to ensure a continued supply of cheap labour. Developed areas will be forced to upgrade from labour-intensive to high value-added manufacturing to offer high wages. In the long term, many migrant workers should be encouraged to settle down in developed areas if sustainable social and economic development is to be achieved. Third, large-scale migration to developed areas has also led to a rise in crime and threats to public security. In an era of high mobility, concerted efforts should be made to combat crime. Success in this regard would improve the general well-being of local residents and also facilitate labour migration for the common good.

Acknowledgement

The chapter was based on research funded by a direct research grant from The Chinese University of Hong Kong, project code 4450119.

Notes

1. The Pan-PRD region accounted for 34.57% of the total population of 1,322.16 million in China in 2003, if the population in Taiwan is also included. In 2003,Taiwan had a population of 22.60 million. See Xingzhengyuan zhujichu 行政院主計處, *02-01 TaiMin diqu hukou shu, xingbili yu renkou midu* 02-01臺閩地區戶口數、性比例與人口密度 (02-01 Number of Households, Gender Ratio and Population Density in Taiwan and Fujian Area), http://www. stat.gov.tw/public/data/dgbas03/bs7/yearbook/ch2/2-1.xls#a2, accessed on 22 July 2005.

2. For example, Guangdong had a population of 86.42 million in 2000 according to the 2000 census and 83.04 million according to annual statistics in 2004. The negative growth indicated by the data is not accurate, and stems from problems in the compilation of the 2004 annual statistics.

3. Shen Jianfa, "Population and Migration Trends in Hong Kong," *Geography*, Vol. 82 (1997), pp. 269–71.

4. Tien H. Yuan, *China's Strategic Demographic Initiative* (New York: Praeger, 1991).

5. You Yunzhong 游允中 and Zheng Xiaoying 鄭曉瑛, *Zhongguo renkou de siwang he jiankang: 20 shiji 80 niandai yilai renkou siwang shuiping leixing yuanyin he fazhan qushi* 中國人口的死亡和健康: 20世紀80年代以來人口死亡水平類型原因和發展趨勢 (Mortality and Health of the Chinese Population: Levels, Patterns, Causes and Trends since the 1980s) (Beijing: Peking University Press, 2005), pp. 40 and 56–57.

6. In the period 1991–1999, the total number of births in China as reported by family planning authorities was 25–30% less than the total estimated by a sampling survey conducted by the National Bureau of Statistics (NBS). See Cai Fang 蔡昉 (ed.), *Renkou lüpishu 2000 nian: Zhongguo renkou wenti baogao — nongcun renkou wenti jiqi zhili* 人口綠皮書2000年：中國人口問題報告—— 農村人口問題及其治理 (Green Paper on Population in 2000: A Report on China's Population Problem — The Problem of the Rural Population and Solutions) (Beijing: Shehui kexue wenxian chubanshe 社會科學文獻出版社, 2000), p. 12; Huang Rongqing 黃榮清 and Zhao Xianren 趙顯人 et al., *20*

shiji 90 niandai Zhongguo geminzu renkou de biandong 20世紀90年代中國各民族人口的變動 (Population Change of Various Ethnic Nationalities in China in 1990s) (Beijing: Minzu chubanshe 民族出版社, 2004), pp. 141–45.

7. The non-*hukou* population in this chapter refers to usual residents who have no local *hukou* (household registration). They comprise only part of the "floating population" or "temporary population," which also includes other people without local *hukou* but who were not considered to be usual residents in the census. In the 2000 census, the non-*hukou* population referred to those who were living in a township (*xiang* 鄉), town (*zhen* 鎮) or street (*jiedao* 街道). Their *hukou* registration was elsewhere and they had been away from their place of *hukou* registration for over half a year. Guangdongsheng renkou pucha bangongshi 廣東省人口普查辦公室, *Guangdongsheng 2000 nian renkou pucha liudong renkou ziliao* 廣東省2000年人口普查流動人口資料 (Tabulation on Floating Population of the 2000 Population Census of Guangdong) (Guangzhou: Guangdong jingji chubanshe 廣東經濟出版社, 2002), pp. 716–18.

8. Tu Jowching 涂肇慶 and Yuan Xin 原新, "Liuqian renkou dui Guangdongsheng renkou fazhan de tidai xiaoying" 流遷人口對廣東省人口發展的替代效應 (The Replacement Effect of Migration and the Floating Population on Guangdong), *Nanfang renkou* 南方人口 (South China Population), No. 4 (2002), pp. 34–40.

9. R. D. Hill, "People, Land, and an Equilibrium Trap: Guizhou Province, China," *Pacific Viewpoint*, Vol. 34, No. 1 (1993), pp. 1–24; Shen Jianfa, "Population Growth, Ecological Degradation and Construction in the Western Region of China," *Journal of Contemporary China*, Vol. 13, No. 41 (2004), pp. 637–61; Shen Jianfa and Wang Guixin 王桂新, "Population Distribution and Growth," in *Developing China's West: A Critical Path to Balanced National Development*, edited by Y. M. Yeung and Shen Jianfa (Hong Kong: The Chinese University Press), pp. 213–49.

10. CSD, *Demographic Trends in Hong Kong* (Hong Kong: Government Printer, 2002), p. 53.

11. Shen Jianfa, "Modelling National or Regional Grain Supply and Food Balance in China," *Environment and Planning A*, Vol. 32 (2000), pp. 539–57.

12. Yuan Xin and Tu Jow Ching, "Zhongguo chusheng xingbiebi piangao ji yuanyin fenxi" 中國出生性別比偏高及原因分析 (Analysis of the High Gender Ratio in China and Its Causes), paper presented at the Conference on Twenty-first Century Population Changes in Mainland China, Taiwan, Hong Kong and Macao: Challenges and Opportunities, organized by the Social Science Division of the Hong Kong University of Science and Technology, 19–21 November 2004, Hong Kong.

13. See also Daniel M. Goodkind, "China's Missing Children: The 2000 Census Underreporting Surprise," *Population Studies*, Vol. 58, No. 3 (2004), pp. 281–95.

14. Zhang Feng 張楓, "Guangdong chusheng renkou xingbiebi piangao de xianzhuang, yuanyin yu duice" 廣東出生人口性別比偏高的現狀、原因與 對策 (The Unbalanced Birth Sex Ratio in Guangdong: Causes and Countermeasures), *Nanfang renkou*, Vol. 18, No. 72 (2003), pp. 31–38.

15. Guowuyuan renkou pucha bangongshi 國務院人口普查辦公室 and Guojia tongjiju renkou he shehui keji tongjisi 國家統計局人口和社會科技統計司, *Zhongguo 2000 nian renkou pucha ziliao xiace* (Beijing: China Statistics Press, 2002), pp. 1681–83.

16. Zhang, "Guangdong chusheng renkou xingbiebi piangao de xianzhuang, yuanyin yu duice" (see note 14); Yong Cai and William Lavely, "China's Missing Girls: Numerical Estimates and Effects on Population Growth," *China Review*, Vol. 3, No. 2 (2003), pp. 13–29; Y. Zeng, P. Tu, B. Gu, L. Xu, B. Li and Y. Li, "Causes and Implications of the Recent Increase in the Reported Sex Ratio at Birth in China," *Population and Development Review*, Vol. 19 (1993), pp. 283–302.

17. Zhongghua renmin gongheguo renkou yu jihua shengyufa 中華人民共和國 人口與計劃生育法 (Population and Family Planning Law of PRC), passed by the 25th meeting of the Standing Committee of the 9th National People's Congress, China, on 12 December 2001. It became effective in September 2002.

18. CSD, *Thematic Report-Persons from the Mainland having resided in Hong Kong for less than 7 Years* (Hong Kong: Government Printer, 2002), p. 10.

19. CSD, *Demographic Trends in Hong Kong* (Hong Kong: Government Printer, 2002), p. 13.

20. CSD, *2001 Population Census Main Tables* (Hong Kong: Government Printer, 2002), pp. 12–13.

21. CSD, *Thematic Report-Ethnic Minorities* (Hong Kong: Government Printer, 2002), p. 5; *South China Morning Post*, 21 November 2002.

22. Census Service of the Macao SAR, "EXCEL File (Statistical Tables)," http://www.dsec.gov.mo/english/html/save.asp?fn=/english/pub/excel/ e_cen_pub_2001_y.xl, accessed on 24 July 2005.

23. Department of Economic and Social Affairs Population Division, *World Population Ageing: 1950–2050*, http://www.un.org/esa/population/ publications/worldageing19502050/, accessed on 13 July 2005.

24. Shen Jianfa, "Counting Urban Population in Chinese Censuses 1953–2000: Changing Definitions, Problems and Solutions," *Population, Space and Place*, Vol. 11, No. 5 (2005), 381–400.

25. C. Mackerras, *China's Minorities: Integration and Modernization in the Twentieth Century* (Hong Kong: Oxford University Press, 1994); Information Office of the State Council of the PRC, *National Minorities Policy and Its Practice in China*, Beijing, 1999; Yan Tianhua 嚴田華, *Guizhou shaoshu minzu renkou fazhan yu wenti yanjiu* 貴州少數民族人口發展與問題研究 (A Study

on the Development and Problems of the Population of Minority Nationalities in Guizhou) (Beijing: Zhongguo renkou chubanshe 中國人口出版社, 1995).

26. CSD, *2001 Population Census Main Tables*, pp. 20–21.

27. Census Service of Macao SAR, EXCEL File (Statistical Tables), Table 4 (see note 22).

28. Hubei 湖北 and Chongqing 重慶 were also the main settlement areas of Tujia nationality.

29. J. Shen, K. Y. Wong and Z. Feng, "State-sponsored and Spontaneous Urbanization in the Pearl River Delta of South China, 1980–1998," *Urban Geography*, Vol. 23, No. 7 (2002), pp. 674–94.

30. Shen Jianfa, "A Study of the Temporary Population in Chinese Cities," *Habitat International*, Vol. 26 (2002), pp. 363–77.

31. L. J. C. Ma and M. Fan, "Urbanization from Below: The Growth of Towns in Jiangsu, China," *Urban Studies*, Vol. 31, No. 10 (1994), pp. 1625–45. Shen Jianfa, "Rural Development and Rural to Urban Migration in China 1978–1990," *Geoforum*, Vol. 26 (1995), pp. 395–409; L. Zhang and X. B. Zhao, "Re-examining China's 'Urban' Concept and the Level of Urbanization," *The China Quarterly*, No. 154 (1998), pp. 331–81.

32. Shen, "Counting Urban Population in Chinese Censuses 1953–2000" (see note 24); Shen Jianfa, "Estimating Urbanization Levels in Chinese Provinces in 1982–2000," *International Statistical Review*, Vol. 74, No. 1 (2006), pp. 89–107. The data set is available at http://ihome.cuhk.edu.hk/~b890706/publish.html, accessed on 28 July 2005.

33. For a justification of the use of these indicators, see Shen, Wong and Feng "State-sponsored and Spontaneous Urbanization in the Pearl River Delta of South China, 1980–1998" (see note 29).

34. NBS, *China Statistical Yearbook 1983* (Beijing: Zhongguo tongji chubanshe, 1983), p. 208; Benshu bianweihui 本書編委會, *Zhongguo xiangzhen qiye nianjian 1991* 中國鄉鎮企業年鑒 (China Townships and Village Enterprises Yearbook 1991) (Beijing: Nongye chubanshe 農業出版社, 1992), p. 140.

35. Shen Jianfa, "A Study on the Dual Track Urbanization in China." Paper presented at the 8th Asian Urbanization Conference, 20–23 August 2005, Kobe.

36. Shen, "A Study of the Temporary Population in Chinese Cities" (see note 30).

37. CSD, *Thematic Report-Persons from the Mainland Having Resided in Hong Kong for Less Than 7 Years* (see note 18), p. 72. Legal migrants from Mainland China to Hong Kong were controlled by a quota, which was set at 150 a day in 2005. Each legal migrant was issued a one-way permit by the mainland authorities, allowing that person to migrate to Hong Kong.

38. Census Service of the Macao SAR, "EXCEL File (Statistical Tables)," Table 13 (see note 22).

39. C. Fan, "The Elite, the Natives, and the Outsiders: Migration and Labour Market Segmentation in Urban China," *Annals of the Association of American*

Geographers, Vol. 92, No. 1 (2002), pp. 103–24; Shen, "A Study of the Temporary Population in Chinese Cities" (see note 30).

40. Fan Zhusanjiao quyu hezuo yu fazhan luntan zuweihui mishuchu 泛珠三角區域合作與發展論壇組委會秘書處 (eds.), *Hezuo fazhan gongchuang weilai: Fan Zhusanjiao quyu hezuo yu fazhan luntan yanjianglu* 合作發展共創未來：泛珠三角區域合作與發展論壇演講錄 (Cooperative Development for Future: Collection of Speeches in the Cooperation and Development Forum in the Pan-PRD Region), Hong Kong, 1 June 2004.

41. Guowuyuan renkou pucha bangongshi and Guojia tongjiju renkou he shehui keji tongji si, *Zhongguo 2000 nian renkou pucha ziliao shangce* (see note 15), p. I.

42. C. C. Fan, "Interprovincial Migration, Population Redistribution, and Regional Development in China: 1990 and 2000 Census Comparisons," *Professional Geographer,* Vol. 57, No. 2 (2005), pp. 295–311.

43. Shen Jianfa, "Urban and Regional Development in Post-reform China: The Case of Zhujiang Delta," *Progress in Planning,* Vol. 57, No. 2 (2002), pp. 91–140.

44. G. J. Hugo, "Migration as a Survival Strategy: The Family Dimension of Migration," in *Population Distribution and Migration* — Proceedings of the United Nations Expert Group Meeting on Population Distribution and Migration, Santa Cruz, Bolivia, 18–22 January 1993, edited by the Population Division of the Department for Economic and Social Affairs, United Nations (New York: United Nations, 1998), pp. 49–65; Q. Cai, "Migrant Remittances and Family Ties: A Case Study in China," *International Journal of Population Geography*, Vol. 9, No. 6 (2003), pp. 471–83.

45. Zhu Yu 朱宇, "The Floating Population's Household Strategies and the Role of Migration in China's Regional Development and Integration," *International Journal of Population Geography*, Vol. 9, No. 6 (2003), pp. 485–502.

46. Ma Zhongdong 馬中東, "Urban Labour-force Experience as a Determinant of Rural Occupational Change: Evidence from Recent Urban-rural Return Migration in China," *Environment and Planning A*, Vol. 33 (2001), pp. 237–55.

47. Rachel Murphy, "Return Migration, Entrepreneurship and Local State Corporatism in Rural China: The Experience of Two Counties in South Jiangxi," *Journal of Contemporary China*, Vol. 9, No. 24 (2000), pp. 231–47.

48. Hu Wuxian 胡武賢, "Hunan yu Xianggang jingji hezuo de jichu yu weilai" 湖南與香港經濟合作的基礎與未來 (The Basis and Future of Economic Cooperation between Hunan and Hong Kong), in *Fan Zhusanjiao yu Xianggang hudong fazhan* 泛珠三角與香港互動發展 (Interactive Development of the Pan-PRD and Hong Kong), edited by Y. M. Yeung and Shen Jianfa (Hong Kong: Hong Kong Institute of Asia-Pacific Studies, The Chinese University of Hong Kong, 2005), pp. 145–68; Peng Xianwei 彭賢偉 and Dan

Wenhong 但文紅, "Guizhou canyu quyu hezuo de zuoyong yu diwei" 貴州參
與區域合作的作用與地位 (The Role of Guizhou's Participation in Regional
Cooperation), in *Fan Zhusanjiao yu Xianggang hudong fazhan*, edited by
Yeung and Shen, pp. 93–121.

49. Ye Jianfu 葉健夫, Peng Qipeng 彭啟鵬, Huang Chunhong 黃春紅, Liu Jianmin
劉建民 and Zhong Zuoyong 鐘作勇, "Guangdong liudong renkou wenti yanjiu"
廣東流動人口問題研究 (Study on the Problem of the Floating Population in
Guangdong), *Tongji yu yuce* 統計與預測 (Statistics and Forecasting), No. 3
(2003), pp. 4–10.

50. Zhou Guolan 周國蘭, "Jiangxi canyu quyu hezuo de jichu yu qianjing" 江西
參與區域合作的基礎與前景 (The Basis and Prospects of Jiangxi's Participation
in Regional Cooperation), in *Fan Zhusanjiao yu Xianggang hudong fazhan*,
edited by Yeung and Shen, pp. 169–91; Dai Bin 戴賓 and Qian Zhihong
錢志鴻, "Sichuan de shehui jingji fazhan ji quyu hezuo qianjing" 四川的社會
經濟發展及區域合作前景 (Socioeconomic Development and the Prospect of
Regional Cooperation of Sichuan), in *Fan Zhusanjiao yu Xianggang hudong
fazhan*, edited by Yeung and Shen, pp. 123–44.

51. Wu Senfu 吳森富, "Guangdong liudong renkou suzhi jiegou he nianling jiegou
yanjiu" 廣東流動人口素質結構和年齡結構研究 (A Study on the Quality and
Age Structures of the Floating Population in Guangdong), *Nanfang jingji*
南方經濟 (South China Economy), No. 3 (2003), pp. 34–36.

52. Ye et al., "Guangdong liudong renkou wenti yanjiu" (see note 49).

53. Duowei xinwen wang 多維新聞網 (Dwnews.com), Zhusanjiao nanpo laodongli
duanque guaiquan 珠三角難破勞動力短缺怪圈 (It Is Difficult to Overcome
the Problem of Labour Shortages in the Pearl River Delta),
http://www1.chinesenewsnet.com/MainNews/Forums/BackStage/
2006_3_3_2_35_33_48.html, accessed on 28 May 2006.

54. Ye et al., "Guangdong liudong renkou wenti yanjiu" (see note 49).

55. *Ming Pao* 明報, Zhongguo liangjia jinnian shoudu fu zengzhang 中國糧價近
年首度負增長 (Negative Growth in Grain Prices in China for the First Time
in Recent Years), *Jishi xinwen* 即時新聞 (Instant News), 5 August 2005,
http://www.mingpaonews.com/, accessed on 5 August 2005.

56. Guowuyuan renkou pucha bangongshi and Guojia tongjiju renkou he shehui
keji tongji si, *Zhongguo 2000 nian renkou pucha ziliao shangce* (see note 15),
pp. 136–38.

57. For details, see Shen, "A Study on the Dual Track Urbanization in China"
(see note 35).

9

Regional Inequality

Mingjie Sun and C. Cindy Fan

Introduction

The Pan–Pearl River Region (Pan-PRD) 泛珠江三角洲 illustrates a relatively new concept of regional development in China, one that involves spatial entities at very different levels of economic development, traversing the eastern coastal region and the inland region, and straddling the mainland and China's two Special Administrative Regions. The Pan-PRD concept emphasizes regional collaboration and breaking down barriers to the flows of factors of production in the region. Since its inception, the concept has stressed economic growth more than the inequality among the region's members. In this chapter, we aim at to show that regional inequality among the mainland provinces in the Pan-PRD is large and we seek to identify the major determinants of inequality in the region. We argue that in the effort to implement the Pan-PRD concept the issue of regional inequality should be placed at the front and centre.

In the next section, we discuss regional inequality in the context of the evolving regional policy in China, and we explain why addressing the issue of regional inequality is important for achieving the objectives of the Pan-PRD concept and for its successful implementation. Our empirical analysis involves the nine Pan-PRD provinces and excludes Hong Kong 香港 and Macao 澳門. It begins by documenting the level and changes of inequality in GDP per capita since 1978. After a brief review of the literature on the determinants of regional inequality, we estimate a model that includes economic and human capital variables using panel data for the period 1990 to 2003. In addition, in order to supplement output indicators with other measures of well-being, we examine data on rural and urban income and the Human Development Index for the period since 1990.

Regional Inequality and the Pan-PRD Region

Regional inequality has been one of the most hotly debated issues in China over the past several decades. From Maoist policies that emphasized developing the inland region, via, for example, the "Third Front" to Deng Xiaoping's 鄧小平 "Coastal Development Strategy" to the most recent "Western Region Development" programme, the disparity between rich and poor regions has been at the centre of China's regional policy. Since the late 1980s, heightened concerns over the widening gap between the eastern coastal region and the inland region have compelled the central government to rethink its regional policy. Inland provinces, convinced that they have been disadvantaged by the Coastal Development Strategy, are especially discontented and have actively lobbied the central government for change. Such discontent, combined with ethnic tensions in areas that have large non-Han 漢族 populations, has intensified the fear that large-scale conflicts could break out. Scholars, in addition, have contributed to this debate by documenting the extent of, and changes to, regional inequality and by calling attention to the possible consequences of a widening gap in regional development. Wang Shaoguang and Hu Angang, for example, have repeatedly called on the government to address and halt the increase in regional inequality. They warned that a steep rise in regional inequality would exacerbate separatist tendencies, as already illustrated in the breakup of Yugoslavia and the Soviet Union.[1]

To be sure, Deng's thoughts on regional policy did not entirely ignore considerations about regional inequality. While emphasizing that some people and some regions should get rich first, he indicated that future state intervention might be necessary to narrow the regional development gap.[2] The appropriate time, Deng stated, would be the end of the twentieth century when China has reached "a comfortable level of living" (*xiaokang* 小康).[3] Those concerned with the development of the inland region have, indeed, invoked Deng's "time-table" to urge the government to increase its efforts to develop that region.[4] Responding to increased criticisms and concern over regional inequality, the central government formulated plans, including the Ninth Five-year Plan (1996–2000), aimed at narrowing the regional development gap.[5] The Western Region Development programme, which was launched in 1999, is the most well-known example of a new development strategy to "minimize the growing social, economic and developmental gaps between the eastern, especially coastal, region and the western region."[6] Accordingly, the Western Region Development programme became the key regional policy in the Tenth Five-year Plan (2001–2005).[7]

Unlike the Western Region Development programme, the concept of a Pan-PRD region was not initiated by the central government. Rather, it was spearheaded by the province of Guangdong 廣東 which, despite a remarkable head start since the late 1980s, is increasingly threatened by the recent rapid growth of Shanghai 上海 and the Yangtzi River Delta 長江 三角洲 region. Nowhere was the rationale for the regional concept stated more clearly than by Zhang Dejiang 張德江, the then Party Secretary of Guangdong:

"Shanghai has got all the Yangzi River Delta provinces behind it, and the Bohai Bay 渤海灣 region is also showing potential. They both have big enough hinterlands to support them. In a long run, we need to have a European-style common market with five neighbouring provinces in southern China so we can have our own hinterland."[8]

The Pan-PRD region is distinct from most of the prominent regional groupings in the last several decades in at least two respects. First, it was initiated "from below" — specifically, at the provincial level — rather than by the central government. This has two implications. Programmes launched by the central government are typically associated with the administrative demarcation, and sometimes upgrading, of specific spatial entities. Prominent examples are the special economic zones and the elevation of Chongqing 重慶 to a centrally administered municipality. The Pan-PRD region is not, as yet, an administrative entity. It is unclear if the central government would consider giving the region formal administrative status. The second implication involves mechanisms to realize the regional concept. Hitherto, market mechanisms and efforts by provincial governments have played a more important role than investment and preferential policies initiated by the central government. Advocates of the concept have argued that better economic integration and reduced regional protectionism, involving breaking down barriers to the flows of goods, capital, and human resources, are beneficial to the entire region. These thoughts were embodied in Zhang's speech in the First Pan-PRD Regional Cooperation and Development Forum (hereafter the Forum) held in June 2004.[9] Nonetheless, it is entirely possible that the central government will in the future consider using its resources to promote the concept.

The Pan-PRD concept is also distinctive in that the collaboration that is being forged is one between provinces with very different levels of development. Hong Kong and Macao aside, Guangdong is one of the most developed and most rapidly growing provinces in China, while Guizhou 貴州 persists in being dead last, among all of the provinces, in level of economic development. Yet, from the Third Front to the "Three Economic Belts" embodied in the Seventh Five-year Plan (1986–1990) to the Western Region Development programme, most regional policies in China have sought to group together geographically contiguous areas with relatively similar levels of development. Quite differently, the Pan-PRD region encompasses the eastern, central and western regions, and is therefore portrayed as a breakthrough approach in regional development.[10] For the above two reasons, therefore, the concept of a Pan-PRD region is innovative and unique.

Inequality among the Pan-PRD provinces has important implications for the region's goals and their likelihood of being achieved. From the inception of the concept by Zhang in 2003, to the Second Forum held in July of 2005, the dominant goal is seen as being to "enhance the region's overall competitiveness" by "achieving a fusion of advantages and rational division of labour," as stated in the speech by Hong Kong's former Chief Executive Tung Chee-hwa 董建華 in the first Forum.[11] Tung stressed further the importance of "realizing mutual benefits and a win-win situation all-around." Reducing the development gap within the Pan-PRD region is, however, not an explicit goal of the regional collaboration. To be sure, Sichuan 四川, Guizhou, Yunnan 雲南 and Guangxi 廣西 — four of the least-developed Pan-PRD provinces — are part of the Western Region Development programme and they have indeed benefited from the increased state investment and preferential policies associated with the programme.

Skeptics of the Pan-PRD concept have voiced concerns over the possible negative impacts of regional collaboration on less-developed provinces. They argue that collaboration would widen the development gap between Guangdong (and Hong Kong and Macao) and poorer provinces.[12] Increased migration from Jiangxi 江西, Hunan 湖南, Sichuan, Guizhou and Yunnan to Guangdong since the 1980s is clear evidence that resources are concentrating in the core of the Pan-PRD rather than diffusing to its hinterland.[13] Indeed, regional collaboration is expected to increase Guangdong's access to a larger pool of cheap labour from surrounding provinces, which is especially urgent given the recent labour shortages in the Pan-PRD as a result of competition from the Yangzi River Delta region.[14] While optimists anticipate the eventual diffusion of industrial production from Guangdong, critics caution that this may take the form of a large-scale migration of polluting industries to other provinces.[15] The vastly different levels of development may, at the same time, constrain the degree of collaboration among provinces. Less-developed provinces may be protective of their industries and refuse to remove barriers to market integration, especially if they are not convinced of the benefits of regional collaboration.[16] Provinces whose economic ties with Guangdong are relatively weak — Fujian 福建, Sichuan and Yunnan — are less enthusiastic than other provinces about regional collaboration.[17] Moreover, the provinces differ considerably in their pace of marketization, integration with the global economy and "mindset" towards development.[18] These differences are further barriers to a full-fledged collaboration among the Pan-PRD provinces and to the successful implementation of the regional concept. Most official and news reports about the Pan-PRD region tend to gloss over rather than fully address the issue of regional inequality. Typically, writers and scholars depict the large gap in regional development in a positive light, emphasizing the complementarity rather than the inequality among the provinces.[19]

In our view, however, it is of critical importance, if the Pan-PRD concept is to succeed, for provincial governments and other agents to fully understand and address the levels, trends and determinants of inequality in the region. Much like the discontent and tension that eventually left the central government with no choice but to adjust its regional policies and develop the western region, a large gap among the Pan-PRD provinces may threaten the soundness and feasibility of the very concept of regional collaboration. In the next sections, therefore, we turn to an empirical analysis of the inequality among the Pan-PRD provinces.

Inequality in GDP Per Capita

Our empirical analysis focuses on the nine mainland Pan-PRD provinces and excludes Hong Kong and Macao, as the latter's levels of economic development are considerably higher than those of the former.[20] We analyze data from the beginning of the economic reforms — 1978 — to the most recent year for which relevant data are available — 2003, and we pay special attention to the period since 1990. In the analysis, we consider Hainan 海南, which became a province in 1988, a separate unit from Guangdong. However, as Chongqing was administratively part of Sichuan until early 1997, we combine the two into one unit.[21]

Using GDP per capita as an indicator of the level of economic development and the coefficient of variation (CV) as a measure of inequality,[22] Figure 9.1 portrays the inequality in development among the nine Pan-PRD provinces from 1978 to 2003. While inequality increased during the 1980s, it was not until the 1990s that it rose sharply. Table 9.1 shows that the CV for the Pan-PRD provinces increased by about 30% from 0.26 in 1978 to 0.34 in 1990, and then by more than 60% from 0.34 in 1990 to 0.55 in 2003. Interestingly, for the country as a whole, inter-provincial inequality declined during the period 1978 to 1990. This did not constitute long-term convergence, however, as it was a result of the rapid growth of previously less-developed provinces, especially Shandong 山東, Zhejiang 浙江, Fujian and Guangdong in the eastern region, which offset the slower growth of the traditional economic core in the north and northeast, including Beijing 北京, Tianjin 天津, Liaoning 遼寧 and Heilongjiang 黑龍江.[23] During the 1990s, however, the eastern region continued to grow faster than the inland region, thus widening the gap between them.[24] The CV for all provinces rose from 0.58 in 1990 to 0.65 in 2003. Many researchers found that the increase in regional inequality had to do with a renewed emphasis on developing coastal areas, which was in no small part due to Deng's 1992 "southern tour," during which he reaffirmed the legitimacy of coastal areas getting rich first.[25] To a large extent, the increase in inequality among the Pan-PRD provinces since 1990 has reflected the national trend.

Wherever appropriate, the tables in this chapter show the Pan-PRD provinces in descending order of their GDP per capita in 2003, thus identifying the region's leaders and laggards. In Table 9.1, we chose to look at three cross-sections: 1978, when economic reforms were first launched; 1990, after which inequality rose sharply; and 2003, the most recent year for which data are available. In all three selected years, Guangdong ranked first and Guizhou ranked last among the Pan-PRD provinces. In fact, Guizhou ranked last among all Chinese provinces throughout the period 1978 to 2003. Guangdong, meanwhile, improved its rank from 8th to 5th. Other noticeable changes include Fujian, which rose from 22nd to 7th; Hunan, which dropped from 14th to 20th; and Hainan, which fell from 10th to 16th.

The "deviation from mean" columns in Table 9.1 quantify how far each province was above or below the average of the Pan-PRD provinces.

Figure 9.1 Inter-provincial Inequality in GDP Per Capita in the Pan-PRD Region, 1978–2003

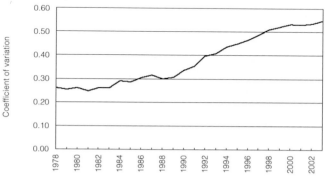

Sources: NBS, *China Statistical Yearbook* (see note 20) and *Comprehensive Statistical Data* (see note 21).

Table 9.1　Level and Growth of GDP Per Capita, 1978–2003

	GDP per capita (2003 constant RMB)			Rank (among all provinces)			Deviation from mean (mean=1)			Average annual growth Rate (%)		
	1978	1990	2003	1978	1990	2003	1978	1990	2003	1978–1990	1990–2003	2000–2003
Pan–Pearl River Delta												
Guangdong	1,497	3,894	17,130	8	5	5	1.41	1.71	2.05	7.97	11.40	10.55
Fujian	1,017	2,799	15,000	22	13	7	0.96	1.23	1.79	8.44	12.92	10.11
Hainan	1,390	2,661	8,278	10	15	16	1.31	1.17	0.99	5.41	8.73	8.44
Hunan	1,264	2,277	6,962	14	21	20	1.19	1.00	0.83	4.91	8.60	7.59
Jiangxi	995	1,934	6,653	23	25	21	0.94	0.85	0.80	5.54	9.50	11.60
Sichuan	1,047	1,530	6,514	21	28	23	0.99	0.67	0.78	3.16	11.14	10.39
Yunnan	811	2,205	5,634	27	22	26	0.76	0.97	0.67	8.34	7.22	7.88
Guangxi	883	1,796	5,631	25	26	27	0.83	0.79	0.67	5.92	8.79	10.19
Guizhou	644	1,418	3,504	29	29	29	0.61	0.62	0.42	6.57	6.96	10.15
Mean	1,061	2,279	8,368							6.37	10.00	9.77
CV	0.26	0.34	0.55									
All provinces												
Mean	1,752	3,189	11,432							4.99	9.82	10.91
CV	0.99	0.58	0.65									

Sources: NBS, *China Statistical Yearbook* (see note 20) and *Comprehensive Statistical Data* (see note 21).
Note:　Chongqing is combined with Sichuan except for 1978–1984. Tibet is excluded.

They are the basis for Figures 9.2 to 9.4, which illustrate the spatial patterns of inequality. The gaps among the provinces have clearly widened over time. In 1978, most provinces were within 25% of the mean (i.e., "deviation from mean" between 0.75 and 1.24), with the exception of Guangdong and Hainan, which were more than 25% above the mean, and Guizhou, which was more than 25% below the mean. In 1990, Guangdong's upward deviation and Sichuan's downward deviation increased significantly, and Fujian shifted from below the mean to above the mean. By 2003, the distance between the leading provinces of Guangdong and Fujian and the laggard provinces grew further. While four provinces were at or above the mean in 1990, in 2003 only Guangdong and Fujian were above the mean. Guizhou fell considerably behind. Its GDP per capita was, respectively, 61% and 42% of the mean in 1978 and 2003 (Table 9.1). In 1978, 1990, and 2003, Guangdong's GDP per capita was, respectively, 2.32, 2.75, and 4.89 times that of Guizhou.

An examination of the average annual growth rates of GDP per capita further reinforces the observation of an increase in inequality (Table 9.1).

Figure 9.2   Spatial Pattern of GDP Per Capita in the Pan-PRD Region, 1978

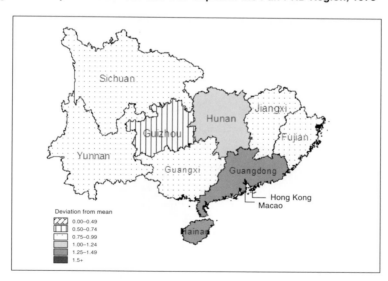

Sources: NBS, *China Statistical Yearbook* (see note 20) and *Comprehensive Statistical Data* (see note 21).

Figure 9.3   Spatial Pattern of GDP Per Capita in the Pan-PRD Region, 1990

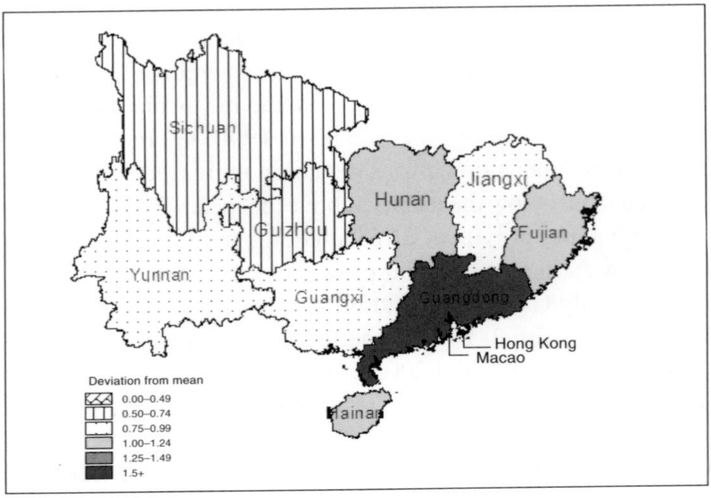

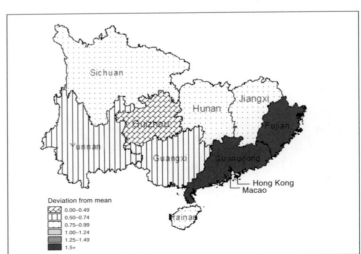

Sources: NBS, *China Statistical Yearbook* (see note 20).

Figure 9.4   Spatial Pattern of GDP Per Capita in the Pan-PRD Region, 2003

Sources: NBS, *China Statistical Yearbook* (see note 20).

For both the Pan-PRD region and the country as a whole, higher growth rates were seen in the period since 1990 than in the previous period. Between 1990 and 2003, among the Pan-PRD provinces, Guangdong and Fujian had the highest average annual growth rates (respectively, 11.40% and 12.92%) and Guizhou the lowest (6.96%). Thus, the rich were getting richer and the poor were getting poorer. Sichuan did also experience double-digit growth (11.14%), but its GDP per capita in 2003 was still below the mean. Figure 9.5 further illustrates the differentials in growth. Since about 1990, both Guangdong and Fujian began to experience sharp growth, widening the gaps between them and other Pan-PRD provinces and firmly establishing themselves as the leaders in economic development in the region. Hainan was a distant third throughout the 1990s. The remaining provinces experienced some growth, but not to a remarkable degree, with Guizhou being distinctly in last place.

It is worth noting, however, that the increase in inequality appears to have slowed down since 2000 (Figure 9.1). Between 2000 and 2003, four of the five lowest-ranked provinces — Jiangxi, Sichuan, Guangxi and Guizhou — all grew at double-digit rates, surpassing or equalling those of Guangdong and Fujian (Table 9.1). Although this is not a sufficient basis upon which to project a trend towards convergence, it does hint at possible

Figure 9.5 GDP Per Capita by Province in the Pan-PRD Region, 1978–2003

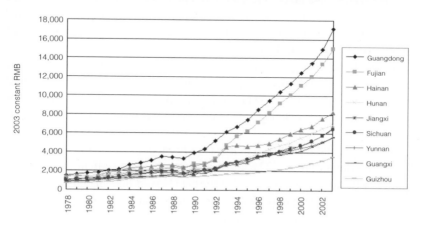

Sources: NBS, *China Statistical Yearbook* (see note 20) and *Comprehensive Statistical Data* (see note 21).

processes at work that have accelerated the growth of the less-developed provinces in the Pan-PRD region. As suggested earlier, increased investment as a result of the inclusion of some Pan-PRD provinces in the Western Region Development programme may have contributed to their more rapid growth in recent years.

Explanations for Inequality in GDP Per Capita

Research on regional development in China has convincingly shown that the persistence of regional inequality and the changes to it, involve multiple factors.[26] The most prominent of these can be collapsed under the headings of economic capital and human capital.

Economic capital refers to both capital input and economic structure. Capital input is largely a function of investment, which can be from domestic or foreign sources. Many studies have shown that investment is a major explanation for the rapid economic growth and high levels of output in China's more developed regions.[27] In addition, research has stressed that government policy is a main reason for the regional differentials in investment.[28] In particular, preferential policies on the part of the government have played an important role in attracting foreign investment to coastal provinces such as Guangdong. Thus, investment is a commonly used indicator of regional policy.[29] Economic structure, especially in the context of a transitional economy, is often linked to the degree of marketization and privatization in a place. The positive relationship between marketization and economic growth in China is well documented.[30] Specifically, the non-state sector's share of the economy has been found to be an important explanation of differentials in regional development.[31] Government policy, again, has shaped the speed and extent of marketization in China.[32] Recent research has also examined the relationship between privatization and economic growth in China. Han and Pannell, for example, showed that provinces that have a stronger private sector experienced faster rates of economic growth.[33]

Human capital is included in most studies that examine multiple factors of regional development. The most commonly used indicator of human capital is educational attainment. Demurger showed that an educated labour force improves economic performance, and Gustafsson and Li linked level of education to earnings inequality.[34] Other studies examined variants of educational attainment such as the proportion of technical workers in the labour force.[35] In addition to education-based explanations, labour migration is shown to be another important factor in regional development. The relationship between migration and regional development is generally thought of as a situation of "chicken-and-egg."[36] For example, economic and employment growth induces labour in-migration, which in turn boosts economic growth. When central planning dominated the Chinese economy and strict control was imposed over labour flows (1949–1978), the role of migration in the regional economy was generally weak. Since the mid-1980s, however, controls over migration have been relaxed, unleashing a torrent of migrants from rural areas into urban ones. These migrants have become the main source of cheap labour facilitating industrialization in more developed regions, thus accelerating the growth in the latter.[37] Foreign investment and employment opportunities in Guangdong, for example, have attracted large numbers of migrants from across the country; and migrants from poorer, rural areas have particularly contributed to the growth of labour-intensive manufacturing in that province. Bao and colleagues and Hu found that labour migration contributes to enlarging the gap between coastal and inland regions.[38] Hare and West argued that the migration of low-wage labour to the coastal region reduces the incentive for labour-intensive manufacturing to move inland, thus reinforcing industrial agglomeration in the coast.[39] In addition, it has been found that the relationship between migration and regional development has become stronger since the 1990s.[40]

There is a growing body of research on the geographic factors of regional development,[41] emphasizing locational attributes such as access to the coast and favourable topography. Location-based explanations (via, for example, regional dummy variables), however, are not mutually exclusive from the economic and human capital factors described earlier. For example, coastal provinces tend to have higher levels of economic and human capital.[42] Because of the conceptual and empirical difficulties in disentangling locational and non-locational factors, we have decided not to include locational factors per se in the analysis.

Employing the framework of economic and human capital as explanations for regional development, we have selected four indicators to explain the inequality in development among the Pan-PRD provinces. We focus on the period from 1990 to 2003 for two reasons. First, as described earlier, inequality among the Pan-PRD provinces increased most notably after 1990. Second, data prior to the mid-1980s, for at least some of our indicators, are not available. Table 9.2 shows the indicators and their values for 1990 and 2003, except for MIGRATION, which is shown for 1990 and 2000.

INVESTMENT represents capital input and is our first indicator of economic capital. It refers to fixed assets investment per capita and includes all ownership types and both domestic and foreign sources. As described earlier, regional policy in the post-Mao period has overwhelmingly favoured the eastern coastal region, which has received large amounts of state investment as well as foreign investment. Among Pan-PRD provinces, Guangdong, Hainan and Fujian were, in that order, the leaders in investment per capita in 1990 (Table 9.2). By 2003, their leading ranks persisted, but Fujian replaced Hainan as the second leading province. In both years, Guizhou and Guangxi ranked the lowest among all PPRD provinces (and among all provinces in China). The above distributions appear similar to those of GDP per capita, described earlier, and they reinforce the notion that investment is an important factor of regional development and has contributed to the uneven development in the PPRD region. Yet, a closer examination of the investment data indicates that some of the laggard provinces have experienced rapid growth in investment in recent years. Jiangxi, Guizhou, and Sichuan were among those with the lowest levels of investment per capita, and had average or near-average growth during the 1990s. Between 2000 and 2003, however, all three had above-average growth in investment per capita (not shown in a table). Remarkably, Jiangxi and Guizhou's average annual growth was, respectively, 30.96% and 20.90%, compared with an average of 16.55% for all of the Pan-PRD provinces. Guizhou and Sichuan's rapid growth in investment suggests that they have benefited from being included in the recent Western Development programme.[43]

STATE refers to the share of state-owned units in fixed assets investment. It is used as a proxy for the importance of the state sector in the regional economy and is our indicator of economic capital that depicts the economic structure.[44] A small state sector indicates that marketization and privatization have exerted significant influence on the economy. We expect STATE to negatively relate to level of development. In 1990, STATE ranged from 56.66% in Hunan to 79.28% in Guizhou, with a range of about 23% (Table 9.2). By 2003, not only did the share decline in every province, but the gap between the highest share — Guizhou (60.33%) — and the lowest share — Guangdong (29.55%) — increased to about 31%. Hainan and Fujian had the second and third lowest shares, respectively, at 32.70% and 34.26%. In short, the data show that the share of the state sector is generally lower in more developed provinces and higher in less developed provinces, and that this relationship appears to have strengthened over time.

Our first indicator of human capital is EDUCATION, measured as the proportion of the population aged six or above whose educational attainment is at or above the junior secondary level. All Pan-PRD provinces showed considerable improvement in this indicator between 1990 and 2003 (Table 9.2). Unlike the economic indicators described earlier, neither Guangdong (55.01%) nor Fujian (51.85%) ranked the highest in 2003, although the differences between them and the leading provinces of Jiangxi (59.76%) and Hainan (59.54%) were in the order of only several percentage points. Yunnan was a negative outlier, however, as its level in 2003 was only 29.45% and was almost 13% points below that of Guizhou and more than 30% points below that of Jiangxi. These data suggest that the relationship between educational attainment and level of development is not straightforward, although the least-developed province of Guizhou did have lower levels of educational attainment than most other provinces.

MIGRATION is our second indicator of human capital. It refers to the inter-provincial net migration rate, which is computed by dividing net migration by the population aged five and above, and which identifies the

Table 9.2   Economic and Human Capital Indicators, 1990–2003

	Investment (2003 constant RMB)		State (%)		Education (%)		Migration (%)	
	1990	2003	1990	2003	1990	2003	1990	2000
Guangdong	1,016	6,051	66.25	29.55	38.38	55.01	1.62	13.88
Fujian	580	4,290	59.60	34.26	29.04	51.85	0.25	2.22
Hainan	1,018	3,455	78.02	32.70	39.43	59.54	0.38	1.25
Hunan	368	2,387	56.66	43.71	36.33	57.70	−0.47	−4.82
Jiangxi	319	3,063	66.73	45.76	31.04	59.76	−0.15	−6.49
Sichuan	371	2,957	73.40	38.08	31.25	49.64	−0.91	−4.17
Yunnan	403	2,286	61.06	52.85	21.49	29.45	−0.12	0.86
Guangxi	274	1,897	60.03	48.02	31.07	53.23	−1.04	−3.78
Guizhou	248	1,933	79.28	60.33	22.38	42.38	−0.38	−3.03

Sources: NBS, *China Statistical Yearbook* (see note 20); *Comprehensive Statistical Data* (see note 21); *China Population Statistical Yearbook* (see note 48) and NBS, 2002. *Zhongguo 2000 nian renkou pucha ziliao* 中國2000年人口普查資料 (Tabulation on the 2000 Population Census of the People's Republic of China), Vol. I and III (Beijing: Zhongguo tongji chubanshe, 2000).

Notes: Investment: Fixed assets investment per capita.
State: Share of state-owned unites in fixed assets investment.
Education: Proportion of the population aged six or above with a junior secondary level of education.
Migration: Inter-provincial net migration rate.

most prominent destinations and donors of migrants.[45] It is important to point out that the Pan-PRD region consists of Guangdong — the most attractive destination to inter-provincial migrants — as well as several of the most prominent donors of inter-provincial migrants — Jiangxi, Hunan, Sichuan, Guangxi, and Guizhou.[46] According to the 1990 census, Guangdong, Fujian, and Hainan were the only Pan-PRD provinces that had net gains in population from migration, whereas all of the other provinces in the region had negative net migration rates (Table 9.2). The 2000 census data show that except for Yunnan, whose net migration rate shifted from negative to positive, gainers remained gainers and losers remained losers. The differentials among the provinces grew bigger, however, as depicted by more positive and more negative net migration rates than those in 1990, indicating that gainers were gaining more and losers were losing more.[47] In particular, Guangdong's net migration rate in 2000 was extremely high (13.88%).

In order to ascertain, assess, and quantify the effects of the above four factors on the level of development of the Pan-PRD provinces, we now conduct a regression analysis where GDP per capita is the dependent variable and the above indicators constitute the independent variables. The analysis focuses on the period since 1990. Regression analyses of yearly cross-sections are constrained by the small number of observations (nine provinces). Rather, we make use of panel data for the period 1990 to 2003. The total number of observations is, therefore, 126.

We considered four issues prior to deciding how to evaluate the variables for the panel data analysis. First, data for EDUCATION for 1991, 1992, 1994, and 2001 are not available and thus we estimate the data for these years by assuming that the value changed uniformly between the years for which we have data.[48] Second, as migration data at the national level and for all provinces are only available in censuses and national sample surveys, we are unable to assemble data for migration rates for every year. Instead, we use the 1990 and 2000 censuses as our main sources of migration data.[49] To estimate the migration rates for years other than 1990 and 2000, we assume that the rate changed uniformly between the two years and we also use the yearly change to estimate the rates for 2001–2003.[50] Third, we express all variables as natural logs, so that the regression coefficient estimates the percentage change in the dependent variable associated with a one per cent change in the independent variable. As net migration rates may be negative, we transformed all rates by adding 100 to them, so that the values would always be positive. Fourth, the period spans only 13 years.

This, in our judgement, is too short to identify changes in coefficients over time. Rather than assessing temporal changes, therefore, we focus on the relationships between the independent variables and the dependent variable over the entire period. Finally, in order to eliminate possible autoregressive effects associated with panel data, we use the fixed effects transformation by time-demeaning all of the data.[51]

Table 9.3 summarizes the ordinary least-squares estimations of the fixed effects model. The adjusted R^2 indicates that the independent variables as a whole account for 94% of the variation in GDP per capita across the Pan-PRD provinces during the period 1990 to 2003. All the signs of the coefficients are as expected. The variance inflation factors show that the estimations are not unduly affected by multi-collinearity. The standardized regression coefficients show that INVESTMENT, which is positively related to GDP per capita, is the most important predictor. The second most important independent variable is STATE, whose coefficient is negative. Ranked third is EDUCATION. All of the above three variables have coefficients that are significant at the 0.001 level. MIGRATION is associated with the expected positive sign, but its small standardized regression coefficient and a relatively weak significance level (0.01) indicate that it is the least important of the four independent variables. In short, the regression

Table 9.3   Ordinary Least-squares Estimates of the Fixed Effects Model

Independent variable	Regression coefficient	Standardized regression coefficient	T-value	VIF
Investment	0.43	0.59	13.71**	4.04
State	−0.53	−0.24	−6.96**	2.63
Education	0.45	0.23	5.96**	3.19
Migration	1.32	0.07	2.79*	1.27

$R^2 = 0.95$

Adjusted $R^2 = 0.94$

$F = 156.99$**

Degree of freedom (regression) = 13

Degree of freedom (residual) = 113

Notes: Dependent variable = Time-demeaned natural log of GDP per capita.
All independent variables are expressed in natural log and are time-demeaned (see text for Migration).
VIF: Variance inflation factor.
*: significant at the 0.01 level.
**: significant at the 0.001 level.

results confirm our expectation that both economic capital — as represented by input and economic structure — and human capital — as represented by educational attainment and migration — are important explanations for the inequality of development among the Pan-PRD provinces. As a whole, economic capital variables have been more powerful explanations than human capital variables.

Inequality in Income and Human Development

Despite the popularity of output indicators such as GDP per capita, researchers have argued that livelihood and quality of life measures should also be employed in order to generate a more comprehensive picture of regional inequality.[52] Thus, in this section, we examine two additional indicators — income and the Human Development Index (HDI) — both of which reflect aspects of well-being in a region.

We consider only the period since 1990, again because of data limitations for earlier years and because of inequality among the Pan-PRD provinces in GDP per capita, as shown earlier. Inequality among the provinces has increased sharply since the 1990s. We examine rural and urban households separately, as it is well documented that rural-urban inequality in China is large and that rural inequality is higher than urban inequality.[53] Table 9.4 shows rural household net income per capita and urban household disposable income per capita[54] (hitherto rural income and urban income, respectively), both based on national sample surveys conducted by the National Bureau of Statistics, for 1990 and 2003. The CVs show that the levels of inequality were lower among the Pan-PRD provinces than among all provinces in China; however, in both cases, rural and urban income inequalities increased between 1990 and 2003. While rural income was lower than urban income, regional inequality in rural income was higher than that of urban income.

In both 1990 and 2003, Guangdong ranked first and Guizhou ranked last in rural income among the Pan-PRD provinces. The rankings in 2003, except for the positions of Yunnan and Guangxi, were the same as those of GDP per capita (Table 9.1) for that year. The "deviation from mean" columns reinforce the observation about the rise in inequality. In 1990, all Pan-PRD provinces, except Guangdong (42% above the mean) and Guizhou (33% below the mean), were within 25% of the regional mean; by 2003, Fujian (46% above the mean) pulled further upward and Yunnan (33% below the mean) fell further behind so that both were no longer within 25% of the

Table 9.4 Rural and Urban Household Income Per Capita, 1990–2003

	Rural household net income per capita				Urban household disposable income per capita			
	Income (2003 constant RMB)		Deviation from mean (mean=1)		Income (2003 constant RMB)		Deviation from mean (mean=1)	
	1990	2003	1990	2003	1990	2003	1990	2003
Pan–Pearl River Delta								
Guangdong	1,653	4,055	1.42	1.59	3,650	12,380	1.33	1.52
Fujian	1,242	3,734	1.07	1.46	2,841	10,000	1.03	1.22
Hainan	1,339	2,588	1.15	1.01	2,840	7,259	1.03	0.89
Hunan	1,245	2,533	1.07	0.99	2,983	7,674	1.08	0.94
Jiangxi	1,152	2,458	0.99	0.96	2,042	6,901	0.74	0.84
Sichuan	1,007	2,226	0.86	0.87	2,690	7,320	0.98	0.90
Yunnan	984	1,697	0.84	0.67	2,758	7,644	1.00	0.94
Guangxi	1,090	2,095	0.94	0.82	2,468	7,785	0.90	0.95
Guizhou	775	1,565	0.67	0.61	2,492	6,569	0.91	0.80
Mean	1,165	2,550			2,752	8,170		
CV	0.21	0.33			0.16	0.23		
All provinces								
Mean	1,288	2,902			2,590	8,295		
CV	0.35	0.45			0.18	0.29		

Sources: NBS, *China Statistical Yearbook* (see note 20) and *Comprehensive Statistical Data* (see note 21).
Note: Chongqing is combined with Sichuan. Tibet is excluded.

mean. In terms of urban income, Guangdong again ranked first in both 1990 and 2003, and Jiangxi and Guizhou ranked last, respectively, in 1990 and 2003. Five provinces were above the mean in 1990 but, by 2003, only Guangdong and Fujian remained above the mean. Guangdong was more than 50% above the mean in 2003. Thus, even though all Pan-PRD provinces except Guangdong were within 25% of the mean in 2003, the overall inequality that year was higher than that in 1990. A closer examination of the data shows that the CVs for both rural and urban income increased most rapidly before the mid-1990s and became more stable afterwards (not shown in Table 9.4). Thus, similar to an earlier observation about GDP per capita, the rise in regional inequality in rural and urban income has slowed down in recent years.

Table 9.5 shows the HDI for the Pan-PRD provinces in 1990 and 2001, the latter being the most recent year for which HDI at the provincial level is available. HDI, developed by the United Nations Development

Table 9.5   Human Development Index (HDI), 1990–2001

	HDI		HDI change
	1990	2001	
Guangdong	0.69	0.80	0.11
Fujian	0.63	0.78	0.15
Hainan	0.64	0.75	0.11
Hunan	0.62	0.74	0.13
Jiangxi	0.59	0.72	0.13
Sichuan	0.59	0.72	0.13
Yunnan	0.55	0.67	0.11
Guangxi	0.62	0.73	0.11
Guizhou	0.53	0.63	0.10

Sources: UNDP, *China Human Development Index* (see note 55) and *China Human Development Report 1999* (see note 56).

Note: For the calculation of HDI, see the text and note 56. Chongqing is combined with Sichuan.

Programme (UNDP), is a summary measure of the average level of human development in three basic dimensions: longevity, educational attainment, and standard of living.[55] Longevity is measured by life expectancy at birth. Educational attainment is represented by a combination of the adult literacy rate (two-thirds weight) and combined enrolment rates at the primary, secondary, and tertiary levels (one-third weight). Standard of living is measured by real GDP per capita adjusted by purchasing power parity (PPP). As such, HDI seeks to evaluate overall well being. The HDI for 1990 published in UNDP (1999a) was based on a slightly different method from that used for the HDI for 2001 published by the UNDP (2002).[56] Thus, we recalculated the HDI for 1990 using the new method, so that the data shown in Table 9.5 for the two years are directly comparable. Similar to what has been observed earlier for GDP per capita and rural and urban incomes, Guangdong was ranked first and Guizhou was ranked last in both 1990 and 2001. The ranking stayed almost the same between the two years. The 2001 ranking is very similar to that of GDP per capita in 2003 (Table 9.1), except for Guangxi, which ranked eighth for GDP per capita but fifth in HDI. As indicated by the change in the HDI between 1990 and 2001, all of the Pan-PRD provinces improved and the degree of improvement seemed quite uniform, suggesting that inequality in HDI did not increase. It is notable, however, that Fujian, which was ranked second in 2001, showed the biggest change in HDI (0.15) and Guizhou the smallest change (0.10).

In summary, both income and human development indicators show that inequality among the Pan-PRD provinces remains large. Regional inequality in rural income is larger than that of urban income. Income indicators show that regional inequality has increased since 1990 but that the increase appears to have slowed down since the mid-1990s. HDI, on the other hand, does not show a clear trend of divergence or convergence.

Summary and Conclusion

The premise of this chapter is that although the Pan-PRD concept does not explicitly embody goals for reducing regional inequality, the large disparity among the Pan-PRD provinces and its trend have important roles to play in determining whether the concept of regional collaboration can be successfully implemented. Our empirical analysis has focused on documenting the level of inequality and identifying its determinants in the Pan-PRD region.

Employing GDP per capita as an indicator of the level of economic development in a province, we found that inequality among the Pan-PRD provinces has increased since 1978, and that the rise was especially sharp during the 1990s. With the exception of Guangxi, coastal provinces remain the leaders and inland provinces the laggards. The gap between the leaders and laggards has grown; for example, Guangdong and Fujian have pulled ahead of the other provinces, while Guizhou has fallen further behind. Since 2000, however, most of the lower-ranked provinces have grown more rapidly than the leading provinces. Our examination of data on rural and urban incomes also supports the finding of large and growing inequality. The regional gap in rural income is larger than that of urban income, and both had widened since 1990. Yet, the rise of inequality in both rural and urban incomes seems to have stabilized since the mid-1990s. This, together with the slow rise in inequality in GDP per capita since 2000, suggests that the Western Region Development programme — which includes four of the nine Pan-PRD provinces — may have already proven effective in boosting the economic development of the region's less-developed provinces. HDI — which addresses overall well-being and includes not only economic but also health and education dimensions — again depicts a persistent gap among the Pan-PRD provinces since 1990, but it does not reveal a widening of the gap over time. Thus, even though regional inequality in economic terms (output and income) has clearly increased since 1990, there is not as much evidence of a widening gap in other dimensions of well-being.

Using panel data for the period 1990 to 2003, we have estimated a fixed effects model for the purpose of identifying and assessing the determinants of regional inequality among the Pan-PRD provinces. Both economic and human capital variables are included in the model. We have argued that both input and economic structure are important components of economic capital. Input, in the empirical analysis, is represented by investment in fixed assets; and the share of the non-state sector in investment is used to evaluate the extent to which the regional economy is marketized and privatized. Human capital refers to both educational attainment and migration. The findings confirm that both economic and human capital explanations are important and, as a whole, economic capital explanations are more powerful.

The above findings suggest that in both empirical and conceptual terms, regional inequality among the Pan-PRD provinces reflects what has been observed in the literature for the entire nation. This is, in fact, not surprising, as the Pan-PRD region, by accident or by design, includes provinces with very different levels of economic development and those from both the eastern coastal region and the inland region. The challenge facing the central government of reducing regional disparity is, therefore, in essence the same challenge that faces the various constituencies — provincial governments, enterprises and investors, and others — that are expected to implement the Pan-PRD concept. In this light, understanding and resolving regional inequality is a key to achieving collaboration among the Pan-PRD provinces and warrants much greater attention than it has hitherto been given.

Acknowledgements

This research was supported by a Faculty Research Grant from the Council on Research, UCLA Academic Senate.

Notes

1. Wang Shaoguang and Angang Hu, *The Political Economy of Uneven Development: The Case of China* (Armonk, New York: M. E. Sharpe, 1999), p. 202.
2. Deng Xiaoping, "Jiefang sixiang, shishi qiushi, tuanjie yizhi xiangqiankan" 解放思想，實事求事，團結一致向前看 (Liberate Ideas, Be Practical, United Towards the Future), in *Deng Xiaoping Wenxuan* 鄧小平文選 (Selected Works of Deng Xiaoping) (1975–1982) (Beijing: People's Publishing House, 1983);

Deng Xiaoping, "Na shishi lai shuohua" 拿事實來說話 (Speaking in Truth) (Speech on 28 March, 1986), in *Deng Xiaoping Wenxuan,* Vol. III (Beijing: People's Publishing House, 1993a).

3. Deng Xiaoping, "Zai Wuchang, Shenzhen, Zhuhai, Shanghai deng di de tanhua yaodian" 在武昌、深圳、珠海、上海等地的談話要點 (Summary of Speeches in Wuchang, Shenzhen, Zhuhai and Shanghai) (Speeches on 18 January – 21 February 1992), in *Deng Xiaoping Wenxuan,* Vol. III (Beijing: People's Publishing House, 1993b).

4. Such as Liu Shiqing and Ling Lin, "The New Challenges Facing the Development of West China," in *China's West Region Development: Domestic Strategies and Global Implications*, edited by Lu Ding and William A. W. Neilson (Singapore: World Scientific Publishing Co., 2004), pp. 333–43.

5. C. Cindy Fan, "Uneven Development and Beyond: Regional Development Theory in Post-Mao China," *International Journal of Urban and Regional Research*, Vol. 21, No. 4 (1997), pp. 620–39; Yao Shujie and Zongyi Zhang, "On Regional Inequality and Diverging Clubs: A Case Study of Contemporary China," *Journal of Comparative Economics,* Vol. 29 (2001), pp. 466–84.

6. Y. M. Yeung, "Introduction," in *Developing China's West: A Critical Path to Balanced National Development*, edited by Y. M. Yeung and Jianfa Shen (Hong Kong: The Chinese University Press, 2004), pp. 1–25.

7. Bai Hejin 白和金 (ed.), *Shiwu jihua shiqi Zhongguo jingji he shehui fazhan de ruogan zhongda wenti yanjiu* 十五計劃時期中國經濟和社會發展的若干重大問題研究 (Research on the Important Questions on China's Economic and Social Development during the Tenth Five-year Plan) (Beijing: Renmin chubanshe 人民出版社, 2001), p. 27.

8. Delegations of German Industry and Commerce (GIC), "Pan-Pearl River Delta (Pan-PRD): A New Common Market emerges in the Booming Southern China," *GC. Comm.,* Issue 8 (2004), http://www.china.ahk.de/gic/publications/gccomm/0408_gc.comm.htm, accessed on 14 September 2005.

9. Pan–Pearl River Delta Cooperation (Pan-PRD Cooperation), "Zhonggong Zhongyang Zhengzhiju weiyuan, Guangdong shengwei shuji Zhang Dejiang: hezuo fazhan gongchuang weilai" 中共中央政治局委員、廣東省委書記張德江：合作發展 共創未來 (Zhang Dejian, Party Secretary of Guangdong: Cooperative Development, Jointly Creating the Future), 1 June 2004. http://61.144.25.119/gate/big5/www.Pan-PRD.org.cn/quanwei/jianghua/2005 03090948.htm, accessed on 15 August 2005.

10. People's Daily Online, "Pan-Pearl River Delta Marks New Breakthrough in China's Regional Cooperation," 24 May 2004. http://english.people.com.cn/200405/28/eng200405258_144646.html, accessed on 28 November 2004.

11. Tung Chee-hwa, "C. E.'s Keynote Speech at Pan-PRD Regional Cooperation and Development Forum," 2004. http://www.info.gov.hk/gia/general/200406-

01/0601252.htm, accessed on 24 November 2004; GIC *GC. Comm.*, (see note 8).

12. Some critics have likened the concentration of resources in more-developed areas as a "blood transfusion" from less-developed areas. See Pan-PRD Cooperation, "Fanzhu hezuo: Xiangyue xieshou gongchuang weilai" 泛珠合作：湘粵攜手共創未來 (Pan–Pearl River Delta Cooperation: Hunan and Guangdong Jointly Create the Future), 13 April 2005a. http://61.144.25.119/gate/big5/www.Pan-PRD.org.cn/yanlun/fangtan/200504130618.htm, accessed on 15 August 2005; Pan-PRD Cooperation, "'Fan Zhusanjiao' jingji fazhan zhanlüe jiexi" "泛珠三角"經濟發展戰略解析 (Analysis of the Strategies for "Pan–Pearl River Delta" Economic Development) 13 April 2005b. http://61.144.25.119/gate/big5/www.Pan-PRD.org.cn/yanlun/fangtan/200504130624.htm, accessed on 15 August 2005.

13. C. Cindy Fan, "Inter-provincial Migration, Population Redistribution and Regional Development in China: 1990 and 2000 Census Comparisons," *The Professional Geographer*, Vol. 57, No. 2 (2005a), pp. 295–311; C. Cindy Fan, "Modelling Inter-provincial Migration in China, 1985–2000," *Eurasian Geography and Economics*, Vol. 46, No. 3 (2005b), pp. 165–84.

14. Denise Yam, "China: Pan-Pearl River Delta — From Diversity to Cooperation," 2004. http://www.morganstanley.com/GEFdata/digests/20040908-wed.html#anchor3, accessed on 24 November 2004.

15. Pan-PRD Cooperation, Pan-Pearl River Delta Cooperation, (see note 12).

16. Yam, "China: Pan-Pearl River Delta — From Diversity to Cooperation" (see note 14).

17. GIC, *GC. Comm.* (see note 8).

18. Yam, "China: Pan-Pearl River Delta — From Diversity to Cooperation" (see note 14).

19. Pan-PRD Cooperation, Pan-Pearl River Delta Cooperation (see note 12); Pan-PRD Cooperation, Yi kexue fazhanguan tuidong Fan-Zhu quyu hezuo 以科學發展觀推動泛珠區域合作 (Promoting Pan–Pearl River Delta Cooperation through a Scientific Development Perspective), 13 June 2005c. http://61.144.25.119/gate/big5/www.Pan-PRD.org.cn/yuannian/200506130668.htm, accessed on 15 August 2005.

20. In 2003, Hong Kong and Macao's GDP per capita was RMB189,815 (HK$179,308) and RMB147,560 (143,000 MOP), respectively, whereas the GDP per capita of the highest ranked Pan-PRD province — Guangdong — was only RMB17,130. See National Bureau of Statistics (NBS), *Zhongguo tongji nianjian* 中國統計年鑒 (China Statistical Yearbook, 1986–2004) (Beijing: Zhongguo tongji chubanshe 中國統計出版社, 1986–2004), Table 1.

21. For 1978–1984, however, our source, NBS 1999, does not report data for Chongqing. Thus, in our analysis of the period 1978 to 1984, Chongqing is excluded from Sichuan. NBS, *Xin Zhongguo wushinian tongji ziliao huibian*

新中國五十年統計資料彙編 (Comprehensive Statistical Data and Materials on 50 Years of New China) (Beijing: Zhongguo tongji chubanshe, 1999). Chongqing became the fourth centrally administered municipality on 14 March 1997.

22. GDP per capita is a widely accepted indicator of the overall level of economic development in a region. Its popularity among studies of inter-provincial inequality in China also facilitates comparison. For example, Sylvie Demurger, "Infrastructure Development and Economic Growth: An Explanation for Regional Disparities in China?" *Journal of Comparative Economics*, Vol. 29 (2001), pp. 95–117; Deng Xiang 鄧翔, *Jingji qutong lilun yu Zhongguo diqu jingji chaju de shizheng yanjiu* 經濟趨同理論與中國地區經濟差距的實證研究 (Empirical Research on Theories of Economic Convergence and Regional Economic Disparity in China) (Chengdu 成都, China: Xi'nan caijing daxue chubanshe 西南財經大學出版社, 2003), p. 85; Ron Duncan and Tian Xiaowen, "China's Inter-provincial Disparities: An Explanation," *Communist and Post-communist Studies*, Vol. 32 (1999), pp. 211–24; Han Fengqin 韓鳳芹, *Diqu chaju: zhengfu ganyu yu gonggong zhengce fenxi* 地區差距：政府干預與公共政策分析 (Regional Disparity: Analysis of Government Intervention and Public Policy) (Beijing: Zhongguo caizheng jingji chubanshe 中國財政經濟出版社, 2004), p. 48; Jian Tianlun, Jeffrey D. Sachs and Andrew M. Warner, *Trends in Regional Inequality in China* (Cambridge, M. A.: National Bureau of Economic Research, 1996), Working Paper 5412; Tang Wing-shing, *Regional Uneven Development in China, with Special Reference to the Period between 1978 and 1988*, Occasional Paper No. 110 (Hong Kong: Department of Geography, The Chinese University of Hong Kong, 1991); Wang and Hu, *The Political Economy* (see note 1); Yao and Zhang, *Journal of Comparative Economics* (see note 5). In the analysis, we have converted all GDP per capita and other economic data into 2003 constant prices. The coefficient of variation (CV) is a straightforward and convenient tool to assess the level of inequality and is also widely employed in research on regional inequalities in China, such as in Ahmad Ehtisham and Yan Wang, "Inequality and Poverty in China: Institutional Change and Public Policy, 1978 to 1988," *The World Bank Economic Review*, Vol. 5, No. 2 (1991), pp. 231–57; Duncan and Tian, 1999; Carl Riskin, *China's Political Economy: The Quest for Development since 1949* (New York: Oxford University Press, 1987); Tsui Kai-yuen, "China's Regional Inequality, 1952–1985," *Journal of Comparative Economics*, Vol. 15 (1991), pp. 1–21; Kenneth Walker, "40 Years on: Provincial Contrasts in China's Rural Economic Development," *China Quarterly*, Vol. 119 (1989), pp. 448–80; Wang and Hu, *The Political Economy*, (see note 1); Wei, Yehua Dennis and Kim Sunwoong, "Widening Inter-county Inequality in Jiangsu Province, China, 1950–1995," *Journal of Development Studies*, Vol. 38, No. 6 (2002), pp. 142–64.

23. Demurger, *Journal of Comparative Economics* (see note 22); Deng, *Empirical Research on Theories of Economic Convergence* (see note 22), p. 97; C. Cindy Fan, "Of Belts and Ladders: State Policy and Uneven Regional Development in Post-Mao China," *Annals of the Association of American Geographers*, Vol. 85, No. 3 (1995b), pp. 421–49; Han, *Regional Disparity* (see note 22), p. 61.

24. Bao Shuming, Gene Chang Hsin, Jeffrey D. Sachs and Woo Wing Thye, "Geographic Factors and China's Regional Development under Market Reforms, 1978–1998," *China Economic Review*, Vol. 13, No. 1 (2002), pp. 89–111; Deng, *Empirical Research on Theories of Economic Convergence* (see note 22), p. 93; Fan, *The Professional Geographer* (see note 13); Han, *Regional Disparity* (see note 22), p. 52; Hare, Denise and Loraine A. West, "Spatial Patterns in China's Rural Industrial Growth and Prospects for the Alleviation of Regional Income Inequality," *Journal of Comparative Economics*, Vol. 27, No. 3 (1999), pp. 475–97; Lu, Max and Enru Wang, "Forging Ahead and Falling Behind: Changing Regional Inequalities in Post-reform China," *Growth and Change*, Vol. 33, No. 1 (2002), pp. 42–71; Wei, Yehua Dennis, *Regional Development in China: States, Globalization, and Inequality* (London: Routledge, 2000); Yao and Zhang, "On Regional Inequality and Diverging Clubs" (see note 5).

25. Deng, *Selected Works of Deng Xiaoping*, Vol. III (see note 3).

26. Bao et al., "Geographic Factors" (see note 24); Sylvie Demurger, Jeffrey D. Sachs, Woo Wing Thye, Shuming Bao and Gene Chang, "The Relative Contributions of Location and Preferential Policies in China's Regional Development: Being in the Right Place and having the Right Incentives," *China Economic Review*, Vol. 13, No. 4 (2002), pp. 444–65; Hare and West, "Spatial Patterns" (see note 24); Shen Xiaoping, "Spatial Inequality of Rural Industrial Development in China, 1989–1994," *Journal of Rural Studies*, Vol. 15, No. 2 (1998), pp. 179–99; Wei, *Regional Development* (see note 24); Wei, Yehua Dennis and C. Cindy Fan, "Regional Inequality in China: A Case Study of Jiangsu Province," *Professional Geographer*, Vol. 52, No. 3 (2000), pp. 455–69; Wei and Kim, *Journal of Development Studies* (see note 22).

27. Peter S. K. Chi and Charng Kao, "Foreign Investment in China: A New Data Set," *China Economic Review*, Vol. 6, No. 1 (1995), pp. 149–55; Demurger, *Journal of Comparative Economics* (see note 22); Wei, Yehua, "Spatial and Temporal Variations of the Relationship between State Investment and Industrial Output in China," *Tijdschrift Voor Economische En Sociale Geografie*, Vol. 86, No. 2 (1995), pp. 129–36.

28. Wang and Hu, *The Political Economy* (see note 1).

29. Chen Chung, Lawrence Chang and Yimin Zhang, "The Role of Foreign Direct Investment in China's Post-1978 Economic Development," *World*

Development, Vol. 23, No. 4 (1995), pp. 691–703; C. Cindy Fan, "Developments from Above, Below and Outside: Spatial Impacts of China's Economic Reforms in Jiangsu and Guangdong Provinces," *Chinese Environment and Development*, Vol. 6, No. 1 and 2 (1995a), pp. 85–116; Fan, *Annals of the Association of American Geographers* (see note 23); Leung Chi-kin, "Foreign Manufacturing Investment and Regional Industrial Growth in Guangdong Province, China," *Environment and Planning A*, Vol. 28 (1996), pp. 513–36; Lu and Wang, *Growth and Change* (see note 24).

30. Jian et al., *Trends in Regional Inequality in China* (see note 22); Shen, *Journal of Rural Studies* (see note 26); Gregory Veeck, "Development, Regional Equity, and Political Change in China," *Bulletin of Concerned Asian Scholars*, Vol. 25, No. 3 (1993), pp. 73–43.

31. Demurger, *Journal of Comparative Economics* (see note 22); Hare and West, *Journal of Comparative Economics* (see note 24); Wei and Kim, *Journal of Development Studies* (see note 22).

32. Demurger et al., *China Economic Review* (see note 26).

33. Han Sunsheng and Clifton W. Pannell, "The Geography of Privatization in China, 1978–1996," *Economic Geography*, Vol. 75, No. 3 (1999), pp. 272–96.

34. Demurger, *Journal of Comparative Economics* (see note 22); Bjorn Gustafsson and Shi Li, "The Anatomy of Rising Earnings Inequality in Urban China," *Journal of Comparative Economics*, Vol. 29 (2001), pp. 118–35.

35. Wei and Kim, *Journal of Development Studies* (see note 22).

36. Michael J. Greenwood, *Migration and Economic Growth in the United States: National, Regional, and Metropolitan Perspectives* (New York: Academic Press, 1981), pp. 143–68; Harry W. Richardson, *Regional Economics* (Urbana, IL: University of Illinois Press, 1978), pp. 108-9.

37. Yang Yunyan 楊雲彥, Xu Yangmei 徐映梅 and Xiang Shujian 向書堅, "Jiuye tidai yu laodongli liudong: yige xinde fenxi kuangjia" 就業替代與勞動力流動：一個新的分析框架 (Employment Replacement and Labour Migration: A New Analytical Framework), *Jingji yanjiu* 經濟研究 (Economic Research) (2003), No. 8, pp. 70–75.

38. Bao et al., *China Economic Review* (see note 24); Hu Dapeng, "Trade, Rural-urban Migration, and Regional Income Disparity in Developing Countries: A Spatial General Equilibrium Model inspired by the Case of China," *Regional Science and Urban Economics*, Vol. 32, No. 3 (2002), pp. 311–38.

39. Hare and West, *Journal of Comparative Economics* (see note 24).

40. Fan, *The Professional Geographer* and *Eurasian Geography and Economics* (see note 13).

41. Bao et al., *China Economic Review* (see note 24); Demurger et al., *China Economic Review* (see note 26).

42. C. Cindy Fan and Lu Jiantao, "Foreign Direct Investment, Locational Factors

and Labour Mobility in China, 1985–1997," *Asian Geographer*, Vol. 20, Nos. 1–2 (2001), pp. 79–99.

43. A prominent feature of the Western Region Development Programme is a significant increase in state investment in fixed assets, especially in infrastructure. See Jie Fan, "Western Development Policy: Changes, Effects and Evaluation," in *Developing China's West: A Critical Path to Balanced National Development*, edited by Y. M. Yeung and Shen Jianfa (Hong Kong: The Chinese University Press, 2004), pp. 79–105; Ling Lin and Liu Shiqing, "Measuring the Impact of the 'Five Mega-projects'," in *China's West Region Development: Domestic Strategies and Global Implications*, edited by Ding Lu and William A. W. Neilson (Singapore: World Scientific Publishing Co., 2004), pp. 261–89; Yeung, *Developing China's West* (see note 6).

44. Wei and Fan, *Professional Geographer* (see note 26).

45. For a detailed definition of migration in the Chinese census, see Fan, *The Professional Geographer* (see note 13). Broadly speaking, much like the U.S. census, the Chinese census compares where one lives at the time the census is taken with one's residence five years ago. Thus, the net migration rate refers to a period of five years.

46. Fan, *The Professional Geographer* (see note 13).

47. Fan, *Eurasian Geography and Economics* (see note 13).

48. NBS, *Zhongguo renkou tongji nianjian, 1992–1996* 中國人口統計年鑒 1992–1996 (China Population Statistical Yearbook, 1992–1996) (Beijing: Zhongguo tongji chubanshe, 1992–1996). Our source for the 1994 data reports only the educational attainment of the 15+ population rather than the 6+ population. As far as we know, publications by the NBS do not report educational attainment data for 1991, 1992 and 2001.

49. We decided not to use the 1995 One Per Cent Population Sample Survey, as several scholars have noted that the survey had seriously underestimated the volume of migration. See Chan Kam-wing and Ying Hu, "Urbanization in China in the 1990s: New Definition, Different Series, and Revised Trends," *China Review*, Vol. 3, No. 2 (2003), pp. 48–71; Liang Zai and Ma Zhongdong, "China's Floating Population: New Evidence from the 2000 Census," *Population and Development Review*, Vol. 30, No. 3 (2004), pp. 467–88.

50. Based on the census definition, these "yearly inter-provincial net migration rates" refer to the five years prior to the year for which the rates are estimated. See also note 45.

51. The model is referred to as a fixed effects model; and the ordinary least-squares estimators based on the time-demeaned variables are called the fixed effects estimators. See Jeffrey M. Wooldridge, *Introductory Econometrics: A Modern Approach* (Cincinnati, Ohio: South-Western College Publishing, 2000), pp. 441–43. The test statistics we reported in Table 9.3 are corrected statistics as required by the fixed effects transformation.

52. Duncan and Tian, *Communist and Post-Communist Studies* (see note 22); Lu and Wang, *Growth and Change* (see note 24); Tsui, *Journal of Comparative Economics* (see note 22).

53. Economist, "To Each according to his Abilities; Income Distribution in China; Inequality Rises in China," (2001) 2 June, p. 5; Ravi Kanbur and Zhang Xiaobo, "Which Regional Inequality? The Evolution of Rural-urban and Inland-coastal Inequality in China from 1983 to 1995," *Journal of Comparative Economics*, Vol. 27 (1999), pp. 686–701.

54. Rural household net income refers to the total income of rural households from all sources minus all corresponding expenses. Urban household disposable income refers to the actual income at the disposal of members of the households which can be used for final consumption, other non-compulsory expenditure and savings.

55. United Nations Development Programme (UNDP), *China Human Development Index 2002 (Updated Statistical Annexes of CHDR2002)* (Beijing: United Nations Development Programme, 2002), p. 9. http://www.undp.org.cn/modules.php?op=modload&name=Downloads&file=index&req=MostPopular (last accessed on 16 September 2005).

56. UNDP, *China Human Development Report 1999* (Beijing: United Nations Development Programme, 1999a). http//hdr.undp.org/reports/view_reports.cfm (last accessed on 14 September 2005). Income — represented by GDP per capita — is used in the calculation of HDI as a proxy for a decent standard of living. Prior to 1999, the UNDP discounted income above the threshold level of the world average income, based on the rationale that a respectable level of human development does not require unlimited income. Beginning in 1999, a new formula has been used, which does not discount income as severely. See UNDP, *Human Development Report 1999* (New York: Oxford University Press, 1999b), pp. 159–60. http://hdr.undp.org/reports/global/1999/en/ (last accessed on 14 September 2005) for the old and new formulas.

PART II

INDIVIDUAL PROFILES

10

Guangdong

Liang Guiquan, You Aiqiong and Gordon Kee

Guangdong 廣東, located at the southern end of China (Figure 10.1), possesses many economic, social, and geographic advantages. Since 1978, Guangdong was destined to be a pioneer in the reform and opening up of China. High-flying Guangdong has become an economic leader among the provinces of China. Its success has become a much-told tale in the world.

Entering the twenty-first century, Guangdong has come to a new stage of development, full of global and regional challenges. Over 25 years of cooperation with Hong Kong have contributed to Guangdong's present economic strength. Guangdong's economy is as strong as Hong Kong's, and even out performs the latter in some sectors. The ways in which Guangdong and Hong Kong have cooperated, and the relationship between them are subjects that are constantly being reviewed by the Guangdong provincial government and society at large. Given China's accession to the World Trade Organization (WTO) in 2001, it is necessary for Guangdong to participate in the global market by fully adopting international rules. Hong Kong is undoubtedly still a key partner with Guangdong. However, Guangdong is in period of transition. The province is facing rising operating costs, a changing industrial structure, spatial limitations, and economic challenges from the Yangzi River Delta (YRD) 長江三角洲. It has to explore new paths of development in order to maintain its leading role in economic reforms.

One of the important strategic decisions that Guangdong has made is to push for a further opening up of its economy, such as by advocating wider regional cooperation. The Guangdong issue caught the attention of the central government and the Chinese Communist Party (CCP); they responded by sending a central CCP cadre, Zhang Dejiang 張德江, to Guangdong in 2002. With his strong experience in regional development, Zhang initiated the setting up of a regional framework for Guangdong to enhance its connections with neighbouring provinces. Zhang and Guangdong officials promoted this regional framework by carrying out numerous visits to neighbouring provinces and holding discussions with officials from those places. They received positive feedback. In June 2004, after a year of negotiations and preparations, Guangdong signed the "Pan–Pearl River Delta 泛珠三角洲 Regional Cooperation Framework Agreement" with Fujian 福建, Jiangxi 江西, Hunan 湖南, Guangxi 廣西, Hainan 海南, Sichuan 四川, Guizhou 貴州, Yunnan 雲南, Hong Kong 香港, and Macao 澳門. Thereafter, Guangdong has continued its utmost to foster the growth of this regional cooperation framework and significant achievements have

Figure 10.1   Prefecture-level Administrative Divisions of Guangdong, *c.* 2004

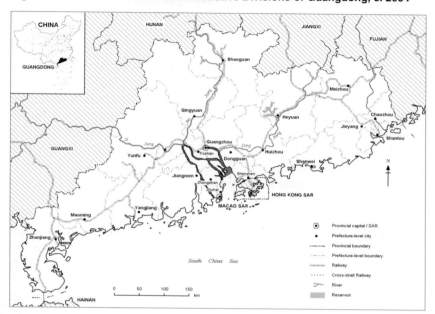

been made. Indeed, without Guangdong's initiative, the framework of Pan–Pearl River Delta (Pan-PRD) regional cooperation would not have come about. Guangdong has played a strategic leading role in the Pan-PRD regional cooperation process.

The Leading Economy

Trajectory of Guangdong's Development and Its Advantages

Guangdong covers an area of 179,800 sq km, a mere 1.87% of the country's land area. The province's major topographic features are hills and mountains, with the exception of the PRD, the Hanjiang River Delta 韓江三角洲, and the Western Guangdong Coastal Plain. In 2004, there were 83.04 million permanent inhabitants in the province.[1] Since the launching of the process of opening up and reforming the economy, the province has experienced rapid industrialization. Guangdong's GDP (gross domestic product) increased from RMB18.59 billion in 1978 to RMB1,603.95 billion in 2004, for an average annual growth rate of 13.4%. Its GDP in 2004 made up one-tenth of the nation's GDP.[2] The province's per capita GDP also rose from RMB369 in 1978 to RMB19,707, or US$2,381 in 2004.[3] The per capita GDP was US$366 higher than the median of middle income-level countries in 2003.[4]

Guangdong's powerful economic performance is demonstrated in many ways. For example, Guangdong accounts for the largest proportion of the nation's total fiscal revenues (one-seventh), total amount of imports and exports (one-third), accumulated amount of utilized foreign capital (one-fourth), and people's savings and deposits (one-seventh). Meanwhile, the global economy has been growing strongly and is increasingly feeling the impact of a resurgent China. According to some estimates, it will be possible for Guangdong to continue to experience steady and rapid economic growth for another 15 to 25 years.[5]

Guangdong's very rapid development over the past 25 years contrasts with the much slower growth in the developed countries and the post-war newly industrializing economies. The province has leaped past the primary stage of industrialization; it is now at the middle stage and is moving towards a higher stage of industrialization (Figure 10.2).

The proportion of primary, secondary, and tertiary industries in Guangdong changed from 29.8:46.6:23.6 in 1978 to 7.8:55.4:36.8 in 2004. Table 10.1 shows the changes in these three economic sectors, indicating rapid industrialization. Guangdong's secondary sector is now transforming itself from light processing and manufacturing industries to heavy chemical industries and high-tech industries. In recent years, the following nine industries have been identified as the pillar industries of Guangdong: the three new industries of electronic information, electric equipment and special purposes equipment and the petroleum and chemical industries; the three potential industries of logging and paper-making, medicine and motor vehicle manufacturing; and the three traditional industries of textiles and garments, food and beverages and building materials. In 2004, the output value of these nine industries totalled RMB2,005.87 billion, an increase of 24.2% over the previous year, accounting for 75.1% of Guangdong's gross industrial output value (above the designated size).[6] The high-tech industry, in particular, is playing a significant role. In 2004, the industry contributed 26% of the province's industrial output value and 40% of the nation's export value of high-tech products.[7]

The basic characteristic of Guangdong's economy is its orientation towards exports. Guangdong has been driven into becoming part of the international business cycle through its high utilization of foreign capital,

Figure 10.2   The Process of Guangdong's Economic and Social Development

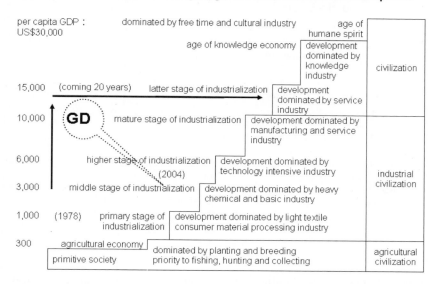

Source: Liang Guiquan and You Aiqiong, "Chayi, hubu, gongying — Fan Zhusanjiao quyu hezuo de jichu yu qushi" 差異，互補，共贏 —— 泛珠三角區域合作的基礎與趨勢 (Differences, The Foundation and Trend of Pan-PRD Regional Cooperation), *Guangdong shehui kexue* 廣東社會科學 (Social Sciences in Guangdong), 2005 (1), p. 29.

Table 10.1   The Trends in Guangdong's Economic Growth as Seen from Changes in the Three Economic Sectors

Year	Primary sector	Secondary sector	Tertiary sector
1978	29.8	46.6	23.6
1980	33.2	41.1	25.7
1985	29.8	39.8	30.4
1990	24.7	39.5	35.8
1995	15.1	50.2	34.7
2000	10.3	50.4	39.3
2001	9.4	50.2	40.4
2002	8.8	50.6	40.6
2003	8.0	53.6	38.4
2004	7.8	55.4	36.8

Source: Guangdong Statistics Bureau, *Guangdong Statistics Yearbook 2005* (see note 1), p. 76.

Table 10.2   Comparison of Degree of External Openness between Guangdong and China, 2004

	Degree of dependence on foreign trade[1] (%)	Degree of dependence on foreign capital[2] (%)	Degree of external openness[3] (%)
Guangdong	184.29	5.17	189.46
China	69.95	3.67	73.62

Notes: 1. Degree of dependence on foreign trade = total value of imports and exports/ GDP.
2. Degree of dependence on foreign capital = utilized amount of foreign direct investment/GDP.
3. Degree of external openness = degree of dependence on foreign trade + degree of dependence on foreign capital dependence.

Sources: Authors' calculation, based on NBS, *China Statistical Yearbook 2005* (see note 2), pp. 51, 626 and 643, and Guangdong Statistics Bureau, *Guangdong Statistical Yearbook 2005* (see note 1), pp. 57, 70 and 432.

inter-regional and international industrial transfers, and participation in international markets. For example, the total value of exports from Guangdong rose from US$1.38 billion in 1978 to US$191.56 billion in 2004,[8] for an average annual growth rate of 20.89%. Over the past 25 years, Guangdong has been the recipient of a vast amount of capital and many industries from Hong Kong, Taiwan 台灣, Japan, and Korea; these have helped to transform the province's economy. One reason for this is that, of all China's provinces, Guangdong has the most open economy. In 2004, Guangdong led the country in the degree of dependence on foreign trade, at 184.29%; with an export dependence degree of 98.85% and a foreign capital dependence degree of 5.17% (Table 10.2).

Through transfers of technology from Europe and America and specifically from Taiwan since the 1990s, Guangdong has been steadily developing a high-tech economy. As a result, the economy is gradually shifting from one based on labour-intensive industries to one based on capital-intensive and technology-intensive industries.

More than economic growth, industrialization has fostered an interactive relationship between industrialization and urbanization in Guangdong. A PRD city-region, with Guangzhou, Shenzhen and Hong Kong as core cities, has taken shape gradually under such conditions. Years of industrialization have provided Guangdong with superior conditions to carry out industrial transfers to peripheral provinces and to cooperate regionally in complementary areas. This superiority is accompanied by relatively well-established infrastructure facilities. The Guangdong government has made great progress in building transport infrastructure. By the end of 2004, the total length of expressways in the province was 2,519 km, ranking Guangdong second in the country.[9] All 21 of Guangdong's prefecture-level cities are now connected by inter-city expressways. From Guangzhou, cities in the PRD region can be reached within an hour, while other cities in the province can be reached within four hours. Besides inter-city expressways, Guangdong also is focusing on constructing inter-provincial expressways, railways and waterways. Regional transport networks are taking shape.

Last, but not least, the opening up and development of Guangdong has enhanced the pioneering reform and innovation of systems in China. Over the past 25 years, by emphasizing the reform of state-owned enterprise, changes to governmental functions, and the normalization of market conditions, Guangdong has realized the transformation of its economic system and has taken the lead in establishing the basic structure of a socialist market economy and the allocation of resources under market mechanisms. For instance, out of 6,000 share-holding enterprises in Guangdong, more than 130 are listed in the stock market, which has put the province in the forefront nationwide. Also, most of the large-scale and medium-scale state-owned enterprises and state-holding enterprises in the province have set up the beginnings of a modern enterprise system and have been improving the role of legal persons. In order to establish better market control, 601 items requiring administrative approval have been abolished.[10] The transition from the traditional system to macro control and market supervision has been completed. Guangdong has sped up these improvement and innovation works after China's entry to the WTO.

Guangdong's Development Aims and Strategic Measures in the Period of the Eleventh Five-year Plan

The Eleventh Five-year Plan (for short, the 11th FYP) is China's economic and social development plan for the period 2006 to 2010. It is regarded as an important FYP for the early period of the twenty-first century that will guide the nation's economic and social development after passing the mark of US$1,000 in per capita GDP and facing severe external and internal challenges. The recent international environment and China's own circumstances have created ambivalent conditions for Guangdong's development during the 11th FYP period. Internationally, although globalization is forcing Guangdong to restructure its economy, the global economy also comes into an accelerated resurgence stage. This is providing Guangdong with opportunities to undertake international industrial transfers and to optimize its industrial structure. China's economic prospects are encouraging, and this is forcing Guangdong to adopt new strategies and approaches to development, in order to achieve further all-round regional cooperation. Moreover, the rich experience and economic strength the province has gained from the past quarter-century of development and its current prosperity are the advantages it brings as it enters the 11th FYP period. The aim of the "11th FYP and Blueprint 2020 of Guangdong" is to make Guangdong into an economic powerhouse, as well as into a moderately well-off society in 5 to 15 years. According to the Blueprint, the per capita GDP of Guangdong will exceed US$3,500 in 2010 and US$7,000 in 2020; while that of the PRD region should be US$7,000 and US$18,000 in 2010 and 2020, respectively,[11] which will approach the level of Europe and America. In order to achieve these goals, 5 development strategies have been proposed and 10 short to long-term measures will be implemented (Table 10.3).

Sustainable Development of Guangdong's Economy and Society and Pan-PRD Regional Cooperation

Both globalization and regionalization are related to the development and enlargement of productivity. According to James Mittelman's definition, two manifestations of globalization include the spatial reorganization of production and the interpenetration of industries across administrative borders.[12] Therefore, the continuous development of an economy will result in the breaking through of spatial limitations; and expansion to a mutually inclusive and neighbouring region will be the first priority. As previously mentioned, by breaking through spatial limitations it is estimated that Guangdong can have a further 15 to 25 years of high-speed sustainable development.[13] There are four directions in which Guangdong can expand its economy.

The first is to develop its internal economic power, especially to strengthen the capacity of an inward-oriented economy. The second is to expand into new fields of development and space by expanding, optimizing, and upgrading its internal industrial structure. Third, is to expand its international markets and enhance international cooperation. Last, is to

Table 10.3   Development Strategies and Measures for Guangdong in the 11th FYP

Development strategies
1. Economic internationalization
2. Emphasis on science and education
3. Emphasis on innovation and reformation
4. Balanced development among the economy, society and environment; and coordinated regional development.
5. Green Guangdong strategy

Measures
1. Speed up the process of transition in the pattern of Guangdong's economic growth
2. Maintain the development of agriculture and the rural economy by strengthening the support given to "agriculture, the countryside and peasants" 三農 —— 農業、農村、農民.
3. Accelerate adjustments to the structure of production to raise competitiveness
4. Execute the strategy of internationalization
5. Energetically expand county economies
6. Strengthen regional cooperation and coordinate development
7. Carry out system reformation and autonomous innovation strategy to raise the regional comprehensive competitiveness.
8. Establish a "green" Guangdong by creating a green culture and a sustainable physical environment and economy.
9. Emphasize the building of a culturally rich province and the promotion of social services
10. Construct a "harmonious Guangdong"

Source: Development and Reform Commission of Guangdong Province et al., *The Eleventh Five-year Plan and Blueprint 2020 of Guangdong* (draft), 2004 (internal document).

promote economic cooperation with neighbouring provinces and to speed up the growth of the regional business cycle. The formation of complementary relationships for development and the expansion of the hinterland for development are anticipated. Therefore, the launching of the Pan-PRD regional cooperation effort is an important strategy for Guangdong.

New Geo-economic Advantages under Globalization and Regionalization

After the Second World War, and especially from the last decade onwards, the pace of globalization and regionalization has accelerated. China's entry to the WTO, participation in the Asia-Pacific Economic Cooperation, the signing of the Treaty of Amity and Cooperation and the formation of the

ASEAN-China Free Trade Area (ACFTA), indicate that China is actively participating in various global and regional affairs. These efforts mark a new phase in the opening of China. China's economic development and industrial growth are now closely bound up with global economic changes and industrial restructuring efforts.

Over the past two decades, Guangdong made heavy use of its geo-economic advantages to develop economically. With the help of Hong Kong's international business networks and with improvements in the inter-provincial transport network, Guangdong is actively participating in the industrial cycles of both national and international markets. Guangdong has profited from the obvious disparity between the global industrial cycle and the national industrial cycle. Along with the successful implementation of the Closer Economic Partnership Arrangement (CEPA) and the establishment of ACFTA, the Pan-PRD regional cooperation is creating new geo-economic advantages for Guangdong. On the one hand, Guangdong should further make use of disparities between the global industrial cycle and the national industrial cycle by expanding regional cooperation to maintain its economic strength. On the other hand, Guangdong should strengthen interactions with the region by expanding its own influence to sustain the development of the region. The emergence of regional economies is thus an inevitable global phenomenon. In China, Guangdong is still one of the most prominent players in global economic competition and in the international economic cycle; in these efforts, Pan-PRD regional cooperation is the most important step.

Specifically, Guangdong's traditional industries, which are now facing increasing constraints and likely to become barriers to the establishment of new high-tech industries, should be relocated to peripheral provinces in order to make room for new industries. As Hong Kong is still the major source of investment in Guangdong, the signing of CEPA has not only allowed Guangdong to continue benefiting from its geo-economic advantages, but will also enable the regional economy and industrial structure to be further unified and upgraded. One major industry that is being relocated from Hong Kong to Guangdong is the service sector. By developing the related upper-stream and lower-stream services to manufacturing industries, an industrial clustering effect can be created by which the tertiary sector in Guangdong can be further modernized, and the regional economic advantages of neighbouring Hong Kong and Macao can also be incarnated.

Breaking the Resource Bottleneck

Over the past 25 years, the increase in Guangdong's GDP has surpassed that of the province's energy consumption, which has allowed its economy to grow at high speed. Nevertheless, as Guangdong is not a resource-rich province, it has been experiencing a shortage of resources in recent years. This is proving to be a challenge to the achievement of sustainable development in Guangdong. For example, the per capita amount of cultivated farmland in Guangdong is only 0.46 *mu* (0.027 ha), which is lower than the critical line — 0.8 *mu* (0.053 ha) — defined by the United Nations.[14] While most of the energy consumed in China is imported, the total amount of energy consumed in Guangdong in 2004 was 7.36% of the national total.[15] Guangdong has been experiencing shortages of electricity since 2002.

Experts have predicted that a larger quantity of energy must be consumed if economic development is to proceed as forecasted in the coming years. A shortage of resources will likely result in a deterioration in the economic performance of enterprises in Guangdong and in the province's economic security and development. Enhancing Pan-PRD regional cooperation is a strategic way to alleviate such a condition. The peripheral provinces have an abundance of water, electricity, minerals, land, manpower and biological and tourism resources. These can be jointly developed by utilizing Guangdong's capital, technology, management, information, and so on. This cooperation can turn the resource advantages of these provinces into economic advantages. It can also break the resource bottleneck and allow Guangdong to break through the constraints on its economic development.

Need to Develop a New Endogenous Power

Guangdong is an outward-oriented economy, for example, the value of its exports reached 98.77% of its GDP in 2004. However, it does not have a healthy economic structure. Comparable figures for developing countries such as South Korea and Thailand are less than 40% and for developed countries only about 10%.[16] After two decades of development, Guangdong's traditional advantages have been lost. The province is experiencing increasing production costs, and the poor quality of the manpower is catching up with Guangdong. Consequently, low value-added and labour-intensive industries are losing ground in Guangdong.[17] Nevertheless, China is a large developing market with much room for development. In addition to encouraging Guangdong's enterprises and industries to develop overseas, the "Japan-Taiwan-Southeast Asia" model of industrial transfers can be adopted.[18] The model was developed after the Second World War, to enable firms to invest in and establish markets in inland regions. From this perspective, the Pan-PRD region would be the best choice. Such a move should make it possible to balance and coordinate the development of the outward and inward economies in Guangdong, lower the relevant risks and possibly maintain economic development at high speed. New opportunities of development can also be created for Pan-PRD members.

Moreover, the development of the Pan-PRD region can serve as a new paradigm for other regions. With the radiation of the Pan-PRD region and the YRD region, economic development of the regions south of the Yangzi River and the upper Yangzi River can be fostered.[19] In short, opportunities arising from CEPA, the Western China Development scheme, ACFTA, and so on, can be found provided that they confine their observations on a prosperous scenario to Pan-PRD regional development. Guangdong's economic development can then make a new breakthrough.

Guangdong's Status and Roles in Pan-PRD Regional Cooperation Framework

As the advocate and key member of the Pan-PRD regional cooperation framework, Guangdong is going to play the following critical roles of radiation, absorption, acceleration and transmission; it will also function as a regional hub and as an example of what can be accomplished in the Pan-PRD region. Guangdong's superiority and its importance can serve the Pan-PRD well in its development.

The Functions of Radiation and Absorption

With more than two decades of experience in pioneering economic reforms and development, Guangdong is at a different stage of industrialization from the eight mainland members of the Pan-PRD. While Guangdong is at the middle to higher stage of industrialization, other Pan-PRD provinces are at the primary stage. Prior to the formation of the Pan-PRD regional cooperation framework, Guangdong had been, after Hong Kong, the largest source of incoming investment in many provinces. Guangdong capital can be found in various fields such as communication and transportation, energy, technology, commodities and tourism, to name a few. The investments have established a close and cross-boundary relationship between Guangdong and these provinces. In recent years, there has been a noticeable emphasis on setting up businesses in the tertiary sector, in technology and research and development.

After the initiation of the concept of Pan-PRD regional cooperation in 2003, official visits, bilateral businesses and other interactions among the Pan-PRD provinces have increased significantly. For instance, an official delegation from Hunan visited Shenzhen in October 2003, immediately followed in November and December 2003 by two delegations to Guangzhou from Jiangxi. In February 2004, a Guangxi delegation visited Guangdong and signed a number of cooperation contracts. In the other direction, a high-profile official delegation from Guangdong visited Guangxi and Hunan in April 2004, contracts on business and trade, technological cooperation and infrastructure development were signed. The total amount of investment was over RMB80 billion and most of the projects involved investments in Guangxi and Hunan by Guangdong.[20] With the implementation of the regional framework agreement and successful visits and cooperation, the pace at which Guangdong capital and expertise is radiating to the inland provinces is intensifying, by means of the transfer of products, expansion of brands, re-ordering of assets, and so forth. In particular, Guangdong is going to enhance cooperation among the Pan-PRD provinces in the following ways:

1. by optimizing the integration of regional resources;
2. by promoting regional investment and industrial development;
3. by bringing about enhanced integration in the trading market;
4. by expanding cooperation in infrastructure projects;
5. by widening cooperation in science, education, culture, hygiene and environmental protection, and
6. by coming up with an innovative mechanism for cooperation.

For its part, Guangdong relies heavily on various resources from neighbouring provinces and areas to maintain its position as a major manufacturing base in the world. For example, Guangdong relies on the financial resources of Hong Kong and Macao. It also depends on the various natural and human resources of other Pan-PRD provinces as well as on their markets. This absorption of resources not only supports the development of Guangdong's manufacturing industries, but can also turn the potential advantages of Pan-PRD provinces into real economic advantages and foster local economic development.

The Function of a Regional Hub

Guangdong, specifically the PRD region, is the regional hub of the Pan-PRD region. The ports of Guangzhou 廣州, Shenzhen 深圳 and Zhuhai 珠海 are three major national coastal ports. The ports of Guangzhou and Shenzhen, coupled with the port of Hong Kong, are world renowned. They are among the busiest ports in the world as they serve at the intersection of two major international shipping routes — the Far East-Europe line and Far East-North America line — and function as the major gateway to the vast landlocked interior of the Pan-PRD region, which can be accessed via expressways, railways, and the waterways of the Pearl River.

According to the customs statistics, the value of the goods imported and exported by the eight Pan-PRD provinces through Guangdong's ports reached US$10.39 billion in 2004, an increase of 43.4% from the previous year.[21] A good regional hub relies on excellent infrastructure. At present, Guangdong is rapidly constructing more infrastructure. There will be 12 expressways connecting Guangdong with the peripheral provinces, and when these expressways are in operation, it will only take one day to go from Guangdong to any major city in the Pan-PRD region. The many projects that are underway on waterways and railways will be discussed in the next section. In addition, port services and management have been improving and are gradually becoming consistent with international codes of practice. All of these efforts will provide a better channel for capital, technology and population to flow from Guangdong, Hong Kong, and Macao to the Pan-PRD provinces. At the same time, they will facilitate the flow of goods from the Pan-PRD provinces to Guangdong, Hong Kong and Macao. Guangdong will become even more prominent as a regional hub.

The Function of Accelerating the Opening up of the Region

Given the rich experience of opening up, Guangdong will continue to promote regional cooperation with Hong Kong and Macao under CEPA and other new and favourable arrangements. In addition, both spatially and functionally, Guangdong can help to foster further cooperation among Hong Kong, Macao and the eight Pan-PRD provinces by, for example, creating opportunities and giving assistance.

Guangdong is also accelerating cooperation between the Pan-PRD region and the Association of Southeast Asian Nations (ASEAN), and the

Greater PRD (GPRD) region will become a primary bridging region between the Pan-PRD and the ASEAN countries. Guangdong has advantages that cannot be replicated by Guangxi, Yunnan and the YRD region, stemming from the implementation of CEPA, the admission of China to the WTO, the establishment of ACFTA, its geographical advantages, the strong cultural and family ties with Guangdong of Chinese inhabitants in ASEAN countries and complementarities between Guangdong and ASEAN countries in the manufacturing sector and in technological structure. Guangdong's advantages are reflected in the statistics cited below.

In 2004, bilateral trade between China and the ASEAN countries totalled US$105.87 billion, with 30.50% of that contributed by Guangdong alone. ASEAN accounted for 9.04% of Guangdong's total trade value, with imports comprising 13.91%.[22] From 2000 to 2004, the value of imports and exports between Guangdong and the ASEAN countries increased by almost 250%.[23] Over the past 25 years, direct investment in Guangdong from ASEAN countries has totalled US$5,094.62 million.[24] Meanwhile, Guangdong enterprises are steadily increasing their investments in ASEAN countries. Eighty-four enterprises have been set up in ASEAN countries with Guangdong capital, for a total investment of US$134 million.[25]

Inevitably, the YRD will play an increasingly larger role in the China-ASEAN bilateral relationship with China's entry to the WTO, which will pose a challenge to Guangdong.[26] But Guangdong's established superiority and the new strategies that are being employed, combined with the rising links between the ASEAN countries and the other Pan-PRD provinces, will still allow Guangdong to capitalize on its geographical and international economic advantages in regional cooperation. Grasping the opportunities for cooperation with ASEAN countries and the world, Guangdong will push forward with regional economic cooperation and exchanges between the Pan-PRD region and Southeast Asian countries, the Asia-Pacific region, and the Pacific Rim economies.

The Function of Transmission

As mentioned earlier, Guangdong is now at the middle to higher stage of industrialization. On the one hand, Guangdong is receiving international inflows of industrial investment in areas such as information technology; on the other hand, Guangdong is diverting its traditional labour- and resource-intensive industries to peripheral provinces, where industrialization is still at the primary stage. Through this process of industrial relocation, those provinces can greatly accelerate their industrialization efforts, or with Guangdong as an intermediary, attract advanced industries that are suitable for local development and realize potential resource advantages.

In fact, the cost of land and labour in Guangdong has risen after years of development. Many traditional labour-intensive and high energy consuming industries have been transferred from Guangdong to other regions that offer comparative advantages in land and labour. The electronic information industry and the petrochemical industry have gradually become the major sectors in Guangdong's development. For instance, two Guangdong-based clothing and knitting companies each recently invested about RMB10 million in Guangxi. In the Guangdong-Guangxi Economic Cooperation Agreement signed in April 2004, almost 70% of the investment projects were items of industrial transfer.[27] Along with the growth of the Pan-PRD economic region, complementary industrial transfers are increasingly becoming a major focal point. It is believed that, with time, a complete industrial chain will be established within the Pan-PRD region.

The Function of Exemplar

As a pioneer in China's opening and reform efforts, Guangdong's development offers the country valuable experience on how to change from a highly centralized planned economy to a market economy. While the basic framework of the socialist market economy has been established, it is still far from a mature system. Guangdong is still the forerunner in providing new experience on how to spearhead development to perfect China's economic system. Moreover, Guangdong can demonstrate, especially to neighbouring provinces, how to engage in sustainable development and participate in cyclical economic development, to build a harmonious society and implement political structural reforms.

The Role of Regional Gateway and Transport Hub

Transport has been recognized as the key to pushing forward cooperation in the Pan-PRD region. Guangdong is the region's main gateway to the sea and is also the artery connecting mainland China with Hong Kong and Macao. Guangdong's transport facilities are playing an irreplaceable role in constructing the Pan-PRD regional economic system, where there is an immediate need to perfect networks of highways, railways and waterways. Guangdong has set up programmes to speed up the construction of transport infrastructure. Besides aiming to complete the construction of an intra-provincial highway and waterway networks in the shortest possible time, Guangdong is determined to speed up the process of building transport infrastructure to peripheral provinces and the Special Administrative Regions (SARs).

Expressway Network

By the end of 2004, Guangdong had 111.45 thousand km of highways, with 2,519 km of expressways. This ranks it second to Shandong 山東 and first in Grade A highways.[28] In addition, there are over 700 inter-provincial passenger bus lines in service between Guangdong and other Pan-PRD provinces.[29] However, it is necessary to strengthen the expressway network and services for to expand regional development; towards this end, the Guangdong government has set up a "three-stage" scheme. First, the construction of expressways linking all municipal cities; this was completed on schedule in 2004. Second, the construction of the Yu-Zhan Expressway 渝湛高速公路 (Chongqing 重慶 to Guangdong) and the Yue-Gan Expressway 粵贛高速公路 (Guangdong to Jiangxi), both of which were completed at the end of 2005. All neigbouring provinces and SARs, with the exception of Hainan, are now connected by expressways. Third, the construction of other inter-provincial expressways will be finished after 2006, with about 12 to be completed by 2008. By 2010, the expressway network, centred on Guangzhou, will be further perfected and Guangdong will become a major transport hub and centre in South China. Table 10.4 is a list of recent highway projects in Guangdong.

Railway Network

Railways are superior in that they save space, run at high speeds and are highly efficient. They are also energy-saving, offer regular schedules, are safe and comfortable and operate at a lower average cost than other forms of transport. The current provision of inter-city railways and inter-provincial railways in Guangdong can no longer keep up with demand. Poor inter-city railway connections are slowing down communication between cities and are acting as a drag on regional development, especially in the PRD region. Insufficient and backward inter-provincial railway connections, especially to Southwest China, are also holding back Pan-PRD economic cooperation.

Table 10.4   Highway Projects in Guangdong

Intra-provincial expressway network

- National highways were upgraded to a Grade B or higher standard in 2005.
- Grade B or higher standard highways will be constructed, linking cities and counties in mountainous and less-developed regions.
- An expressway network in the PRD region will be formed by 2007.

Inter-provincial expressway network

Guangdong—Fujian

- The Shan-Fen expressway section 汕汾段 of the Tongjiang—Sanya National Highway 同江—三亞國道 (Heilongjiang 黑龍江 to Hainan), opened in 2001.
- Mei—Long Expressway 梅龍高速公路, expected to open by the end of 2006.

Guangdong—Jiangxi

- Yue-Gan Expressway, construction started at the end of 2003; opened in December 2005.

Guangdong—Hunan

- The Xiaotang—Gantang section 小塘—甘塘段 of the Beijing—Zhuhai Expressway 北京—珠海高速公路, opened in March 2005.

Guangdong—Guangxi

- The Suixi—Gaoqiao section 遂溪—高橋段 of the Yu-Zhan Expressway, construction started in 2003, opened in December 2005.
- The Hekou—Cangwu section 河口—蒼梧段 of the Guang—Wu Expressway 廣梧高速公路, construction started in 2004, expected to open by the end of 2007.

Guangdong—Hong Kong and Macao

- Shenzhen—Hong Kong Western Corridor 深港西部通道, opened in July 2007.
- The Zhuhai—Macao section of the Beijing—Zhuhai Expressway, undergoing planning.
- Guangzhou—Shenzhen Coastal Expressway, undergoing planning.
- Hong Kong—Zhuhai—Macao Bridge, undergoing final feasibility studies.

Guangdong—Hainan

- Zhan—Xu Expressway 湛江—徐聞高速公路 connects the Qiongzhou Strait 瓊州海峽, an important channel for people and vehicles travelling between Guangdong and Hainan.

Source: Liu Man, "*Lingqi nian Zhusanjiao jiancheng 'banri gongzuoquan,' lingwu chu sheng gaosu tong Fan Zhusanjiao*" 07年珠三角建成 "半日工作圈," 05出省高速通泛珠三角 (PRD forms "1/2 Day Working Circle" in 2007, Inter-provincial Expressway to Pan-PRD Provinces in 2005), *Guangzhou Daily*, 26 December 2003; Feng Yiju, "*Guangdong chu sheng tongdao jianshe quanmian tisu, Yue-Gan Gaosu jiang jiuyue kaigong*" 廣東出省通道建設全面提速，粵贛高速將9月開工 (Guangdong speeds up the Construction of Inter-provincial Highways, Guangdong-Jiangxi Expressway starts Construction in September), *Nanfang Daily*, 5 June 2003; *Yue-Gan, Yu-Zhan he xibu yanhai gaosu gonglu tongshi tongche*" 粵贛、渝湛和西部沿海高速公路同時通車 (Guangdong-Jiangxi-Chongqing-Zhanjiang Expressway and the Western Coastal Expressway open to Traffic), *Xinhua Net*, 28 December 2005, http://news.xinhuanet.com/travel/2005-12/28/content_3980612.htm.

Only by pushing forward the construction of inter-city high-speed and high-capacity railways, raising the proportion of railway services in urban transport, and constructing an interlocking modern railway network, can favourable conditions for the development of core cities and the PRD region be created. Therefore, the most important target is to construct an inter-city high-speed railway system that will integrate all major cities in the PRD region with Hong Kong and Macao, so that the economic integration of the GPRD can be enhanced. According to Guangdong's development plan, from 2005 onwards, nine new railway projects worth RMB139 billion, including the Wuhan-Guangzhou Passenger Line 武廣客運專線, will be constructed. By 2020, 2,164 km of new railways will be added, bringing Guangdong's total railway mileage to 4,000 km.[30] A railway network covering the whole PRD region will be established. Guangzhou will be the centre of the railway network and a "one-hour circle" will be created in the GPRD region (Table 10.5 and Figure 10.3).

For the inter-provincial railway, five new lines are planned and Guangdong will have a total of ten inter-provincial lines. Again, Guangzhou will be the major terminus of these 10 lines. Besides raising the running speed of the current train services, passenger express lines will be constructed and the proposed maximum speed of the passenger trains will be 200 km/hour. Starting from Guangzhou, all major cities in the Pan-PRD region will be reachable within 24 hours. Table 10.6 lists some major inter-provincial railway projects.

Table 10.5 The PRD Inter-city High-speed Railway System (in 2020)

Line	Proposed length	Remarks
Axis Lines		
• Guangzhou—Zhuhai Line	117.5 km	will be completed by 2010
• Guangzhou—Shenzhen Line	132.5 km	will be completed by 2010
Radial Lines		
• Guangzhou—Zhaoqing 肇慶 Line	109.7 km	
• Zhongshan 中山—Jiangmen 江門 Line	28 km	
• Dongguan 東莞—Huizhou 惠州 Line	75 km	
Bridge Lines		
• Shunde 順德—Dongguan Line	59.6 km	
• Zhongshan—Humen 虎門 Line	64 km	will be completed by 2010

Source: Liu Qian, "*Xin Guangzhou huochezhan donggong, tielu si da keyun zhongxin hu zhi yu chu*," 新廣州火車站動工，鐵路四大客運中心呼之欲出 (New Guangzhou Station starts Construction, Four Passenger Railway Hubs formed), *Nanfang Daily*, 30 December 2004.

Figure 10.3   Existing Railways and Current Railway Development in Guangdong

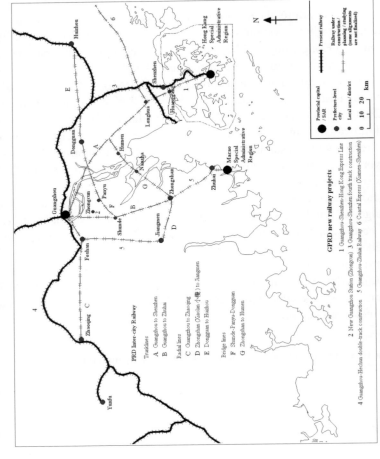

Source: Yeung and Kee, *Basic Infrastructure Development... Railways* (see note 30), p. 18.

Besides new railway lines, a new Guangzhou Railway Station in Zhongcun 鍾村 of Panyu 番禺 is now being built. It will be one of four major railway passenger transport centres in China and a modern, comprehensive transport interchange for railway trunk lines, inter-city railways, tubes, expressways, and roads. It is also a major component of the Wuhan-Guangzhou Passenger Line project.

Table 10.6 Some Major Inter-provincial Railway Projects

Guangdong—Guangxi
- Luozhan Railway 洛湛鐵路, Guangdong section, 116 km in length, RMB2.3 billion investment.
- Lizhan Railway 黎湛鐵路, project to double-track the Hechun—Zhanjiang section 河唇—湛江段, 62 km in length.

Guangdong—Jiangxi
- Ganshao Railway 贛韶鐵路, Guangdong section, 128 km in length.
- Wuhan—Guangzhou Passenger Line, Guangdong section, 320 km in length. (This high-speed railway will shorten travelling distances between major cities in the Pan-PRD region).

Guangdong—Fujian
- Zhangchaoshan Railway 漳潮汕鐵路, undergoing planning, a major section of the planned Southeastern Coastal Railway 東南沿海鐵路.

Guangdong—Hainan
- Cross-strait railway, opened in December 2003.

Guangdong—Hong Kong
- Guangzhou—Shenzhen—Hong Kong High-speed Railway 廣深港高速鐵路, Guangdong section, started construction in December 2005.
- Guangzhou—Shenzhen fourth line, opened in April 2007.

Other
- Southeastern Coastal Railway (from Ningbo 寧波 to Shenzhen), Guangdong section, 423 km in length, from Raoping 饒平 to Shenzhen.

Source: Chen Hanhui et al., "*Liuyue er ri huati: jichu sheshi jianshe yu xietiao*" 6月2日話題：基礎設施建設與協調 (June 2 Topic: Construction and Coordination of Infrastructure), *Nanfang Daily*, 2 June 2004.

Waterway Network

Emphasis will be placed on constructing the West River trunk waterway and the PRD high-class navigable waterway network, and on perfecting existing waterways for large vessels and cargo ships so as to establish the core navigable waterway network of the PRD. As part of the project, from 2004 to 2010, Guangdong will invest over RMB4.6 billion[31] in constructing navigable waterways with the aim of modernizing the navigable waterways in the PRD region and the West River. There are 17 projects, 7 of them on-going and 10 new. By completing these 17 projects, the Guangdong navigable waterway network, with 3 major west-east waterways and 3 major north-south waterways, will be fully upgraded, and will cover a larger hinterland. Moreover, the interaction and integration of inland water transport and sea transport can be gradually enhanced.

Conclusion

The environment, which is full of challenges and opportunities, is always changing. Guangdong must face up to the changes and respond if it is to keep developing in an environment of global competition. Guangdong's traditional mode of development can no longer result in further growth in the province, but will damage its economic development, environment, competitiveness, and so on. Guangdong officials and think-tanks must come up with possible solutions such as finding new sources of internal growth and expanding regionally to overcome the constraints. Therefore, it is prudent for Guangdong to enhance cooperation with peripheral provinces. During the 11th FYP, Pan-PRD regional cooperation will accelerate. There will be two ways to access the sustainable development of Guangdong.

First, there should be a successful internal transformation. The 11th FYP aims to restructure Guangdong's economy by enhancing industrial transfers and by strengthening the province's internal economic structure. But the question is how to achieve successful implementation. We believe that Guangdong must attend to at least three points. Sound and feasible measures must come first. Without practical plans and programmes, no policies, however ideal, can ever be realized and all development goals can only come to nothing. Adjustable policies and regular adjustments come second. In an ever-changing economic world, adjustable policies should be adopted and regular examinations and adjustments should be made. Achieving a good public-private-society relationship comes third. Although some industries and factories contributed to the rise of Guangdong, they have become a burden and are being forced to relocate or to close down. It is suggested that negotiations be carried out between the government and enterprises and that the government provide help with industrial relocations. The government also needs to deal with a large number of unskilled workers who will be laid off once industrial relocations increase.

Second, there should be a desirable external expansion. In the 11th FYP period, Guangdong will embark on various transport and communication infrastructure projects to enhance its linkages with Pan-PRD members. Guangdong will also benefit from various regional cooperation agreements such as CEPA and ACFTA. Infrastructure will help to increase regional interaction. We should pay attention to the amount of infrastructure that is constructed in order to avoid excesses or inadequacies. Comprehensiveness, high quality and high efficiency should also be the focus. Smooth physical links should also be supported by a barrier-free environment. Guangdong should try to free itself from protectionist policies and practices and encourage both Guangdong companies to go out and non-Guangdong companies to come in. Only in this way will there will be some likelihood of Guangdong's strategy of expansion being fulfilled.

Notes

1. Guangdong Statistics Bureau, *Guangdong Statistical Yearbook 2005* (Beijing: Zhongguo tongji chubanshe 中國統計出版社, 2005), p. 53.
2. Ibid., pp. 52–53; National Bureau of Statistics (NBS), *China Statistical Yearbook 2005* (Beijing: Zhongguo tongji chubanshe, 2005), pp. 51 and 59. In early 2006, the National Bureau of Statistics of China announced revised national GDP figures from 1993 to 2004, which were raised. The revised GDP of Guangdong in 2004 was RMB1,886.46 billion and the figure for 2005 was RMB2,236.65 billion.
3. Guangdong Statistics Bureau, *Guangdong Statistical Yearbook 2005* (see note 1), p. 81. The average exchange rate of RMB against the US$ in 2004 was RMB827.68 to US$100. Unless otherwise noted, this is the exchange rate that is adopted in this chapter.
4. United Nations Development Programme (UNDP), *Human Development Report 2005* (New York: UNDP, 2005), p. 269. The GDP per capita of middle-income countries in 2003 was US$2,015.
5. Liang Guiquan 梁桂全 and You Aiqiong 游靄琼, "Guangdong de quyu hezuo zhanlüe: chayi, hubu, gongying" 廣東的區域合作戰略：差異，互補，共贏 (Guangdong's Strategies in Regional Cooperation: Diversity, Complementary and Mutual-benefit), in *Fan Zhusanjiao yu Xianggang hudong fazhan* 泛珠三角與香港互動發展 The Pan–Pearl River Delta and Its Interactive Development with Hong Kong, edited by Yeung Yue-man 楊汝萬 and Shen Jianfa 沈建法 (Hong Kong: Hong Kong Institute of Asia-Pacific Studies, The Chinese University of Hong Kong, 2005), p. 17.
6. Guangdong Statistics Bureau, *Guangdong Statistical Yearbook 2005* (see note 1), pp. 301 and 307.
7. "Quyu chuangxin nengli Hu Jing Yue lie sanjia, Yue gaoxin jishu chanpin nian chanzhi chao wanyi" 區域創新能力滬京粵列三甲，粵高新技術產品年

產值超萬億 (Shanghai, Beijing and Guangdong Rank Top in Regional Innovation Capability, Guangdong's Hi-tech Products Valued at Over 100 Billion), *Hong Kong Commercial Daily*, 12 January 2006, B06.

8. Guangdong Statistics Bureau, *Guangdong Statistical Yearbook 2005* (see note 1) p. 57.

9. NBS, *China Statistical Yearbook 2005* (see note 2), p. 551.

10. "Guangdongsheng jihua weiyuanhui Huang Weihong: Guangdong 18 nian yao shixian xiandaihua" 廣東省計劃委員會黃偉鴻：廣東18年要實現現代化 (Huang, Member of the Guangdong Planning Commission: Guangdong to Realize the Modernization in 18 Years) Southcn.com (南方網), 31 December 2002, http://www.southcn.com/news/gdnews/hotspot/czmhwl/tzft/ 200301020264.htm, accessed on 6 December 2005.

11. "Guangdongsheng quanmian jianshe xiaokang shehui zongti gouxiang" 廣東省全面建設小康社會總體構想 (A General Framework of the Construction of a Moderately Well-off Society in Guangdong), 2004. Retrieved from the homepage of Guangdong Social Sciences on 8 November 2005, http://www. gdass.gov.cn/news_view.jsp?cat_id=1001479&news_id=1598&keyword= 廣東省全面建設小康社會總體構想.

12. James H. Mittelman, *Globalization: Critical Reflections* (Boulder, Colo.: Lynne Rienner Publishers, 1996), p. 2.

13. Liang and You, "Guangdong's Strategies in Regional Cooperation" (see note 5).

14. "Yue renjun gengdi jin 0.46 mu, jinnian jixu yan ba tudi 'zhamen'" 粵人均耕 地僅0.46畝，今年繼續嚴把土地"閘門" (Guangdong's Per Capita Amount of Farmland Is Only 0.46 Acres; Strict Control of Farmland to Continue), Southcn. com, 25 March 2005, http://www.southcn.com/news/gdnews/gdzw/zwlb/gtzy/ 200503250033.htm, accessed on 7 November 2005.

15. Total energy consumption in Guangdong and China are, respectively, 145.03 million tonnes of SCE and 1,970.00 million tonnes of SCE in 2004.

16. Liang and You, "Guangdong's Strategies in Regional Cooperation" (see note 5), p. 21

17. You Aiqiong, "Jianshe Fan Zhusanjiao: shun shi ying shi de jingji fazhan xin zhanlüe," 建設泛珠三角：順時應勢的經濟發展新戰略 (The Pan-PRD: A Well-timed Strategy for Economic Development), *Nanfang jingji* 南方經濟 (Southern Economics), No. 6 (2004), p. 37.

18. See Liang and You, "Guangdong's Strategies in Regional Cooperation" (note 5), p. 21, for further details of the "Japan-Taiwan-Southeast Asia" industrial model.

19. You, "The Pan-PRD" (see note 17).

20. "358 yi! Yue Xiang qianding ju'e hezuo dadan" 358億！粵湘簽訂巨額合作 大單 (35.8 Billion! Guangdong-Hunan's Surprising Cooperation in Investment) *Minying jingji bao* 民營經濟報, 20 April 2004.

21. "Fan Zhusanjiao diqu jinchukou maoyi dafu zengzhang" 泛珠三角地區進出

口貿易大幅增長 (Large-scale Growth in the Import and Export Trade of the Pan-PRD), in the homepage of the Ministry of Commerce of the People's Republic of China, Special Commissioner's Office in Guangzhou, 31 January 2005, http://gztb.mofcom.gov.cn/aarticle/shangwxw/200501/2005010 0341264.html, accessed on 8 December 2005.

22. NBS, *China Statistical Yearbook 2005* (see note 2), p. 631; Guangdong Statistics Bureau, *Guangdong Statistical Yearbook 2005* (see note 1), p. 413.

23. Guangdong Statistics Bureau, *Guangdong Statistical Yearbook* (see note 1), 2002 to 2005.

24. Guangdong Statistics Bureau, *Guangdong Statistical Yearbook* (see note 1), p. 436. The figure is the sum of utilized capital from six ASEAN countries (the Philippines, Thailand, Malaysia, Singapore, Indonesia and Brunei) between 1979 and 2004.

25. "Guangdong jiji tuidong yu Dongmeng jingmao hezuo" 廣東積極推動與東盟經貿合作 (Guangdong Actively Promotes Trade with ASEAN), *Xinhuanet* (新華網), 1 January 2005, http://news.xinhuanet.com/newscenter/2005-01/01/content_2404093.htm, accessed on 8 December 2005.

26. "Guanzhu rushi hou Guangdong yu Dongmeng maoyi youshi ruohua wenti" 關注入世後廣東與東盟貿易優勢弱化問題 (Following the Weakening of Guangdong's Advantage in Trade with ASEAN after WTO), *Nanbo wang* (南博網), http://219.159.68.69/gb/news/hotnews/t20050823_47253.html, accessed on 16 November 2005.

27. Hou Ying 侯穎, "Fan Zhusanjiao chanye zhuanyi shi zai bi xing" 泛珠三角產業轉移勢在必行 (Industrial Shifts Are Going to Occur in the Pan-PRD), *Minying jingji bao* 民營經濟報 (Privately-run Economic Daily), 14 July 2005.

28. Guangdong Statistics Bureau, *Guangdong Statistical Yearbook* (see note 1), p. 389; NBS, *China Statistical Yearbook 2005*, (see note 2), p. 551.

29. You, "The Pan-PRD" (see note 17), p. 39.

30. Yeung Yue-man and Gordon Kee Wai-man 紀緯紋, *Fan Zhusanjiao jichu jianshe fazhan yanjiu xilie, II. Tielu* 泛珠三角基礎建設發展研究系列, II. 鐵路 (Basic Infrastructure Development in the Pan–Pearl River Delta Research Series, II. Railways) Occasional Paper No. 155 (Hong Kong: Hong Kong Institute of Asia-Pacific Studies, The Chinese University of Hong Kong, 2005), p. 19.

31. "Fan Zhusanjiao hezuo jiaotong jichu sheshi zhuan'an zhankai, Guangdong hangdao jianshe guihua zhuan'an jiben qiaoding" 泛珠三角合作交通基礎設施專案展開,廣東航道建設規劃專案基本敲定 (Pan-PRD Transport Infrastructure Cooperation Starts, Construction of Guangdong Navigation Channels Confirmed), *Nanfang dushi bao* 南方都市報 (*Nanfang Daily*), 14 June 2004.

11

Guangxi

Huang Yefang

Introduction

Guangxi 廣西 is a very special provincial unit of Pan–Pearl River Delta region (Pan-PRD) 泛珠江三角洲. A high proportion of the population consists of ethnic minorities and the province is one of five autonomous regions in China.[1] It lies along one of China's borders and shares a long land and sea border with Vietnam. It is both a coastal provincial unit and a part of the western provincial region. The province occupies a unique position in the campaign to develop the western region of China launched in 1999, in the development of the Association of Southeast Asian Nations (ASEAN) — China Free Trade Area (ACFTA for the 10 ASEAN nations plus China or simply "10+1") initiated in 2001, in the Closer Economic Partnership Arrangement (CEPA) established in 2003 and in regional cooperation in the Pan-PRD region announced in 2004. It is the least developed of China's coastal provinces. Yet, it is not the least developed among the 9+2 areas of the Pan-PRD region. It has abundant water, agricultural and mineral resources. With many geographical and natural advantages, Guangxi is clearly a region with a great deal of economic potential.

Many regional cooperation initiatives have been adopted in Guangxi. But cooperation between Guangxi and Guangdong 廣東 has been very limited in the past. Guangdong has focused on developing the Pearl River Delta (PRD) region 珠江三角洲. Guangxi has also rarely looked to the east, although Guangdong is the most prosperous province in South China and is located right next to Guangxi. The gap in development between Guangxi and Guangdong has widened significantly during the reform period.[2]

There have been very few studies conducted on Guangxi, especially in the English language. Hendrischke's interesting study on Guangxi focused on the relationship between Guangxi and the central government, the process of reforms and the socioeconomic changes in the region. Hendrischke and Brantly also examined the province's growing border trade with Vietnam.[3] In 1990, Ye considered the urban reform strategies followed by cities in Guangxi.[4] The changing relationship between urbanization and development in Guangxi was also examined by the present author in a previous study.[5]

This chapter examines Guangxi's regional advantages, economic foundation and regional cooperation in the context of the Pan-PRD regional cooperation and development concept.[6] The province's population, resources and environment are first briefly examined to assess its regional advantages.

Then, Guangxi's existing economic foundation is examined to provide a context for Pan-PRD regional cooperation. Previous regional cooperation arrangements involving the province will then be reviewed, followed by a consideration of the opportunities for regional cooperation in the Pan-PRD region for Guangxi.

Population, Resources and Regional Advantages

Since the founding of the People's Republic of China (PRC) in 1949, the country has experienced continuous population growth in every region. Guangxi is no exception. Its population increased from 19.43 million in 1952 to 36.42 million by 1982 and 48.57 million by 2003.[7] With a territory of 236 thousand km^2, population density in Guangxi increased by 87.44% in the period 1952–1982 and 33.36% in the period 1982–2003, reaching 206 persons per km^2 in 2003, close to the average of 228 persons per km^2 in the Pan-PRD region.

The quality of human resources is a major problem due to the inadequate provision of education. According to the 2000 population census, only 3.24% of population aged 15 years and over had received an education at the junior college level or above, lower than the national average of 4.60% for Mainland China as a whole in 2000.[8] On the other hand, it is encouraging that the percentage of the population aged 15 years and over with only a primary level of education or less was 6.93%, lower than the national average of 10.97% in 2000. Clearly, more educational opportunities both at the elementary and university levels need to be provided, so that people will be better prepared for the challenges of on-going development.

Another main feature of Guangxi's population is its large minority population. There are 37 ethnic nationalities in Guangxi, 12 of which are aboriginal nationalities and the other 25 of which are nationalities that have migrated from elsewhere.[9] The minority population increased from 12.72 million to 18.54 million in the period 1978–2003. Its share of the total population of Guangxi increased from 37.39% to 38.17% in the same period. Guangxi had the largest minority population among all of the provinces of China, and in terms of the minority population's share of the total population, the province ranked fourth highest after Tibet 西藏, Xinjiang 新疆 and Qinghai 青海. The largest minority nationality in Guangxi was the Zhuang 壯, with a population of 15.89 million[10] and accounting for 32.72% of the province's total population in 2003. The Han 漢 population, 30.30 million in total, was still the largest, accounting for 62.38% of the total population of Guangxi.

With its large minority population, Guangxi has enjoyed a high level of autonomy in its status as a Zhuang autonomous region since 1958. The governor of Guangxi is required by law to be a member of the Zhuang nationality. Guangxi is also empowered to make its own laws relating to political elections, society, the economy, education, labour protection and the environment. Special attention is paid to the education and training of the minority population. Over 1.5 million minority nationalities are currently appointed as government officials, teachers, scientists and technical personnel in Guangxi.[11]

Guangxi's geographical location is a major asset. First, the province has direct access to sea transport, which is not the case for five other provinces in the Pan-PRD region. Guangxi is becoming a major sea passage for the greater southwestern region, which includes Sichuan 四川, Chongqing 重慶, Guizhou 貴州, Yunnan 雲南 and Tibet.[12] In 2003, exports from these four provincial units to international markets via Guangxi increased by 55.4%, to US$704 million.[13] Second, many cities of Guangxi are linked with Guangdong by the Xijiang 西江 channel of the Pearl River, providing convenient river transport. Third, sharing a 1,020 km long border with a foreign country, Vietnam, gives Guangxi another major advantage in the age of globalization. As Vietnam is a member of ASEAN, the relationship of economic cooperation and trade between China and Vietnam offers huge potential. The growth of the border trade has been a significant phenomenon since the early 1990s (Figure 11.1).[14] Guangxi has four border-crossings at state level I and eight other border-crossings. There are also 25 sites for border trading. Exports and imports in the border trade amounted to US$418 million and US$282 million, respectively, in 2003. Two border cities, Pingxiang 憑祥 and Dongxing 東興, have benefited most from border trade. Their total imports and exports reached US$2,132 million and US$1,677 million, respectively, in 2003. For Guangxi as a whole, international trade has rebounded after a decline in the late 1990s. The province's total exports declined from US$2,246 million in 1995 to US$1,236 million in 2001, along with a decline in foreign investment. Exports then recovered to US$1,970 million in 2003. Total imports declined from US$965 million in 1995 to US$545 million in 2000. They then recovered to US$1,222 million in 2003.[15]

Guangxi has a favourable natural environment. As much as 41.3% of its territory was covered by forests in 2003. A beautiful landscape is a valuable resource, especially in the present period when tourism has become an important economic sector. The karst landscape in Guilin 桂林 is one of

Figure 11.1 Guangxi in Its Geographical Setting

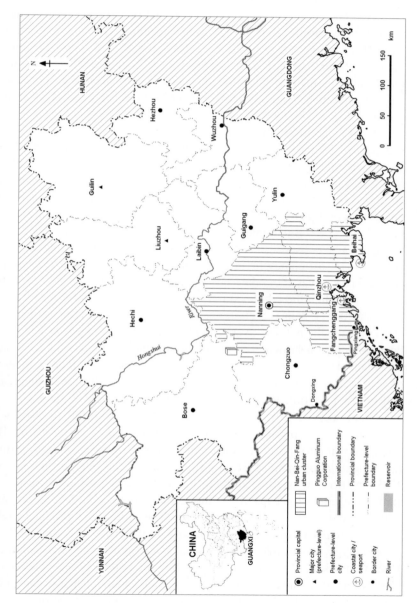

the most famous attractions in the province to tourists from China and abroad.[16] The culture of the minority nationalities, the province's natural reserves and coastal resorts are also quite appealing. The number of tourists from Hong Kong 香港, Macao 澳門, Taiwan 台灣 and foreign countries increased from 0.42 million in 1995 to 1.30 million in 2002. This declined to 0.65 million in 2003, due to the impact of an outbreak that year of Severe Acute Respiratory Syndrome (SARS). The province attracted 45.40 million domestic tourists in 2003.[17]

A subtropical climate has made Guangxi the biggest producer of sugarcane in China. In 2003, 6.01 million tonnes of sugarcane were produced there, accounting for 55.48% of the national total. However, 68% of the province's land is made up of hilly area. This includes rocky hills, which comprise 18.4% of the total land area in Guangxi and which pose a serious environmental problem. There were 4.41 million ha of arable land in Guangxi in 2003. But arable land per capita was only 0.091 ha, lower than the national average of 0.101 ha. As a result, Guangxi has not been able to achieve self-sufficiency in grain production. Guangxi's grain output per capita, 318 kg, was about the same as the national average of 317 kg in the year 1978, when the whole country was struggling with food shortages. By year 2003, Guangxi's grain output per capita had declined further, to 302 kg, while the national average had increased to 333 kg.[18] As China has been producing a sufficient amount of grain since 1996, it is not necessary for Guangxi to achieve self-sufficiency in grain production. Indeed, in terms of agriculture, the province should specialize in the production of sugarcane and subtropical fruits to take advantage of its favourable climate.

Guangxi is rich in water resources. Annual rainfall in 2003 was 1,432 mm, which produced a large streamflow of 178 billion cu m. The most significant natural resource in Guangxi is water energy, with a theoretical endowment of 21.33 million kw.[19] It has been estimated that 17.52 million kw of this can be utilized. As many as 856 hydro-power stations, each with a capacity of more than 500 kw, can be constructed, with a total capacity of 15.62 million kw. They could then produce a total of 78.8 billion kwh of electricity annually. In the year 2003, about 22% of water energy was utilized. In that year, hydro-power stations generated 19.29 billion kwh of electricity,[20] accounting for 53.04% of the total amount of electricity generated in Guangxi. Of the total amount of energy consumed in Guangxi in 2003, 17.3% was provided by hydro-power stations.

One major project of the strategy to develop the western region is to develop water energy in Guangxi for transfer to developed areas such as

Guangdong. One section of the 1,050 km long Hongshui River 紅水河 is particularly rich in water energy, as the water level drops by 756.5 m. A project has been proposed to build a series of 10 hydro-power stations on the Hongshui River, with a total capacity of more than 11.05 million kw.[21] Five of these stations have been constructed since 1978. When it is completed, the Longtan hydro-power station 龍灘水電站 will be the second biggest hydro-power station in China after the Three-Georges 三峽 hydro-power station. The Longtan project is one of 10 strategic projects in the strategy of developing the western region. Its power generation capacity will be 4.2 million kw in phase one, for an annual production of 15.6 billion kwh of electricity.[22] The project involves an investment of RMB23.3 billion. The Longtan Hydro-power Development Ltd 龍灘水電開發有限公司 was formed with an initial capital of RMB4.86 billion contributed by the National Power Cooperation 國家電力公司 (33%), Guangxi Electric Power Ltd. 廣西電力有限公司 (32%), Guangxi Development and Investment Ltd. 廣西開發投資有限責任公司 (30%) and the Infrastructure Investment Cooperation of Guizhou Province 貴州省基本建設投資公司 (5%). The remaining capital came from a loan of RMB19.44 billion provided jointly by the National Development Bank 國家開發銀行, China Construction Bank 中國建設銀行, the Bank of China 中國銀行 and the Agricultural Bank of China 中國農業銀行. Carried out in a mountainous area, the project will submerge 5,613 ha of arable land and involve the resettlement of 80,500 people. Construction started in late 2001 and the river was closed on 6 November 2003 for the construction of a dam. It is expected that power will begin to be generated in 2007 and that the project will be fully completed by 2009. Over 50% of the electricity produced will be exported to Guangdong.

Guangxi is also rich in mineral resources, especially in non-ferrous metal resources. Guangxi ranks among the top 10 provincial regions in China in recoverable reserves of 52 kinds of minerals. It has the largest reserves in the country of 15 kinds of minerals such as tin ore. It is among the top six provinces in reserves of 27 kinds of minerals, such as aluminium. Some mineral resources, such as aluminium and tin, are highly concentrated in one site, up to 67.5% and 78% of reserves, respectively, facilitating large-scale exploitation. Guangxi is also endowed with the best and largest reserves of limestone, which is the main raw material for cement production.[23]

Clearly, a high proportion of minority nationalities, a coastal location, and a shared border with Vietnam give Guangxi tremendous geo-political advantages. Guangxi also has rich natural resources. If they can be fully utilized, urbanization and development will proceed rapidly. The next section will assess the province's economic foundation for development and cooperation in the context of Pan-PRD regionalization.

Economic Foundations for Development and Cooperation

Guangxi has long been considered an economically backward peripheral area of China.[24] The industrial foundations of the province were laid mainly during the period from the late 1960s to the early 1970s, when China implemented the "Third Front" policy. Although, as a coastal province, Guangxi has been allowed since 1984 to implement open policies to encourage investment and economic development, real progress in the carrying out of economic reforms, opening up and economic development took place only in the early 1990s. The adoption of the western region development strategy has also boosted Guangxi's economy in the twenty-first century. Over 1,200 enterprises enjoyed a total of RMB1.1 billion in tax concessions in the period 2001–2003, equivalent to 25% of the total profits tax collected by the government or 3.5% of the total local tax revenue of Guangxi.[25] Table 11.1 presents the per capita Gross Domestic Product (GDP) in Guangxi, Guangdong and China, for an overview of Guangxi's relative position in China.

In the period 1978–2003, per capita GDP in Guangxi increased from RMB225 to RMB5,969. Economic growth has improved the province's economic base and the living standards of its people. In the same period, average per capita GDP in China rose from RMB379 to RMB10,778, while the per capita GDP in Guangdong rose from RMB369 to RMB17,213. Per capita GDP in Guangxi lagged behind the average for China, while Guangdong's overtook the national average in 1980. Since then, Guangdong has become a leading province in economic development.

The relative per capita GDP of Guangxi is defined as its per capita GDP as a percentage of the per capita GDP of China or Guangdong. Using China's average GDP per capita as a benchmark, Guangxi's relative per capita GDP remained remarkably stable in the range of 55–68% over the period 1978–2003. This means that Guangxi remained a less-developed region during that whole period and its situation neither worsened nor improved significantly in that time. There were two short periods in the early 1980s and early 1990s, when relative per capita GDP increased due to rising prices for agricultural goods in the early years of the reforms and to the economic boom associated with the designation of Guangxi as the

Table 11.1   GDP per Capita in Guangxi, Guangdong and China, 1978–2003

Year	GDP per capita (RMB)			Guangxi's GDP per capita as a percentage of	
	Guangxi	Guangdong	China	China	Guangdong
1978	225	369	379	59.37	60.98
1980	278	480	460	60.43	57.92
1982	354	631	526	67.30	56.10
1985	471	1,025	855	55.09	45.95
1986	525	1,168	956	54.92	44.95
1989	927	2,307	1,512	61.31	40.18
1990	1,066	2,537	1,634	65.24	42.02
1992	1,490	3,815	2,287	65.15	39.06
1994	2,675	6,795	3,923	68.19	39.37
1995	3,304	8,495	4,854	68.07	38.89
2000	4,319	12,885	7,078	61.02	33.52
2003	5,969	17,213	10,778	55.38	34.68

Sources: NBS, *China Statistical Yearbook 2001* (see note 42), pp. 49 and 51; Statistical Bureau of Guangdong (ed.), *Guangdong Statistical Yearbook 2001* (Beijing: Zhongguo tongji chubanshe, 2001), p. 119; Guangxi Zhuangzu zizhiqu tongjiju (ed), *Guangxi tongji nianjian 2001* 廣西統計年鑒 2001 (*Guangxi Statistical Yearbook 2001*) (Beijing: Zhongguo tongji chubanshe, 2001), pp. 28 and 30; NBS, *China Statistical Yearbook 2004* (see note 7).

sea passage for Greater Southwest China in 1992. However, Guangxi's economic performance lagged behind the national average in the period 1994–2003, as its share of per capita GDP in the average per capita GDP in China declined from 68.19% to 55.38%. In the whole period, the gap in per capita GDP between Guangxi and Guangdong widened significantly as the economy of the latter took off.[26]

Although Guangxi's economic performance was not outstanding in comparison with other provinces such as Guangdong, its economic development was still significant in the early years of the twenty-first century. In the remainder of this section, Guangxi's economic performance in the period 2000–2003 will be examined. Table 11.2 presents the main economic indicators in Guangxi in 2000–2003.

Economic Growth

Based on constant prices, the GDP of Guangxi increased 9% annually in the period 2000–2003. In 2003, the province's GDP grew by 10.2%, to

Table 11.2 Main Economic Indicators in Guangxi, 2000-2003

Indicator	Value				Growth rate (%)			
	2000	2001	2002	2003	2000	2001	2002	2003
GDP (RMB billion)	205.01	223.12	245.54	273.51	4.95	8.83	10.05	11.39
GDP growth rate at comparable prices	na	na	na	na	7.3	8.2	10.5	10.2
GDP per capita (RMB)	4,319	4,668	5,099	5,969	4.12	8.08	9.23	17.06
Agricultural output (RMB billion)	82.90	87.29	91.65	103.09	-1.87	5.30	4.99	12.48
Industrial output (RMB billion)	180.02	190.31	203.66	235.42	7.97	5.72	7.01	15.59
Share of primary sector in GDP (%)	26.3	25.2	24.3	23.8	na	na	na	na
Share of secondary sector in GDP (%)	36.5	35.5	35.2	36.9	na	na	na	na
Share of tertiary sector in GDP (%)	37.2	39.3	40.5	39.3	na	na	na	na
Total fiscal revenue (RMB billion)	22.00	28.75	30.55	34.14	9.40	30.68	6.26	11.75
Investment in fixed assets (RMB billion)	66.00	73.13	83.50	98.73	6.42	10.80	14.18	18.24
Retail sales (RMB billion)	85.92	93.59	102.55	85.77	8.58	8.93	9.57	-16.36
Exports (US$ billion)	1.49	1.24	1.51	1.97	19.2	-16.78	21.77	30.46
Consumer price index (%)	99.7	100.6	99.1	101.1	na	na	na	na
Disposable income per urban resident (RMB)	5,834	6,666	7,315	7,785	3.83	14.26	9.74	6.43
Net income per rural resident (RMB)	1,865	1,944	2,013	2,095	-8.93	4.24	3.55	4.07

Sources: *Guangxi tongji nianjian 2001-2004* (see note 9).

RMB273.51 billion. That year, its GDP in the primary sector increased by 4.0% (reaching RMB65.23 billion), in the secondary sector by 14.6% (reaching RMB100.80 billion) and in the tertiary sector by 9.9% (reaching RMB107.49 billion). The contributions of the three sectors to economic growth were 10.02%, 51.30% and 38.68%, respectively. The secondary sector was the engine of economic growth. Clearly, Guangxi's is experiencing steady economic growth in the twenty-first century. In year 2004, there was further economic growth. The Guangxi government's objectives of achieving a GDP of over RMB300 billion, fiscal revenues of over RMB40 billion and net profits of over RMB10 billion for manufacturing enterprises of a designated scale for statistical purposes were realized in 2004. Some large and strong enterprises with an output value of over RMB0.1 billion have emerged in Guangxi. There were two enterprises with an output value of over RMB10 billion.

Changing Economic Structure and Pillar Industries

In 2003, the primary, secondary and tertiary sectors accounted for 23.8%, 36.9% and 39.3% of the province's GDP, respectively. Compared with the year 2000, the shares of the tertiary sector and the secondary sector increased by 2.1 and 0.4 percentage points, respectively, while the share of the primary sector declined by 2.5 percentage points (Table 11.2). The growth of the tertiary sector was noticeable. The traditional service industries, including commerce, transportation, tourism and restaurants, grew further, while new service industries, including the communications and real estate industries, developed rapidly.

Further improvements were seen in the province's industrial and agricultural structures. In the agricultural sector, outputs from the farming, animal husbandry and fishery sub-sectors all increased in 2003. The quantity and quality of the main agricultural products rose at the same time. The shares of the farming, animal husbandry and fishery sub-sectors in the total agricultural output were 48.6%, 33.3% and 11.2%, respectively, in 2003. The scale of agricultural production units expanded further. The development of township and village enterprises (TVEs) sped up.

The industrial value added reached RMB81.2 billion in 2003, an increase of 15% from the previous year. Manufacturing enterprises reaching designated scales for statistical purposes made a net profit of RMB66.4 billion in 2003, an increase of 86.52% from the previous year, representing the best performance in the history of the province. The net profit of domestic manufacturing firms increased from RMB21.69 billion in 2002 to RMB48.59 billion in 2003. The effective supply of various sub-industries was increased. Substantial progress was made in the development of new industries, such as aluminium manufacturing and the integrated processing of forestry-paper and pulp-paper in which Guangxi has comparative advantages. Various industries, including power generation, vehicle manufacturing, machinery, non-ferrous metals, sugar processing, instruments and food processing, were the major sources of manufacturing growth.

In Guangxi, the pillar industries of the economy include non-ferrous metals, machinery, vehicle manufacturing, building materials, food processing, medicine and power generation. Most of these will be examined briefly below.

Non-ferrous metals industry. Guangxi has established a large and comprehensive non-ferrous metals industry with a mining capacity of 7.32 million tonnes, an ore dressing capacity of 6.83 million tonnes, a smelting capacity of 0.77 million tonnes and a manufacturing capacity of 60,000 tonnes a year. Non-ferrous metals, especially tin, antimony and zinc, are also important staples for export. There are large enterprises, such as the Pingguo Aluminium Corporation 平果鋁業 and the Huaxi Group 華錫集團 in Liuzhou 柳州. The Pingguo Aluminium Corporation has a production capacity of 0.85 million tonnes of aluminium hydroxide and 0.13 million tonnes of electrolytic aluminium. Construction has started on phase one of the Guixi aluminium hydroxide factory 桂西氧化鋁廠, with production capacity of 1.60 million tonnes of aluminium hydroxide.

Machinery and vehicle manufacturing industry. The industry has a comparative advantage in the production of vehicles, engineering machinery and internal combustion engines for vehicles. The industry has the largest industrial output, and makes the largest profits and tax contributions in Guangxi. There are several strong enterprises in the industry that are well known within and outside of China. Their technology and management are relatively more advanced than their counterparts in China.

Building materials industry. This important industry has developed because of the high-quality and rich local resources. There are over 10 sub-industries in this industry. Products in this industry that are produced on the mainland include ordinary cement, special cement, flat glass, marble slabs, bathroom China, talc and gypsum. The production capacity of cement in Guangxi is close to 40 million tonnes, which is greater than the production capacity of other provinces in Southwest China and which ranks the province tenth in China. Cement products are among the high-quality products produced in Guangxi.

Food processing industry. This is the most diversified pillar industry in Guangxi given the rich raw materials available in the province. The industry comprises a comprehensive food processing system involving over 20 sub-industries such as the production of sugar, cigarettes, canned food, alcohol, soft drinks, salt and starch. Over 50% of China's sugar is produced in Guangxi. Cutting-edge technology is employed in the sugar industry. The cost of producing sugar in Guangxi is RMB100–200 per tonne lower than in other sugar production areas in China.[27]

Medicine industry. Guangxi is rich in medicinal resources. In varieties of medicinal resources, the province ranks second in the country. Some varieties can grow in Guangxi with both high yield and high quality. A relatively complete industrial system has formed after several decades of development. It consists of R&D, medicine manufacturing and commerce. Currently, Guangxi is an important production base of Chinese medicine. The industry has several strong enterprises such as Guilin *sanjin* 桂林三金, Yulin *zhiyao* 玉林製藥 and Liuzhou *huahong* 柳州花紅.

Capital Investment and Infrastructure Construction

Investment in fixed assets in Guangxi increased by over 10% annually in the period 2000–2003. In 2003, the growth rate was 18.24%, the largest during that period. Such investment (RMB14.80 billion) contributed to 52.9% of the GDP growth (RMB27.98 billion) that year according to GDP estimated using the expenditure approach. Along with an expansion in the scale of investment, the investment structure has also improved in recent years. In 2003, investment in manufacturing amounted to RMB30 billion, an increase of 37% from the previous year. Investment in infrastructure and production facilities, in technical updating and in real estate increased by 20.5%, 35.3% and 59.8%, respectively. As was the case elsewhere during the reform period, investment projects were mainly driven and financed by local units. Local investment accounted for 76.6% of the total investment in Guangxi in 2003.

Many major investment projects have been completed or have started construction. Phase two of the Pingguo Aluminium Corporation's facilities and the expressway section between Liujing 六景 and Xingye 興業 have been completed and are now operating. Construction has started in recent years on a number of large projects, including the Longtan hydro-power station, the Bose 百色 water complex project and phase one of the Guixi aluminium hydroxide factory. The Qinzhou 欽州 project for the integrated processing of forestry-paper and pulp-paper, and the Changzhou 長州 water complex project, have been initiated. Expanding investment is providing a sound foundation for continued economic growth in Guangxi.

Significant improvements have been made in the construction of infrastructure such as transportation and communication facilities. Since 1992, Guangxi has adopted a strategy of "constructing major transport routes to serve the great southwest." It aims to become a transport hub to link domestic and international markets and to facilitate economic cooperation between China and ASEAN. By 2003, railways in the province reached a total length of 3,400 km. In the same year, highways reached a length of 58,451 km, including 1,011 km of expressways, 482 km of first-class highways and 5,351 km of second-class highways.

There are currently three main seaports in Guangxi: Beihai 北海, Qinzhou and Fangchenggang 防城港. The history of Beihai dates back to 1876. It was one of 14 cities designated open coastal cities by the Chinese government in 1984. Its handling capacity has expanded since then, especially after 1992. In the period 1992–2003, capacity increased from 1.90 million tonnes to 5.30 million tonnes.[28] In the same period, the throughput of goods in Beihai increased from 1.31 million tonnes to 4.33 million tonnes. The construction of Fangchenggang only began in 1968, but the expansion has been dramatic since 1992. The port's handling capacity increased from 3.25 million tonnes to 16.04 million tonnes in the period 1992–2003.[29] The throughput of goods also increased from 2.20 million tonnes to 13.20 million tonnes. Fangchenggang is now the largest seaport in Guangxi.[30] Qinzhou was only a minor port in 1992, when it could only handle ships of 500 DWT (dead weight tons). The port has been expanded dramatically and can now handle ships of 30,000 DWT. Its total handling capacity was 3.52 million tonnes in 2003 and this will reach 11.58 million tonnes when all of the planned construction is completed.[31] Its goods throughput reached 2.63 million tonnes in 2003. Currently, the total throughput capacity of the three seaports is 25.86 million tonnes. The total goods throughput of river ports increased from 7.81 million tonnes to 20.05 million tonnes in the period 1990–2003.

Three big transport routes have formed. The first is the sea passage led by three seaports, and consists of a dense highway and railway network. The second is the sea passage along the "golden channel," the Xijiang, with supporting highways from Nanning 南寧, Laibin 來賓, Liuzhou, Guilin, and Guigang 貴港 to Wuzhou 梧州 to reach the PRD, Hong Kong and Macao. The third is the most convenient border passage from Pingxiang to Southeast Asia. Furthermore, there are two international airports in Nanning and Guilin that provide air services to major cities in China and various countries of ASEAN. Thus, a comprehensive transport system has been established in Guangxi consisting of seaports, railways, highways, a river channel and air aviation. Guangxi has become the transport hub and a convenient passage from inland areas of China, especially Southwest China to Guangdong, Hong Kong, Macao and ASEAN. It is also the most convenient international passage from various countries of ASEAN to inland areas of China.

Urban Development and Human Resources

Cities are symbolic of contemporary civilization and also the powerhouse of a modern economy. There has been rapid urban development in Guangxi in recent years. The level of urbanization increased from 15.10% in 1990 to 29.06% in 2003. Important urban areas include large and medium-sized cities, designated towns of county seats and some key designated towns. There are 14 prefecture-level cities. Nanning and Liuzhou are the largest and most powerful cities in Guangxi. Guilin is a well-known city in China and abroad. Wuzhou is well known in Guangdong, Hong Kong and Macao. Five new prefecture-level cities including Yulin 玉林, Guigang, Chongzuo 崇左, Laibin and Hezhou 賀州 have good development potential. Bose and Hechi 河池 are located in old revolutionary areas. They are enhancing their economic bases to increase their status in the region. Beihai, Qinzhou and Fangchenggang are coastal cities with the greatest potential for further development. These cities, which have their own characteristics, form the nodes (growth poles) in Guangxi's development network that are distributed evenly in space. The functioning of these cities, led by the regional capital of Nanning, ensures rapid and coordinated development in Guangxi.

To speed up economic development, various cities are making strenuous efforts to improve their infrastructure and enhance their urban function. Various "half-hour economic circles" are being formed. Central cities will play an important role in leading the economic development of their respective hinterland. The relations among the central city, and counties and towns in the hinterland will be enhanced.

More importantly, on the basis of close economic relations and cooperation among Nanning, Beihai, Qinzhou and Fangchenggang, a Nan-Bei-Qin-Fang urban cluster 南北欽防城市群 is emerging. These four cities are striving to make the urban cluster an important one in South China within a short time.

Technology and human resources are important in economic development. Guangxi has a good foundation in science, technology and human resources. There were 0.36 million professionals and technical experts in Guangxi. They have made notable achievements in scientific research and R&D. In 2003 alone, about 1,834 innovation projects were conducted. There were some 305 achievements in science and technology, including over 280 applied technical innovations and over 1,331 patents. A total of 748 contracts for technology transfers involving RMB418 million were signed in 2003.[32] The development of high technology and new technologies has sped up, and the number of firms in the industry reaching almost 400. In the high and new technology development zones of Guilin, Nanning, Liuzhou and Beihai, total revenues, total profits and taxes, and total exports reached RMB34.04 billion, RMB3.62 billion and US$0.188 billion, respectively, in 2003. The increase was 30.8%, 48.3% and 20.2%, respectively, in 2003 over the previous year. The total industrial output and the output value of high and new tech products increased by 32.5% and 29.2%, respectively, in 2003.[33]

There is stable development in education to train quality human resources. There were 45 institutes of higher education in Guangxi in 2003. Degree courses were offered in 14 of those institutes. Together, they admitted 82,537 students that year, an increase of 20.5% over the previous year. The total number of students enrolled in institutes of higher education reached 227,300, an increase of 22.0% over the previous year. Nine institutes were accredited to train postgraduate students. They admitted 2,643 postgraduates in 2003, an increase of 50.5% over the previous year. The total number of postgraduate students reached 5,774 in 2003.[34] Clearly, higher education and postgraduate training have been expanding rapidly in Guangxi. There is much room for educational cooperation between Guangxi and other developed regions in Pan-PRD region to enhance the quality of education. This, in turn, will boost economic development in Guangxi.

Rising Income of Urban and Rural Residents

The income level of residents reflects the outcome of economic development. The disposable income per urban resident in Guangxi increased by 33.44% in the period 2000–2003. It reached RMB7,785 in 2003. The income growth of rural residents was slower than that of urban residents. The net income per rural resident increased by 12.33% in the period 2000–2003 to RMB2,095 in 2003. Clearly, the incomes of both urban and rural residents have increased over time, although the gap between them has grown. For structural reasons, net income per rural resident was less than 30% of the disposable income per urban resident. The percentage of rural income relative to urban income declined from 31.97% in 2000 to 26.91% in 2003.

With incomes on the rise, the number of people living in poverty decreased from 8,000,000 in 1993 to 1,500,000 in 2000 and 960,000 in 2003.[35] Rural poverty improved, as the Engle index[36] of peasant households declined to 51.3% in 2003, down by 0.6% from 2002. Urban employment also improved. Urban employment increased by 175,000 persons. About 70,000 people who had previously lost their jobs due to economic restructuring were re-employed in 2003. As an indicator of consumption power, total retail sales in Guangxi reached RMB10.26 billion in 2002. They then declined to RMB8.58 billion in 2003, along with the slump in tourism that year.

Regional Cooperation: Previous Experience and Review

A less-developed autonomous region in China, Guangxi, as a recipient of development aid and assistance, has a long history of economic cooperation with other provinces in China. Domestic and international economic and technological exchanges and cooperation could help to introduce advanced technology, capital, talent and good management experience from China and elsewhere to Guangxi, facilitate the importation of raw materials and goods that are in short supply in Guangxi, help the province achieve an optimal and rational distribution of production capacities, and eventually stimulate economic development there. Regional cooperation would result in the joint effect of "one plus one is more than two" and help a weak and stand-alone province, prefecture, department, industry and firm to tap into the resources of larger economies. It will help the region to make full use of its resources and to convert these resource advantages to development advantages to promote regional economic development.

Overview of Regional and International Economic and Technological Cooperation

The government of the Guangxi autonomous region has promoted efforts to achieve regional and international economic and technological cooperation. Given the above understanding of the positive role of regional cooperation, government officials have long promoted regional cooperation. The regional and international efforts at economic and technological cooperation over the past 20 years can be divided into three stages.

In the first stage in the 1980s, regional cooperation started with various provinces in Southwest China. The cooperation was then extended to provinces in Central China, and Guangdong became an important partner. Later, Jiangsu 江蘇 was matched with Guangxi for regional cooperation. Regional cooperation between Jiangsu and Guangxi was formulated according to the model of paired assistance 對口支援, in which a developed province is paired with a less-developed one, in a move usually coordinated by the central government. Such a model has been successfully applied in other areas of China such as Tibet.[37]

In the second stage of development after 1992, various forms of domestic and international cooperation flourished when the central government made the decision in 1992 to construct a sea passage in Guangxi for Southwest China, as part of a bold strategy to revitalize economic reforms and the open policy in China. Both domestic and international cooperation were promoted. First, cooperation between Guangxi and various provinces in Southwest China was stepped up, with a focus on the construction of a sea passage for Southwest China. Second, international cooperation between Guangxi and countries in Southeast Asia was initiated, as areas along the border, the coast and the river were opened up as part of efforts to promote the further opening of China to the outside world. In this period, economic relations between Guangxi and other parts of China, especially Guangdong became closer than ever. Products from other parts of China were shipped to Guangxi, both for the domestic market and for export to Southeast Asian countries, notably Vietnam.[38]

In the third stage, since 2000, regional cooperation in Guangxi has been further stepped up, along with major initiatives such as the state's strategy of developing western China, the Pan-PRD cooperation arrangement and the proposed formation of ACFTA. Given its special location in the Pan-PRD region and ACFTA, Guangxi is expected to play an important role in regional and international cooperation in the coming years. Further details will be explored in the next section after a review of previous agreements and the results of regional cooperation.

Evolution of Regional Cooperation

Major projects and agreements will be outlined in this sub-section to illustrate the varieties and forms of regional cooperation. In April 1984, "The economic coordinating conference of four provinces/regions and five parties" was held in Guiyang 貴陽 by Guangxi, Sichuan, Yunnan, Guizhou, and Chongqing to form the Southwest Economic Cooperation Area at the national level. In March 1985, "The first joint conference on economic cooperation" was held in Guangzhou 廣州 by the five provinces/regions of Guangxi, Guangdong, Hubei 湖北, Hunan 湖南 and Henan 河南, and the two cities of Guangzhou and Wuhan 武漢 to form the Zhongnan 中南 Economic and Technological Cooperation Area at the national level. In June 1986, three provinces/regions jointly established the 10 Neighbouring Prefectures, States (*zhou* 州) and Cities Economic Cooperation Area in Guangxi, Yunnan and Guizhou.

In 1980, the State Council approved paired assistance between Guangxi and Jiangsu. "A roundtable on the paired assistance of Jiangsu to Guangxi" was held in 1986, which promoted paired assistance along with developing horizontal economic linkages. There is a long history of cooperation between Guangdong and Guangxi. In 1982, Guangxi and Guangzhou jointly launched the two designated tourist routes of Guilin-Wuzhou-Guangzhou and Guiping 桂平-Wuzhou-Guangzhou. In May 1986, the governments of Guangxi and Guangdong signed "The agreement to establish long and stable economic and technological cooperation" in Guangzhou. In 1990, representatives from Wuzhou city, Wuzhou prefecture and Yulin prefecture in Guangxi and the cities of Guangzhou and Zhaoqing 肇慶 in Guangdong met to establish the "Coordinating conference on the joint development of the economic corridor in the Xijiang river basin." In November 1990, "The second joint conference on economic and technological cooperation between Guangdong and Guangxi" was held in Nanning.

After the release of Deng Xiaoping's 鄧小平 speech during his tour to southern China in 1992, economic and technological cooperation between Guangxi and other provinces intensified. In 1992, delegations from Shenyang 瀋陽 and Heilongjiang 黑龍江 visited Guangxi, and a set of agreements were signed on the establishment of friendship cities and cooperation in joint projects. The Economic and Technological Cooperation Committee of Guangxi and the former Chinese General Company of Astronautics Industry 中國航天工業總公司 held their first meeting in Nanning in 1993. Some agreements for potential cooperation were signed during that meeting. In July 1996, the State Council formally designated the relationship of paired assistance between Guangdong and Guangxi. Under this scheme, Guangzhou city would help and support Bose, while Dongguan 東莞 city would help and support Hechi prefecture. Since 1992, Guangxi has also signed a series of cooperation agreements with Thailand, Singapore, Myanmar, Vietnam and Cambodia. Real progress has been made in cooperation with foreign countries through various forms and channels.

Regional cooperation was sped up early in the twenty-first century. In April 2001, the first joint conference of the cities of Nanning, Guiyang and Kunming 昆明 was held in Guiyang to discuss the establishment of the Nanning-Guiyang-Kunming Economic Region. An "agreement on enhancing economic and technological cooperation" was signed during the meeting. In November 2001, a working conference was held in Nanning by relevant ministries of the central government, the Guangxi, Yunnan and Guizhou provincial governments, and the Nanning, Guiyang and Kunming city governments. Regional cooperation between Guangxi and Guangdong was further enhanced. Various forums on cooperation were held and many agreements for cooperation were signed.

After the introduction of the Pan-PRD concept, Guangxi has been actively engaged in various seminars and cooperation forums. In June 2004, Guangxi signed the Agreement on Pan-PRD Regional Cooperation 泛珠三角區域合作協議 with other provincial regions and Hong Kong and Macao. In 2005, Guangxi held an investment promotion fair in Hong Kong. In 2004 and 2005, with the support of the central government and other provinces, the first and second China-ASEAN Expo was held successfully in Nanning. This marked the beginning of a new era of profound and wide regional and international cooperation for Guangxi.

Achievements of Previous Regional Cooperation Efforts

Regional cooperation between Guangxi and other areas has yielded substantial results. Friendly relationships of technological cooperation have been established with other cities and regions. For example, in the 1980s, Guilin and Guangzhou, Nanning and Maoming 茂名 in Guangdong established a friendly relationship for economic and technological cooperation. Nanning and Nanjing 南京; Liuzhou, Beihai and Wuxi 無錫; Guilin, Guilin prefecture and Suzhou 蘇州; Wuzhou, Wuzhou prefecture and Changzhou 常州; Liuzhou prefecture and Zhenjiang 鎮江; Yulin prefecture, Hechi prefecture and Yangzhou 揚州; Nanning prefecture, Bose prefecture and Nantong 南通 formed pairs for paired assistance. In the 1990s, Nanning and Fushun 撫順 in Liaoning 遼寧 became friendship cities. Guangzhou provided paired assistance to Bose prefecture in Guangxi, while Dongguan and the administrative departments of the Guangdong provincial government provided paired assistance to Hechi prefecture.

Many cooperation projects have been launched and much investment made. During the period from the early 1980s to 1992, Guangxi established relationships of cooperation with 25 provinces and cities. A total of 12,500 cooperation projects were completed, including over 7,500 projects of economic cooperation, over 4,600 projects of technological cooperation and 400 other projects. These projects attracted capital investments totalling RMB4.3 billion, including RMB2 billion from other provinces. About 1,000 cooperation projects were completed with provinces in Southwest China, attracting capital of RMB1.1 billion. Further cooperation has been achieved since 1992. In 2003, over 2,007 domestic cooperation projects were signed by Guangxi, involving a contracted capital of RMB52.21 billion from outside Guangxi. Some 1,782 cooperation projects were implemented and the inflow of actual capital reached RMB10.93 billion.[39]

The cooperation between Guangdong and Guangxi is outstanding. In 2003, the governments of Guangdong, Guangzhou and Dongguan, and others donated RMB61.43 million to Guangxi for poverty alleviation. In that year, 413 projects of economic and trade cooperation were implemented. Guangdong contributed RMB3.37 billion to these projects.[40] Top provincial leaders of Guangdong and Guangxi exchanged visits in 2004. They signed 100 cooperation projects in Nanning. Of the contracted capital of RMB48.631 billion, Guangdong would contribute RMB42.370 billion.

Some large cooperation projects have been constructed. Some examples are a coke factory with a capacity of 600,000 tonnes that is to be jointly constructed by Guangxi and Guizhou, the Nanning-Kunming railway, the Panxian 盤縣-Bose highway, the Changzhou hydro-power hub jointly developed by Guangdong and Guangxi, and the Longtan Hydro-power station. The Meiyan Group 梅雁集團 from Guangdong invested in the construction of the Honghua Hydo-power station 紅花水電站 in Liuzhou in 2003. The project involved a total investment of RMB1.76 billion.[41]

Due to the long-standing support and cooperation of Jiangsu, new production technology for a set of new or famous and high-quality products and a large amount of capital has been introduced. Traditional industries and firms have upgraded their technology, and the technical and management skills of their staff have improved. Various companies

have been able to manufacture products that are competitive in the
market.

Capital from various provinces such as Yunnan, Guizhou and Sichuan
has been introduced to construct berths for vessels up to 10,000 DWT,
50,000 DWT and 100,000 DWT, transfer storage facilities, logistics hubs,
and export bases along the coastal ports and the inland golden river channel.
The current strength of the coastal ports in Guangxi has much to do with
the cooperation and support that it has received from various provinces.

Guangxi was not a major destination for foreign/external investment
in Mainland China until recently. Actual foreign/external investment
declined from US$964 million in 1995 to US$576 million in 2001 due to
the impact of the Asian financial crisis in 1997.[42] It recovered to US$690
million in 2003. Hong Kong, Macao and Taiwan contributed 56.1% of the
actual foreign/external investment (Table 11.3). On 26 August 2005,
Guangxi held an investment promotion fair in Hong Kong. A total of 65
projects were signed involving an investment of US$1.454 billion. Some
46 were manufacturing projects. By the end of June 2005, Hong Kong had
invested in 5,694 enterprises in Guangxi, involving a total contracted
investment of US$8.06 billion.[43]

In Guangxi, the cities of Nanning, Wuzhou, Guilin and Liuzhou were
the main destinations of foreign/external investment. They received an actual
investment of US$89.03 million, US$75.60 million, US$63.54 million and
US$55.96 million, respectively, in 2003.[44]

By 2003, actual investment from ASEAN countries amounted to
US$125.35 million. Singapore was the largest investor from ASEAN.
Investors from Malaysia and Thailand have also invested in Guangxi.[45]
One example is the Xinhai Oil and Fat Industrial Ltd. 新海油脂工業有限公
司 in Fangchenggang owned by Singapore investors. It was established in
1993. It is the largest oil and fat company in Southwest China, involving a
total investment of US$22 million. Its factory occupies an area of 10 ha

**Table 11.3   Major Origins of Actual Foreign/External Investment in Guangxi in
2003 (US$ million)**

Area	Hong Kong	British Virgin Islands	U.S.A.	Singapore	Taiwan	Macao	Malaysia
Actual investment	209	66	35	33	24	23	10

Source: Guangxi nianjianshe, *Guangxi nianjian 2004* (see note 10), p. 215.

with a production capacity of 250,000 tonnes of vegetable oil.[46] Another example is Lida (Liuzhou) Chemicals Ltd. 利達 (柳州) 化工有限公司, also owned by Singapore investors. Its main product is sorbitol. It was established in 1993 and expanded in 2001 and 2003. Its production capacity reached 80,000 tonnes with a registered capital of US$16.67 million.[47]

On the other hand, Guangxi has also invested in ASEAN countries, establishing a textile factory in Thailand, a cigarette factory in Myanmar, and a premixed feed company in Vietnam. One major overseas project is by the Haining Group 海寧集團 in Cambodia, established by the Guangxi Beihai Corporation for Overseas Technoeconomic Cooperation in 1996. The Haining Group rented an area of 23,000 ha in Cambodia for agricultural development and food processing.[48] In 2003, there were nine outward investment projects in Cambodia involving a total investment of US$9.83 million, of which US$6.58 million had been contributed by Chinese investors.[49] These projects represent an initial attempt by Guangxi companies to invest overseas. Their economic performance, especially those involving state-owned enterprises, should be closely monitored to prevent large losses of state assets.

Overall, after many years of regional and international cooperation, Guangxi has accumulated useful experience and lessons on how to engage in such cooperation. They provide great insights on future regional cooperation in the Pan-PRD region.

Opportunities for Regional Cooperation in the Pan-PRD Region

In the past several decades, economic development in Guangxi has experienced ups and downs, and some good opportunities have been lost. Regional cooperation has made a positive contribution to economic development in Guangxi. Economic cooperation among six provinces and seven partners in Southwest China, the China-ASEAN free trade zone framework, and regional cooperation under the Pan-PRD concept, all provide excellent opportunities for Guangxi.

Total trade between China and ASEAN increased by 38.9% annually in 2002–2004. In 2004, it reached US$105.9 billion in 2004, and ASEAN had become China's fourth largest trading partner. Nanning was chosen to host the annual China-ASEAN Expo, the first of which was held on 3–6 November 2004. Over 18,000 businessmen, including about 4,000 businessmen from overseas, joined the event. It generated a total trading value of US$1.03 billion, including US$0.826 billion in exports. A total of

129 foreign investment projects with US$4.968 billion were signed, including outward investment of US$0.493 billion from China. A total of 102 domestic cooperation projects involving RMB47.54 billion were also signed. The second China-ASEAN Expo was held on 19–22 October 2005, attended by 20,000 businessmen.[50]

It would be in Guangxi's interest to make use of the above opportunities to enhance its economy through regional and international cooperation. The overall development objective is to make Guangxi a prosperous region with beautiful landscapes and a clean environment. Guangxi's regional cooperation should be based on the realities of the province and the national development strategy. Guangxi should implement the strategy of "expansion towards the east, cooperation with the west and development towards the south" for effective results in three directions. The focus will be on participation in Pan-PRD cooperation (including "expansion towards the east and cooperation with the west") and on enhancing cooperation with Guangdong and Hong Kong. Guangxi should make use of the strengths of Guangdong and Hong Kong to promote "development towards the south" (developing trade and cooperation with ASEAN).

Industrial Cooperation and Transfers

Unbalanced socioeconomic development is a commonplace phenomenon in the world. Some countries/regions have more advanced economic sectors than other countries/regions. For example, even the United States, the most advanced economy in the world, has various cities and regions with different economic strengths. Since 1932, when Franklin D. Roosevelt became president, the U.S. federal government has changed its policy on the development of the western part of the country. There has been much progress in industrial and urban development in the west. The approach of the federal government was to influence local governments and enterprises to invest in the region by providing guidance and incentives; government intervention was applied where necessary. The approach was effective in promoting the development of backward areas through the transfer of financial resources. It also resulted in better industrial locations. The American western region now has a strong manufacturing capacity.

It is clear that industrial cooperation and transfers are important to achieving balanced regional development. Industrial cooperation means the formation of a reasonable division of labour in various industries to avoid the duplication of similar industries in different regions. One way to achieve this is to transfer some uncompetitive industries in developed regions to less-developed regions. The "flying geese" model provides a sound theoretical basis for such a strategy of industrial cooperation and transfer.[51]

To participate in Pan-PRD regional cooperation and to enhance economic cooperation with Guangdong and Hong Kong, Guangxi should promote the linkages of industries and markets between Guangxi and Guangdong/Hong Kong to stimulate economic development. The comparative advantages and complementarity of resources and industries between Guangxi and Guangdong/Hong Kong mean that all regions will benefit through innovative forms and mechanisms of cooperation on an equal basis.

According to the principle of "the competitive advantage of nations" developed by Michael E. Porter, the following industries are identified as pillar industries of Guangxi that have some degree of competitiveness. They are the non-ferrous metals industry, the food processing industry, the medicine industry, the building materials industry, machinery, power generation and the vehicle manufacturing industry. All of these are traditional industries and need technological upgrading. On the other hand, most of these traditional industries have become sunset industries in Guangdong and Hong Kong, especially in the PRD region. They have lost their competitive advantage and should be transferred to other regions such as Guangxi. Thus, there is a perfect match between the shortage of capital, technology, and management in some regions and the availability of capital, technology, and management in Guangdong and Hong Kong. Industrial transfers would realize such a perfect match to explore the comparative advantages of both regions. Such opportunities for cooperation should not be missed by any region. The following are details of how to realize industrial cooperation and transfers for various industries.

Non-ferrous metal industry. The focus should be on extending the industrial chain by horizontal cooperation in aluminium pressing and processing. A large industrial group involving various departments, areas and ownership can be established in Guangxi with inputs of capital and technology from Guangdong and Hong Kong. The group would conduct R&D, production and trade, targeting markets in Guangdong, Guangxi and ASEAN.

Food processing industry. Guangxi could provide unused factory space and land while Guangdong and Hong Kong could provide advanced equipment and technology for the food processing industry. The management system of the industry could also be reformed. Another possibility is to relocate whole factories that are facing the problem of rising costs in Guangdong to Guangxi. Such factories include those that produce instant food, biscuits, white liquor, canned food and candied fruit. Capital and management could be introduced from Guangdong and Hong Kong to upgrade the sugar processing industry in Guangxi, to increase the level at which comprehensive use is made of raw materials. Guangxi, Guangdong and Hong Kong can also jointly establish a standardized food logistics system to explore the domestic and ASEAN markets. The system should include logistics firms, a wholesale market, redistribution centre and information network.

Medicine industry. The focus should be on cooperation in the planting and processing of Chinese medicine. Guangdong and Hong Kong can use their capital, R&D institutes and modern production equipment to cooperate with Guangxi to enhance R&D on Chinese medicine to develop new products. Guangdong and Hong Kong firms can also use their new technology and good management to introduce good management practices (GMPs) to large and medium-sized pharmaceutical firms in Guangxi to promote modernization and standardization and increase the scale of the production of Chinese medicine. Together, Guangxi, Guangdong and Hong Kong can promote integrated operations in the redistribution, wholesaling and retailing of Chinese medicine to explore the markets of ASEAN, Europe and America.

Building materials industry. The focus is on cooperation in rock materials and cement production. Investment from Guangdong and Hong Kong is welcomed for this sector. Investors from Guangdong and Hong Kong can engage in cooperation in various forms such as renting, contracting, or buying. It is expected that old cement production facilities will be replaced by advanced cement production lines to produce quality cement products. Large-scale development cooperation in the production of rock materials can be established by using capital and technology from Guangdong and Hong Kong. High-quality and super-thin rock products with special patterns and artistic effects can be produced. Attempts can be made to export such products to markets in ASEAN

Machinery industry. Guangxi has a strong heavy machinery industry. It should cooperate with firms in Guangdong and Hong Kong to compete in international markets. Guangxi may become an important manufacturing centre and export base for China's heavy machinery industry. The vertical division of labour in the general metal processing and machinery manufacturing industries can be enhanced. The general machinery industry in Guangxi can be upgraded with the help of Guangdong and Hong Kong firms in the areas of investment, stock holding, joint procurement, joint manufacturing and assembly contacts.

Vehicle manufacturing industry. The focus is to speed up cooperation in vehicle manufacturing. The vehicle manufacturing industries of Guangdong and Guangxi have their own characteristics and comparative advantages. Cooperation between them would be like one strong partner working with another strong partner. Hong Kong has abundant capital and advantages in international trade. Hong Kong's participation in the vehicle manufacturing industries can expand Guangxi's development opportunities in this area. One important objective is to achieve cooperation in the integration of R&D, production and trade to enhance product quality and the competitiveness of the whole vehicle manufacturing industry of Guangxi in the international market.

Integrated processing of forestry-paper and pulp-paper. Guangxi can learn much from Guangdong on how to stimulate the development of the forestry industry by recognizing property rights in forestry. Guangxi can also make use of investment from Guangdong and Hong Kong. Further marketization should be introduced in the forestry industry to diversify ownership and investors. The construction of an economic base for the integrated processing of forestry-paper and pulp-paper in Guangxi should be speeded up to make the industry a leading one in China and ASEAN.

In addition to above key industries, there are also many opportunities for cooperation the in petroleum, chemical, rubber, electronics and power generation industries for Guangxi, Guangdong and Hong Kong. There is also great potential in cooperation in tourism and modern agriculture.

Conclusion

This chapter has examined the regional advantages, economic foundation and regional cooperation in Guangxi in the context of Pan-PRD regional cooperation and development. A high proportion of minority nationalities, a coastal location and a shared border with Vietnam have given Guangxi tremendous geo-political advantages. Guangxi also has rich natural resources, especially mineral and water energy resources.

However, Guangxi has long been a backward peripheral region of China. In the period 1978–2003, the province's per capita GDP increased from RMB225 to RMB5,969, but remained below the average for China.

Foreign investment and exports were still small. The province's economic development was still significant in the early years of the twenty-first century. GDP in Guangxi increased by 9% per year based on constant prices in the period 2000–2003. In Guangxi, the pillar industries of the economy include the non-ferrous metals, machinery, vehicle manufacturing, building materials, food processing, medicine and power generation industries.

Guangxi, as a recipient of development aid and assistance, has a long history of economic cooperation with other provinces in China. After 2000, regional cooperation in Guangxi was further stepped up along with major initiatives, such as the national strategy of developing western China, Pan-PRD cooperation and the future formation of ACFTA. After the introduction of the Pan-PRD framework, Guangxi has been actively engaged in various seminars and cooperation forums. In 2005, Guangxi held an investment promotion fair in Hong Kong. In 2004 and 2005, the first and second ASEAN-China Expo was held successfully in Nanning. This marked the beginning of a new era of profound and wide regional and international cooperation for Guangxi. Both domestic and foreign investment in Guangxi has grown. Under an emerging market economy in China, private and foreign investment has become more important in the economic development of the province.

To participate in Pan-PRD regional cooperation and to enhance economic cooperation with Guangdong and Hong Kong, Guangxi should promote linkages of industries and markets between Guangxi and Guangdong/Hong Kong to stimulate economic development. The comparative advantages and complementarity of resources and industries between Guangxi and Guangdong/Hong Kong mean that all regions will benefit from cooperation.

It is argued that cooperation is only a way to achieve regional economic development. Most regions still compete against each other for their own interest. In a market economy, competition is the cornerstone for enterprises and, to some extent, for cities and regions. Cooperation is for enhancing the competitiveness of the region as a whole. Thus, mutual respect, equal treatment, mutual benefit and mutual trust are the foundation for successful cooperation in the Pan-PRD region.

Notes

1. Guangxi Tong 僮 Autonomous Region was established on 3 March 1958 to replace the previous Guangxi. In 1965, it was renamed the Guangxi

Zhuang 壯 Autonomus Region. Its border with Guangdong was also finalized in 1965. See Xiao Yongzi 肖永孜 (ed.), *Zhongguo xibu gailan: Guangxi* 中國西部概覽：廣西 (Introduction to the Western Region of China: Guangxi) (Beijing 北京: Minzu chubanshe 民族出版社, 2000), pp. 8–9.

2. Y. Huang and J. Shen, "Guangxi," in *Developing China's West: A Critical Path to Balanced National Development*, edited by Y. M. Yeung and Jianfa Shen (Hong Kong: The Chinese University Press, 2004), pp. 463–502.

3. See Hans Hendrischke, "Guangxi: Towards Southwest China and Southeast Asia," in *China's Provinces in Reform: Class, Community and Political Culture*, edited by David S. G. Goodman (London: Routledge, 1997), pp. 21–47; Womack Brantly, "Sino-Vietnamese Border Trade: The Edge of Normalization," *Asian Survey*, Vol. 34, No. 6 (1994), pp. 513–28.

4. S. Ye, "Guangxi Cities: New Strategies for In-between Regions," in *Chinese Urban Reform: What Model Now?*, edited by R. Y. Kwok, W. Parish, A. G. Yeh and X. Xu (New York: M. E. Sharpe, 1990), pp. 213–29.

5. See note 2.

6. In addition to various other sources, some materials and observations were obtained for this study during two field trips to Guangxi, in 15–25 May 2001 and 11–19 May 2005, with the help of two professors in the Department of Environment and Urban Sciences of the Teachers' College of Guangxi, Nanning.

7. Department of Comprehensive Statistics of the National Bureau of Statistics (NBS), *Comprehensive Statistical Data and Materials on 50 Years of New China* (Beijing: Zhongguo tongji chubanshe 中國統計出版社, 1999), p. 112; Guojia tongjiju renkou he shehui keji tongjisi 國家統計局人口和社會科技統計司 (ed.), *Zhongguo renkou tongji nianjian 2001* 中國人口統計年鑑2001 (China Population Statistics Yearbook 2001) (Beijing: Zhongguo tongji chubanshe, 2001), p. 53; NBS, *China Statistical Yearbook 2004*, http://www. stats.gov.cn/english/statisticaldata/yearlydata/yb2004-e/indexeh.htm, accessed on 18 July 2005.

8. Guowuyuan renkou pucha bangongshi 國務院人口普查辦公室 and Guojia tongjiju renkou he shehui keji tongjisi, *Zhongguo 2000 nian renkou pucha ziliao shangce* 中國2000年人口普查資料上冊 (Tabulations on the 2000 Population Census of the People's Republic of China, Vol. 1) (Beijing: Zhongguo tongji chubanshe, 2002), pp. 593–602.

9. For a detailed history of the minority population, see Xiao, *Zhongguo xibu gailan: Guangxi* (see note 1), pp. 194–213. Data in this chapter, unless specified, are drawn from the Guangxi Zhuangzu zizhiqu tongjiju 廣西壯族自治區統計局 (ed.), *Guangxi tongji nianjian 2004* 廣西統計年鑑 2004 (Guangxi Statistical Yearbook 2004) (Beijing: Zhongguo tongji chubanshe, 2004).

10. Guangxi nianjianshe 廣西年鑑社, *Guangxi nianjian 2004* 廣西年鑑 2004 (Guangxi Yearbook 2004) (Nanning: Guangxi nianjianshe, 2004).

11. Xiao, *Zhongguo xibu gailan: Guangxi* (see note 1), p. 208.

12. See note 2.

13. Guangxi nianjianshe, *Guangxi nianjian 2004* (see note 10), p. 212.

14. Brantly, "Sino-Vietnamese Border Trade: The Edge of Normalization" (see note 3); Huang and Shen, "Guangxi" (see note 2).

15. Guangxi nianjianshe, *Guangxi nianjian 2004* (see note 10), pp. 216–17.

16. Sites other than Guilin are also very attractive. Field observations, 15–25 May 2001 and 11–19 May 2005.

17. See note 10.

18. Arable land and grain output per capita have been calculated by the author based on data from the NBS, *2004 China Statistical Yearbook* (see note 7).

19. Xiao, *Zhongguo xibu gailan: Guangxi* (see note 1), pp. 17–18.

20. Guangxi nianjianshe, *Guangxi nianjian 2004* (see note 10), p. 296.

21. Xiao, *Zhongguo xibu gailan: Guangxi* (see note 1), pp. 70–73.

22. For information on the project, see http://www.gx.xinhua.org/jdda/longtan/sdzh/jjyy102.htm, accessed on 13 August 2005.

23. Xiao, *Zhongguo xibu gailan: Guangxi* (see note 1), pp. 18–20.

24. Hendrischke, "Guangxi" (see note 3).

25. Guangxi nianjianshe, *Guangxi nianjian 2004* (see note 10), p. 211.

26. See Y. M. Yeung and D. K. Y. Chu (eds.), *Guangdong: Survey of a Province Undergoing Rapid Change* (Hong Kong: The Chinese University Press, 1998); J. Shen, "Urban and Regional Development in Post-Reform China: The Case of Zhujiang Delta," *Progress in Planning*, Vol. 57, No. 2 (2002), pp. 91–140.

27. *Wen Wei Po* 文匯報, 24 August 2005.

28. Guangxi nianjianshe, *Guangxi nianjian 2004* (see note 10), p. 506.

29. Ibid., p. 570.

30. Its port facility was very impressive (field observation, 15–25 May 2001).

31. Guangxi nianjianshe, *Guangxi nianjian 2004* (see note 10), p. 573.

32. Ibid., pp. 409–15 and 661.

33. Ibid., p. 219.

34. Ibid., p. 427.

35. Ibid., p. 211.

36. The Engle index refers to the share of food expenditure in the total household income.

37. Ng Wing-fai 吳永輝 and Zhou Yixing 周一星, "Tibet," in Yeung and Shen, *Developing China's West* (see note 2), pp. 549–79.

38. For details, see note 2.

39. Guangxi nianjianshe, *Guangxi nianjian 2004* (see note 10), p. 212.

40. Ibid., pp. 210 and 215.

41. Ibid., p. 212.

42. Similarly, foreign direct investment in China also declined from US$91.28

billion in 1995 to a low of US$41.22 billion in 1999; see NBS, *China Statistical Yearbook 2001* (Beijing: Zhongguo tongji chubanshe, 2001), p. 602.

43. *Ming Pao* 明報, 27 August 2005.

44. Guangxi nianjianshe, *Guangxi nianjian 2004* (see note 10), p. 215.

45. Ibid.

46. See Fangchengang shi shangwuju 防城港市商務局 (Bureau of Commerce, Fangchenggang city), Fangchengang xinhai youzhi gongye youxian gongsi 防城港新海油脂工業有限公司 (Xinhai Oil and Fat Industrial Ltd. in Fangchenggang), http://fangchenggang.mofcom.gov.cn/aarticle/gqfb/200507/20050700156123.html, accessed on 2 September 2005.

47. Lida (Liuzhou) huagong youxian gongsi 利達 (柳州) 化工有限公司 (Lida (Liuzhou) Chemicals Ltd), http://www.investchina.com.cn/market/qiye/my/417873.htm, accessed on 2 September 2005.

48. Guangxi Beihai haiwai jingji jishu hezuo gongsi 廣西北海海外經濟技術合作公司 (Guangxi Beihai Corporation for Overseas Technical and Economic Cooperation), http://www.beihai.gov.cn/qybl/gbcot/gbcot.htm, accessed on 2 September 2005.

49. Guangxi nianjianshe, *Guangxi nianjian 2004* (see note 10), p. 218.

50. Shangwubu: Zhongguo—Dongmeng bolanhui zhuyao you si tedian 商務部：中國—東盟博覽會主要有四特點 (Ministry of Commerce: The China-ASEAN Expo has Four Main Characteristics), http://www.caexpo.org/gb/news/hotnews/t20050915_49843.html; Zhongguo Dongmeng bolanhui xian juda shangji 中國東盟博覽會顯巨大商機 (The China-ASEAN Expo Reveals Great Business Opportunities), http://www.caexpo.org/gb/news/caexponews/t20041109_18524.html; Zhongguo-Dongmeng bolanhui chengguo fengshuo: touzi Dongmeng zhengshi shihou 中國—東盟博覽會成果豐碩：投資東盟正是時候 (The Great Success of the China-ASEAN Expo; It Is the Right Time to Invest in ASEAN), http://www.caexpo.org/gb/news/caexponews/t20041109_18488.html; Dierjie Zhongguo-Dongmeng bolanhui zhanwei luoshi keshang yu liangwan ren 第二屆中國—東盟博覽會展位落實客商逾兩萬人 (Over 20,000 Businessmen Have Taken Booths in the Second China-ASEAN Expo), http://www.caexpo.org/gb/news/hotnews/t20050920_50130.html, accessed on 25 September 2005.

51. K. Kojima, "The 'Flying Geese' Model of Asian Economic Development: Origin, Theoretical Extensions, and Regional Policy Implications," *Journal of Asian Economics*, Vol. 11 (2000), pp. 375–401.

12

Yunnan

Yang Xianming and Ng Wing-fai

Introduction

Yunnan 雲南 is an inland province situated on the Yun-Gui (Yunnan-Guizhou) Plateau 雲貴高原 in the southwest of China. It shares a border with several countries and is China's gateway to Southeast Asia and South Asia. Westward, along the Dian-Mian (Yunnan-Myanmar) Highway 滇緬公路, the Zhong-Yin (China-India) Highway 中印公路 and the railway from Kunming 昆明 to Dali 大理, both Bangladesh and India can be reached. Along the Lancang River 瀾滄江 and the Mekong River, and the highway from Kunming to Daluo 打洛, and from Xishuangbanna 西雙版納 Airport, there is a passage to Laos, Myanmar and Thailand, ending in Malaysia and Singapore. Eastward, Vietnam is accessible via the Dian-Yue (Yunnan-Vietnam) Railway 滇越鐵路 and Kun-He (Kunming-Hanoi) Highway 昆河鐵路 (Figure 12.1).

Due to its geo-political significance, Yunnan is an important factor in the economic cooperation of the Greater Mekong Sub-region (GMS) involving six countries, namely Cambodia, Laos, Myanmar, Thailand, Vietnam and China (Yunnan). Furthermore, the GMS can be connected to the Pan–Pearl River Delta (Pan-PRD) 泛珠江三角洲 region via Yunnan by developing regional trade through speeding up exchanges in capital, technology and manpower. Not only can transportation and communication costs be reduced due to geographical proximity, but the GMS and Pan-PRD region can also complement each other with respect to the importation of resources and industrial output. By sharing a common market, Yunnan is bound to have a great impact on the Association of Southeast Asian Nations (ASEAN)-China Free Trade Area (ACFTA) 中國與東盟自由貿易區 as well.

By analyzing Yunnan's comparative advantages with regard to resource endowment and location, the aim in this chapter is to highlight Yunnan's unique position in its potential to foster economic cooperation between the GMS and the Pan-PRD region. The conclusion here is that, in order to enhance Yunnan's significance in sub-regional economic cooperation, there should be more conscious efforts to narrow the gap in regional capabilities and to promote regional trade, so as not to rely on the exploitation of natural resources as a prime tool in activating economic cooperation.

Resources and Comparative Advantages

Natural Resources

Commonly known as "the water tower of Asia," Yunnan has the most

Figure 12.1 Yunnan in Its Geographical Setting

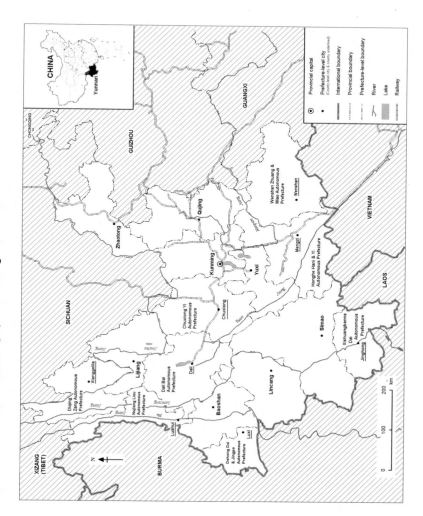

important hydropower reserves in Southeast Asia. The province's total proven hydropower reserves amount to 103.64 million kw. Under the West-East Power Transmission Project 西電東輸, Yunnan started to transmit power to Guangdong 廣東 in 1993. By the end of 2004, 7 billion kw hours of electricity had been transmitted. During the duration of the Eleventh Five-year Plan (FYP), the aim is to transmit 110 billion kw hours of power, averaging 22 billion kw hours per annum. It is expected that, with the completion of the Guangdong project, electricity will be transmitted to Hong Kong 香港, Macao 澳門 and Fujian 福建.

Moreover, under the Yunnan-Foreign Countries Power Transmission Project 雲電外送, Yunnan has already been transmitting electricity to Vietnam, Laos and Myanmar, to the tune of a total of 400 million kw hours of electricity by the end of 2005. Furthermore, with the completion of the Jinghong Power Station 景洪電站, which is a joint venture between Yunnan and Thailand, 3 million kw and 1 million kw will be transmitted annually to Thailand and Vietnam, respectively. By 2020, with a power capacity of 80 million kw, Yunnan will continue to send power to Southeast Asian countries.

Mineral Resources

Yunnan is rich in mineral resources, with some 142 kinds of minerals found in the province. For example, Yunnan has the country's largest reserves of plumbum, zincum, chromium, and thallium; and its second-largest reserves of titanium, stannum, nickel, and germanium. As the nation's most important non-ferrous metal mines such as plumbum and zincum are found in Yunnan, the province has also been dubbed the "kingdom of non-ferrous metals" and a "major producer of phosphorous chemicals."

Biological Resources

Yunnan is remarkably rich in biological resources and diversity. As of the end of 2004, natural forest coverage in the province was 52%, 12.17 million ha of which consisted of community forests and 12 million ha of commodity forests. Some 6,500 kinds of medicinal plants, 200 kinds of wild oil seeds and 2,100 kinds of wild flowers have thus far been identified. There are also numerous species of wild animals, among which are 1,671 kinds of amniotes. Fifty percent of the wild animals in the province are endangered species. Yunnan has long been a supplier of timber, herbal medicine, powder and resinous materials to the Pan-PRD region.

Tourist Resources

Due to its particular geographical and climatic conditions and socio-historical development, Yunnan is remarkably rich in tourist resources. With its mild weather and numerous scenic spots, Kunming, the provincial capital, is known as the "spring city." There are now 10 national tourist districts, 1 national tourist park, 48 provincial tourist districts and 6 provincial tourist parks in the province, in addition to five national and three provincial historical cities. With rich natural and human resources and strategic access to Southeast Asia, Yunnan is bound to become a significant tourist destination.

Ethnic Culture

In 2004, Yunnan had a population of 44.15 million, with an annual growth rate of 0.9%. Ethnic minorities make up one-third of the culturally diverse population. Yunnan has also been influenced by Chinese, Indian and Southeast Asian cultures, adding to the cultural richness of the province.

Location

Yunnan shares a border of over 4,000 km with three ASEAN countries: Vietnam, Laos and Myanmar. The province has about 20 Grade 1 and Grade 2 permanent ports. With the formation of ACFTA, Yunnan will be further opened to ASEAN countries through exchanges in capital, information and commodities. Since Yunnan is the only province in China that is accessible by land to Southeast Asia and South Asia, it plays a strategic position in connecting the markets of the Pan-PRD region, Southeast Asia and South Asia. Yunnan is also contiguous with Bangladesh and India, providing those countries with a land passageway to China. In 1999, China, India, Myanmar and Bangladesh signed the "Kunming Declaration," aimed at fostering closer economic cooperation in the region.

In connecting China with Southeast Asia and South Asia, Yunnan provides an international passageway for China's eastern and central provinces to export their products to neighbouring countries and to import natural resources, such as petroleum, mineral ore, timber, and so forth. This will also provide a chance for those provinces to develop their secondary and tertiary industries.

Pillar Industries

Tobacco Industry

China is the biggest producer of tobacco in Asia and in the world. Yunnan's output of tobacco and the province's tax revenues from the product account for 25% of the national total and is an important part of the national economy. After nearly 20 years of development, Yunnan's tobacco industry has been transformed from a capital-intensive to a knowledge-based industry. With reforms in production and distribution, the competitive advantage of China's tobacco industry will be further improved, leading to a bigger market share for Yunnan's tobacco industry in the Pan-PRD region.

Tourist Industry

Yunnan is playing a leading role in fostering tourism into a pillar industry, and the province is now a well-known destination for overseas and domestic tourists. In 2004, 1 million overseas and 51.68 million domestic tourists visited Yunnan, generating revenues of US$340 million and RMB30.66 billion. Tourism made up 10.3% of the province's GDP, ranking Yunnan seventh nationally in tourism revenues as a percentage of provincial GDP. The Pan-PRD region has been a major source of tourists to Yunnan and vice versa. With closer cooperation in tourism, it is expected that still more tourist routes will be opened.

Floral Industry

Supported by its rich biological resources, Yunnan's floral industry has attained a certain economy of scale. In 2004, 13,600 ha of land was devoted to the floral industry, producing 3,600 million fresh flowers and accounting for 50% of the domestic market. About 80% of the flowers were sold to 70 mainland Chinese cities, and about 10% were exported to Japan, Thailand, Singapore, Korea, Taiwan and Hong Kong. Due to its favourable climate and relatively low cost of production, Yunnan has a comparative advantage in the floral industry. Moreover, Yunnan possesses numerous species of wild flower resources. Both Guangdong and Hong Kong are major consumers and importers of Yunnan's flowers and closer cooperation between Yunnan and these places can be expected.

Non-ferrous Metal Industry

In the mining industry, Yunnan has a national comparative advantage in non-ferrous metals and phosphorus chemicals. Since 1949, a huge amount of capital has been invested in the exploration and research of non-ferrous metals, ferrous metals and non-metals. At present, Yunnan possesses a mineral industry with sizable plants and comprehensive composition. In 2003, there were 80 plants in Yunnan's mining industry, and the gross industrial output of these plants was RMB51.5 billion. In 2004, the province's output of 10 kinds of non-ferrous metals was 1.25 million tonnes, accounting for 8.7% of the national total, although only one-third of it was processed within the province. The production of yellow phosphorus was 329,900 tonnes, accounting for 50% of the national total. The Pan-PRD region is a major destination for Yunnan's mineral output and is also located on its export route.

Relationship between Yunnan, the Pan-PRD Region and ASEAN Countries

Geographically, Yunnan is contiguous with three ASEAN countries. A more convenient trade route over land, instead of one that circumscribes the Malacca Strait, can be formed between China's southwest and mid-west and the ASEAN countries, shortening the current distance by 1,000 km to 1,500 km. Moreover, the cultural affinities among Yunnan, Southeast Asia and South Asia are an advantage in achieving economic cooperation. Yunnan can make use of these factors to win itself a competitive advantage in cooperation between the Pan-PRD region and ASEAN countries.

Comparison of the Capability Structures of Yunnan and the Pan-PRD Region

There are five elements to take into consideration when defining the capability of a particular region: the allocation of resources, sectoral structure, technological development, trade development and economic openness.[1] The results of the calculation of these elements for the members of the Pan-PRD grouping are listed in Table 12.1.

Resources allocation capability refers to the levels of economic development, investment and expenditure, government fiscal situation, degree of marketization and allocation efficiency of a particular region.[2]

Table 12.1 Comparison of Capability Structures within the Pan-PRD Grouping

Regions	Resources allocation index	Sectoral structure index	Technological development index	Trade development index	Economic openness index
Guangdong	1	0.5538	1	1	1
Fujian	0.2954	0.4779	0.6652	0.1899	0.3105
Guangxi	0.1944	0.1805	0.5650	0.0672	0.0455
Hainan	0.0181	0.2276	0.2271	0.0839	0.1870
Jiangxi	0.1687	0.2974	0.4883	0.0798	0.0310
Hunan	0.3194	0.2259	0.7028	0.1187	0.0216
Sichuan	0.3631	0.2092	0.7523	0.1411	0.0179
Guizhou	0.1015	0.0744	0.3132	0.0004	0.0015
Yunnan	0.1978	0.0004	0.5325	0.0336	0.0231
National average	0.30	0.34	0.64	0.19	0.18

Source: *Statistical Yearbook of China, 2003.*

According to Table 12.1, there are three tiers of resources allocation capability in the Pan-PRD region. In the first tier is Guangdong, whose capability factor is far above the national average of 0.3. Included in the second tier are Sichuan 四川, Hunan 湖南, Fujian, Yunnan, Guangxi 廣西, Jiangxi 江西 and Guizhou 貴州, whose capability factors are about the national average. Falling under the third tier is Hainan, whose capability factor is far below the national average. The discrepancies in resources allocation capability among the members of the Pan-PRD grouping are mainly due to the size of economy and the degree of marketization of particular regions. Since the market mechanism plays a major role in the allocation of resources in Guangdong, the substitution effects of technology, capital and manpower are more effective. As a result, the capability structure can be improved, leading to the faster agglomeration of production factors.[3]

Sectoral structure capability refers to the sectoral structure, labour structure, ownership structure (including the level of private ownership of enterprises) and level of industrialization of a particular region. As Table 12.1 shows, there are three tiers of sectoral structure. Occupying the first tier are Guangdong and Fujian, whose capability factors are far above the national average of 0.34. In the second tier are Sichuan, Hunan, Jiangxi, Hainan and Guangxi, whose capability factors are slightly below the national average. Among the third tier are Guizhou and Yunnan, whose capability factors are far below the national average. With regard to the share of the

GDP occupied by the secondary and tertiary industries, the figures are 83.39%, 90.6% and 84.7% for the whole nation, Guangdong and Fujian, respectively. The figure for Yunnan is far below the national average, indicating a sectoral structure that will be more difficult to transform than that of many of the other members of the Pan-PRD grouping.

Technological development capability refers to the technological innovations (including the application and transformation of technology through foreign direct investment (FDI)) and technological transformation of a particular region. Again, Table 12.1 indicates the existence of three tiers of technological development in the country. In the first tier is Guangdong, whose capability factor is again the highest. Sichuan, Hunan, Fujian, Guangxi, Yunnan and Jiangxi are in the second tier, with capability factors at about the national average of 0.64. Guizhou and Hainan fall into the third tier, with capability factors far below the national average.

Trade development capability refers to international, domestic and regional trade. As seen in Table 12.1, there are three tiers of trade development. In the first tier is Guangdong, whose capability factor is once again the highest among the members of the Pan-PRD grouping. Fujian, Sichuan and Hunan are in the second tier, with capability factors at about the national average of 0.19. Hainan, Jiangxi, Guangxi, Yunnan and Guizhou occupy the third tier, with capability factors far below the national average. The scale of a province's trade and the composition of its exports are the major reasons accounting for discrepancies among them. The scale of Guangdong's trade and the share comprised by mechanical, electrical and hi-tech products in its output have significantly enhanced that province's capability in trade development.

Economic openness capability refers to foreign direct investment and international trade. Table 12.1 again shows three tiers of economic openness. Once again, Guangdong, whose capability factor is the highest, occupies the first tier. In the second tier are Fujian and Hainan, whose capability factors are slightly above the national average of 0.18. Guangxi, Jiangxi, Yunnan, Hunan, Sichuan and Guizhou are in the third tier, with capability factors far below the national average. In 2003, Guangdong's degree of openness was judged to be 70.1%, a figure far higher than the national average of 13.8%. In addition, Guangdong's degree of openness to international trade was assessed at 174.4%, far above the national average of 73.7%. Its degree of openness to FDI was 18.3%, compared to the national average of 3.7%.

As a whole, Guangdong's capability structure is outstanding. With the exception of its sectoral structure index, which lags behind Beijing 北京, Shanghai 上海, Tianjin 天津 and Zhejiang 浙江, its capability index in the allocation of resources, technological development, trade development and economic openness ranks first in the nation. Therefore, it is natural to find Guangdong placing itself at the centre in the formation of any plans for regional economic cooperation.

In the Pan-PRD region, where there are great discrepancies in capability structure among the provinces, Yunnan's capability structure is relatively low. The province ranks fifth in the region in the allocation of resources, ninth in sectoral structure, sixth in technological development, eighth in trade development and sixth in economic openness. However, Yunnan is comparatively well endowed in natural resources. The natural resources index for individual provinces in the Pan-PRD can be calculated in the range of 0–1 for hydropower capacity, coal reserves and mineral reserves (including minerals that have a significant impact on economic development, such as iron, manganese, copper, zinc, aluminum, tin, nickel, gold, phosphorus and so forth).

According to the indices in Table 12.2, in the Pan-PRD region the figures for a province's endowment of natural resources and the status of its capability structure are basically opposite to each other (Figure 12.2). While capability structure is changeable, a province's endowment of natural resources will decrease in the long term. Generally, there are two possibilities for economic cooperation in the Pan-PRD region. First, the existing model

Table 12.2   Natural Resources Index within the Pan-PRD Grouping

	Water resources index	Coal reserve index	Coal resources index	Natural resources total index	Capability structure total index
Guangdong	0.0573	0.0999	0.1569	0.1047	0.9108
Fujian	0.0727	0.1214	0.0196	0.0712	0.3878
Hainan	0.0511	0.1301	0.1176	0.0996	0.1487
Guangxi	0.1218	0.0002	0.1961	0.1060	0.2105
Jiangxi	0.0474	0.2533	0.4902	0.2636	0.2130
Hunan	0.1065	0.6222	0.3137	0.3475	0.2777
Sichuan	1.0000	1.0000	0.5294	0.8431	0.2967
Guizhou	0.1303	0.6382	0.5294	0.4326	0.0982
Yunnan	0.7204	0.3192	1.0000	0.6799	0.1575

Source: Websites of Provincial Governments and China Natural Resources Data (www.data.ac.cn).

Figure 12.2 General Index of Capability Structure and Natural Resources of the Pan-PRD Provinces

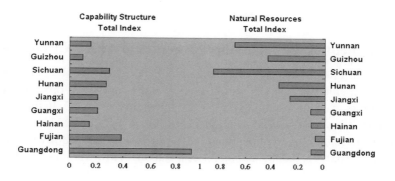

of regional economic cooperation can be maintained by placing the emphasis on the endowment of natural resources of the various provinces, but neglecting differences in their capability structures. As shown in Figure 12.2, economic cooperation will focus on the exploitation of natural resources. In such case, not only will the scope of cooperation be limited, but both the current industrial and trading relationships will be fixed. Second, economic cooperation can focus on capability structure. If differences in the capability structure of individual provinces can be narrowed, both the scope and depth of cooperation can be expanded, facilitating the free flow of factors and resources, and leading to closer region-wide economic linkages. This is an economic cooperation model with accelerating returns and sustainability.

Yunnan is also faced with the above two possibilities. Most current cooperation projects focus on the exploitation of natural resources, with limited scope for other aspects of cooperation. The second possibility of strengthening the regional capability structure and expanding the scope of cooperation is, of course, preferable for Yunnan. Here, the province's comparative advantage can be improved by external investment. As internal linkages in the region are strengthened, economic cooperation will improve and a united economic entity could emerge.

Why is the second option in economic cooperation more promising? The answer is that it is not only the comparison of accelerating and decelerating returns that is important. What is more important is the consideration that if the exploitation of natural resources dominates in economic cooperation between Yunnan and other provinces, the resulting trade deficit will inevitably be detrimental to Yunnan's enthusiasm for participating in economic cooperation efforts.

Assessment of the Capability Structure of ASEAN Countries

The results of the assessment based on levels of GNP, economic development, sectoral structure, investment, exports, savings, and the development of information systems are shown in Table 12.3. In the GMS, the capability structure of Thailand is the strongest, at 0.2331. Yunnan, Vietnam, Cambodia, Myanmar and Laos follow, with a capability structure of 0.1094, 0.0992, 0.0383 and 0.022, respectively. However, in comparison with China and other ASEAN countries, Thailand ranks only slightly above the Philippines and Indonesia, but far below Singapore.

As shown in Figure 12.3, those ASEAN countries with a relatively lower capability structure are situated in the GMS. Moreover, the differences in capability structure in the GMS are relatively large, with a 50-fold difference between the strongest and the weakest entities in the region. By comparison, in the old ASEAN grouping, there was only a six-fold difference between the strongest and the weakest countries.

In developing economic cooperation with the ASEAN, Yunnan has a comparative advantage in certain sectors, such as metallurgy and in exploration for metals and minerals. There is already cooperation in these areas, and such cooperation is increasing. In agriculture and husbandry, Yunnan and ASEAN are natural partners, as similar animal and plant species are found in the two areas. Moreover, all major universities in Yunnan provide training for students from ASEAN countries.

Another aspect of cooperation between Yunnan and ASEAN arises from complementarities in economic structure and commodity trading. On the one hand, as Yunnan is located in China's western region, its level of

Table 12.3   China-ASEAN Capability Structure in 2002

Countries/regions	Laos	Myanmar	Cambodia	Vietnam	Yunnan, China	Thailand
Capability structure index	0.0022	0.0383	0.0466	0.0992	0.1094	0.2331
Countries/regions	Philippines	Indonesia	Malaysia	China	Brunei	Singapore
Capability structure index	0.1434	0.1545	0.3109	0.4261	0.513	0.8184

Sources: *ASEAN Statistical Yearbook, China Statistical Yearbook*, www.worldbank.org.

Figure 12.3   China-ASEAN Capability Structure

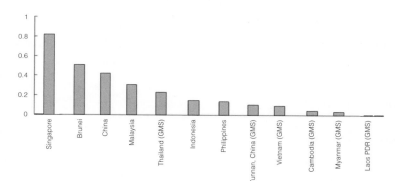

economic development is lower than the more developed coastal region of the country. However, Yunnan is more economically advanced than some ASEAN countries. The province's geographical location and economic conditions enable both the economically less developed and the more developed countries of ASEAN to find markets in Yunnan for their primary commodity and hi-tech products, respectively. Both primary commodities produced domestically and hi-tech products produced nation-wide can find markets in Yunnan as well.

Vietnam, Laos, Cambodia and Myanmar are less-developed countries in the GMS. Both their levels of development and degree of openness are relatively low. As these countries share no common foreign economic policy and concentrate on the production of low-end products, with the exception of Thailand the scale of trade between Yunnan and the countries of the GMS is small.

Infrastructure

By developing a passageway to Southeast Asia and South Asia over the years, Yunnan is currently covered by infrastructure that connects the province to the outside world. By the end of 2002, there were 164,852 km of roads in Yunnan, ranking the province first in the nation in this respect. There were also 2,016 km of railway, 1,824 km of inland waterway and 148,114 km of civil airline routes. With regard to railway engines, vehicles and ships, 338, 699,400 and 1,062, respectively, were registered as being owned in the province. In addition, the province is relatively developed in terms of the coverage of information technology (IT) communications, with nearly 20,000 km of optical fibre cables and 10,000 km of long-distance microwave lines, covering over 90% of the province. Yunnan is relatively well placed nationally in the development of modern logistics.

Land Transport

Highway Transport

There are six national-grade highways in Yunnan. These are connected to provincial-grade highways, linking the province to Sichuan in the north, Guizhou and Guangxi to the east, Vietnam and Laos to the south and Myanmar to the west. Road mileage in Yunnan accounted for 10% of the national total, more than any other province in the nation. By the end of 2002, there were 107,615 km of provincial-grade highways and 746 km of national-grade highways in Yunnan. To accord with the requirements of the Western Development Plan, 6,341 km of highway are being planned, which will make Yunnan China's passageway to Southeast Asia. The key projects include:

(1) Kunming-Bangkok Highway
    The total length of this will be 1,855 km. By the end of 2009, all sections within Yunnan will be completed. The northern section in Laos was constructed with financial aid from China and was completed in 2006. The remaining sections will be built with aid from the Asian Development Bank (ADB) and Thailand. Starting from Nongkai in Thailand, it will be possible to travel by highway through Malaysia to Singapore. It is expected that, by 2007, it will take only 24 hours to drive from Kunming to Bangkok.

(2) Kunming-Lashio Highway
    The total length of this highway will be 952 km. By the end of 2009, the sections within Yunnan will be completed. The section from Ruili 瑞麗 to Lashio is as yet relatively undeveloped and will be improved through a bilateral agreement between China and Myanmar.

(3) Kunming-Hanoi Highway
    The total length of this highway will be 775 km. By the end of 2009, all sections connected to Hekou 河口 will be completed.

(4) Kunming-Chengdu 成都 and Chongqing 重慶
   The total length of this highway in Yunnan will be 661 km. It is to be connected to the Chengdu-Chongqing Highway, forming the Kunming-Chengdu and Kunming-Chongqing Highway.
(5) Kunming-Nanning 南寧 Highway
   The total length of this highway in Yunnan will be 636 km. Through cooperation with Guangxi, the Kunming-Nanjing Highway will be completed by 2009.
(6) Kunming-Guiyang 貴陽 Highway
   The total length of this highway in Yunnan will be 212 km. Through cooperation with Guizhou, the Kunming-Guiyang Highway will be completed by 2009.
(7) Yunnan-Tibet 西藏 Highway
   The total length of this highway in Yunnan will be 594 km. This high-grade road will be completed by the end of 2009.
(8) Passenger and goods services
   China has signed passenger agreements with both Laos and Vietnam. Since 1 May 2002, there have been three passenger routes serving both China and Laos, namely the Kunming to Vientiane, Simao 思茅 to Vientiane and Jinghong 景洪 to Vientiane routes. China has already opened negotiations with the Myanmar government to open passenger services across the border. A GMS agreement regarding cross-border passenger services was signed in September 2003 and will become effective in 2007.

The number of vehicles in Yunnan has increased with the improvements in highway transport. By the end of 2002, there were 699,400 public vehicles in the province, including 381,800 for passengers and 314,200 for goods, and 3,400 for other purposes. The number of private vehicles totalled 368,700, including 189,200 for passengers and 77,300 for goods. Both the expansion of highways and the increase in the number of vehicles had improved modern logistics in Yunnan.

Railway Transport

Yunnan has a total of 2,016 km of railway, linking the province to Nanning, Chengdu, Guiyang, Chongqing, Hekou, Yuxi 玉溪 and Dali 大理, and greatly enhancing Yunnan's capability in national logistics.

The Pan-Asia Railway, which is under construction, will become a main passageway from Yunnan to the ASEAN countries, forming a continental bridge for sea transport and enabling less-developed areas in Yunnan to become part of ACFTA. The feasibility report for the Kunming-Singapore Railway, written by a Malaysian consultancy company, was completed in June 2001. Three alternatives (east, central, west) were proposed. During the Sixth ASEAN Transport Ministers meeting, these and a further three alternatives were discussed. Eventually, the eastern line was recommended, after taking into account the countries being covered and the cost of construction. Currently, China has completed a study on a railway plan for Yunnan, reviewing three of the proposed alternatives. Both the State Council and the Yunnan government have arrived at a consensus to begin with the section from Yuxi to Hekou, making it a priority project that will link up with the Pan-Asia Railway. The Chinese government's attitude towards the central and east proposals is open, encouraging domestic enterprises to participate. China will expedite the construction of the Kunming-Hekou Railway by using the existing Kunming-Yuxi Railway and upgrading the Yuxi-Hekou Railway, which needs to be re-gauged. A section of railway from Hanoi to Laojie 老街 is also being planned. Although the transport of both passengers and goods between China and Vietnam has recovered from the disruption that resulted from the uneasy relations that existed between the two countries for some decades, the current annual rail transport capacity between the two countries is only about 1,500,000 tonnes due to operational difficulties.

By the end of 2002, Yunnan had 338 railway machines, 1,045 passenger trains and 1,380 cargo trains. In order to meet the needs of the ACFTA and the requirements for an international passageway to Southeast Asia and South Asia, and to pave the way for a modern logistics industry, the renovation of the existing railway stations in Yunnan has been speeded up.

Waterway Transport

Yunnan is linked to the Yangzi River 長江 and the Pearl River 珠江. On the other hand, the waterways of the Lancang, Salween, Nu 怒江 and Hong 紅河 Rivers link Yunnan to Southeast Asia through to the Pacific and Indian Oceans. International transport has been opened to Laos, Myanmar, Thailand and Vietnam through the Lancang, Hong, Lixian 李仙江, Daying 大盈江 and Nanding 南定河 Rivers, with a total length of about 2,200 km. However, cross-border transport has been impeded due to the lack of adequate investment and coordination among bordering countries and provinces. As of the end of 2002, the total length of inland waterway transport in Yunnan was 1,824 km, linking Jinshajiang 金沙江 at Suijiang 綏江 Port and Shuifu 水富 Port, through to Sichuan, Hubei 湖北, Hunan, Jiangxi, Jiangsu 江蘇 provinces and Bangbu 蚌埠 City in Anhui 安徽. At present, Shuifu Port is the most important port for Yunnan on the Yangzi River for domestic river transport, while international waterway transport is conducted mainly through the Lancang-Mekong River.

The international waterway of the Lancang-Mekong River is over 1,000 km long. It links Yunnan to ASEAN countries, and contains nine ports and terminals of over 100,000 DWT capacity each.

Since 1990, there have been only a few major attempts to investigate the transport capacity of the Lancang-Mekong River at different seasons. The Ministry of Transport and the Yunnan government have invested RMB189.79 million on the construction of Simao Port, Jinghong Port and Guanlei 關累 Terminal, enhancing the transport capacity to 400,000 tonnes per annum. The waterway from Simao to Myanmar has also been significantly improved. In April 2000, an agreement was signed by China, Laos, Myanmar and Thailand, opening 14 ports along the "Golden Waterway" of the Lancang-Mekong River to cross-border transport. There are also standard concessions for customs and port charges, following another agreement signed in December 2003.

The early phase of an international waterway transport system has been completed, but major difficulties exist in realizing its full capacity to deliver Chinese goods into the hinterland of the ASEAN countries. According to the plan, the 593 km of waterway from Simao Port to Huishen in Laos will be improved to allow access for ships of over 300 DWT. Plans for cooperation have also been drawn up with Laos, Myanmar and Thailand to improve the 774 km waterway from Huishen to Vientiane, as well as to construct port facilities at Kampot Waterfall through cooperation with Laos and Cambodia. It is expected that, by 2009, all bottlenecks along the Lancang Waterway will be removed, realizing the full integration of Yunnan with the hinterland of ASEAN.

By the end of 2002, there were 1,062 cargo ships operating in inland waterways in Yunnan. The river ports in Yunnan include Shuifu, Shuijiang, Jinghong and Simao. The lake ports include Kunming, Xiaguan 下關, Jiangchuan 江川 and Chengjiang 澄江. With the improvement of the waterway facilities, the capacity of Yunnan in modern logistics can be significantly enhanced.

In addition, both the Hong River and the Salween River are important waterways. In the past, the Hong River was an important waterway for Yunnan. Both the ADB and the Vietnamese government have suggested making joint efforts to develop the waterway, with technical support provided by the ADB. The Ministry of Transport has also headed a feasibility study on the internationalization of transport on the Hong River. However, as the development of Hong River for transport is at the planning stage, its use as an international waterway is still pending further discussion. The same applies to the Salween River, which cannot be easily transformed into a major waterway linking Yunnan to ASEAN and South Asia because a cross-border agreement on the issue will take at least five to ten years to materialize.

Air Transport

At present, an air-transport network has been established in Yunnan, with over 80 air routes radiating from Kunming to other cities in the province and to other provincial capitals. Kunming Airport, which can handle 12 flights per hour, with an annual passenger capacity of over seven million, is the fourth-largest airport in the country after Beijing, Shanghai and Guangzhou. There are international flights from Kunming to Bangkok, Singapore, Hanoi, Ho Chi Minh City, Kuala Lumpur and Mandalay in Southeast Asia, and to Delhi in South Asia, as well as to Seoul, Tokyo, Hong Kong and Macao. A project to expand Kunming Airport is being studied, while the construction of 9 branch flight routes covering 16 prefectures, counties and cities has been completed. With the completion of the airports at Honghe, Wenshan 文山 and Nujiang, all of the main border regions in the province are accessible by air. In addition, the Xishuangbanna Airport was upgraded into an international airport in January 1997.

As of the end of 2002, there were a total of 148,114 km of civil aviation routes in Yunnan, accounting for 9.04% of the distance of China's domestic and 5.05% of its international flight routes. The province's fast-growing airline network will provide Yunnan with the infrastructure covering the ACFTA area for express mail services and to transport time-sensitive cargo. The flows of air cargo and air passengers will be further facilitated with the completion of the new international airport at Songming 嵩明, which will be connected to peripheral regions with light rail and highway transport. It is expected that 500,000 to 1,000,000 tonnes of cargo can be handled by the international airport at Songming by 2020. Furthermore, with the completion of its new airport, Kunming can aspire to be an international city with well-equipped with logistics facilities.

Ports

At present, there are 10 national-grade and 10 provincial-grade ports open for air, land and water transport. In 1992, Kunming, Wanding 畹町, Ruili and Hekou were opened to foreign trade; there were also 86 border trade townships, enabling Chinese goods to be exported to neighbouring countries.

Energy Development

Efforts at cooperation in the development energy resources have been formalized by China with Thailand and Laos at both the national and provincial levels. Feasibility study reports concerning the construction of a joint venture — the Jinghong hydropower station — were approved in 1997 and 1999. Similarly, in accordance an agreement signed with Laos in December 1997, Yunnan will transmit electricity through a 10 kw and a 35 kw power station to four counties in Laos. With the development of the water resources at the middle and lower streams of the Lancang River, clean energy can be supplied to the GMS countries.

Development of IT Infrastructure

By employing advanced technology, a communication network has been developed consisting of digital microwaves, satellite communications, optical fibre transmission cables, and so forth. In 1992, Kunming was the first city in Southwest China to adopt an automated communications system. By the end of 2002, long-distance telecommunications within the province had been digitized, with the laying of 19,989 km of optical fibre cables and 9,380 km of microwave lines. In 1998, in order to strengthen the development of a multi-media communication network, phase 1 of the Yunnan digital port was completed, providing nine nodal points for installation and commissioning. In addition, both the digital data network (DDN) and hierarchical exchange network were completed, covering a total of 1.03 million multi-media users.

In order to support the development of a communication network in the GMS, a forum involving six countries, was held on this subject to discuss the feasibility of developing cross-border cooperation in IT development in two phases. There are 13 optical fibre cable transmission projects in

Phase 1, connecting six countries in three transmission circuits: east, west and north. Five of these transmission projects are connected to Yunnan. There are four fibre cable transmission projects in Phase 2, connecting Cambodia, Yunnan, Laos and Vietnam. In 2001, a China-ASEAN undersea cable system was constructed, linking up Singapore, China (Shanghai and Guangzhou 廣州), Vietnam (Hanoi), Laos (Vientiane), Thailand (Bangkok) and Malaysia (Kuala Lumpur).

The fast-developing telecommunications facilities in Yunnan and the cross-border development plans that are in the planning stages board will definitely enable Yunnan to speed up the modernization of its logistics industry to meet the demands of ASEAN countries.

Emergence of a New Economy

Although Yunnan enjoys no advantages in its capability structure, it is becoming more important geographically with the formalization of ACFTA in July 2003. As Yunnan is geographically contiguous with some ASEAN countries and is China's only province participating in the GMS, cooperation can be greatly enhanced by the lowering of tariffs between Yunnan and ASEAN. The regional cooperation efforts of the Pan-PRD grouping and those of the GMS grouping overlap in Yunnan, which will be favourable for trade and investment in the province. With the speeding up of regionalization, some potential industries in Yunnan will attract foreign direct investment, further advancing the cause of regionalization.

Logistics

In accordance with the development plan to connect Yunnan to Southeast Asia and South Asia, a logistics network will be completed by the end of 2010. By 2007, it will take only 24 hours to travel between Kunming and Bangkok by highway. For the transport of goods that are not time-sensitive and volume-sensitive, the sea route from Shanghai and Shenzhen to the ASEAN countries will still cost less. However, if there are constraints, the Kunming-Bangkok Highway will be preferred. Other alternatives include the Pan-Asia Railway and the Lancang-Mekong River. With regard to the Pan-PRD region, Kunming will join Shenzhen as the other logistics centre of ACFTA. With the opening of the central line of the Pan-Asia Railway, both the relative cost and efficiency of transport from major cities in various provinces in China to Bangkok are shown in Table 12.4:

Table 12.4 Comparison of the Cost and Efficiency of Transport from Major Cities and Provincial Cities in China to Bangkok

	Transport routes	Mode of transport	Cost (RMB per 20-foot container)	Time (day)
Scenario 1	Harbin—Kunming—Mohan 磨憨—Bangkok	railway and highway	22,874.10	11
Scenario 2	Harbin—Kunming—Hekou—Bangkok	railway	14,632.48	14
Scenario 3	Harbin—Kunming—Vientiane—Bangkok	railway	9,382.49	11
Scenario 1	Beijing—Kunming—Mohan—Bangkok	railway and highway	21,137.48	9
Scenario 2	Beijing—Kunming—Hekou—Bangkok	railway	12,895.87	12
Scenario 3	Beijing—Kunming—Vientiane—Bangkok	railway	7,645.88	9
Scenario 1	Shanghai—Kunming—Mohan—Bongkok	railway and highway	20,982.43	9
Scenario 2	Shanghai—Kunming—Hekou—Bangkok	railway	12,740.82	12
Scenario 3	Shanghai—Kunming—Vientiane—Bangkok	railway	7,490.83	9
Scenario 1	Wuchang 武昌—Kunming—Mohan—Bangkok	railway and highway	19,477.73	6
Scenario 2	Wuchang—Kunming—Hekou—Bangkok	railway	11,236.12	9
Scenario 3	Wuchang—Kunming—Vientiane—Bangkok	railway	5,986.12	8
Scenario 1	Lanzhou 蘭州—Kunming—Mohan—Bangkok	railway and highway	19,907.84	7
Scenario 2	Lanzhou—Kunming—Hekou—Bangkok	railway	11,666.22	10
Scenario 3	Lanzhou—Kunming—Vientiane—Bangkok	railway	6,416.23	8
Scenario 1	Chengdu—Kunming—Mohan—Bangkok	railway and highway	18,327.63	5
Scenario 2	Chengdu—Kunming—Hekou—Bangkok	railway	10,086.02	8
Scenario 3	Chengdu—Kunming—Vientiane—Bangkok	railway	4,836.03	6
Scenario 1	Chongqing—Kunming—Mohan—Bangkok	railway and highway	18,330.33	5
Scenario 2	Chongqing—Kunming—Hekou—Bangkok	railway	10,088.71	8
Scenario 3	Chongqing—Kunming—Vientiane—Bangkok	railway	4,838.72	6

Notes:

(1) The transport cost is the sum of the actual mileage and standard charges: recipient charges (RMB149.50) plus operating cost (mileage × RMB0.6603/container km) plus railway construction fund (mileage × RMB0.528/container km) plus electrification charges (mileage × RMB0.16/container km).

(2) The cost from Yunnan and Guangxi after leaving China is an estimate based on two 10-tonne trucks, which is roughly equivalent to one 20-ft container. Both the railway and highway costs are based on domestic charges. In the sea transport cost from Shenzhen to Bangkok, all customs charges have been included.

The cost of transporting one 20-foot container worth of freight from Harbin to Bangkok through Kunming and Vientiane will be about RMB 9,000 to RMB10,000, which is only half the existing transport cost. The development of logistics between Northeast China and ASEAN countries will, therefore, be greatly facilitated. Similarly, the cost of sending the same amount of freight from Beijing through Kunming to Bangkok will be below RMB8,000, again cutting the present cost of transport by half. The same applies to Shanghai and Wuhan. As the cheapest way to transport goods between major cities in China to Bangkok is via Kunming, there is great scope for the development of logistics between Northeast and Southeast China and ASEAN countries centering on Kunming.

From these comparative statistics, it is apparent that, whenever the ASEAN hinterland is to be reached (taking Bangkok as the destination) from China, with the exception of the route via sea from the Yangzi River Delta and the Pearl River Delta to Bangkok, the transport of freight from all other regions in China to Bangkok is cheapest via Kunming. Provided that the capacity of the Lancang-Mekong waterway can be improved, transport costs from Northeast and Southeast China to ASEAN countries can be greatly reduced. At the same time, transport costs from Northeast and Central West China to ASEAN countries are comparable with those of the sea route, but the transport time is significantly reduced. Although the transport cost from Shenzhen to ASEAN countries through the sea route is cheaper than from Kunming, the transport time is longer. Therefore, it can be expected that, within the next 5 or 10 years, Yunnan will eventually become an irreplaceable hub for the regional logistics industry. A two-hour air freight network will enable Yunnan to be the centre of the air logistics industry for freight transported by air between China and the countries of the GMS. A 24-hour travelling distance through the Kunming-Bangkok Highway will enable fresh goods from Yunnan to be distributed internationally. Similarly, a three-day travelling distance through the Lancang-Mekong waterway will enable bulky goods from Yunnan to be exported at low cost and within a short time. Yunnan has great potential as a logistic centre for ACFTA.[4]

Development of Biological Resources

The development of a modern biological industry in Yunnan, especially the pharmaceutical industry, can be founded on the province's bio-diversity. With Yunnan participating in the development of the Pan-PRD region and

ACFTA, the market prospects are promising for biological products. At present, 4,758 plant species for herbal medicine are found in Yunnan, ranking the province first in the nation in this aspect. Among the numerous species, there are 1,300 kinds for normal use and 300 kinds for production purposes. In addition, there are nearly 200 kinds of wild oilseeds and 2,100 kinds of wild flowers in Yunnam. In recent years, the pharmaceutical industry in Yunnan has been developing rapidly. Well-known enterprises in Yunnan that produce a large volume of pharmaceuticals under competitive brand names include Kunming Pharma, Panlong Yunhai, Kunming Yunhai, Kunming Baker Norton, Tianhong Pharma, Jida Pharma and Yunnan Baiyao. Not only is market demand for such pharmaceuticals stable, but the reserves of herbal medicine in Yunnan are also huge. The next phase of growth is to achieve an economy of scale and a level of industrialization compatible with the province's comparative advantage in herbal medicine reserves. As a long-term goal, natural medicine can become a modern industry and a new growth pole for Yunnan.

There is great potential for regional economic cooperation in Yunnan's biological industry. Through continuous support given to this industry in the 1990s, Yunnan has established a biological industry that is rich in resources, and that is advanced and in the process of becoming fully integrated. Among the neighbouring ASEAN countries, Yunnan's biological industry, including its pharmaceutical industry, is the most developed. Provided that the resources in Yunnan and the relevant technology in the Pan-PRD region are integrated, Yunnan's biological industry can be further developed.

Electricity Industry

Yunnan has 103.64 million kw of hydropower reserves, accounting for 15.3% of the national total. The annual output is 907.8 billion kw hours. At present, the province's development capacity is 90 million kw, accounting for 21.8% of China's total. Although the development ratio of water energy reserves is as high as 87.1%, ranking the province second after Sichuan, in reserves per square metre the province ranks first in the nation. At present, the utilization ratio of water energy resources in Yunnan is only 5.5%, much lower than the national level of 18.5% and the world level of 32.6%, indicating great potential for future development.

Conditions for the development of hydropower in Yunnan are superior, with good geological conditions and concentrated distribution. About 85%

of the province's hydropower is concentrated along the main streams of the Jinsha 金沙江, Lancang and Nu Rivers, which together can accommodate 35 large-scale hydropower stations with a capacity larger than 250,000 kw each. The total capacity is estimated at 670.7 million kw, accounting for 88% of the provincial total. The areas of inundation and the number of relocated people are only, respectively, one-half and one-third of the national average, greatly limiting the cost of development. Besides hydropower, Yunnan also has rich coal reserves, with open cast coal mines in 16 prefectures. Yunnan is one of 11 provinces with proven reserves of coal of over 15 billion tonnes, ranking the province eighth nationwide and second among the provinces of the southwest. There is great potential in Yunnan for developing large-scale open-cast coal mines to provide resources for coal-fired power stations.

In the Pan-PRD region, Guangdong's demand for electricity is the most acute. That province is the main destination for Yunnan's electricity. Most of the ASEAN countries are also short of electricity. In the next 20 years, the gap in Thailand, Vietnam, Laos, Myanmar and Cambodia between the demand for electricity and the supply will total 53 million kw per year. Moreover, the price of the electricity produced in Yunnan is only one-third that of Myanmar, one-fourth that of Thailand and two-thirds that of Vietnam. The market prospect for Yunnan's electricity has attracted large-scale overseas investment, including in the Jinghong Power Station, 70% of which is owned by Thailand, and investment from China Light and Power of Hong Kong.

Rubber Industry

Hainan, Yunnan and Guangdong are the three main regions in China where rubber is grown. Yunnan is the country's second-largest centre for the production of rubber, after Hainan. Although the conditions for growing natural rubber are inferior to those in ASEAN countries, the production technology in Yunnan is relatively advanced, resulting in a significant cost advantage and market competitiveness. From an analysis of direct production costs in rubber plantations, it can be seen that costs in both Hainan and Guangdong are slightly higher than costs in overseas countries (Table 12.5). However, Yunnan's direct production cost is significantly lower than those overseas, primarily due to the expansion since 1994 of the size of its plantations and its higher per acre output, which averages 110 kg. Yunnan's low cost and high productivity in the production of rubber have

Table 12.5 Comparison of Average Costs and the Relative Shares of the Costs of the Three Rubber Producing Regions in China, 1996–2001

	Hainan		Yunnan		Guangdong	
	Cost (RMB)	Share (%)	Cost (RMB)	Share (%)	Cost (RMB)	Share (%)
Direct cost	5,742	57.34	4,886	52.63	6,038	60.3
Indirect cost	4,272	42.66	4,398	47.37	3,970	39.6
Total cost	10,014	100	9,284	100	10,008	100

led to market competitiveness within China in the product. The direct cost of producing rubber in Yunnan can be further reduced through higher productivity and efficiency.

However, China has no comparative advantage in international competition in the rubber industry. Over 85% of the world's rubber is produced in Thailand, Indonesia and Malaysia. About 50% of China's needs in rubber have to be met by imports from these three ASEAN countries. An important theme in economic co-operation in the Pan-PRD region, therefore, is to improve China's competitiveness through integrating resources in Hainan, Yunnan and Guangdong with a wider region of rubber production.[5]

Tourist Industry

With the exception of seaside resorts, Yunnan is well-endowed with all kinds of tourist attractions. Since the 1990s, Yunnan's tourist industry has been developing rapidly, at an annual average growth rate of 27.09% for international tourists and 32.65% for foreign currency tourist income.

As shown in Table 12.6, the interflow of tourists between China and ASEAN has been steady, with 5–6% of ASEAN's international tourists coming from China, 17% of China's international tourists and 25% of Yunnan's coming from ASEAN. The Pearl River Delta is also an important source of tourists for Yunnan. However, there is still room to expand Yunnan's tourist industry. For example, a Greater Shangri-la region can be created by cooperating with Sichuan and Tibet. Yunnan can also cooperate with other provinces in the Pan-PRD region to integrate Yunnan's natural tourist resources with the cultural and international tourist resources of neighbouring provinces. Thus, the development of the tourist industry is one feasible way of boosting links within the Pan-PRD region.

Table 12.6   Interflow of Tourists among China, Yunnan and ASEAN

Year	China to ASEAN (1,000 tourists)	Share (%)	ASEAN to China (1,000 tourists)	Share (%)	ASEAN to Yunnan (1,000 tourists)	Share (%)
1991	—	—	291.5	10.76	6.9	7.57
1992	—	—	437.9	10.93	36.2	22.63
1993	—	—	499.9	10.74	117.6	43.79
1994	—	—	580.5	11.20	161.4	40.12
1995	794.9	2.68	1,039.1	17.65	172.0	36.31
1996	1,275.7	4.12	1,159.6	17.19	189.4	33.16
1997	1,337.9	4.31	1,270.6	17.11	150.0	26.05
1998	1,512.3	5.09	1,121.9	15.78	97.8	17.78
1999	1,919.3	5.61	1,413.0	16.76	167.6	23.12
2000	2,312.5	5.91	1,666.0	16.40	165.6	24.87
2001	2,433.6	5.77	1,814.2	16.16	166.3	23.91

Notes: (1) % share refers to the percentage of international tourists of the respective
                countries or regions.
            (2) With regard to tourists from ASEAN to China, only those from Singapore,
                Thailand and Philippines are included for the period 1991–1994, while
                those from Singapore, Malaysia, Thailand, Philippines and Indonesia are
                included for the period 1995–2001.
            (3) With regard to tourists from ASEAN to Yunnan, only those from Singapore,
                Thailand, Philippines and Indonesia are included.

Sources: (1) http://www.aseansec.org;
            (2) *China Statistical Yearbooks*;
            (3) *Yunnan Statistical Yearbooks*.

Deepening the Relationship between the GMS and the Pan-PRD Region

Yunnan can play a significant role in synthesizing the economic regions of the GMS and the Pan-PRD region. In the Pan-PRD region, not only are there regional variations in economic conditions but also political diversities, such as the unique political roles in China of Hong Kong and Macao. Furthermore, even as Guangdong's productive capacity is well developed, the remaining eight provinces are endowed with rich natural and manpower resources. Through matching the needs of the GMS and the Pan-PRD region, Yunnan's strategic position in ACFTA can be further strengthened.

First, the international passageway linking China, Southeast Asia and South Asia can be built using different types of infrastructure. Second, through regional economic cooperation with the Lancang-Mekong River

Sub-region, ACFTA and the Bangladesh-China-India-Myanmar Economic Cooperation grouping, a multi-tier open economy can be built for exchanges in information, trade, finance, manpower and affairs of common interest in promoting economic development in agriculture, tobacco, energy, mining and tourism. Third, in restructuring its economy, Yunnan's competitiveness can be improved by joining the regional division of labour in both the GMS and the Pan-PRD region. On the one hand, processing industries can be relocated to speed up the development of the hydropower, tourism, biological and chemical industries. On the other hand, Yunnan can become a logistics centre for the hinterland of Southeast Asia and South Asia. Fourth, new products can be developed in the Pan-PRD region to meet the new market demands of the various Southeast Asian countries. Fifth, the technological content of exports from Yunnan can be improved to strengthen Yunnan's position in trade. The existing customs system should also be improved. Sixth, Yunnan's export capability can be improved by branding its products. Seventh, the carrying capacity of Yunnan's environment can be improved by constructing an ecological barrier at the upper reaches of the Lancang, the Pearl and the Hong Rivers. At the same time, a compensation mechanism should be implemented for compensating people who need to be relocated and for those whose livelihoods depend on exploiting the environment. Eighth, the urban system of Yunnan must be improved to upgrade its urban function so that its large and middle-sized cities can better participate in regional and sub-regional cooperation, while making Kunming an international regional city. Last, there should be stronger exchanges and cooperation in technology, education, health, culture and environmental protection in the form of the development and training of human resources.

Conclusion

Under a market economy, both the scope and efficiency of regional cooperation depend upon the capability structure of individual regions. Since great discrepancies in capability structure exist among the Pan-PRD provinces, regional economic cooperation must proceed in stages. Such cooperation cannot be sustained if the exploitation of natural resources is a primary platform of economic cooperation between the developed and the less-developed regions, since the terms of trade would not be mutually beneficial. Moreover, the capability structure of a less-developed region can be improved by direct investment of a certain scale, since there will be a wholesale transfer of capital, technology, managerial skills and market networks to narrow the gap in capability. Therefore, a special meaning is attached to direct investment from Hong Kong and Macao in the Pan-PRD. Not only is direct investment a preferable mode of regional cooperation, but the scope of cooperation can also be expanded on the basis of an improved capability structure. To realize such a strategy, it is important to establish an effective mechanism within the cooperation framework of the Pan-PRD region and to improve the investment environment of the particular region.

With the involvement of enterprises, market efficiency will be a major concern in regional economic cooperation. Discrepancies in regional capability structure are not only the result of economic cooperation, but also the basis upon which to achieve market efficiency. Therefore, a capability-based form of economic cooperation in the Pan-PRD region should focus on an inter-regional operational model so as to protect the interests of the respective parties. In this new form of regional economic cooperation it is important for the local governments to develop their respective capability structures, while leaving the enterprises to select the projects on which they wish to cooperate.

In pushing ahead with economic cooperation with both the Pan-PRD region and the GMS, Yunnan must strive to construct an international land passageway to strengthen its unique geographical position and to serve the ASEAN countries, the Lancang-Mekong River Sub-region and China as a whole. Yunnan should also do the following:

First, in order to profit from the advantage of being close to various neighbouring sub-regional countries, it is important to speed up the development of an "information highway" for facilitating the transmission of information on economic growth, industrial development, investment and regional cooperation, so that Yunnan can become a centre for the provision of information and consultancy services to the GMS and ACFTA. Second, in order to promote cooperation, facilities should be developed at Kunming, Hekou, Mohan and Ruili to facilitate trade, exhibitions and exchanges between provinces in China's interior and ASEAN countries. Third, a practical, convenient and mutually beneficial cash flow and banking system should be established to facilitate investment, financing and the development of joint ventures among Yunnan, the members of the Pan-PRD grouping and the GMS countries. Fourth, Yunnan should avail itself of the education facilities of the members of the Pan-PRD grouping, to train its residents in all kinds of skills necessary to meet the needs of the

ASEAN countries. Fifth, Kunming can be developed into a centre to host offices of official representatives from ACFTA, Southeast Asia and South Asia. At the same time, commercial and trading offices can be set up at border cities such as Ruili, Mohan and Hekou to promote trade between China and ASEAN countries.

Notes

1. Michael E. Porter, *The Comparative Advantage of Nation* (New York: Free Press, 1990); D. Teece, G. Pisano and A. Shuen, "Dynamic Capabilities and Strategic Management," *Strategic Management Journal*, Vol. 18, No. 7 (1997), pp. 509–33.
2. Cui Weiguo 崔衛國 and Liu Xuehu 劉學虎, *Quji jingjixue* 區際經濟學 (Regional Economics) (Beijing: Jingji kexue chubanshe, 2004).
3. Fan Gang 樊綱, Wang Xiaolu 王小魯 et al., "Zhongguo shichanghua zhishu: ge diqu shichanghua xiangdui jincheng baogao" 中國市場化指數：各地區市場化相對進程報告 (China's Marketization Index: A Report on the Comparative Progress of Marketization in Each Region), *Jingji yanjiu* 經濟研究 (Economic Review) (2003), Issue 3, pp. 9–18.
4. Liang Shuanglu 梁雙陸, "Yunnan zai Zhongguo: dongmeng ziyou maoyiqu jianshe zhong de xiandai wuliuye fazhan yanjiu" 雲南在中國 —— 東盟自由貿易區建設中的現代物流業發展研究 (A Study of Yunnan in the Development of Modern Logistics in the China-ASEAN Free Trade Area) (Kunming: Yunnan University Development Research Institute 雲南大學發展研究所, 2004).
5. Ke Youpeng 柯佑鵬 and Guo Jianchun 過建春 (eds.), "Dui woguo sanda zhijiao kenqu tianran xiangjiao de chengben bijiao fenxi" 對我國三大植膠墾區天然橡膠的成本比較分析 (A Comparative Analysis of the Cost of Producing Natural Rubber in China's Three Major Plantation Areas), *Zhongguo nongken jingji* 中國農墾經濟 (China's Agricultural Economy), Issue 4 (2003), pp. 31–33.

13

Guizhou

Peng Xianwei and Maggi W. H. Leung

Introduction

Guizhou 貴州, also known as Qian 黔 or in abbreviation as Gui 貴, is situated in southwest China, on the eastern slope of the Yunnan-Guizhou Plateau 雲貴高原, adjoining Sichuan 四川 and Chongqing 重慶 to the north, Yunnan 雲南 to the west, Guangxi 廣西 to the south, and Hunan 湖南 to the east. The province has nine cities (prefectures) including three prefecture-level cities (Guiyang 貴陽, Zunyi 遵義, and Liupanshui 六盤水), three prefectures (Anshun 安順, Tongren 銅仁, and Bijie 畢節), and three autonomous prefectures of minority nationalities (the Qiandongnan 黔東南, Qiannan 黔南 and Qianxinan 黔西南), respectively. There are 87 counties (cities, special zones, and prefectsures) in Guizhou. The capital, Guiyang, is the political, economic, and cultural centre of the province. Guizhou is home to 36 million people, 34.7% (12.5 million) of which are members of 49 ethnic groups.

The province has a land area of about 176,000 km², which accounts for 1.84% of the nation's territory. Guizhou is a largely mountainous area, with an average altitude of about 1,100 metres. Of the total area, 61.7% are mountains, 30.8% hills, and 7.5% flat land between the mountains. The annual temperature averages 15 degree Celsius and the annual rainfall between 1,100–1,300 mm. Guizhou has spectacular natural scenery and a temperate climate, with warm winters, mild summers, and little contrast between the seasons.

As shown in Figure 13.1, Guizhou is an inland province bordering the affluent coastal, southern provinces as well as provinces in the west that are a new target for development. It also serves as a hub for inland transport. Guizhou's infrastructure has improved noticeably in recent decades. Five main railway lines currently pass through the province, namely the Guiyang-Kunming 昆明, Hunan-Guizhou, Sichuan-Guizhou, Guizhou-Guangxi 廣西, and Nanning 南寧-Kunming lines. Guizhou has five national highways and 30 provincial-level trunk roads, for a total of 33,000 km of highway. Air transport has also improved greatly. Guiyang's Longdongbao 龍洞堡 Airport opened in May 1977. In recent years, more airports have also been put into service, including the Tongren Daxing 銅仁大興 Airport (since 2001), the Guizhou Xingyi 興義 Airport, and the Guizhou Anshun 安順 Huangguoshu 黃果樹 Airport (both since 2004).

Guizhou has a predominantly agriculture-based economy. Over the last decades, the conditions for agricultural production gradually improved, and the output of both staple and market crops also increased greatly. The major crops that are produced, and their by-products, are paddy rice, maize,

Figure 13.1 Guizhou in Its Geographical Setting

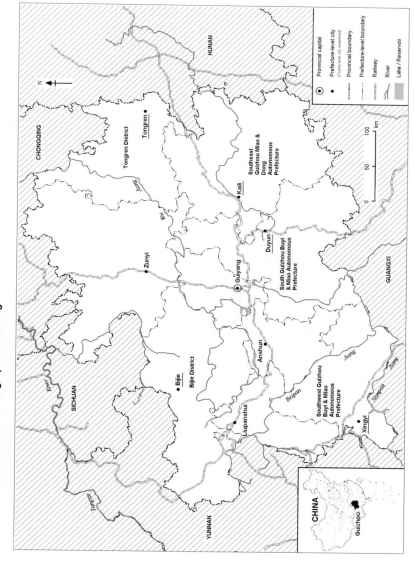

rapeseed, tobacco, tung oil, Chinese tallow, raw lacquer, tea, and the materials for medicine. Guizhou leads the country in the production of these products. There has also been a fair amount of industrial development in the province. Based on the province's resource base, priority has been given to the development of the iron and steel, coal, metallurgical, chemical, machinery, electricity-generation, cigarette, and papermaking industries. It is worth noting that Guizhou possesses three specialized manufacturing bases, in aerospace, aviation and electronics.

In relative terms, however, Guizhou's economic development lags that of other member provinces of the Pan–Pearl River Delta (Pan-PRD 泛 珠江三角州) region, especially those in the coastal area. It might not be apparent to observers that Guizhou was once at the forefront of the nation during the agrarian reform in the 1980s. Even in the 1990s, some of the enterprise and urban reforms that were implemented in Guizhou made contributions at the national level. As a result of the reform of the past few decades, systems relating to enterprises, agriculture, investment, urban management, housing, education and tourism in Guizhou have made noticeable progress — even leading in the nation in some aspects. Nevertheless, due to the province's long isolation arising from its geographical remoteness and lack of connectivity with other provinces and rest of the world, coupled with its short history of economic openness and market development, Guizhou still trails behind the nation in economic development. In measures of both economic and social development, it ranks among the lowest in the country. The provincial government views integration into the Pan-PRD region as a golden opportunity to push forward the development of the province.

This chapter explores the opportunities and constraints in Guizhou's pursuit of a more sustainable form of development within the Pan-PRD framework. Sustainability is a particularly important concept for Guizhou as the province has a fragile economy based on valuable natural resources and a still pristine environment that calls for extra attention in the drive for development. There are seven million people in Guizhou who are living in poverty (10% of the country's total), and who will need special support in the course of economic change and development.[1] This chapter provides an analysis of the province's opportunities and constraints as viewed broadly from the economic, environmental, and social perspectives. Finally, we conclude with recommendations on how to foster a more sustainable form of development in Guizhou as its connections with its counterparts in the Pan-PRD grouping strengthen.

Opportunities for Development

Guizhou is endowed with rich natural resources that can, with careful planning and sustainable utilization, be turned into a valuable base for development. The primary sector has traditionally dominated Guizhou's economy. Its vast forest coverage (34.9%) is a source of high-quality timber (e.g., China fir, pine, beech and oak). There are over 600 kinds of wild plants in the province producing products for industrial use including tung oil, natural lacquer, nan bamboo and rosin. Furthermore, there are over 500 kinds of plants such as chestnut trees, oriental white oaks, chestnut rose, fungi and so on, that yield edible products. In spite of the relative dearth of fertile soil — yellow earth and yellow-brown soils being the major soil types, a vast range of food crops are produced including rice, maize, wheat and potatoes, and marketable crops such as tobacco and rape seeds. A vast area of high-quality and abundant grassland for grazing (more than 2,500 types) supports over 30 types of livestock. In addition to the abovementioned more traditional ways of exploiting the natural resource base, in the following we shall highlight a few areas that have been identified as strategic sectors for development within the Pan-PRD framework, namely tourism, energy and mineral resources, and the processing of medicinal herbs and specialty foods.

Tourism

Guizhou has some of the best tourism resources in China. The province's humid sub-tropical climate, together with its spectacular natural scenery and the diverse folk customs and cultures of its different ethnic groups, are all attractions for domestic and international tourists. The province contains 12 state-level scenic areas, 67 provincial-level scenic areas, 6 state-level natural reserves, 9 national historical and cultural sites, 11 national forest parks, 4 national geological parks (the Fanjing Mountain Botanic Garden 梵淨山植物公園, the Maolan Karst Primeval Forest 茂蘭喀斯特原始森林, the Chishui Primeval Forest 赤水原生林 and the bird reserve 鳥類棲息衍生地 at Caohai 草海), and 2 national historical and cultural cities. Such endowments qualify Guizhou to become the back garden of the Pan-PRD region and a pleasant place to spend the summer holidays.

Natural wonders are abundant in Guizhou. Most representative of the province is the karst landscape that covers 61.9% of the provincial territory, which includes spectacular mountains, gorges, waterfalls, stone forests, caves, hot springs and lakes. The Dragon's Palace 龍京 City is a splendid underground karst cave; the Huangguoshu Waterfall is the biggest in China and one of the famous waterfalls of the world; while the Zhijin Cave 織金 洞 area has been dubbed "the Miracle of the Nature" and "King of Caves" because the patterns of accumulated karst are rich in shapes and formations. Other natural wonders include the Hongfeng Lake 紅楓湖, which covers an area of 57 km^2 and contains more than 170 islands; and the Wuyang River 舞陽河 scenic area, which is full of green bamboos, rugged peaks and intriguingly-shaped stones lining the river banks. There are 130 nature reserves in the province, covering a total area of 961,000 hectares (5.5% of the province's territory). Some virgin forests and ancient plant species, including some from the Jurassic Age, have survived in this pristine corner of China.

In addition, the province has rich biodiversity. Some 70 kinds of plants in Guizhou are listed as rare and precious, including the first-class protected plants of China silver fir, the dove tree, the bare China fir and the Spinulosa tree fern, of which 50% of China's supply are found in the province. Guizhou is also home to over 1,000 species of wildlife, 83 of which have been listed as state-protected animal species. Among these precious species, 14 are first-class state-protected animal species, including the Guizhou golden-haired monkey, black-leaf monkey, South China tiger, clouded leopard, leopard, white stork, black-necked crane, Chinese goosander, golden eagle, white-shouldered eagle, white-tailed sea eagle, white-headed crane and boa. Thirteen per cent of all animals in this category in the country are found here. With careful planning and management, such biodiversity can be tapped and developed to be a tourism product.

Other than natural resources, cultural diversity is also another valuable asset for tourism. Guizhou is home to 48 ethnic minority groups who account for more than 37% of the province's total population. They include the Yao 瑤, Miao 苗, Yi 彝, Shui 水, Dong 侗, Zhuang 壯, Bouyei 布依, Bai 白, Tujia 土家 and Gelao 仡佬. Over half of the province's area is designated as autonomous regions for these populations. There are as many as 1,000 ethnic festivals held in the province in a year, which would be attractive to a significant number of domestic and international tourists. The main festivals for ethnic minorities include the 6th June Singing Festival of the Dong people, the Dragon Boat Festival, the New Rice Tasting Festival, and Sister's Meal Festival of the Miao; the Duan Festival and Mao Festival of the Shui, and so on. In addition to festivals, many of the minority groups are well known for their singing and dancing, opera, architecture and handicrafts. The southeastern corner of the province is known for the unique culture of the Dong minority. Their tradition, culture, and agricultural practices reflect their long interactive relationship with the karst natural landscape. The combination of natural and cultural treasures in Guizhou provides invaluable resources for tourism. Experts in France, England and Norway have also concluded that the minority population's achievements in conserving Guizhou's environment, culture, and art represent rare examples in today's world. After years of effort, Guizhou has become an increasingly popular tourist destination offering hotels that suit the needs of tourists with different demands. In 2004, the number of domestic tourists reached 24.8 million, bringing RMB16 billion of revenue to the provincial; while the number of overseas tourists exceeded 230 thousand, generating an income of US$80 million.

In the context of the Pan-PRD development concept, Guizhou aims to coordinate with other provinces to enhance its tourism assets. The province has, to cite a good example, put a strong emphasis on developing four tourist routes that extend beyond its boundaries in four directions, with Guiyang as the centre: The first route comprises 10 sites featuring the Miao and Dong cultures; the second covers karst virgin forest and villages inhabited by the Bouyei, Yao and Shui nationalities; the third features historic sites in commemoration of the Long March conducted by the Red Army led by the Chinese Communist Party between 1934 and 1936, and finally, the fourth is characterized by karst landscape including the famous Hongfeng Lake, Anshun, Dragon's Palace City, and the Huangguoshu Waterfall. It is hoped that through networking with the partner provinces of Sichuan, Yunnan, Hunan and Guangxi, new energy will be generated that will bring more fresh ideas and incentives for the development of tourism in the region. In addition, Guizhou province also plans to intensify its tourism-related connections with Guangdong 廣東, Hong Kong 香港 and Macao 澳門 in order to stabilize and upgrade its tourism sector.

The task of developing tourism is not always an easy one. Due to the fragile nature of the tourism assets in Guizhou, a fine balance has to be struck between exploitation for tourism and conservation. Furthermore, the infrastructure for the development of tourism such as transportation and communication facilities, urban facilities, water and electricity supply, and tourism management, all need to be enhanced if tourism is to be boosted.

Energy and Mineral Resources

The province has the largest coal reserves in South China, and the fifth largest in the country. Guizhou is also rich in natural resources for the generation of hydro-electricity, supported by the ample precipitation (1,000–1,300 mm per annum). Guizhou's rainy weather has led to the popular Chinese saying that "There are never three days of clear skies or three dry feet of earth to be seen in Guizhou." The greater portion of the province's land area belongs to the watershed area of the Yangzi River 長江 and Pearl River 珠江. Due to Guizhou's mountainous terrain, many of its rivers offer great potential for the generation of hydropower. Its abundant water and coal reserves make it possible for the province to develop hydro- and coal-based power generation at the same time. The low production costs in Guizhou enable electricity to be sold for RMB0.12/kwh cheaper than the national average. In 2004, Guizhou had an electricity generating capacity amounting to 11 million kwh. It exported 3 million kwh to Guangdong, a figure expected to exceed 8 million kwh by 2010.

Guizhou is also a major base from which electricity can be supplied from the western to the eastern part of China (西電東送), and Guangdong (黔電粵送) in particular. The government has invested heavily in power generation and coal mining. The generation of electricity rose from 2.9% of GDP in 1999 to 5.1% in 2003 — a 2% increase that has been maintained in the last three consecutive years. Coal mining and electricity generation have become engines of growth in 2004. In the coming years, the province will focus on utilizing its abundant coal and inexpensive electricity to become the power base of south China, supplying the power required in the Pan-PRD region. The development of energy production has also strengthened the growth potential for related industries such as the coal mining, machinery, transport and chemical industries among others. A general picture of the energy infrastructure in Guizhou may be gained in Table 13.1.

As shown in Table 13.2, Guizhou is rich in mineral resources. Of the 110 kinds of minerals found in the province, the amount of the reserves for 76 kinds is known. Guizhou ranks among the top 10 in the nation for reserves of 42 kinds of minerals and in the top 3 for 22 kinds. It has particularly abundant reserves of coal, phosphorus, mercury, aluminium, manganese, antimony, gold, barite, the raw materials for cement and bricks, dolomite, sandstone, and limestone. Rich mineral resources provide immense opportunities for the smelting and processing of various kinds of metals, for the development of the chemical industry, and for the production of construction materials, among others.

Table 13.1 Energy Infrastructure in Guizhou

Indicator	1999	2000	2001	2002	2003	2000 to 2003 total	Average growth rate % (2000–2003)
1. Added value from electricity production (RMB million)	2,623	3,223	4,207	5,735	6,905	20,070	21.1
Total profit tax (RMB million)	1,268	1,710	1,672	1,979	2,234	7,595	15.2
Investment in electricity (RMB million)	3,243	6,492	9,046	10,947	14,729	41,214	
Added capacity in electricity production (thousand kw)	10,300	337.4	657.2	426.4	2,693.7	4,114.7	
Added power lines (km) (0.11 million kw and above)	387	493.6	1,893.2	1,098.4	1,149	4,634.2	
Electricity exported (million kwh)	2,120	2,650	3,490	5,940	9,150	21,230	
2. Added value from coal production (RMB million)	714	741	713	942	1,372	3,768	14.4
Total profit tax (RMB million)	103	193	236	335	484	1,248	47.3
Investment in coal (RMB million)	594	538	477	501	1,272	2,788	
Added capacity in coal production (thousand tonnes)	3,890	1,827	1,500	980	3,792	8,099	
Coal production (thousand tonnes)	40,250	36,770	37,310	50,010	78,160	202,250	

Sources: Various official statistics.

Table 13.2 Major Reserves in Guizhou (2003)

	Reserve unit	Total reserve	National ranking
Coal	10^{12}kg	492.12	5
Manganese	Ore 10^6kg	76,327	3
Aluminium	Ore 10^6kg	395,471	2
Mercury	Mercury 10^3kg	33,000	1
Antimony	Antimony 10^3kg	244,500	4
Magnesium	Ore 10^6kg	32,131	3
Gold (deposits)	Gold 10^3kg	165.81	10
Rare earth (oxide)	10^3kg	1,446,037	2
Phosphorus	Ore 10^{12}kg	26.87	2

Sources: *Guizhou Statistical Yearbook 2004* and the Geological Bureau of Guizhou.

Medicinal Herbs and Specialty Food Processing

As many as 4,290 kinds of Chinese *materia medica* (plants, animals, and minerals) are found in Guizhou — 3,924 herbs, 289 kinds of animals, and 77 kinds of minerals. This rich resource base makes Guizhou the fourth leading producer province of Chinese medicine. Of the 363 major ingredients of Chinese medicine, 326 (or 89.9%) are available in Guizhou. The province's reserve capacity of Chinese *materia medica* is estimated to reach 65 billion kg. The quality of its medicinal herbs is also high; products such as tianma 天麻 (*Rhizomn Gastrodiae*), duzhong 杜仲 (*Cortex Eucommiae*), houpo 厚朴 (*Cortex Magnoliae Officinalis*), heshouwu 何首乌 (*Polygonum multiflorum Thunb*), and dangshen 黨參 (*Radix Codonopsis Pilosulae*) from Guizhou are well known nation-wide. The province's rich biodiversity provides fertile ground also for the development of three-dimensional farming, bio-pharmaceutics, and specialty food processing.

In addition to the tangible resources mentioned above, the traditional knowledge of the ethnic population in Guizhou also provides invaluable resources for further research and development. For instance, the healing culture of the Miao group has been studied in the last few decades. More than 150 recipes of Miao medicines have been upgraded to national standard.

In its drive to enhance development in the western provinces, the central government has invested heavily in improving the research infrastructure, technology, capital and human resources for the Chinese medicine industry in Guizhou. In 2001, the province was designated one of the national bases for the modernization of the Chinese medicine industry. There are currently 14 tertiary and research institutions, 8 privately owned Chinese and ethnic medicine research corporations, and 8 pharmaceutical companies in the province. The province's potential to become a major source of ethnic medicine and "organically grown food" for the Pan-PRD region has been identified, and its authorities also aim to seek opportunities to cooperate with Hong Kong in its plan to develop its production of Chinese traditional medicine.

However, Guizhou's pharmaceutical industries need to find solutions to an array of challenges if they are to expand in the future. The following problems in the sector have thus far been identified: (1) a lack of unique products and sub-standard corporate management; (2) the small scale and unsophisticated nature of production, the lack of capital and, thus, competitiveness; (3) a lack of diversity in the products, low skill levels in the industry, and unstable product quality; and (4) a lack of professional skills and technological input, a backward informational network, and poor service quality. In addition to the above structural problems, the industry also needs to confront a series of issues related to its medicinal resource base including: (1) a lack of research on the quality of the *materia medica*; (2) insufficient quality control; (3) the lack of longitudinal data regarding changes in the quality of the *materia medica*; (4) the lack of a professional workforce; and (5) insufficient knowledge of national standards and regulations. The Guizhou government hopes that through integration with the economy of the Pan-PRD region, it can tap into the rich resources of its partners, namely Guangdong, Hong Kong, and Macao, in order to enhance its capital base, production, research, and technology in this field.

Development Constraints

Poor Economic Structure

Being one of the poorest provinces in the country, Guizhou compares particularly poorly with its counterparts in the Pan-PRD region. In 2004, Guizhou ranked last or second last in all measures of economic comparison. Its GDP was only 9.2% that of Guangdong and its per capita GDP amounted to only 39.9% of the country's average, or 21.4% that of Guangdong. Table 13.3 charts the difference in per capita GDP between Guizhou and other provinces in the Pan-PRD region. The data further show that the gap widened from 2003 to 2004.

Primary production dominates Guizhou's economy. Guizhou did not develop modern industries during the beginning phase of liberation, and adopted a nature-based economy. After 50 years of development, Guizhou's primary and secondary production comprise as much as 66% of its economy.

Table 13.3   Comparison of Per Capita GDP in Guizhou and Other Provinces in the Pan-PRD Region

Year	Compared to Guangdong		Compared to the second lowest income		Compared to the fourth lowest income	
	Absolute difference	%	Absolute difference	%	Absolute difference	%
2003	RMB13,387	371	RMB2,044	56.7	RMB2,815	78.1
2004	RMB15,494	368	RMB2,518	59.7	RMB3,898	92.5

Source: Relevant provincial statistical yearbooks.

The ratio of the three sectors of economy in 2004 was: primary 20.99; secondary 44.89; tertiary 34.12. While the development strategy adopted by the province can be justified by its rich natural resource base, Guizhou's comparative advantage in this area has declined over the course of time as competition has intensified. For instance, while Guizhou exploits its mineral resources, the higher value-adding industrial processing takes place in the eastern and central provinces. This regional division of labour has created a highly disproportional distribution of the profits generated. The province's lack of capital has, in turn, constrained the further development of its economic structure and human capital. The vicious cycle of underdevelopment acts as a trap preventing Guizhou from enhancing its competitiveness as compared to other provinces. As a consequence, Guizhou's economy is increasingly dependent upon external forces.

Following national development strategies, Guizhou has focused on heavy industries. In 2000, the ratio of light industries vs heavy industries as indicated by the value of the industrial products sales of industrial enterprises above a designated size in the province was 37.9: 62.1. This emphasis on heavy industries is, however, not favourable for the overall economic development of the province. As shown by the development path of the coastal provinces, light industries are much more profitable than heavy industries. Guizhou must move away from heavy industries in its drive to more speedy development.

Another problem with Guizhou's economy is that it is very heavily dependent on external inputs. After liberation, Guizhou experienced three phases of intensive "input phases," namely the First Five-year Plan (1953–1957) and Third Five-year Plan (1966–1970) (when the state poured in immense resources for the development of the aviation and aerospace industries as well as the electronic industry) and, since 1999, most the China's Western Development Strategy. All of these three phases can be explained by Guizhou's important role in the central state's development plans. During those times when Guizhou is not important to the central state's development plans, the province would then be marginalized. During such phases, this passive characteristic of Guizhou's economic development style is less than optimal. For instance, during the period of the Third Five-year Plan, Guizhou received a large sum of investment in the military and heavy industrial sectors that had little to do with the livelihood of the common people in the province, and failed to lead to any sustainable contribution to the betterment of the living standards of the people. The current push to export electricity to the east mirrors, to a certain extent, the above concern. The singularly externally led and passive characteristics of the current development approach should be regarded with caution, especially when the central state reorients its general development strategy.

The gap in development between rural and urban areas is greater in China than anywhere else in the world. The situation is most severe in the poorer regions (including Guizhou). In 2003, the average per capita disposable income of urban residents in Guizhou was RMB6,569, while the average income of the rural population was RMB1,565, for a ratio of 4.19:1. In 2004, the average per capita disposable income of urban residents in the province was RMB7,322, while the average income of the rural population was RMB1,722, for a ratio of 4.25:1. While it should be apparent that there is an urgent need to reduce the economic gap between urban and rural areas, the provincial government has chosen to adopt policies that might exacerbate the imbalance. More specifically, the provincial communist party committee has announced its plan to create a system in which economic activity in the province is led by, and centred on, the capital, Guiyang.[2] While the Greater Guiyang concept presents theoretically the potential to diffuse development into less-developed regions, there is also a realistic risk that it will induce further imbalances between the "head of the dragon," Guiyang, and other cities in the province.

Poverty in rural Guizhou is severe. In 1993, there were 10 million people in the province living in poverty. In 2000, 3.1 million of the rural population earned less than RMB650, comprising 9.74% of the total rural population (Table 13.4), while about 5.6 million of the rural population earned between RMB625 and 865, making up 17.5% of the whole rural population. In total, there were 2.3 million poor people in 48 poor counties, constituting a poverty rate of 12.13%. Also noteworthy is the high proportion (over 80%) living

Table 13.4   Rural Population by Per Capita Income, 2000 (million)

Population living in poverty	Below RMB 625	RMB 625– 865	RMB 865– 1,000	RMB 1,000– 1,200	Above RMB 1,200	Prevalence of poverty %	% of population with an income below RMB625	% of population with an income below RMB825
3.1346	2.961	5.578	3.4559	4.4417	15.51	9.74	9.27	26.73

Source: Guizhou Provincial Poverty Alleviation and Development Office, *Guizhou nongcun fupin gongjian gongzuo shouce* 貴州農村扶貧攻堅工作手冊 (Working Manual for Poverty Alleviation in Rural Guizhou). Unpublished.

in extreme poverty. At the end of 2004, there were still 2.77 million people earning below RMB625, and living in extreme poverty, while 4.77 million people earned between RMB625 and 865, accounting for an average 6.88% of poverty rate in the province (while the poverty rate for some counties was as high as 30%), exceeding the national average of 3%. Furthermore, poor people in Guizhou also have a higher tendency to relapse into poverty; where the national average rate of relapse into poverty is around 9%, Guizhou's is as high as 15%.

Low income levels, coupled with the low quality of the labour force, mean that local government revenues and the average savings rate are low. This, in turn, leads to a low level of capital formation and difficulty in enhancing the productivity of the workforce. Guizhou's economy can be classified as having fallen into the trap of the "vicious cycle of poverty," as expressed by U.S. economist R. Nurkse (1953) in his book *Problems of Capital-Formation in Underdeveloped Countries.*[3] According to Nurkse's concept, low-income levels lead to low-saving rates. This, in turn, causes a low rate of capital formation and, consequently, low productivity, which contributes to low levels of income. In addition to this vicious cycle on the supply side, there is also a cycle on the demand side. Low income leads to low purchasing power, which in turn makes investment unattractive and consequently leads to a low level of productivity and, in turn, low levels of income. These vicious cycles do indeed characterize Guizhou's current economic system.

When viewed from another perspective, however, the backwardness of Guizhou's economy can also be considered an opportunity. According to regional development theories, the complementarity of two or more regions increases when the difference in economic development between these units increases. In this sense, Guizhou's potential to contribute to the broader economic development drive in the Pan-PRD region is huge. As other provinces in the Pan-PRD region strive to develop their high value-added production and related services, Guizhou's natural resources and cheap workforce are valuable assets that its counterparts lack.

Natural Environment at Risk

The health of Guizhou's natural environment directly affects economic activities in the lower Yangzi Delta and Pearl River Delta. The fragile karst landscape in the area is particularly sensitive to threats from unsustainable practices. Previous agricultural and industrial practices have led to serious pollution and natural resource depletion in Guizhou. The ecological deficit and deterioration has widely been documented. Population pressure and malpractices in land use have intensified the processes of rock desertification. In Guizhou, the annual rate of rock desertification in the karst areas was as high as 933 ha in the 1980s. This has led to the following environmental problems:

(1) Soil erosion

Soil erosion in Guizhou has accelerated in the last half century, increasing from 25,000 ha in the 1950s to 50,000 ha in the 1970s and, in 1995, to 76,700 ha or 43.5% of the total area of the province. The current estimate is as high as 50% of the total area.

(2) Loss of soil fertility

Rock desertification reduces the fertility of the soil, making intensive agriculture impossible. In many of the affected areas, agriculture is still performed in a slash and burn manner. Maize production in these areas is only 750 kg/ha, which is only one-tenth of the capacity on the plains.

(3) Drought hazard

Rock desertification has altered the chemical content and hydrological paths in the soil, which in turn has exacerbated the problem of drought, making the events more intensive, more frequent, and more widespread. Water shortages affect as many as 3.5581 million people and 2.5481 million livestock. Statistics help to illustrate the extent to which the problem of drought has intensified. During the 36 years of the period 1951 to 1987, natural hazards affected crop growth in 34 of those years, with an average affected area of 700,000 ha/year, accounting for 25% of the total crop area. The problem has accelerated to such an extent that in 1996 alone, natural hazards covered 1.947 million ha of agricultural land and affected a further 1.2 million ha, reducing agricultural production by 1.5 billion kg and thus causing a direct economic loss of RMB16.282 billion.

(4) Deterioration of ecological systems

Large volumes of sand are being deposited in the Yangzi River and the Pearl River as a result of rock desertification. As much as 66.25 million tonnes of sediment eroded into Guizhou's river systems in the 1980s, that is, an annual transporting sediment module of $376t/km^2$. By 1998, a total of 0.28 billion tonnes of sediments were estimated to have been eroded. Silting in the middle and lower reaches of the Yangzi and Pearl River has caused lakes and river surfaces to shrink, which in turn is contributing to the deterioration of ecological systems in the area. Ecological deterioration can be visualized clearly from the worsening deforestation (forest coverage has now been reduced to less than 10%) and decline in biodiversity in the region.

Lack of Infrastructure

The density and standard of the transportation network in Guizhou is below the average of the Pan-PRD region. The total mileage of motorways, railways, and river ways reached 52,853 km in 2004, which converts to a density of 0.3 km/km^2 as compared to the average of 0.4 km/1,000 km^2 in the Pan-PRD region. Classified highways only make up 73.3% of the total network (6.2% lower than the national average), and only half of the 3,010 km of railway is electrified. Such a relatively backward transportation network is not capable of handling the rapid rise in demand that is expected to result from economic growth in the Pan-PRD region.

Agricultural infrastructure represents another aspect of infrastructural weakness in Guizhou. The per capita area of irrigated farmland is only 0.3 mu, that is, only 35% of the national average and the lowest in the Pan-PRD region (see Table 13.5). In addition, the province is also lagging in basic healthcare and social welfare facilities. For instance, over 50% of the village clinics in the province did not have enough rooms, and 90% of the village clinics were sub-standard. Cultural facilities are also lacking: There are no libraries or cultural centres in 13 of the counties, and 34% of the villages do not have any cultural stations. If the basic infrastructure of the villages is not improved, there would be serious constraints to sustainable cooperation between Guizhou and other partner provinces in the Pan-PRD grouping.

Table 13.5   Classified Highways and Irrigated Farmland in Guizhou

	PRC	Guangxi	Sichuan	Guizhou	Yunnan
Proportion of classified highways (%)	79.5	77.5	66.9	73.3	65.8
Per capita area of irrigated farmland (mu)	0.86	0.58	0.55	0.3	0.59

Lack of Connection with External Areas

Guiyang, the capital city, is about 500 km from Beihai 北海 in Guangxi and over 300 km from Chongqing 重慶 along the Yangzi River. Thus, it can be characterized as inaccessible in three ways: from the river, the sea and the border.[4] Because of its physical isolation, coupled with its hitherto low level of economic development and poor infrastructure, Guizhou's connection with external areas has been weak. Up until now, development initiatives in Guizhou have mainly been funded by the central government; the outward expansion of the province's economic activities and its efforts to attract foreign investment have been limited and conducted in an ad hoc manner, without a well-defined objective. Most (70%) of Guizhou's trade goes to Asia, notably to Japan, Korea, Hong Kong and countries in Southeast Asia which account for about 50%. Such a market structure poses a potential limitation to the scale of further growth in the province, and represents a big risk from lack of diversification.

Lack of accessibility to basic services is particularly serious for rural people. Much of Guizhou's population consists of ethnic minorities who live in hilly areas where living conditions are poor and basic infrastructure such as transportation and communications is lacking. A survey conducted in 2001 found that residents in 50% of the villages needed to walk 5 km to reach the nearest motor pick-up point. The power supply and communications network are also unstable, limiting interaction between the rural population and the outside world.

On the other hand, successful connections could also give rise to problems. Rapid development in the PRD in the last 20 years has attracted many migrant workers from Guizhou. These connections can, therefore, be understood to have contributed to the dilemma of a brain drain. While migrant workers send large remittances back to their home areas, much of the money is channelled to more economically active areas rather than used to develop the very poor areas. Thus, Guizhou actually suffers a net loss from its existing connections with the PRD. If the fundamental nature of development is not changed, Guizhou will remain a loser rather than become a winner in the Pan-PRD development process.

Lack of a Conducive Structural Context for Development

The market environment in Guizhou is still at the stage of infancy. Facing the problems of a small economy, population pressure, and a large ethnic minority population, the state remains the key player in the reform period. The low level of private participation in the economy sets Guizhou apart from its counterparts in the Pan-PRD region, making smooth integration a challenge. As of the year 2000, Guizhou had 3,741 state-owned enterprises, producing a total gross output value of RMB126.2 billion and accounting for 79.28% of all industrial enterprises above a designated size.

Sustainable Development in Guizhou: Policies and Institutional Structures

Guizhou is firm in its objective to promote economic growth that adheres to the principle of sustainable development. In the above sections, we have offered an analysis of the province's opportunities and challenges with regard to its economic development. Guizhou suffers from a whole array of constraints to development, including its geographical isolation, lack of good transport linkages and basic infrastructure, a market that is unstable and still in an early stage of development, a lack of competitiveness among its industrial enterprises, the low level of its human capital, as well as environmental changes such as rock desertification, desertification, and ecological deficits. On the other hand, Guizhou is endowed with development opportunities, including a high potential in hydro- and coal-power production, mining industries, phosphorus and coal-based chemical industries, as well as nature-based and cultural tourism. In order to build up its position and harness the potential benefits of Pan-PRD integration, Guizhou needs to improve its policy and institutional structures in the following aspects:

Economic Aspects

(1) Intensify its linkages and cooperation with other provinces in the Pan-PRD region, in order to increase the province's attractiveness for investors.

(2) Strengthen the legal framework and hence improve the investment environment in order to create a fair competitive context that is well integrated to the Pan-PRD context.

(3) Provide better support, leadership, coherent planning, structuring, and management to the major industrial sectors, in order to increase their competitiveness. In particular, the Guizhou government should accelerate the development of the power industry, which would help to energize the raw materials production industries (e.g., the

aluminium industry, and the phosphorus and coal-based chemical industries) while paying keen attention to the environmental threats these industries pose. Second, the development of hi-tech industries (such as the aerospace and mechanical sectors) should be speeded up. The private sector should also be encouraged to invest in technological developments of this kind. Third, light industries such as the pharmaceutical, tobacco, liquor, and food processing industries should be encouraged. Fourth, the tourism sector should also be fostered.

(4) Improve the relationship between the state and the market. In order to catch up and keep pace with the development of the Pan-PRD region, Guizhou needs to handle the state-market relationship well. In any system of governance, the state remains a key actor. Decision-making can be conducted on the basis of repeated negotiations among different state actors, and respecting the principle of the market economy. Mechanisms should also be set up to monitor the functioning of such a system of governance.

Ecological and Environmental Aspects

Efforts to regenerate the ecological environment of the area suffering from rock desertification should be intensified. Policies should be implemented to encourage farmers to convert farmland to forest and grass cover, which will in turn enhance the sustainability potential of the area. Rock desertification has posed serious threats to the cattle industry and to the hydrological and ecological environment, consequently endangering the basic livelihoods of people living in the area and the economic development potential of the area. Guizhou is an important ecological defence for the Yangzi and Pearl River regions. Improving the ecological environment of the province will, therefore, contribute to the sustainable development of the whole Pan-PRD area.

Social Aspects

(1) Control population growth and improve the educational level of the population

Human capital is the most crucial factor in determining a society's competitiveness. To this end, current family planning policies and strict controls over population should continue to be implemented. Furthermore,

more efforts to enhance education levels and to improve the general living conditions of the minority populations are important steps in helping to solve Guizhou's population problem. In order to achieve these goals, the province must raise its investment in education and implement nine years of compulsory education. The structure and quality of tertiary education also need upgrading. In addition, professional education and vocational training, as well as further education for adults, should be developed. Vocational training and labour export arrangements should also be organized for the surplus agrarian workforce in Guizhou.

(2) Improve basic infrastructure

The backwardness of the basic infrastructure is the bottleneck that in Guizhou's economic development. Both road and air transport infrastructure and networks are insufficient and of poor quality. It is essential for Guizhou to improve its basic infrastructure if it is to create a better investment environment.

Institutional Aspects

In order to successfully tap its resource base for economic development, Guizhou needs to attract additional capital, technology, skills, and talent. To this end, institutional reforms are necessary to modernize the existing obsolete and protectionist policies and regulations, in order to attract potential investors and talent by providing them with a sense of security. Specific policy implications include the following:

(1) Establish an infrastructure for the free movement of capital

In order to realize China's Western Development Strategy, abundant external capital is necessary. Guizhou is in particular need of external investment due to its weak economic base. In this regard, the establishment of the Pan-PRD economic region provides a good opportunity for Guizhou. In order to make good use of this chance, the provincial government must establish necessary regulations and eliminate unnecessary structural and policy constraints on the flow capital between various administrative units. This would help to create a system that is conducive to the free movement of capital.

(2) Encourage entrepreneurship

The out-migration of people with capital and talent from the central and western provinces to the eastern part of the country has been a trend since the onset of economic reforms. Following the example of its counterparts in the eastern region, Guizhou should remove institutional blockages in order to retain its local talent and potential entrepreneurs, and attract those from the eastern region as well as from overseas.

(3) Establish a barrier-free environment for technological flows

Advanced, appropriate, and practical scientific knowledge and technology are important for Guizhou's development. The elimination of all regulatory barriers that work against the free and efficient flow of technology and related talent is, therefore, vital.

Conclusion

In this chapter, we have provided an overview of the development opportunities for Guizhou and the constraints on such development. Geographically, Guizhou can be considered to be the junction between eastern and southern China and the southwestern part of the country. Guiyang is the nodal centre for roads and railways that connect Guizhou with all parts of China, in particular Sichuan, Yunnan, Guangxi, Guangdong and Hunan. The existing and planned railway, road and air transport networks through Guizhou can provide invaluable connections between different parts of the country. In the context of the Pan-PRD development, Guizhou displays immense potential in energy generation, mineral production, biodiversity-related industries and tourism. In the past few decades, substantial progress has also been made in the aviation and aerospace industries, electronics, energy generation, mineral mining and processing, construction materials production, and machinery and auto parts production. In addition, the province is also well endowed to develop such sectors as organic food and tourism. Armed with an abundant and relatively cheap workforce, power, and land as compared to other regions in the Pan-PRD region, Guizhou can strive to be a productive partner for other provinces, and become the power base and back garden of the economic region.

Nevertheless, as discussed in the chapter, Guizhou's future development path is also not smooth. The development constraints considered above are all grave ones and cannot be corrected or improved without political commitment from the province and central state. While the central tenor of the development strategies is rapid economic growth, the impact of such economic projects on the environment, natural resource base, and livelihood of the people, especially the poor, should not be ignored. Only by the careful planning and implementation of policies that also attach value to these other aspects can development in Guizhou be sustainable.

Notes

1. Xinhua, "Guizhou to Eliminate Poverty in Next Five Years," 2 April 2006, http://english.gov.cn/2006-04/02/content_243045.htm, accessed on 29 May 2006.
2. Views on implementing the "decision of the central committee of the Chinese communist party to improve the system of the socialist market economy." It was a recent provincial strategy to build a "large Guiyang."
3. R. Nurkse, *Problems of Capital-formation in Underdeveloped Countries* (New York: Oxford University Press, 1953).
4. This highlights the awkward geographical position of Guiyang: "三不沿" (not linked in three ways), "不沿邊、不沿海、不沿江" (not along border, the sea or river).

References

Gao Guilong 高貴龍, Deng Zimin 鄧自民 and Xiong Kangning 熊康寧, *Karst de huhuan yu xiwang* 喀斯特的呼喚與希望 (The Current Situation and Future Prospects of Karst) (Guiyang: Guizhou Science and Technology Press, 2003).

Guizhou Development and Reform Commission 貴州省發展和改革委員會, *Guizhou gaikuang 2004* 貴州概況 2004 (Profile of Guizhou 2004) (internal document) (Guizhou: Guizhou Development and Reform Commission, 2004).

Guizhou People's Government 貴州省人民政府, *Guizhousheng guomin jingji he shehui fazhan shiyiwu guihua gangyao* 貴州省國民經濟和社會發展十一五規劃綱要 (The 11th Five-year Plan of Guizhou Province) (Guiyang: Guizhou People's Government, 2006).

Guizhou Statistics Bureau 貴州省統計局, *Guizhou tongji nianjian* 貴州統計年鑒 2005 (Guizhou Statistical Yearbook 2005) (Beijing: China Statistics Press, 2005).

Peng Xianwei 彭賢偉, "Guizhou shengcun tiaojian elie de Karst huanjing yu quyu pinkun" 貴州生存條件惡劣的喀斯特環境與區域貧困 (Adverse Circumstances of the Karst Environment and Regional Poverty in Guizhou), *Guizhou minzu yanjiu* 貴州民族研究 (Research in Guizhou Tribe), Vol. 23, No. 4 (2003), pp. 96–101.

Rong Li 容麗 and Yang Long 楊龍, "Guizhou de shengwu duoyangxing yu Karst huanjing" 貴州的生物多樣性與喀斯特環境 (Biodiversity and the Karst

Environment in Guizhou), *Guizhou shifan daxue xuebao (ziren kexue ban)* 貴州師範大學學報 (自然科學版), Vol. 22, No. 4 (2004), pp. 1–6.

Tu Yulin 屠玉麟, *Dute de wenhua yaolan — Karst yu Guizhou wenhua* 獨特的文化搖籃——喀斯特與貴州文化 (A Unique Cultural Hearth: Karst and Guizhou's Culture) (Guiyang: Guizhou Education Press, 2000).

Wang Shijie 王世杰 and Zhang Dianfa 張殿發, *Guizhou fanpinkun xitong gongcheng* 貴州反貧困系統工程 (Guizhou's Poverty Alleviation System and Programme) (Guiyang: Guizhou People's Press, 2003).

Xiong Kangning 熊康寧, Li Ping 黎平 and Zhou Zhongfa 周忠發, *Karst shimohua de yaogan — GIS dianxing yanjiu, yi Guizhousheng weili,* 喀斯特石漠化的遙感——GIS典型研究——以貴州省為例 (Classic Remote Sensing — G.I.S. Study on Desertification in a Karst Landscape, with Guizhou as an Example) (Beijing: Geological Publishing House, 2002).

Yang Long 楊龍, *Guizhou lüyou dili* 貴州旅遊地理 (Guizhou's Tourism Geography) (Guiyang: Guizhou Science Press, 1998).

14

Sichuan

Dai Bin, Qian Zhihong and Chung Him

Sichuan 四川 is one of China's landlocked inland provinces. Unlike the coastal region, which has experienced remarkable changes in the past couple of decades under the interplay of global and local forces, Sichuan appeared to have been excluded from globalization's reach. The promotion of the Western Development Strategy in 1999, however, has provided golden opportunities for the province to open up and develop its economy. Sichuan has been chosen by the central government to be the "dragonhead" of the inner region. As a result, transportation, infrastructure, and energy facilities for the province have been planned under integrated master plans. The provincial government of Sichuan has also leveraged on the new central government policy by offering concessions to foreign investors to speed up economic development. High-priority policies have been introduced to attract foreign investment. For instance, investors are being offered tax holidays of up to 10 years. Good concessions, including favourable land-leasing terms, are given to investors involved in key projects such as the construction of highways, bridges, and power plants, the exploitation of minerals, and the development of high technology.[1]

Sichuan's offer has attracted investors looking beyond the coastal area for investment opportunities. In 1999, the total value of foreign direct investment actually utilized in the province amounted to US$454 million.[2] The figure soared to US$659 million in 2002, a 51% increase when compared with 2000.[3] In 2003, the province received another US$582 in foreign investment, in 334 major projects. Most of these investments went to the manufacturing industry (60%) and the service industry (18%).[4] The result was an impressive 12% growth rate for Sichuan in 2003, the third consecutive year that the province had experienced growth of over 10%.[5]

The opening of the Pan–Pearl River Delta (Pan-PRD) 泛珠江三角洲 Regional Cooperation and Development Forum in 2004 has brought Sichuan new opportunities to bridge the global economy. The forum has constructed a cooperation framework between coastal and inland provinces, allowing Sichuan to participate actively in development and cooperation with Guangzhou 廣州, Hong Kong 香港, and Macao 澳門. What, then, are the comparative advantages of Sichuan? How can the province use these advantages to benefit from the regional economy of the Pan-PRD grouping? Investigating regional cooperation between Sichuan and the Pan-PRD, this chapter first highlights local conditions in Sichuan and development trends in the province since the promotion of the Western Development Strategy. This is followed by a discussion of the dynamics of spatial integration and the urban agglomerations arising from these forces. In the last section,

Sichuan's cooperation with other provinces, including members of the Pan-PRD grouping, is discussed. The potential areas for cooperation are highlighted and their possible impact on both Sichuan and the Pearl River Delta (PRD) 珠江三角洲 region, particularly Hong Kong, is analyzed.

Sichuan — the Settings and Development

Sichuan has a total area of 485,000 sq km. It is the fifth largest province in China, accounting for 5.1% of the country's territory. In economic capacity the province ranked first out of the 12 provinces and provincial-level cities in western China.[6] In 1999, Sichuan's GDP was RMB372 billion.[7] The figure rose to RMB488 billion and RMB656 billion in 2002 and 2004, respectively, for an impressive annual growth rate of 12%.[8] This robust development stemmed from the booming of the secondary and tertiary sectors, which grew 12% and 11%, respectively, in 2004.[9] In 1999, the province's GDP per capita was RMB4,473; in 2003 the figure soared to RMB6,418.[10] Sichuan's per capita GDP reached RMB8,114 in 2004, ranking it 24th among all provinces in China (Table 14.1).[11]

Since the mid-1990s, Sichuan has become one of the most attractive provinces for foreign investment in western China. In 2003, there were 6,174 foreign investors in Sichuan, including 40 of the world's top 500 enterprises. For instance, Motorola of the U.S.A. has set up a development centre in Sichuan; Toyota Motor of Japan has formed a joint-venture to manufacture automobiles; Lafarge of France is jointly investing in the building of a cement plant with a production capacity of 1.2 million tonnes; Vivendi Waterworks of France and Marubeni of Japan are carrying out build-operate-transfer (BOT) waterworks projects in the city of Chengdu

Table 14.1   Major Economic Indicators of Sichuan, 1995–2004

	1995	2000	2002	2004
Total population (in millions, excluding migrants)	82	84	85	86
GDP (RMB billion)	250	401	488	656
GDP per capita (RMB)	3,081	4,784	5,766	8,114
Total amount of foreign capital utilized (US$ million)	N.A.	956	1,066	1,001
Foreign direct investment (US$ million)	N.A.	436	659	701

Source: Sichuan tongjiju, 2005, pp. 12–13, 18–19 (see note 5).

成都; and Alcatel of France is setting up an Optical Communications R&D Centre there. Other international financial and insurance giants, such as the International Finance Corporation, the Asian Development Bank, Citibank, OCBC Bank, New York Life, and Aviva, are also setting up offices in Sichuan.[12]

Sichuan's rapid pace of economic growth has been fostered by its abundant resources. The province has long been regarded as a land of abundance. The province's huge population and rich resources, such as arable land, mineral resources, hydropower, and biological resources, has provided a solid material basis for the realization of the strategic objective of developing western China. In 2004, Sichuan had a total population of 86 million.[13] This ranked the province the third most populous of China's 31 provinces, and first in the 12 western provinces. Unlike other inland provinces, Sichuan has a large pool of well-trained technical workers. This is the result of the pursuit in the 1960s of the strategy of the "Third Front 三線," when enormous state investments were injected to the inner regions to diffuse industries away from the coast to reduce the country's vulnerability in the event of military attacks. Many heavy industries, as well as military factories, were established in Sichuan and technological research institutions were built to train technical workers. These developments have consolidated Sichuan's position as a solid industrial centre. Since the introduction of economic reforms, these industrial facilities and trained workers have been made available to commercial industries. Moreover, wages in Sichuan are about one-third of those in the coastal cities.

In Sichuan, there is a total of 60.9 million *mu* of arable land, ranking the province first in China.[14] The Sichuan Basin, covering an area of 170,000 sq km, is one of the most fertile regions in the country. However, the average amount of land per capita is only 8.9 *mu*, and the average amount of arable land per person is 0.7 *mu*. So far, as much as 11.8% of the total land area is not being utilized. Many tracts of land in the urban areas have been expropriated by local governments and enterprises, but not all of them have been developed.

Sichuan is abundant in mineral resources, energy resources, biological resources, and tourist attractions. Sichuan boasts 132 verified kinds of mineral resources and ranks first in the county in reserves of vanadium, titanium, and other 11 minerals. Of these, its reserves of titanium comprise 69% of the nation's reserves, and are the second richest in the world. Moreover, Sichuan has 93% of the vanadium in China and one-third of the world's resources of that mineral. The Panzhihua region 攀枝花地區 and southern Sichuan 川南 are the province's biggest mineral bases. Sichuan is also one of the most important hydropower bases in China. In theory, the province possesses 143 million kw of hydropower, accounting for about 20% of the nation's total. The exploitable figure is estimated at 110 million kw, which again tops the country. A series of hydropower stations have been or will be constructed in Sichuan, and in 2005 12% of the province's hydropower was converted into electricity, according to a provincial research report.[15] So far, Sichuan has been the base for the exploitation of hydropower and the base of the export of hydroelectricity to the eastern region. In addition, Sichuan is a major tourism destination in China, with seven national-level historical and cultural cities. There are 41 relics under special preservation by the government, 9 state-level scenic spots, and 11 national forest parks. Some historical and cultural sites, such as Jiuzhaigou 九寨溝, Huanglong Temple 黃龍寺, the Leshan Giant Buddha 樂山大佛, Mountain Emei 峨眉山, the Qingcheng Mountain–Dujiangyan Irrigation System 青城山—都江堰, the Sanxindui Relics 三星堆遺址, and the Hailuogou Glacier 海螺溝冰川, are known worldwide.

While located in an inland region, Sichuan's transportation facilities have improved significantly during the past decade. This has helped the province to overcome the disadvantages of its location. Five trunk railway lines have been constructed, connecting Sichuan to its neighbouring provinces. Moreover, an expressway network with Chengdu city as its centre has already been built in Sichuan. It is mainly made up of seven expressways: the Chengdu-Chongqing 重慶 line, the Chengdu-Mianyang 綿陽 line, the Chengdu-Ya'an 雅安 line, the Chengdu-Leshan line, the Chengdu-Dujiangyan line, the Chengdu-Nanchong 南充 line, and Chengdu-Wenjiang 溫江-Qionglai 邛崍 line. A new circular expressway is also being planned, which will connect Chengdu, Ya'an, Leshan, Yibin 宜賓, Luzhou 瀘州, Chongqing, Suining 遂寧, Mianyang, and Chengdu. In general, these improvements have made Sichuan into a regional transport centre for southwest China. The city of Chengdu, in particular, has developed into a transport hub, connecting the north to the south in western China (Figure 14.1)

Moreover, two seaward transport lines, connecting Sichuan to the central area of the PRD, have been planned to facilitate integration between the two regions. The southwest seaward roadway, which was completed in 2001, stretches a full length of 451.8 km within the territory of Sichuan. The roadway merges with the Arongqi 阿榮旗-Beihai 北海 section of the western passage, and then emerges to pass through Longchang 隆昌, Luzhou,

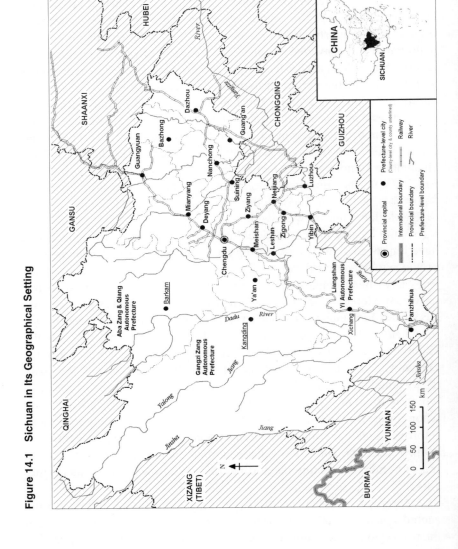

Figure 14.1 Sichuan in Its Geographical Setting

Naxi 納溪, and Xuyong 敘永 in Sichuan. It then enters Guizhou 貴州 along the Dafang 大方-Bijie 畢節-Liupanshui 六盤水 stretch, and finally stops at Beihai in Guangxi 廣西. At the same time, a second seaward roadway in Sichuan is also being planned. This roadway will pass from Chengdu to Panzhihua, then to Yunnan 雲南 and end in Vietnam. The project is scheduled for completion in 2010. Once the roadway is completed and connected to Sichuan's expressway network, it will greatly enhance Sichuan's economic partnership with the Pan-PRD region. This, in turn, will facilitate regional cooperation between Sichuan, Guizhou, and Guangxi. In addition, a southwest seaward railway is planned. It will be built upon the existing Longchang-Luzhou railway, and go on to Xuyong and Gulan 古藺, passing over the Chishui River 赤水河 to enter Bijie and Dafang in Guizhou, and finally merging with the Huangtong 黃桶-Bose 百色 railway. When the railway is completed, it will provide Sichuan with another effective link with the coastal area.

In sum, Sichuan's social and economic development has taken a quantum leap forward during the past decades. Its solid economic base, the availability of various resources, and the improvements in its infrastructure have made Sichuan an exciting alternative for investors.

Regional Dynamics in Sichuan

Sichuan is a large province in both size and population. Generally, regions with better infrastructure and a solid economic base are competitive and have recorded rapid rates of growth. Yang has classified Sichuan into four areas with different levels of development: most developed, relatively developed, low level of development, and underdeveloped (Table 14.2, Figure 14.2).[16] The city of Chengdu, the province capital of Sichuan, is the mostly developed area in the province. It is located in the Chengdu plain and its municipal area represents the economic core of Sichuan. Four prefecture-level cities — Panzhihua, Deyang 德陽, Mianyang, and Leshan — belong to the category of relatively developed area. They are located at the edge of the Chengdu plain, surrounding Chengdu city. The area of low development includes seven cities located in the hilly area between the Chengdu plain and the plateau areas, while the underdeveloped area consists of nine cities and autonomous prefectures located in the western and eastern mountainous areas. In these areas are concentrated some of the nation's most impoverished counties. Transport infrastructure is inadequate and accessibility is poor. Energy and mineral resources are scarce. Traditional

Table 14.2   Comprehensive Development Levels of Regions in Sichuan, 2003

Category of area	Municipality or prefecture	Population (1,000 persons)	Area (1,000 sq km)
Most developed	Chengdu	1,044.3	12
Relatively developed	Panzhihua, Deyang, Mianyang, Leshan	13,619	46
Low level of development	Zigong (自貢), Ya'an, Meishan (眉山), Yibing, Luzhou, Neijiang (內江), Suining	25,900	61
Underdeveloped	Nanchong, Aba (阿壩), Guangyuan (廣元), Guang'an (廣安), Dazhou (達州), Ziyang (資陽), Bazhong (巴中), Liangshan (涼山), Ganzi (甘孜)	35,332	366

Source: Yang, 2004, p. 123 (see note 16).

Figure 14.2   Regional Economic Development Pattern in Sichuan

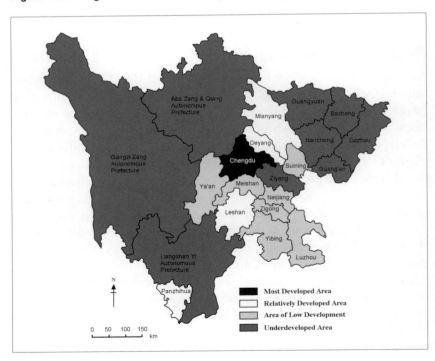

agriculture and animal husbandry remain the economic mainstays of these areas.

The development pattern demonstrated by Yang is a classic one, with Chengdu at the centre and cities and towns circling around it.[17] This geographical distribution is highly conductive to diffusing Chengdu's influence and resources to neighbouring areas. Indeed, the city of Chengdu has played a vital role in the province's spatial development strategy. For instance, the following strategies have emphasized the polarization effects of Chengdu: the "one line and two wings" strategy in 1992; the strategy of "leading the province by two cities, two lines, two wings" in 1995; the "one point, one circle, two patches and three areas" strategy in 1997; the strategy of "accelerating the development of the Chengdu plateau and the Panzhihua area" in 2000; and the "five economic regions" strategy of the current Eleventh Five-year Plan (2006–2010). Thus, Chengdu has constituted the economic engine of Sichuan. Further, urban agglomerations stemming from the polarization effects of Chengdu are perceived as important for the future development of the province. It is to a discussion of these urban systems that this chapter now turns.

Chengdu City and Metropolitan Region

The city of Chengdu is the provincial capital of Sichuan. It is one of the mega cities in western China, and the transport, postal, and communications hub of the region. In recent years, Chengdu has expanded at an astounding speed, and its all-round economic strength and competitiveness have skyrocketed. Some statistics will help to illustrate its economic power (Table 14.3). In 2003, Chengdu ranked fourth in GDP, fifth in terms of total

Table 14.3   Economic Development of Chengdu City

Indicators	2000	2003	Percentage of growth
Total areas of the city proper (km²)	207.8	382.5	84
Total population in urban districts (million)	3.4	4.5	34
GDP (RMB billion)	131.3	187.1	42
Total investment in fixed assets (RMB billion)	47.6	86.3	81
Financial income (RMB billion)	11.9	21.6	82
Total retail sales of consumer goods (RMB billion)	55.4	77.2	39

Source: Chengdu tongjiju, 2004, pp. 6–7, 72, 112 (see note 18).

investment in fixed assets, and fourth in total retail sales of consumer goods compared to 15 other sub-provincial cities in the inland area.[18] In 2004, Chengdu's strong economic growth repeatedly earned rave reviews within China. For instance, on 4 November, the city was rated one of the 10 most economically dynamic cities in China. On 3 December, it was given the "China City Branding Award." On 7 December, it was voted one of the top 10 cities for businesses in China. At the end of the year, it was ranked fifth among "China's Most Livable Cities," and first in western China. On 18 February 2005, Chengdu was named the "National Model City for Environmental Protection" by the State Environmental Protection Administration of China. It was the first subordinate province-level city in western China to receive such an award. Clearly, Chengdu has been making impressive progress in recent years. Germany opened a consulate in Chengdu on 5 December 2004, while Korea and Thailand also opened consulates in Chengdu in 2005. This will elevate Chengdu's international status and influence to a new level.

Indeed, Chengdu has become a favourite among foreign investors, including those from Hong Kong, Macao, and Taiwan 台灣. In September 2003, Intel built in Chengdu its first Solution Centre in western China, which is also its 12th such centre in the world. US$375 million was invested to build a microprocessor assembly and test plant. Intel's Chengdu centre is its fourth Solution Centre in China, after Beijing 北京, Shanghai 上海, and Shenzhen 深圳.[19] In July 2004, The city of Chengdu and the Semiconductor Manufacturing International Corporation (SMIC) signed an official investment agreement on the corporation's plan to invest US$175 million to build a testing and assembly facility (AT2) in Chengdu. This will be the corporation's fourth largest investment in the mainland, after Shanghai, Beijing, and Tianjin 天津.[20] The two major investments by Intel and SMIC in Chengdu it is giving the city an even more competitive edge in the electronic information industry. In September 2004, Chengdu was voted the third "Most Recommended City" by Taiwan investors.[21]

Chengdu's rapid development has given its neighbouring cities and towns an economic boost, and leading to the formation of a highly integrated Chengdu metropolitan region. Within the 12,400 km^2 of Chengdu's administrative territory, there are 1 mega city, 4 small cities, and 251 towns. The density of cities is 4.03/10,000 km^2 and the density of towns is 167/10,000 km^2. Situated in the Chengdu plain around the Min River 岷江, these cities and towns are scattered on a gentle slope stretching from the northwest to the southeast. They are centred on Chengdu in a circular distribution. This geographical distribution is highly conductive to the diffusion of Chengdu's influence and resources to neighbouring cities and towns. The highly integrated area of the metropolis of Chengdu (whose geographical coverage is roughly equal to that of the Chengdu administrative region) accounts for 2.6% of Sichuan's total area but over one-third of its economic volume. In the next 5 to 10 years, the metropolis of Chengdu may develop into the main centre for Sichuan's modern industries, population, towns, and economic life, and be the source of over 40% of the province's total economic volume.[22]

Cheng-Yu Economic Region

The Chengdu metroplex extends to the east and forms part of the Cheng-Yu Economic Region 成渝經濟區. This region has developed alongside Chengdu and Chongqing — a mega city which was subordinate to Sichuan before 1997 — and is composed of the cities of Zigong, Neijiang, Nanchong, Suining, and Deyang. The Cheng-Yu region is a core economic belt along the upstream area of the Yangzi River 長江. It is a region characterized by a dense population, rich agriculture, and a concentration of heavy industries. Its fertile farmland, moderate weather, and well-developed irrigation network have made it one of the most important agricultural bases in China in general and in the southwest in particular. Its food, meat, and fruit products accounted for 40%, 51%, and 33%, respectively, of the production of Southwest China in 2003. As noted, the Cheng-Yu region was one of the most critical areas in the national development strategy during the First and Second Five-year Plans and the Third Front Construction. The national development strategy resulted in this region becoming a base for heavy machinery, military aircraft, the electronics and IT industry, automobiles, the nuclear industry, and other military industries. However, the promotion of Chongqing to a municipality has aroused strong competition between Chengdu and Chongqing in attracting foreign investment, and in convincing the central government that it should be accorded priority in national development as the leading city in western China.[23]

Chengdu-Deyang-Mianyang Region

The Chengdu-Deyang-Mianyang region 成德綿城市帶 is situated west of the Sichuan plain. It is comprised of the three most important municipal areas of Sichuan and forms one of the main development axes in the province. These cities are connected by the Baocheng 寶成 railway and the Chengmian expressway, and the distance between them is only a little over 90 km. This region is the most economically developed and dynamic in Sichuan. Chengdu has notable advantages in the electronics and information technology communication (ITC) industries, and Deyang's strength is in heavy equipment manufacturing, while Mianyang is prominent in the electronics and information industries, the nuclear industry, and the aviation and aerospace industries. Besides the above industries, this urban region has also incubated hi-tech industries. Today, there are 1,952 state-owned enterprises and sizable private industrial enterprises in the region, accounting for 42.5% of such enterprises in the entire province, and over half of Sichuan's total industrial output. During the period of the Eleventh Five-year Plan, the region will become a target area for planning and development in Sichuan. In the next 5 to 10 years, it may develop into an interlocking metropolitan area, becoming a development zone in Sichuan with a high agglomeration of industries and comprehensive infrastructure, and characterized by high innovation, competitiveness, and economic vigour. It will be the main region supporting the economic development of Sichuan, and is expected to account for over 60% of the province's total economic volume.[24]

The Southern Sichuan Urban Agglomeration

The urban agglomeration in southern Sichuan is composed of four medium-sized cities — Zigong, Yibin, Luzhou, and Neijiang. It is actually a polycentric urban region, totalling roughly 50 to 100 km, and connected by expressways and the Neijiang-Kunming 昆明 railway line. In the past few decades, southern Sichuan was perceived as a region rich in natural resources, and resources-based industries were emphasized. However, the urban agglomeration effects were ignored. With the completion of modern transport infrastructure, economic linkages have been strengthened and urban economies have been growing at a much more rapid pace than the surrounding hinterlands. Therefore, urban agglomerations with multiple centres are being highlighted by academics in Sichuan. A policy of creating a self-organizing economic dynamism is being intentionally introduced by the government to the urban regions, so that urban agglomeration can work as an economic engine for the rapid development of the regional economy in southern Sichuan.[25]

The abovementioned four urban zones of integration are the most economically advanced in Sichuan. They are not mutually exclusive but overlap spatially, and together make up the economic engine of Sichuan. With the best infrastructure, the most concentrated industries, good development potential, financial services, import-export trade, logistics, advanced technology, and management, these zones also offer big opportunities for cooperation with the PRD region, especially Hong Kong, Guangzhou, and Shenzhen.

Cooperation with Regions outside Sichuan

The expansion of urban economic power and the emergence of urban agglomerations in Sichuan have triggered regional integration. At the same time, the further engagement of China in the world economy has facilitated active cooperation and integration between Sichuan and other important cities, provinces, and national municipalities. The following are key economic alliances between Sichuan and other provinces and cities.

Organization for the Economic Coordination of Six Provinces, One Municipality and One Autonomous Region

Similarities in their natural and economic conditions have caused four southwestern provinces — Sichuan, Yunnan 雲南, Guizhou, and Guangxi — to band together to formalize cooperation efforts, in order to overcome constraints stemming from their disadvantageous locations and administrative barriers. In 1984, these provinces, which have many large hydropower stations, tourist resources, and important mineral resources, established an organization for regional economic coordination. The involvement of Tibet 西藏 in 1986 and the promotion of Chongqing as a city directly under state administration in 1997 extended the membership into six provincial-level units.[26]

The objectives of this organization mainly focus on six aspects: (1) to collectively construct transport and communication infrastructure; (2) develop resources with an emphasis on energy and minerals; (3) establishing a regional market system; (4) promote progress in minority nationality areas; (5) conduct surveys on territorial resources and; (6) carry out research on development strategies.

Since the formation of the organization, there has been an increase in investment in industries related to the exploitation of resources, and in the manufacturing and service industries. For example, collaborating with other members of the organization, Guizhou carried out 628 economic projects in 2004, with about RMB35.29 billion having been utilized. These projects are concentrated in the following sectors: energy, the chemical industry, metallurgy, construction materials, light industry, urban infrastructure, real estate, and tourism.[27]

Two economic sub-regions — the Nan-Gui-Kun Economic Region 南貴昆經濟區 and the Economic Region of the Upper Reaches of the Yangzi River 長江上游經濟區 — have been formed under this cooperation framework. The former accommodates three metropolitan regions, Nanning 南寧, Guiyang 貴陽, and Kunming, which are rich in tourism resources and reserves of nonferrous metals. As a result, an industrial system with a pillar of resource-based industries has been established. These industries are of great significance at the national level for hydropower, for the steel and automobile industries, and for tourism. The economic region of the Upper Reaches of the Yangzi River is comprised of the cities of Chongqing, Chengdu, Panzhihua, and Lhasa 拉薩. Since it is situated at the upper reaches of the Yangzi River, its development is subject to the national policy on the Yangzi River, which places an emphasis on ecological protection and the reduction of soil erosion. Given the considerable degree of policy restriction, cooperation among the members of this organization is mainly driven by top-down forces. Government institutions at various levels have played a dominant role in facilitating cooperation, while local enterprises have shown little enthusiasm for participation. Thus far, the progress on regional integration has not been satisfactory, and significant achievements are yet to be seen.

Cooperation between Sichuan and Chongqing

Sichuan and Chongqing are geographically nestled next to each other and share the same central Sichuan plain, a similar culture, and intensive population flows. Both have excellent infrastructure and the essential factors for regional cooperation are in place. However, as noted, the promotion of Chongqing as a special municipality has institutionally separated it from Sichuan and created structural constraints for regional cooperation — a classic example of China's administrative separation.[28] This has led to economic disjunction and, in many cases, economic battles, dearly costing Sichuan and Chongqing many golden chances for spatial and economic integration. Recently, senior officials of the Sichuan and Chongqing governments have reached the consensus that Sichuan and Chongqing in general, and Chengdu and Chongqing in particular, are both competitors and partners. Therefore, the two entities should strengthen their ties, increase communication, overcome regional administrative constraints, and utilize the free flow of talent, funds, materials, and other resources for their mutual development. In 2003, the Chongqing government proposed a "1 + 2" cooperation framework to Sichuan. The aim is to establish "1" interactive mechanism for general planning, and initiate a close partnership in "2" areas: (1) tourism and (2) transport and energy infrastructure. The "1 + 2" proposal was eventually extended to "1 + 6" for a more comprehensive effort at cooperation. In 2004, an agreement — the *Agreement on Strengthening Socioeconomic Cooperation and Striving for Regional Development in the Economic Region of the Upper Reaches of the Yangzi River* — was reached to endorse this partnership. The agreement includes a commitment to share resources and hold regular meetings on the development of transport and energy infrastructure; to promote cultural activities, agricultural production, public security, and the broadcasting industry; and to promote tourism.[29] The "1 + 6" agreement symbolizes broader, deeper, higher-level, and more concrete efforts at communication and cooperation between Sichuan, Chengdu, and Chongqing. It will also have significant implications for the relationship between Sichuan and the PRD region in the future.

Recent Cooperation among the Members of the Pan-PRD Grouping

The initiation of the Pan-Pearl River Delta Forum in 2004 has brought new opportunities for Sichuan. As noted, the province's solid industrial base, large reserves of manpower, and rich natural resources give it strong comparative advantages in the PRD region, including Hong Kong. This is particularly the case during a time when rising costs of production and industrial restructuring are challenging the economic sustainability of the Delta. In the case of Hong Kong, since the outbreak of the regional economic crisis in the late 1990s, the former colony has recognized that its prosperity cannot be sustained without the support of the mainland. The development of Southwest China has provided Hong Kong with a great opportunity to extend its economic hinterland beyond the Delta area. At the same time, Hong Kong's position in the world economy and its strength in international trade are all essential to helping inland provinces enter international markets.

From the perspective of Sichuan, the Pan-PRD is significant for the development of the province. First, it will provide an opportunity for Sichuan to upgrade its industrial structure and speed up its industrialization, because Sichuan is expected to absorb the industries that are moving out from the PRD. Second, the formation of the Pan-PRD grouping is making it easy for Sichuan's enterprises and products to gain access to international markets through Hong Kong. Third, both the Sichuan government and local enterprises are expected to improve their public administration techniques and managerial skills in response to the challenges from new ideas and styles from Hong Kong. Fourth, the Pan-PRD grouping will attract the central government's attention and will help Sichuan gain more policy support from national and international agencies and organizations.[30]

A number of areas for cooperation have been suggested in the Pan-PRD agreement. They widely cover the areas of information, transportation, logistics, industries, investment, financing, tourism, science and education, culture and health, and human resources. The expectation is that a series of trans-provincial unified markets will be created. Sichuan's cooperation with the Pan-PRD, Hong Kong, and Macao has mainly concentrated in the following fields: industrial development, the utilization of labour and human resources, tourism and trade, and logistics.[31] It is to an examination of these areas that the remaining sections turn.

Promote Project-driven All-round Cooperation in the Industrial Sector

Sichuan has the most comprehensive mix of industries in western China and produces a large number of competitive products. As noted, the "Third Front" strategy during the 1960s laid an excellent foundation for Sichuan's industrialization. Many advanced science and technology enterprises were established, with a focus on equipment manufacturing. Nowadays, Sichuan's major industries concentrate on six sectors: hydropower, machinery and metal refinement, the pharmaceutical and chemical industries, electronic information, food and beverages, and tourism, for all of which the province is highly regarded nationwide. During the first "Pan-Pearl River Delta Regional Cooperation and Development Forum," Sichuan, based on its natural resources and economic development needs, launched dozens of projects ranging from the development of infrastructure, to the processing industry, the processing of agricultural products, culture and tourism, the restructuring of state-owned enterprises, the service trade, and so forth. A large number of prominent enterprises participated in the projects in order to seek external cooperation. They include the Chengdu Aircraft Industrial (Group) Co., Ltd, Panzhihua Iron & Steel (Group) Co., Chengdu Diao Pharmaceutical Group Co., Ltd, Dongfang Electrical Machinery Co., Ltd, Changhong Electric Co., Ltd, and the Wuliangye Group. At the end of the Forum, contracts for 542 projects, worth a total of over RMB97 billion, were signed.[32]

Emphasis on Labour Training and the Fortification of Cooperation in Labour Service

The upgrading of Hong Kong's industries and the northward shift of its manufacturing industry has made the PRD region the most attractive place for migrant labourers. In recent years, the demand for labour in the Delta region has not only been increasing in terms of quantity but also in quality. It is anticipated that Guangdong's demand for migrant labour will increase by 10% annually (the current demand is 1.5 million workers per annum) in the next three to five years. According to the *Yangcheng Evening News* 羊城晚報, some areas of the PRD are suffering from a serious shortage of labourers, including mechanical workers, maintenance workers, tailors and seamstresses, waiters, salesmen, domestic helpers and, in particular, technical workers.[33]

As noted, Sichuan's population of 86 million represents a huge pool of labour. In 2003, as many as 13.7 million people were engaged in different kinds of labour, and 6.6 million migrated to other provinces in search of work. *Economic Information Daily* suggests that over 3 million went to the PRD.[34] In 2003, Sichuan spent RMB4 million to provide training for 1.5 million migrant workers via the internet, according to the demands of the market and hiring units. This practice has substantially improved the quality of migrant workers.[35] There are also plans to provide training for 10 million migrant workers in 2004 and 2005.[36] The Sichuan Provincial Development and the Reform Commission, the Sichuan Provincial Labour and Social Security Department, and the Sichuan Provincial Finance Bureau have teamed up to invest in and develop an online interview system. The system allows applicants to conduct face-to-face negotiations with faraway potential employers through computers and on-line cameras. At the end of 2004, this system was installed in 50 labour-base counties in Sichuan, 50 training bases, and towns/villages with better infrastructure than most towns/villages.[37] The system was in service after the Spring Festival of 2005, the traditional high season for migrant workers to hunt for jobs. This far-sighted project will greatly help migrant labourers in Sichuan.

Tourism Development: Improve Facilities for Tourists, Consolidate Tourism Resources, and Promote Cooperation

As an important tourism region in China, Sichuan boasts spectaular landscapes, a rich ancient history, and cultures as well as a unique local civilization. Three of the province's most renowned tourist attractions are (1) the fairyland — Jiuzhaigou; (2) the national treasure — the giant panda; and (3) the ancient Sichuan city of Sanxingdui. In addition, there are 15 national-level scenic spots in the province, as well as four sites that have been designated World Natural Hertiage Sites by the United Nations Educational, Scientific and Cultural Organization (UNESCO). These rich, diverse, and unique tourism resources have tremendous development potential. In view of this, Sichuan has adjusted its tourism development strategy and is opting to pour resources into the continual development of the industry. The infrastructure for tourism has been boosted, and tourism is being promoted, both nationally and internationally, around two main themes: (1) the natural landscape; and (2) the local history and culture. For instance, five internationally renowed tourism attractions are being redeveloped and promoted. They include "China's Number One mountain — Emei — international tourism region," the "Greater Jiuzhaigou international tourism site," "Wolong 臥龍, the Great China Panda tourism site," the "Ancient Archaeological Site, Sanxingdui," and the "Dujiangyan-Qingcheng Mountain tourism site."

Sichuan and cities in the PRD, such as Hong Kong, Guangzhou, and Shenzhen, are mutually assisting in tourism development. The attractions of the latter mainly lie in their urban appeal, while the former lures with its natural landscape. This makes Guangdong 廣東 and Hong Kong extremely attractive to the visitors from Sichuan, and vice versa. In 2003, about four million people from Guangdong visited Sichuan while three million people from Sichuan visited Guangdong.[38] Close connections between travel-related institutions and agencies in Sichuan and their counterparts in Hong Kong and Macao have hence been established. In addition, Sichuan has actively assisted the Hong Kong Tourism Board in promoting tourism in Sichuan, and has even helped it set up an office in Chengdu. Indeed, Sichuan has already begun an extremely beneficial cooperation with the PRD. Together, they will build a circuit for tourism.

Developing the Logistics and Exhibition Sectors by Learning from Hong Kong and Well-developed Cities in the PRD

Sichuan, with the highest density of national expressway networks and the biggest railway traffic hub in the country, an important aviation hub, and a cargo terminal in Southwest China, is the ideal place for developing logistics industries. This is particularly the case with Chengdu, which, with its strategic location and competitive edge in science and technology, finance, trade, transport, and communications has all of the necessary conditions to nurture a modern logistics industry. Indeed, as early as the 1990s, Chengdu formulated the strategy of "letting circulation drive the city's economic development." The aim was to promote trade to invigorate commodity flows and expand markets in particular products. Since 2000, many world-renowned retail companies, such as PriceSmart, Metro, and Auchan, have set up stores in Chengdu and brought with them advanced logistics processes, business models, information technology, modern business practices, management practices, and customer services. This has boosted economic growth and diversification in Chengdu's business operation models. Some of the examples include department stores, supermarkets, megastores, convenience stores, professional stores, specialty stores, shopping malls and hypermarkets, and so forth.

Sichuan's agenda to develop Chengdu into a logistics centre in western China also draws on the experience of Hong Kong — a cosmopolitan, international aviation hub and port city. In the short term, efforts are being made to create a favourable environment for development, by integrating logistics bases and centres. The goal is to create two to four major "Third Party Logistics" (3PL) corporations with the capacity to serve the whole of western China. The target for the logistics industry is to create RMB30 billion in 2005, accounting for 15% of Chengdu's GDP, while lowering the ratio of logistics cost to GDP to around 25%. An interim plan (2006–2010) is to establish modern logistics corporations (協作群體). Special assistance will be given to five to eight leading corporations. They will be made the leading players in the region and their businesses will be diffused to the entire nation. A preliminary modern logistics framework has been drafted, with modern logistics industry parks, functional logistics centres, and multi-level distribution centres as nodes. The aim is to push up the market share of third party logistics to over 30% and lower the ratio of cost to GDP to around 15% in 2010. In the long run (2011–2015), a western China logistics centre with sophisticated operation networks, service delivery systems, and an international outlook will be established. It will be a regional leader with great influence nationwide.[39]

The plans to transform Chengdu into a logistics base, southwestern logistics centre, logistics park for imported goods, aviation logistics park, and Sichuan expressway international logistics centre have already been completed. Construction will soon begin. In the next 20 years, four major logistics parks will be built. They include the Xindu Taixing 新都泰興 Railway Scheduling Station Logistics Park, the Longquanyi 龍泉驛 East Railway Station Logistics Park, the Baijia 白家 Passenger Terminal Logistics Park, and the Shuangliu 雙流 Southwestern Aviation Logistics Park. Hong Kong can provide strong back-up support and valuable guidance on constructing logistics centres/parks and designing logistics systems. A flourishing logistics industry will then bring an influx of businesses to the PRD in general, and Hong Kong in particular. This will sustain and elevate Hong Kong's standing as an international logistics centre.

The plan to develop Chengdu as a logistics centre in west China will give the city extraordinary potential to develop its exhibition economy. Indeed, as one of the three national centres for commodity distribution in China, Chengdu has already conceived the idea of developing an exhibition economy. From 1997 to 2001, in the four years after the opening of the Chengdu International Conference and Exhibition Centre, 144 exhibitions were held; over 4.2 million people attended the functions and a transaction amount of over RMB84.2 billion was recorded.[40] In 2002 alone, Chengdu hosted over 140 commodity fairs and exhibitions, attracting over 30,000 enterprises. In August 2003, members of the Tenth Party Representative Meeting in Chengdu formed the following resolution: "Emphasize the development of an exhibition economy. Build an exhibition city with national research and an international outlook."

Chengdu plans to devote 10 years to transforming itself into the nation's top "exhibition city" and gain international recognition. The three major platforms for exhibitions include the Chengdu International Conference and Exhibition Centre, the Century City New International Exhibition Centre, which is the largest in western China, and the Jiuzhai International Resort and Convention Centre. Efforts will also be devoted to nurturing and creating branded exhibitions by considering Chengdu's industrial mix. According to relevant proposals, the government will concentrate on six types of exhibition themes: medical and healthcare (Chinese medicine fairs, medical equipment and machinery exhibitions), ecological and environmental conservation (the Wenjiang flora expo, the world environment and development forum), culture and tourism (the Longchuan peach blossom festival, a tourism exchange forum), fine wine and fine food (a confection and wine fair, a fine food cultural festival), electronic information (the Chengdu computer festival, the Sichuan television fair, software meetings), and automobiles and real estate (an international automobile exhibition, a real estate exchange forum, a residential property expo).[41]

The cooperation framework that was established by the Pan-Pearl River Delta Forum has allowed Sichuan to learn directly from the Hong Kong experience. Hong Kong is regarded as Asia's top-notch exhibition city, and the exhibition industry has brought the city tremendous profits and unprecedented prosperity. Hong Kong reaps substantial profits by hosting various major conferences and exhibitions every year. As China's only free port city and modern logistics base, Hong Kong is highly experienced in logistics management and in hosting international exhibitions. It boasts world-class talent in conference planning and in logistics management and services. Hong Kong can help Sichuan develop a logistics and exhibition economy according to Sichuan's characteristics and comparative advantages. At the same time, the development of a logistics and exhibition economy in Sichuan can help corporations in Hong Kong and the PRD region to penetrate the western China market. This will create a good investment environment and exchange platform, thereby expanding industry development possibilities in Hong Kong and the PRD region. In short, Sichuan and the PRD region, particularly Hong Kong, have good prospects for future cooperation in the logistics and exhibition industries.

Conclusion

Sichuan is a very important province in western China because of its comparatively well- developed economy, good infrastructure, and huge development potential. Within the province, the Chengdu metropolitan region, the Chengdu-Deyang-Mianyang megalopolis, and the southern Sichuan urban agglomeration have the best infrastructure and enjoy very robust economic growth. They are not only Sichuan's economic growth poles but also the centres for the province's regional trade as well as windows for attracting foreign investment. The formation and development of these urban economic systems have produced optimum locations for Sichuan to cultivate inter-regional trade. The close partnership between Sichuan and

Chongqing, the plans to establish an economic zone as well as the construction of a western roadway have created favourable conditions for Sichuan to extend its economic alliances beyond western China.

The "Pan-Pearl River Delta Regional Cooperation and Development Forum" and the establishment of the Pan-PRD cooperation framework have provided a stable and reliable platform for Sichuan to interact with the Pan-PRD region in general, and Hong Kong in particular. Sichuan's unique and rich resources (hydropower resources, tourism resources, and mineral resources), its large rural labour force and highly qualified urban talent, good infrastructure, the development of new industries (tourism, exhibitions, and logistics) and its active participation in regional affairs, have not only created new opportunities for collaboration, but also invigorated Sichuan's existing relationships with Hong Kong, Macao, Guangzhou, and other members of the Pan-PRD region. Without doubt, the Pan-PPD cooperation framework is one of the most important achievements in China's regional economic development. Such cooperation will not only sustain the growth of the PRD, but also integrate western China, including Sichuan, into the global economic system.

Notes

1. See Sichuansheng renmin zhengfu 四川省人民政府, *Sichuansheng renmin zhengfu guanyu yinfa sichuansheng guli waishang touziyouhui zhengce de tongzhi* 四川省人民政府關於印發四川省鼓勵外商投資優惠政策的通知 (Notice from the Sichuan Provincial Government on the Distribution of Incentive Policies for Foreign Investment in Sichuan), Document No. 50 (1999).
2. Sichuan tongjiju 四川統計局, *Sichuan tongji nianjian 2004* 四川統計年鑒 2004 (Sichuan Statistical Yearbook 2004) (Beijing: Zhongguo tongji chubanshe 中國統計出版社, 2004), p. 427.
3. Ibid.
4. Sichuan nianjianshe 四川年鑒社, *Sichuan nianjian 2004* 四川年鑒 2004 (Sichuan Yearbook 2004) (Chengdu: Sichuan nianjianshe 四川年鑒社, 2004), p. 210.
5. Sichuan tongjiju, *Sichuan tongji nianjian 2005* (Beijing: Zhongguo tongji chubanshe, 2005), pp. 12–13.
6. The 12 provinces and provincial-level cities are Inner Mongolia 內蒙古, Guangxi, Chongqing, Sichuan, Guizhou, Yunnan, Tibet, Shanxi 陝西, Gansu 甘肅, Qinghai 青海, Ningxia 寧夏 and Xinjiang 新疆. See Liu Qingquan and Gary M. C. Shiu, "Sichuan," in *Developing China's West: A Critical Path to*

Balanced National Development, edited by Y. M. Yeung and Shen Jianfa (Hong Kong: The Chinese University Press, 2004), p. 418.

7. Sichuan nianjianshe, *Sichuan nianjian 2001* 四川年鑑 2001 (Sichuan Yearbook 2001) (Chengdu: Sichuan nianjianshe, 2001), p. 583.

8. *Sichuan tongji nianjian 2005* (see note 5).

9. Ibid.

10. Data from *Sichuan nianjian 2001* and *Sichuan tongji nianjian 2005* (see notes 7 and 5).

11. *Sichuan tongji nianjian 2005* (see note 5).

12. See Xinhua wang Shanghai pindao 新華網上海頻道, *Sichuan kuoda kaifang gei waishang tigong juda shangji* 四川擴大開放給外商提供巨大商機 (Sichuan Opens Further and Provides Great Business Opportunities to Foreign Investors), 2003. http://www.sh.xinhuanet.com/2003-04/09/content_380012. htm, accessed on 25 April 2005.

13. See note 5.

14. 1 *mu* = 1/15 ha.

15. See Sichuansheng fazhan yu gaige weiyuanhui 四川省發展與改革委員會, *Guanyu jiakuai Sichuan jichusheshi jianshe de yanjiu* 關於加快四川基礎設施建設的研究 (A Study on Speeding up the Construction of Infrastructure in Sichuan), 2001. http://info.sc.cei.gov.cn/2001/20010424031955.htm, accessed on 16 September 2006.

16. Yang Xichuan 楊西川, "Sichuan quyu jingji chayi yu xietiao fazhan" 四川區域經濟差異與協調發展 (Regional Economic Disparities and Coordinated Development in Sichuan), in *Sichuan jingji zhanwang* 四川經濟展望 (Prospects for Sichuan's Economy), edited by Cui Xinheng 催新桓, Lai Qi 賴齊 and Zhao Xi 趙西 (Chengdu: Sichuan renmin chubanshe 四川人民出版社, 2004), pp. 121–29.

17. Ibid.

18. Chengdu tongjiju 成都統計局, *Chengdu tongji nianjian 2004* 成都統計年鑑 2004 (Chengdu Statistical Yearbook 2004) (Beijing: Zhongguo tongji chubanshe, 2004).

19. See Sichuan zaixian 四川在線, *Yingte'er jiejue fang'an zhongxin luo hu Chengdu* 英特爾解決方案中心落戶成都 (Intel Solution Centre Located in Chengdu), 2003. http://www.scol.com.cn/nsichuan/sccj/20030918/ 2003918101400.htm, accessed on 19 April 2005.

20. See ICAD Shijie 世界, *Shiwuyi yuan touzi xibu, Chengdu chengwei disan da IT zhizao* 15億元投資西部，成都成為第三大IT製造 (RMB1.5 Billion Investment in the Western Region: Chengdu Becomes the Third IT Manufacturing Base), 2004. http://www.icad.com.cn/html/2004-7-16/ 200471695145.asp, accessed on 19 April 2005.

21. See Huaxia jingwei wang 華夏經緯網, *Taishang jili tuijian Chengdu, cheng xibu weiyi ruxuan chengshi* 台商極力推薦成都，成西部唯一入選城市

(Chengdu is Recommended Strongly by Taiwan Investors, Becoming the Only City in the Western Region to be Selected by Them), 2004. http://www.huaxia.com/sw/rdtz/3/00243601.html, accessed on 19 April 2005.

22. See Dai Bin 戴賓, *Chengdu dushiquan zhanlüe guihua yanjiu* 成都都市圈戰略規劃研究 (A Study on the Strategic Planning of the Urban Region of Chengdu) (unpublished report, 2003); Dai Bin and Qian Zhihong 錢志鴻, *Chengdu chengshihua zhanlüe yanjiu* 成都城市化戰略研究 (A Strategic Study on the Urbanization of Chengdu) (unpublished report, 2004).

23. Lin Ling 林凌 (ed.), *Gongjian fanrong: ChengYu jingjiqu fazhan silu yanjiu baogao* 共建繁榮：成渝經濟區發展思路研究報告 (Striving for Prosperity: Report on Thoughts about the Development of the Chengdu-Chongqing Economic Region) (Beijing: Jingji kexue chubanshe 經濟科學出版社, 2005); Yanjiuzu 研究組, *ChengYu jingjiqu fazhan silu yanjiu* 成渝經濟區發展思路研究 (A Study on Strategic Ideas on the Development of the Chengdu-Chongqing Economic Region) (unpublished report, 2004).

24. Dai Bin, "Sichuan quyu fazhan zhanlüe de xin silu" 四川區域發展戰略的新思路 (New Thoughts on the Regional Development Strategy of Sichuan), *Jingji xuejia* 經濟學家 (Economists), No. 1 (2004), pp. 120–21; Dai Bin, *Sichuan shengchanli buju yu kongjian jiegou fazhan zhanlüe yanjiu* 四川生產力佈局與空間結構發展戰略研究 (A Study on the Strategic Development of the Economic Distribution and Spatial Structure in Sichuan) (unpublished report, 2004).

25. Dai Bin, *Sichuan shengchanli buju yu kongjian jiegou fazhan zhanlue yanjiu* (see note 24).

26. Shi Xiushi 石秀詩, "Luoshi kexue fazhanguan, gongmou hezuo xinkuayue" 落實科學發展觀，共謀合作新跨越 (Implement the Approach of Scientific Development and Seek New Advances in Cooperation), *Jinri Guizhou* 今日貴州 (Guizhou Today), No. 16 (2005), pp. 6–7.

27. Xiang Yongdong 向永東, "Ershiyi nian licheng daxinan quyuxiezuo jingjiquan yueshang xintaijie" 21年歷程大西南區域協作經濟圈躍上新臺階 (New Progress in the Regional Economic Cooperation Group of the Greater Southwest after 21 Years), 18 August 2005. http://www.chinawestnews.net/gb/westnews/xbkf/yw/userobject1ai483611.html, accessed on 17 September 2006.

28. The notion of the "administrative region economy" was developed by Prof. Liu Junde 劉君德 to describe a special form of regional economy in China. See Liu Junde, Jin Runcheng 靳潤成 and Zhou Keyu 周克瑜, *Zhongguo zhengqu dili* 中國政區地理 (Geography of the Administrative Regions of China) (Beijing: Kexue chubanshe, 1999).

29. Yanjiu zu, *ChengYu jingjiqu fazhan silu yanjiu* (see note 23).

30. Zhang Jiangong 張建功, *Sichuan zai Fan Zhusanjiao quyu hezuo zhong de jiyu yu tiaozhan* 四川在泛珠三角區域合作中的機遇與挑戰 (Opportunities and Challenges for Sichuan in Regional Cooperation in the Pan-Pearl River Delta),

2006. http://www.pprd.org.cn/yanlun/200605/t20060509_6468.htm, accessed on 17 September 2006.

31. Ibid.

32. See Nanfang Wang 南方網, *Shengzhang fangtan Sichuan pian: jiakuai maixiang xibu gongye qiang sheng* 省長訪談四川篇：加快邁向西部工業強省 (Interview with the Provincial Governor: Speed up and Become an Industrially Strong Province in the Western Region), 2004. http://www.southcn.com/panprd/qth/zymt/200407130808.htm, accessed on 26 April 2005.

33. See Yangcheng wanbao 羊城晚報, *Jiu sheng qu qianyue tiaokong laodongli gongqiu* 九省區簽約調控勞動力供求 (Nine Provinces Have Signed an Agreement to Regulate the Supply of Labour), 2004. http://www.ycwb.com/gb/content/2004-07/16/content_725213.htm, accessed on 26 April 2005.

34. See Jingji cankaobao 經濟參考報, *Fan Zhusanjiao hezuo Sichuan dayou kewei* 泛珠三角合作四川大有可為 (Sichuan Has Great Opportunities in Pan-PRD Cooperation), 2004. *http://202.84.17.25/www/Article/2004121085919-1.shtml*, accessed on 26 April 2005.

35. See Hong wang 紅網, *Sichuan jiang chuzi sibaiwan yuan dui yibai wushiwan laowu renyuan jinxing peixun* 四川將出資400萬元對150萬勞務人員進行培訓 (Sichuan will Spend RMB4 Million to Train 1.5 Million Labourers), 2003. http://news.rednet.com.cn/Articles/2003/02/394883.htm, accessed on 19 April 2005.

36. See note 30.

37. See Zhongguo laodongli shichang 中國勞動力市場, *Sichuansheng zai quanguo shouchuang yanhai dagong wangshang mianshi* 四川省在全國首創沿海打工網上面試 (Sichuan is the First to Introduce On-line Interviews for People Seeking Jobs in Coastal Areas of the Country), 2004. http://www.lm.gov.cn/gb/employment/2004-09/24/content_48370.htm, accessed on 19 April 2005.

38. See note 32.

39. See Zhongguo gongshang wang 中國工商網, *2015 nian Chengdu gouzhu xibu wuliu zhongxin* 2015 年成都構築西部物流中心 (Chengdu will Become the Logistics Centre of the Western Region by 2015), 2003. http://www.icncn.com/west/ShowWest.asp?id=116820, accessed on 26 April 2005.

40. See Chengdu zhichuang 成都之窗, *Huizhan jingji fangxing weiai* 會展經濟方興未艾 (The Flourishing Exhibition Economy), 2005. http://www.cdw.gov.cn/html/sdfc31.htm, accessed on 26 April 2005.

41. See Zhongguo jingji wang 中國經濟網, *Daidong xiaofei chao baiyi, Chengdu liang huizhan zhi du mingpian* 帶動消費超百億，成都亮會展之都名片 (Stimulating Consumption of over RMB10 Billion, Chengdu Emerges as the City of Exhibitions), 2003. http://www.ce.cn/cyse/sylt/gdxw/t20031222_259649.shtml, accessed on 21 April 2005.

15

Hunan

Hu Wuxian and Joanna Lee

Introduction

The world economy underwent rapid changes in modes of production and consumption in the early 1980s. Industrialization spread as companies sought to capture the comparative advantages of producing in different countries and regions. With a relatively low cost of production, the Pearl River Delta (PRD) region[1] has witnessed unprecedented growth in trade and investment. The forces of globalization have bolstered the prosperity of some regions in China.

Due to its geographical location, Hunan 湖南 is well positioned to facilitate the transformation of the PRD by serving as its economic hinterland. Although Hunan had long been lacking an impetus to boost its economic development, the Pan–Pearl River Delta (Pan-PRD) regional collaboration proposed by Guangdong is now acting as a catalyst to expedite the development of Hunan. Hunan's government has vigorously responded to changing economic conditions by coming up with a series of measures to integrate the province with the Pan-PRD economic region.

After the signing of the Pan-PRD Regional Cooperation Framework Agreement in 2004, Hunan's government began to formulate plans for Hunan's trade and development with the Pan-PRD region. Since then, a series of investment promotion activities have to be held with a view to attracting foreign investors. The Hunan Investment and Trade Fair held in 2004 was one such activity. In the aftermath of the fair, the Hunan government announced the launching of 1,050 provincial-level projects spanning various sectors and amounting to US$30.35 billion. Unlike previous investment promotion activities, this was an outward-looking move that highlighted the development potential of the Pan-PRD region. As with the participants of this trade fair, about one-quarter of the investors in those projects were from Hong Kong, Macao and Taiwan. There were also investors from other provinces in the Pan-PRD region.

All of these moves have furthered the integration of Hunan with the Pan-PRD region. In order to fully capitalize on development opportunities, Hunan should build on its rich resources and locational advantages. Strategically, Hunan has the potential to become the main supplier of agricultural products and migrant labour as well as to be the receiving destination of industries relocating from the PRD. The ways in which Hunan is capitalizing on the opportunities offered by the structural shift taking place in the PRD region will be the main focus of this chapter.

Overview of Hunan

Geographical and Administrative Setting

Situated at the middle reaches of the Yangzi River 長江 (108°47'E–114°15'E, 24°38'N–30°08'N), Hunan has an area of 211,800 km² or about 2.2% of the total area of China. Its cities had a total area of 9,158.73 km² in 2005. As most of the province is located south of Dongting Lake 洞庭湖, it was named "Hunan" (meaning south of the lake, abbreviated as "Xiang" 湘). Hunan is surrounded by mountains to the east, south and west. The central and northern parts of the province are relatively flat. This unique topography has resulted in a U-shaped basin, open in the north, with Dongting Lake as its centre. The Zijiang 資江, the Yuanjiang 沅江, the Lishui 澧水 and the Xiangjiang 湘江 converge on the Yangzi River at Dongting Lake (Figure 15.1). The highest point in Hunan is at Lingfeng 酃峰 with an elevation of 2,122 m, while the lowest point is at Huanggai *zhen* 黃蓋鎮 with an elevation of 21 m. Blessed with a sub-tropical climate characterized by adequate sunshine, high humidity and a long frost-free period, Hunan is a major producer of agricultural products in China.

Hunan has 13 prefecture-level cities and 1 autonomous prefecture (the Xiangxi Tujia and Miao Autonomous Prefecture 湘西土家族苗族自治州). The prefecture-level cities include Changsha 長沙, Zhuzhou 株洲, Xiangtan 湘潭, Hengyang 衡陽, Shaoyang 邵陽, Yueyang 岳陽, Changde 常德, Zhangjiajie 張家界, Yiyang 益陽, Chenzhou 郴州, Yongzhou 永州, Loudi 婁底 and Huaihua 懷化 (Figure 15.1). Changsha is the capital of Hunan. In 2005, Changsha's GDP was RMB151.99 billion, and the per capita GDP was RMB23,968.

Social Landscape

Hunan is one of the most populous provinces in China, and the population has continued to grow steadily in recent years (Table 15.1). In 2005, the total population was 67.32 million, ranking the province seventh in China. Among them, 24.91 million people lived in cities and towns, up from 17.24 million in 1999, while 42.41 million people lived in rural areas. The level of urbanization in Hunan was 37% in 2005, an increase of 1.5% from 2004. Population density in Hunan was about 317.85 people/km², more than double the national average.

Hunan is a province with many ethnic groups. According to the Fifth

414   Hu Wuxian and Joanna Lee

Figure 15.1 Hunan in Its Geographical Setting

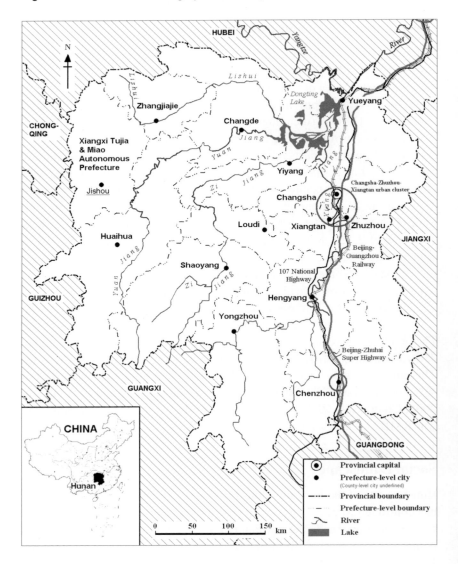

Table 15.1   Population Changes in Hunan, 1999–2005

	1999	2000	2001	2002	2003	2004	2005
Total population (10,000 persons)	6,532.00	6,562.04	6,595.85	6,628.50	6,662.80	6,697.70	6,732.10
Urban	1,724.00	1,952.21	2,031.52	2,121.12	2,232.04	2,377.68	2,490.88
(%)	26.39	29.75	30.80	32.00	33.50	35.50	37.00
Rural	4,808.00	4,609.84	4,564.33	4,507.38	4,430.76	4,320.02	4,241.22
(%)	73.61	70.25	69.20	68.00	66.50	64.50	63.00

Source: Hunansheng tongjiju (ed.), *Hunan tongji nianjian 2006*, p. 35 and *Hunan tongji nianjian 2002*, p. 27.

National Population Census of 2000, there were 56.86 million Han Chinese in Hunan, accounting for 89.9% of Hunan's total population. Minority groups comprised about 6.41 million, or 10.1% of the province's total population. The major ethnic minority groups include the Tujia 土家族 (2.64 million), the Miao 苗族 (1.92 million), the Dong 侗族 (0.84 million) and the Yao 瑤族 (0.7 million). They are widely distributed over the entire province, but the majority of them are concentrated in the western and southern parts of Hunan.

General living standards in Hunan have improved continuously in recent years. In 2005, the annual per capita disposable income of urban households was RMB9,524, an increase of 8.2% over the previous year. There was also an increase in the annual per capita net income of rural households, to RMB3,118 in 2005. The province's basic infrastructure, such as its various urban public facilities, have improved rapidly (Table 15.2). For example, the total length of liquefied petroleum gas pipelines increased from 119 km in 1999 to 1,261 km in 2005. The length of paved roads also reached 5,978 km in 2005. Other basic infrastructure such as water supply pipelines increased to total 9,862 km in length in 2005.

Economic Development

The province's GDP has increased substantially over the past few years, from RMB332.68 in 1999 to RMB651.13 billion in 2005 (Table 15.3). Of this, the secondary and the tertiary sectors accounted for RMB259.67 and RMB264.05, respectively. The per capita GDP of permanent residents reached RMB10,426 in 2005. With a total GDP of RMB151.99 billion and a per capita GDP of RMB23,968 in 2005, Changsha's economic performance topped that of all other cities and prefectures in the province

Table 15.2   Selected Indicators of Basic Urban Infrastructure in Hunan, 1999–2005

	1999	2000	2001	2002	2003	2004	2005
Length of water supply pipelines (km)	7,487	7,650	9,665	8,563	9,342	9,117	9,862
Length of coal gas pipelines (km)	953	1,116	1,156	1,220	1,141	1,590	695
Length of liquefied petroleum gas pipelines (km)	119	216	462	507	626	907	1,261
Length of public transportation lines (km)	3,065	3,713	3,169	3,559	8,839	5,938	11,453
Number of passengers carried in public transport vehicles (10,000 person-times)	91,835	106,227	101,835	105,522	117,635	175,137	212,507
Length of paved roads (km)	4,739	4,739	4,837	4,979	5,369	5,540	5,978
Length of sewer pipelines (km)	4,922	3,754	3,854	4,090	4,404	4,946	5,594
Rate of sewage disposal (%)	18	27.31	22.05	18.93	26.81	38.13	40.55

Source: Hunansheng tongjiju (ed.), *Hunan tongji nianjian 2006*, pp. 201–2 and *Hunan tongji nianjian 2002*, pp. 193–94.

Table 15.3   Gross Domestic Product (GDP) in Hunan, 1999–2005

(Unit: 100 million RMB)

	1999	2000	2001	2002	2003	2004	2005
GDP	3,326.75	3,691.88	3,983.00	4,340.94	4,659.99	5,641.94	6,511.34
Primary industry	778.25	784.92	825.73	847.25	886.47	1,156.80	1,274.15
Secondary industry	1,297.74	1,461.86	1,573.00	1,737.20	1,777.74	2,190.54	2,596.71
Tertiary industry	1,250.76	1,445.10	1,584.27	1,756.49	1,995.78	2,294.60	2,640.48

Source: Hunansheng tongjiju (ed.), *Hunan tongji nianjian 2006*, p. 35 and *Hunan tongji nianjian 2002*, p. 27.

(Table 15.4), particularly in secondary and tertiary industries. In per capita GDP, Changsha (RMB23,968), Zhuzhou (RMB14,497) and Xiangtan (RMB13,604) were the top three cities in 2005. Their combined GDP that year was RMB241.26 billion, an increase of 12.4% over the previous year. As a designated growth area under the Tenth Five-year Plan (2001–2005), it is envisaged that the Changsha-Zhuzhou-Xiangtan urban cluster will continue to grow in the future.

Industrial development in Hunan has accelerated. In 2005, the ratio between light and heavy industries was 30:70. That year, the total value-added of the industrial sector was RMB219.99 billion, an increase of

Table 15.4   Gross Domestic Product (GDP) and Its Composition by Cities and Prefecture in Hunan, 2005

(Unit: 100 million RMB)

Cities and prefecture	GDP	Primary industry	Secondary industry	Tertiary industry	Per capita GDP (RMB)
Changsha	1,519.90	113.98	624.15	763.77	23,968
Zhuzhou	524.14	70.50	264.61	189.03	14,497
Xiangtan	366.84	56.61	158.94	151.29	13,604
Hengyang	590.86	150.49	224.35	216.02	8,899
Shaoyang	360.09	111.07	101.21	147.81	5,399
Yueyang	634.87	126.75	294.35	213.77	12,532
Changde	634.17	167.02	254.78	212.37	11,811
Zhangjiajie	110.63	19.58	26.85	64.20	7,588
Yiyang	294.76	82.92	84.18	127.66	7,130
Chenzhou	477.69	84.16	226.59	166.94	11,073
Yongzhou	361.22	110.59	94.57	156.06	7,139
Huaihua	295.21	70.21	91.18	133.82	6,564
Loudi	311.11	58.21	143.61	109.29	8,193
Xiangxi	123.32	26.69	42.48	54.15	5,026

Source: Hunansheng tongjiju (ed.), *Hunan tongji nianjian 2006*, p. 79.

15.3% from 2004. The total number of state-owned and non-state-owned industrial enterprises with sales revenues of over RMB 5 million in the 13 prefecture-level cities was 6,966 in 2004.[2] The majority of these enterprises was domestically funded (6,596 units). However, there was also a considerable number of industrial enterprises with investment from Hong Kong 香港, Macao 澳門 and Taiwan 台灣 (223 units). The Gross Industrial Output Value of the 13 prefecture-level cities was RMB352.43 billion, of which the city of Changsha accounted for RMB70.61 billion.

As Hunan has proactively adopted an outward-looking development strategy to attract foreign investment, the amount of foreign capital utilized in Hunan increased from US$1.07 billion in 1999 to US$2.07 billion in 2005 (Table 15.5). Moreover, foreign trade totalled US$5.2 billion in 2004, a 40% increase over 2003.[3] This was the first time that Hunan's foreign trade had exceeded US$5 billion. The total value of exports and imports in Hunan has also grown considerably over the past few years (Table 15.6). In 2005, it amounted to US$6.005 billion.

Table 15.5   Utilization of Foreign Capital in Hunan, 1999–2005

(Unit: US$10,000)

	1999	2000	2001	2002	2003	2004	2005
Amount of foreign capital for utilization through signed contracts or agreements	94,351	109,370	133,063	165,759	237,610	260,728	424,465
Amount of foreign capital actually utilized	106,945	110,843	118,747	137,689	179,041	141,806	207,235

Source: Hunansheng tongjiju (ed.), *Hunan tongji nianjian 2006*, p. 39 and *Hunan tongji nianjian 2002*, p. 27.

Table 15.6   Foreign Trade in Hunan, 1999–2005

(Unit: US$100 million)

	1999	2000	2001	2002	2003	2004	2005
Total exports and imports	19.56	25.13	27.58	28.76	37.36	54.38	60.05
Imports	6.74	8.60	10.04	10.81	15.90	23.40	22.58
Exports	12.82	16.53	17.54	17.95	21.46	30.98	37.47

Source: Hunansheng tongjiju (ed.), *Hunan tongji nianjian 2006*, p. 41 and *Hunan tongji nianjian 2002*, p. 29.

Hong Kong is the province's main trading partner. In 2003, the total value of Hunan's imports and exports through Hong Kong was about US$0.39 billion, of which exports accounted for US$0.38 billion. Hong Kong has been an important gateway for Hunan to the western market since the late 1970s, when the country began to open up to the outside world. At present, more than half of the foreign investment in Hunan is from Hong Kong. In 2003, there were 4,146 Hong Kong-invested enterprises in Hunan, for a total investment of US$0.79 billion. They accounted for 53% of total foreign investment in Hunan.

Apart from Hunan's comparative advantage in different factors of production, such remarkable economic growth has partly been due to the government's efforts to improve the investment environment in an endeavour to make Hunan a major destination for local and foreign investment. In the past few years, Hunan has successfully transformed itself and is well prepared to host those labour-intensive and traditional industries that moved away from the PRD region due to the increasing cost of production. In the following sections, the ways by which Hunan is capitalizing on the opportunities offered by the structural shift in the PRD region will be examined.

Main Reasons for the Relocation of Industries to Hunan

In the 1950s and 1960s, massive cross-border flows of industrial activity have taken place. Since the mid-1980s, the world economy has undergone rapid globalization, ushering in a new phase of massive economic restructuring.[4] The increasing cross-border flow of different factors of production and the reorganization of resources have had a profound impact on China's economy. On the one hand, the acceleration in economic restructuring of developed countries, coupled with the massive outflow of capital, have created valuable opportunities for the emerging coastal regions in China.[5] On the other hand, these coastal regions are themselves also undergoing rapid economic restructuring. China has ushered in a new phase of development — an east-west and coastal-inland transfer of industries.

The relocation of industries from coastal to inland regions is an outcome of the global shift of capital. Since China adopted the epoch-making decision to open up to the world, coastal cities along the eastern coast have successfully attracted massive inflows of labour-intensive industries from Hong Kong, Taiwan, and a number of developed regions and countries. This favourable external force led to the mushrooming of enterprises, which formed the basis of capital accumulation. With the rapid development of the coastal region, the pressure has been growing for a structural shift in the economy. Confronted by escalating costs of production, the coastal cities are hard pressed to compete with other low-cost regions. The result has been the increasing relocation of labour-intensive and resource-intensive industries to the central and western regions. With the improvement in the investment environment as well as an increase in consumption, the central and western regions are well prepared to receive foreign investment.

Given Hunan's geographical location, the PRD is the main source of industrial transfers to the province. In the 1980s, Guangdong proactively opened itself up for foreign investment. Given plenty of land and an almost inexhaustible supply of cheap labour in the PRD, many labour-intensive industries in Hong Kong were relocated across the border to the PRD. In recent years, the PRD has been facing the challenges of increasing costs of production and vicious competition with other low-cost areas. Many labour-intensive industries have started to further relocate to the outer regions of the Pan-PRD. This, in brief, is a description of the main causes underlying the industrial relocation process in the Pan-PRD region.

Loss of the Comparative Advantage of Low Production Costs in the PRD

Industries located in the PRD have long enjoyed the advantage of low production costs. Prior to the Asian financial crisis in 1997, labour and land costs in the PRD were well below those of Southeast Asian countries. In order to capitalize on these advantages, multinational corporations relocated their manufacturing plants from Southeast Asia to the PRD. This led to the rise of the PRD as China's "global factory." An unprecedented economic boom occurred and the region prospered. However, the outbreak of the Asian financial crisis led to the depreciation of the currencies of Southeast Asian countries. As a result, various factors of production in these countries have become comparatively lower than in the PRD, threatening the position of the PRD as a leading manufacturing centre in Asia.

Manufacturing industries in the PRD are also facing intense competition from other Chinese cities and regions, such as the Yangzi River Delta region, the Northeast industrial region and some neighbouring provinces in the PRD. Both endogenous and exogenous threats have greatly affected the attractiveness of the PRD to foreign investors.

Rapid Growth of Technology-based and Capital-intensive Industries

The rapid development of high-tech and capital-intensive industries in the PRD has crowded out traditional industries. Since the mid-1990s, high-tech industries have become the largest contributor to Guangdong's economic growth. The number of high-tech enterprises in the province grew steadily from 693 in 1997 to 1,407 in 2002, and the output value of these industries grew at an annual average rate of 33%. In 2003, Guangdong's high-tech industrial output value was RMB350 billion, which was 43 times that of 1991 and 3 times that of 1997. The output value of high-tech industries as a proportion of total industrial output value increased from 3.3% in 1991 to 19.4% in 2003. Most of these high-tech products produced in Guangdong were manufactured in the PRD. At present, the output value of electronics and telecommunications products in the PRD comprises more than 30% of the total output value of these products in China. Other high-tech products produced in the PRD, including advanced ceramic electronic components, biomedical output, intelligent environmentally friendly appliances and electric medical equipment, account for more than half of the total output value of these products in China. Apart from the development of high-tech industries, the PRD region is also benefiting from the relocation of capital-intensive heavy industries and petrochemical industries to China from developed countries. The automobile and petrochemical industries have developed rapidly in recent years.[6] The mushrooming of technology-based and capital-intensive industries has upgraded the industrial structure of the PRD. Such a structural shift has crowded out traditional industries to the outer provinces of the Pan-PRD region, where production costs are lower.

Environmental Considerations in the Upgrading of Guangdong's Industrial Structure

The industrial restructuring that occurred in Hong Kong during the 1980s led to a massive relocation of manufacturing industries to the PRD that were generally polluting and of low-added value. In recent years, environmental awareness has grown, as has the eagerness of the Guangdong government to tackle the problem of environmental pollution. The result is a series of stringent measures to protect the environment. "Guangdong's Scheme to Upgrade the Industrial Structure" includes a proposal to transfer 804 types of polluting and low value-added industries out of the PRD. Recently, the scheme was further amended to include 341 additional industries, including electronic toys and beverages. Thus, low value-added manufacturing industries are unable to meet the new basic requirements of the PRD. At the same time, the developed core of the PRD has begun to transform itself into a modern industrial centre for high-tech industries. This has further pushed those low value-added industries towards other areas of the Pan-PRD region such as Hunan. However, this could simply transfer problems faced in the PRD to Hunan. While Hunan has experienced rapid economic growth in the past few years, it suffers from serious environmental pollution.[7] Untreated industrial wastewater and urban sewage is threatening to pollute the province's sources of drinking water. As for air pollution, national standards have been exceeded with regard to SO_2 and TSP. In particular, the problem of acid rain is very serious in Hunan. Two acid rain belts have been formed around Yuanjiang and Xiangjiang.

Government Support

In order to accelerate the structural shift that is taking place in Guangdong and to boost the province's economic growth, the Guangdong government has formulated a plan for adjusting the province's industrial structure.[8] They have stipulated the need for an outward decentralization of industries to the less-developed eastern and western wings of the PRD region. Under this development framework, the developed core of the PRD will become the leading producer of electronics and telecommunications products. The eastern and western wings will move along the strategic direction of leveraging on the central PRD and build on their own resources. While the eastern and western wings, as well as other provinces in the Pan-PRD region, are the preferred destinations for the labour-intensive industries that are relocating from the central PRD, they have the potential to develop industries with local characteristics. Mountainous and less-developed regions have to create favourable conditions for attracting industries from the central PRD.[9] In response to changing market conditions, industrial activities have recently spread along major transport links to areas outside Guangdong.

Favourable Conditions for Attracting Investment

Many neighbouring jurisdictions are competing among themselves to attract outward investments from the core PRD region. It is noteworthy that Hunan possesses a number of comparative advantages, a fact that makes it a favourable destination for those labour-intensive industries moving out of the central PRD region.

Efficient Transportation Network

As can be seen from the existing transportation network, the east-west connectivity of the PRD region is not so well developed. Rather, the PRD region is better linked with its northern hinterland because of a number of strategic links, including the Beijing–Guangzhou Railway 京廣鐵路; the Beijing–Zhuhai Expressway 京珠高速公路 and 107 National Highway 一零七國道. Hunan is strategically located along this north-south transport corridor. Blessed with an efficient transportation network, it only takes 6.5 hours to travel from Changsha 長沙 to Guangzhou 廣州, and 8 hours from Changsha to Shenzhen 深圳.

Massive investments have been made in the development of infrastructure since the establishment of the Pan-PRD grouping in 2004. Hunan's accessibility will be further strengthened by a number of proposals. First, there is a plan to build an expressway linking Yongzhou with Qingyuan 清遠, Guangzhou and Zhanjiang 湛江. Such a proposal is supported by the central government. Second, there is a proposal to construct an express passenger rail line (250km/hour) connecting Hunan directly with the PRD. With this railway, passengers from Changsha can reach Guangzhou in three hours.[10] These two proposed links, together with the Hong Kong-Zhuhai-Macao bridge, will further enhance the accessibility of Hunan within the PRD region. The journey between Changsha and other major cities in the PRD will be under four hours. This will sharpen Hunan's competitive edge as a major destination for industries relocating from the PRD and Hong Kong.

Low Production Costs

Hunan has an almost inexhaustible supply of land and cheap labour. Every year, 8 million people from Hunan go work in other provinces. Guangdong alone is the destination of 5 million of these workers. It has been noted that Hunan is the most important source of migrant workers in Guangdong.[11] After several years, these workers will return to Hunan and constitute a significant pool of trained labour. Moreover, wage levels in Hunan are relatively lower than other places in the PRD. The average annual income of a manager is about RMB16,500, while that of an average worker is about RMB8,000. Given the low labour costs, Hunan's investment environment is very attractive to foreign investors.

Land resources are also available at very low prices. The land development fees for paddy fields and un-irrigated farmland are RMB12 – 18/m² and RMB7.5 – 12/m², respectively. The land transfer fee is based on the land price, which varies according to land use and, therefore, to location.[12] Apart from the availability of cheap land resources, a series of preferential policies have recently been introduced to attract foreign investment. Under the existing policy, foreign-invested enterprises in China are entitled to a three-year period of tax reductions and exemptions. With the aim of supporting the development of the central and western regions of the country, however, the central government has granted those investing in the central and western regions further tax incentives (for example, another three years of preferential tax rates). This is making Hunan popular with foreign investors. Moreover, special policies have also been adopted for all development zones in Hunan.

Thus, it is clear that labour and land costs in Hunan are much lower than that of the coastal regions. These comparative advantages, together with a series of favourable policies, have paved the way for Hunan to become the preferred destination of industries relocating from the PRD.

Abundant Resources

Natural Resources

Hunan is rich in both natural resources (land, mineral deposits and water) and tourism resources. Blessed with a favourable climate, Hunan is one of the largest producers of rice in China. It is, therefore, known as the "Land of Fish and Rice." In addition, Hunan is the country's third largest producer of tea, and the fourth largest producer of citrus fruit, tobacco and meat.[13] It has a unique topography, with 70% of the province comprised of mountains and hills. Plains make up 20% of Hunan and water bodies 10%. About 15% of its land area is farmland. A total of 3.25 million ha of farmland are scattered around Dongting Lake and the eastern and central parts of Hunan. Woodlands occupy 10.81 million ha.

Apart from agricultural resources, Hunan is rich in rare animals (about 40 species) and plants (about 70 species). It has a forest coverage of 51%, ranking the province fourth in China in this respect. Several rare species with primitive traits are found there, including the *Maiden-hair Tree*, the *Water Pine*, the *Dawn Redwood*, the *Dovetree*, and others. Abundant water resources are another one of Hunan's comparative advantages. The whole province is drained by rivers, with a total of 164 billion m³ of water resources. The great part of Hunan lies within the basin of the four major tributaries of the Yangzi River — the Zijiang, Yuanjiang, Lishui and Xiangjiang. Most of the lakes in Hunan are distributed around Dongting Lake, the second largest freshwater lake in China.

Due to its rich reserves of minerals, Hunan is also known as the "land of non-ferrous metals" and the "land of non-metal minerals." Of the 168 types of minerals in the world, 141 are found in Hunan. The distribution of minerals in Hunan is highly concentrated, but widely spread over the entire province. There are a total of 94 types of minerals (with known reserves) in Hunan, accounting for 61% of all mineral deposits in China. The province's reserves of tungsten, antimony, zinc and bauxite are among the richest in the country. Other major deposits of minerals found in Hunan include lead, tin, barite and graphite mineral. A large share of Hunan's industrial output is related to its rich mineral deposits, such as the smelting and pressing of ferrous and non-ferrous metals. In short, Hunan's non-ferrous metal industry occupies an important position in China.

With regard to hydropower (HP) reserves, Hunan is one of the leaders in southern China, possessing 2.3% of the country's total. It has reserves of 15.3 million kWh, with a generating capacity of 134.2 billion kWh per year, ranking it ninth in China. There are a total of 1,024 HP stations in Hunan[14] capable of generating a total of 48.9 billion kWh per year. At present, 35% of the energy supply in Hunan comes from HP. As Hunan is well drained by rivers, the province has great potential to further increase its supplies of HP.

Tourism Resources

Hunan is a popular tourist destination in China, with places of historic interest and scenic beauty. Natural scenic spots include Hengshan 衡山 and Yuelu Mountain 嶽麓山; Dongting Lake, one of the top four freshwater lakes in China; 22 national parks and 23 nature reserves. In particular, Wulingyuan 武陵源 in Zhangjiajie 張家界 has been included in the Almanac of World Historical Cultural Relics since 1992. The Wulingyuan scenic area is famous for spectacular rock pinnacles as well as exquisite waterfalls and streams. Hunan's cultural heritage is equally appealing to tourists. There are over 200 historic sites in the province, including Yueyang Tower 岳陽樓 (one of the three historical monuments in South China), the Yuelu Academy of Classical Learning 嶽麓書院 (one of the largest academies during the Song 宋 dynasty) and Aiwan Pavilion 愛晚亭 (one of the four most famous pavilions in China). Hunan was also the birthplace of many Chinese leaders such as Mao Zedong 毛澤東 and Liu Shaoqi 劉少奇. It is, therefore, not surprising that the total number of domestic and overseas tourists has been growing at a rate of more than 8% per year. In 2005, 71.8 million tourists visited Hunan, generating sizeable revenues for the province. Foreign exchange earnings from tourism increased from US$0.2 billion in 2000 to US$0.4 billion in 2005.

Strong Economic Base

Hunan has achieved a relatively high level of economic development. Since the Eighth Five-year Plan (1991–1995), the province has ranked twelfth in

GDP in China and the third among the provinces of Central China, with annual growth rate of 9% or more. In 2005, Hunan's GDP was RMB 651.1 billion, with a growth rate of 11.6%.

Hunan's economic structure is well defined. The primary sector accounted for almost 19.6% of the province's GDP in 2005. In 2003, the value-added output from the primary sector reached RMB88.6 billion, with a growth rate of 3.6%. Animal husbandry and the production of diary products are important primary activities in Hunan. As shown in Table 15.7, both the secondary (39.9%) and tertiary (40.5%) sectors contribute a significant portion of Hunan's GDP. In 2004, Hunan's value-added industrial output reached RMB178.1 billion, with a growth rate of 12.6%. A modernized and diversified industrial system has evolved in Hunan over time. In particular, there has been rapid development in heavy industries. For example, electrical equipment and machinery occupy an important position in China. Due to its rich mineral deposits, a large share of Hunan's industrial output is related to the processing of minerals. The non-ferrous metal industry is an important one in China, with the smelting and pressing of ferrous and non-ferrous metals accounting for 14.3% of the country's total industrial output in 2004. Metallurgy, machinery and electronics, household ceramics, food and building materials are some of Hunan's pillar industries. All state-owned enterprises have recently undergone ownership restructuring. During the process of industrial relocation, enterprises in the PRD are finding it rewarding to reform and invest in Hunan's traditional industries through different ownership arrangements such as acquisition and share holdings.

Table 15.7   Composition of Hunan's GDP by Industrial Sector (%), 1999–2005

	1999	2000	2001	2002	2003	2004	2005
Primary industry	23.4	21.3	20.7	19.5	19.0	20.5	19.6
Secondary industry	39.0	39.6	39.5	40.0	38.1	38.8	39.9
Tertiary industry	37.6	39.1	39.8	40.5	42.9	40.7	40.5

Source: Hunansheng tongjiju (ed.), *Hunan tongji nianjian 2006*, p. 45 and *Hunan tongji nianjian 2002*, p. 40.

A Well-structured Urban Hierarchy

Cities are the basis for accelerated industrial development in Hunan. With a well-developed hierarchy of cities and towns, Hunan has successfully become the preferred destination of industries relocating from the developed core of the PRD. There are currently a total of 29 cities in Hunan, with 1 mega-city, 3 large cities, 25 medium-sized and small cities, as well as 1,098 towns. In recent years, the agglomeration of industries and economic activities has resulted in a number of newly formed urban clusters, development corridors and economic belts. These have not only upgraded the existing spatial structure of Hunan but also form the backbone of Hunan's urban hierarchy.

Driven by Hunan's urbanization strategy, cities and towns have become magnets that attract investment as well as engines of economic growth. In 2003, the total GDP of the 13 prefecture-level city regions accounted for 40.98% of the province's GDP. In particular, the urban cluster formed by Changsha, Zhuzhou and Xiangtan is playing a critical role in spearheading economic development in Hunan. Although the three cities only accounted for 13.3% of Hunan's total area and 18.6% of the total population, they altogether contributed 33.8% of the province's economic growth. Their GDP per capita was RMB15,038, while the provincial average was RMB5,921. With an urbanization level of 44.5%, the Changsha-Zhuzhou-Xiangtan urban cluster was designated as a growth area under the Tenth Five-year Plan (2001–2005). It is envisaged that the Changsha-Zhuzhou-Xiangtan urban cluster will continue to take an active role in spurring development in the rest of the province. On the other hand, it is also worth noting that towns that are county seats have also become increasingly important in the overall economic development of Hunan. Such towns contributed 10–20% of the county's economy. This has furthered the economic integration of Hunan.

Advanced Technological Development

As the foundation to support economic development, continuous investments have been made in the area of technological innovation since the beginning of economic reforms in 1978. Local companies have shown a keen interest in establishing business relationships with companies in other parts of the world. Several advanced technological products developed in the province are of international standard, including the Yinhe series of supercomputers, the maglev train, hybrid rice and genetically engineered products. Ascending the technological ladder, many high-tech products from Hunan have continued to gain a larger share of the market in China. Hunan has equipped itself with the necessary technological skills to advance and develop high-tech industries relocating from the PRD region.

Improvement in the Investment Environment

In recent years, Hunan has gradually adopted an outward-looking strategy with a view to enhancing an open and efficient investment environment. Efforts have been made to provide a comprehensive infrastructure, preferential policies, flexible mechanisms and low investment costs. These will be further discussed below.

Recent Efforts to Improve the Investment Environment

Hunan has been able to sharpen its competitive edge and move up the ladder of success because of the provincial government's continued proactive efforts to improve Hunan's investment environment.

In the province's Tenth Five-Year Plan,[15] the government highlighted two main directions for growth, namely cooperating with coastal regions and attracting foreign investment. Immediately after the signing of the Pan-PRD Regional Cooperation Framework Agreement in 2004, the Hunan government formulated its Plan for Pan-PRD Business Cooperation in the Development of Hunan.[16] There are eight major areas of work, including establishing mechanisms for business and trade in the Pan-PRD; improving the investment environment; attracting foreign investment; building a platform for business cooperation between Hunan and the Pan-PRD; establishing an open and competitive market for trade; enhancing cooperation with Guangdong, Hong Kong and Macao in developing a services industry; facilitating agricultural industrialization in Hunan and enhancing the exchange of business information in the Pan-PRD.

In order to enhance administrative efficiency, the government has recently announced a set of rules to expedite the process of industrial development. Investment service centres providing a one-stop service to investors are being set up in Hunan. These centres offer different kinds of services, including fee-collection, the issuance of permits, project approval and all necessary administrative services. With the establishment of these centres, investment procedures have been streamlined. Investors in Hunan no longer have to contact individual government departments separately to settle investment matters. The provincial government has also delegated power to individual departments to grant permits, as well as streamlined the entire decision-making process. With a simplified procedure, investors do not need to wait a long time for their investment applications to be processed. A free service is offered for those seeking to obtain approval for development projects.

Apart from introducing efficient and effective administrative procedures, the government is also drawing up special preferential policies to attract investors. At present, Hunan has three national development zones and many provincial-level key development zones. These zones are supported by comprehensive infrastructure and other ancillary facilities. Priority will be given to those key industries with good development potential and the ability to make a significant contribution to the local economy. The preferential policies include lower administrative fees and competitive prices for basic infrastructural facilities such as electricity and water supplies. The aim is to meet the needs of individual investors with a view to lowering their overall cost of production. In sum, the favourable policies offered in Hunan are comparable to those in the coastal regions and are more attractive than in neighbouring provinces.

To further assist enterprises in Hunan to cope with problems in production and operation, a service platform with a liaison officer responsible for each firm has been set up. An open society, a fair market, a sound legal system, an efficient administrative structure as well as a comprehensive infrastructure system have together contributed to a good investment environment. In short, the government's recent efforts to upgrade both the province's hardware and software have brought about a transformation in the province over the past few years.

Locational Choices for Industrial Development

As strategically situated along the Beijing-Guangzhou Railway, Hunan has benefited tremendously from its geographical location and is the ideal province to receive investment and industries relocating from the PRD. Taking into consideration different factors affecting locational choices, such as distance, regional development strategy, industrial structure and development threshold, two growth poles have been identified as the most favourable locations in Hunan for such industries. They are the Changsha-Zhuzhou-Xiangtan urban cluster and Chenzhou.

Changsha-Zhuzhou-Xiangtan City Region

Changsha, Zhuzhou and Xiangtan are three major industrial cities in Hunan. Lying at the middle and lower reaches of the Xiangjiang, the three cities are arranged in a triangular pattern. Located within the same catchment area, they are only about 50 km apart from each other.[17] From the perspective

Table 15.8 Key Indicators of Changsha, Zhuzhou and Xiangtan, 2004

City	Total population (10,000 persons)	Non-agricultural population (10,000 persons)	GDP (billion RMB)	Per capita GDP (RMB)	Growth rate of GDP (%)	Urbanization level (%)
Changsha	610.38	212.57	113.38	18,036	15.0	51.19
Zhuzhou	370.93	99.22	45.25	12,635	12.4	41.50
Xiangtan	282.82	81.59	33.28	12,475	13.4	40.90
Total	1,264.13	393.38	191.91	—	—	—

Source: Hunansheng tongjiju (ed.), *Hunan tongji nianjian 2005*, pp. 206–15.

of urban competitiveness, no one city can take the lead in spearheading Hunan's economic growth. It would be highly beneficial for the three cities to merge together to form a mega-city region (Table 15.8). In this way, the Changsha-Zhuzhou-Xiangtan city region will be able to go from strength to strength and face down the growing competition from neighbouring provinces.

The formation of the Changsha-Zhuzhou-Xiangtan city region is one of the regional development strategies of Hunan. In the mid-1980s, there was already a strategic plan to develop a Changsha-Zhuzhou-Xiangtan economic zone. Taking into consideration the peculiar strengths and weaknesses of each city, resources were directed towards the development of a multi-functional city region. This region has served as the financial, industrial, transport, information and technological centre of Hunan. In 2000, the provincial government proactively expedited the planning of the Changsha-Zhuzhou-Xiangtan city region by inviting experts from the World Bank[18] and the China Urban Planning and Design Institute[19] to formulate a long-term development strategy that maximizes the comparative advantages of the three cities. The long-term vision for Changsha-Zhuzhou-Xiangtan is based on the principle of economic integration. The trans-boundary flow of resources is strongly encouraged. In the years ahead, the Hunan government will prioritize the development of a "one point, one line" (一點一線) region, that is, the Changsha-Zhuzhou-Xiangtan city region (*point*) and the Beijing-Guangzhou Railway growth axis *(line)*. It is envisaged that the Changsha-Zhuzhou-Xiangtan city region will play a critical role in moving Hunan up the ladder of success.

Cooperation among the three cities in infrastructural provision and economic development has further facilitated the expansion of the Changsha-Zhuzhou-Xiangtan city region. At present, electricity supplies and transport and communication facilities are being planned under a regional framework. Further unification in the development of Changsha, Zhuzhou and Xiangtan is moving Hunan towards a mature stage of development with an emphasis on specialized industrial clusters. It is an undeniable fact that the Changsha-Zhuzhou-Xiangtan city region shows great promise as a zone for receiving Hong Kong investment and industries relocating from the PRD. The two cities have seen double-digit growth in GDP. Considerable resources have been directed towards nurturing of four main industry groups, namely the manufacturing of transport equipment; education and culture; food and medicine, and the manufacturing of electronic equipment.

Building on the strengths of its geographical proximity to the PRD and lower cost of production, the Changsha-Zhuzhou-Xiangtan city region in Hunan is an ideal location for Hong Kong investors. In particular, Hunan's industrial structure fits well with the industries in the PRD. It has the capability to nurture new industries and enhance specialized industrial clusters.

Chenzhou Border City

Chenzhou is located in the southern part of Hunan and is within four hours from Guangzhou and Changsha. Lying close to the border of Guangdong, Hunan and Jiangxi, it occupies a strategic location where inland economies and coastal economies meet.

Even in the era of the planned economy, Chenzhou had a strong wish to experiment the outward-looking move of integrating with the PRD region. In the early 1980s, Guangdong and Chenzhou were aware of the benefits of a market exchange in food commodities and coal. However, during the 1980s, all basic necessities were still being rationed by the central government and free market exchanges were strictly forbidden. With no official channel for exporting and selling goods to Guangdong, smuggling activities were rife at that time. In order to control the illegal transaction of commodities, the government was vigilant about dampening market activities by setting up different types of inspection stations at the border between Chenzhou and Guangdong.

With the changing economic conditions in the past decade, Chenzhou has adopted the outward-looking strategy of integrating itself with the PRD. In 1988, the State Council approved the setting up of an experimental zone in Chenzhou that was not subject to policies adopted in Hunan. The signing of CEPA (內地與香港關於建立更緊密經貿關係的安排) and the Pan-PRD Regional Cooperation Framework Agreement has further accelerated the integration of Chenzhou and the PRD. Similar to Dongguan 東莞, Chenzhou has introduced measures to attract labour-intensive industries from the PRD.[20] A large number of such enterprises can be found in Chenzhou. The amount of utilized FDI in Chenzhou rose by 30.3% to RMB0.2 billion in 2003 over 2002. Chenzhou ranks second in Hunan in the utilization of foreign capital.

Historical legacies, economic strengths, geographical proximity and cultural ties with the PRD are some of the factors that have helped Chenzhou to become the forerunner of Hunan's integration with the PRD. In order to maximize development opportunities, Chenzhou has to continue its structural shift so that its policy framework, industrial structure, as well as cultural mindset can be smoothly integrated with those of the PRD region. In addition, the government should support the development of Chenzhou by granting preferential treatment in project approval and utilization of foreign capital. As the processing business is one of the major contributors to Hunan's foreign trade, the government should set up processing and trade zones, customs checkpoints and other ancillary facilities in Chenzhou to accelerate the development of this border city.

Conclusion

With China on a trajectory of rapid growth, the PRD will continue to be the economic powerhouse of the country, although it faces intense competition from other regions as its cost of production rises. The PRD is also undergoing a structural shift as it upgrades its industrial structure. The rapid development of high-tech and capital-intensive industries is crowding out traditional industries. Many low value-added industries that cannot meet new environmental standards in the PRD have been pushed to the outer regions of the Pan-PRD. Given government support as well as geographical proximity to the PRD, Hunan possesses a number of comparative advantages, a fact that makes it a favourable destination for those industries that are moving out of the central PRD region. These advantages include an efficient transportation network, low production costs, abundant natural and tourism resources, a strong economic base, a well-structured urban hierarchy, advanced technology, as well as an improved investment environment.

Taking into consideration different factors that affect choices of location, the Changsha-Zhuzhou-Xiangtan urban cluster and Chenzhou are two growth poles that have been identified as the most favourable locations in

Hunan for industries relocating from the PRD. The formation of the Changsha-Zhuzhou-Xiangtan city region is one of the Hunan provincial government's regional development strategies. In the mid-1980s, there was already a strategic plan for the development of a Changsha-Zhuzhou-Xiangtan economic zone. In the years ahead, Hunan government will prioritize the development of "one point, one line," that is, the Changsha-Zhuzhou-Xiangtan city region (*point*) and the Beijing-Guangzhou Railway growth axis (*line*). Chenzhou, for its part, has become the forerunner of Hunan's integration with the PRD due to historical legacies, economic strengths, geographical proximity and cultural ties with the PRD.

It is difficult for Hunan to link up with the Yangzi River Delta and the Western Region because of the great distances involved. With its geographical location, the chosen strategy for the future development of Hunan is to leverage on the PRD, capitalizing on its advantages and moving up the value chain. Through better cooperation with other provinces in the Pan-PRD region, there will be ample opportunities for Hunan to further develop its industries and attract foreign investment. However, careful consideration should be made to protect the natural environment. Sustainable development will be the key to economic success.

Notes

1. In this chapter, PRD refers to the PRD Economic Region which consists of nine prefecture-level cities, namely Guangzhou 廣州, Shenzhen 深圳, Zhuhai 珠海, Foshan 佛山, Huizhou 惠州 (part), Dongguan 東莞, Zhongshan 中山, Jiangmen 江門 and Zhaoqing 肇慶 (part).
2. All of the statistics on the industrial development of Hunan have been extracted from Hunansheng tongjiju 湖南省統計局 (ed.), *Hunan tongji nianjian* 湖南統計年鑒 (Hunan Statistical Yearbook) (Beijing: Zhongguo tongji chubanshe 中國統計出版社, various years).
3. Source: Hong Kong Trade Development Council.
4. Wang Bin 汪斌 and Zhao Zhangyao 趙張耀, "Guoji chanye zhuanyi lilun shuping" 國際產業轉移理論述評 (Discussion on the Theory of International Transfer of Industries), *Zhejiang shehui kexue* 浙江社會科學 (Zhejiang Social Sciences), Vol. 6 (2003), p. 47.
5. Hu Xinghua 胡興華, "Xin yi lun guoji chanye zhuanyi yu Zhongguo fazhan jiyu" 新一輪國際產業轉移與中國發展機遇 (A New Cycle of International Transfer of Industries and Development Opportunities for China), *Jiage yuekan* 價格月刊 (Prices Monthly), Vol. 3 (2004), pp. 9–10.
6. Wu Weiping 吳偉萍, "Guangdong chengjie xin yi lun guoji chanye zhuanyi

de celue yanjiu" 廣東承接新一輪國際產業轉移的策略研究 (Guangdong's Strategy on Hosting the New Cycle of International Transfer of Industries), *Guoji jingmao tansuo* 國際經貿探索 (International Economics and Trade Research), Vol. 19, Issue 3 (2003), pp. 73–77.

7. He Renyu 賀仁雨, *Hunan maixiang 21shiji fazhan zhanlüe* 湖南邁向21世紀發展戰略 (The Development Strategy of Hunan in the Twenty-first Century) (Changsha 長沙: Hunan renmin chubanshe 湖南人民出版社, 1998).

8. This refers to Guangdongsheng renmin zhengfu bangongting dang 廣東省人民政府辦公廳檔 (2001), *Guangdongsheng gongye chanye jiegou tiaozheng shishi fang'an* 廣東省工業產業結構調整實施方案 (The Implementation of Industrial Adjustment in Guangdong).

9. Ibid. *Yuefuban* 粵府辦 (Guangdong Government Paper) No. 74. http://www.gd.gov.cn/gov_files/wj_title.

10. Zhao Yong 趙勇, "Yu Youjun tan Xiang-Yue jingji hezuo shi hubu da yu jingzheng" 于幼軍談湘粵經濟合作是互補大於競爭 (Economic Cooperation of Guangdong and Hunan: Complementarity More Than Competition, Discussion by Yu You-jun), *Nanfang dushibao* 南方都市報 (Nanfang Daily). Cited from *Xinhua wang* 新華網 (Xinhua Net), 13 March 2004. http://www.southern.com/news/gdnews/hotspot/fzsj.

11. He Cheng 賀成, "Guanzhu Fan Zhusanjiao jingji quan" 關注泛珠三角經濟圈 (The Pan-Pearl River Delta Economic Zone), *Ningbo jingji* 寧波經濟 (Ningbo Economy), Vol. 2 (2004), p. 23.

12. Hunansheng shangwu ting 湖南省商務廳 (Business Department of Hunan Provincial Government), reference material, October 2004.

13. Source: Webpage of the Trade Development Council, Hong Kong.

14. The generating capacity of each of these stations is above 500 kWh.

15. This refers to the *Hunansheng guomin jingji he shehui fazhan di shi ge wu nian jihua gangyao* 湖南省國民經濟和社會發展第十個五年計劃綱要 (The Tenth Five-year Plan of Hunan National Economic and Social Development).

16. This refers to the *Fan Zhusanjiao quyu shangwu hezuo fazhan Hunan guihua* 泛珠三角區域商務合作發展湖南規劃 (Pan-Pearl River Delta Regional Business Cooperation in the Planning of Hunan Development).

17. Spatially, Changsha, Zhuzhou and Xiangtan formed a triangle with Changsha at the top. The distance between Changsha and Zhuzhou is 52 km, between Changsha and Xiangtan 54 km, and between Zhuzhou and Xiangtan 48 km.

18. Experts from the World Bank have conducted a study on the development strategy for the Changsha-Zhuzhou-Xiangtan city region.

19. The China Urban Planning and Design Institute has formulated the Changsha-Zhuzhou-Xiangtan Regional Plan.

20. Wang Haiyan 王海燕, "Chenzhou: Gulai liufang di, jinzuo hou huayuan" 郴州：古來流放地，今做後花園 (Chenzhou: Exile in the Past and Leisure Garden of Today), *Nanfang dushibao*, 19 March 2004.

16

Jiangxi

Zhou Guolan, Huang Shuhua and Lin Hui

Salient Characteristics

Physical Geography

Jiangxi 江西省 lies in the lower-middle reaches of the southern flank of the Yangzi River 長江 and borders Zhejiang 浙江 and Fujian 福建 to the east, Guangdong 廣東 to the south, Hunan 湖南 to the west, and Hubei 湖北 and Anhui 安徽 to the north. In ancient times, Jiangxi was called: "the head of Wu 吳 (Hubei) and the tail of Chu 楚 (Hunan), the gate of Yue 粵 (Guangdong) and the courtyard of Min 閩 (Fujian)," so it is "the area of good shape." Jiangxi was part of the Jiangnanxi administration area 江南西 道 in the Tang dynasty 唐代 (618–907), from which the name of the province is derived. The Zhang River 章江 joins the Gong River 貢江 to become the Gan River 贛江 (Figure 16.1). The character "Gan" 贛 is a combination of the two Chinese characters "Zhang" 章 and "Gong" 貢. The Gan River is the longest river in the province, stretching all the way to the south. Therefore, the province is also referred to as, "Gan." There are 11 cities and 99 counties in the province, with Nanchang 南昌 as the capital. As of the end of 2004, the province had a total population of 42.83 million.

The province has an area of 166,900 sq km, making up 1.74% of the country's territory and ranking it first among China's eastern provinces.[1] Jiangxi has rolling hills and broad plains, and is surrounded by mountains on three sides and the Yangzi River on the other. The land gradually tilts from south to north, leading to the largest fresh water lake in China, Poyang Lake 鄱陽湖, which forms a large open basin. Topographically, the province is characterized by mountains and hills. The mountainous areas make up 36% of the total land area of the province, the foothills 42%, and the plains, hillocks and water 22%.

Jiangxi is part of the Yangzi River valley. The river flows from the northern part of the province. There are 152 km of deep-water shoreline. There are more than 2,400 rivers in the whole province, the five largest of which are the Gan River, the Fu River 撫河, the Xin River 信江, the Xiu River 修河 and the Rao River 饒河. Poyang Lake is the biggest fresh water lake in China, as well as the largest habitat in the world for migratory birds.

Jiangxi is close to the Tropic of Cancer, and thus has a warm climate and abundant rainfall, with an annual precipitation of 1,341 to 1,940 mm. The subtropical moist conditions are favourable to the growth of a wide variety of plant life, and to the raising of crops.

Figure 16.1   Jiangxi in Its Geographical Setting

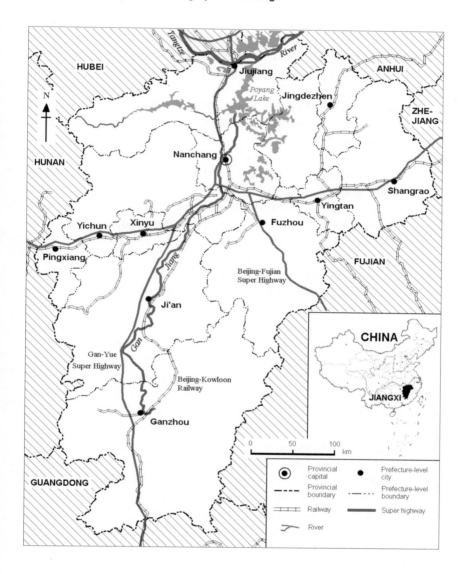

Historical and Cultural Features

Rice was already being planted paddies in Jiangxi some 5,000 years ago.[2]
After the Sui 隋 (581–618) and Tang dynasties, as the economic centre of
the nation shifted south, Jiangxi's land was further exploited and the province
became an important base for food production. Its economy prospered. Tea
plantations developed rapidly, and the province's tea ranked first in the
country for quantity and quality. Pottery making, shipbuilding, and silver
and copper smelting also became important industries. Much of the recently
unearthed bronze ware of the Shang 商 (16th – 11th centuries B.C.) and
Zhou 周 (11th – 256 B.C.) dynasties clearly showed the high level of
Jiangxi's civilization at that time and further proved that the cultures of
Jiangxi were also a part of Chinese civilization. In the Ming 明 (1368–
1644) and Qing 清 (1644–1911) dynasties, Jiangxi was still one of the most
prosperous areas in China. The province became the national centre for the
production of paper and cloth, as well as the granary for the middle and
lower areas of the Yangzi River and the southeastern coast. Large quantities
of grain were exported from Jiangxi to other provinces. Cash crops such as
tobacco, indigo, sugar cane, oil-tea camellias, bamboo and fruit trees were
planted extensively. Industries focusing on the processing of various
agricultural products flourished, as did handicraft industries. Many cities
and towns emerged that were hubs of industry and commerce.

Jiangxi's long history and rich cultural traditions mean that there are
many interesting and well-known sites in the province. Nanchang,
Jingdezhen 景德鎮 and Ganzhou 贛州 have been named national historical
and cultural cities. One of the "Three Famous Pavilions in South China,"
the Tengwang Pavilion 滕王閣 in Nanchang, was the subject of Wang Bo's
王勃 "The Preface of Tengwang Pavilion." The ancient porcelain kilns of
Jingdezhen, the eight scenery platform of Ganzhou, Liukeng Village of
Le'an County 樂安流坑村 and the ancient villages of Anyi County 安義古
村落 bear witness to the glorious history of Jiangxi. Even today, the
porcelains of Jingdezhen, which has been called the "porcelain capital of
China," are famous for their fine quality, being "white as jade, bright as a
mirror, thin as paper, and in sound like a bell." The porcelain collection in
the British Museum is mostly from Jingdezhen. Jiangxi is the cradle of
Taoism and the Three Sects of Buddhism. There are five national important
temples in the province: the Donglin Temple in Lushan 廬山東林寺, the
Nengren Temple of Jiujiang 九江能仁寺, the Zhenru Temple of Yunshan 雲
山真如寺, the Jingju Temple of Ji'an 吉安淨居寺 and the Tianshifu Temple

of Longhushan 龍虎山天師府. The academies of Jiangxi were once well known, with the White Deer Cave Academy 白鹿洞書院 in Lushan being one of the four greatest academies in China. Many famous personalities lived in Jiangxi, among them Tao Yuanming 陶淵明 (the idyllist of the Jin 晉 dynasty), Ouyang Xiu 歐陽修, Zeng Gong 曾鞏 and Wang Anshi 王安石 (three of the Eight Masters of the Tang and Song 宋 (960–1279) dynasties), Zhu Xi 朱熹 and Lu Jiuyuan 陸九淵 (philosophers), Tang Xianzu 湯顯祖 (a great drama master), Wen Tianxiang 文天祥 (a national hero), Huang Tingjian 黃庭堅 and Yang Wanli 楊萬里 (poets), Song Yingxing 宋應星 (a scientist) and Badashanren 八大山人 (a painter).

Jiangxi was a famous revolutionary base during the period of the Chinese Revolution. The Communist Party of China saw many "first" events in Jiangxi: The first gunfire erupted during the August 1st Nanchang Uprising; the first red revolutionary base was set up in Jinggang Mountain 井岡山, which has been praised as the cradle of the Chinese Revolution; the central government of the first Red Army was established in Ruijin 瑞金 in southern Jiangxi, and the first steps in the Long March were taken from here.

However, in the past several decades, Jiangxi's development has lagged far behind that of the eastern coastal areas.

Locational Advantages

Geographically, Jiangxi lies in the central part of both the Yangzi River economic zone and the Beijing 北京-Kowloon 九龍 economic zone. It is the only province that abuts the Yangzi River Delta 長江三角洲, the Pearl River Delta (PRD) 珠江三角洲 and the southern Fujian economic zone at the same time. The region within a six-hour distance from Nanchang has a population of 450 million, accounting for one third of the total population of China. With many metropolises, such as Wuhan 武漢, Nanjing 南京, Shanghai 上海, Xiamen 廈門, Guangzhou 廣州, Hong Kong 香港 and Macao 澳門, lying within 600 or 700 km of the province, Jiangxi has comparative locational advantages.

From the viewpoint of transportation, a convenient and high-speed network has been built. In terms of the construction of transport infrastructure, the past four years have been the most important period in Jiangxi's history. To date, there are 1,500 km of expressways in the province, ranking Jiangxi ninth in the country. Highways from Nanchang, the provincial capital, to other municipalities have been rebuilt into expressways. The provincial "four-hour economic circles" and inter-provincial "eight-hour economic circles" have come into being. Meanwhile, the construction of a comprehensive transport system, including railways and airports, has made communication between Jiangxi and neighbouring areas faster and more convenient. To the Pearl River Delta, the Ganyue 赣粤 Expressway (Jiangxi-Guangdong) and the No. 105 State Highway are connected by the Jingjiu 京九 Railway line (Beijing-Kowloon); to the Yangzi River Delta, the Hurui 沪瑞 Expressway (Shanghai-Ruili 瑞丽) and the No. 302 State Highway cross Jiangxi and reach the Zhegan 浙赣 Railway line (Zhejiang-Jiangxi); to Fujian, the Jingfu 京福 Expressway (Beijing-Fuzhou 福州), the Changxia 昌厦 Highway (Nanchang-Xiamen) and the Yingxia Railway (Yingtan 鹰潭-Xiamen) will be linked to the future Ganlong 赣龙 Railway line (Ganzhou-Longyan 龙岩, currently under construction); to Hunan, Hubei and Anhui, the Wujiu 武九铁路 Railway line (Wuhan-Jiujiang) and the Wan'gan 皖赣 Railway line (Anhui-Jiangxi) join many expressways. As for air transport infrastructure, there are five airports in the province, located in Nanchang, Jiujiang, Jingdezhen, Ji'an and Ganzhou. Flights from Nanchang to Hong Kong and Singapore have been launched, while flights from Nanchang to Tokyo will soon be available. Moreover, Jiangxi has a good inland waterway system, which totals more than 5,500 km, including 133 km along the Yangzi River. The 55 harbours in Jiangxi, each with an annual cargo-handling capacity of more than 1,000 tonnes, contribute to the formation of a large water transport network based on the Yangzi and the Gan Rivers.

Thus, in geographical location and transport infrastructure, Jiangxi clearly connects east and west, north and south, and many harbours at home and abroad.

Ecological Advantages

In regional ecology and environmental conditions, Jiangxi ranks sixth and eighth, respectively, in the country. Lush vegetation carpets its mountains, giving the province a green appearance and spectacular scenery. Its forest area amounts to 143 million *mu* 亩 (1 ha = 15 *mu*), for a forest coverage rate of 60.5%, which is second in China.[3] Jiangxi has eight national scenic resorts: Lushan Mountain, the Jinggang Mountains, Sanqing (Pure Trinity) Mountain 三清山, Longhu (Dragon and Tiger) Mountain 龙虎山, Sanbai Mountain 三百山, Fairy Maiden Lake 仙女湖, the Meiling Mountain Range 梅岭 and Turtle Mountain 龟峰. It also has 5 nationally protected natural regions such as Poyang Lake, and 14 national forest parks.[4] Large stretches of marshland, including 6.9% of natural marsh, cover 21.8% of the province's total area. Poyang Lake has been listed as one of the important marshes in the world and is a nationally protected natural region for migratory birds. For every winter, 95% of the white cranes in the world come and live here. With more than 140 species of fish, Poyang Lake is an important fishing and fish-reproducing base in China.

Resource Advantages

Jiangxi has many resource advantages. First, it is rich in forest resources. The province has a forest area of up to 9.31 million ha, ranking it seventh in the country. With regard to timber reserves, it is ninth in China, with 370 million cu m. It is second in the country in resources of bamboo and oil-tea camellia. Second, Jiangxi has abundant mineral resources, especially of nonferrous metals, rare metals and rare earth metals. To date, more than 160 kinds of minerals have been found there. The province has proven reserves of 101 of these kinds, the most abundant reserves in the country of 12 kinds, and is among the top five provinces with the most plentiful reserves of 35 kinds. Copper, tungsten, uranium, tantalum, gold, silver and rare earth have been called the "seven golden flowers" of Jiangxi's mineral resources. The largest copper smelter base in Asia is found in Jiangxi, Guixi 貴溪, while southern Jiangxi is sometimes called the world capital of tungsten. Third, the province has the third most plentiful supply of fresh water in the country, with a total fresh water area of 25 million *mu*. The fine quality of Jiangxi's fresh water is favourable for aquaculture. Fourth, Jiangxi has been and still is one of the most agriculturally developed provinces in China producing large quantities of high-quality grain, oil plants, vegetables, oranges, pigs, freshwater fish and other products. Thus, Jiangxi is in an ideal position to export such products to the southern coastal area of the country, especially to Guangdong, Hong Kong and Macao. Fifth, manpower resources are abundant. In 2004, Jiangxi had a labour force of 30.76 million, or 71.8% of its total population. In addition, 72.0% of the labour force was employed, while 8.61 million were unemployed, representing mainly surplus labour in the countryside. Since the launching of economic reforms, millions of farmers and workers in Jiangxi have gone to Guangdong, Fujian, Hainan 海南 and other coastal provinces to engage in business or find manual work.

General Information on Economic Development

In the post-1949 period, Jiangxi's economy underwent a phase of large-scale socialist construction. During the First Five-year Plan, 156 key state projects were initiated in Jiangxi, laying the initial basis for the industrialization of the province. Many new military industrial enterprises were launched during the "Small Third Line 小三線 Construction" period in the late 1960s and the early 1970s, when some factories were moved into Jiangxi from the coast or from the nation's large cities. At the beginning of the period of economic reforms and the opening up of the country in the late 1970s, Jiangxi's industries remained at a low-to-middle level in comparison to the rest of the country. The first China-made planes, motorbikes and non-fluorine refrigerator compressors were produced in Jiangxi, and Jiangxi was the second province in China to start producing instant noodles, washing machines, down clothes, television sets and refrigerators. However, in the reform period, Jiangxi gradually lagged behind in nation-wide economic development because of its weak open economy. Among the six provinces in Central China (Shanxi 山西, Hebei 河北, Hubei, Hunan, Jiangxi and Anhui), Jiangxi compared poorly in industry, finance and general economic development.

In the new century, Jiangxi has learned much from the experiences of other provinces in the areas of opening up and reforming its economy. It is focusing more attention on industrialization than in the past. With the aim of opening up the province, provincial authorities are determined to turn Jiangxi into "three bases and a back garden": that is, a base for taking over the industries that are gradually being transferred from developed coastal developed areas to inland areas, a base for processing and supplying agricultural and side products, a base for exporting labour, and a "back garden" for tourism and entertainment for people from coastal areas. Jiangxi has quickened its pace to catch up with developments in the Yangzi River Delta, the Pearl River Delta and the Minjiang 閩江 Economic Development Zone, to benefit from globalization. With the implementation of a series of new strategic measures in opening up and modernizing its economy, Jiangxi has taken on a new look. The media have dubbed the rapid pace of its open economic development and its increasing attractiveness to domestic investment in the "Jiangxi phenomenon."

Great Leap Forward in Economic Development

Since 1949, Jiangxi has undergone three major phases in economic development: The first phase was from 1949 to 1978 before China opened up; the second phase, from 1978 to 2000; and the third phase, from 2001 to 2004. The average annual economic growth rates of the three phases were 4.3%, 9.4% and 11.5%, respectively.

In the past few years, Jiangxi's economy has been advancing at a rapid pace. In 2004, Jiangxi ranked fifth in GDP in the Pan-PRD 泛珠江三角洲 region. Since 2002, the province's GDP has been increasing for three successive years at double digits annually, at 13% in 2003 and 13.2% in 2004, ranking it first and third, respectively, among the provinces of Central China in terms of growth. In 2004, the value of Jiangxi's GDP was RMB350 billion. The province's fiscal revenues rose from RMB17.17 billion in 2000 to RMB34.92 billion in 2004, an annual increase of 19.42%. Total investment in fixed assets went from RMB54.8 billion in 2000 to RMB182 billion, up by 232%. With the steady progress in the economy, personal incomes also grew rapidly. The average disposable income of urban residents was RMB7,560 in 2004. Jiangxi has also made great adjustments to its economic infrastructure. The provincial GDP ratio of the three industry sectors has been adjusted from 24.2: 35.0: 40.8 in 2002 to 20.3: 45.7: 34.0 in 2004. The dominant status of industry in the provincial economy has been singled out, and pillar industries and industrial parks have become the main force in Jiangxi's industrial economic growth (Table 16.1).

An open economy is taking shape in Jiangxi. From 2001 to 2004, actually utilized foreign capital in Jiangxi increased at the highest rate among all of the provinces in Central China to total US$5.5 billion. In 2004 alone, actually utilized foreign capital in Jiangxi was US$2.05 billion, ranking the province eighth in the whole country. At present, more than 20 Fortune 500 companies have invested in Jiangxi. Foreign trade has also grown. The total value of provincial imports and exports in 2004 reached US$3.532 billion, up by 39.7% over the previous year, and 4% higher than the national average (35.7%). Exports were US$1.995 billion, up by 32.5% and imports were US$1.537 billion, up by 50.3%. Jiangxi has also strengthened its cooperation with other provinces. In 2004, it received as much as RMB117.1 billion in investment from other provinces, up by 67.4% over the previous year. Also, 21 out of 200 largest enterprises in China have investments in Jiangxi. The Pan-PRD region is the main focus of the province's economic cooperation efforts, and 56% of the virtually utilized investment in Jiangxi was from Hong Kong and Macao, and 70% of the 5,000 enterprises in its industrial parks are from Hong Kong, Macao, Guangdong and Fujian. On the other hand, 60% of the labourers who have

Zhou Guolan, Huang Shuhua and Lin Hui

Table 16.1 Key Economic Indicators of the Pan-PRD Region and the Position of Jiangxi, 2004

Province	GDP (RMB billion)	Growth rate (%)	GDP per capita (RMB)	Fixed assets value (RMB billion)	Growth rate (%)	Local revenue (RMB billion)	Growth rate (%)	Urban resident income (RMB)	Growth rate (%)	Farmers' net income (RMB)	Growth rate (%)
Jiangxi	349.6	13.2	8,189	182.0	31.9	20.58	22.4	7,560	9.5	2,953	20.1
Guangdong	1,603.9	14.2	19,313	598.3	19.9	141.687	N.A.	1,362	10.1	4,365	7.7
Guangxi	332.0	11.8	7,196	125.4	27.1	23.769	16.7	8,690	11.6	2,305	10.1
Hainan	79.0	10.4	9,669	32.2	16.7	6.939	21.0	7,736	6.6	2,818	8.9
Sichuan	655.6	12.7	7,514	237.7	22.7	38.41	N.A.	7,709	9.5	2,580	14.5
Guizhou	159.1	11.4	4,215	86.7	15.0	14.904	19.7	7,322	7.7	1,721	5.6
Yunnan	295.9	11.5	6,733	133.1	30.3	26.33	15.0	8,870	9.4	1,864	6.0
Hunan	561.2	12.0	9,117	198.1	27.3	31.652	26.4	8,617	7.9	2,838	8.0
Fujian	605.3	12.1	17,218	189.9	25.9	33.336	20.0	11,175	11.8	4,089	9.5
Rank of Jiangxi	5	2	5	5	1	7	N.A.	7	4	3	1

Source: Provincial statistical bulletins for 2004.

left Jiangxi to find work elsewhere are working in Guangdong, Fujian and Hainan.

Economic Strengths

Compared with other provinces, Jiangxi is still a relatively backward place, despite its rapid economic development in recent years. It has not yet fought its way out of its underdeveloped status. Its GDP remains small and its economic development limited. In the year 2004, for example (Table 16.2), out of five economic indicators, Jiangxi has only one item ranked at a relatively high 13th, leaving the other four ranked at a lower-middle or low level.

Compared with the five other provinces in Central China, Jiangxi is still lagging economically, although its economy has struggled to rise from the "bottom of the valley" and is beginning to show a trend towards growth. The difference in the per capita GDP of Jiangxi and that of the nation as a whole has narrowed, but Jiangxi's is still remained small relative to the other provinces of Central China (Table 16.3).

Jiangxi's Special Industries and Regional Cooperation

Stable Agriculture and Great Potential

Jiangxi, which was one of the first paddy planting regions in the middle reaches of the Yangzi River, is among the 13 top suppliers of food in the country.

Table 16.2 Key Economic Indicators in Jiangxi and Jiangxi's National Ranking, 2004

Indicator	GDP (RMB billion)	GDP per capita (RMB)	Local revenue (RMB billion)	Local revenue per capita (RMB)	Urban residents' income per capita (RMB)	Farmers' net income per capita (RMB)
Value	349.59	8,189	20.58	480.5	7,560	2,935
Rank	16	22	22	24	23	13

Note: The rank is based on the statistics of 31 provinces and municipalities, excluding Hong Kong, Macao and Taiwan.

Source: Provincial statistical bulletins.

Table 16.3   Jiangxi's Key Economic Indicators and Jiangxi's Rank in Central China, 2004

Indicator	Unit	Hubei	Hunan	Henan	Shanxi	Anhui	Jiangxi	
							Value	Rank
GDP	RMB billion	632.0	561.2	881.5	304.2	481.2	349.59	5
Per capita GDP	RMB	10,519	9,117	9,470	9,121	7,768	8,189	5
Local revenue	RMB billion	30.37	31.65	42.86	25.53	27.44	20.58	6
Revenue per capita	RMB	504.8	472.5	441.0	765#	427.8	480.5	3
Increased value of large-scale industries	RMB billion	166.47	119.8	233.27	124.29	108.2	61.78	6
Urban residents' income	RMB/ per capita GDP	8,023	8,617	7,704	7,902	7,511	7,560	5
Farmers' net income	RMB/ per capita GDP	2,897	2,838	2,553	2,589	2,499	2,953	3
Fixed assets investment	RMB billion	2,356	198.1	309.9	145.8	191.4	182.0	5
Utilized foreign capital	US$ billion	2.071	1.418	0.874	0.09	0.55	2.05	2

Source: From provincial statistical bulletins for 2004.

Its superior natural conditions and fine ecological environment are suitable for the production of grain and timber, and for animal husbandry and fisheries. Jiangxi has been exporting foodstuffs without interruption since 1949. During the period 1990–2003, Jiangxi sent a total of 17.81 million tonnes of rice to other provinces, for an annual average of 1.37 million tonnes.[5] Even in "the three-year natural disaster" period in the late 1950s when the country experienced a severe famine, Jiangxi still supported other provinces with 2.175 million tonnes of food.[6] Jiangxi is still contributing to the stability of the country's food supply. In 2004, the total food supply amounted to 18.15 million tonnes, up by 25.1% over the previous year, for an increase of 3.65 million tonnes. Jiangxi also regularly exports large quantities of other agricultural products, such as cooking oil, pigs, fowl and fresh eggs.

With regard to agricultural production, the province has the following advantages in the Pan-PRD region. First, it is the main supplier of agricultural products to Guangdong and Fujian, and since the 1950s, has also been one of the main suppliers of fresh food to Hong Kong and Macao. In 2004, the per capita food supply in Jiangxi amounted to 421 kg, ranking the province first in the Pan-PRD region, and over Guangdong and Fujian by 254 and 212 kg, respectively. Jiangxi exports several million tonnes of food to Guangdong and Fujian every year. Recently, the organic food industry has been developing rapidly in Jiangxi. In 98 organic food products, the province ranks first in China, and in 302 green food products and 188 healthy agricultural products, it ranks eighth in the country, leading the Pan-PRD region. Clearly, Jiangxi has the potential to become a major supplier of high-quality food for the coastal regions of the country (Table 16.4).

In recent years, the Jiangxi government put forward a new approach to development based on the province's relative advantages in agriculture – that of "setting up a 'green bank' up in the hills and a high-quality granary below the hills," to enhance overall agricultural productivity.

Greater efforts are also being made to develop an outward orientation in agriculture, essential for promoting agricultural modernization and accelerating development.

In 2004, there were 150 foreign enterprises in Jiangxi with agricultural investments totalling US$3.9 billion. In 2003, there were 1,141 agricultural

Table 16.4 Agricultural Gross Output and Per Capita Grain Output of the Nine Provinces, 2004

Province	Grain gross output (million tonnes)	Per capita grain output (kg)	Oil (thousand tonnes)	Fruit (thousand tonnes)	Meat (thousand tonnes)	Aquatic products (thousand tonnes)
China	469.47	361	30,570.0	152,430	72,600.0	48,550.0
Jiangxi	180.34	421	401.0	1,024.0	2,200.3	1,573.4
Guangdong	139.00	167	775.1	7,878.5	3,653.2	6,713.8
Guangxi	147.32	301	N.A.	5,264.0	383.0	2,743.0
Fujian	73.60	209	N.A.	N.A.	1,837.5	5,912.1
Hunan	281.02	419	1,396.1	N.A.	596.15	1,672.1
Sichuan	332.65	381	1,650.0	5,073.0	8,635.0	850.0
Yunnan	150.95	342	330.0	1,155.0	2,778.0	221.0
Guizhou	115.00	294	827.1	828.9	1,710.5	88.5
Hainan	19.66	240	N.A.	1,434.5	587.2	1,362.6

Source: Based on national and provincial statistical bulletins for 2004.

projects in the province involving contracted foreign and domestic capital worth RMB12.5 billion, and actually utilized capital of RMB4.26 billion. In 2004, there were 880 agricultural projects involving foreign capital and capital from other provinces with a total contractual amount of RMB12.6 billion and an actually utilized amount of RMB4.4 billion. The foreign funds came mainly from Hong Kong and Macao while the domestic investments came from three provinces: Zhejiang, Fujian and Guangdong. The processing of agricultural products is increasing and agricultural development is becoming more comprehensive as investment increases. In 2004, the value of livestock products made up 11.25% of all agricultural production, cash crops 27.84%, marine products 13.29%, the processing of agricultural products 13.86%, and integrated development 16.02%. Projects worth more than RMB50 million made up 20% of the total foreign capital attracted.

Recently, the potential for agricultural development and the increase in the income of farmers can be summed up as follows: "Hope lies in mountains, potential in the waters, the emphasis is on farmland, there is stamina in the livestock, a way forward in industry." From now on, Jiangxi will concentrate its external cooperation efforts in agriculture on adjusting its agricultural structure and on modernizing the industry. The key points in its approach are: to make full use of the province's ecosystem resource advantages and agriculture resource advantages; and to develop high-quality agricultural products and organic food, as well as the processing of products in the agriculture, forest, animal husbandry and fishery industries. Specific points for departure are the development of an organic rice industry, a high-quality fruit industry, a forest products processing industry, the raising of grass-fed livestock and the deep exploitation of the resources of Poyang Lake. Leading enterprises will be encouraged to promote the continual opening up of the agricultural sector.

Grain production has always been the key to an agricultural economy. Jiangxi has established high-quality rice (dominated by organic rice) producing and processing bases in more than 20 counties in the northwestern, northeastern, and southwestern areas of the province and established some leading processing enterprises such as the China Grain Group. In 2004, the only braise-rice processing project in China began production in Jiangxi's Jinxian county 進賢縣. China Grain Enterprise (Jiangxi) has a processing capacity of 400,000 tonnes, or 2.2% of the grain output of Jiangxi. There is much room for the development of a grain processing industry in Jiangxi.

Development of forest resources. Forests are Jiangxi's first resource advantage. Recently, the province has emphasized the exploitation and utilization of forest resources. It has been striving to convert its resource advantage into an economic one by systemic reforms and by promoting the forestry industry. The focus is on fruit production, the processing of wood and bamboo, the production of edible mushrooms and the production of organic green tea. Jiangxi's forestry industry is already developed to some extent, as its total output ranks among the top ten in China and the value of its products in the top eight. Some of main forest products in Jiangxi are: artificial planks (represented by fine-quality, environmentally friendly and resource-saving medium-density fiberboards), paper pulp and bamboo products. In general, the scale of forest enterprises in Jiangxi is small and the province's forest advantages have not been brought into full play. Greater results can be achieved in outward cooperation in the aspects of the production of functional synthetic planks, timber, research and development of bamboo-wood synthetic planks, compound material of bamboo and the chemical uses of bamboo.

High-quality fruit industry. Jiangxi's fruit industry is characterized by an "oranges in the south and pears in the north" layout. Fresh fruits from Jiangxi are sold to 25 nations in Asia, Africa and Europe. They have a reputation for fine quality throughout country, including Hong Kong and Macao and in international markets. Strategies for developing Jiangxi's outwardly oriented agriculture include placing more importance on the cultivation of pears and oranges in northern and southern Jiangxi, respectively, and striving to further raise their quality. Currently, nationally known fruit processing companies such as the Huiyuan Beverage & Food Group Co. 匯源果汁 have established a presence in Jiangxi, as well as shareholding companies such as the Gannan Fruits Co. 贛南果業. Nevertheless, the fruit industry is still at the stage of infancy. Therefore, it is very important to encourage the leading fruit processing enterprises to set up operations in the province and to develop techniques for preserving fresh fruit if the industry is to expand.

Aquacultural industry. Jiangxi has 25 million *mu* of water area, which make up 10% of the total area of the province and 9.34% of the nation's inland water area. In 2004, 1.56 million tonnes of aquaculture products were produced, ranking Jiangxi first among the inland provinces. To date, nearly 80% of the water area is not being fully utilized. The development of fresh water aquaculture has enormous potential.

Livestock breeding industry. In Jiangxi's agriculture economy, animal husbandry occupies an important place. It is a main focus in the drive to increase the incomes of farmers. In 2004, RMB33 billion worth of livestock were raised, accounting for 33% of the total value of the province's agricultural production. Livestock products worth more than US$54 million were exported, doubled that of the year before. Jiangxi has 36 species of local livestock, including some that are well-known internationally, such as the black-boned chickens of Taihe 泰和烏雞 and some that are famous throughout the nation, such as the yellow chicken of Ningdu 甯都黃雞, the sesame chicken of Chongren 崇仁麻雞, the green hull egg chicken of Dongxiang 東鄉綠殼蛋雞 and the gray goose of Xingguo 興國灰鵝. The black pigs of Yushan 玉山黑豬, also well known nationally, can be raised on a larger scale. In 2004, 2.36 million tonnes of meat were produced in Jiangxi, from the raising of 22 million pigs (an increase of 9.5% over 2003) and 0.9 million cows (an increase of 24.1% over 2003). But the number and scale of processing enterprises, particularly advanced processing enterprises, are small.

Rapid Industrial Development

Jiangxi's industrial system was established after 1949 and has been developing rapidly in recent years. In 2004, there were 3,445 large industrial enterprises in 38 areas: coal, nonferrous metals, steel, machinery, building materials, food, medicine, electronics information, and so forth. Industrialization has become an important aspect of the provincial economy.

Since the Jiangxi government formulated a clear development strategy of "taking industrialization as the core, extensive opening as the main strategy" in 2001, progress on industrialization in the province has been speeding up. The economy has already shifted from one based on agriculture to one based on industry. The incremental value of large-scale industrial enterprises has been increasing rapidly. From 2001 to 2004, it increased by 10.29%, 16.16%, 18.5% and 26.1% in each successive year. The value of industrial output accounted for 27.4%, 28.3%, 30% and 31.77% of the province's GDP in those four years, respectively.

Automotive industry. Jiangxi has laid a good foundation for an automotive industry. First, its products sell well. Since 2004, the Jiangling 江鈴 Motor Company has developed more rapidly than many other national automotive companies. Quanshun 全順 currently has 10% of the domestic light trucks market and Baodianpika 寶典皮卡, 20%. Exports of vehicles to international markets have grown rapidly, with a marketing network extending from the Middle East to Central America. In terms of the total number of diesel light trucks exported and foreign currency earned, Jiangxi ranks first in China. In May 2005, the first batch of 200 Lufeng 陸風 trucks were exported to Europe, becoming the first Chinese automobiles made available in the European market. Second, the province's automotive industry has now attained a certain level of production capacity and scale. Currently, Jiangxi has whole-vehicle production bases in Jiangling, Changhe 昌河, Shangrao 上饒 and Pingxiang 萍鄉, and components industries such as the Jiujiang Components Industry Park and the Jiangling Component Production Group. Jiangxi's automotive industry has already engaged a series of outward cooperation efforts in capital and techniques. The Jiangling Component Production Group plans to produce three series of automobiles of 20 varieties. The production capacity will be 300,000 vehicles and a large quantity of vehicle parts and components. The Changhe Group, for its part, intends to have a production capacity of 200,000 vehicles and 300,000 engines.

Aviation manufacturing industry. Jiangxi is one of the few provinces in the country in which airplanes are manufactured. There are two large airplane manufacturing enterprises in Jiangxi: the Hongdu 洪都 Aviation Industry Group Company and the Changhe Airplane Industry Company. Hongdu ranks first in the country in foreign currency earnings from the export of planes. The company produces one-third of the airplanes made in China. It has begun to make helicopters through subcontracting arrangements with foreign companies. The first MD600N helicopter jointly made by the Hongdu Aviation Industry Group Company and the MD Helicopter Company of the RDM Group of Holland was assembled on 21 October 2004. It was featured at the Fifth Zhuhai 珠海 International Aviation and Aerospace Exposition, greatly strengthening Jiangxi's position as an aviation manufacturing centre.

Metallurgy industry. Jiangxi has a large variety of nonferrous metals, valuable metals, rare metal minerals and rare earth. The potential to develop the mining and processing of these metals is great. There are now copper smelting, production and processing bases in Yingtan and Guixi, a tungsten smelting and deep-processing base in Ganzhou and some other bases for the separating and smelting of rare-earth products. The Jiangxi Copper Group is the biggest copper production company in China and was one of the top ten in the world in 2003, having mined 400,000 tonnes of copper in that year alone. Its goal is to be among the top ten copper producers in the world by 2010. The metallurgy industry is growing fast, and the market potential is huge. In 2004, the profits of Jiangxi's nonferrous metals industry amounted to 5.54% of the country's total, ranking the province sixth in the nation. In the first few months of 2005, the sale and profits of the provincial nonferrous metals industry increased by 46% to 66%, with a production sales rate of 100%.

Medicine. Jiangxi's Chinese traditional medicine is one of the strongest in the country. Jiangxi was one of five provinces allowed to set up national production and technology centres for Chinese pharmaceuticals. In 2004, the sales revenues from these centres in Jiangxi ranked fifth in the country and the profits twelfth. Many Chinese medicine enterprises based in Jiangxi are among the 50 largest such enterprises in the country. They include the Jiangzhong 江中 Group, the Huiren 彙仁 Group, the Jimin 濟民 Group and the Sanghai 桑海 Group. Among them, they have many well-known brands such as Huiren Shenbao 腎寶, the Wujibaifeng pill 烏雞白鳳丸, the Caoshanhu 草珊瑚 tablet, Jinshuibao 金水寶 and the Jianweixiaoshi tablet 健胃消食片. Meanwhile, the medical instruments industry in Jiangxi is developing rapidly. The province leads the country in the production scale of one-off injectors and transfusion instruments.

Fine chemical engineering and the new building materials industry. Jiangxi is rich in such nonmetal mineral resources as sulphur-iron, phosphorite, snake-vein stones, dolomite, and so on, and has some leading large-scale enterprises that produce products that are in high demand in the country. The Jiangxi Xing Huo 星火 Organic Silicon Factory has an annual production capacity of 200,000 tonnes, making it one of the largest organic silicon monomer producing enterprises in Asia and one that is internationally competitive. It possesses equipment enabling it to produce 10,000 tonnes annually of thionyl chloride by the full circulation of sulfur dioxide and 20,000 tonnes of AC vesicant.

Electronic information and the modern household electronic appliances industry. The electronic information and modern household electronic appliances industries have been developing rapidly in the past two years and have a bright future. By 2004, the sales revenue of the industries in Jiangxi quadrupled in two years. The province leads the country in the techniques and production scales of some sub-sectors of the industry. Now, Jiangxi has developed a "Nanchang industrialization base for a national semi-conductor illumination project" and the optoelectronic industry has been brought into the national macro layout. The project is thus set to receive priority in policy and funding support from the state. The Jiangxi Lianchuang 聯創 Optoelectronic Company ranks first among the inland provinces in the production scale of semi-conductor irradiant materials and SMOS chips, and Nanchang University leads the country in research on semi-conductor irradiant materials. The software industry in Jiangxi also has great potential. The Pioneer Software Company, the Jiangxi Jiede 捷德 Intelligent Company and the Taihao 泰豪 Software Company are among the 100 largest software enterprises in China. Clusters of companies involved in the electronic information and modern household electrical appliances industries are taking shape: 181 Hi- and New-Tech enterprises (over 60% of those in the province) and 150 software companies (80% of those in the province) are congregated in the Nanchang National Hi- and New-Tech Industrial Development Zone; and two leading household electrical appliances enterprises — the Greencool 格林柯爾 Group, the AUX 奧克斯 Group and 50 other components-producing factories are located in the Jiangxi Economic and Technology Development Zone.

In addition, many electronic and household electrical appliance industries such as Phoenix Optical Instrument Group and Jiujiang Optical 3T Projector Factory have been attracted to set up a presence in other development zones in the province.

Food industry. Jiangxi made the food industry one of its pillar industries early in the period of the Ninth Five-year Plan (1996–2000). As a result, the province's food industry has reached an advanced stage of development: 359 products have received fine-quality awards from the province, 213 have been recognized by state ministries and 17 have won national awards. There are 35 brands that are well known within the province, 2 brands that are nationally famous and 2 nationally known trademarks. By the end of 2004, more than 20 enterprises in Jiangxi's food industry had passed the ISO9000 quantity control test. In 2004, sales revenues in the food industry amounted to RMB18.43 billion, an increase of 32.6% over the previous year. The agriculture by-product processing industry, in particular, has grown rapidly. Relying on local advantages in special agricultural products, a large number of intensive-processing projects of agricultural products have been launched. These projects have greatly promoted the development of the food processing industry.

Jiangxi's industries are comparatively backward relative to the rest of the country. First, its industries tend to be small in scale. In 2004, the value-added component of Jiangxi's industry was RMB111.07 billion, ranking the province 19th in China. Second, industry plays a weaker supporting role in Jiangxi's economy than it does in that of many other provinces. In 2004, the incremental value-added component of Jiangxi's industry made up 31.77% of the province's GDP, 14.24% lower than the national average.

The development gap between Jiangxi's industries and the manufacturing industries in Hong Kong, Guangdong and Fujian is favourable to the gradual transfer of industries from the latter to the former. Jiangxi's level of industrial development, from the viewpoint of economic structure (Table 16.5), is behind that of Guangdong and Fujian but above the other provinces in the Pan-PRD region. According to theories of economic structure transfer, the economic structure of a place is upgraded when there is a gradual transfer of industries from an area with a higher economic structure to the area with a lower structure. Jiangxi is in the good position to receive such transfers. Currently, the total production values of the technical and capital-intensive industries in Guangdong and Fujan amount to 62.26% and 46.81% of the total industrial output of these provinces, respectively; in Jiangxi, the figure was 33.79%, only 28% and 13% lower than the figures for Guangdong and Fujian, respectively (Table 16.6). In the Pan-PRD region, Guangdong and Fujian rank first and second, respectively, and Jiangxi third in terms of industrial level. According to the Mainland and Hong Kong Closer Economic Partnership Arrangement (CEPA) and the Pan-PRD Regional Cooperation Framework Agreement, the structural change among the three industries has occurred, with secondary and tertiary industries having gained importance. Industries in the Pan-PRD region are being re-oriented. Guangdong will mainly concentrate on developing a manufacturing industry, with supporting components and a services system, to become one of the most important manufacturing bases in the world. Hong Kong will give priority to finance, trade, shipping, logistics and high value-added services to become one of most important modern services centre globally; Macao will become one of the world's most attractive gambling and tourism centre with regional commercial services. Mindful of these different roles, Jiangxi will play a supporting role and serve as "three bases and a rear garden" for the developed areas (Yangzi River Delta, Pearl River Delta and Minjiang Economic Zone), namely as a base for the transfer of industries, for the supply of high-quality agricultural products, and for the export of labour, and as a rear garden for tourism and entertainment.

There are outstanding economic advantages to setting up an international headquarters in Hong Kong. Jiangxi should strive to become not only the "back factory" of Guangdong but also the "back factory" of the Greater PRD region. Towards this end, continuous efforts should be

Table 16.5 The Relative Weight of Three Economic Sectors in the Pan-PRD, 2004

Provinces	Relative weight of three economic sectors
Jiangxi	20.40: 45.60: 34.00
Guangdong	7.76: 55.43: 36.80
Guangxi	24.40: 38.80: 36.80
Hainan	36.36: 25.46: 38.18
Fujian	12.90: 48.70: 38.40
Hunan	20.60: 39.50: 39.90
Yunnan	20.40: 44.40: 35.20
Guizhou	20.99: 44.89: 34.12
Sichuan	21.27: 41.03: 37.70

Source: Based on the 2004 provincial statistical bulletins.

Table 16.6 Total Production Value and Their Proportion in Large-scale Industrial Sectors in Guangdong, Fujian and Jiangxi

Regions / Industrial sectors	Guangdong		Fujian		Jiangxi	
	Total production value (RMB billion)	Share %	Total production value (RMB billion)	Share %	Total production value (RMB billion)	Share %
General and special equipment manufacturing	53.077	2.47	19.604	3.96	4.552	3.09
Transportation equipment manufacturing	91.860	4.27	27.814	5.61	16.453	11.18
Electrical and machinery manufacturing	216.043	10.04	19.903	4.02	4.298	2.92
Apparatus and office instrument manufacturing	65.431	3.04	7.713	1.56	0.985	0.67
The metal products industry	86.675	4.03	9.799	1.98	1.704	1.16
Communication, computer and other electronics manufacturing	593.221	27.57	90.143	18.20	3.196	2.17
Chemistry industry	233.19	10.84	56.868	11.48	18.563	12.61

Sources: Calculated from provincial statistical yearbooks of Guangdong, Fujian, and Jiangxi, 2004.

made to attract investment from Guangdong and to convince leading enterprises and multinational enterprises to establish a presence in Jiangxi. Second, cooperation should be further strengthened with enterprises and especially with manufacturing enterprises in Hong Kong, where many manufacturing companies with processing bases mostly in the mainland, including Jiangxi, have their headquarters. With the implementation of CEPA, trade and investment between Hong Kong and the mainland has become more convenient, and the exchanges of funds, personnel, goods and information easier and more frequent. With the rapid economic development in the province in recent years, Jiangxi's ability to attract industries from developed areas has been considerably enhanced. There is a bright future for cooperation between Hong Kong and Jiangxi in the processing and manufacturing industries. With encouragement from the state, further cooperation can be achieved in the hi-tech sector. Jiangxi has a certain foundation and scientific research capability in the fields of the integral digital televisions, back-projected televisions, third-generation mobile communication equipment, green and efficient air-conditioners, energy-saving refrigerators, the development of software, satellite-orientation incept equipment, automobile electronics, machinery electronics, new parts for apparatuses, and so forth. Third, with the help of Hong Kong, cooperation with overseas enterprises should be further strengthened. After the adoption of "zero tariffs" under CEPA, more overseas enterprises will make use of Hong Kong, which is a free port and connects mainland and overseas countries. Jiangxi and Hong Kong can strengthen cooperation in this aspect by transferring foreign-invested high-cost manufacturing in Hong Kong to Jiangxi to form new production bases.

Judging from the current industrial development and Jiangxi's existing advantages, the province should place the emphasis on the following with regard to industrial cooperation. First is the construction of a copper industry base to introduce copper processing technology. This will ensure that after the Jiangxi Copper Group has implemented the fourth phase of its expansion of the Guixi Smelting Company, it will be possible to process 600,000 tonnes of electrolysis copper within the province. Numerous copper processing projects should then be launched to lay a strong foundation to enable the company to become one of the top three copper enterprises in the world. Second, efforts should be made to expand and strengthen the electronic information and household electronic appliance industries. Jiangxi should take advantage of its good foundation and low costs to promote the transfer of IT industries from the PRD region to Jiangxi. At the same time, it should develop the components industry based on core products such as Greencool and AUX air-conditions, LCOS digital displays and 3T optoelectronics, and form a research and development base for the IT industry. Third, Jiangxi needs to strengthen the construction of an automobile industry base. Based on the Jiangling and Changhe automobile enterprises, and with the development of new vehicle models and the enforcement of the whole vehicle production, Jiangxi should join hands with Guangdong and Shenzhen 深圳 in the production of vehicle parts and components and make new breakthroughs in developing the automobile spare parts industry. Jiangxi and Guangdong share a common foundation in the production of automobile spare parts, although Guangdong mainly produces Japanese-brand vehicles. With full cooperation, the automobile accessories industries of both provinces will form an industrial group cluster that will be highly competitive at home and abroad.

In the long run, Jiangxi can bring its advantages in aviation manufacturing into full play, attract more investment and technology, and cooperate with big enterprises in Hong Kong, Macao and Guangdong to produce "branch-route" airplanes. In the Eleventh National Five-year Plan period, the state may issue some policies to encourage the production of branch-route airplanes. Jiangxi and Guangdong both intend to manufacture branch-route airplanes. In Guangdong, the desirability of developing an aviation manufacturing industry has been voiced for a long time in academic and political circles, and the launching of such an industry is regarded as one concrete measure that should be taken to upgrade the province's industrial structure. There are more than 10 domestic and foreign enterprises in Zhuhai that manufacture airplane parts. Jiangxi should further strengthen the mutual utilization of capital and technology with other areas of the Pan-PRD region, focus on developing civil branch-route airplanes, launch efforts to achieve cooperation in the aviation manufacturing industry, and seek support from the state.

Recently, Jiangxi has set up the Golden Hi-Tech Industry Delta, which is based in the cities of Nanchang, Jiujiang and Jingdezhen. The Pan-PRD regional cooperation grouping has brought new opportunities for Jiangxi to develop hi-tech industries with the help of Hong Kong. To make use of these opportunities, Jiangxi first of all needs to cooperate with Hong Kong's research institutes in those fields of high-technology that are relatively developed in Jiangxi. In key projects, the province can benefit from the highly trained research personnel and fine laboratory equipment in Hong Kong by working on joint projects to solve technical problems. Relevant experts can be invited to act as consultants, not necessarily as long-term employees. In this way, it will be possible to get around the problem of high-level talents being unwilling to live and work in Jiangxi because they are not used to inland living conditions, and the goal of technical cooperation. Second, Jiangxi has to take advantage of its relatively low costs in manufacturing to promote industrialization of related new high techniques and shorten the period of research and development. Hong Kong can do much to help Jiangxi in this regard. For example, the Advanced Manufacturing Research Institute in Hong Kong has succeeded in developing techniques for large-scale customization and individual design and manufacturing of high value in industrial applications. Because of the higher costs involved in the techniques, some of the research results could not be applied for use in production in a timely manner. On the other hand, Jiangxi has the advantage of low costs and inland markets; it needs these techniques urgently to speed up its adoption of new industrialization processes. If Jiangxi steps up cooperation with Hong Kong, and converts research results in time, the province will be able to quicken the pace of its industrialization and narrow the gap in development between it and the outside world.

Tourism Resources

Tourism is a pillar industry for the provinces of the Pan-PRD region. Jiangxi possesses abundant tourism resources and a fine ecological environment. The province has unprecedented opportunities to develop its tourism industry to improve the standard of living of its people and to bring about other positive changes.

Jiangxi's tourist industry is well positioned to become a new lever of economic growth. First, an increasing number of tourists are visiting Jiangxi. From 2000 to 2004, the number of tourists grew from 25.54 million to 41.18 million, for an annual increase of 14.33%. Since 2004, the number of inbound tourists has grown rapidly, reaching a total of 0.29 million, 73.8% more than 2003. In the first four months of 2005, the province received a total of 95,754 inbound tourists, 69.1% more than the same period in 2004. At the same time, the average number of days that tourists have spent in the province has also been rising, from 2.22 days in 2000 to more than 2.5 days in 2005. Second, income from tourism has also grown. Since 2000, gross earnings from tourism in Jiangxi increased by more than 18% annually, even with the outbreak of the Severe Acute Respiratory Syndrome

(SARS) in 2003. In 2004, gross earnings from tourism in Jiangxi increased by 22%. Third, the tourist industry has contributed much to economic growth. Gross earnings from tourism made up 6.72% of the province's GDP in 2000, exceeding 5% for the first time. In 2004–2005, the corresponding figure was over 7%. At the same time, the province's share of gross earnings from tourism in relation to that of the whole country has increased yearly, from 2.98% in 2000 to 5.11% in 2004 (Table 16.7).

Abundant tourism resources. Jiangxi has abundant tourism resources, with 8 famous national scenic spots, 7 AAAA class national scenic spots, 14 national forest parks, 128 conservation areas of various kinds, 3 national historic cities like Jingdezhen, Nanchang and Ganzhou, 26 key national relic protection units in Nanchang, Jingdezhen, Pingxiang, and other places. With respect to historical and religious sights, Jiangxi has various shrines and places of worship that go back to the origin of Chinese Buddhism, Taoism and Confucianism. Chinese Zen Buddhism is divided into "five schools and seven sects," of which "three schools and five sects" originated in Jiangxi.

Tourism infrastructure. In recent years, Jiangxi has strengthened its tourism infrastructure by improving its "eating, living, transport, travel, shopping and playing" conditions. First, the travel environment and conditions have greatly improved, with the upgrading of airports, railroads, highways and waterways. Fast, safe and comfortable transportation is available to all of the scenic areas in the province. Second, accommodation and the quality of services have improved. By the end of 2004, the province has already established 207 star-class hotels and 376 domestic and international travel agencies. Along with the improvement of tourism hardware, the software is continually being strengthened: from basic

Table 16.7   Basic Indicators of Tourism Income in Jiangxi, 2000–2004

Year	Total tourism income (RMB billion)	Growth rate (%)	Proportion in the country (%)	Share GDP (%)	Share of the tertiary sector (%)
2000	13.460	20.95	2.98	6.72	16.47
2001	16.139	19.90	3.23	7.41	18.31
2002	19.106	18.38	3.45	7.95	19.85
2003	19.747	3.40	4.04	6.98	18.93
2004	24.081	22.00	5.11	6.89	20.61

language skills and the provision of guides to the management of hotel and restaurant services, and even to the establishment of a set of rules for the tourism market as a standardized management system to suit the development of tourism in Jiangxi. Comfortable travel conditions and low-cost food and entertainment are bringing Jiangxi's tourism advantages into full play.

Tourism as a pillar industry. In 2003, in order to support tourism, the Jiangxi provincial government issued a document entitled Opinions on Further Quickening the Development of Tourism, and set the following goal. By 2007, the gross income from tourism should amount to 12% of the province's GDP, making tourism a pillar industry of the province's economy; by 2010, the figure should rise to 15%. With the aim of becoming a top tourist destination, Jiangxi has set aside special funds to develop tourism. At the same time, all levels of government in the province have attached great importance to developing tourism, working jointly and in a unified manner and investing heavily in key projects.

Red tourism. Jiangxi has abundant red tourism resources that are highly popular in the whole country. People associate Jiangxi with the origins of communism in China, calling to mind such places as Nanchang, Jinggangshan, Pingxiang and Ruijin. Nanchang is the place where the flag of Chinese People's Liberation Army (PLA) was first raised. The "August 1st Nanchang Uprising" took place in this city, as did the founding of the PLA. Jinggangshan is a world-renowned revolutionary place and the first revolutionary base of the Chinese Communist Party. Ruijin, the "red capital, " saw the establishment of the First Chinese Soviet Provisional Central Government of China and was the starting point of the Chinese Red Army's Long March. The state governmental departments concerned plan to set up 10 major "red tourism" bases in five years, the first of which will be "the cradle of New China — the Chinese Soviet Central Government." This will mainly comprise the red scenic spots of Jinggangshan city, Ruijin city, Yongxin county 永新縣, Xingguo county and Yudu county 於都縣 in Jiangxi.

Green tourism. Jiangxi has both rich tourism resources and abundant ecological resources, with its green hills and clear waters playing an important role in tourism. Very popular with both domestic and foreign visitors are such scenic areas and spots as Lushan, Jinggangshan, Sanqingshan, Poyang Lake, Wuyuan 婺源 — called "the most beautiful country in China" — and the village of Baohulu 寶葫蘆 in Ganzhou, a national model of ecological agricultural tourism. The world-famous Lushan, in particular, has been included in UNESCO's list of world cultural heritage and natural heritage sites. It is considered one of the foremost geological parks in the world. It was named the only "Excellent Ecological Touring Area" at the 2005 Conference of the World Environmental Day and Global Green Ecology sponsored by the UN Environment and Planning Committee and organized by the UN International Exchange and Cooperation Committee.

Ancient cultural tourism. Jiangxi is also attractive for historical cultural tourism, as represented by its Confucian academies, porcelain and ceramics culture, Taoist culture, Hakka customs and "Nuo culture 儺文化." Some of the most advanced and renowned Confucian academies were established in the province. They are famous for their long history, large numbers of students and great influence, having taking the lead many times in the country's intellectual life during a history of more than 1,000 years. The most famous of them was the Bailudong (White Deer Cave) academy, Jingdezhen is the country's thousand-year-old capital for the production of porcelain. Longhusha is generally accepted as the place where Taoism originated. Sanqingshan is known as having "the most wonderful view in southern China." Also well known in China are the Tengwang pavilion — one of the three most famous pavilions in South China, Bajingtai 八境台 in Ganzhou, circle-shaped Hakka houses 客家圍屋, the Tianshi Temple in Guixi, Liukeng Village in Anle and the newly-discovered origins of the "Nuo culture" in Nanchang.

Cooperation in tourism with other provinces in the Pan-PRD region. Jiangxi has established a good platform for cooperation with the provinces of the Pan-PRD region, and various efforts at cooperation in tourism are ongoing among them. Jiangxi has signed agreements or memos of cooperation in tourism with Hong Kong, Guangdong, Fujian, Hunan and Guangxi; organized promotional activities for the expansion of each other's tourism resources; and jointly put forward especially attractive inter-provincial "red" tour routes, and tours with natural-ecological and cultural themes. The following two aspects are main ones to be considered in the further promotion of cooperation in tourism with other provinces of the Pan-PRD region: the exploitation of Jiangxi's tourism resources and the expansion of tourism markets in the provinces concerned.

Comparatively speaking, Jiangxi's tourism economy is falling behind that of other areas in the Pan-PRD region. Its "red" and ecological tourism resources are obviously outstanding, but they are not being put into full use. Table 16.8 shows the weak-supporting role played by tourism in Jiangxi's economy in 2004. Compared with other eight provinces of the

Table 16.8 The Tourism Economy in the Nine Pan-PRD Provinces, 2004

Province	Total tourism revenue (RMB billion)	Rate of increase (%)	Share of GDP (%)	Foreign exchange revenue (US$ billon)	Rate of increase (%)	Tourists from abroad (thousand)	Rate of increase (%)	Domestic tourists (thousand)	Rate of increase (%)
Jiangxi	24.081	22.0	6.89	0.08	68.1	287.7	73.8	40,892.2	20.6
Guangdong*	166.39	24.3	10.37	5.38	26.1	15,620.3	31.6	88,242.0	17.6
Guangxi	N.A.	N.A.	N.A.	0.238	79.7	1,125.0	74.4	55,175.0	21.5
Hainan*	11.101	18.7	14.05	0.677	2.6	308.6	5.2	13,720.3	13.9
Fujian	55.074	42.2	9.1	1.065	13.4	1,729.0	15.5	46,430.0	25.0
Hunan	37.159	26.4	6.62	0.313	N.A.	553.4	N.A.	64,310.0	N.A.
Yunnan	36.927	20.4	12.48	0.422	24.2	1,101.0	10.1	60,110.0	16.3
Guizhou	16..6	43.5	10.52	N.A.	N.A.	N.A.	N.A.	N.A.	N.A.
Sichuan	56.62	34.6	8.64	0.29	93.1	966.0	110	114,256.0	36.0

Note: The number of tourists * excludes day tourists.
Source: The data are from the communiqués of the provinces in 2004.

region, the economic impact of tourism in Jiangxi is small, particularly with regard to the amount of foreign exchange earned.

Most of Jiangxi's tourism resources are unexploited and not being efficiently utilized. Even in the famous scenic spots, development is limited and there is much room for the exploitation and construction of tourist resources. First, better methods of management should be introduced from Hong Kong and Macao in key national-level tourist areas, such as scenic spots, protected natural areas, forest parks and geological parks. There should be more investment in the construction and management of amusement facilities, cabaret facilities and projects for holiday tours to bring up to international standards. There should also be efforts to promote tourism to the province. Second, based on the length of the tourist routes between Jiangxi and the Yangzi Delta, Pearl River Delta and Minjiang Economic Development Zone, special leisure tours should be devised, with an emphasis on natural ecology, folk-customs and farmhouses, particularly on resources unknown to the outside world and suitable for weekend holidays. Efforts should be made to encourage investment in infrastructure, amusement facilities, local food and the construction of related projects. The principle should be adopted that "those who invest benefit and those who exploit protect" in order to promote the setting up of short to medium-distance tour routes. Third, in the effort to reform government-owned tourism enterprises, foreign investment in various forms should be encouraged, such as stake-holding, mergers and acquisitions. The formation of some big tourism enterprise groups can help to strengthen the province's tourism economy.

The scenic areas in the nine provinces of the Pan-PRD region and Hong Kong and Macao all have their own special features with regard to the advantages of mutual cooperation. To date, Jiangxi has six tourism specialties — "a unique and special landscape, a reputation as the cradle of communism in China, porcelain arts, Taoist culture, a special ecosystem, and Hakka customs." These form the basis for further cooperation in tourism with the other provinces of the Pan-PRD region. First, Jiangxi's travel agencies should be encouraged to actively participate in the market for regional tours and to help expand the tourism markets of other provinces. Other provinces should also be encouraged to take part in the development of Jiangxi's tourism market, make joint efforts to promote exchanges of tourists, share information, associate with each other in sales promotions, and develop a mutual understanding so as to minimize obstacles to developing tourism. Second, cooperation with other provinces should be strengthened to exploit the potential of tourism by presenting the most attractive tour routes with such themes as sightseeing, shopping and playing, and holidaying. Third, joint efforts should be made to expand the market for long-tour routes that involve more than one province and that feature multiple scenic spots. Jiangxi can work together with the eight other provinces to create a huge tourist market of "a string of beads type" or the "network type" centred on one city and connecting to others. In the development of long-tour routes, Jiangxi should take advantage of the rich overseas tourism resources of Hong Kong, Macao, Guangdong and Fujian, and cooperate with them to expand the market for international tourists.

Conclusion

This chapter has introduced the geographical, historical, economic and resource characteristics of Jiangxi and discussed its role and advantages in the Pan-PRD region. Although Jiangxi has lagged behind most of its neighbours in economic development since the end of the Cultural Revolution (1966–1976), in the last ten years, this central province has been seizing its opportunity as foreign investment began to move inland from the coastal special economic zones. Undoubtedly, Jiangxi will have a great opportunity to win back its historic glory with its six specialties, "a unique and special landscape, the cradle for communism in China, porcelain arts, Taoist culture, a special ecosystem and Hakka customs."

There have been many "firsts" in the long history of Jiangxi and its people have contributed a great deal to the construction of a New China. Although in the 1980s and 1990s Jiangxi lagged behind neighbouring provinces, the province is now beginning to move forward economically. It is playing a supporting role for the developed regions of the Yangzi Delta, the Pearl River Delta and the Minjiang Economic Development Zone.

Since the beginning of the new century, Jiangxi has made further the opening up of its economy as its main strategy in economy development, and its investment and management conditions have improved. On 3 June 2005, the Jiujiang Export Processing Zone was formally set up after approval by the State Council. On 14 May 2006, the State Council approved the establishment of the Nanchang Export Processing Zone (NEPZ) in the Nanchang High and New-Tech Industry Development Zone. The establishment of these zones will be a milestone in attracting foreign capital. In addition, customs procedures in Jiangxi have been improved greatly in efficiency, helping to lower the business cost of investors. In July 2005, the Longnan Office of the Nanchang Customs became the first county-level customs office in the inland provinces of China. It is in charge of customs procedures for six counties and is implementing a "fast customs-procedure" service. In June 2006, compared with the same period last year, the total volume of the province's import and exports in foreign trade increased by over 70%.

In order to strengthen support for related industries, Jiangxi is constructing 10 large manufacturing bases and many special industry bases. Jiangxi has been trying hard to improve its investment environment and its efforts have been praised by investors throughout the country.

In 2006, according to the economic status and development trend of new metropolises, the popular English Journal *Newsweek* selected 10 big cities, such as London, as the most dynamic cities in the world. Nanchang — the capital of Jiangxi, was the only city in China that was selected.[7] In 2005, in the List of Competitive Cities compiled by China Institute of City Competitiveness, Nanchang ranked 23rd out of 287 big Chinese cities including Hong Kong, Macao, and cities in Taiwan, and ranked second among the cities of six provinces in central China.[8] Regarding the investment environment of inland cities, the Trilect Group of France has chosen Nanchang as the key city for investment and has moved its headquarters to that city.

Under the impetus of industrialization, urbanization and an open economy, Jiangxi's economy has ended years of stagnation and entered a period of rapid development. In 2005, the province's per capita GDP exceeded US$1,000, indicating that its essential development index has risen or reached high level. This is a historic leap forward in Jiangxi's economic and social development. Jiangxi has successfully transformed its closed and agriculture-based economy into an open and industry-dominant one. The province has rapidly enhanced its economic strengths and the disparities in economic development between Jiangxi and other provinces in the country are narrowing.

With great expectations for its future, Jiangxi is implementing the major tasks outlined in the provincial Eleventh Five-year Plan and making great efforts to achieve agricultural modernization in rural areas, a new type of industrialization, a new type of urbanization, and to expand its international trade and market economy so as to turn Jiangxi into a province characterized by harmony, innovation and a green ecological environment. In a new cycle of economic growth, Jiangxi aspires to achieve an economic and social renaissance.

Notes

1. The data for this chapter were mainly drawn from the following sources. The data for 1949–1998 came from *Xin Zhongguo wushinian — Jiangxi* 新中國五十年 —— 江西 (50 Years of New China — Jiangxi) (Beijing: Zhongguo tongji chubanshe 中國統計出版社, 1999); other data are from Jiangxisheng tongjiju 江西省統計局, *Jiangxi tongji nianjian 2000–2004* 江西統計年鑑 2000–2004 (Jiangxi Statistics Yearbook 2000–2004) (Beijing: Zhongguo tongji chubanshe, 2000–2004).

2. Zhu Naicheng 朱乃誠, *Zhongguo shiqian daozuo nongye gailun* 中國史前稻作農業概論 (An Outline of Paddy Agriculture in Prehistoric China), *Nongye kaogu* 農業考古 (The Archaeology of Agriculture), No. 1 (2005), p. 26.

3. Jiangxisheng linyeting 江西省林業廳, *Jiangxisheng shiwu senlin ziyuan erlei diaocha chengguo* 江西省"十五"森林資源二類調查成果 (The Results of the Investigation into Second-class Forest Resources for the Tenth Five-year Plan in Jiangxi), April 2005.

4. According to data on listed national-class scenic spots announced by the State Council in 1982, 1988, 1994 and 2002.

5. Tang Weidong 唐衛東, *Jiangxi liangshi zonghe shengchan nengli baohu jizhi yanjiu* 江西糧食綜合生產能力保護機制研究 (Research on a Protection Mechanism for Integrating Jiangxi's Foodstuff Production Capacity), Sannong ziliao wang 三農資料網 (Website for Data on Agriculture, Villages and Farmers), http://www.sannong.gov.cn/fxyc/zzysc/200409070482.htm (30 August 2004), accessed on 23 August 2006.

6. He Youliang 何有良 et al., *Dangdai Jiangxi nongshi yaolüe* 當代江西農史要略 (Summary of Modern Agriculture in Jiangxi), *Nongye kaogu*, No. 3 (2003), p. 22.

7. Cited from Jinshi wang 今視網, http://jiangxi.jxnews.com.cn/system/2006/06/28/002285310.shtml (28 June 2006), accessed on 23 August 2006; also Quindlen Krovatin, 2006, "Welcome, World" in *The Ten Most Dynamic Cities, Newsweek International*, at the website (http://www.msnbc.msn.com/id/13528949/site/newsweek/page/6/).

8. *Nanchang ribao* 南昌日報 (Nanchang Daily), 9 January 2006.

References

Jiangxi sheng nongye gaikuang 江西省農業概況 (Outline of Agriculture in Jiangxi), Jiangxi nongye ting 江西省農業廳, May 2005.

Meng Jianzhu 孟建柱, Speech at the meeting of the leading cadres of the entire province in July 2005.

Zhou Shaosen 周紹森 and Yin Jidong 尹繼東, *Jiangxi zai zhongbu diqu jueqi fanglue* 江西在中部地區崛起方略 (The Strategy for Jiangxi's Rise in Central China) (Jiangxi: Jiangxi renmin chubanshe 江西人民出版社, 2002).

17

Fujian

Zheng Daxian, Hu Tianxin, Tang Xiaohua and
He Chenggeng

Geographical and Historical Background

Located along the southeastern coast, Fujian 福建 is adjacent to Zhejiang 浙江 on the northeast, to Jiangxi 江西 on the northwest, Guangdong 廣東 on the southwest, and opposite to Taiwan 台灣 across the Taiwan Strait. The province has an area of 121,400 sq km and a population of 35 million.

With regard to physical geography, some 85% of Fujian is mountainous, dominated by two mountain ranges — the Wuyi Mountain Range 武夷山 and the Jiufeng-Daiyun-Boping Mountain Range 鷲峰山—戴雲山—博平嶺. Most of its rivers empty into the sea in a northwest-to-southeast direction. East Fujian has a zigzag coastline of 2,120 km dotted with 1,202 offshore islands, and the province's plains are concentrated in a narrow strip along its eastern coastline.

Fujian's physical geography has had a significant impact on the historical and socioeconomic development of the province. Although its sub-tropical climate is conducive to agriculture, the lack of flat land has limited crop production to support what eventually became a large population. Historically, large numbers of Fujianese have thus sought a living outside the province. The mountains made communications with inland provinces, including adjacent ones, difficult. However, thanks to the fact that Fujian's long coastline has an abundance of excellent natural harbours, the Fujianese were able to forge maritime trade links with foreign and domestic traders (Figure 17.1).

The long tradition of engagement in maritime trade also led many Fujianese to emigrate to other parts of Asia and the rest of the world to pursue opportunities and means of making a living. More than 33 million overseas Chinese and people of Chinese ancestry are estimated to be living outside of Mainland China, Hong Kong 香港, Macao 澳門 and Taiwan. Around two-thirds of the ethnic Chinese population in Southeast Asia and four-fifths of Taiwanese originated from Fujian. Not surprisingly, Fujian is often described as the main home of overseas Chinese.

Fujian's skilled navigators enabled the province to achieve prosperity in what was a maritime trade-oriented economy. An Office for Oceangoing Ships was established in 1087 in the city of Quanzhou 泉州, which was one of the most important seaports in China's history. During the Song 宋 (960–1279) and Yuan 元 (1279–1368) dynasties, Quanzhou was perhaps the largest and busiest port in the world. Foreign trade brought prosperity to Fujian's agricultural and handicraft industries. Early in the Ming 明 dynasty (1368–1644), in response to constant and devastating incursions by Japanese

Figure 17.1   Fujian in Its Geographical Setting

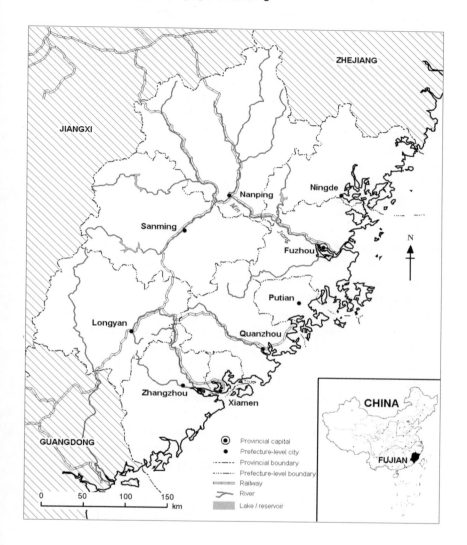

pirates, the government implemented a policy of maritime restrictions. Quanzhou was one of only three ports in China which foreign trade could legally be conducted. During the mid-Ming period, Quanzhou declined due to the silting up of the Jin River 晉江. In its place, Zhangzhou 漳州 and Xiamen 廈門 port emerged as important new ports. Early in the Qing 清 dynasty (1644–1912), as part of its efforts to suppress the anti-Qing forces in Taiwan, the government ordered those living within a certain distance along the coast to move away. Maritime trade was strictly forbidden, and the status of Fujian in foreign trade declined.

After the Opium War (1840–1842), Fuzhou 福州 and Xiamen were two of five treaty ports forced open to trade with Western nations. Foreign trade and Western civilization attracted new industries, such as sugar refining, tea processing and textile manufacturing. These tended to concentrate in Fuzhou and Xiamen, which became early leaders in modern industrialization in the province. Also of particular importance in the industrialization of the province was the central government's decision in 1866 to establish in Mawei 馬尾 in Fuzhou a Shipping Affairs Bureau and the largest shipyard in China. During the first half of the twentieth century, Fujian's economy was further stimulated by investments by overseas Chinese of Fujianese origin. Modern industries were set up in Fujian, including the shipbuilding, electricity, printing and canning industries, and factories for the production of soap, candles and soft drinks. Fuzhou, Xiamen, Jinjiang and Longxi 龍溪 became significant industrial cities.

In 1950–1978, the period of the centrally planned economy, the central government dominated every aspect of the local economy. For much of this period, China adopted a strategy of self-reliance in developing its economy. Since foreign trade was controlled and foreign investment was avoided for ideological reasons, Fujian lost its important role in trade and industry. Furthermore, because of its proximity to Taiwan, Fujian actually suffered from disinvestment, because the central government wished to keep losses to a minimum in case of any outbreak of war between the mainland and Taiwan. Thus, from 1950 to 1980, the central government did not permit any large industrial and infrastructural projects to be constructed in Fujian, with the exception of such projects as the Yingtan 鷹潭-Xiamen railway and Laizhou 來舟-Fuzhou railway, which were designed and constructed mainly for military use. As a result, Fujian's economy was stagnant from the 1960s to 1978. Its per capita GDP decreased from 86% of the national average in 1952 to 72% in 1978, ranking Fujian last among the coastal provinces.[1]

Since the launching of China's open-door policy in 1978, Fujian's geographical and historical background has turned out to be advantageous for economic development. Due to its strategic situation as an outpost, and its close socio-cultural relations with overseas Chinese, Fujian was one of two provinces (along with Guangdong) selected for the implementation of comprehensive experimental reforms. To explore and demonstrate the effectiveness of the reform process, these two provinces were authorized to adopt special policies and flexible measures to develop their economies. The result has been tremendous growth in both places.

Economic Growth and Industrial Restructuring in Fujian

Thanks to the success of the reforms, Fujian's economy has been maintained a high growth rate since 1978. During the period 1978-2004, average annual GDP growth in the province was 12.9%. In total GDP, Fujian's ranking in the country rose from 22 to 11; and in per capita GDP from 23 to 7. With the rapidity of industrialization in the province, the ratios of the primary, secondary and tertiary industries have changed markedly from 36:42.5: 21.5 in 1978 to 13.2:47.7:39.1 in 2004. The rapid transition of Fujian's economy is revealed in Table 17.1.

Table 17.1   Main Economic Indicators of Fujian's Economy, 1978–2004

Item	1978	1990	2000	2004
Gross domestic product (RMB billion)	6.64	52.23	392.01	605.31
Primary industries (RMB billion)	2.39	14.70	64.06	78.73
Secondary industries (RMB billion)	2.82	17.45	171.12	295.03
Tertiary industry (RMB billion)	1.43	20.08	156.83	231.55
GDP per capita (RMB)	271	1,720	11,496	17,241
Output value of industry (RMB billion)	6.31	53.15	529.61	885.65
Total exports (US$ billion)		2.45	12.91	28.95
Total imports (US$ billion)		1.89	8.32	18.13
Number of agreements on FDI		1,043	1,463	2,277
Value of actually utilized foreign capital (US$ million)		290	3,804	5,318

Sources: Fujiansheng tongjiju 福建省統計局, *Fujiansheng tongji nianjian 2005* 福建省統計年鑒2005 (Fujian Statistical Yearbook 2005) (Beijing 北京: Zhongguo tongji chubanshe 中國統計出版社, 2005).

As a vanguard in developing an outward-oriented economy, Fujian has been one of the greatest beneficiaries of China's open policy. The achievements of an outward-oriented economy in Fujian have been proven by the rapid growth in utilized foreign direct investment (FDI) and foreign trade. Mainly stimulated by substantial investment from Hong Kong, Taiwan and Southeast Asia, in 2004 Fujian had more than US$5.3 billion of utilized FDI, ranking the province third in the nation in this respect; and US$4.7 billion of foreign trade, ranking it seventh. In that same year, exports reached US$29.0 billion and imports US$18.1 billion, but a significant portion of it involved the processing trade, which accounted for 46.5% of Fujian's total foreign trade (Table 17.1).

The outward-oriented economy in Fujian obviously dominates the province's economic structure, as can be seen by the fact that in 2004, foreign-invested enterprises (FIEs) accounted for 59% of Fujian's gross industrial output and 63% of exports. The growth of the economy has transformed the once self-sufficient industrial structure to a modern one that is conducive to Fujian's participation in the global economy.

FDI has mainly been focused in manufacturing industries (72% of the utilized amount), in such areas as electronics, telecommunications, electrical equipment and machinery, and construction materials, and in such traditional industries as textiles and garments. Because of this, the leading industrial sectors in Fujian are electronics and telecommunications, machinery and equipment, petrochemicals, textiles and garment, food, leather, plastics, building materials and metallurgy. The electronics industry in particular has become a new growth pole in Fujian, with the value-added component of the electronics and telecommunications industry amounting to RMB34 billion in 2004, for a growth rate of 32.4% over 2003.

As of 2004, major export items include non-metal mineral products, office machinery and automatic data processing equipment, power machinery and parts, garments and related parts and footwear. Major export markets include the U.S.A., the European Union (E.U.), Japan and Hong Kong. Major import items include plastics of primary pattern, steel, special industry equipment, power machinery and parts, clerical machinery and automatic data processing equipment and specialized, scientific and controlled instruments and equipment, and so forth. Major sources of imports were Japan, the U.S.A. and the E.U.

Industrial restructuring in Fujian has reflected the fact that some newly industrialized economies (NIEs) such as Taiwan and Korea have moved their capital-intensive industries to the mainland in the process of shifting away from labour-intensive industries.

The Challenges of Inter-provincial Competition

The open policy led Fujian to achieve rapid progress in developing labour-intensive industries in the 1980s and the 1990s, when the ratio of light industrial output in its economy was quite high. FDI in Fujian was mainly derived from overseas Chinese from Hong Kong, Taiwan and Southeast Asia. In order to pursue low-cost labour, their investments have been concentrated in small-scale and labour-intensive processing enterprises, which have relatively limited backward and forward industrial linkages with domestic enterprises. As the recent restructuring of the outward-oriented economy in Fujian has shown, such economic growth based on low-cost and labour-intensive processing cannot be sustained in the face of rising competition from other inland provinces. Fujian's comparative advantages in attracting labour-intensive FDI are gradually beginning to decline.

With the rapid economic growth of coastal China and industrial restructuring, Fujian's economy will face more severe provincial competition from neighbouring coastal provinces. Compared to coastal neighbours such as Guangdong, Jiangsu 江蘇, Zhejiang and Shanghai 上海, Fujian is a laggard in terms of GDP and per capita GDP (Table 17.2). The growth index shows that the province's economic growth rate has been lower than these places in recent years (Table 17.3).

Since it has now almost 30 years since China launched its reform programme, the pioneer's advantages of being the recipient of special

Table 17.2   Per Capita GDP and Local Fiscal Incomes in Fujian and Selected Provinces, 2003

	Fujian	Guangdong	Shanghai	Jiangsu	Zhejiang
GDP(RMB billion)	523.22	1,362.59	625.08	12,460.8	9,395.0
GDP per capita (RMB)	14,979	17,213	46,718	16,809	20,147
Local fiscal income (RMB billion)	30.471	131.552	88.623	79.811	70.656

Source: Guojia tongjiju 國家統計局, *Zhongguo tongji nianjian 2004* 中國統計年鑒2004 (Statistical Yearbook of China 2004) (Beijing: Zhongguo tongji chubanshe, 2004).

Table 17.3 Comparisons between Fujian and Neighbouring Coastal Provinces in GDP Growth Rates

Year	Fujian	Guangdong	Shanghai	Jiangsu	Zhejiang
1997	114.6	110.6	112.7	112.0	111.1
1998	111.4	110.2	110.1	110.0	110.1
1999	110.0	109.5	110.2	110.1	110.2
2000	109.5	110.8	110.8	110.6	111.0
2001	109.0	109.6	110.2	110.2	110.5
2002	110.5	111.4	110.9	111.6	112.5
2003	111.6	114.3	111.8	113.6	114.4

Source: *Zhongguo tongji nianjian 2004.*

policies have disappeared. Since China's admission to the World Trade Organization (WTO) in 2001, inflows of FDI have increased. Yet Fujian has obviously lagged behind Guangdong and Jiangsu in developing an outward-oriented economy. In 2003, Fujian attracted only 6.2% of the FDI in China, because the growth rate of utilized FDI has slowed since 1996.[2]

Unlike Guangdong and Jiangsu, Fujian is less likely to attract the kind of large-scale, capital-intensive and technology-intensive industrial investments that come mainly from Western countries and Japan, which are believed to play a much more important role than other kinds of industrial investments in stimulating the local economy. Since these investments are focused less on the pursuit of low labour costs and more on the capturing of market share, such drawbacks in Fujian as low technical skills, weak infrastructure and a small hinterland have constrained investments not only from the Western countries and Japan, but also from Taiwan.

Compared with the three new industrial economies of Hong Kong, Singapore and Korea, Taiwan has achieved greater success in developing high-tech industries. In recent years, outward investments from Taiwan have shifted from labour-intensive industries to technological industries. However, the flow of investment from Taiwan to Mainland China has mainly gone to Jiangsu, Guangdong and Zhejiang, while Taiwanese investments in Fujian have decreased dramatically despite the province's close geographical and cultural relations with Taiwan, which was believed to be a comparative advantage of Fujian.

Regionalization: The Strategic Choice of Fujian

In the 1980s and 1990s, Fujian proposed a series of policies on regional development. In the early 1980s, the provincial government decided to construct eight economic bases to stimulate the economies of both the mountainous areas and the coastal areas of Fujian. A regional development strategy put forward in the early 1990s was presented as "expanding the economic scale of Fuzhou and Xiamen, stimulating economic take-off in the main cities of middle Fujian, and enhancing cooperation between the mountainous areas and the coastal areas in order to push the economic development of the whole Fujian."[3] The strategy was adjusted in 1995 to focus on "constructing the prosperous coastal belt on the west bank of the Taiwan Strait."

Such policies for regional development played a significant role in guiding economic growth in Fujian. However, the policies emphasized the importance of the outward economy and intra-provincial economic linkages, while ignoring inter-provincial economic linkages. Influenced by the policies, Fujian did not make any progress in luring investment from other provinces and expanding the inland market by means of inter-provincial cooperation. Statistical data on the sale of industrial products in 2001 shows that intra-provincial sales made up 46% of sales, and exports 32%, and sales to other provinces only 22%. The intra-provincial market and the foreign market seemed much more important than the markets of other provinces; hence, in the 1980s and 1990s, there were few policies in Fujian to attract investment from other provinces. It is, therefore, not surprising to see that during the period 1996–2000, the amount of investment from other provinces totalled RMB6 billion, while the outflow of investment from Fujian to other provinces accounted for RMB100 billion. Fujian's share of all inter-provincial investments in fixed assets was only 1% in 2001.[4]

The competitiveness of the Yangzi River Delta (YRD) 長江三角洲 and the Pearl River Delta (PRD) 珠江三角洲, both of which have a huge hinterland, has had a severe impact on Fujian. The rapid growth of the YRD in particular has diverted such resources as investment funds, enterprise capital and R&D institutes from Fujian.

Since the acceleration of globalization in the new century, Fujian's government has proposed the construction of "three strategic channels"[5] and the "West Bank Economic Zone." Approved by the central government, the "West Bank Economic Zone" has become a major theme in Fujian's Eleventh Five-year Plan (FYP) (2006–2010). The economic zone, including the whole of Fujian and parts of Guangdong, Jiangxi and Zhejiang, was designed with the hope that it will develop into one of the country's most important economic growth poles, along with the PRD and the YRD regions.

The new strategy, based on a macro-level regional approach, is believed to meet the requirements of the accelerated regional integration stimulated by China's entry to the WTO in 2001.

An illustration of the recent progress of the West Bank Economic Zone is the exemplary development of the small but dynamic border county town of Zhao'an 詔安, located between Guangdong and Fujian. Zhao'an is a five-minute drive from Guangdong on National Highway Number 324. Entering Zhao'an, one is greeted with a huge billboard with the words "West Bank Economic Zone — Pan–Pearl River Delta (Zhao'an) Open District." This hitherto obscure border town has grown rapidly after the birth of the West Bank Economic Zone strategy, having become a beachhead for the development of the Pan-PRD region. Along the national highway, the government has created a 15-sq km border economic zone. To date, investors from the PRD region have poured RMB2 billion in 150 projects of various sizes (*Wen Wei Po* 文匯報 (Hong Kong), 13 March 2007, p. A08).

Participation in the Pan-PRD grouping is regarded as beneficial for Fujian in that it is expected to improve the province's competitiveness in several ways. First, it is believed that cooperation will help to advance industrial restructuring in Fujian through a division of labour and by creating more efficient and effective channels to attract investment from Hong Kong, Taiwan and Macao. Second, cooperation could expand the market for Fujian products in the PRD and surrounding regions. In other words, the hinterland of the West Bank Economic Zone could be expanded by strengthening linkages with such provinces as Jiangxi, Hunan 湖南, Guangdong, Guangxi 廣西, Hainan 海南, Sichuan 四川, Guizhou 貴州 and Yunnan 雲南.

Bases of Cooperation within the Pan-PRD Region

With regard to regional cooperation between Fujian and the Pan-PRD region, three levels of operation have their own contributions to make. They refer to the economic relations between Fujian and the Hong Kong/Macao Special Administrative Regions (SARs), then between Fujian and Guangdong and, finally, between Fujian and seven other provinces of the Pan-PRD grouping.

Fujian and Hong Kong/Macao

Fujian and Hong Kong/Macao are geographically proximate and have enjoyed close economic and trade relations since the launching of China's economic reforms in 1978. Together, Hong Kong and Macao are the largest source of foreign investment in Fujian. Moreover, trade between Fujian and Hong Kong/Macao has grown steadily, because of the two SARs' unrivalled geographical position and widely recognized strengths as trade, financial, logistics and entertainment centres. They have greatly fostered Fujian's economic development and trade over the past two decades.

Hong Kong is by far the largest source of FDI in Fujian. Between 1979 and 2002, contracted FDI from Hong Kong amounted to US$40.6 billion, with US$21.27 billion realized, representing 55.8% and 50.8%, respectively, of Fujian's total FDI.[6] By the end of 2004, there were some 20,000 Hong Kong-invested enterprises in the province, with a cumulative contracted and utilized investment of US$45.8 billion and US$23.4 billion, respectively. The share of Hong Kong's investment in total foreign investment in Fujian accounted for 49% in 2004, far higher than the share of investment from such major sources of investment as Taiwan, Southeast Asia and the U.S.A.[7]

Hong Kong is also one of Fujian's main trading partners. The SAR is the fourth-largest importer of products made in Fujian. Two-way trade between Fujian and Hong Kong totalled US$3.3 billion in 2004, accounting for 7% of Fujian's total trade. Hong Kong is also Fujian's third-largest export market, with the value of exports to the SAR having increased by 44.2% in 2004 over the previous year. Imports from Hong Kong reached US$266 million in 2004, accounting for 10.5% of Fujian's total exports.[8]

On the other hand, Fujian's investments in Hong Kong have also increased. In 2003 alone, China's Ministry of Commerce gave approval to eight enterprises to set up companies in Hong Kong. By the end of 2003, 16 Fujian enterprises were listed in the Hong Kong Stock Exchange, for a cumulative total of over 40 such companies, involving a cumulative investment of HK$9 billion.[9]

It is clear from the figures cited and trends described above that Hong Kong, as an international centre for trade, finance, shipping and tourism, can provide crucial financial services to advance Fujian's industrial structure towards capital-intensive industries. Towards this end, a large delegation of over 70 from the financial and related sectors in Hong Kong visited Fujian in September 2005. Led by the Secretary for Financial Services and the Treasury, the delegation was the first one focused on the financial sector to visit any province under the rubric of the Pan-PRD grouping. This shows the high expectations of Hong Kong's financial sector for mutually beneficial outcomes in cooperating with Fujian in financial services. The delegation visited enterprises in Fujian and sized up opportunities there, in addition to introducing the range and advantages of the financial services that Hong Kong can offer.[10]

Fujian and Guangdong

Fujian and Guangdong are provinces that are adjacent to each other. They share a similar culture, and a history of openness since 1978. The two provinces also share a relatively advanced economic status compared to other provinces within the Pan-PRD, as attested to by comparative economic indicators shown elsewhere (Table 3.4, p. 73). At present, Guangdong's output in electronics and telecommunications, household appliances, everyday petrochemicals, food and beverages, clothing and construction materials occupy a large share of the market in Fujian. Conversely, more than 10,000 Fujian enterprises have invested in Guangdong, with more than 3,600 of them located in Guangzhou alone.[11]

Fujian and Guangdong are connected by the Tongjian-Sanya 同江－三亞 Expressway. In addition, the Meizhou-Yongding-Kanshi 梅州－永定－坎市 Railroad links the western part of Fujian with the northeastern part of Guangdong. Both land links highlight the importance of regional cooperation between the two provinces. In addition, Fujian spearheaded the Fujian-Guangdong-Jiangxi (Min-Yue-Gan 閩-粵-贛) Economic Coordination Zone joined by 13 cities at the prefecture level in the three provinces. As noted above, the provincial government has also approved Zhao'an as a development zone and market for border trading activities between Fujian and Guangdong.

Fujian possesses similar economic characteristics as Guangdong: a high growth rate, high dependency on labour-intensive industries and foreign trade, large disparities between its coastal areas and less-developed mountainous inland areas, relatively low levels of state ownership, a large number of foreign-invested enterprises and private companies. However, Fujian's economy differs from that of its neighbour in several respects: Fujian has a higher ratio of light industry and more small-scale enterprises, weak industrial linkages, a lack of high-tech industries, and a lack of technological skills and advanced equipment in most industrial enterprises. A summary of the comparative industrial structures of the two provinces is shown in Table 17.4.

A close examination of Table 17.4 reveals that there are many

Table 17.4 Comparison of the Industrial Structure of Fujian and Guangdong, 2004

Guangdong			Fujian		
Industrial sector	Value (RMB billion)	%	Industrial sector	Value (RMB billion)	%
Electronic and telecommunications equipment manufacturing	599.2	34.18	Electronic and telecommunications equipment	69.0	18.79
Electric equipment and machinery	198.4	11.32	Leather, fur, down and related products	20.3	5.54
Raw chemical materials and chemical products	87.3	4.98	Garments and other fibre products	18.7	5.10
Metal products	77.7	4.44	Transport equipment manufacturing	18.4	5.01
Transport equipment manufacturing	69.9	3.99	Non-metallic mineral products manufacturing	17.7	4.83
Plastic products	65.9	3.76	Textile products	17.2	4.68
Garments and other fibre products	63.5	3.62	Food processing	15.5	4.22
Textile mill products	59.8	3.41	Electric equipment and machinery	15.1	4.11
Non-metallic mineral products manufacturing	59.4	3.39	Plastic products	14.3	3.91
Instruments, metres and office machinery	45.2	2.58	Chemical raw materials and chemical products	13.3	3.62

Sources: Fujiansheng tongjiju, *Fujian tongji nianjian 2005*; Guangdong tongjiju 廣東統計局, *Guangdong tongji nianjian 2005* 廣東統計年鑒 2005 (Guangdong Statistical Yearbook 2005) (Guangzhou: Guojia tongji chubanshe, 2005).

similarities in the economic structures of the two provinces and, hence, that competition is inevitable in their industrial development. In the ten largest manufacturing industries as shown, eight exhibit different degrees of structural overlap. Nevertheless, some industries have formed their own system, such as Fujian's electronics and telecommunications industries, which produce their own products and enjoy economies of scale. Likewise, the footwear clothing and building materials industries are strong enough to form their own production chains, and are thus well positioned to compete with Guangdong products. In terms of leading industries, in both provinces, these are the electronics and telecommunications, heavy machinery and petrochemical industries. Consequently, there is a clear need for coordination and a division of labour between the two provinces.

Leading industries such as electronics and telecommunications manufacturing, and the electric equipment and machinery industries are very significant in Guangdong, accounting for 45% of that province's total industrial output. In contrast, Fujian is weaker not only in the two abovementioned sectors, but also in the following industries: instruments; meters; office machinery; medical and pharmaceutical products; cultural, educational and sports goods; and food processing

Guangdong and Fujian were the first two provinces on the mainland to open up to the world. These provinces are close to Taiwan, Hong Kong and Macao geographically as well as in history and culture. Their high dependence on international trade and lower proportion of state-owned enterprises compared to other provinces have enabled them to more easily align themselves with international rules and standards. They have been better prepared to build contacts and to cooperate with Hong Kong and Macao, in ways that make use of the latters' free port status and sound market systems. In this respect, the outward-oriented economies of Fujian and Guangdong have been boosted by their relative proximity to Southeast Asia and links with ethnic Chinese from that region whose origins lie largely in the two provinces.

Fujian and Other Provinces

In the context of the Pan-PRD region, geographically Fujian is located in its fringes, but the province's level of economic development is the highest in the grouping after Guangdong. With its high level economic growth, Fujian's economic strength stands it in good stead in regional cooperation efforts. The construction of infrastructure for inter-provincial linkages enables Fujian to play a sub-central role in the regional economy. However, the province's lack of economic linkages with the inland provinces has limited its potential role in establishing closer economic ties with other provinces in the region. Considering its advantages in ports and its coastal location, the participation of Fujian in the Pan-PRD framework could offer opportunities for the provinces to strengthen linkages with the other provinces.

In fact, Fujian's economic structure is highly complementary with that of the other provinces within the Pan-PRD grouping, with the exception of Guangdong. Hainan stands out with its distinctive tourism advantages. Jiangxi, Hunan, Sichuan, Yunnan and Guizhou are rich in natural resources such as mineral and hydropower, and food products, and also have large populations and markets. By and large, these provinces are laggards in development and would form outstanding complementaries with Fujian, which is a step ahead of them in economic development and exposure to global markets.

To the other provinces within the Pan-PRD, the strengths of Fujian lie in its manufacturing, financial services, tourism, marine economy and construction of regional infrastructure.[12] It is thus not surprising that since the Pan-PRD came into being in mid-2004, Fujian has signed with the other 10 spatial units a total of 1,055 projects at a total investment of RMB40.3 billion. Fujian enterprises have fully utilized the new platform to "go out" and to encourage other investors to "come in" (*Wen Wei Po*, 12 March 2007, p. A08).

Fujian can also provide an important platform for the other seven provinces to cooperate with Taiwan in economic development. Since the relaxation of the tension between the mainland and Taiwan, there has been significant progress in developing economic relations between the two places. Investment from Taiwan in the mainland has rapidly expanded. The mainland has become the biggest recipient of Taiwan's exports and the site of the greatest number of Taiwan's overseas production bases. Investment from Taiwan has been concentrated in the PRD, the YRD and Fujian. Taiwan has undergone industrial restructuring, from a labour-intensive to capital-intensive and technology-intensive focus. Such industries as the iron and steel, petrifaction, automobile, electronics, textile and agricultural industries need to further shift to locations with greater comparative advantages. As a result, in recent years, investment from Taiwan to such provinces as Jiangxi, Sichuan and Liaoning 遼寧 has increased.

Infrastructure and the Economic Development of Fujian

Fujian's transport infrastructure had long been regarded as a bottleneck to growth. Its poor state was mainly due to the province's rugged terrain and to its role as a military front line. To improve inter-provincial linkages, Fujian has had to focus on developing its transport network. Transport infrastructure may be divided into three stages of rapid growth.

In the first stage, 1978–1989, Fujian emphasized the upgrading of its previous transport infrastructure, which had been built with investment from the central and provincial governments. Fuzhou-Xiamen Highway and the Yingtan-Xiamen Railway were upgraded, and the airports and ports of Fuzhou and Xiamen were expanded with the aim of attracting FDI. In the second period of 1979–1997, the province decided to accelerate the pace of construction of transport infrastructure by seeking to attract FDI in priority areas. During this period, the following were built: the Xiamen-Fuzhou and the Xiamen-Zhangzhou Expressway, the Hengfeng 橫峰-Nanping 南平 and Zhangping 漳平-Quanzhou-Xiaocuo 肖厝 Railways, the port of Qingzhou 青州 in Mawei, the Wuyishan and Jinjiang Airports and the Changle 長樂 Airport in Fuzhou. To deal with the temporary shock to Fujian's outward economy caused by the Asian financial crisis in 1998, the central government decided to stimulate demand in the domestic market by investing in large projects. In the third period, the years since 1998, the financial policies of the central government have facilitated a large amount of investment in infrastructure. The Luoning 羅寧-Zhanglong 漳龍-Funing 福寧-Zhangzhao 漳詔, the Sanming 三明-Fuzhou-Shaowu 邵武 and the Longyan 龍岩-Changding 長汀 Expressways were constructed, as was the Meizhou-Yongding-Kanshi Railway. The Waiyang 外洋-Fuzhou Railway was electrified and deep-water berths were constructed in the ports of Fuzhou and Xiamen.

Even though Fujian made rapid progress in improving its transport infrastructure, the province still lags behind the nation in the condition of its current transport infrastructure. The gaps are reflected not only in the length and density, but also in the distribution, of its railway and highway networks (Table 17.5). The lack of rail linkages between the main cities in southeastern Fujian has caused the highways connecting them to become overloaded. The fact that there are no rail connections to most of Fujian's ports has limited the expansion of hinterland areas.

Table 17.5 Comparison of Fujian and the Nation in Transport Infrastructure, 2004

	Total length of railways (km)	Total length of highways (km)	Density of railways (km/1,000 sq km)	Density of highways (km/1,000 sq km)	Length of railways/ 1,000 persons (km)	Length of highways/ 1,000 persons (km)
Fujian	1,453	56,208	12	463	2.25	87
Nation	74,408	1,870,661	78	1,949	5.72	144

Source: Zhang Qianhong 張千紅 and He Yue 何躍, *Fujian quyu jingji xietiao fazhan xianzhuang yu duice* 福建區域經濟協調發展現狀及對策 (Current Situation and Policies for Coordinated Regional Development in Fujian), *Fuzhou dangxiao xuebao* 福州黨校學報 (Journal of the Party School of Fuzhou), Vol. 4 (2006), p. 56.

Ports

With its abundant natural deep-water harbours, Fujian has an obvious advantage in the development of ports. In 2003, Fujian had more than 500 berths in its ports, over 50% of which were deep-water berths. Benefiting from its coastline of 154 km, and a water area of 300 sq km, Xiamen port now has 80 berths, 18 berths of which are deep-water berths that can accommodate 10,000 DWT-cargo vessels. In 2004, the port had a container throughput of more than 2.87 million TEUs, and a cargo throughput of more than 42 million tonnes, ranking Xiamen port seventh in the mainland. Fuzhou was also among the top 10 busiest ports in China that year. It had 119 productive berths, among which 19 were deep-water berths of over 10,000-DWT. Its cargo throughput was 23.35 million tonnes and its container throughput was 360,000 TEUs.

However, with competition from ports in neighbouring provinces, from a macro-level regional point of view, the roles of such hub ports as Xiamen and Fuzhou ports are not as significant as those played by the ports of Shanghai and Yantian 鹽田, and Beilun 北侖 port in Ningbo 寧波.

The construction of coastal ports is considered vital for supporting an outward-oriented economy. Fujian's rapid embrace of globalization has enabled ports to become more strategically important not only in the province, but also in the West Bank of the Strait Zone. In recent years, the functions of Fujian's ports were further strengthened because of two significant opportunities that arose. First, improvements in the inter-provincial linkages promoted by the Pan-PRD grouping has caused the hinterland of the ports to expand to such interior provinces as Jiangxi and

Hunan. In addition, the inter-provincial linkages could cause seaports in Fujian to act as engines for the diffusion of development in the context of regional economic development. Second, port development is urgently required if industries are to be restructured. That Fujian is currently undergoing industrial restructuring is reflected by the transformation of its leading industries from light industries to such heavy industries as metallurgy, petrochemicals and machinery. The rise of heavy industries has not only led to rapid growth in such imports as oil and raw materials, but also caused the new heavy industries to concentrate near seaports for the purpose of minimizing transport costs.

To meet increasing demand, Fujian's ports need to keep expanding. Investment in port construction in Fujian in 2004 was RMB1.51 billion. Construction in such ports as Xiamen and Fuzhou is highlighted in Fujian's Eleventh FYP. Accordingly, Xiamen and Fuzhou ports are to be built to become international, multifunctional and comprehensive trade and logistics hubs. The government has approved the expansion of Xiamen port through mergers with the ports of Zhaoyin 招銀 and Houshi 后石 in Zhangzhou and through the construction of the Haicang 海滄 and Songyu 嵩嶼 deep-water berths. The construction efforts will focus not only on berths for containers and petrochemical liquids, and on coal and ore terminals, but also on the industrial complexes that will be encouraged to be located around the ports.

Fujian's Eleventh FYP does not only envisage improvements to the competitiveness of its ports to come from strengthening coordination between different ports/cities to ensure the competitiveness of the whole port system and of hub ports such as Fuzhou and Xiamen in the province, but also from the construction of a ports-oriented land transport system that will make the ports of Xiamen, Fuzhou and Quanzhou hubs in the system. Here, special emphasis will be placed on the construction of railways and highways to link the interior provinces to the ports.

Highways

By the end of 2003, Fujian had a total of 54,876 km of highway. Of these, 727 km were expressways, 279 km were first-grade highways, and 5,756 km, 3,600 km and 12,935 km were second, third and fourth-grade highways, respectively. At present, Fujian's highways consist of 5 national highways, 17 provincial main highways (5,522 km) and country highways (12,578 km).

Highway construction in previous years focused on the construction of high-quality roads. Such expressways as the Fuzhou-Quanzhou-Xiamen-

Zhangzhou-Zhao'an, Luoyuan 羅源-Ningde 寧德, Fuzhou-Ningde and Luoyuan-Changle Expressways are well constructed. The Fujian portion of the Beijing-Fuzhou Expressway, the Zhangzhou-Longyan Expressway and an expressway to Fuzhou Airport are currently under construction. A main issue is the high percentage of low-quality roads in the province, below the third-grade. Expressways make up only 1.32% of all roads in Fujian.

The proposals in the Eleventh FYP are to accelerate the construction of main artery highways and the upgrading of low-quality highways. There are to be eight horizontal (east-west) expressways and three vertical (south-north) expressways. Also to be constructed are the ring roads in cities and lateral highways.

The so-called three-vertical expressway system includes the national trunk line expressway from Tongjiang in Heilongjiang 黑龍江 to Sanya in Hainan (with a section running through in Fujian), the national key arteries expressway from Tianjin 天津 to Shantou 汕頭 in Guangdong (with a section through Fujian), and the two lines or sections of the Fuzhou-Xiamen-Zhangzhou-Zhao'an expressway. The last two road lines have yet to be constructed.

The so-called four-horizontal expressway system refers to the national trunk line from Beijing 北京 to Fuzhou (with a section in Fujian), the national key expressway from Xiamen to Kunming 昆明 (with a section running through Fujian), the main line from Quanzhou to Guizhou (the Fujian section) and the Ningde coastal expressway to Nanping 南平, a mountainous region. The first of these projects has been completed, and the second and the fourth have been partly completed.

In the period 2006–2010, Fujian will strengthen transportation network. The four ports of Ningde, Fuzhou, Meizhouwan 湄州灣 and Xiamen will be selected as the terminals for the highways linking the inland provinces. All of the cities at the county level and the famous resorts will be connected to expressways by convenient highways. After the construction completed, there will be a total of 2,450 km of highway in Fujian in 2010.

Since the plan is to construct some highways to connect Fujian with adjacent provinces such as Guangdong, Jiangxi and Zhejiang, inter-provincial transport will improve.

Railways

By the end of 2003, there were five main railways linking neighbouring provinces with Fujian: the Yingtan-Xiamen, Waiyang-Fuzhou, Hengfeng-Nanping, Zhangping-Quanzhou-Xiaoji and Meizhou-Kanshi Expressways. In addition, the rail network made up of the five railways was an offshoot of the national network. There were also eight lateral intra-provincial railroads connecting cities within Fujian: the Zhangzhou, Zhanglong 漳龍, Longkan 龍坎, Yongjia 永嘉, Nanpingdong 南平東, Fuma 福馬, Tianhushan 天湖山 and Haicang railroads. The total length of the railroads in Fujian was 1,573 km, ranking the province twentieth in China.

Rail transport is still weak, as reflected by the low share occupied by rail transport in the province's total transport infrastructure, even though the government has paid more attention in the last couple of decades to building more railroads. Until now, the capacity of the Yingtan-Xiamen, Waiyang-Fuzhou and Zhangping-Quanzhou-Xiaoji railroads is low because they are terminal railroads. The distribution of railroads in Fujian is not efficient due to the low density of the railway network. Moreover, inter-provincial linkages are still inconvenient because the railroads in Fujian are not part of the national railroad arteries, which carry large volumes of traffic.

In the Eleventh FYP, the construction of railways is to be guided by a focus on trans-provincial rapid mass rail transit lines. These will be part of the national railway network, in which lateral railroads connect harbours with hinterlands. To promote inter-provincial rail linkages, the plan is to build three new railways, namely the Longyan-Ganzhou 贛州, Fuzhou-Xiamen and Wenzhou 溫州-Fuzhou railways, to link Fujian with neighbouring provinces. The Longyan-Xiamen high-speed railway will be constructed to connect western Fujian with the middle parts of the province.

Airports

Fujian has two international air terminals, namely the Fuzhou Changle and Xiamen Gaoqi 高歧 Airports, which ranked twelfth and twentieth, respectively, in China in terms of passenger throughput. The two airports aim to upgrade their services and facilities to international standards. In addition, there are four airports that serve regional airlines, namely Jinjiang, Wuyishan, Liancheng 連城 and Sanming. Together, Fujian's airports are open to more than 200 domestic and international flight routes. The passenger throughput of these airports reached 11.78 million in 2004.

Telecommunications

Fujian leads the country in telecommunications services. International call services are available in all urban and rural areas of the province to over 180 countries and regions. A mobile phone network covers the whole province. The density of fixed-line telephones and mobile phones reached 76.93 lines/100 persons with a total of 27.01 million subscribers. The number of internet subscribers totalled 3.19 million.

Fujian was the first province of the country to install the international direct dial (IDD) system. Its switch-board capacity reached 3.963 million terminals by the end of 1996. It was also the first province in China to digitalize its telephone network above the county level; more than 60% of Fujian's rural areas are equipped with an automatic telephone system. A radio pager service is now available in all cities and counties in the province.

In terms of postal services, there are seven central bureaux in the postal areas of Xiamen, Quanzhou and other places, but Fuzhou functions as their hub within the province. There is a personal computer (PC) network for subscriptions to province-wide newspapers and magazine subscriptions. The setting up of a comprehensive postal PC system in all cities and prefectures and in some counties in the province has greatly improved the efficiency and quality of postal services. The delivery of mail, newspapers, and magazines has been further speeded up and an Express Mail Service (EMS) offering next-day delivery is now available in all cities and counties within the province.

Power

To meet the challenges raised by rapid industrial growth and restructuring, Fujian has placed an emphasis in recent years on the construction of power plants. Short of coal reserves, Fujian has encouraged new thermal power projects to be located around the province's ports to reduce the cost of transporting coal. The large power stations that are currently under construction include the pithead power plant in Longyan, the Nanpu 南埔 Power Plant in Quanzhou, the Datang 大唐 Power Plant in Ningde, the Huaneng 華能 Power Plant (Phase III), the Kemen 可門 Plant in Fuzhou, the Jiangyin 江陰 Plants in Fuzhou, the Houshi Power Plant in Zhangzhou (Phase III) and the Songyu Power Plant in Xiamen (Phase II). In addition, the Luoyuan Thermal Power Project in Fuzhou and a nuclear power project are in the design stage. Large thermal power projects under construction include a comprehensive liquefied natural gas (LNG) project for Fujian. Located in the city of Xiuyu 秀嶼, Phase I of the LNG regasification terminal has a capacity of 2.6 million tonnes per year; Phase II is in the planning stage. The natural gas from this terminal will be provided to gas-fired power plants that will be built during the project's first phase and piped to households in five cities in the province, namely Fuzhou, Putian, Quanzhou, Xiamen and Zhangzhou. The hydropower projects include the Jiemian Power Station in Youxi 尤溪, the Hongkou Power Station in Ningde and pumped storage projects in Xianyou 仙游.

Some big power stations, with a total loading capacity of 13.5 million kw, were constructed in Fujian in previous years. In 2005, the total installed capacity for the generation of electricity was 17.58 million kw. This increasing capacity will enable Fujian to export electricity. Meanwhile, its connection with the East China Power Grid has guaranteed a rich power supply for the Fujian Power Grid.

According to the Eleventh FYP, the installed capacity of all forms of power in Fujian will reach 30 million kw in 2010, with 33% coming from hydropower, 54% from thermo-power, 11% from gas power and 2% from wind power.

Conclusion

This chapter has highlighted Fujian's special geography and history, and the strategic role the province can play in the emergence of China as a global power that must strive to balance the forces of globalization and regionalization.

As a province tasked with experimenting with new directions for development when China launched its open policy in 1978, Fujian, together with Guangdong, pioneered new ground and seized the opportunity to forge ahead economically. This demonstrated to other parts of China and the world that openness and economic reforms could bring highly positive results. In the 1980s and 1990s, competition from other provinces, especially from those in the YRD and the PRD regions, prompted Fujian authorities to devise regionalization programmes for implementation within the province. The West Bank Economic Zone was one such strategy to strengthen the regional role of Fujian, with the issue of Taiwan always clearly in the picture.

The policies pursued by the Fujian authorities since the early 1980s have kept focused on the need to overcome the province's geographical drawbacks, which have traditionally caused it to be isolated from other provinces. They saw the development of infrastructure as a strategic way of speeding up economic development. This emphasis has been given renewed support during the Eleventh FYP that commenced in 2006. Enhancing the development of infrastructure across a broad front will prepare the province well in its efforts to accelerate regional development and cooperation.

Indeed, this focus on developing the province's infrastructure has come on the heels of the establishment of the Pan-PRD framework in mid-2004, which has created for Fujian an unprecedented opportunity to accelerate development with the aid of its traditional trading partners of Guangdong, Hong Kong and Macao. In addition, expanded cooperation with seven other provinces within the regional grouping has opened up new vistas of growth and cooperative development. In the past two decades, Taiwan has been an active participant in the mainland market in terms of investment and industrial production, especially in the YRD and the PRD regions. Now, Fujian can provide a much larger platform for it to extend its economic reach, while catering to Taiwan interests at the same time, to tap a greatly expanded hinterland in the rest of the Pan-PRD region.

In sum, together with Guangdong, Fujian reaped an early harvest from China's open policy and economic reforms. With the formation of the Pan-PRD framework, it is expected that Fujian will continue to play a vital and special role vis-à-vis Taiwan in the context of a broader regional setting. An emerging, strong Pan-PRD region will add to the competitive strength of not only this part of China, but of the country as a whole in the age of globalization.

Notes

1. Maruya Toyojiri, "An Economic Overview," in *Fujian: A Coastal Province in Transition and Transformation*, edited by Y. M. Yeung and D. K. Y. Chu (Hong Kong: The Chinese University Press, 2000), pp. 169–90.
2. Huang Tingman 黃庭滿, "Liangguo waiyi jiasu Fujian bianyuanhua" 兩國外移加速福建邊緣化 (Two Shifts Accelerate the Trend of Fujian Becoming a Peripheral Region), *Kaifang chao* 開放潮 (Opening Tide), Vol. 1 (2004), pp. 10–13.
3. The three strategic channels refer to channels to develop outward economy, to strengthen inter-provincial coordination and to improve intra-provincial cooperation.

4. Fujiansheng tongjiju 福建省統計局 (ed.), *Fujian tongji nianjian* 2004 福建統計年鑑2004 (Fujian Statistical Yearbook 2004) (Beijing: Zhongguo tongji chubanshe 中國統計出版社, 2004).

5. "Caijing shiwu ji kuwuju juchang zai Xianggang jinrongjie Fujian fangwentuan Xianggang wanyan shang zhici quanwen" 財經事務及庫務局局長在香港金融界福建訪問團香港晚宴上致辭全文 (Address by the Secretary of Financial Services and the Treasury at the Banquet in Honour of the Visit to Fujian by Members of the Hong Kong Financial World). http://www.info.gov.hk/gia/general/200509/29/P200509290233.htm. Accessed on 13 March 2007.

6. Ibid.

7. Fujian News Net 福建新聞網, *Zongshu: Min'gang hezuo, shuoguo leilei* 綜述：閩港合作，碩果累累 (Plentiful Results in Fujian-Hong Kong Cooperation) 24 June 2004. http://www.fjcns.com/Zhuanti/detail.asp?id=9509. Accessed on 25 May 2005.

8. "Caijing shiwu ji kuwuju juchang zai Xiamen juxing jizhehui de fayan yaodian" 財經事務及庫務局局長在廈門舉行記者會的發言要點 (Main Points of the Address by the Secretary for Financial Services and the Treasury at a Press Conference in Xiamen). http://www.info.gov.hk/gia/general/200509/30/P200509300244.htm. Accessed on 12 March 2007.

9. *"9+2" Hupeng youren jingmao da dan'gao* "9+2"互捧誘人經貿大蛋糕 ("9+2" Mutually Praising the Attractively Large Economic and Trade Pie), *Yangcheng wanbao* 羊城晚報 (Yangcheng Evening News), 14 July 2004. http://www.ycwb.com/gb/content/2004-07/14/content_723818.htm. Accessed on 24 May 2005.

10. For a detailed description of Fujian's strengths in these leading domains as the basis for regional cooperation with the Pan-PRD framework, see Zheng Daxian 鄭達賢, Tang Xiaohua 湯小華 and He Chenggeng 何承耕, *Fujian canyu quyu jingji hezuo de sikao* 福建參與區域經濟合作的思考 (Thoughts on Fujian and Its Participation in Regional Cooperation), in *Fan Zhusanjiao yu Xianggang hudong fazhan* 泛珠三角與香港互動發展 (Interactive Development of the Pan–Pearl River Delta and Hong Kong), edited by Y. M. Yeung and Shen Jianfa (Hong Kong: Hong Kong Institute of Asia-Pacific Studies, The Chinese University of Hong Kong, 2005), pp. 208–11.

11. This section should be read in conjunction with Chapter 5 (Y. M. Yeung and Gordon Kee).

12. Some points of review considered the linkage with inland areas and the coastal areas by the construction of transport infrastructures to be helpful to shorten the regional disparity. However, in terms of the theories of regional economy on "back wash effect," it is more possible that the new highways and railways lead the southeast Fujian to draw off resources from the northwest Fujian.

18

Hainan

Yang Guanxiong and Matthew Chew

Hainan 海南 is located in the South China Sea along the southwestern coast of Guangdong 廣東. It occupies approximately 3,500 sq km of land, and is mainly composed of a tropical maritime island and a surrounding sea area of approximately 2 million sq km.[1] Administratively, Hainan was originally a part of Guangdong. It gained the status of a province in 1988. At the same time, Hainan was designated a Special Economic Zone (SEZ). In 1999, the significant decision was made to have Hainan officially developed as an EcoProvince 生態省, that is one to develop on an ecologically sustainable basis.

By the end of 2005, Hainan had a population of 8.28 million, 45.2% of which were urban and 17.9% ethnic minorities. Historically, Hainan was mainly composed of immigrants. Three of the four indigenous peoples of Hainan were originally from the Pan–Pearl River Delta (Pan-PRD) 泛珠江三角洲 region. The *Li* 黎 arrived 5,000 years ago from Southeast China, accounting for over 1 million of Hainan's present population. *Han* 漢 Chinese began to migrate to Hainan over 2,000 years ago, mainly from Guangdong, Guangxi and Fujian. The *Miao* 苗 and *Hui* 回 are the two other major ethnic groups in Hainan.

Characteristics of Hainan's Economic Development

Among the 11 spatial units within the Pan-PRD region, Hainan occupies a lower-middle ranking in a range of indicators of economic development, including total GDP, per capita GDP, investment in infrastructure, level of urbanization, industrial structure, and so forth. Nonetheless, Hainan, as a part of the Pan-PRD region, can play a special role that strongly and profitably complements the other parts of the region.

Hainan is the only maritime province in the Pan-PRD as well as the second largest island province in China. The ocean provides enormous potential and opportunities for marine fishing, oil and gas extraction, and tourism.[2] Marine fishing yields reached a total of 1.26 million tonnes in 2005, a 9.5% increase over 2004.

Hainan is unique as the only tropical province in the Pan-PRD and in China, and has been dubbed the "tropical treasure island." It represents 42.5% of China's tropical land mass. An oceanic monsoon climate is felt throughout most of the province's land and marine areas, and the island has rich agricultural resources. After years of development, Hainan is at present the largest producer of tropical agricultural products in China, particularly in such products as coconuts, mangoes and rubber.

Located at the southernmost part of the Pan-PRD as well as China, Hainan's neighbours are the Philippines, Malaysia, Indonesia, Vietnam, Singapore and other Southeast Asian countries. Hainan can potentially serve as a link between the Pan-PRD region and ASEAN countries (Figure 18.1).[3] There are significant historical ties between Hainan and Southeast Asia, some of which directly promote transnational business relations between Hainan and specific ASEAN countries.[4] Hainan is the native place of the third largest number of overseas Chinese, many of whom live in Southeast Asia.

Hainan is particularly rich in mineral resources. It supplies high-quality iron ore to dozens of steel-makers in China. More recently, Hainan's titanium ores (the province is estimated to contain 70% of China's reserves), high-quality silicon ores, natural spring water, medicinal hot springs, and its large reserve of natural gas has attracted national and global attention. A part of Hainan's natural gas is currently transported to Hong Kong through underwater pipelines.

Hainan is the only province in the region with a tourist industry that promotes the themes of tropical ecology and scenery. Besides its tropical natural scenery, the province's tropical weather is especially conducive to tourism. Hainan enjoys summer sunshine nine months of the year, and pleasant spring and autumn weather in the remaining months. During winter in the northern hemisphere, tourists from China and Northeast Asia in particular find Hainan to be an attractive resort.

On the whole, Hainan's economic potential is founded on its special geographical circumstances (e.g., its location, climate and ecology) and resource base (e.g., its water, tourism, agricultural, oceanic and mineral resources). As a maritime island, Hainan clearly has a different economic structure than all other parts of the Pan-PRD region. Because of this, Hainan can potentially play a strong complementary role in the region's economy. In the following two sections, two specific industries in Hainan that demonstrate the potential of this complementarity will be discussed.

Agriculture in Hainan

Between 1990 and 2003, Hainan's primary sector contributed 40% of the province's GDP. The figure has fluctuated over the years and also between 2004 and 2005. In 2005, it accounted for RMB30.11 billion out of Hainan's GDP of RMB90.36 billion. Within the sector, fishing and forestry are relatively underdeveloped (compared to animal husbandry, for example),

Figure 18.1 Hainan in Its Geographical Setting

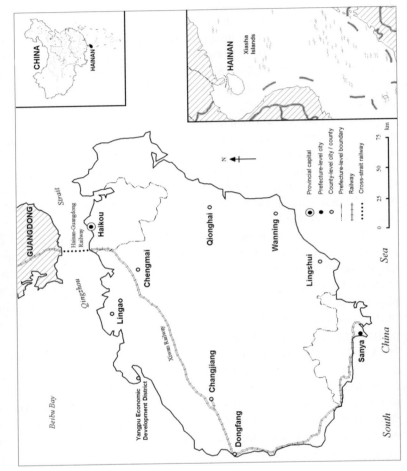

so that there is much room for growth.[5] Current representative products include tropical fruits (mangoes, lychees and coconuts), sugar, natural rubber and timber. For example, Hainan's production of natural rubber accounted for 56% of national production in 2004.[6]

Agricultural production has taken on a new significance since Hainan's establishment as an EcoProvince and its adherence to the "one province, two sites" 一省兩地 development strategy in the 1990s.[7] It was then realized that Hainan does not necessarily need to follow the conventional route of diminishing the primary sector before expanding its secondary and tertiary sectors. Hainan is well-positioned and well-suited to focus on developing its primary sector in creative ways that contribute to development of the other two sectors.

A successful example of this is the province's forest resource industry and related industries. Between 1998 and 2003, a total of 3.9 million acres of forest were planted and 0.8 million acres of land were earmarked for the purpose of cultivating forests. The province's forest coverage soared from 48.7% in 1997 to 54.5% in 2003, 51.3% of which was for commercial uses.[8] Around 2 million more acres of forest were planted between 2003 and 2005. In 2002, a preliminary estimate of Hainan's "Green GDP" was made. It was found that forestry and related industries made up a significant part of the province's GDP.[9] At the same time that forests were being successfully cultivated, large-scale industrial and commercial services projects were being completed to make profitable use of forest resources. For instance, the world's largest paper pulp production plant was built in 2004 in Hainan, realizing the formation of a forest, pulp and paper recycling production chain in China.[10] Another example was the establishment in 2002 of the Nongken Electronic Transactions Centre 海南農墾電子商務交易中心, which provides a national platform for the purchase and sale of natural rubber. In its first years of operation, turnover amounted to 70% of China's total rubber production.[11]

In the context of a development-oriented focus on agriculture as advocated by the government, the diversification of agricultural production into medical herbs, flowers, palm trees and other profitable products is being pursued. The systematic industrialization of flower production, for example, promises profit for Hainan as well as opportunities for cooperating with members of the Pan-PRD grouping. Flowers are one of the most lucrative cash crops in the contemporary world, and Hainan's tropical weather, many flower species, and abundance of low-cost labour together give the province a considerable competitive edge in the global market.

Yet, Hainan's productivity in the flower industry is currently low and its production potential very underutilized.[12] The main causes of such underutilization are said to be a lack of government institutional support and incentive programmes, highly trained personnel, adequate financial support and advanced logistics support.[13] Apart from government support, all of the other missing elements of success can be readily gained through business cooperation with the highly-developed members of the Pan-PRD grouping.

Tourism in Hainan

Tourism became a main contributor to the province's GDP in the 1990s. As Table 18.1 shows, income from tourism grew sharply in the first part of the 1990s. In 1996, Hainan's officials formally designated tourism as one of the province's three main industries in Hainan's Ninth Five-year Plan (FYP) and in its 2010 Long-term Target Objectives. In the past five years, the number of tourists visiting Hainan has been increasing at a rate of over 10% annually and tourism income at 9.7% annually.[14] Tourism's contribution to the province's GDP was 13% in the past few years and averaged 17% between 1988 and 2003, demonstrating its critical value to the province's economy.[15]

Within China, Hainan is a leader in the establishment tourism-related legislation and ordinances. As early as 1992, the Tourist Bureau of Hainan announced an *Outline of Hainan's Tourism Planning* 海南省旅遊規劃大綱. In 1995, Hainan was a pioneer in drawing up a local tourism ordinance, the *Hainan Tourism Management Ordinance* 海南省旅遊管理條例. The comprehensive *Hainan Tourism Ordinance* 海南省旅遊條例 was formulated in 2001 and announced in 2002 to regulate the fast-growing tourism industry. Hainan has also convinced the central government to pass numerous special legal provisions to facilitate its tourism business. For example, citizens

Table 18.1   Hainan's Income from Tourism

(Unit: RMB100 million, 1990 value)

Year	1990	1991	1992	1993	1994	1995	1996	1997	1998	1999	2000	2001	2002	2003
Income from tourism	4.09	4.97	8.36	27.10	27.20	26.16	27.40	29.29	32.68	35.94	38.58	43.82	47.80	46.84

Source: Data adopted from Lu, Zhang and Guo, 2005 (see note 15).

from over 20 countries are allowed to enter Hainan without having to obtain a Chinese visa if they come as part of a tour group and stay for less than 15 days.

Hainan's tropical climate is its main drawing card. Apart from its climate, however, Hainan offers much to tourists who are looking for natural scenery and ecological attractions. Outstanding attractions include beaches with fine sand and clear water, lush off-coast islands, coral reefs with marine ecology, mangroves, mountainous tropical forests and volcanic lava sites. Sanya's Yalong Bay 三亞亞龍灣, for example, has been elected by domestic tourists as the third most attractive tourist destination in the nation.[16] Perhaps less obviously, Hainan also offers much in terms of cultural tourism. Hainan culture has historically borrowed substantially from China's central areas and yet developed its own cultural characteristics in its maritime and tropical settings. There are numerous heritage spots and points of interest for cultural tourists. The four main ethnic groups in Hainan also contribute much to enhancing the cultural experience for tourists.

Beginning in the early 2000s, Hainan's tourism industry began to face problems. As a result, its growth rate lagged the national average and income from international tourists stalled for three years.[17] Among the problems are a lack of new tourist products, heightened and unregulated competition among local travel agencies, and insufficient transportation infrastructure.[18] Hainan's much flaunted tourism specialty, ecotourism, has not yet generated profits for local communities and businesses.[19] At a deeper level, there are the problems of the financial weakness and unreasonable business structure of many local travel business firms, the uncoordinated development of tourist products, and the lack of tourism marketing efforts.[20]

Officials and business leaders are proactively dealing with the above-mentioned problems. Policy-makers are advocating a strategy of veering away from the sightseeing type of tourism that depends on spectacular scenic spots to developing the kind of resort and cultural tourism that draws tourists for longer and more frequent stays. A common opinion is that a tropical climate and "natural scenery are not sufficient, [...] Hainan needs to make use of "culture" to retain tourists."[21] The strategic diversification and specialization of tourist products, such as convention travel and sports tourism, is also being encouraged for the same reasons.[22] Hainan is being marketed and packaged as a choice tourist destination in China. Hainan's authorities have designed the year 2007 as the province's Tourism Promotion Year. A broad range of marketing events is planned, with attention being paid to details such as the building of 125 "five-star" quality toilets at major tourist sites.[23] Cooperating with large transnational travel corporations as well as sharing Hainan's tourism market with them can help the local industry in the long run. Hainan's Tourist Bureau has recently put much effort in this direction and, in 2006, successfully arranged long-term contracts with giants such as the United Kingdom's Mytravel, Russia's PTS, the United States' RCI, Hong Kong's Kingway and China's Tuichina.[24] Authorities in Haikou 海口 recently announced a bold scheme to make direct grants totalling RMB30 million to local travel agencies.[25]

Members of the Pan-PRD grouping possess a wealth of tourist resources. Guangdong, Guangxi 廣西, Hong Kong 香港, Macao 澳門, Sichuan 四川, Yunnan 雲南 and Hainan are among the most developed tourist areas in China. However, efforts to develop tourism have thus far been carried out independently in each of these areas. There is, as yet, no effort to develop tourism on a regional scale. The lack of regional cooperation has hindered the full realization of the region's tourism potential. For example, there is an urgent need to design regional tourist routes to complement independent province/city-based ones. A considerable amount of coordination would be required in planning and carrying out such an operation. Marketing the Pan-PRD region as a whole to potential tourists is also clearly beneficial to all members of the region. In November 2006, tourism planning officials from the nine provinces of the Pan-PRD met in Guangzhou to sign an agreement to coordinate efforts to develop region-wide tourism. The agreement focuses on developing sustainable regional tourism, the branding of Pan-PRD tourism, integrating tourism resources within the region, building an internet base of tourism information on the region, dismantling provincial obstacles to tourist flows and coordinating the training of specialized personnel.[26] With such comprehensive efforts at cooperation among the provinces, tourism in the Pan-PRD region should be entering a new era.

Transportation

Since the 1990s, Hainan has viewed transportation as a major priority and invested heavily in it. Although the province started the effort somewhat later than other highly-developed parts of the Pan-PRD region, it has recently completed important projects and begun numerous ambitious ones. The most important development within the past few years has been the linking of the Guangdong and Hainan railways over the Qiongzhou Strait 瓊州海

峽 in 2004. This has allowed Hainan to be connected directly by railway to almost all provinces in China. A new Hainan-Guangzhou 廣州 line has been launched, helping to strengthen travel flows between Hainan and the rest of the Pan-PRD region. The renovation of the Xihuan Railway 西環 鐵路 was completed in December 2006. This can facilitate direct rail travel between Sanya and Shanghai 上海, Beijing 北京 and Shenzhen 深圳.[27] The building of a new and large-scale Donghuan Railway 東環鐵路 commenced in 2006.[28] There is also an ambitious and controversial plan to build a bridge across the Qiongzhou Strait which, if it is realized, will greatly facilitate travel flows between the Pan-PRD region and Hainan.[29]

Hainan during the Tenth Five-year Plan (2001–2005)

Hainan's economy has undergone a circuitous path to development since the founding of the province and its establishment as an SEZ. Between 1988 and 1993, a real estate bubble made it possible for economic growth to reach double digits. Between 1994 and 1998, however, real estate prices tumbled, numerous national enterprises retreated from Hainan; the cancelling of large-scale government projects undermined many local businesses, and the Asian financial crisis indirectly affected Hainan. The province's economy reached a nadir in 1999, before rebounding through adherence to the "one province, two sites" strategy, the pursuit of sustainable growth, and a reorganization of Hainan's industrial structure. From 1999 to the end of the Tenth FYP, Hainan managed to achieve an economic growth rate of above the national average.

During the Tenth FYP, Hainan's leaders and policy-makers attempted to raise the province's overall competitiveness, income levels, and local government revenue through strategic industrialization and urbanization projects. These took the form of attracting large enterprises to Hainan, initiating large-scale local projects and regrouping state-owned businesses. The industrial structure was transformed from a ratio of primary, secondary and tertiary industries of 36.5:19.7:43.8 in 2000 to 33.3:25.2:41.5 in 2005, showing the success of industrialization and balanced development.

The above efforts gradually attracted a large number of nationally and internationally known corporations to invest in Hainan, including Petro China 中石化, China National Offshore Oil Corporation 中海油, Huaneng Power 華能, Guodian 國電, Yiqi 一汽, South Korea's Samsung, Indonesia's Jinguang 金光, and Hong Kong's PCCW, Hang Lung, New World and Hutchison Whampoa. Many large-scale projects were commenced and/or completed during the Tenth FYP, including the Dongfang 1-1 natural gas field, an 8 million-tonne oil refinery, the Hainan-Guangdong Railway, the second phase of the Bo'ao Special Planned Zone 博鰲特別規劃區二期, the Jinhai paper and pulp factory, the second phase of Yangpu Harbour 洋浦港二期, the Dalong reservoir 大隆水庫, the Muladong reservoir 毛拉洞水庫, and other projects.[30] The province's GDP has grown at an average rate of 10% per year during the Tenth FYP period, with per capita GDP reaching RMB10,980 in 2005.

Aside from economic growth, there was significant progress in welfare and environment affairs during the period of the Tenth FYP. For example, Hainan was the first province in China to implement policies cancelling the levying of miscellaneous school fees for children of compulsory school age. As a result, high school attendance rates doubled and junior high school rates tripled during the Tenth FYP.

Development Plans in the Eleventh FYP (2006–2010)

Under the Eleventh FYP, Hainan's economic goals are to reach a yearly growth rate of 10% during the period and a per capita GDP of RMB16,000 by 2010. In order to accomplish these goals, the amount of fixed investment will need to exceed RMB200 billion. The Hainan government will pay special attention to speeding up the development of industrial infrastructure, cultivating new tourism destinations and exploiting oceanic resources. Another target is to continue adjusting the industrial structure by strengthening the secondary sector, raising its ratio from 33.3:25.2:41.5 (2005 figures) to the vicinity of 29:32:39 by 2010. One aim of the Eleventh FYP is to complete the reform of state-owned enterprises — essentially all large state-owned enterprises will be co-owned by private businesses, while all small and medium-sized stated-owned enterprises will be dismantled or privatized.[31]

With regard to the development of industrial infrastructure, Hainan plans to focus on developing a Yangpu economic development district 洋浦經濟開發區, a Haikou national hi-tech industry development district 海口國家高新技術產業開發區, a Chengmai old city development district 澄邁老城開發區, a Lin'gao golden development district 臨高金牌開發區, a Changjiang industrial district 昌江工業區, a Dongfang chemical industrial city 東方化工城, a Sanya Meishan industrial district 三亞梅山產業園, and other projects. The building of the Western Industrial Corridor 西部工業走廊 will be accelerated.

Industrial development will focus on six core industries: natural gas and chemicals; oil extraction and petrochemicals; forestry, pulp and paper; automobiles; biochemical pharmaceutics; and mining.[32] To date, the potential of natural gas and chemical production in the province has not been realized. Several large-scale projects to be launched during the Eleventh FYP will help make natural gas and related chemical production industries one of the pillars of Hainan's economy. For instance, the Fudao Chemical Fertilizers Plant, which has recently started operation, is the largest fertilizer plant in China. The building of an 8 million-tonne oil refinery was commenced in the Tenth FYP and is scheduled for completion during the period of the Eleventh FYP. This plant is expected to contribute RMB20 billion worth of industrial production and RMB2 billion in tax revenues to the province. The integration of the forestry industry and the pulp and paper industry will continue to directly contribute to GDP and indirectly stimulate growth in the Yangpu area. The development of an automobile industry will focus on the localization of the manufacturing of automobile parts, an example of which is the building of an engine manufacturing plant with an annual production capacity of 15,000 engines. Haikou is building a "pharmaceutics valley" to attract investment by pharmaceutics manufacturers. The first phase of construction has been completed, and several enterprises have already set up operations there. The second phase has already attracted applications from 23 pharmaceutics companies. The development of the mining industry will enhance the province's capacity to mine high-quality minerals (such as silicon) as well as to cooperate with global players in the establishment of plants that specialize in high value-added processes (such as glass-making).

The Eleventh FYP's overall strategic plan for tourism focuses on the pursuit of quality over quantity in the development of tourism, and on the transformation of Hainan from a sightseeing tourist destination into a globally branded tropical resort. Specific steps to achieve these two goals include the cultivation of high-quality resort facilities and sites in the Shenzhou Peninsula in Wanning 萬寧神州半島, Haitang Bay in Sanya 三亞海棠灣, Qingshui Bay in Lingshui 陵水清水灣, the second phase of Bo'ao Special Planned Zone, Tongguling in Wenchang 文昌銅鼓嶺, Meilisha in Haikou 海口美麗沙, Xinfudao 新埠島, Qizi Bay in Changjiang 昌江棋子灣 and uninhabited islands among the Paracel Islands 西沙群島. Sanya has been strategically designated as the centre of the South Hainan tourism economic belt to integrate tourism resources in southern Hainan. It will become a base for the development of new tourist routes. Innovative real estate developments are being designed in coordination with tourist development projects. Some 30 new five-star hotels are being planned; 20 boutique resorts will be built; 30 scenic tourist spots will be cultivated; and 10 new tourist routes will be formulated within the next three years.

As for the utilization of oceanic resources, Hainan plans to build up its deep-sea fishing teams; support technology-based fish breeding; develop Hainan into a base for South Sea oil and gas explorations; speed up the construction of seaside tourist resorts; develop shipping in order to transform Hainan into a regional logistics centre; launch research projects to develop pharmaceutical products based on oceanic life forms; restructure the sea-salt industry; and accelerate the development of mining industries that focus on oceanic minerals.[33] The Hainan authorities are formulating strategic regional plans to designate coastal areas in northern Hainan as an integrated production belt, in southern Hainan as a tourist resort belt, in western Hainan as an industrial belt, and in the eastern part of the province as a fishing and tourism belt. The placement of new harbours will be coordinated with the province's development as a whole, with an emphasis to be placed on providing supply lines for deep-sea fishing.

Under the Eleventh FYP, the aim is to coordinate urbanization and urban development with Hainan's industrialization, tourism development and utilization of oceanic resources. The general goal is to reach a 50% urbanization level by 2010. Haikou will continue to strengthen its role as the economic, political, cultural and logistics centre of the province. Sanya's development will emphasize its central economic role in the economy of southern Hainan as well as its position as an Asian/global tourist destination. Yangpu and Qionghai 瓊海 will gradually be developed into the regional economic centre for western and eastern Hainan, respectively. Two or three towns in each county-level administrative area will be given priority in urban development efforts. In these towns, a South Sea style of architecture and urban landscape will be added or preserved to enhance the local culture and the development of tourism.[34]

To help realize the goals specified in the Eleventh FYP, the Hainan government signed a Strategic Financial Cooperation Agreement with the China Construction Bank in December 2005. The Agreement specifies that the China Development Bank will offer RMB50 billion in loans and comprehensive banking services to Hainan to finance the development of infrastructure, core industries, education, health, research and other social sectors.[35]

Under the Eleventh FYP, the scale of development and the province's

GDP will be 50% larger than that planned under the Tenth FYP. Moreover, the number of large-scale projects planned under the Eleventh FYP is significantly larger than those in the Tenth FYP. The need for investment in fixed assets and other development projects is thus correspondingly larger. These circumstances offer much room for complementary economic cooperation between Hainan and other areas of the Pan-PRD region. This especially applies to the highly-developed areas of Hong Kong, Macao and Guangdong, as the financing of Eleventh FYP projects will offer a new round of investment opportunities for these areas.

Hainan's Development: Strategies and Issues

When Hainan was established as a province and an SEZ in 1988, officials were already advocating coordination between economic development and environmental protection. After years of adhering to such a policy direction, Hainan went a step further in 1998 to formally pursue the path of an EcoProvince. Hainan has been a pioneer among Chinese provinces in placing a priority on environment protection. On the whole, it has been able to reach a comparatively better balance between development and ecological protection than most other places in China.

At the same time, there have been places in Hainan in the past decade where environmental protection has been ignored for the sake of economic development. The result has been severe destruction of the local ecology or serious cases of pollution, which has negatively affected Hainan's economy in the long run. In the face of such a persistent problem, some scholars and officials formulated a new development strategy for Hainan: to focus almost exclusively on tourism and agriculture and relegate industrialization to a strictly secondary place. The proposal partly adheres to the "one province, two sites" policy by emphasizing the "two sites" (i.e., sites of agricultural production and sites of tropical tourism) part, but it contradicts the "one province" (i.e., new industrial province) part by de-emphasizing the development of the secondary sector.

Such a development strategy proposal has attracted support as well as a great deal of controversy. Detractors claim that if Hainan were to completely give up developing the secondary sector, then the province's goals of achieving rapid economic development and comprehensively raising the living standards of its citizens could be seriously undermined, and that an exclusive focus on agriculture and tourism is uni-dimensional thinking. Proponents argue that rapid economic development does not necessarily rely on a highly-developed secondary sector, that agriculture and tourism offer a stronger national, regional, and global competitive edge for Hainan than any industries in the secondary sector, and that strategic planning for Hainan should be coordinated with national and regional development rather than focusing exclusively on the economic performance of the province itself.[36]

The debates over development strategy partly reveal a genuine clash of interests and perspectives regarding the direction of Hainan's development. While the priorities of the Hainan authorities are understandably to raise the general standard of living in the province and to increase government revenues and income, those from outside the province may be more interested in seeing Hainan remain an affordable tropical resort and a supplier of food and raw materials. Such conflicts of interest will have to be recognized and dealt with in the course of Hainan's dealings with the Pan-PRD region in the near future.

Nonetheless, when considered from the point of view of development practices and tactics, part of this dilemma over development becomes moot. Take the example of the development of the flower industry. Hainan's policy planners have always envisioned developing Hainan into a "flower and fruit store" for the Pan-PRD region. But, as discussed earlier, Hainan is currently unable to supply an abundant quantity of high-quality and affordable flowers because production technology and management systems are underdeveloped. In order to be able to modernize Hainan's floral agriculture, the requisite related industries, technology, infrastructure and financial arrangements have to be developed. This will inevitably facilitate the development of industrialization and the secondary sector. In practice, therefore, an emphasis on developing high-value agriculture and tourism will not necessarily displace the secondary sector but support its development in indirect ways.

Hainan and Pan-PRD Regional Cooperation

Hainan's Role in Pan-PRD Cooperation

As a member of the Pan-PRD region, Hainan is positioned to cooperate with other members of the region in the following ways. First, the province has been consciously advertising and playing the role of a "vegetable basket," "fruit and flower store," "backyard garden" and "second home" to developed areas in China.[37] With its tropical agricultural resources, pleasant climate and geographic position, Hainan is going to play the same role in the Pan-PRD region. In addition, Hainan differs from other less-developed areas in the Pan-PRD in that of the ratio of the income that it draws from the tertiary sector is relatively high with respect to the primary and secondary sectors. In this, it more closely resembles such places as Hong Kong and Macao than Sichuan and Guizhou 貴州.[38] Therefore, while in many economic aspects Hainan differs from and lags behind the developed areas of the Pan-PRD region, with regard to some aspects of economic structure, the province may have something in common with them.

Second, Hainan will further utilize its local advantages to open up venues of cooperation. More specifically, the province's authorities are increasingly realizing that Hainan's tropical agriculture, climate and other local resources could help Hainan to attract industrial investment and spur economic growth in areas other than its conventionally recognized role as a backyard garden or fruit basket. The vertical integration of the forestry, timber and paper industries that is presently taking place in Hainan is a good example. The creative and strategic utilization of local resources for economic development will depend on a revision of the conventional strategic designation of Hainan as a mere fruit basket, on the creative marketing of local resources to attract new investment, as well as on the establishment of special economic policies to help create a new regional economic role for Hainan.

Third, the establishment of a government on Hainan that is oriented towards providing public services would greatly contribute to future regional cooperation. As early as Hainan's initial establishment as an SEZ, officials have emphasized the administrative principle of "minimizing government and maximizing society." Such a governmental structure would seem to fit well with China's transition from a socialist-planned economy to a socialist market economy. Moreover, it is suitable for Hainan as a provincial-level political unit. Nonetheless, it may not be the most appropriate development for Hainan as an SEZ. Consequently, while the administration of Hainan as a provincial-level political unit has been very successful in the past two decades, the administration of Hainan as an SEZ leaves much to be desired. Hainan has made limited headway in functioning as an SEZ, with the results falling far short of what had been expected. The lack of special planning, administration and policies for the province's economic development has disappointed many local observers.

Re-adjusting Hainan's government functions in the direction of providing public services and a special economic administration would provide Hainan with a strong footing for future efforts at regional cooperation. It would help to invigorate Hainan's government structure and place Hainan in a pioneering political role within the region. In addition, it would provide Hainan with economic advantages that are currently being utilized with great success in Hong Kong and Macao. Such a change would help to speed up economic growth within Hainan as well as strengthen the linking of the Pan-PRD region to the world.

Recent Progress

Both Hainan officials and scholars have argued that the province should aggressively seek opportunities for regional cooperation.[39] At the First Pan-PRD Regional Cooperation and Development Forum held in Hong Kong, Hainan's provincial governor gave a presentation entitled "Seize the Historic Opportunity, Realize Mutually Beneficial Development" and formally stated Hainan's sincere wish for cooperation. He emphasized that given complementary strengths and geographic proximity, the prospect of cooperation is bright.[40]

A few days before participating in the Forum, Hainan sent a 60-person official delegation on a five-day study tour of the Pearl River Delta region.[41] The delegation was led by 6 former province-level leaders and 18 township-level leaders, and joined by the provincial governor and party secretary. The mobilization of such a large number of high-level officials to visit an out-of-province area was unprecedented. The Guangdong government took the visit very seriously. The Hainan delegation did not simply concentrate on learning from Guangdong's successful experience in economic development. Rather, Hainan's mobilization of all of its higher-level officials signalled a new recognition of the importance of Hainan's joining the Pan-PRD grouping and a consensus on the issue. After the study-tour, Hainan government sent a 400-person delegation to the First Pan-PRD Regional Economic and Trade Cooperation Seminar.

In June 2004, immediately after the beginning of Pan-PRD cooperation efforts, Guangdong sent a delegation to Hainan consisting of representatives from 50 enterprises. Within five days of holding negotiations and meetings in different parts of Hainan, 38 cooperation agreements involving a total of RMB2.68 billion were signed.[42] In November 2004, Hainan organized a (Hong Kong) Hainan Trade and Investment Cooperation Convention. Over a hundred projects, involving a range of products and services were offered, from agricultural products to human resource training. During the meeting, partners were found to cooperate in nine large-scale projects totalling RMB27 billion.[43] The highlight of the convention was the enthusiasm shown by the Cheung Kong and China International Trust and Investment Company (CITIC) group in investing in Hainan. CITIC signed a 10-year development contract to build a high-quality resort and convention centre as the second phase of the development of the Bo'ao district.[44]

In 2005, the Hainan government put two major new objectives on its agenda: building Hainan into a key national site for the production and processing of natural gas, and laying undersea wires in the Qiongzhou Strait to supply electricity to the continent. These projects will certainly be an instance of the utilization of complementary strengths, with Hainan's rich gas fields in the South China Sea benefiting power-hungry areas in the Pan-PRD region.

Conclusion

We opened this chapter with a discussion of Hainan's unique resources that show that the province has great potential for development in the long term. We then explored the prospects of two main pillars of Hainan's economy — agriculture and tourism. We identified a range of current problems in the two industries, and then showed that local governments and businesses are taking steps to solve them and that cooperation with the developed members of the Pan-PRD region will also help to solve those problems. We then briefly described the main infrastructural projects that are being completed or that were commenced during the Tenth FYP, demonstrating how heavily corporations and government have invested in Hainan. Details of economic development plans in the Eleventh FYP were also discussed, with an emphasis on the prospects and direction of development. We found that while there may be contending views on the direction that Hainan should take in development, the "one province, two sites" principle seems to have been broadly embraced and is being successfully implemented. Lastly, we explored the various roles that Hainan can assume in Pan-PRD regional cooperation efforts and the eagerness with which Hainan officials are seeking regional cooperation.

Although Hainan is currently one of the less-developed provinces in the Pan-PRD region, given its unique resources, Hainan has a great deal of economic potential and possesses the capacity to contribute significantly to the success of the Pan-PRD region. Its rich primary resources such as oil, gas, timber, water and minerals guarantees that the province will experience a certain level of growth in its primary and secondary sectors. Hainan's tourism and agricultural advantages provide a significant basis for sustainable development in the province, especially within the context of a strong national and local political will to making Hainan China's leading province in ecologically sustainable development. Hainan's attractive climate, diverse cultures and geographical location will directly and indirectly allow it to participate in cultural and economic globalization. As the Hainan government searches for ways to integrate itself into the Pan-PRD region as an active contributor, the developed members of the region should also make use of the opportunity to cooperate with Hainan for mutual benefit.

Notes

1. Hainan Encyclopedia Editorial Board 海南百科全書編纂委員會 (ed.), *Hainan Encyclopedia* 海南百科全書 (Beijing: China Encyclopedia Publisher, 1999), p. 2.
2. Zha Daojiong, "Localizing the South China Sea Problem: The Case of China's Hainan," *The Pacific Review*, Vol. 14, No. 4 (2001), pp. 575–98.
3. Wang Zhifang 王志方, "Cong dongya quyue jingji hezuo kan Hainan jingji fazhan zhanlüe" 從東亞區域經濟合作看海南經濟發展戰略 (A View of Hainan's Economic Development Strategies from the Perspective of Southeast Asian Regional Economic Cooperation), from the Statistical Bureau of Hainan 海南省統計局 (28 July 2004), http://statistic.hainan.gov.cn/ReadNews.asp? NewsID=ID=740.
4. Tan Chia-zhi and Henry Yeung Wai-chung, "The Regionalization of Chinese Business Networks: A Study of Singaporean Firms," *Professional Geographer*, Vol. 52, No. 3 (2000), pp. 437–54.
5. Zhang Yumei 張玉梅, Xu Haiping 許海平 and Guo Jianchun 過建春, "Hainan nongye fazhan yu jingji zengzhang de shizheng fenxi" 海南農業發展與經濟增長的實証分析 (A Positive Analysis of Agricultural Development and Economic Growth in Hainan), *Humanities and Social Sciences Journal of Hainan University* 海南大學學報 (人文社會科學版), Vol. 23, No. 2 (2005), pp. 142–44.
6. Jiang Shaowei 蔣紹惟, "Hainan: Woguo zuida de tianran xiangjiao shengchan jidi" 海南:我國最大的天然橡膠生產基地 (Hainan: The Nation's Largest Natural Rubber Production Base), *China Tropical Agriculture* 中國熱帶農業, Vol. 1, No. 1 (2004), p. 12.
7. The "one province, two sites" strategy refers to the resolve to simultaneously transform Hainan into a site for the production of high-value tropical

agricultural products, a site of tropical ocean island resorts, and a newly developed industrialized province.

8. Han Jianzhun 韓劍准, "Hainan senlin de shengtai gongneng yu lüse GDP" 海南森林的生態功能與綠色GDP (Hainan's Forest Ecological Functions and Green GDP), *Tropical Forestry* 熱帶林業, Vol. 32, No. 2 (2004), pp. 9–15.

9. Ibid.

10. Miao Hong 繆宏, "Hainan jiancheng shijie zuida zui huanbao de danyi zhijiang shengzhan xian" 海南建成世界最大最環保的單一制漿生產線 (Hainan Has Built the World's Largest and Most Environment Friendly Pulp and Paper Production Plant), *Green China* 綠色中國, Vol. 7 (2005), pp. 68–69.

11. Jiang, "Hainan," (2004) (see note 6).

12. Zhou Qiliang 周其良, "Hainan huahui chanye hua daolu de tantao" 海南花卉產業化道路的探討 (Exploration of How to Industrialize Hainan's Flower Production), *Journal of Qiongzhou University* 瓊州大學學報, Vol. 11, No. 5 (2004), pp. 82–83.

13. Wu Yougen 吳友根 and Wang Jian 王健, "Ershiyi shiji Hainan huahui ye fazhan de jiyu yu tiaozhan" 21世紀海南花卉業發展的機遇與挑戰 (Opportunities and Challenges for the Flower Industry in Hainan in the 21st Century), *Chinese Agricultural Science Bulletin* 中國農學通報, Vol. 21, No. 1 (2005), pp. 245–77.

14. "2005 nian Hainansheng jingji he shehui fazhan tongji gongbao" 2005年海南省經濟和社會發展統計公報 (Hainan Economic and Social Survey Report, 2005), from Homepage of The People's Government of Hainan Province, http://www.hainan.gov.cn/data/news/2006/03/18.

15. Lu Jiangyong 盧江勇, Zhang Yumei and Guo Jianchun, "Hainan lüyou jingji zengzhang de shizheng fenxi" 海南旅遊經濟增長的實證分析 (A Positive Analysis of the Growth of Hainan's Tourist Industry), *Journal of Anhui Radio & TV University* 安徽廣播電視大學學報, February 2005, pp. 39-42.

16. Zhang Jie 張傑 and Wu Hao 吳昊, "Zhongguo qingnian xi'ai de lüyou mudidi jiexiao, Yalongwan lie disan" 中國青年喜愛的旅遊目的地揭曉, 亞龍灣列第三 (Yalong Bay is Listed as the Third Favourite Tourist Spot of Chinese Youths), *Hainan Daily* 海南日報, 24 December 2006.

17. Wang Jianpu 王建樸, "Hainan disan chanye de wenti ji zhengce" 海南第三產業的問題及政策 (Problems and Policies of Hainan's Tertiary Sector), *China Economist* 經濟師, Vol. 1 (2005), pp. 242–43.

18. Yan Miaozheng 嚴妙政, "Shixian sange zhuanbian cujin Hainan lüyouye jiankang fazhan" 實現三個轉變促進海南旅遊業健康發展 (Realize the Three Transformations, Promote the Healthy Development of Hainan's Tourism Industry), *Hainan renda* 海南人大, February 2004, pp. 20–21.

19. Stone, Mike and Geoffrey Wall, "Ecotourism and Community Development: Case Studies from Hainan, China," *Environmental Management*, Vol. 33, No. 1 (2004), pp. 12–24.

20. Li Ping 李萍 and Li Yong 李勇, "Hainan lüyou chanye fazhan xianzhuang ji qianjing yanjiu" 海南旅遊產業發展現狀及前景研究 (A Study of the Development of Hainan's Tourism Industry and Its Prospects), from the Statistical Bureau of Hainan (5 December 2006), http://statistic.hainan.gov. cn/ReadNews.asp?NewsID=2231.

21. Quoted from a news reporter's interview with Sanya's Mayor in Xie Hongling 謝紅玲, "Sanya lüyou sanbu qu: laikan, laidujia, laiyanglao" 三亞旅遊三部曲: 來看、來度假、來養老 (A Trilogy of Tourism in Sanya: Sightseeing, Vacationing, Retirement), *Zhongguo jingying bao* 中國經營報, 30 December 2006, www.hainantour.com. See also Hong Baoguang 洪寶光, Xu Ji 徐吉 and Liang Changjun 梁昌軍, "Anxian lüyou yi shengtai wei jichu yi wenhua wei linghun" 安縣旅遊以生態為基礎以文化為靈魂 (Anxian's Tourism Takes Ecology as Its Basis and Culture as Its Soul), *Hainan Daily*, 28 December 2006.

22. Li Ping and Li Yong, "Hainan," (2006) (see note 20).

23. Zeng Miao 曾苗, "Wosheng ge lüyou jingqu(dian) liangnian jianshe 125 zuo xingji lüyou cesuo" 我省各旅遊景區 (點) 兩年建設125座星級旅遊廁所 (Our Province Aims to Build 125 Five-star Tourist Washrooms in Various Scenic Spots), *Nanguo dushibao* 南國都市報, 1 April 2006.

24. Zhao Manli 趙曼莉, "Nianzhong zongjie: guoji caituan yuanhe 'chuiyan' Hainan lüyouye?" 年終總結：國際財團緣何"垂涎"海南旅遊業？ *Zhongxinshe* 中新社, 29 December 2006, from www.hainantour.com; "'Lüyou hangmu' shijin Hainan, lüyouye tian huoli" "旅遊航母" 駛進海南, 旅遊業添活力 ("Tourism Flagships" Sail into Hainan and Empower Hainan's Tourism Industry), *Hainan tequbao* 海南特區報, 25 October 2006, from www. hainantour.com.

25. Zhang Chi 章馳, "Haikou chuzi 3,000 wan yuan 'zhutui' lüyouye re zhengyi" 海口出資3,000萬元'助推'旅遊業惹爭議 (Haikou Grants RMB30 Million to "Facilitate" Tourism and Arouses Controversy), *Nanfang dushibao*, 20 December 2006.

26. Cui Zhongren 崔忠仁, "Tuidong quyu hezuo tisheng Fan Zhusanjiao quyu lüyou jingji shuiping" 推動區域合作提升泛珠三角區域旅遊經濟水平 (Promote Regional Cooperation and Raise the Level of the Pan-PRD's Regional Tourism), *Guangxi zhuangzu zizhiqu renmin zhengfu fazhan yanjiu zhongxin jianbao* 廣西壯族自治區人民政府發展研究中心簡報 (Bulletin of Development Research Centre, The People's Government of Guangxi Zhuang Autonomous Region), No. 15, 11 December 2006.

27. Lin Zhimeng 林志猛, "Hainan xihuan tielu zuo quanxian putong mingnian sanyue touru yunying" 海南西環鐵路昨全線鋪通 明年3月投入運營 (Hainan's West-ring Railway was Completed Yesterday and will Begin Operating in March of Next Year), *Sanya chenbao* 三亞晨報, 14 December 2006.

28. "181 yiyuan jianshe donghuan tielu tiedao bu yu wosheng hezi jianshe, zhengqu

jinnian niandi kaigong, jihua yu 2010 nian jiancheng" 181億元建設東環鐵路鐵道部與我省合資建設, 爭取今年年底開工, 計劃於2010年建成 (RMB18.1 Billion to be Spent on the East-ring Railway; the Hainan Government and the Ministry of Railways will Jointly Fund It; An Attempt will be Made to Begin Construction this Year and Completion is Planned for 2010). *Hainan Daily*, 21 June 2006, from www.hainan.gov.cn.

29. Yang Chunhong 楊春虹 "Kaishi qianqi yanjiu hangtai fashe zhongxin Qiongzhou haixia kuahai daqiao deng teda zhuan'an" 開始前期研究航太發射中心瓊州海峽跨海大橋等特大專案 (Research has been Started on a Space Launching Centre, the Qiongzhou Strait Bridge and Other Super Projects), *Hainan Daily*, 23 December 2004. He Jingwen 何靜文, "Qiongzhou haixia nijian suidao huo daqiao; Yue nijiu 500 yi gongcheng fangan" 瓊州海峽擬建隧道或大橋；粵擬就500億工程方案 (Tentative Plans to Build a Bridge or a Tunnel across the Qiongzhou Strait; Guangdong Formulates a RMB50 Billion Construction Plan), *Southern Daily* 南方日報, 31 January 2005.

30. Bo Bin 柏彬 and Zhou Lingjun 周領軍, "Xin taijie, xin jiyu, xin tiaozhan: Hainan 'shiwu' jingji jianshe chengjiu pingshu" 新臺階, 新機遇, 新挑戰—海南 '十五' 經濟建設成就評述 (New Steps, New Opportunities, New Challenges: A Commentary on Hainan's Tenth FYP Economic Achievements), *Hainan Daily*, 15 November 2005.

31. Wei Liucheng 衛留成, "Guanyu Hainansheng guomin jingji he shehui fazhan di shiyi ge wunian guihua gangyao de baogao" 關於海南省國民經濟和社會發展第十一個五年規劃綱要的報告 (A Report on the Economic and Social Development Plans in Hainan's Eleventh FYP), 16 January 2006, from Homepage of The People's Government of Hainan Province, www.hainan.gov.cn.

32. "Shiyi wu: liuda gongye 'yinqing' qianghua jingji kangzhen nengli" 十一五：六大工業"引擎"強化經濟抗震能力 (The Eleventh FYP: Six Major Industrial "Engines" Strengthen the Anti-shock Capacities of Hainan's Economy), 23 March 2006, from Homepage of The People's Government of Hainan Province, www.hainan.gov.cn/data/news/2006/03/91551.

33. "Zhonggong Hainan shengwei guanyu zhiding guomin jingji he shehui fazhan di shiyi ge wunian guihua de jianyi" 中共海南省委關於制定國民經濟和社會發展第十一個五年規劃的建議 (Proposals of the CCP Hainan Committee on the Eleventh FYP), *Hainan Daily*, 29 November 2005.

34. Ibid; also Wei Liucheng, 2006 (see note 31).

35. Shan Jinggang 單憬崗, "Hainan huo Jianhang 500 yiyuan xindai zhichi" 海南獲建行500億元信貸支持" (Hainan Gains Support of RMB50 Billion in Loans from the China Construction Bank), *Hainan Daily*, 24 December 2005.

36. Yan Jia'an 顏家安 and Yan Min 顏敏, "Cong jingji tequ dao shengtai tequ: Hainan tequ fazhan mianlin de di erci lishi xing jueze" 從經濟特區到生態特區—海南特區發展面臨的第二次歷史性抉擇 (From Special Economic Zone

to Special Ecological Zone: Hainan's Development Faces Its Second Historical Turning Point), *Zhongguo keji luntan* 中國科技論壇, Vol. 3 (2005), pp. 29–33.

37. Peng Jingyi 彭京宜, "Fanzhusanjiao hezuo zhong de Hainan dingwei" 泛珠三角合作中的海南定位 (The Positioning of Hainan in Pan-PRD Regional Cooperation), *Journal of Shenzhen Polytechnic* 深圳職業技術學院學報, Vol. 3 (2004), pp. 5–7.

38. Jiang Guozhou 蔣國洲 and Wang Zhifang, "Yituo 'Fan Zhusanjiao' shixian Hainan jingji kuayue shi fazhan" 依託"泛珠三角"實現海南經濟跨越式發展 (Relying on the Pan-PRD to Realize a Leapfrogged Economy for Hainan), *Hainan Finance* 海南金融, Vol. 210 (2005), pp. 32–34.

39. For example, see Wang Zhifang, "'Fan Zhusanjiao' hezuo yu Hainan jingji fazhan jiyu" "泛珠三角"合作與海南經濟發展機遇 (Pan-PRD Cooperation and Hainan's Economic Development Opportunities), *Journal of Hainan Radio and TV University* 海南廣播電視大學學報, Vol. 22 (2006), pp. 66–67.

40. Wang Jun 王軍, "Wei Liucheng zai Fan Zhusanjiao quyu hezuo yu fazhan luntan shang fabiao yanjiangshi biaoshi Hainan ying zhuazhu lishi jiyu" 衛留成在泛珠三角區域合作與發展論壇上發表演講時表示海南應抓住歷史機遇 (In the Pan-PRD Cooperation and Development Forum, Wei Liucheng says that Hainan should Grasp a Historic Opportunity), *Hainan Daily*, 2 June 2004.

41. Liu Mi 劉甯, "Fabing 'Zhujiang xue' laoguang" 發兵"珠江學"老廣 (Sending Troops to Zhujiang to Learn from Guangdong), *Hainan Today* 今日海南, Vol. 8 (2004), pp. 7–9.

42. Yang Chunhong, "Guangdong jingmao kaocha tuan manzai ergui" 廣東經貿考察團滿載而歸 (The Guangdong Commerce Study Group Returns with Rich Gains), *Hainan Daily*, 19 June 2004.

43. Yang Chunhong, "Xiangjiang caifu jujiao Hainan" 香江財富聚焦海南 (Hong Kong Tycoons Turn Their Focus on Hainan), *Hainan Daily*, 17 November 2004.

44. Yang Chunhong, "Zhongxin jiang touzi kaifa Bo'ao" 中信將投資開發博鼇 (CITIC will Invest in Developing Bo'ao), *Hainan Daily*, 17 November 2004.

19

Hong Kong

Y. M. Yeung and Shen Jianfa

Introduction

Hong Kong 香港 has an area of 1,099 km², and a population of 6.90 million in 2004.[1] It is largely surrounded by the sea, and has a land border with Shenzhen 深圳 in the New Territories 新界 in the north. It was only a tiny fishing village when it was seized by Britain in 1841 and made a colony. Thereafter, Hong Kong acquired increasing significance as an entrepôt. A free port for many years, Hong Kong was ranked the freest economy in the world by the Heritage Foundation in the period 1995–2005 and by the Fraser Institute in the period 1970–2004. The success of Hong Kong as a global city in Asia has much to do with its status as a free port and its role in international trade.

The implementation of economic reforms and open-door policies in Mainland China 中國內地 has brought many development opportunities to Hong Kong investors since 1978. Economic cooperation between Hong Kong and the Pearl River Delta (PRD) 珠三角 created the famous model of "front shop, back factory" in the period 1978–1997. Hong Kong reached a high level of development with a significant expansion of its services sector, in areas related directly with outward investment and the re-export trade.[2]

Currently, Hong Kong is a Special Administrative Region (SAR) of China. "One country, two systems" has been practised in Hong Kong since July 1997. Under the impact of the Asian financial crisis and a global economic slow down, Hong Kong has been struggling since 1997 to restructure its economy. China's economy is becoming increasingly integrated with the global economy and the country has been accepted to World Trade Organization (WTO). These developments have raised questions about Hong Kong's role as a bridge between Mainland China and the world. There have also been significant changes in Hong Kong's position on close cross-border integration with the PRD and Mainland China in general after 2001. Since 2001, Hong Kong has enhanced its cooperation with the PRD and Pan–Pearl River Delta (Pan-PRD) 泛珠江三角洲. The debates of these issues involve both economic and political dimensions.[3]

This chapter focuses on the economic development in Hong Kong, especially on regional cooperation within the Greater Pearl River Delta (GPRD) 大珠江三角洲 region and the Pan-PRD region since 1997 (Figure 19.1). It also examines the challenges and crises in post-1997 Hong Kong, regional cooperation between Hong Kong and the PRD, and Hong Kong's participation in regional development and cooperation in the Pan-PRD.

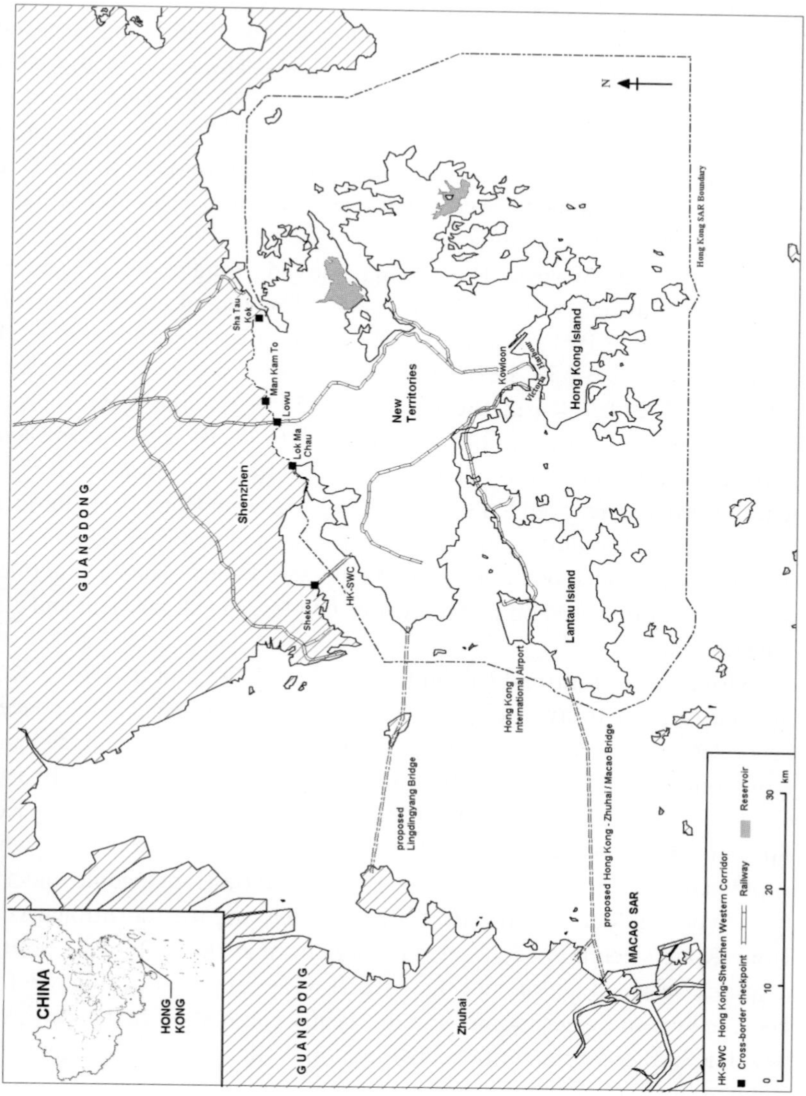

Figure 19.1   Hong Kong in Its Geographical Setting

Challenges and Crises in the World City of Hong Kong

Hong Kong had a per capita GDP (gross domestic product) of only US$410 in 1961. Prior to the 1980s, rapid economic growth in Hong Kong was based on industrialization within Hong Kong. The share of the labour force employed in manufacturing was as high as 47.8% in 1978 and was still 41.0% in 1984.[4] However, during the period 1979–1997, Hong Kong transferred the majority of its manufacturing operations to the PRD and itself became a prominent service centre. By 1996, only 18.9% of its labour force was engaged in manufacturing.[5]

Except for a few years, Hong Kong enjoyed a long period of economic growth from the early 1960s to 1997, and a low rate of unemployment of below 5% (Table 19.1). As the data show, Hong Kong's annual real GDP growth rate was 8.65% in the period 1962–1977, 8.26% in the period 1978–1984 and 5.8% in the period 1985–1997. The territory's per capita GDP tripled during the period 1975–1997. By 1997, Hong Kong had become a well-established world city. Its per capita GNP (gross national product) reached US$25,280 in 1997, ranking Hong Kong thirteenth in the world.[6] The emergence of Hong Kong as a major world city in the region has depended on various complementary factors, such as the rule of law, competition based on free market principles, and an efficient and clean government.

Hong Kong returned to China on 1 July 1997 and the Hong Kong Special Administrative Region (HKSAR) was established. The peaceful handover of Hong Kong was unprecedented in history. China and the United Kingdom worked closely in the transitional period 1984–1997. In 1990, China's People's Congress passed the "The Basic Law of the Hong Kong Special Administrative Region of the People's Republic of China," which stipulated that Hong Kong would be ruled by Hong Kong people under the framework of "one country, two systems."[7] During the transitional years, Hong Kong's economy continued to grow even as the diplomatic/political disputes between China and the United Kingdom over political reform became ever more acrimonious in the 1990s. Soon after the handover, the new HKSAR government faced two major challenges: an economic crisis and a political challenge.

Economic Crisis after 1997

As an important node in the global economy, Hong Kong's economy is particularly susceptible to external economic shocks. As shown in Table 19.1, the GDP growth rate rose and fell even in the period 1978–1997. For example, it was only 2.8% in 1982 and 3.9% in 1995. The 1984 Joint Declaration of China and Britain on the future of Hong Kong also contributed to the lowest growth rate during that period of 0.5% in 1985.

However, the worst economic crisis was the Asian financial crisis, which hit Hong Kong in October 1997 and decimated the city's stock and property markets. The price index on private housing dropped by 46.8% and the rental index by 27.1% in the period 1997–2000.[8] The Hang Seng index dropped from over 16,000 in 1997 to a low of 6,600 in August 1998. Hong Kong's domestic exports dropped from HK$211.4 billion in 1997 to HK$170.6 billion in 1999. The consumption power of Hong Kong residents also declined significantly. Hong Kong registered a GDP growth rate of –5.0% in 1998. The unemployment rate rose from only 2.2% in 1997 to 6.2% in 1999 (Table 19.1).

In 2000, Hong Kong's economy seemed to be on its way to recovery with a positive GDP growth rate of 10.2%. However, it worsened again after the 9/11 tourist attacks in New York. The GDP growth rate was only 0.5% and 1.9% in 2001 and 2002, respectively (Table 19.1). Some people lost their jobs and many suffered wage cuts. Consumer confidence and the investment atmosphere in Hong Kong fell to a low in those years.

The outbreak of SARS (Severe Acute Respiratory Syndrome) in March–June 2003 was another blow to Hong Kong's tourism industry and further weakened domestic consumption. Tourist arrivals dropped by 67.9% in May 2003 compared to the same period a year before. Retail sales dropped by 12.2% in real terms in April 2003 from April 2002. The SARS outbreak pushed the seasonally-adjusted unemployment rate to a peak of 8.8% in June-August 2003.[9] As can be seen in Table 19.1, Hong Kong's annual real GDP growth rate was 3.08% in 1998–2004.

There are various explanations for the economic crisis and poor economic performance in Hong Kong after 1997.[10] Some scholars, referring to the problem of an economic structure based on finance and property, believe that the roots of the problems lay in the pre-1997 years; while others, pointing to the problem of governance, hold the new HKSAR government and the first Chief Executive responsible. Li argued that the run-up to 1997 induced short-term investment behaviour in the transitional period of 1984–1997.[11] Inflows of global capital and large investments in public infrastructure by the government, such as the 10 airport core programmes, created many jobs and increased the income of local residents. This resulted

Table 19.1   Growth Rates of GDP and GDP Per Capita and the Unemployment Rate in Hong Kong, 1978–2004 (%)

Year	GDP	GDP per capita	Unemployment rate
1978	8.5	6.5	2.8
1979	11.5	5.6	2.9
1980	10.2	7.3	3.8
1981	9.2	6.7	3.9
1982	2.8	1.2	3.6
1983	5.8	4.2	4.5
1984	10.0	8.9	3.9
1985	0.5	−0.6	3.2
1986	10.8	9.4	2.8
1987	13.0	11.9	1.7
1988	8.0	7.1	1.4
1989	2.6	1.6	1.1
1990	3.7	3.4	1.3
1991	5.6	4.8	1.8
1992	6.6	5.7	2.0
1993	6.3	4.5	2.0
1994	5.5	3.1	1.9
1995	3.9	1.8	3.2
1996	4.3	−0.2	2.8
1997	5.1	4.2	2.2
1998	−5.0	−5.8	4.7
1999	3.4	2.4	6.2
2000	10.2	9.2	4.9
2001	0.5	−0.4	5.1
2002	1.9	1.0	7.3
2003	3.1	2.9	7.9
2004	8.1	6.9	6.8

Note: GDP and GDP per capita are at 2000 market prices.
Sources: The GDP data are from CSD, "Gross Domestic Product (GDP)"; see note 15. Data on the unemployment rates in 1982-2004 are from CSD, "Statistics on Labour Force, Unemployment and Underemployment"; see note 9. Data on unemployment in the period 1978-1981 are from CSD, *Hong Kong Annual Digest of Statistics 1982 Edition* (Hong Kong: Government Printer, 1982), p. 38.

in two economic spirals. The first was the wealth spiral. The rise in income drove up the yearly average of the Hang Seng Index from 933 in 1983 to 13,295 in 1997. Such growth also spread to the property market. The average price index of private domestic premises grew by 20.91% per year in the period 1985–1997.[12] Strong economic growth and a rising cost of living led to the second wage-inflation spiral. The nominal wage level in both the private and public sectors increased sharply. Price inflation was 7.59% per year in the period 1982–1997. An economic bubble had formed in Hong Kong by 1997. While some people felt the pressure of high living costs and expensive housing, many people did not notice the economic bubble as their real income had still improved in this high-inflation period. With a negative real interest rate of –3.44% in the period 1982–1997, enterprises recorded positive profits while the government accumulated huge fiscal reserves mainly due to the sale of land at high prices. Kwong and Miscevic argued that such affluence came with a cost.[13] The territory's previously diverse economic activities narrowed to the finance and service industries. In any financial crisis, such an economy would be hit hard.

Indeed, Sung and Wong pointed out that Hong Kong's economic growth had slowed down in the early 1990s even before the outbreak of the Asian financial crisis.[14] The territory's annual growth rate in per capita GDP was only 3.27% in the period 1991–1996, much lower than 5.31% seen in the period 1981–1990.[15] Hong Kong's growth became increasingly reliant on the profits from outward processing and the re-export trade, while the TFP (total factor productivity) of manufacturing actually declined by 13% in 1984–1993.[16]

With the outbreak of the Asian financial crisis and the departure of international capital, Hong Kong's economic bubble burst. The economic policies of the colonial government may also have been partly responsible for the problem of the economic structure in 1997, such as the high land price policy. But it is more important to examine whether the policies of the new HKSAR government have contributed to the poor economic performance of Hong Kong after 1997.

The new HKSAR government's policies have been widely criticized. The following are some key arguments. First, the government's plan, announced in July 1997, to provide 85,000 flats a year of government-subsidized housing was considered a major blow to the housing market. Second, there were some concerns about the transparency of government decision-making, especially regarding the Cyberport project, which was awarded without a competitive bid. Third, government efficiency was low and the government was slow to take action on various issues. For example, the government administration was crippled by drawn-out disputes between the government and the Legislative Council, and sometimes by disagreements among senior government officials. These were also related to the political challenge faced by the HKSAR after 1997. Other scholars have argued that "the rule of law" had deteriorated in Hong Kong both before and after 1997. The central government was also blamed: "The minds of China's policy makers seem to be firmly set on not allowing Hong Kong to maintain its supremacy."[17]

Political Challenge after 1997

To better understand the issue of governance in cooperation between Hong Kong and the PRD, it is useful to scrutinize the political challenge that faced Hong Kong immediately after the handover. Due to the disputes between the Chinese and British governments on political reforms in Hong Kong, the old legislative council was disbanded, and replaced by a new provisional legislative council on 1 July 1997.[18] But almost all of the previous civil servants stayed on in the new government, including the Chief Secretary for Administration. The first Chief Executive of the HKSAR, Tung Chee-hwa 董建華, was elected by an election committee and appointed by the central government of China.

The main political challenge for Mr Tung and the HKSAR government was to ensure the implementation of "one country, two systems," as Hong Kong residents initially had little confidence in the new political model and in the central government. Many Hong Kong people have a strong Hong Kong identity. According to public surveys, over 59.7% of Hong Kong residents considered themselves to be Hong Kong people or Chinese Hong Kong people, while about 38.7% considered themselves to be Chinese people or Hong Kong Chinese people in August 1997. These percentages changed to 45.2% and 51.1% in June 2005, when more residents identified themselves as Chinese people or Hong Kong Chinese people than as Hong Kong people or Chinese Hong Kong people for the first time after 1997.[19] According to Lau's 1997 survey, "Middle-class Hongkongers were alienated from Tung's administration right from the very beginning." Tung's publicly perceived pro-Beijing stance "turned him off from the middle-class of the SAR."[20] Hong Kong people were concerned about possible interference in the internal affairs of Hong Kong by the central government.

In the early days, Mr Tung enjoyed a high rating in various polls.[21] His popularity decline soon after a number of controversial issues arose. His ratings in the monthly poll conducted by the Hong Kong Institute of Asia-Pacific Studies (HKIAPS) dropped from a peak of 63.7 in July 1997 to 49.7 in July 2000 and 38.9 in July 2003. It recovered to 48.6 in February 2005, just before his resignation, but was still below 50.[22] Society in Hong Kong was then polarized politically into the pro-Beijing and anti-Beijing camps (also called the pro-government camp and the democratic camp, respectively). The disputes between the two camps dominated the Legislative Council debates and the local media. A group of politicians, officials and organizations, exemplified by the Democratic Party, focused on promoting a "Hong Kong first" mentality to bolster its legitimacy. Various activities and policies of the HKSAR government were scrutinized, and the government was often accused of sacrificing Hong Kong's interests to the interests of the central government. Three interpretations of the Basic Law by the Standing Committee of the National People's Congress on the right of abode issue in 1999, the political reforms of 2004, and the term of service of the new Chief Executive following the resignation of Mr Tung in 2005, were considered to have reduced Hong Kong's autonomy. Interestingly, the key disputes between the two camps centred on the political autonomy/interests of Hong Kong rather than on Hong Kong's economic interests. Indeed, the first interpretation of the Basic Law was meant to relieve the new HKSAR from the pressure of an imminent influx to Hong Kong of the 1.67 million mainland children of Hong Kong residents.

The democratic camp did a successful job of mobilizing the support of residents, especially the middle-class, in their political campaigns. The poor economic conditions and various unpopular reforms in such areas as education and the civil service further reduced the popularity of Mr Tung and his government. The introduction of a bill on Article 23 of the Basic Law finally caused half-a-million people to march in central Hong Kong on 1 July 2003. After the demonstration, the HKSAR government suspended its attempts to legislate the Article 23 bill. The democratic camp then campaigned for the next Chief Executive and the Legislative Council in 2007/2008 to be elected by universal suffrage, in a demonstration held on 1 July 2004 in which about 0.2 million participated.[23] Ironically, these two demonstrations came at a time when Hong Kong and the mainland had signed CEPA (the Closer Economic Partnership Arrangement), and Hong Kong's economy had begun to recover strongly.

Clearly, Mr Tung and the new HKSAR government failed to adequately address the political issues. This contributed to the mounting political crises of 2003 and 2004. There were four main reasons for this failure of the government. First, the severe economic crisis that broke out after 1997 plus controversial economic policies weakened the confidence of residents in the HKSAR government. Second, the disputes over the interpretation of the Basic Law and the Article 23 bill reinforced residents' concerns about Hong Kong's autonomy and freedom, as confidence was fragile over the 1997 handover. Third, Mr Tung, as a former businessman, had no political experience. He actually declared several times during his term that he would focus on economic matters rather than on political issues. This proved to be fatal, as he was the key man in the relationship between the HKSAR and the central government. He should have put more time into engaging with the grassroots, the middle class, legislators and even the various democratic camps to build a consensus in the community. Nor did Hong Kong's poor economic situation increase his popularity. Fourth, the democratic camps and the middle class had a solid political base under the banner of "Hong Kong's interests." This base was further strengthened by the mainstream media, which, as indicated by their editorials, were sympathetic and/or supportive of their political campaigns.[24] Mr. Tung was in short of this kind of strong political support, as even his government machinery and some senior officials might not have given him full support.

With the full support of the central government and nominations from 714 members of the election committee, in 2002, Mr. Tung won a second term as Chief Executive without contest. Mr. Tung's most significant contribution was in economic matters, especially in reaching the CEPA agreement with the mainland and promoting regional cooperation in the GPRD. These measures were instrumental to the strong economic recovery experienced in Hong Kong since late 2003. Mr. Tung resigned from his post on 12 March 2005 for health reasons.

Donald Tsang 曾蔭權 was appointed his successor on 21 June 2005 after an uncontested election, supported again by 714 members of the election committee. With popular support from the Hong Kong people and the full support of the central government, Mr. Tsang is expected to lead Hong Kong into a new era.[25] The critical challenge remains the same, i.e., to deal with the relations between the HKSAR and the central government for the best interests of the nation and Hong Kong. These relations may also have important implications for regional cooperation in the GPRD and the Pan-PRD regions.

Hong Kong's Participation in the GPRD Region: Lessons in Regional Cooperation

TSEs in Regional Cooperation: A Conceptual Framework

Trade and economic links between Hong Kong and the mainland have existed for a long time. But large-scale economic integration began in the late 1970s when China adopted an open-door policy and special economic zones were established in South China. Until recently, economic integration in the GPRD region was dominated by private companies in Hong Kong and local governments in the PRD region. No significant progress at the government level was made on regional cooperation in the GPRD region in the period 1997–2001.[26] Hong Kong's cross-border relations with the PRD region have been subject to serious criticisms in recent years.[27] It is claimed that the HKSAR government has adopted a so-called Fortress Hong Kong policy towards regional integration of the Hong Kong-PRD region in stark contrast to its famous liberal and positive non-intervention policy towards global capital and globalization.[28] This section attempts to explain such an impasse in regional cooperation using the framework of time-space envelopes (TSEs).

A TSE is a nexus of social and political relations that projects a coherent identity to a space.[29] A TSE is considered a system of meaning that is produced through an articulation of personal, public and meta-narratives. At the risk of over simplification, the chapter proposes that there are two competing geoeconomic TSEs (the pro-economic-integration TSE and the anti-economic-integration TSE) and two competing geopolitical TSEs (the nationalist TSE and the politically distancing TSE) in Hong Kong with different economic interests and political agendas. The interaction and dynamics of these TSEs will determine Hong Kong's path in its cross-border relationship with the PRD region and Mainland China in general.

Regional Cooperation before 1997

As a British colony until 1997, a colonial geopolitical TSE dominated Hong Kong, although a nationalist TSE always existed there. Politically, the Hong Kong government and Hong Kong politicians were accountable to the British government, and it was natural for them to keep some distance from the Chinese government.

There were no government controls at the border in the period 1841–1949, with free trade and the free movement of people. After 1949, an anti-economic-integration TSE emerged to sever economic links with the mainland and to serve the geopolitical TSE following the United Nations' embargo on China. A pro-separation political TSE and an anti-economic-integration TSE dominated Hong Kong. The political, economic and social distance between Chinese in Hong Kong and the mainland grew significantly.

After the opening of Mainland China in 1978, a pro-integration TSE emerged in Hong Kong, with the active participation of the territory's business sector and residents. Rapid growth was seen in re-exports and in the number of passengers going through the border-crossing at Lowu 羅湖. Hong Kong's re-exports to Mainland China increased from HK$153.3 billion in 1992 to HK$417.8 million in 1996.[30] Recognizing the huge economic benefits of cross-border investment, the dominant colonial geopolitical TSE did not intervene in cross-border investments from Hong Kong. In the period 1978–1997, the central government of China and local governments in the PRD region took many measures to attract investment from Hong Kong. Throughout this period, Hong Kong has been the main source of external investment in the PRD.[31]

But there was very limited contact or cooperation between Hong Kong and the PRD at the official level before 1997. A new border-crossing was built at Lok Ma Chau 落馬洲 and opened to goods vehicles on a 24-hour basis and for passenger traffic between 7 am–9 pm in November 1994. With the signing of the Sino-British Joint Declaration in 1984, various liaison groups between the Chinese government and the British government were set up to ensure a smooth transition to the 1997 handover. The Hong Kong government had little say in the whole process except on technical matters.[32]

Overall, the role of Hong Kong's colonial government in the GPRD regionalization efforts was very limited, being at most a passive one.[33] The Hong Kong government made no serious attempts to consolidate cross-border infrastructure. This was a serious lapse that became clear after 1997.[34] The Fortress Hong Kong mentality had already been formed in the colonial period.

Regional Cooperation 1997–2001

The return of Hong Kong to China in 1997 was expected to be the catalyst for the development of a close economic relationship between Hong Kong and Mainland China, especially at the governmental level. Indeed, the first

Chief Executive indicated as much in his first policy address in 1997.[35] A high-level framework, "Hong Kong/Guangdong 廣東 Cooperation Joint Conference," was established in March 1998. The plan was to hold half-yearly meetings. But this failed to happen due to the economic and political crises that beset Hong Kong soon after the handover. There was little progress in cross-border cooperation until 2001.

The pro-economic-integration TSE clashed with the politically distancing TSE in the initial period after 1997. The emergence of the politically distancing TSE was rooted in concerns about potential interference in Hong Kong's internal affairs by the Chinese government. As mentioned before, a group of senior officials and the middle class focused on promoting a "Hong Kong first" mentality.

The nationalist TSE and the politically distancing TSE had a quite different approach towards the central government and Hong Kong-PRD integration. Participants in the politically distancing TSE were keen to safeguard the autonomy of Hong Kong. Many of them also participated in the anti-economic-integration TSE, as they were worried that economic integration would eventually undermine political autonomy. Some scholars argued that the initial insulation of the HKSAR from the mainland system actually deprived Hong Kong of the leverage to defend local interests in the central-local bargaining framework.[36] They believed that a set of more democratic institutions is needed to maintain Hong Kong's autonomy and forestall a qualitative change towards a merging of the Hong Kong and mainland systems.

Indeed, the return of Hong Kong to China in 1997 marked the beginning of a period of cross-border protectionism. The conservative policy of the HKSAR government towards cross-border development was partly due to its potentially negative economic impact on Hong Kong. The participants in the anti-economic-integration TSE included some real estate developers, homeowners and retailers in Hong Kong. With the presence of a politically distancing TSE, their complaints were well noted by government officials.

The HKSAR government was sceptical about most of the suggestions coming from the Shenzhen side and did not actively move forward to cooperate, and in fact showed resistance against the idea of closer cross-border integration. By delaying improvements in cross-border facilities for passengers and the 24-hour operation of the border-crossings, HKSAR officials hoped that the border would act as an effective barrier to constrain Hong Kong's residents from buying cheap housing in the PRD and shopping in Shenzhen. Many policy suggestions from businessmen and the public were stalled even before a serious policy study could be conducted. For example, Shenzhen proposed to construct a building at the Lok Ma Chau checkpoint designed for joint inspections, to save the trouble of two inspections.[37] But the HKSAR government was not initially very interested in this idea. Before 2002, the government did not give serious consideration to the construction of the Lingdingyang Bridge 伶仃洋大橋, proposed in the early 1990s.[38] Disregarding the over-crowded border-crossing, the government insisted that there was no need for the bridge before 2016. The HKSAR government, often jointly with the central government, was also careful to limit the number of migrants and tourists from the mainland to Hong Kong. The aim was to limit the potential social burdens on Hong Kong of such an influx, and to maintain public security.

Given the above concerns on Hong Kong's part, only limited progress was achieved in cooperation between the HKSAR and Guangdong/Shenzhen at the government level during the period 1997–2001. The following examples illustrate the limited nature of such progress:

1. A Hong Kong/Guangdong Cooperation Joint Conference was inaugurated by Chief Executive Tung Chee-hwa of the HKSAR and the governor of Guangdong Lu Ruihua 盧瑞華 on 30 March 1998. This conference was to be held regularly and to facilitate and expand cooperation in economy and trade; education, science, technology and the exchange of skilled persons; and the construction and management of ports to ensure the smooth flow of travellers, vehicles and freight. But this joint conference was stalled soon after 1998.

2. From mid-October 1998, the opening times of two main border-crossings for passengers were extended by one hour at Lowu and Lok Ma Chau.

3. A decision was made in 1998 to construct the Lok Ma Chau spur line to link the Lok Ma Chau border-crossing with the East Rail to relieve passenger congestion at Lowu. The scheme of the spur line was formally approved on 14 June 2002.

4. An "Admission of Talents Scheme" was adopted on 17 December 1999 allowing skilled mainland people (usually with a Ph.D. degree) to work in Hong Kong. Another "Admission of Mainland Professionals Scheme" was adopted on 1 June 2001. It was replaced in June 2003 by the "Admission Scheme for Mainland Talents and Professionals."

Regional Cooperation after 2001

The situation of impasse in regional cooperation in the GPRD changed dramatically after 2001. The entry of China into the WTO on 11 December 2001 brought both opportunities and challenges. Some people were worried that Hong Kong would lose its middleman role in the near future as the mainland might move to deal directly with foreign countries. Such a sense of crisis was enhanced by the rapid rise of Shanghai 上海, which is positioning itself as the international economic, financial, trading and shipping centre of China. A research report of the Hong Kong Trade Development Council even projected that Shanghai will overtake Hong Kong in terms of total GDP by 2015 and in terms of per capita GDP by 2020 if the current growth rates of both cities continue.[39] Although this is an over-optimistic projection for Shanghai, the city does present a challenge to Hong Kong.

The argument that Hong Kong will suffer from close economic integration has been outweighed by the argument that close economic integration will benefit the city-state. It seems that a consensus has been reached in Hong Kong to pursue a closer economic relationship with the PRD and Mainland China in general. According to a survey conducted by the HKIAPS of 1,004 residents in Hong Kong in September 2002, 77.1% supported the construction of a Hong Kong-Zhuhai 珠海-Macao 澳門 Bridge 港珠澳大橋 and 54.2% supported the 24-hour operation of the border-crossings.[40]

Following suggestions from the Hong Kong General Chamber of Commerce, the Chief Executive of the HKSAR made the proposal to establish a free trade zone (later named CEPA) between the HKSAR and the mainland on 20 December 2001.[41] The government of HKSAR adopted a strategy of strengthening cooperation and development with the PRD region for the sustained long-term growth of the GPRD. The development of four pillar industries — financial services, logistics, tourism and producer services — depends on achieving a closer economic relationship with the PRD and Mainland China in general. In his 2003 policy address, Mr. Tung argued that:

> Today, much of the global competition is a contest of integrated strengths among different economic regions. A city is simply not strong enough to compete on its own. To advance its competitive edge, Hong Kong must pool its strengths with other cities in the region. Hong Kong has the advantage of being a world-class international centre of finance, business and logistics. On the other hand, the PRD is the fastest-growing processing base in the

world. It will further develop its modern manufacturing and high technology industries.[42]

Since late 2001, the central government has also been more active in facilitating the negotiations and arrangements for cross-border development. The nature of cross-border cooperation has been transformed to the point where the HKSAR government is now assuming as a leading and active role in cross-border development, while the central government acts as a facilitator and coordinator. These developments mark the beginning of a new era of cross-border regional cooperation. The following examples illustrate the rapid progress in cross-border cooperation and development since 2002. Many issues, which in the past would have taken years to resolve, have been settled quickly.

1. The "Hong Kong/Guangdong Cooperation Joint Conference" was upgraded during its sixth meeting, held on 5 August 2003. The joint conference would henceforth be led directly by the governor of Guangdong and the Chief Executive of the HKSAR.[43] More concrete projects for cooperation have been identified and implemented.

2. Following the "Hong Kong/Guangdong Cooperation Joint Conference" in August 2003, cooperation in the GPRD (nine prefecture-level cities plus Hong Kong and Macao) was stepped up. The Greater Pearl River Delta Business Council was established in Hong Kong in March 2004 as the business committee of the "Joint Conference." The business committee of the Guangdong side is led by the Guangdong Sub-Council of the China Council for the Promotion of International Trade.

3. CEPA was signed between the HKSAR and the mainland on 29 June 2003.

4. Twenty-four-hour operation of the border-crossing for passengers was introduced at the Lok Ma Chau checkpoint on 27 January 2003.

5. The daily quota of 2,000 tourists per day from the mainland to Hong Kong was abolished on 1 January 2002. Since July 2003, individual tourists from various cities and regions have been allowed to apply for travel permits to visit Hong Kong. See Table 19.2 for details.

6. In early 2004, Hong Kong banks were given approval by the State Council to handle personal RMB (*renminbi*) banking services in

Table 19.2 The Arrangements of the Mainland's Individual Visit Scheme

Date of opening	Cities covered by the scheme
28 July 2003	Foshan 佛山, Dongguan 東莞, Jiangmen 江門 and Zhongshan
20 August 2003	Guangzhou, Shenzhen, and Zhuhai
1 September 2003	Beijing 北京and Shanghai
1 May 2004	Guangdong (the remaining cities)
1 July 2004	Fujian (Fuzhou 福建 urban district, Xiamen 廈門 and Quanzhou 泉州)
	Jiangsu 江蘇 (Nanjing 南京, Suzhou 蘇州 and Wuxi 無錫)
	Zhejiang 浙江 (Hangzhou 杭州, Ningbo 寧波 and Taizhou 台州)

Sources: Various news channels.

Hong Kong.[44] This will consolidate Hong Kong's position as an international financial centre.

7. The case of the Hong Kong-Zhuhai-Macao Bridge (previously, the Lingdingyang Bridge) was re-opened in 2002. Since then, the HKSAR government has worked closely on the issue with the Macao SAR and the mainland authorities.

Perhaps it is the CEPA agreement and the introduction of the individual travel scheme that have had the most significant effect thus far on Hong Kong's economy. Hong Kong's business sector should benefit from the abolition, from January 2004, of customs duties on 273 categories of products manufactured in Hong Kong and exported to the mainland, accounting for 60% of the value of Hong Kong's exports.[45] This is in addition to 30% of Hong Kong's exports to the mainland that were already exempt from customs duties. The mainland market would also be opened to Hong Kong in 18 kinds of business and professional services. CEPA II, signed on 27 October 2004, provided more incentives for Hong Kong companies. Hong Kong's business sector should benefit from zero customs duty on the export of a further 713 categories of products manufactured in Hong Kong to the mainland. Eleven kinds of business and professional services included in the first stage of CEPA are to be opened further. Eight more kinds of business and professional services have been opened to Hong Kong enterprises. CEPA II became effective from January 2005. It should be noted that the average customs duty imports to China from the rest of the world would still be 8.9%. CEPP III came into being in January 2006, in which all finished goods of Hong Kong origin would be tariff free in their export to the mainland. From January 2007, further liberalization measures were put in place, in which the mainland further relaxed the market access to 10 areas in sectors already under CEPA.

It has been argued that CEPA would help to expand the mainland market for Hong Kong service providers and overcome the problems of the separation between manufacturing and producer services, the separation of production and consumption, and the mismatch between the regional economy and the previous constraints of "one country, two systems."[46] CEPA helps to remove some constraints on economic integration and represents further improvement arrangement of "one country, two systems."

Since mid-2003, Hong Kong economy has shown a steady trend of recovery. Hong Kong's GDP grew by 8.1% and the rate of employment dropped to 6.8% in 2004 (Table 19.1). This is due to both the direct and indirect impact of CEPA on the Hong Kong economy. A total of 720 locally registered enterprises have obtained the Certificate of Hong Kong Service Supplier under CEPA. Six local service sectors will make an additional investment of HK$4.2 billion in Hong Kong. At the end of December 2004, 68 mainland enterprises had been approved to invest in Hong Kong. About 42.5% of the enterprises came to Hong Kong between August and December 2004, and their investment reached US$470 million.[47] The total number of tourists to Hong Kong increased from 12.97 million in 1996 to 13.06 million in 2000 and 21.81 million in 2004. Tourists from Mainland China numbered 2.39 million in 1996, 3.79 million in 2000 and a magnificent 12.25 million in 2004.[48] The indirect impact of CEPA has also been substantial. CEPA has had the psychological impact of restoring the confidence of businesses and residents in the Hong Kong economy, boosting both local investment and consumption.

This section reveals that regional cooperation between Hong Kong and the PRD has strengthened since 2001. The establishment of "Hong Kong/ Guangdong Cooperation Joint Conference" in 1998 marked the formation of a formal institutional framework for cross-border cooperation between Hong Kong and Guangdong. Although it was not very effective in the first five years, it was upgraded and revitalized in 2003 to promote regional cooperation in the GPRD region. The signing of CEPA between Hong Kong and Mainland China in June 2003 represents a significant step in the setting up of a formal, legal and institutional framework for cooperation between Hong Kong and the mainland. CEPA is particularly instrumental for further cooperation in the GPRD region, where most of Hong Kong's outward investment and trade is conducted.

The "Hong Kong/Guangdong Cooperation Joint Conference" and CEPA are also indications of the complicated institutional arrangement for regional cooperation in the GPRD region. Although nine prefecture-level cities were the main partners for cooperation for Hong Kong, it was the Guangdong provincial government and the central government who really dealt with the HKSAR government on issues of economic cooperation (Figure 19.2). One drawback to this arrangement is that the interests of these PRD cities may have been overlooked, as they were not able to participate in these higher-level talks. It is suggested that the HKSAR government should strength its interaction with PRD cities (Figure 19.3).[49]

Hong Kong and the Pan-PRD Region

Hong Kong's Participation in the Pan-PRD Region

Regional integration in the Pan-PRD region is a response to the double challenges of globalization and regionalization. In the past years, China has taken dramatic steps to engage in regional development and globalization such as launching the Western Region Development Strategy (1999), joining the WTO (2001), initiating the formation of the ASEAN (Association of Southeast Asian Nations)-China free trade area (ACFTA) (2001), and formulating policies catering specifically to Hong Kong such as CEPA and the individual travel scheme (2003). These measures are consistent with the move to develop a more open and liberal economy.

Rapid economic growth in China has made the country the growth engine of the world economy in the twenty-first century. However, China is a large country where a mature market economy has yet to be established. Along with economic reforms and decentralization, excessive inter-city/inter-regional competition has hampered national economic integration. Local protectionism is rampant and market fragmentation is pronounced.[50] CEPA established a formal regulatory framework for economic relations between Hong Kong and the mainland. Further institutional reforms and cooperation are needed for national and regional market integration among provinces/cities in Mainland China as well as between them and Hong Kong. The Pan-PRD regional development and cooperation framework founded in June 2004 is a new project to integrate the "9+2" regions (nine provincial regions plus Hong Kong and Macao) in South China.[51]

Regional cooperation in the Pan-PRD can be compared to the 250 regional trade arrangements reported to the WTO. But it is different from

Figure 19.2   Current Mode of Hong Kong and PRD Cooperation at the Government Level

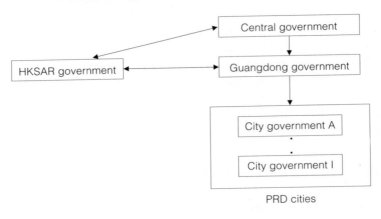

PRD cities

Figure 19.3   Proposed Mode of Hong Kong and PRD Cooperation at the Government Level

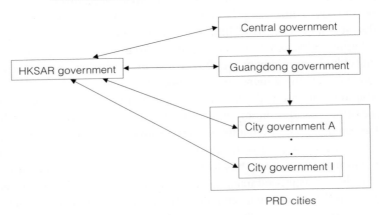

PRD cities

regional trade arrangements, as the 9+2 regions involved are within one single country. On the other hand, Hong Kong and Macao are independent customs areas and it is not possible for them to form a common market with the nine provinces in the Pan-PRD that are part of the large customs area of Mainland China. The case is similar to the situation between Hong Kong and Shenzhen or the PRD. Thus, the framework of 9+2 regional cooperation is very flexible and includes cooperation on projects and the formal liberalization of unnecessary regulations and procedures.[52] The designation of the Pan-PRD region is an innovative initiative in regional development in China.

The Pan-PRD framework would not only help to implement the opening of markets as specified by CEPA, but also nurture regional cooperation in infrastructure construction, economic promotion, resource development and environmental protection that is beyond the scope of normal trade agreements. Thus, the Pan-PRD can be seen as a tool to implement CEPA and also an extension of CEPA for broader regional cooperation.

Hong Kong's participation in the Pan-PRD region is a natural extension of existing regional cooperation efforts in the GPRD region. As an important member of the Pan-PRD region, this spatial regionalization strategy has enormous implications for Hong Kong's role in South China as well as Southeast Asia. After China's entry into the WTO in 2001, the country's next strategy in globalization is to develop the "10+1" ACFTA (10 ASEAN nations plus China). The Pan-PRD region is located strategically between Central China and Southeast Asia. The region is expected to play an important role in the regionalization and globalization of the Chinese economy. With consolidation and growth, the Pan-PRD region will become the focal point of economic integration and cooperation between Hong Kong and the mainland. Figure 19.4 illustrates the position of Hong Kong and the Pan-PRD region in the wide spatial framework of China and the ACFTA.

Figure 19.4   Hong Kong and the Pan-PRD Region in the Spatial Framework

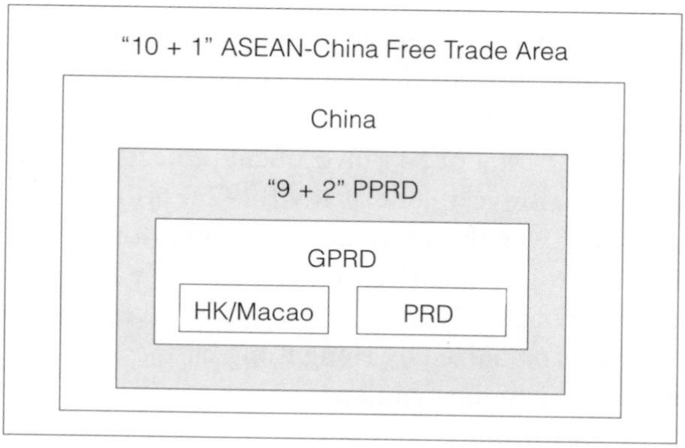

Different from CEPA, the Pan-PRD development and cooperation framework is a regional initiative driven by governments in nine provincial regions plus Hong Kong and Macao. These governments have adopted a strategy of regionalism to promote regionalization in the Pan-PRD. Indeed, it will work as a regional cooperation network, similar to the "Hong Kong/ Guangdong Cooperation Joint Conference," under the trading regulations set up by CEPA. It also enjoys the full support of the central government and active participation from the business sector and the general public. Ten areas for cooperation in the Pan-PRD region have been identified, including the construction of infrastructure, industries and investment, commerce and trade, tourism, agriculture, labour flows, science, education and culture, extended IT application, environmental protection, and health and disease control. Hong Kong is expected to play important roles in the financial sector, logistics, tourism and professional services.[53]

Hong Kong is keen to participate in the Pan-PRD regional cooperation effort. On 1 June 2004, the first high-profile "Pan-PRD Regional Cooperation and Development Forum 泛珠三角區域合作與發展論壇" was opened in Hong Kong and then held in Macao and Guangzhou 廣州 in the second and third days of the conference, respectively. This arrangement indicates Hong Kong's important role in the Pan-PRD regional cooperation framework. After the agreement on Pan-PRD cooperation was signed, the HKSAR government, the business sector and various sections of society engaged in various activities ranging from investment, trade and business cooperation to cultural and social exchanges.

First, formal meetings and trade fairs were staged in the Pan-PRD region. In July 2004, representatives of the HKSAR government attended The First Coordination Meeting of Secretaries 秘書長協調會議, held in Sichuan 四川. This was an important meeting to define the mode of cooperation, which was vital to the successful operation of Pan-PRD cooperation in the future. In the same month, the Pan-PRD Regional Economy and Trade Cooperation Fair 泛珠三角區域經貿合作洽談會 was held in Guangzhou. A total of 847 investment projects were signed in this fair, involving a total investment of RMB292.6 billion in the Pan-PRD region. Hong Kong was the second-largest investor after Guangdong, accounting for 313 projects and HK$56.3 billion.[54] The Hong Kong business sector was also very actively involved in many investment promotions, exhibitions and visits organized by Hong Kong businesses and trade bodies, and their counterparts on the mainland.

Second, various promotional and exploratory activities have been organized by the business sector, various chambers of commerce, academic circles and professional associations. The aim of these activities was to seek out more development opportunities and facilitate the entry of the Hong Kong business sector and professionals into the mainland market as well as to help mainland enterprises reach out to the world via Hong Kong. For example, Hong Kong's chambers of commerce held many seminars on Pan-PRD development jointly with the media. The Hong Kong General Chamber of Commerce and the South China Morning Post have held annual conferences on the PRD and the Pan-PRD jointly since 2002, and the participation and discussions in these conferences have been active. The Third Pearl River Delta Conference titled "Evolution, Enhancement, and Expansion — The Delta within the Pan-PRD" was held in Zhongshan 中山 on 1 November 2004. The Hong Kong Institute of Asia-Pacific Studies and the Central Policy Unit of the HKSAR government held "The Pan-PRD Development Forum" in December 2004. Scholars from Hong Kong and the mainland discussed the opportunities and prospects for regional cooperation in the Pan-PRD region.

Third, exchange visits between Hong Kong and regions and cities in the mainland have increased. These visits have often been led by government officials. For example, the mayor of Guangzhou, Mr Zhang Guangning 張 廣寧, led a large delegation consisting of over 300 people from 250 state-owned enterprises and private enterprises in Guangzhou to Hong Kong in August 2004.[55] The delegation was warmly welcomed and the visit reflected the close economic cooperation that has developed between Guangzhou and Hong Kong. In subsequent months, many cities in the Pan-PRD region conducted investment promotion activities in Hong Kong in response to the Pan-PRD cooperation effort. Such promotional activities were taking place almost every week.

Hong Kong's Role and Opportunities in the Pan-PRD Region

This section will discuss the role of Hong Kong in the Pan-PRD region, in light of Hong Kong's strengths and the comparative advantages of other regions in the Pan-PRD. As an important member in the large Pan-PRD region consisting of both developed and less-developed provinces in China, one important issue is Hong Kong's role in the region and how Hong Kong and other provinces in the region could benefit from mutual cooperation in an era of rapid economic growth and globalization. In considering this issue, it is illuminating to assess the current economic relationship between Hong Kong and the nine mainland provinces in the Pan-PRD grouping. Hong Kong and Macao have a close economic relationship in business, trade and tourism; and Macao has a special role to play in the Pan-PRD region. The relationship between Hong Kong and Macao will not be further discussed here.

As shown in Table 19.3, exports from the nine provinces to Hong Kong more than doubled from US$27.036 billion in 1993 to US$57.865 billion in 2003. In 2003, they accounted for 75.86% of the total exports from Mainland China to Hong Kong. Clearly, the bulk of the exports from the nine provinces to Hong Kong came from Guangdong due to the close economic relationship between the two. On the other hand, exports to Hong Kong accounted for 31.12% of the total exports from the nine provinces of the Pan-PRD to the world. As much as 35.24% and 27.99% of the exports from Guangdong and Hainan 海南 went to Hong Kong. It is clear that Hong Kong is the main destination for exports from the Pan-PRD region, especially those from Guangdong. Hong Kong has great potential to help the other eight provinces in the Pan-PRD grouping to expand their exports, a role that Hong Kong has been playing in the past two decades for Guangdong.

Table 19.4 presents Hong Kong's investments in the nine provinces of the Pan-PRD. Actually utilized foreign investment increased from US$16,003 million in 1993 to US$27,960 million in 2003. Hong Kong contributed over 40% of the actually utilized foreign investment, although its share declined from 66.82% in 1993 to 51.64% in 2003. In Guangdong and Guangxi, over 59.40% and 45.91%, respectively, of actually utilized foreign investment came from Hong Kong. Among Hong Kong's total investments in the mainland, 73.98% went to the Pan-PRD region. Guangdong received the lion's share of Hong Kong's investment in the mainland, and Fujian was next in the Pan-PRD region.

The data presented above underline Hong Kong's significant contribution to international trade and investment in the Pan-PRD, especially in Guangdong. There is great potential for Hong Kong to go beyond Guangdong and to expand its investment and trade activities to other provinces of the Pan-PRD.

As mentioned before, there are still many formal and informal barriers to investment, trade and services among local economies in the mainland. CEPA is helping to eliminate tariff barriers for many Hong Kong products and to open the market for many service providers from Hong Kong. On

Table 19.3 Exports from the Nine Provinces of the Pan-PRD Region to Hong Kong, 1993-2003 (US$ billion)

Province	1993	1995	1997	1999	2000	2001	2002	2003	Share of Hong Kong in the total exports of the area in 2003
Guangdong[1]	22.951	21.567	29.185	26.370	31.530	33.683	42.386	53.858	35.24%
Guangxi[2]	0.547	1.196	1.220	0.239	0.220	0.182	0.257	0.276	14.00%
Fujian[3]	2.700	4.085	2.254	1.440	1.509	1.469	1.822	2.181	10.32%
Jiangxi[4]	0.387	0.751	0.435	0.156	0.160	0.127	0.185	0.311	20.63%
Hunan[5]	n.a.[11]	0.349	0.283	0.191	0.225	0.251	0.291	0.380	17.71%
Sichuan[6]	n.a.	n.a.	n.a.	0.161	0.237	0.179	0.294	0.379	11.79%
Yunnan[7]	n.a.	n.a.	n.a.	0.174	0.211	0.200	0.243	0.237	14.13%
Guizhou	n.a.	n.a.	n.a.	n.a.	n.a.	n.a.	n.a.	n.a.	n.a.
Hainan[8]	0.451	0.444	0.279	0.318	0.302	0.283	0.312	0.243	27.99%
Total exports of the nine provinces to Hong Kong[9]	27.036+	28.392+	33.656+	29.049+	34.394+	36.374+	45.790+	57.865+	31.12%+
Total exports of Mainland China to Hong Kong[10]	22.064	35.984	43.781	36.863	44.518	46.541	58.463	76.274	17.41%
Total exports of the nine provinces to the world	39.191	73.658	93.532	94.774	112.963	117.422	145.586	185.949	n.a.
The share of the nine provinces in the total exports of Mainland China to Hong Kong[9]								75.86%+	n.a.
The share of Mainland China in the total imports of Hong Kong[12]								43.51%	n.a.

Notes:
1 Guangdong: The 1993 figure is from the foreign trade department; customs statistics are used since 1995. Hong Kong was the top destination of exports from Guangdong in 2003.
2 Guangxi 廣西: The 1993–1997 figures are from the Foreign Trade Department; customs statistics are used since 1999. Hong Kong was the top destination after Vietnam for Guangxi's exports in 2003.
3 Fujian 福建: The 1993–1995 figures are from the Foreign Trade Department; customs statistics are used since 1997. Hong Kong was the top destination after Japan for Fujian's exports in 2003.
4 Jiangxi 江西: The 1993–1995 figures are from the Foreign Trade Department; customs statistics are used since 1997. Hong Kong was the top destination for Jiangxi's exports in 2003.
5 Hunan 湖南: The 1993 figure is from the Foreign Trade Department; customs statistics are used since 1995. Hong Kong was the top destination for Hunan's exports in 2003.
6 Sichuan 四川: Hong Kong was the top destination after the U.S.A. for Sichuan's exports in 2003.
7 Yunnan 云南: Hong Kong was the top destination after Myanmar 緬甸 for Yunnan's exports in 2003.
8 Hainan: Hong Kong was the top destination for Hainan's exports in 2003.
9 As the data from Guizhou 貴州 are not available, the total exports from the nine provinces to Hong Kong and its share should be larger than the figures in this table.
10 The "Total exports of Mainland China to Hong Kong" are based on "customs statistics," which differ from some of the figures for the provinces from the foreign trade department. Therefore, two data sets in the early years are not comparable.
11 "n.a." means that a figure is not available or not applicable.
12 This figure is from the CSD of the HKSAR government, while other data are from various statistical yearbooks of China.
Sources: *1994–2004 China Statistical Yearbook* and the statistical yearbooks of the nine provinces; CSD, "Imports from Ten Main Suppliers," http://www.info.gov.hk/censtatd/eng/hkstat/fas/ex-trade/trade1/country/trade1_std3_index.html, accessed on 11 July 2005.

Table 19.4 Hong Kong Investment in the Nine Provinces of the Pan-PRD Region, 1993–2003

(US$ million)

Province	1993	1995	1997	1999	2000	2001	2002	2003	Share of Hong Kong in total foreign investment in 2003
Guangdong	7,372	8,990	9,787	8,561	8,780	8,647	8,618	1,1251[7]	59.40%
Guangxi	509	372	240	270	202	192	216	2097	45.91%
Fujian1,[2]	1,586	2,401	2,287	1,784	1,517	1,709	1,693	1,936[7]	47.50%
Jiangxi3	n.a.[4]	n.a.	n.a.	n.a.	n.a.	n.a.	n.a.	n.a.	n.a.
Hunan[1]	453	323	425	310	324	396	477	789[7]	53.00%
Sichuan	n.a.	n.a.	n.a.	n.a.	n.a.	n.a.	n.a.	202[6]	34.78%
Yunnan[1]	n.a.	n.a.	n.a.	61	75	23	47	51[7]	30.31%
Guizhou	n.a.	n.a.	n.a.	n.a.	n.a.	n.a.	n.a.	n.a.	n.a.
Hainan	773	564	386	142	132	141	224	n.a.	n.a.
Total Hong Kong investment in the nine provinces[5]	10,693+	12,650+	13,125+	11,128+	11,030+	11,108+	11,275+	14,439+	51.64%+
Total Hong Kong investment in Mainland China	18,893	20,402	21,651	17,402	16,729	17,935	19,170	19,516	34.76%
Total actually utilized foreign investment in the nine provinces	16,003	17,324	23,255	23,399	22,553	23,996	26,045	27,960	n.a.
The share of the nine provinces in total Hong Kong investment in Mainland China								73.98%+	n.a.

Notes:

1. The figure for Fujian, Hunan, and Yunnan refers to foreign direct investment from Hong Kong.
2. Since 2002, the figure for Fujian has been based on a new statistical coverage.
3. In the *Jiangxi Statistical Yearbook 2003*, only data for seven Asian countries (US$181.6 million in total) are listed and account for 15.17% of the total amount from Asia (US$1,196.92 million). The remaining amount was likely from Hong Kong, which was the largest source of foreign investment in Jiangxi.
4. "n.a." means not available or not applicable.
5. As the figures from Jiangxi, Guizhou and Hainan are not available, the total amount of Hong Kong investment in the nine provinces should be larger than the figure in this table.
6. This is the foreign direct investment from Hong Kong. See Sichuan nianjianshe 四川年鉴社 (ed.), *Sichuan Nianjian 2004* 四川年鑒2004 (Sichuan Almanac 2004) (Chengdu 成都: Sichuan nianjianshe, 2004), p. 210.
7. In Guangdong, Guangxi, Fujian, Hunan and Yunnan, Hong Kong was the largest source of foreign investment in 2003.
Sources: *1994–2004 China Statistical Yearbook* and the statistical yearbooks of the nine provinces.

the other hand, regional cooperation in the Pan-PRD would help to remove some of the formal and informal barriers set up by provincial and local governments to protect local markets. Indeed, some substantial policies and actions for cooperation have already been taken, especially among the nine provinces of the Pan-PRD grouping. For example, the nine provinces and Chongqing 重慶 signed the "2003 development and cooperation agreement on highway transport integration among the nine provinces in the Pan-PRD and Chongqing municipality" on 29 November 2003. The agreement would abolish the principle that scheduled inter-province vehicular passenger services be offered by both sides equally, and the territorial and site restrictions on chartered inter-province tourism vehicles.[56]

While CEPA and Pan-PRD regional cooperation would help Hong Kong companies and individuals to enter the mainland market, especially in the services sector, Hong Kong is also expected to play an important role in the development of the other provinces in the Pan-PRD region. First, Hong Kong has many advantages in providing financial services to various provinces and cities in the Pan-PRD region. This includes Macao, which has constraints on the development of its financial and insurance services.[57] As a well-established international financial centre, Hong Kong offers professional services of international standard. The rule of law, clean and institutionalized government administration, and the free flow of information are all well-known advantages of Hong Kong. Hong Kong's far-reaching international network would play an important role in engaging the Pan-PRD with the world economy. Hong Kong was the second-largest destination of foreign direct investment (FDI) in Asia, just after Mainland China. FDI in Hong Kong reached US$34.6 billion in 2004.[58] Hong Kong has been playing a bridging role for mainland enterprises to engage in global operations and for foreign investors to invest in the mainland. The share of capital raised by listed companies in the Hong Kong Stock Exchange of the total capital raised in the Greater China area increased from 48% in 2002 to 55% in 2003 and 74% in 2004.[59] In 2004, mainland enterprises accounted for 28% of the total of 1,096 listed companies and 30% of the total capitalization of HK$858.5 billion in the Hong Kong stock market.[60] Companies incorporated outside Hong Kong had set up 1,098 regional headquarters (RHQs) and 2,511 regional offices (ROs) in Hong Kong by 1 June 2004.[61] Table 19.5 presents the number of regional headquarters, regional offices and local offices in Hong Kong by the country/territory of incorporation of the parent company in 2004. The table is arranged in order

Table 19.5   Regional Headquarters, Regional Offices and Local Offices in Hong Kong by the Country/Territory of Incorporation of the Parent Company, 2004

Country/territory of incorporation of overseas parent companies	Number of regional headquarters	Number of regional offices	Number of local offices
United States	256	557	401
Japan	198	515	402
Mainland China	106	156	373
United Kingdom	105	211	164
Germany	67	135	80
France	47	106	87
Netherlands	46	52	51
Switzerland	39	70	58
Singapore	35	97	132
Taiwan	29	128	140
Australia	18	57	69
Sweden	16	33	20
Canada	15	29	29
Republic of Korea	15	67	59
Denmark	15	0	0
Italy	15	54	0
Malaysia	0	0	30
Thailand	0	0	20

Note: A regional headquarters is an office that has control over the operations of offices in the region (i.e., Hong Kong plus one or more other places) and manages the business. A regional office is an office that coordinates offices/operations in the region, and manages the business but with frequent referrals to its parent company or its regional headquarters. A local office is an office that only takes charge of the business in Hong Kong on behalf of its parent company outside Hong Kong.

Source: InvestHK, "Local or Regional Operations,"–http://www.investhk.gov.hk/content1q.aspx?id=864&code=IHK2-RESULTS-RL&lang=1, accessed on 7 July 2005.

of the number of regional headquarters. The United States, Japan, Mainland China and the United Kingdom ranked among the top four countries/territories that had set up regional headquarters, regional offices and local offices in Hong Kong. The expanded hinterland of the Pan-PRD region would provide even more opportunities for Hong Kong.

Second, Hong Kong also has tremendous advantages in the logistics and tourism industries. Integration with the Pan-PRD region will further enhance Hong Kong's role in logistics services. Hong Kong needs to expand its links with the transportation system in the Pan-PRD. In recent years, Guangdong has constructed a land transport network that links the province with surrounding provinces. This network will further improve through regional cooperation under the Pan-PRD framework.[62] Hong Kong should try to ensure that Guangdong's transport network is well linked with Hong Kong. The completion of the Hong Kong-Shenzhen Western Corridor in 2007 and the expected construction of the Hong Kong-Zhuhai-Macao Bridge would improve Hong Kong's transport links with the Pan-PRD region. After the formal opening of Hong Kong Disneyland on 12 September 2005, Hong Kong will be able to attract more tourists from the mainland and elsewhere. On the other hand, Hong Kong may face increasing competition from Shenzhen and Guangzhou on container transport and aviation services, respectively. Close cooperation with Guangdong would prevent excessive competition and bring a win-win situation for the GPRD and the Pan-PRD regions.

Third, Hong Kong's business and professional services have a vital role to play in the Pan-PRD region. With China's entry into the WTO, the country is busy upgrading its business and professional services to international standards. As one of the top world cities in Asia with a long history of conducting international business, Hong Kong has the rich human resources and excellent service capabilities to help the Pan-PRD region upgrade the quality of its services and to engage in the world economy. Under CEPA, some professionals have already acquired the professional certification to engage in professional services in the mainland. Many service providers in Hong Kong have also gained access to mainland markets. The expansion of Hong Kong's services sector into the Pan-PRD market seems to be the most promising avenue for further economic growth in Hong Kong.

The aforesaid was also echoed by John C. Tsang 曾俊華, the Secretary of the Commerce, Industry and Technology Bureau of the HKSAR government. He identified the directions for Hong Kong to follow in order to consolidate its advantages in regional cooperation. These include the coordination of infrastructure in the region, creation of an open and fair business environment, expansion of the production bases of Hong Kong businessmen, cooperation on logistics services and the development of diversified tourism.[63] These areas match Hong Kong's strengths and needs very well.

Looking ahead, Hong Kong will have three main foci in Pan-PRD cooperation. One is playing the role of financial centre. The second is to further develop the infrastructure for sea and land transport between Hong Kong and the mainland. The third is to promote the development of Hong Kong service industries in the mainland market.[64] If Hong Kong can move steadily in these directions, it would have a bright future in the Pan-PRD region.

One final note is that the Pan-PRD regional development and cooperation framework provides nothing but a platform for cooperation and for creating a better business environment for all enterprises in the region and elsewhere. It remains for the governments concerned to coordinate the development of infrastructure and the setting up of a regulatory environment. More importantly, the business sector will be the key player in identifying new development opportunities and in making the best decisions regarding the location, scale and forms of business in the region.

Conclusion

This chapter has traced the rise and relapse of Hong Kong and the attendant vicissitudes of the mood of the people prior to and since the return of Hong Kong to China in 1997. Meanwhile, Hong Kong reached a new height of development success and economic prosperity as Asia's world city, as the official appellation would have it, at the time of the handover. This was the build-up from more than a decade of dovetailed regional cooperation between the PRD and Hong Kong in a highly effective development model of "front shop, back factory," highlighting their respective comparative strengths. Consequently, Hong Kong has evolved into a city heavily dependent on its services sector for employment and economic sustenance.

With Hong Kong's return to Chinese sovereignty under the "one country, two systems" formula, the territory was soon to face an unprecedented economic crisis and a raging political challenge. Economically, Hong Kong was almost immediately drawn into the Asian financial crisis in 1997 on the heels of its handover, followed in quick succession by the global economic slowdown triggered by the 9/11 terrorist attacks and the SARS outbreak. A combination of sudden and powerful external shocks coupled with repeated policy fumbles sharply drove down property and stock prices. For most people in Hong Kong, economic euphoria turned into social pandemonium. The economic bubble that had been building up towards the handover had burst.

Politically, Hong Kong was also to face a testing period with the new HKSAR government and the people making their voices heard and society became ever polarized on major issues. Little progress was made on cooperation between Hong Kong and the PRD in the period 1997–2001. This was a period of trial and error, of doubt and uncertainty. This chapter has attempted to explain the economic and political tussle between opposing forces, by employing the conceptual framework of TSEs.

By 2001, the first glimmer of hope appeared with China's admission to the WTO, and a fresh beginning was made in Hong Kong-mainland relations. The central government played a more prominent role in facilitating cross-border cooperation. From the nadir reached in mid-2003 with the SARS outbreak, new policies such as CEPA and the individual travel scheme breathed new dynamism into Hong Kong. Hong Kong was soon on the path of rapid recovery. In early 2006 the city's economic and political health appeared to have recovered to their handover peaks. A new Chief Executive, Donald Tsang, was elected in June 2005 to succeed Tung Chee-hwa.

A new era of regional cooperation has dawned with the establishment of the Pan-PRD region in June 2004. Expectations are high that Hong Kong's success will be disseminated to a much larger region beyond Guangdong. The 9+2 region, indeed, can become a much enlarged hinterland for Hong Kong to play out its positive impact on many of the areas that have not yet experienced rapid economic growth and have not been exposed to the forces of globalization. Together, Hong Kong and the Pan-PRD can add to their regional competitiveness and, ultimately, contribute to the continued rise of the country.

Acknowledgement

Thanks are due to Gordon Kee for collecting data and materials for this chapter.

Notes

1. CSD (Census and Statistics Department), "Population by Sex" (2005), http://www.info.gov.hk/censtatd/eng/hkstat/fas/pop/by_sex_index.html, accessed on 8 July 2005.
2. Yue-man Yeung, "Planning for Pearl City: Hong Kong's Future, 1997 and Beyond," *Cities*, Vol. 14 1997), pp. 249–56; *Guangdong: Survey of a Province*

Undergoing Rapid Change, edited by Y. M. Yeung and David K. Y. Chu (Hong Kong: The Chinese University Press, 1998); Shen Jianfa, "Cross-border Connection between Hong Kong and Mainland China under 'Two Systems' Before and Beyond 1997," *Geografiska Annaler Series B, Human Geography*, Vol. 85, No. 1 (2003), pp. 1–17; V. F. S. Sit, "Industrial Transformation of Hong Kong," in *The Hong Kong-Guangdong Link: Partnership in Flux*, edited by R. Y. Kwok and A. Y. So (Armonk, N.Y.: M. E. Sharpe, 1995), pp. 163–86.

3. T. P. Rohlen, "Hong Kong and the Pearl River Delta: 'One Country, Two Systems' in the Emerging Metropolitan Context," Working paper (Asia/Pacific Research Center, Stanford University, 2000); Shen Jianfa, "Cross-border Urban Governance in Hong Kong: The Role of the State in a Globalizing City-region," *The Professional Geographer*, Vol. 56, No. 4 (2004), pp. 530–43.

4. Y. Sung and K. Wong, "Growth of Hong Kong Before and After Its Reversion to China: The China Factor," *Pacific Economic Review*, Vol. 5, No. 2 (2000), pp. 201–28.

5. CSD, *1996 Population By-census Main Report* (Hong Kong: Government Printer, 1997), p. 94.

6. After adjusting for purchasing power, Hong Kong's per capita GNP was US$24,540, ranked fourth in the world. See The World Bank, *World Development Report 1998/99* (1998), p. 190.

7. For a full text of the basic law, see http://www.info.gov.hk/basic_law/fulltext/index.htm, accessed on 24 June 2005.

8. CSD, *Hong Kong Annual Digest of Statistics 2001 Edition* (Hong Kong: Government Printer, 2001).

9. CSD, "Statistics on the Labour Force, Unemployment and Underemployment" (2005), http://www.info.gov.hk/censtatd/eng/hkstat/fas/labour/ghs/labour1_index.html, accessed on 23 June 2005.

10. Y. C. Wong, "The Asian Financial Crisis, Economic Recession, and Structural Change in Hong Kong," *Journal of Asian Economics*, Vol. 13, No. 5 (2002), pp. 623–34; M. K. Ng, " 'Business As Usual': Root Cause of the Hong Kong Crisis," *Asian Geographer*, Vol. 19, No. 1–2 (2000), pp. 49–62.

11. Li Kui-wai, "The Political Economy of Pre- and Post-1997 Hong Kong," *Asian Affairs: An American Review,* Vol. 28, No. 2 (2001), pp. 67–79.

12. Ibid.

13. Peter Kwong and Dusanka Miscevic, "Globalization and Hong Kong's Future," *Journal of Contemporary Asia,* Vol. 32, No. 3 (2002), pp. 323–37.

14. Sung and Wong, "Growth of Hong Kong Before and After Its Reversion to China."

15. CSD, "Gross Domestic Product (GDP), Implicit Price Deflator of GDP and Per Capita GDP" (2005). http://www.info.gov.hk/censtatd/eng/hkstat/fas/nat_account/gdp/gdp1_index.html, accessed on 23 June 2005.

16. K. Kwong, L. J. Lau and T. Lin, "The Impact of Relocation on the Total Factor Productivity of Hong Kong Manufacturing," *Pacific Economic Review*, Vol. 5, No. 2 (2000), pp. 171–99.

17. Kwong and Miscevic, "Globalization and Hong Kong's Future," p. 326.

18. See "History of the Legislature" at http://www.legco.gov.hk/general/english/intro/hist_lc.htm, accessed on 27 June 2005.

19. HKU Pop Site, "Categorical Ethnic Identity — Per Poll," 15 June 2005, http://hkupop.hku.hk/chinese/popexpress/ethnic/eidentity/poll/index.html, accessed on 28 June 2005. Citizens instead of people were used in the original.

20. S. K. Lau, "Tung Chee-hwa's Governing Strategy: The Shortfall in Politics," in *The First Tung Chee-hwa Administration: The First Five Years of the Hong Kong Special Administrative Region* , edited by S. K. Lau (Hong Kong: The Chinese University Press, 2002), p.8.

21. *Ming Pao* 明報, 11 March 2005.

22. The rating ranged from 0 to 100. A rating of over 50 is considered to be satisfactory. See HKIAPS, "Tequ zhengfu eryue fen minwang yijian diaocha jieguo zhaiyao" 特區政府二月份民望意見調查結果摘要 (Summary of Polling Results of the HKSAR Government in February), 28 February 2005; "Tequ zhengfu shieryue fen minwang yijian diaocha jieguo zhaiyao" 特區政府十二月份民望意見調查結果摘要 (Summary of Polling Results of HKSAR Government in December), 22 December 2003.

23. *Ming Pao*, 25 June 2005.

24. *Apple Daily* 蘋果日報, "Zoushang jietou, yongbao ziyou" 走上街頭，擁抱自由 (Take to the Streets, Embrace Freedom), 1 July 2003.

25. Mr Tsang was nominated by 674 Election Committee members, and received letters of support from 40 Election Committee members; see *Ming Pao*, 16 June 2005. Mr Tsang received a rating of 70.4 in June 2005, the highest since July 1997. See HKIAPS, "Tequ zhengfu liuyue fen minwang yijian diaocha jieguo zhaiyao" 特區政府六月份民望意見調查結果摘要 (Summary of the Polling Results of the HKSAR Government in June), 27 June 2005.

26. Shen, "Cross-border Urban Governance in Hong Kong."

27. E. Ng, "Cross-boundary Planning: The Interface between Hong Kong and the Mainland," in *Building a Competitive Pearl River Delta Region: Cooperation, Co-ordination and Planning*, edited by A. G. Yeh, Y. F. Lee, T. Lee and N. D. Sze (Hong Kong: Centre of Urban Planning and Environmental Management, The University of Hong Kong, 2002), pp. 271–81.

28. Y. Sung, "Re-defining Hong Kong's Strategy of Growth and Development," in *New Challenges for Development and Modernization: Hong Kong and the Asia-Pacific Region in the New Millennium*, edited by Yue-man Yeung (Hong Kong: The Chinese University Press, 2002), pp. 75–100.

29. N. Sum, "A Temporal-spatial Approach on Cross-border Subregions: Time-space Envelopes and Governance," in *Regionalism and Subregionalism in*

East Asia: The Dynamics of China, edited by G. Drover, G. Johnson and P. J. Tao Lai (Huntington, N.Y.: Nova Science, 2001), p. 33.

30. CSD, *Hong Kong Annual Digest of Statistics 2001 Edition*, p. 52.
31. Shen Jianfa, "Urban and Regional Development in Post-reform China: The Case of Zhujiang Delta," *Progress in Planning*, Vol. 57, No. 2 (2002), pp. 91–140.
32. K. Y. Chu, J. Shen and K. Y. Wong, "Shenzhen-Hong Kong as One: Modes and Prospectus of Regional Governance in the Pearl River Delta," in *Resource Management, Urbanization and Governance in Hong Kong and the Zhujiang Delta*, edited by K. Y. Wong and J. Shen (Hong Kong: The Chinese University Press, 2002), pp. 231–48.
33. Shaun Breslin, "Greater China and the Political Economy of Regionalisation," *East Asia: An International Quarterly*, Vol. 21, No. 1 (2004), pp. 7–23.
34. C. Yeung, "Separation and Integration: Hong Kong–mainland Relations in a Flux," in *The First Tung Chee-hwa Administration*, edited by Lau (Note 20), pp. 237–65.
35. Tung Chee-hwa, *Building Hong Kong for a New Era*. Chief Executive Policy Address 1997. Hong Kong.
36. Ian Holliday, Ma Ngok and Ray Yep, "After 1997: The Dialectics of Hong Kong Dependence," *Journal of Contemporary Asia*, Vol. 34, No. 2 (2004), p. 254.
37. Sung, "Re-defining Hong Kong's Strategy of Growth and Development."
38. *Ming Pao*, 14 June 2002; 11 September 2002.
39. Hong Kong Trade Development Council, *The Two Cities: Shanghai-Hong Kong, The Development of Shanghai as a Business Center and Its Implications for Hong Kong* (2001).
40. Sung Yun-wing 宋恩榮 (ed.), "Neidi yu Xianggang geng jinmi de jingmao guanxi anpai" 內地與香港更緊密的經貿關係安排 (Closer Economic Partnership Arrangement between Mainland China and Hong Kong), Occasional Paper No. 135 (Hong Kong: Hong Kong Institute of Asia-Pacific Studies, The Chinese University of Hong Kong, 2003), p. 14.
41. *Ming Pao*, 3 and 21 December 2001.
42. Tung Chee-hwa, *Capitalising on Our Advantages, Revitalising Our Economy*, Chief Executive Policy Address 2003. Hong Kong, p. 19.
43. Yue-man Yeung, "Integration of the Pearl River Delta," *International Development Planning Review*, Vol. 25, No. 3 (2003), pp. iii–viii.
44. HKSAR Government, "CE's Transcript on Personal Renminbi Banking Services," *Press Release*, 18 November 2003, http://www.info.gov.hk/gia/general/200311/18/1118211.htm, accessed on 4 July 2005.
45. Trade and Industry Department, *CEPA Legal Text*, http://www.tid.gov.hk/english/cepa/cepa_legaltext.html, accessed on 6 July 2005; Research Department of Hong Kong Trade Development Council, *CEPA: Opportunities for Hong Kong Services Industries* (2003).

46. Qian Yunchun 錢運春, "CEPA yu Zhujiang Sanjiaozhou yitihua" CEPA 與珠江三角洲一體化 (CEPA and the Integration of the PRD), *Shijie jingji yanjiu* 世界經濟研究 (World Economy Research), No. 9 (2003), pp. 34–38; Wang Chunxin 王春新, "CEPA: Xianggang diqu jingji zhuanxing de xin qiji" CEPA: 香港地區經濟轉形的新契機 (CEPA: New Opportunities for Economic Transformation in the Hong Kong Region), *Guoji jinrong yanjiu* 國際金融研究 (International Finance Research), No. 10 (2003), pp. 12–17.

47. InvestHK, "CEPA Brings 7,200 Jobs to Hong Kong in 2005," http://www.investhk.gov.hk/readarticle.aspx?id=524, accessed on 7 July 2005.

48. CSD, *Hong Kong Annual Digest of Statistics 2001 Edition*, p. 184; CSD, "Hong Kong in Figures: Transport, Communications and Tourism," http://www.info.gov.hk/censtatd/eng/hkstat/hkinf/transport_index.html, accessed on 29 June 2005.

49. Y. M. Yeung, Shen Jianfa and Zhang Li, *The Western Pearl River Delta: Growth and Opportunities for Cooperative Development with Hong Kong*, Research Monograph No. 62 (Hong Kong: Hong Kong Institute of Asia-Pacific Studies, The Chinese University of Hong Kong, 2005).

50. S. Poncet, "Measuring Chinese Domestic and International Integration," *China Economic Review*, No. 14 (2003), pp. 1–21; Shen Jianfa, "Space, Scale and the State: Reorganizing Urban Space in China," in *Restructuring the Chinese City: Changing Society, Economy and Space*, edited by L. J. C. Ma and F. Wu (London: Routledge, 2005), pp. 39–58.; C. E. Bai, Y. J. Du, Z. G. Tao and S. Y. T. Tong, "Local Protectionism and Regional Specialization: Evidence from China's Industries," *Journal of International Economics*, Vol. 63 (2004), pp. 397–417.

51. Yue-man Yeung, "Emergence of the Pan-Pearl River Delta," *Geografiska Annaler*, Vol. 87B, No. 1 (2005), pp. 75–79.

52. Tsang Shu-ki 曾澍基, "Fan Zhusanjiao jingji zhenghe: jiyu haishi tiaozhan" 泛珠三角經濟整合：機遇還是挑戰 (Economic Integration in the Pan-PRD Region, Opportunities or Challenges), *Xinbao caijing yuekan* 信報財經月刊 (Hong Kong Economic Journal Monthly), No. 331 (October 2004), pp. 12–16.

53. Mingpao.com, *Fan Zhusanjiao hezuo xieyi quanwen* 泛珠三角合作協議全文 (Full Text of the Agreement on Pan-PRD Regional Cooperation), http://specials.mingpao.com/htm/Pan-PRD/cfm/index.cfm, accessed on 5 July 2005.

54. *Ming Pao*, 18 July 2004.

55. HKSAR Government, "Xingzhen zhangguan yu Guangzhoushi shizhang huimian tanhua neirong" 行政長官與廣州市市長會面談話內容 (Dialogue of the Meeting between the Chief Executive and the Mayor of Guangzhou), Press Release, 25 August 2004, http://www.info.gov.hk/gia/general/200408/25c.htm, accessed on 6 July 2005.

56. Yu Ning 于寧 (ed.), *Jujiao Fan Zhusanjiao* 聚焦泛珠三角 (Focus on the Pan-

PRD) (Guangzhou: Guangdong jiaoyu chubanshe 廣東教育出版社, 2004), p. 66.

57. Yang Daokuang 楊道匡 and Feng Xiaoyun 封小雲, "Aomen de dingwei yu fazhan celue xuanze" 澳門的定位與發展策略選擇 (Macao's Role and Its Choice of Development Strategy), in *Fan Zhusanjiao yu Xianggang hudong fazhan* 泛珠三角與香港互動發展 (Interactive Development of the Pan-PRD and Hong Kong), edited by Y. M. Yeung and Shen Jianfa (Hong Kong: Hong Kong Institute of Asia-Pacific Studies, The Chinese University of Hong Kong, 2005), pp. 271–93.

58. InvestHK, "FDI Flows Hit US$34 Billion in 2004," http://www.investhk.gov. hk/readarticle.aspx?id=523, accessed on 7 July 2005.

59. *Ming Pao*, 14 August 2005.

60. InvestHK, "Zhongyao shuju" 重要數據 (Key Statistics), http://www.investhk. gov.hk/content1t.aspx?id=1020&code=TC-KEYSTAT&lang=2, accessed on 7 July 2005.

61. InvestHK, "Hong Kong's Investment Promotion Reaches an All-time High in 2004," 6 January 2005, http://www.investhk.gov.hk/readnews.aspx? id=841&parent_id=0&lang=1, accessed on 7 July 2005.

62. Lau Pui-king 劉佩瓊, "Cong '9+2' kan YueGang xin dingwei" 從"9+2"看粵港新定位 (Repositioning Guangdong and Hong Kong from the Perspective of "9+2"), *Xinbao caijing yuekan*, No. 331 (October 2004), pp. 18–21.

63. John C. Tsang, "Wu fangmian bawo Fanzhu hezuo jiyu" 五方面把握泛珠合作機遇 (Grasp the Five Development Opportunities in the Pan-PRD), *Wen Wei Po*, 25 August 2004, p. 26.

64. HKSAR Government, "Zhengzhi shiwu ju juzhang: Xianggang yu neidi quyu hezuo yu fazhan" 政制事務局局長：香港與內地區域合作與發展 (Secretary for Constitutional Affairs: Regional Cooperation and Development between Hong Kong and the Mainland), *Xinwen gongbao* 新聞公報 (Press Release), 24 September 2004, www.info.gov.hk/gia/general/200409/24/0924265.htm, accessed on 11 July 2005.

20

Macao

Kwan Fung and Lee Pak-kuen

This chapter examines the roles that Macao 澳門, a relatively small city of barely half a million people,[1] will play in the Pan–Pearl River Delta 泛珠江 三角洲 (Pan-PRD) regional grouping. Macao's roles and functions in the Pan-PRD are expected to grow, in part because of globalization. What, however, do we mean by globalization and regionalism and what is the relationship between the two concepts and phenomena? What will be their impact on the formation of the Pan-PRD as well as Macao's role in the new grouping?

The structure of this chapter is as follows. First, we will briefly outline the relationship between regionalizing and globalizing tendencies, which are both at work in the world economy. Special reference will then be made to the challenges that the original Pearl River Delta 珠江三角洲 faces in this context and the growth of the Pan-PRD region. Second, we will discuss the factors that contribute to the positioning of Macao in this framework. Finally, we will consider the challenges and outlook for Macao.

Globalization and Regionalism

Globalization can be succinctly defined as the thickening of globalism.[2] Seen from this perspective, an understanding of globalization should start from globalism, which, in turn, has been defined by Keohane and Nye as "a state of the world involving networks of interdependence at multicontinental distances, linked through flows and influences of capital and goods, information and ideas, people and force, as well as environmentally and biologically relevant substances (such as acid rain or pathogens)."[3]

Globalism has two defining features. First, it refers to multiple relationships or networks of connections. In other words, a bilateral relationship between two countries, even between two major powers, is not globalism. Second, the networks of connections must involve multicontinental distances rather than regional networks. Close interactions among countries in Southeast Asia are, therefore, not an instance of globalism. Globalism can be differentiated into economic, military, environmental, and social and cultural dimensions, and the interdependence associated with globalism involves reciprocal costly effects. The consequential effects may offer benefits to the participants by reducing costs, or impose costs on them. The costs may take the form of money that needs to be spent on production or the negative impact on human security as well as on the moral values of a society.

In short, globalization is a process whereby intercontinental networks of economic, military, environmental, and social and cultural connections that generate costly effects to the world become increasingly dense and extensive. As a result of globalization, the significance of geographical distances and boundaries in human affairs is declining. The worldwide spread of the Asian financial crisis, which started in Thailand in July 1997, and spread to as far as Russia, Latin America and the U.S., is often cited as an example of contemporary globalization.

However, if proximate regional relationships are not regarded as part of globalization, then how can we argue that regionalism or regionalization follows from globalization? Regionalism can be conceived in various ways. A working definition for the study of the Pan-PRD is that it is the growth of state-sponsored regional collaboration and integration.[4] In forming the Pan-PRD grouping, the governments in the geographical region are consciously promoting deepening intra-regional economic integration. How can one explain the creation and evolution (and, for some, the resurgence) of regionalism in the epoch of globalization?[5]

Systemic theory emphasizes the impact of external pressures working on a region. Neo-realism, a dominant systemic theory, argues that the development of economic regionalism is a response to external challenges. It is closely related to the intensifying competition and unequal growth among economic entities and the concomitant increase in concern about declining competitiveness on the part of economic and political elites. Wary of being marginalized, regional governments have an incentive to forge ahead with fostering "group-solidarity." From this perspective, it is the fear of competition from provinces and cities in the Yangzi River Delta 長江三角洲 that is prompting those in the Pearl River Delta to develop a larger regional entity.

On the other hand, both neo-functionalism and neo-liberal institutionalism see regionalism as a functional response by states or governments to the problems associated with or created by regional interdependence. Partial integration in functional areas, according to neo-functionalism, would set in motion a self-sustaining process of cooperation. Proponents of neo-liberal institutionalism believe that cooperative institutions are created by states to solve problems requiring collective action and to enhance welfare. Institutions matter and survive because they facilitate the provision of information, promote transparency and monitoring, reduce transaction costs and lead to the development of convergent expectations.

Drawing on the insights of neo-realism and neo-liberal institutionalism, this chapter argues that governments in the micro-region of southern China are compelled to cooperate with each other to form an economic grouping to enhance their bargaining power with multilateral corporations. Second, they expect that an enlargement of the size of "home" market will promote their respective economic welfare.

The end of the Cold War removed a big hurdle to increasing inter-state cooperation at the regional level in both North America and Europe, giving impetus to the signing of the North America Free Trade Agreement as well as the enlargement and deepening of the European Union (EU). In addition, as a result of the collapse of the Soviet Union and the socialist development model, less-developed countries, including Central and East European countries (CEECs), began to embrace export-oriented industrialization. Southern China, which pioneered China's export-oriented industrialization, faced an uphill battle in maintaining the competitiveness of its economy. Another spur to micro-regionalism in southern China was the Asian financial crisis of 1997–1998, which not only highlighted the fragility of Asian economies, but also pushed various Asian countries to devalue their local currencies against the U.S. dollar in order to maintain their competitiveness in the global market.[6] In order not to aggravate the financial crisis, China defused the pressure to devalue its *renminbi* currency. However, while ruling out the possibility of devaluation, it had to grope for other alternatives to reduce production costs. The decision to forge closer economic relations among entities in southern China was a response to the pursuit of regionalism in North America and Europe and to the shift in the Third World towards an outward orientation.[7]

Recent Developments in Macao and Macao's Edge in the Pan-PRD

With a small population living in an area of only 27.5 sq km, Macao is the smallest unit in the Pan-PRD (Figure 20.1). While its population constitutes only 0.1% that of the Pan-PRD region, it produces 1.38% of the region's gross domestic product (GDP). In terms of per capita annual output, Macao's is MOP181,900 (or US$22,671), ranking it second highest, after Hong Kong.[8] Like Hong Kong, Macao lacks natural resources, so 87% of its output is contributed by services. Table 20.1 shows the major economic indicators of Macao.

Gaming (or gambling) forms the backbone of Macao's economy. In

Figure 20.1   Macao's Location and Its Transport Infrastructure

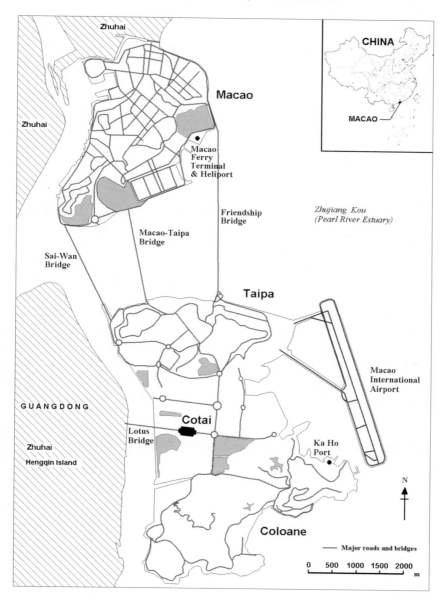

1999, when the territory reverted to Chinese sovereignty, the revenues generated by the industry amounted to about US$1.6 billion; five years later, the figure had jumped to US$5 billion,[9] making Macao the largest gaming market in the world. As a result of the boom, unemployment fell to 4.8% in 2004 from 6.3% in 1999.[10] The city now has 17 casinos, 15 of which are operated by the Sociedade de Jogoes de Macao, S.A. (S.J.M.), controlled by Stanley Ho and his family.[11] According to Manuel Joaquim das Neves, Director of the Gaming Inspection and Coordination Bureau (DICJ), Macao will have more than 20 casinos by 2007.[12]

Concomitant with the rapid expansion of the economy, more infrastructure has been built in the territory since the early 1990s. The domestic transport network between the peninsula, Macao's business hub and Taipa 氹仔, the rapidly growing residential island, improved greatly with the completion of two new cross-harbour bridges, the Friendship Bridge 友誼大橋 and the Sai-Wan Bridge 西灣大橋.[13] Since its opening in 1991, Ka Ho Port 九澳港 has been operating oil tankers and handling container traffic. The plan is to eventually move cargo transportation from the inner harbour to Coloane 路環.[14] In 1993, a new ferry terminal with a maximum annual handling capacity of 30 million passengers was completed to provide better passenger transport between the territory and its next-door neighbour — Hong Kong 香港. With the inauguration of the Macao International Airport[15] in 1995, Macao has been connected to the outside world by air, in addition to sea and land routes. Yet, the airport has drawn criticism for being underutilized, as commercial flights in and out of the airport are mostly only to and from Taiwan 台灣 and several major cities in Mainland China.

Table 20.1   Macao's Major Economic Indicators, 1995–2005 (Selected Years)

Year	1995	1998	1999	2000	2001	2002	2003	2004	2005
Nominal GDP (MOP billion)	52	49	47	49	50	55	64	83	93
Real GDP growth (2002 GDP=100)	n.a.	–4.6	–2.4	5.7	2.9	10.1	14.2	28.3	6.7
Per capita GDP (current US$)	16,032	14,649	13,844	14,171	14,253	15,567	17,805	22,557	24,277
Annual visitors (million persons)	78	70	74	92	103	115	119	167	187
Unemployment (%)	n.a.	4.6	6.3	6.8	6.4	6.3	6.0	4.8	4.1
Inflation (2002 price= 100)	8.3	–2.8	–1.9	–2.1	–1.4	0.2	1.6	1.7	4.7

Note: n.a. = not available.
Source: Statistics and Census Service, Macao SAR Government (DSEC).

The most recent large-scale infrastructure project was the construction of sports facilities for the Fourth East Asian Games held in the city in October 2005. The Macao East Asian Games Dome, which has a seating capacity of 10,990, was the centrepiece of the project. In addition, the Macao Stadium and Pavilion, Macao Olympic Aquatic Centre, Tap Seac Multisport Pavilion, IPM Multisport Pavilion and other supporting facilities[16] cost US$350 million to construct.

The strong economic growth after 1999, supported by healthy government finances, a favourable trade balance, and a promising economic outlook for the gaming industry, caused Moody's to twice upgrade the territory's foreign currency country ceilings for debt and for deposits in 2003, from Baa1 to A3 and then to A1.[17] However, without any government intervention, Macao is not at an advantage over neighbouring cities in promoting industries. Instead, it is positioning itself as a gaming city in East Asia, as a gateway into the less-developed western region of Guangdong 廣東, and as a bridge between Mainland China on the one hand and the Portuguese-speaking world as well as Taiwan on the other.

Favourable Conditions for Macao's Development

The following constitute Macao's niches in the Pan-PRD framework: a unique comparative advantage in the gaming industry and the associated structural changes that have taken place as a result of liberalizing the gaming sector, a fairly established international business network and the endeavour to set up services platforms.

Unique Comparative Advantage and Structural Change in Gaming

Orthodox international trade theory maintains that a country should specialize in producing and exporting goods that it can produce at a relatively lower cost. This principle can be further extended to account for the formation of an internal industrial composition. As the production of different goods requires different combinations of factor inputs, each economy is expected to adopt a structure based mostly on its resource endowment.

The supply of land in Macao is relatively limited, although the land area has more than doubled to 27.5 sq km from 12.7 sq km since the early 1900s.[18] Labour and capital are almost the only available factor inputs. As labour is relatively more abundant than capital, the cost of labour has been kept low relative to that of capital. Macao continues to rely on labour-intensive output, as seen by the dominance of the garment and textile industries in the 1980s. Until the mid-1980s, Macao economy depended heavily on manufacturing (constituting 30 to 40% of total output) and tourism (around 25% of total output).[19] Table 20.2 shows that there has been a significant decline in manufacturing since the early 1980s (Column 2). Manufacturing in Macao has been characterized by (1) labour-intensive production, with most of the producers being small and medium enterprises (SMEs); (2) output concentrating on garments and textiles; and (3) outputs largely exported to foreign markets, mainly the U.S.A. and EU countries. Until the end of 2004, its textile and garment exports had benefited from the Multi Fibre Agreement (MFA).[20]

Because the Pearl River Delta and the newly industrialized economies (NIEs) in Southeast Asia can provide an abundance of inexpensive labour, Macao's low value-added and labour-intensive manufacturing has gradually lost its comparative advantage. In addition, Guangdong is keen to turn itself into a manufacturing base under the Pan-PRD drive.[21] A shift from manufacturing to tourism reflects an ongoing effort by the city to find new comparative advantages, though its outputs are still labour-intensive.

Macao has approximately 50 years of experience in licensed gaming, with unorganized gambling dating from the early 1900s. By offering a number of traditional Chinese games and Western types of gaming, Macao has become known as the "Las Vegas of the Orient." Because Portuguese business interests in Macao were minimal, before the 1999 handover, the colonial government played little role in managing the territory's economic growth. By granting a gambling monopoly to a single local company, the government had almost an assured source of fiscal revenue from various gaming activities. This, in turn, was used to support the basic operations of the Portuguese-administered government and the public sector. Table 20.3 shows the relation between gambling tax and government revenue. The gambling tax accounted for 30% of public revenues in the 1970s and early 1980s. The share hovered around 70% in the early 2000s.

For many years, Sociedade de Turismo e Diversoes de Macao (STDM) held a monopoly on gambling in Macao. In the 1990s, Stanley Ho, the CEO of STDM, reformed his gaming corporation by subcontracting casino rooms to a variety of operators. Far-reaching reforms of the gaming sector began to take place in 2000, the impact of which is expected to be enormous in the coming decades. On the recommendations of an international

Table 20.2 Industrial Composition of Macao, 1981–2004 (Selected Years)

Year	Nominal GDP (MOP billion)	Manufacturing (%)	Construction (%)	Trade, hotel and restaurant (%)	Transportation and communication (%)	Finance (%)	Real estate (%)	Gambling (%)	Social and personal services (%)
	(1)	(2)	(3)	(4)	(5)	(6)	(7)	(8)	(9)
1981	4.6	28.0	16.0	3.0	n.a	5.0	n.a	22.0	n.a
1985	9.1	35.0	8.0	3.0	n.a	5.0	n.a	23.0	n.a
1989	19.9	20.6	4.7	14.0	3.5	19.8	n.a	37.9	n.a
1995	52.3	8.1	6.0	10.8	3.6	7.7	15.4	29.2	n.a
1998	49.4	9.8	3.8	10.7	7.3	11.3	12.6	24.6	19.8
1999	47.3	9.8	3.6	10.5	7.6	11.3	10.9	24.0	20.7
2000	49.0	10.1	2.6	11.2	7.6	12.1	8.3	27.9	19.7
2001	49.7	8.3	2.3	11.8	6.9	11.6	6.8	30.2	20.5
2002	54.8	7.2	2.7	12.7	6.8	11.0	6.3	32.8	19.8
2003	63.6	6.3	4.0	12.0	5.5	10.3	6.0	35.8	18.2
2004	82.7	n.a	n.a	n.a	n.a	n.a	n.a	n.a	n.a

Note: n.a. = not available; For 1989, (6) includes (9); (2) to (9) are stated as a percentage of the total GDP.
Sources: Between 1981 and 1985: R. D. Cremer, "The Industrialization of Macau," in *Economic Development in Chinese Societies: Models and Experiences*, edited by V. C. Jao, V. Mok and L. S. Ho (Hong Kong: Hong Kong University Press, 1989), 227; others from: Statistics and Census Service, Macao SAR Government (DSEC).

Table 20.3 **Economic Significance of Gambling in Macao, 1977–2005 (Selected Years)**

Year	Gross revenue of gambling (MOP million)	Gambling tax (MOP million)	Public revenue (excluding specific account — autonomous agencies) (MOP million)	(2)/(3) (%)
	(1)	(2)	(3)	(4)
1977	420	46	154	30
1980	858	97	369	26
1984	1,965	838	1,443	58
1990		2,044	5,997	34
1995	17,912	5,349	10,776	50
1999	13,947	4,670	10,111	46
2000	17,076	5,523	9,079	61
2001	19,541	6,115	10,090	61
2002	22,843	7,555	11,317	67
2003	29,476	10,426	14,279	73
2004	42,306	14,740	19,345	76
2005	45,800	16,562	22,769	73

Note: All are in current million MOP; the 2005 figures are provisional.
Sources: 1977–1984: Cremer (1989), 227; Other years: Statistics and Census Service, Macao SAR Government (DSEC) and Gaming Inspection and Coordination Bureau, Macao SAR Government (DICJ).

consultant,[22] the government of the Macao Special Administrative Region (SAR) decided to liberalize the sector by offering stakes to three concessionaires. In 2002, the SAR government signed contracts with the following three companies: (1) Sociedade de Jogos de Macao S.A. (a subsidiary of STDM) — with a minimum contracted investment of US$580 million; (2) Wynn Resorts (Macao), S.A. — with a minimum contracted investment of US$500 million; and (3) Galaxy Holdings (which was later split into two sub-concessions: Galaxy Casino and the Las Vegas Sands) – with a minimum contracted investment of US$1,100 million.

The implications of the liberalization of gaming are threefold. First, the influx of foreign capital and know-how in the gaming sector has increased the significance of tourism in the economy, as shown in its share of the territory's GDP and the rising share of gambling taxes in government revenues in the SAR era (Table 20.3). This demonstrates the territory's increasing reliance on the gaming industry.

Second, it represents an attempt to diversify the sources of visitors.

Under the old casino concession system, most of the gamblers were from Hong Kong; thus, there was excessive dependence on a single market. With the Closer Economic Partnership Arrangement (CEPA) with Mainland China,[23] and the related policy of the "Individual Visit Scheme" whereby residents from selected cities in Mainland China are allowed to apply for documents to travel on an individual basis, the number of visitors from the mainland and the associated revenues from tourism have increased significantly. A total of 10.46 million mainland Chinese visited Macao in 2005, accounting for 56% of the total number of tourists. About half of the mainland visitors entered Macao under the Individual Visit Scheme.[24] The gambling expenditures of these mainland Chinese visitors exceeded the initial predictions of all gaming operators. Macao gaming operators are luring mainland visitors to the city's casinos through low-profile promotion campaigns.[25] With two new concessionaires, both highly experienced in running gaming operations, wealthier overseas Chinese and non-Asian gamblers are being targeted. Diversifying the sources of gamblers, with regard to both geographical locations and income levels, is clearly desirable.

Third, the liberalization of gaming represents an even more ambitious attempt by Macao's tourism authorities to promote non-gaming activities over the medium term. Wynns Macao specializes in resort and leisure amusements. The Las Vegas Sands/Venetian focuses on exhibitions and conventions. In Las Vegas, gaming accounts for about 40% of total income; if the experience there is any guide, there is ample room for Macao to expand into non-gaming services. This, in turn, will help Macao's tourism industry to branch out to other entertainment activities. It has been agreed that the China Council for the Promotion of International Trade will hold a trade show in 2007 to inaugurate the Venetian Macao Hotel and Casino.[26]

Since the Singaporean government has already given the green light to gambling, other countries in Southeast Asia are likely to follow suit sooner or later. Macao can safeguard its position as a regional amusement centre only if it provides a variety of tourism products. The development of resort/ leisure and meeting, incentive, convention and exhibition (MICE) facilities would seem to be a viable option. In fact, the 54th Pacific Asia Travel Association (PATA) Annual Conference, held in Macao in April 2005, attracted more than 1,100 delegates from 44 countries. This shows that there is a keen interest among both the government and the private sectors to develop this sector. One of the advantages of holding conferences and symposiums in Macao is the city's capacity to attract participants from Southeast Asia, Mainland China, and elsewhere. Nevertheless, substantial improvements in MICE infrastructure in the short term are desperately required to address the shortage of manpower and MICE venues, a subject to which we will return later.

As a special administrative region of China, Macao's "privilege" and niche lies in the fact that it is the sole Chinese city that allows gambling to operate legally. When Donald Tsang Yam-kuen 曾蔭權 was Hong Kong's financial secretary, he reportedly pondered the possibility of having a casino operate in Hong Kong. James Tien Pei-chun 田北俊, chairman of Hong Kong's Liberal Party, likewise suggested that a casino be built on Lantau to lure more tourists to Hong Kong.[27] However, it is unlikely that the central government would favour the rise of competition between Hong Kong and Macao over gambling. To demonstrate the success of "one country, two systems" in the two SARs, Beijing would prefer to keep intact Macao's "vested interest" in gaming intact. Qian Qichen 錢其琛, whose responsibilities in the central government included Hong Kong and Macao affairs, was openly opposed to the idea of Hong Kong developing gaming businesses.[28] Wary of the risk of relying heavily on gambling and in the face of the pressing need to address worsening unemployment among manufacturing workers, however, the Macao SAR government is sparing no effort to diversify the economy. Measures have been proposed and taken to arrest a rapid decline in the manufacturing sector. Triggered by the signing of CEPA, Macao announced in early 2003 a plan to set up a cross-border industrial zone between Zhuhai 珠海 and Macao. The aim would be to persuade certain manufacturers not to leave Macao by offering lower-cost production opportunities across the border in Zhuhai. Producers would also be offered tariff-free access to Mainland China. More importantly, the incoming international business is expected to bring in new capital, technology and products into Macao. The attractiveness of this zone is that products produced within the zone[29] are registered as goods made in Macao under the preferential treatment of CEPA. Since the zone (on the Zhuhai side) also allows business people from other provinces to visit and make business contacts, Macao is expected to benefit from these business services. Those intending to set up production in this zone include companies that produce garments and textiles, pharmaceuticals and gaming commodities. Discussions on economic cooperation between Hengqin 橫琴, an island next to Taipa with an area of about 80 sq km, and Macao are in progress. In October 2005, the Las Vegas Sands signed a letter of intent to build a 520-hectare resort on Hengqin worth more than US$1 billion. It would be designed to complement Sands' US$6 billion development in Macao.

According to William Weidner, President of Las Vegas Sands, the two projects would not only maximize his company's business potential, but also realize Macao's vision of integration into the Pan-PRD by broadening the appeal of the region as a hub for international conventions, tourism and extended-stay vacations.[30]

Fairly Established International Business Network

Macao is one of the two members of the Pan-PRD grouping to have relatively strong business networks with overseas enterprises.[31] Gross merchandise trade accounted for 70-80% of Macao's GDP between 1998 and 2004. More than two-thirds of exports originated from orders made by importers in the U.S.A. and the EU,[32] signifying the importance of trade relationships between local businesses and foreign enterprises (Table 20.4). The share in GDP of the services trade increased from 63 to 94% in the same period, as a result of huge investments from the three gaming concessionaires. In addition, foreign capital accounts for more than 60% of the assets of financial institutions (banks and insurance companies). Provinces and cities in the Pan-PRD could benefit from such an established network in finding overseas trade partners and gaining access to foreign markets.

Endeavour to Set up Service Platforms

At the end of 2002, the Macao SAR government began to promote the idea of developing Macao into a "platform" for providing three kinds of linkages between China and overseas markets: a service platform for

Table 20.4   Main Destinations of Macao's Merchandise Exports, 2002–2005

	2002	2003	2004	2005
Total (MOP million)	18,925	20,700	22,561	19,823
US (%)	48.4	49.9	48.7	48.7
EU (%)	23.2	22.8	21.6	17.1
China (%)	15.6	13.7	13.9	14.9
Hong Kong (%)	5.8	6.6	7.6	9.8
Others (%)	7.0	7.0	8.2	9.6

Note: A country's share in percentage terms. The 2005 figures are provisional.
Source: Statistics and Census Services, Macao SAR Government (DSEC).

Mainland Chinese businesses, focusing on western Guangdong; a platform for promoting business activities between Mainland China and Portuguese-speaking countries; and a platform for bridging the business activities of overseas Chinese particularly those in Taiwan, and mainland Chinese.

Economic ties between western Guangdong, a relatively under-developed region in the province, and the outside world have been undermined by poor transport infrastructure, low economic growth, and less preferential policies accorded by the central government as compared to those in Shenzhen 深圳 and Dongguan 東莞. Yet, Guangdong, under a large-scale transport development project that includes the construction of an inter-city light rail system[33] and in the midst of an attempt to upgrade major highways and improve the railway system, is making every effort to link up Guangzhou 廣州 and cities in the western part of the province. Upon the completion of this transport project, connections between Macao and such regional cites as Zhanjiang 湛江, Maoming 茂名, Yangjiang 陽江, Yunfu 雲浮, Zhaoqing 肇慶 and Jiangmen 江門 will be greatly improved, leading to more business opportunities in these places. Foreign trade, logistics and business services are potential activities to which Macao can contribute and from which it can benefit.

Promoting a service platform for western Guangdong is also connected to the development of a platform for joining China and Portuguese-speaking countries. The Portuguese-speaking world (Comunidade dos Países de Língua, CPLP, or Community of Portuguese Language Countries) has a population of 220–230 million on four continents. Portugal is a bridge for China to enter the EU market, which has as many as half-a-billion consumers. Brazil, on the other hand, is an entrance to the South American economies of 200 million people. Portuguese-speaking nations in Africa, notably Angola, can serve as a stepping-stone for investing into the resource-rich continent. Table 20.5 summarizes the basic features of all Portuguese-speaking nations.

The ability to speak in Portuguese is essential to doing business in these countries. The Portuguese cultural heritage and personal intimacy are the assets of the locally born Macanese or immigrants from Portugal, who can serve as a bridge between Chinese enterprises and their counterparts in the Portuguese-speaking economies. Macao's privileges lie in having expertise in China's markets, and in the areas of legal, accounting and professional consultancy. More importantly, goods produced in western Guangdong, for example, foodstuffs, beverages, textiles, footwear and

Table 20.5 Selected Indicators of the Portuguese-speaking Countries (2002)

County	Populations (million)	GDP (billion US$)	GDP growth (%)	Per capita GDP (US$)	Exports (million US$)	Trade with China (million US$)	Trade with Macao (million US$)	Major export items
Portugal	10.4	150.5	-1.1	14,471	31,100	380	15	Consumer goods, capital goods
Brazil	177.5	497.2	-0.40	2,801	73,235	4,469	4.8	Transport equipment and parts; metallurgical products
Angola	14.3	13.1	4.4	916	9,618	1,148	N.A.	crude oil
Mozambique	18.9	4.3	7	228	795	48	N.A.	Aluminium
Cape Verde	0.47	0.8	5	1,663	43	1.8	N.A.	Agricultural products
Guinea Bissau	1.3	0.2	-7	160	40	8.3	N.A.	Agricultural products
East Timor	0.83	0.4	18	N.A.	4	N.A.	N.A.	Coffee

Note: N.A. = not available. The CPLP comprise eight countries. In addition to the above seven, there is the Democratic Republic of São Tomé and Príncipe in Africa. However, it has been excluded from any CPLP-China cooperation since it began to recognize the Republic of China in 2002.[34]

Source: Compiled by the principal author.

leather produced in Zhaoqing, are competitive in Portuguese-speaking countries, in terms of price and quality.

In fact, high-level interactions between China and the Portuguese-speaking countries to foster closer economic relations have been in progress. The first ministerial-level Forum for Economic and Trade Cooperation between China and Portuguese-speaking Counties (Macao) was held in October 2003. The second meeting of the Forum is scheduled to be held in Macao in the second half of 2006, and an economic fair for enterprises in China and Portuguese-speaking countries will be held in Portugal in 2006.[35] With China's support, Macao is to host the first ever CPLP games in September 2006.[36] In the first forum, An Min, the Chinese Vice-Minister of Commerce, signed an "Economic and Trade Cooperation Action Plan" with Portugal, Brazil, Angola, Mozambique, Cape Verde, Guinea Bissau and East Timor, covering inter-governmental cooperation, and investment and enterprise cooperation. The Macao Trade and Investment Promotion Institute, the official organization promoting business opportunities to foreign investors, has emphasized that there are plenty of cooperation protocols with commercial associations in Brazil and Mozambique, such as the Portuguese Commercial Association in Macao, Portuguese Business Centre in Asia, Forum for Portuguese-speaking Entrepreneurs (Forum dos Empresarios de Lingua Portuguesa), Portuguese-Chinese Chamber of Commerce and Industry (Camara de Comercio e Industria Luso Chinesa), Portuguese Business Association and Portuguese Trade Commission.

Challenges for Macao's Development under the Pan-PRD Grouping

While maintaining its pre-handover economic policy largely intact, Macao faces several challenges in promoting its economic development and in integrating itself into the regional grouping of the Pan-PRD. First, both its domestic and external transportation networks need significant enhancement. It is true that the internal transport network has improved greatly, with three bridges now connecting the peninsula and Taipa as well as the expansion of roadways in various areas of Macao. Yet, the rapid increase in the number of visitors and a growing population is putting further pressure on the existing traffic system. A light-rail system to provide convenient and fast traffic linkages among major locations in both Macao and Taipa is currently under consideration. Since all prefecture-level cities in Guangdong are now connected by expressways,[37] Macao is expected to develop its network to connect it to cities in Guangdong in order not to be marginalized. The Hong Kong–Zhuhai–Macao Bridge will begin construction once the decision on the building of the bridge is announced, which is expected at any time. The bridge will add to Macao's transport capacity, and help the city integrate economically into the Pan-PRD region. The most obvious advantage of this cross-border bridge to Macao is that it would ease transportation between Macao and Pan-PRD cities and Hong Kong, facilitating the inflow of mainland and overseas visitors. Following the formal *lixiang* 立項 process (the initial registration of the project with the State Council), the project is undergoing a technical analysis, which includes site selection, an environmental impact analysis and an exploration of sources of funding.

Second, a structural change to the economy involving the diversification of tourism in the medium term is crucial to transforming Macao into a significant member of the Pan-PRD. In the 1980s, attempts had been made by local industrialists to produce a wide variety of manufactured goods, including toys, artificial flowers, electronics, ceramics and leather products.[38] Yet, the manufacturing sector stagnated after 1985, revealing the difficulties of this approach. Today, diversification entails the co-existence of gaming, MICE, business services and other supporting services. If this is to be achieved, the Macao SAR government needs to demonstrate a high degree of flexibility to investors, which is allowed by the political and legal framework, and to promote Macao as a unique place for the services industry, especially tourism. In July 2005, the World Heritage Committee of the United Nations Educational, Scientific and Cultural Organization (UNESCO) included a group of cultural sites in Macao on its World Heritage List.[39] Collectively known as the "Historic Centre of Macao, " Macao's historic settlements represent the living traditions of an array of occidental and oriental cultures. Comprising major urban squares and streetscapes, they encompass architectural legacies interwoven in the midst of the original urban fabric.[40] The inclusion of the historical sites on the global heritage list is a positive development in promoting Macao to the international community as a city of culture and entertainment, as this will help it to attract a wide array of visitors — not just gamblers.

Yet, the obstacles to the further expansion of Macao's tourism industry cannot be understated. The average length of a visitor's stay in Macao has been declining since 2002, against the backdrop of an increase in the number of people coming to Macao (Table 20.6). Correspondingly, hotel occupancy rates have hovered around 65% while those in Hong Kong stay above

Table 20.6   Key Indicators of Tourism in Macao, 2002–2005

	2002	2003	2004	2005
(A) Average length of stay (days)	1.28	1.26	1.22	1.10
(B) Hotel occupancy (%)	67.13	64.27	75.55	70.9
(C) Origins of visitors (%)				
Mainland China	37	48	57	56
Hong Kong	44	39	31	30
Others	19	13	13	14

Source: Statistics and Census Services, Macao SAR Government (DSEC).

Table 20.7   Educational Attainment of Labour Employed by Industry in Macao, 2004 (%)

	No schooling or pre-primary education	Primary education	Junior secondary	Senior secondary	Non-degree tertiary education	University degree
All	10	24	31	20	3	12
Manufacturing	12	29	39	15	1	4
Construction	15	34	31	12	1	6
Wholesale and retailing	13	26	33	19	1	7
Hotel and restaurant	12	32	32	19	1	4
Transport and storage	11	24	28	21	3	14
Finance	2	5	22	35	9	26
Real estate	12	27	26	19	3	14
Public administration	2	14	31	24	4	26
Education	1	7	10	16	12	54
Health and welfare	3	12	20	10	17	38
Gaming	4	18	37	33	2	6

Source: Statistics and Census Services, Macao SAR Government (DSEC).

80%.[41] This is partly attributable to an increase in the supply of hotel rooms[42] and, more importantly, to a rising number of "same-day travellers." These same-day visitors tend to spend less in Macao. Therefore, in order to boost Macao's tourism income, it will be necessary to attract more business or MICE tourists. According to the Singapore Exhibition and Convention Bureau (SECB), MICE visitors generally spend more than double the amount that ordinary visitors do.[43] As the new projects currently underway are completed, Macao is likely to gradually be transformed into a city that offers more well-rounded entertainment and that is capable of attracting more conference business.

Third, the overseas experience shows that high-calibre human resources are crucial if a city is to become a regional service centre. Table 20.7 reveals the level of education attained by the labour force in various industries. What is most striking is the low percentage of workers that hold tertiary education qualifications. In the hotel and finance sectors, only a minority could be considered well educated.

A survey on investment in education, as shown in Table 20.8, gives further support to our arguments. One of the common measures of investment in education is the share that the government spends on education occupies in total government expenditure. Here, Macao ranks lowest in the Pan-PRD, with only 11% of its public expenditure going to education in 2004 (Column 4), well below the average for the region and the nation (17.4% and 15.3%), respectively. In terms of the share of educational expenditure in GDP (Column 5 in Table 20.8), Macao is also far behind other Pan-PRD members; its public spending on education accounts for only 1.8%, despite the fact that its per capita GDP is the second highest in the region. It should be noted that even though meaningful, direct comparisons of per capita public spending on education between the two SARs and other Pan-PRD provinces are not available,[44] Macao's students received only approximately 40% of what was spent on their counterparts in Hong Kong.

Another important indicator of human capital is the proportion of the population that possesses at least a university degree out of the total population. It appears that the share in Macao, 5.64%, is below the national average of 5.77%.[45] In the light of the continuous improvement in the government's fiscal revenues, the government should accord a higher priority to investment in education at all levels. There is a particularly high demand for technical and professional training in the territory.

Concluding Remarks

As an intergovernmental drive for regionalism, the Pan-PRD can serve as a "vehicle" for its members to discuss and carve out policies on regional economic cooperation, and negotiate and make compromises among themselves to increase the attractiveness of the regional economy to potential overseas investors.

Table 20.8   Education: Macao's Relative Position in the Pan-PRD Region, 2004

Provinces	Per capita GDP	Government expenditure in education (billion)	Total government expenditure (billion)	(2)/(3)	(2)/ GDP in current prices	Per capita public educational expenditure	Population with university degree (%)
	(1)	(2)	(3)	(4)	(5)	(6)	(7)
Guangdong	19,707	28.80	185.30	15.54	1.80	347	5.19
Fujian	17,218	10.09	51.67	19.53	1.67	288	4.56
Jiangxi	8,189	7.37	45.41	16.23	2.12	173	4.67
Guangxi	7,196	9.05	50.75	17.83	2.74	186	5.18
Hainan	9,450	1.79	12.72	14.07	2.34	220	5.21
Hunan	9,117	10.43	71.95	14.50	1.85	155	5.22
Sichuan	8,113	12.25	89.53	13.68	1.88	141	3.62
Yunnan	6,733	11.18	66.36	16.85	3.79	253	3.84
Guizhou	4,215	7.38	41.84	17.64	4.65	190	4.47
Hong Kong	187,547	55.73	265.30	21.01	4.32	8,072	14.10
Macao	181,900	1.48	13.40	11.04	1.78	3,217	5.64
Pan-PRD total	12,995	155.55	894.23	17.39	2.59	336	—
National	10,561	314.63	2,059.28	15.28	2.30	242	5.77

Note: All prices are in local value without exchange adjustments; HK$100=RMB106, MOP100=RMB103; (7) the figure for Macao is the 1991 figure; (2) and (3) refer to local government budgetary expenditures; (6) refers to budgetary expenditures only; the "National" of (2) and (3) refers to the sum of local government expenditures only.

Sources: *Zhongguo Tongji Nianjian 2005*, Statistics and Census Services, Macao SAR Government (DSEC), Census and Statistics Department, Hong Kong SAR Government.

As a first step in regional economic integration, the Pan-PRD framework aims to channel resources across borders for better utilization. To do so, members of the grouping have to identify their relative strengths and weaknesses and redefine their roles so as to maximize the benefits of cooperation.

Globalization is imposing pressure on Macao, a tiny territory, to remain competitive in the global economy. To achieve this, Macao has to extensively utilize the enlarged market created by the Pan-PRD economic grouping to boost its tourism-related industries. A larger market will enable Macao to produce its services more efficiently due to economies of scale. To attain gains, the small city will need to cooperate more with its neighbouring economies and integrate itself into the Pan-PRD, not the other way round. Undoubtedly, gaming continues to constitute the backbone of the territory's economy. With the central government's tacit support, Macao remains the only city in the Pan-PRD where gaming is legally permitted. With enhanced integration into the Pan-PRD, Macao can expand its tourism reach to dynamic inland and overseas markets. More importantly, as a tiny city, Macao can avoid being marginalized only if it becomes an active member of the Pan-PRD.

In conclusion, under the pressures of globalization, the nine provinces and two SAR cities in the Pan-PRD have formed a regional grouping to strengthen intra-regional cooperation. Macao's principal — if not the sole — niche in the grouping is in gaming-related tourism services. Yet, to maintain its relevance and to encourage an exchange of goods and services within an expanded regional market, Macao has to promote itself as a city of high value-added tourist services. Seen in this perspective, it is imperative for Macao to develop an improved transportation network with regional cities and high-quality human capital if the city is to enjoy sustained economic growth in the twenty-first century.

Acknowledgement

The authors owe a special debt of gratitude to Charles C. L. Kwong, who taught economics at the University of Macau for a couple of years before moving to the Open University of Hong Kong, for his insightful comments and suggestions on two earlier versions of this chapter.

Notes

1. Macao's population was 488,144 as of 31 December of 2005 (Statistics and Census Service, DSEC).
2. Robert O. Keohane and Joseph S. Nye, *Power and Interdependence* (New York: Longman, 2001), Chapter 10.
3. Ibid., p. 229.
4. Andrew Hurrell, "Regionalism in Theoretical Perspective," in *Regionalism in World Politics: Regional Organization and International Order*, edited by Louise Fawcett and Andrew Hurrell (Oxford: Oxford University Press, 1995), pp. 37–73.
5. Louise Fawcett and Andrew Hurrell, "Introduction" (see note 4), pp. 1–6.
6. Shaun Breslin, Richard Higgott and Ben Rosamond, "Regions in Comparative Perspective," in *New Regionalisms in the Global Political Economy*, edited by Shaun Breslin, Christopher W. Hughes, Nicola Phillips and Ben Rosamond (London: Routledge, 2002), pp. 1–19.
7. Andrew Wyatt-Walter, "Regionalism, Globalization, and the World Economic Order" (see note 4), pp. 74–121, especially 1992–1993, 1994–1995.
8. The 2004 figure, subject to revision (Statistics and Census Services, Macao, DSEC). MOP refers to Macao pataca, MOP100 = RMB103.167.
9. From the Gaming Inspection and Coordination Bureau (DICJ).
10. From the Labour Affairs Bureau (DSAL).
11. As at the end of 2005 (Gaming Inspection and Coordination Bureau, DICJ).
12. Jasmine Yap, "A Risk-free Gamble on Macao?" *International Herald Tribune*, Hong Kong edition, 18 November 2004. In fact, by the third quarter of 2006, Macao already had 21 casinos.
13. There are three bridges connecting the peninsula and Taipa. The first, the Governador Norbre de Carvalho Bridge 嘉樂庇總督大橋/澳氹大橋, was opened in 1974. The Friendship Bridge and the Sai-Wan Bridge were opened in 1995 and 2004, respectively.
14. Managed by the Macauport (Sociedade de Administracao de Portos SARL).
15. The airport was designed with a runway long enough (at 3,360 m) to land a Boeing 747-400. It has an initial capacity of 6 million passengers per year and operates around the clock.
16. Other facilities include the Nam Van Lakes Nautical Centre, Macao International Shooting Range, Tennis Academy and Bowling Centre, Macao Hockey Centre, East Asian Hall, Youth Centre, Media Centre, Macao Forum, Press and Information Centre, and the MEAGOG Headquarters.
17. According to the Basic Law, the Macao SAR government is required to achieve a fiscal balance. Article 105 states, "The Macao Special Administrative Region shall follow the principle of keeping expenditure within the limits of revenues in drawing up its budget, and strive to achieve a fiscal balance, avoid deficits

and keep the budget commensurate with the growth rate of its gross domestic product."

18. From the Land, Public Works and Transport Bureau (DSSOPT).
19. V. F. S. Sit, R. D. Cremer and S. L. Wong, *Entrepreneurs and Enterprises in Macau: A Study of Industrial Development* (Hong Kong: Hong Kong University Press and API Press, 1991), p. 13.
20. The quota regime is also known as the Agreement on Textiles and Clothing (ATC).
21. See P. A. Azevedo, "Happy Captain," *Macao Business*, July 2004, p. 15.
22. Arthur Anderson was appointed by the Macao SAR government to review the development of gambling in Macao. Twenty-one companies submitted bids for three licences in December 2001.
23. A total of 311 products were involved in the first stage of tariff-free preferential treatment in January 2004. In the second stage, effective in January 2005, the same status was further extended to 190 products.
24. James Ning, "Macao Government Vows to Boost Tourism Potential," *China Daily*, Hong Kong edition, 12 January 2006, p. 3.
25. Fox Yi Hu, "Casinos Lure Mainlanders with Resort Promotions," *South China Morning Post*, 10 July 2006.
26. *EIU Country Report – Macau*, December 2005, p. 16.
27. Andy Cheng, "Visit 'the City' without Leaving Lantau," *South China Morning Post*, 28 July 2005; Chris Yeung, "Foreign Lessons in Winning," *South China Morning Post*, 10 July 2006.
28. Yeung, "Foreign Lessons in Winning" (see note 27).
29. Now, goods produced outside the zone but inside Macao also enjoy the benefit.
30. Peter Sanders, "Las Vegas Sands will build a resort close to Macau," *Wall Street Journal Asia*, 17 October 2005; press release by Las Vegas Sands on 17 October 2005.
31. International business networking in Hong Kong is probably the most sophisticated in the region.
32. This is the 2004 figure.
33. The system aims to shorten the travelling time from Guangzhou to any city in the Pearl River Delta region to less than one hour.
34. Loro Horta and Ian Storey, "China's Portuguese Connection," *Yale Global Online*, 22 June 2006, http://yaleglobal.yale.edu/display.article?id=7634.
35. "Text of China-Portugal Joint Statement 9 December," *BBC Monitoring Asia Pacific*, 10 December 2005.
36. Horta and Storey, "China's Portuguese Connection" (see Note 34).
37. A target of Guangdong is to build expressways in 21 prefecture-level cities (*Aomen ribao* [*Macao Daily*], 6 August 2005).
38. Sit, Cremer and Wong (1991) (see note 19), p. 184.
39. The list was reviewed and approved during the 29th session of the World

Heritage Committee that opened on 10 July 2005 in Durban, South Africa. See "Mostar, Macao, Biblical Vestiges in Israel are among 17 Cultural Sites Inscribed on UNESCO'S World Heritage List," UNESCO, http://portal.unesco. org/en/ev.php-URL_ID=28372&URL_DO=DO_TOPIC&URL_ SECTION=201.html, accessed on 15 June 2006.

40. The sites include the A-Ma Temple, the Moorish Barracks, the Mandarin's House, St. Lawrence's Church, St. Joseph's Seminary and Church, the Dom Pedro V Theatre, the Sir Robert Ho Tung Library, St. Augustine's Church, the "Leal Senado" Building, the Sam Kai Vui Kun Temple, the Holy House of Mercy, the Lou Kau Mansion, St. Dominic's Church, the Ruins of St. Paul's, the Na Tcha Temple, a section of the Old City Walls, the Mount Fortress, St. Anthony's Church, Casa Garden, the Protestant Cemetery and the Guia Fortress (including the Guia Chapel and the Lighthouse). Together they are known as "The Historic Centre of Macao."

41. These are figures for 2004. See the Hong Kong Tourism Board, 11 July 2005.

42. At the end of August 2005, there were 10,549 rooms available in hotels and similar establishments, an increase of 1,268 rooms (or 13.7%) over August 2004.

43. *Bangkok Post*, 29 July 2005, B3.

44. The purchasing power and the conditions of educational operation vary among Hong Kong, Macao and other provinces in the Pan-PRD.

45. This is the figure for Macao in 2001. The percentage may be higher in recent years as the number of university graduates has been increasing.

Glossary

107 National Highway 一零七國道
administrative zone-based economy 行政區經濟
beiwangji 備忘集
bianzhong 編鐘
bird reserve, the 鳥類棲息衍生地
chama gudao 茶馬古道
circle-shaped Hakka houses 客家圍屋
citang 祠堂
Comprehensive Economic Zones 綜合經濟區
daxue yanyibu 大學衍義補
economic zone based economy 經濟區經濟
economically coordinated regions 經濟協作區
eight North-South and eight East-West Lines 八縱八橫
erji xueyuan 二級學院
fanfang 番坊
five North-South and seven East-West Lines 五縱七橫
hanzu 漢族
hukou 戶口
jingji tequ 經濟特區
liangji 兩基
Lingwai daida 嶺外代答
lixiang 立項
lixue 理學
macro-economic regions 大經濟區
Minxue 閩學
minying 民營
modern logistics corporations 協作群體
mu 畝 (the Chinese acre, equivalent to 0.067 ha or 0.16 acre)
Nan-Bei-Qin-Fang urban cluster 南北欽防城市群
Nanfang caomuzhuang 南方草木狀

Nou culture 儺文化
one point, one line 一點一線
one province, two sites 一省兩地
paired assistance 對口支援
(the) Panzhihua region 攀枝花地區
PRD Economic Zone 珠江三角洲經濟區
rencai 人才
Sanxingdui 三星堆
Shanghan zabinglun 傷寒雜病論
shaoshu minzu 少數民族
shehui fuliyuan 社會福利院
shequ wenhua zhongxin 社區文化中心
shuifei gaige 稅費改革
shuyuan 書院
Sishu jizhu 四書集注
small third line 小三線
third front 三線
tianfuzhiguo 天府之國
Tiangong kaiwu 天工開物
tonggu 銅鼓
West-East Gas Pipeline Project 西氣東輸
West-East Power Transmission Project 西電東輸
xiangzhen 鄉鎮
xiaokang 小康
xingzhengcun 行政村
xinxue 心學
Yunnan-Foreign Countries Power Transmission Project 雲電外送
zhuanye renyuan 專業人員
zirancun 自然村

Editors and Contributors

Y. M. YEUNG (楊汝萬) is Emeritus Professor of Geography, Research Professor of the Hong Kong Institute of Asia-Pacific Studies, The Chinese University of Hong Kong. His wide-ranging research interests have focused on China's coastal cities, South China, globalization and Asian cities. He has published extensively, including, as editor, co-editor or author, *Globalization and the World of Large Cities* (1998), *Fujian* (2000), *Globalization and Networked Societies* (2000), *New Challenges for Development and Modernization* (2002) and *Developing China's West* (2004).

SHEN JIANFA (沈建法) is Professor and Head of Graduate Division in the Department of Geography and Resource Management, The Chinese University of Hong Kong. His research interests focus on urban/regional governance and development, spatial population modelling and migration analysis. He serves in the Editorial Boards of *The China Review*, *Population, Space and Place*, and *Applied Spatial Analysis and Planning*.

MATTHEW M. CHEW (趙明德) graduated from Princeton University in 1997. He has taught courses on sociology, communications and education in Hong Kong and Shanghai, and is currently teaching at the Sociology Department of Hong Kong Baptist University. His research interests include cultural sociology, globalization, cultural policy, Chinese society and social theory.

CHUNG HIM (鍾謙) is Assistant Professor in the Geography Department at Hong Kong Baptist University. His main research areas span across rural and urban geography of China, including rural marketing activities, contesting urban space, migrant workers and state-society relations. He is the author of *China's Rural Market Development in the Reform Era*. He has also published paper on China's rural transport development, illegal construction and the spatial implication of China's administrative hierarchy reform.

DAI BIN (戴賓), Professor, Vice-Dean of School of Public Administration, Director of Research Centre for Regional Economy and Urban Management, Southwest Jiaotong University, Chengdu, China, 610031.

C. CINDY FAN (范芝芬) is Professor of Geography at the University of California, Los Angeles. Her research and teaching interests centre on the regional and social dimensions of transitional economies, focusing on regional policy, inequality, labour migration, marriage migration, gender and urban system in post-Mao China. She has been a consultant for The World Bank and is an editor of *Regional Studies* and a senior contributing editor of *Eurasian Geography and Economics*.

HE CHENGGENG (何承耕) is Associate Professor in the College of Geographical Sciences, Fujian Normal University and holds a Ph.D. in Geography from the Fujian Normal University. His major interest is in regional economy, natural resources and environmental management.

HU TIANXIN (胡天新) obtained his Ph.D. in Geography from The Chinese University of Hong Kong. At present, he is a senior urban planner in the China Academy of Urban Planning and Design, Beijing.

HU WUXIAN (胡武賢) received his Master's degree in economics from Renmin University of China. He was Associate Director of the Department of Economics and Management in Hunan University of Arts and Science before July 2006. He serves as Professor of Economics of the College of Public Management in South China Agricultural University. His research interests include growth of regional economy, rural economic sociology and basic government renovation.

HUANG SHUHUA (黃淑華) is a senior economist of the Jiangxi Provincial Development and Reform Commission Research Centre. She has published many articles on macro-economics and regional economic studies.

HUANG YEFANG (黃葉芳) received her Ph.D. from The Chinese University of Hong Kong. She is currently an instructor in the Department of Geography and Resource Management, The Chinese University of Hong

Kong. Her research interests are in regional development in China, especially in Guangxi and Shanghai, mathematical modelling in Geography and spatial analysis.

GORDON KEE (紀緯紋) is Research Assistant of the Hong Kong Institute of Asia Pacific Studies at The Chinese University of Hong Kong. His major research interests include regional development, regional governance, formation of city-region and infrastructure development. His latest work includes *The Networked Region: Basic Infrastructure Development in the Pan-Pearl River Delta Region* (2007, co-author with Y. M. Yeung, in Chinese). He is also currently a Ph.D. student in the Department of Geography and Resource Management.

KWAN FUNG (關鋒) teaches economics in the Department of Economics, University of Macau. His research interests include development economics, macroeconomics, the modern Macao economy and the Chinese economy, especially labour issues, income inequality and its total factor productivity growth.

LAU YEE-CHEUNG (劉義章), Associate Professor in the History Department at The Chinese University of Hong Kong, holds a Ph.D. from the University of California, Santa Barbara. His research interests cover Republican figures, Hakka studies, Christian philanthropy and Chinese Islam. His recent publications include *The First Fifty Years of the Haven of Hope Christian Service* (2005), an edited volume *Hong Kong Hakka* (2005) and articles published by the Center for Interdisciplinary Study of Monotheistic Religions and the *Republican Archives.*

JOANNA W. Y. LEE (李慧瑩) received her Ph.D. from The Chinese University of Hong Kong. She is a Professional Consultant in the Department of Geography and Resource Management and a Programme Director of the Centre for Environmental Policy and Resource Management at The Chinese University of Hong Kong. She is by profession a chartered town planner. Her research areas include urban planning, globalization and regional development.

LEE PAK-KUEN (李百權) is Lecturer in the Department of Politics and International Relations, University of Kent, Canterbury, United Kingdom. He has previously taught at the Open University of Hong Kong and the

University of Macau. His recent publications have appeared in *Challenges and Policy Programmes of China's New Leadership* (2007), *Journal of the Asia Pacific Economy* (2005) and *Pacific Review* (2005). He is currently working on a joint book project on China's participation in global governance.

MAGGI W. H. LEUNG (梁慧嫻) is a geographer working mainly on Chinese Diaspora, transnationalism, international migration and development, migrant entrepreneurship, cultural identities and heritage. She is currently Assistant Professor in the Department of Geography at The University of Hong Kong. Her current research explores the development of Chinese outbound tourism and tourism-related Chinese migrant businesses in Europe.

LIANG GUIQUAN (梁桂全) is the President of Guangdong Academy of Social Sciences and an economics researcher. His research interests include development economics, development strategy studies, and theories of modernization and sustainable development.

LIAO HAIFENG (廖海峰) is an M.Phil. candidate in the Department of Geography at The University of Hong Kong.

LIN HUI (林琿) is Professor in the Department of Geography and Resource Management and Director of the Institute of Space and Earth Information Science, The Chinese University of Hong Kong. He was elected academician of International Eurasian Academy of Sciences in 1995. His major research interests include virtual geographic environments, cloud-prone and rainy area remote sensing, spatially integrated humanities and social sciences.

NG WING-FAI (吳永輝) received his Ph.D. in Geography from The Chinese University of Hong Kong. His major research interest is poverty alleviation in China's nationalities areas. He is currently working for a Chinese multi-national corporation specializing in turnkey telecommunications projects.

PENG XIANWEI (彭賢偉) is Professor in the School of Geography and Biological Science, Guizhou Normal University. His major research interests include rural regional development, and urban and rural land use.

QIAN ZHIHONG (錢志鴻), Associate Professor, Research Centre for Regional Economy and Urban Management/School of Public Administration, Southwest Jiaotong University.

MINGJIE SUN (孫明潔) is a Ph.D. candidate in geography at the University of California, Los Angeles. Her research interests are population and economic geography, focusing on regional development, inequality and migration in China.

TANG XIAOHUA (湯小華), Associate Professor in the College of Geographical Sciences, Fujian Normal University, holds a Ph.D. in Geography from the Fujian Normal University. His recent research has focused on the eco-environment of Fujian.

TSANG SHU-KI (曾澍基) is a professor at the Economics Department of the Hong Kong Baptist University. His research interests include currency board systems, economic transition and monetary integration. He was a former Hong Kong Affairs Advisor to the Chinese government and is presently a member of the Currency Board Sub-committee of the Exchange Fund Advisory Committee of the Hong Kong SAR government.

XIAO JIN (肖今) is Associate Professor in the Department of Educational Administration and Policy, Faculty of Education, The Chinese University of Hong Kong. She holds a Ph.D. from Michigan State University. Her research interest lies mainly in human resource development in China. She has conducted surveys of employees in business and industry firms in Shenzhen, Shanghai, Chongqing, and of employees, school teachers and students in 12 counties across China.

YANG CHUN (楊春) is currently a visiting scholar at Harvard University after serving the Department of Geography, The University of Hong Kong, as a Research Assistant Professor and a policy think-tank in Hong Kong Special Administrative Region (HKSAR) as a research officer. Her research interests focus on Hong Kong-Mainland China relations, urban and regional development, and cross-straits relations in the Greater China region.

YANG GUANXIONG (楊冠雄) is former Professor in the Institute of Geography, Chinese Academy of Science and former Deputy Director-General, Department of Environment and Resources of Hainan. Currently, he is a member of the Commission of Environment and Resource, the Standing Committee of the Hainan People's Congress. Tourism geography is his main study field. He has published such books as *Xinan luyou ziyuan kaifa* 西南旅遊資源開發 (Development of Tourist Resources in the Southwest China) in the field.

YANG XIANMING (楊先明) is Professor of Economics, member of the 10th and 11th CPPCC National Committee, and Dean of the School of Development Studies at Yunnan University. He graduated with a Ph.D. from the Institute of International Economy at Nankai University. His research interests focus on economic development and regional development. He is the author of six books and more than 30 articles on economic development.

YOU AIQIONG (游霭瓊) is Researcher in Guangdong Academy of Social Sciences. Her major research interests include regional economy, international trade, foreign investment, industrial economy and modernization.

ZHANG LI (張力) is Assistant Professor in the Department of Geography and Resource Management, The Chinese University of Hong Kong. His research areas include migration, urbanization and regional development in China. He has published articles in international journals, including *China Quarterly, International Journal of Urban and Regional Research, Urban Studies, Geoforum, Habitat International, International Regional Science Review, Asian Survey* and *China Economic Review*.

ZHENG DAXIAN (鄭達賢), Professor and former Director of the School of Geographical Sciences, Fujian Normal University. He is a council member of the Geographical Society of China and President of the Geographical Society of Fujian. His research interests cover physical geography, eco-environment and regional development of Fujian. He has published many papers and books in these fields.

ZHOU GUOLAN (周國蘭) is a researcher and the Director of the Jiangxi Provincial Development and Reform Commission Research Centre. She is also a general council member of *Jiangxi jingji xuehui* (Jiangxi Economic Society). Her research interests include macro-economy and policy research, and she has published over 50 articles and 8 books.

Index